NINTH EDITION

QUANTITATIVE ANALYSIS FOR MANAGEMENT

Charles P. Bonini
William R. Timken Professor of Management Science
Graduate School of Business
Stanford University

Warren H. Hausman
Professor of Industrial Engineering and Engineering Management
Department of Industrial Engineering and Engineering Management
Stanford University

Harold Bierman, Jr.
Nicholas H. Noyes Professor of Business Administration
Johnson Graduate School of Management
Cornell University

IRWIN

Chicago • Bogotá • Boston • Buenos Aires • Caracas
London • Madrid • Mexico City • Sydney • Toronto

To Barbara, Joan, and Florence

The previous edition of this book was Bierman, Bonini, and Hausman: *Quantitative Analysis for Business Decisions,* Eighth Edition

Irwin Book Team

Publisher: *Tom Casson*
Sponsoring editor: *Colleen A. Tuscher*
Marketing manager: *Colleen J. Suljic*
Project supervisor: *Karen M. Smith*
Production supervisor: *Pat Frederickson*
Designer: *Crispin Prebys*
Prepress buyer: *Jon Christopher*
Compositor: *Weimer Graphics, Inc., Division of Shepard Poorman Communications Corp.*
Typeface: *10/12 Times Roman*
Printer: *R. R. Donnelley & Sons Company*

Library of Congress Cataloging-in-Publication Data

Bonini, Charles P.
Quantitative analysis for management / Charles P. Bonini, Warren H. Hausman, Harold Bierman. — 9th ed.
p. cm. — (The Irwin series in quantitative methods and management science)
Revision of previous editions: Quantitative analysis for business decisions / Harold Bierman.
Includes index.
ISBN 0-256-14021-9
1. Industrial management—Mathematical models. 2. Decision-making—Mathematical models. 3. Management—Problems, exercises, etc. I. Hausman, Warren H. II. Bierman, Harold. III. Bierman, Harold. Quantitative analysis for business decisions. IV. Title. V. Series.
HD30.25.B664 1997
658.4′033—dc20 96-36779

Printed in the United States of America
2 3 4 5 6 7 8 9 0 DOC 3 2 1 0 9 8 7

PREFACE

For Managers and Future Managers

The first edition of this book in 1961 was the pioneering text in the application of quantitative analysis to management. It attempted to bridge the gap between the newly developed analytic methods and applied business disciplines. Over the years we have maintained this focus through eight subsequent editions.

In recent years the popularity of quantitative methods might appear to be declining. The current business press touts approaches such as *Reengineering, Total Quality Management (TQM)*, or *Supply Chain Management* as the keys to business success. But all this is somewhat misleading as it relates to the value of quantitative analysis. First of all, in many instances the implementation of these heralded approaches relies partially on using the tools and methods presented in this book. And while these new approaches have been in the limelight, the continuing success of quantitative analysis in making business and other organizations more efficient and effective has been overlooked. Because quantitative methods have been so widely utilized over the years, they have become routine and are taken for granted in many organizations. They just do not get the same press coverage as the newer ideas.

We think it is important for you, the reader, to be aware of the continuing successful use of quantitative methods. Hence we have included material in each chapter describing a recent application of the techniques in that chapter. These often involve savings of millions of dollars to the companies involved. We call these "Motivating Examples," and our aim is to make you aware that there is still ample opportunity for successful use of these methods. You should also briefly review the problems, and especially the cases, at the end of each chapter. These represent real applications—usually greatly simplified into problem format.

We authors have kept our enthusiasm for the value and role of quantitative analysis over the 36 or so years of the life of this text. We hope some of the enthusiasm will be contagious.

For Instructors

This book is the ninth edition of *Quantitative Analysis for Business Decisions*. This edition is a major revision—sufficiently major that the title has been changed to *Quantitative Analysis for Management*. Major changes include format, chapter coverage, motivating examples, and spreadsheet friendliness.

The first edition, over 35 years ago, was a pioneering approach to applying quantitative techniques to managerial problems. As stated in the original preface, one purpose of the book was to "act as a connecting force between the mathematical courses on the one hand and the applied business courses on the other." Over the years courses in Quantitative Analysis have served that role. But in recent times, business curricula have changed and that "connecting force" has often been merged into the applied courses themselves—especially into the Operations or Production course. It is with this change in mind that we undertook this revision.

The format has been altered so that each chapter is as self-contained as possible. We anticipate that some professors will use this book in its entirety but others may select a subset of chapters to be included in a "course reader", possibly with material from other Irwin texts or that of other publishers. We have eliminated virtually all chapter cross-references and have moved the "answers" section of the book, "Practice Problems," to the end of each chapter. The new one-color format has been selected with this use in mind.

We have also made most chapters substantially larger, by combining smaller chapters in the previous edition. This results in fewer chapters, more cohesion within each chapter, and again ease of use if an instructor wishes to create a unique course reader by selecting among different materials.

Each chapter now opens with one or more Motivating Examples which are brief vignettes of applications of quantitative models to real-world decision situations. These are designed to show the reader that these methods of analysis can and do have real payoff in actual business settings, hence providing motivation to undertake the effort to understand them.

The entire book has been made "spreadsheet-friendly" throughout. We have focused on Excel® and have added many examples of the use of spreadsheets in quantitative modeling. We have also added Appendixes with more detail on the use of Excel for both simulation and the solution of linear programming problems using Solver®.

We have also added a new chapter on Forecasting, covering Exponential Smoothing, Regression, New Product Forecasting, and Forecast Error Measurement.

The Decision Analysis material has been combined into two chapters, and discussion of stock options and bias in estimating probabilities has been added.

The Inventory Control and Management material has been combined into a single chapter and now includes material on Tradeoff Curves for Customer Service vs. Inventory Investment and a brief discussion of Supply Chain Management issues, including risk pooling effects.

The Queuing chapter has been extensively revised to include modern treatment of arrivals and services, focusing on the interarrival time and service time distributions and including treatment of general service times, loss systems, and a brief introduction to networks of processing systems.

Many new problems have been added to this edition. One major strength of previous editions was the quality and quantity of the problems, and we have retained the best of the best in this edition.

As always, we have attempted to make changes that are consistent with an objective described in the preface of the first edition—to make the material understandable to a reader who does not have an extensive mathematical background.

We thank the many users of previous editions who have taken the time to point out errors and inconsistencies and have offered suggestions for improvement. This assistance is greatly appreciated.

Although Lawrence Fouraker and Robert Jaedicke are no longer listed as authors, we acknowledge that a considerable percentage of the book carries forward their words and ideas.

Charles P. Bonini
Warren H. Hausman
Harold Bierman, Jr.

ACKNOWLEDGMENTS

We would like to thank these reviewers who, for recent editions, have made many helpful suggestions. We appreciate your contributions.

Steve Achtenhagen, *San Jose State University*

Ray Ballard, *E. Texas State University*

Thomas Boland, *Ohio University*

Fredrick Davidson, *Mary Washington College*

Peter Ellis, *Utah State University*

Warren W. Fisher, *Stephen F. Austin State University*

J. William Gotcher, *California State University–Hayward*

Tim Ireland, *Oklahoma State University*

Raj Jagannathan, *University of Iowa*

Prem S. Mann, *California State University–Fullerton*

Mike Middleton, *University of San Francisco*

G. John Miltenburg, *McMaster University*

W. E. Pinney, *University of Texas–Arlington*

Mary Rolfes, *Mankato State University*

Taj Shahran, *University of Detroit Mercy*

Linda Salchenberger, *Loyola University*

Stephen P. Stuk, *Emory University*

George Vlahos, *University of Dayton*

Mark Walker, *State University of New York–Stonybrook*

C. P. B.
W. H. H.
H. B., Jr.

EXTRACTS FROM THE PREFACE TO THE FIRST EDITION

The administration of a modern business enterprise has become an enormously complex undertaking. There has been an increasing tendency to turn to quantitative techniques and models as a potential means for solving many of the problems that arise in such an enterprise. The purpose of this book is to describe a representative sample of the models and their related quantitative techniques. It is hoped that this book will serve as a basis for a course . . . that acts as a connecting force between the mathematical courses on the one hand and the applied business courses on the other.

This is an introductory work in the application of mathematics to problems of business. It is not an introductory work to the mathematics which are being applied. We have summarized—in a rather rough and ready manner by a mathematician's standards—some of the mathematical tools employed. Our purpose is to get our notation and a few basic relationships before the reader rather than to teach him mathematics.

We have attempted to minimize the amount of mathematical training required to read this book . . . a reader who does not have formal training in these areas should not think that this book is beyond his ability.

The book is an attempt to consider techniques which treat quite sophisticated and difficult problems; so, even though we tried to choose the simplest means of exposition—avoiding proofs and much of the characteristic rigor of such treatments—the essential subtlety of the techniques remains. These attributes can be understood only by patient application of effort over a protracted period of time.

Harold Bierman, Jr.
Lawrence E. Fouraker
Robert K. Jaedicke

BRIEF CONTENTS

CONTENTS

PART III

Application Areas

PART

I MODELING AND OPTIMIZATION

Motivating Example

Modeling Coast Guard Operations[1]

The United States Coast Guard has responsibility to maintain more than 50,000 aids to navigation (including buoys, lights, and day beacons) located on U.S. waterways. Maintenance involves verifying a buoy's location, replacing missing letters or numbers, and repainting; this work is generally carried out once a year.

The Coast Guard uses two types of vessels to perform this maintenance: seagoing tenders and coastal tenders. Seagoing tenders cost nearly twice as much as coastal tenders. The entire fleet was due for replacement, and a quantitative model was developed to analyze both the scheduling of the fleet and its desired composition. The modeling effort used tools described in this book and took into account the required maintenance work, the distance to be traveled to reach each buoy, and the complete life-cycle cost (including acquisition cost of vessels and operating costs) of each type of vessel.

Various complications existed in this study. It was important to allow for the differing capabilities of each type of vessel (seagoing versus coastal tender), and the routing of vessels to buoy locations. The effects of bad weather were modeled by estimating the annual hours lost due to bad weather, depending on whether the buoys being serviced were fully exposed to weather, partially exposed, or protected. Furthermore, since these tenders were also used for other operations such as environmental response, search and rescue, and law enforcement, the Coast Guard had determined that at least 16 seagoing tenders were required.

After the modeling effort was completed, it was validated by "forecasting" current operations and comparing the model's output with actual operations. The model was then used to deal with the question of the optimal composition and operation of a replacement fleet. The model's results were that 16 seagoing tenders, 14 coastal tenders, and one stern-loading buoy boat would provide sufficient coverage, if scheduled efficiently; this configuration has 7 fewer vessels in total, with 10 fewer seagoing vessels (which are the most expensive) compared to the current fleet. Compared with a direct replacement strategy of the existing fleet, the model generated a savings of $350 million in capital acquisition costs.

[1]Mark Bucciarelli and Kip Brown, "A Desktop-OR Success: Modeling Coast Guard Buoy Tender Operations," *Interfaces,* July–August 1995, pp. 1–11.

CHAPTER

1 Introduction to Analysis and Model Building

This book is about managerial decision making. Managerial decision making is a process whereby management, when confronted by a problem, selects a specific course of action, or "solution," from a set of possible courses of action. Since there is often some uncertainty about the future, we cannot be sure of the consequences of the decision that is chosen, and we cannot be sure that the decision chosen will produce the best outcome. Furthermore, the problem may be quite complex because there are either a large number of alternatives to consider or many factors to take into account.

This book presents a general approach for managers to use when faced with decision problems, as well as specific quantitative tools for particular types of problems.

Decisions

A manager wants to choose that course of action that will be most effective in attaining the goals of the organization. In judging the effectiveness of different possible decisions, we must use some criterion or performance measure. The most commonly used performance measure in making decisions is a monetary unit, such as dollars, but we shall see in the following chapters that for some decisions, the use of dollars in judging the relative merits of different courses of action would not be adequate.

The following general process of solution is common to all types of decision situations:

1. Establish the *criterion* to be used. For example, in a simple situation the criterion may be to choose the act that maximizes profit.
2. Select a set of *alternatives* for consideration.
3. Determine the *model* to be used and the values of the parameters of the process. For example, we may decide that an adequate expression for total expenses is:

$$\text{Total expenses} = a + b(\text{units sold})$$

The parameters are a and b, and their values would have to be determined in order to use the model.

a = Fixed cost for the period or project
b = Variable (incremental) cost per unit

4. Determine which alternative *optimizes* (i.e., produces the best value for) the criterion established above in step 1.

Example
We can sell 1,000 units of product to the government at a price of $50 per unit. Should the order be accepted? The firm has excess capacity.

1. We shall use the profit maximization criterion.
2. The alternatives are to (a) accept the order or (b) reject the order. In accordance with our profit criterion, we shall accept the order if it increases profit or reject the order if it does not increase profit.
3. We need to know the incremental expenses of producing the 1,000 units. The relevant expense model is:

$$E = a + 1{,}000b$$

   Assume that special dies costing $5,000 will have to be bought (a is equal to $5,000) and that the variable costs of producing a unit are $30 ($b$ is equal to $30). Then the total relevant expenses of filling the order are $35,000 (equal to $5,000 plus $30,000).
4. A comparison of the incremental revenues, $50,000, and incremental expenses, $35,000, indicates that we should accept the order. Profit will be greater by $15,000 if we "accept" compared with the alternative "refuse the order."

In the above example, we used basic knowledge and simple computational techniques. However, in dealing with more complex problems, we might need to use other tools of quantitative analysis, including calculus, probability, statistics, and mathematical programming.

We shall now consider some aspects of model building.

Abstraction and Simplification

Real-world problems tend to be enormously complex. There are literally an uncountable number of inherent "facts" in any empirical situation. Further, every potential course of action starts a chain of cause, effect, and interaction that logically is without end.

Consider the problem of constructing a building. An endless amount of time could be devoted to gathering factual information about this situation: for example, the precise location and physical characteristics of the building; a detailed study of the climatic conditions of the potential sites and the influence these will have on construction costs; the sources of the funds used and their cost. The decision maker might decide to consider specifically and in detail all other potential uses of the funds in this period and in future periods. If our decision maker adopts a strategy of collecting *all* the facts before acting, it follows that no action will take place. The human mind cannot consider every aspect of an empirical problem. Some attributes of the problem must be ignored if a decision is to be made. The decision maker must determine those factors most relevant to the problem. Abstraction and simplification are necessary steps in the solution of any human problem. Our objective is to improve decision making, not to provide an excuse for not making a decision.

Model Building

After the decision maker has selected the critical factors, or variables, from the empirical situation, they are combined in some logical manner so that they form a *model* of the actual problem. A *model* is a simplified representation of an empirical situation. Ideally, it strips a natural phenomenon of its bewildering complexity and duplicates the essential behavior of the natural phenomenon with a few variables that are simply related. The simpler the model, the better for the decision maker, provided the model serves as a reasonably reliable counterpart of the empirical problem. The advantages of a simple model are:

1. It is economical of time and thought.
2. It can be understood readily by the decision maker.
3. If necessary, the model can be modified quickly and effectively.

The object of the decision maker is not to construct a model that is as close as possible to reality in every respect. Such a model would require an excessive length of time to construct, and then it might be beyond human comprehension. Rather, the decision maker wants the simplest model that predicts outcomes reasonably well and is consistent with effective action.

Solutions

After the model has been constructed, conclusions may be derived about its behavior by means of logical analysis. The decision maker then bases actions or decisions on these conclusions. If the logic in deriving the conclusions from the abstracted variables is correct, and if the relevant variables have been abstracted, then the solution to the model will also serve as an effective solution for the empirical problem. For our example, the decision maker may decide that an interest rate of 15 percent measures the firm's annual opportunity cost of money. The firm can make the decision on construction of the building by computing the net present value of the cash flows and not consider alternative investments in detail.

Errors

Two important sources of error in using models for decision making are the exclusion of important variables and mistakes in defining the relationships among the variables. For example, in the above example involving the government contract, assume that a 40 percent loss in yield during production can be expected due to unusually tight product specifications. If this factor were present but omitted from the analysis, the resulting model would not represent the situation adequately enough for decision purposes (the wrong decision may result).

Model-Building Techniques

Models may be represented in a variety of ways. For simple, repetitive problems, the entire decision-making process may take place in the mind of the decision maker, perhaps in a quite informal, intuitive manner. We walk, eat, and open doors every day without the aid of formal models. If the problem is somewhat more unusual or complex, we spend more time thinking about it.

The appropriate technique for describing and relating selected variables depends to a large extent on the nature of the variables. If the variables are subject to measurement of some form, and particularly if they can be given a quantitative representation, then there are strong reasons for selecting a mathematical representation of the model. First, there is a rigorous inherent discipline in mathematics that ensures an orderly procedure on the part of the investigator: You must be specific about what variables you have selected and what relationships you are assuming to exist among them. Second, mathematics is a powerful technique for relating variables and for deriving logical conclusions from given premises. Mathematics, combined with modern computers, makes it possible to handle problems that require models of great complexity, and it facilitates the decision-making process where quantitative analysis is applicable.

A large number of business problems have been given a quantitative representation successfully, leading to a general approach that has been designated as quantitative analysis, decision science, management science, or operations research. Of course, the quantitative representation and resolution of business problems is much older than these labels—witness the practice of accounting. However, quantitative analysis has been extended to many other areas of the business firm's operations and has become established as an effective way of approaching certain business decision problems. Today's managers have to be as knowledgeable about these techniques and models as they are about accounting reports.

A further word of caution is in order. The business executive should never become the captive of a quantitative model and automatically adopt its conclusions as the correct decision. The conclusion derived from the model contains some degree of error because of the abstraction process. The question of when the error becomes so large that the conclusion must be modified before it can be adopted as a solution is one of judgment. Quantification is an aid to business judgment and not a substitute for it. A certain amount of constructive skepticism is as desirable in considering quantitative analysis of business problems as it is in any other decision-making process.

Qualitative Factors

Many business decisions, particularly the most important ones, involve some variables that are qualitative rather than quantitative in nature. For example, major decisions may affect morale and leadership in the organization or may affect employment, affirmative action, pollution, or other areas of social responsibility. Many of these factors cannot be expressed in dollar terms. How, then, does the decision maker deal with these qualitative variables?

First, two extreme attitudes should be avoided. One such extreme attitude would ignore qualitative factors, on the grounds that factors that cannot be measured are unimportant. An equally extreme attitude would argue that quantitative models have no value given that qualitative factors are important.

A more sensible approach is to accept the idea that the quantitative model can deal effectively with the measurable aspects of the decision problem, and that the decision maker must also deal intuitively with the qualitative variables. The manager must find some appropriate balance between the quantitative and qualitative factors.

Summary

In making business decisions, one should establish the decision-making criterion, select the alternatives, determine a model, and evaluate the alternatives using the model, selecting the best alternative.

A model is an abstraction and simplification of a real problem, ideally incorporating the essential elements and relationships from the real problem. Solving a model means obtaining the logical conclusions that follow, and these conclusions should be an effective guide to decision making if the model is designed and solved properly. Decision making involves integrating the quantitative information obtained from the model with intuitive judgment about qualitative factors.

Classification of Models

There are several types of decision models that we shall discuss in this book; these are classified in Figure 1–1. Models are classified as certain if the major factors are assumed known, and uncertain if some factors are unknown.

Simple Problems

All problems must be simplified in constructing the model for any analysis. If this results in only a small number of factors or variables, and relatively few alternatives, then the model is called **simple.** Simple models may be very useful, even for very important decision problems.

A **case** or **scenario model** is a model of a decision problem that is analyzed by trying out a series of cases (possible outcomes or scenarios) using different alternatives or different assumptions. The model is not programmed to find the "best"

FIGURE 1–1
Types of Models

Decision problem is:	**Major variables in a decision problem are:**	
	Certain	*Uncertain*
Simple	Case models	Decision analysis (decision trees)
Complex	Case models Linear and integer programming	Simulation
Dynamic	Inventory models PERT (critical path) models	Simulation Inventory models Queuing models

solution directly. Rather, the manager uses the model in a trial and error process. Most of the other types of models in Figure 1–1 are **optimization** models, in which the model uses mathematical procedures to find the optimal solution. Case models are described later in this chapter.

Decision analysis models incorporate the use of probabilities in decision making under uncertainty. Part II of the book presents these models.

Complex Problems

Many decision problems involve a large number of important factors or variables, or they may have many alternatives to consider. For example, a firm may have several plants that produce goods for shipment to several hundred customers. The decision problem of scheduling the plants and determining which plants supply which customers in order to minimize cost involves hundreds of variables and constraints and may have millions of possible solutions.

Linear and integer programming models are the most widely used techniques for solving large complex business problems of this type. They use mathematical techniques to find the maximum (or minimum) value of an objective, subject to a set of constraints. These techniques are treated in the next several chapters.

Simulation is a technique for modeling large complex systems involving uncertainty. A model is designed to replicate the behavior of the system. Simulation models are usually analyzed by a case by case (versus optimization) approach. Chapter 10 introduces simulation models.

Dynamic Problems

Dynamic decision problems involve a particular type of complexity—when there is a sequence of interrelated decisions over several time periods. Part III of this book includes several of these types of models: **inventory** models for determining when to order inventory and how much stock to hold; **PERT** or **critical path** models for scheduling projects; and **queuing** models for problems involving congestion.

Decision Support Systems

A *decision support system,* or DSS, is an integrated computer system designed to aid management decision making. A DSS generally incorporates a model that is one of the types described in this text, and the computer system performs the calculations necessary to solve the model. However, a DSS is often more than just a model. It generally involves a database that can be used to provide information directly to the manager (or to the model). A DSS sometimes involves graphics or other reports that are readily understandable by the user. Also, the DSS incorporates computer technology to make it easy to do the analysis needed for the decision problem or to query the database for needed information.

This book is not devoted to developing the computer tools necessary to build DSSs. To the extent that models are a significant part of DSSs, then understanding the models in this book is an important step in building a DSS. Throughout the book, we shall refer to and illustrate computer software to solve particular models. This software might be a part of a DSS.

Summary

Decisions may be characterized as being made under certainty or uncertainty, depending on whether or not the major factors are assumed known. Decision making under uncertainty involves the use of probabilities to express the likelihood of uncertain events.

Decision problems may also be classified as simple (if there are few important variables), complex (if there are many), or dynamic (if the decisions are interrelated over time). Various types of models fitting these categories are described throughout this text.

Computer decision support systems (DSSs) often include, as a major component, a decision model of the kind studied in this book.

Basic Modeling Concepts

As explained earlier, a model is a simplification of a business decision problem. The simplification is accomplished by including only the important elements and omitting the nonessential considerations. A road map is a good example of a model. It excludes most of the detail of landscape, buildings, and so forth in order to show clearly the highway routes. Because it is simplified, it is highly useful. If all the detail of the real world were included, it would be much less useful, since we would be spending a large amount of time trying to sort out the highways from the other detail.

Thus, the first step in model building is to pick out the factors or variables that the decision maker considers important. These may be classified into five categories:

- Decision variables.
- Exogenous variables.
- Policies and constraints.
- Performance measures.
- Intermediate variables.

Decision Variables

The decision variables are those under the control of the decision maker. They represent alternative choices for the manager. Consider a marketing manager deciding on the introduction of a new product. The manager can choose to introduce the product or not; the manager may also choose the price at which to sell the product and the amount to spend on advertising. Since these are the major choices, these are the decision variables.

The manager may also have a number of minor decisions to make, such as the color of the product, the detailed content of the advertising, how the sales force is to be informed about the product, and so on. In order to simplify the analysis, the manager may choose to omit these less important factors from the model.

Exogenous Variables

Exogenous or external variables are those that are important to the decision problem but are controlled by factors outside the purview of the decision maker. Generally, economic conditions, actions of competitors, prices of raw materials, and similar factors are exogenous variables. In the case of the marketing manager considering a new product introduction, the reaction of customers (how much they will buy) is certainly an important exogenous variable. Other exogenous variables are the cost of raw materials and other elements needed to produce the product.

Policies and Constraints

A decision maker often operates within constraints imposed by company policy, legal restraints, or physical limitations. For example, there may be limited capacity available in the plant, and this may restrict the sales that can be made. A company policy may specify that materials are to be procured from certain suppliers or that certain levels of quality must be maintained.

Sometimes, policies or constraints can be modified. For example, plant capacity is a constraint, but management could decide to expand the plant. This means that there may be some confusion between what is considered a decision variable and what is a constraint. It is not important to make too fine a distinction. What is important is that management recognize the presence of constraints, with the understanding that they can be modified if appropriate.

Performance Measures

In making a decision, managers have goals or objectives that they are trying to achieve. Criteria or performance measures are quantitative expressions of these objectives. For example, our marketing manager with the new product introduction decision would have profit as one performance measure. Market share and return on investment may also be performance measures.

Intermediate Variables

A number of other variables are usually needed to include all the important factors in the decision problem. Often these are accounting variables that relate to cost or revenue factors. They are used to relate the decision variables and exogenous variables to the performance measures. They are thus intermediate variables in the sense that they are between the other variables. In our example of a new product decision, total revenue (price times quantity sold) would be an intermediate variable; the components of manufacturing and sales costs would also be intermediate variables.

The Model and Relationships between Variables

Figure 1–2 shows how the various categories of variables are related. The model is in the middle. Decision variables, exogenous variables, and policies and constraints are inputs to the model, and performance measures are outputs. The model itself represents the set of all relationships among the variables. Defining these relationships is the second important step in building a model (the first step, as discussed above, is defining the important variables).

Some relationships are accounting definitions. For example, profit is revenue minus expense, a simple accounting rule. Other relationships depend on physical limits, such as determining the amount of product that can be produced from a batch of raw

FIGURE 1–2
Model Inputs and Outputs

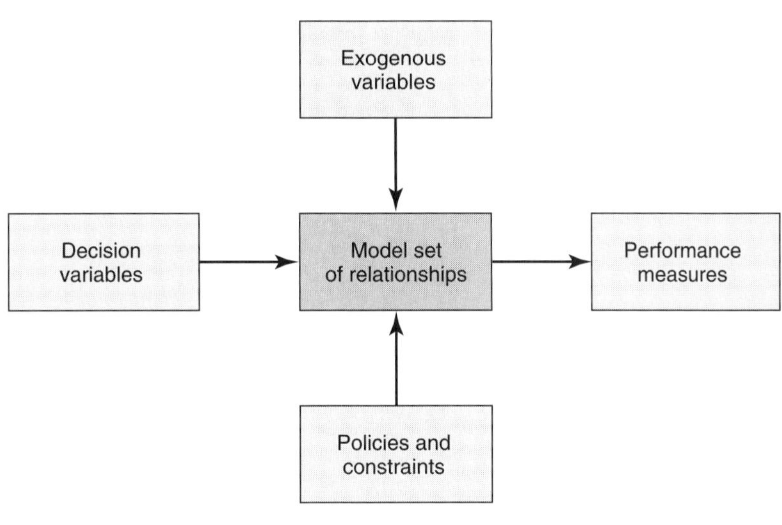

material. Some relationships are judgmental, representing management's understanding of how factors are related. Management's judgment about the reaction of customers to a price change is an example of such a relationship.

The model is the set of all these relationships. It is like a "black box" that transforms decision variables into performance measures for a specified set of exogenous variables and policies and constraints.

An Example: A Model of a Plywood Mill

These concepts are difficult to understand in the abstract. Hence, we introduce an example, a mill that peels logs to make plywood and sells the plywood to wholesale customers. Although the example is based on a real case,[2] it is somewhat simplified in order to show the major points. A real-world model used to make an actual business decision would usually be more complex.

Suppose the managers of a plywood mill are making their plans for next year. They face two decisions: one about plant capacity and another about labor rate. The plant capacity decision involves whether or not the firm should expand the mill, by how much, and when. Let us suppose that if they decide to expand now, additional capacity can be added in any quarter of next year.

The second decision relates to labor negotiations that are about to start with the company's labor union. The company and the union have to agree on a labor rate for the coming year. This is a joint decision, the result of the negotiation process.

The company has prepared forecasts of the prices for the plywood that it will sell next year, as well as projections for how much could be sold (i.e., an estimate of demand). The company has a policy of producing to order, so that no inventory of plywood is maintained. This means that the company can't sell more than it can

[2]See the Puyallup Forest Products case in Charles P. Bonini, *Computer Models for Decision Analysis* (Palo Alto, CA: Scientific Press, 1980), pp. 55–66.

Table 1–1 Important Factors in Model of Plywood Mill

Decision Variables
LABOR RATE. Average wage for mill employees (dollars per hour).
ADDITIONAL CAPACITY. Amount of capacity (MSF or thousands of surface square feet of plywood capacity) added in each quarter.

Performance Measure
PROFIT. Net profit from operating the mill each quarter, and for the year (M$ or $ thousands).

Exogenous Variables
PLYWOOD PRICE. Sales price for plywood each quarter (dollars per MSF).
DEMAND. Demand for plywood each quarter (MSF).
LOG COST. Purchase cost of logs (dollars per MBF—dollars per thousand board feet).
LABOR PRODUCTIVITY. Production output (MSF) per labor hour.

Constraints and Policies
No inventories of plywood. Production of plywood is scheduled to match sales. Analysis is to be done by quarters (i.e., three-month periods).

Intermediate Variables
REVENUE. Revenue from sale of plywood (M$ per quarter).
OPERATING EXPENSE. Expense associated directly with producing plywood (supplies expense, raw material expense, and labor expense—M$ per quarter).
SUPPLIES EXPENSE. Expense for supplies (M$ per quarter).
LABOR EXPENSE. Cost for labor (M$ per quarter).
LOGS REQUIRES. Amount of logs needed for production (MBF per quarter).
PLYWOOD PRODUCTION. Amount of plywood produced (MSF per quarter).
CAPACITY. Actual production capacity of mill (MSF per quarter).
OTHER EXPENSE. Total of other expenses, including sales expense, fixed expense, and equipment expense (M$ per quarter).
SALES EXPENSE. Expense for marketing plywood (M$ per quarter).
FIXED EXPENSE. Fixed expense (M$ per quarter).
EQUIPMENT EXPENSE. Lease cost for equipment (M$ per quarter).

produce in any period. Forecasts have also been made for the price of logs, the raw material from which plywood is made.

In order to produce plywood, the company incurs expenses for labor, supplies, and, of course, raw material (logs). Other expenses are related to sales. The company leases its production equipment and pays fees for these leases. There are also certain fixed (overhead) costs each period.

Table 1–1 shows a list of the important factors in this example. The abbreviation MSF stands for thousands of surface square feet and is the unit of measure for plywood. MBF stands for thousands of board feet, the unit for logs. M$ stands for thousands of dollars.

The list of variables in Table 1–1 may seem rather formidable at first, but you will see that it is really rather simple once the table is examined closely. Although the example is simplified, it is necessary to have enough complexity to illustrate how a model can be used.

Relationships: The Influence Diagram

We now turn to defining the relationships between the variables. Sometimes it is helpful to draw a diagram showing which variables relate to or influence others. For

FIGURE 1–3 Plywood Mill Model—Influence Diagram

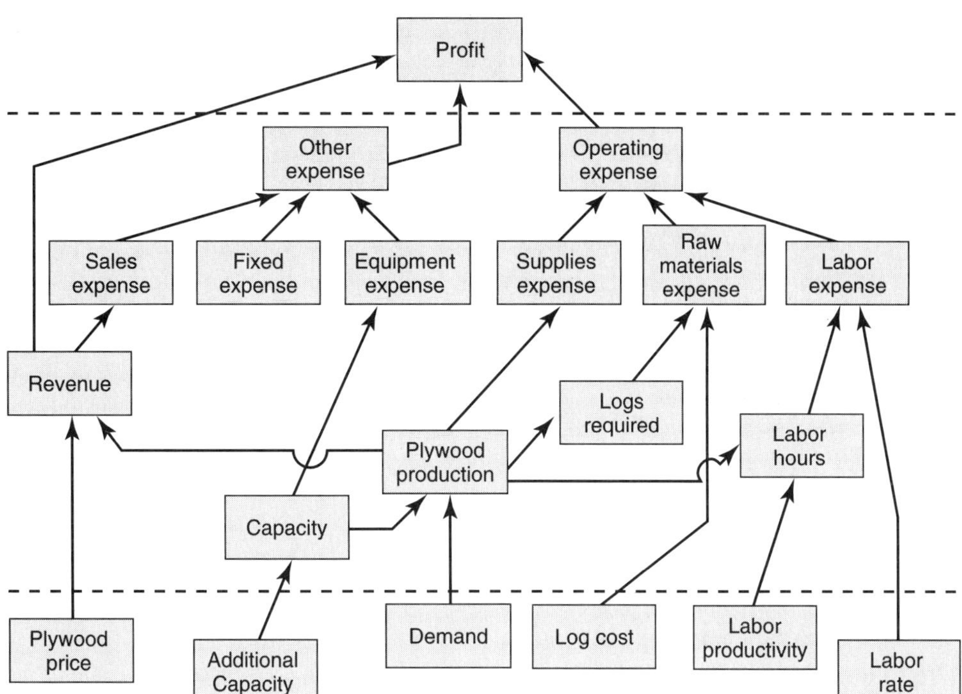

our example, Figure 1–3 is such a diagram, called an **influence diagram.** The lines with arrows indicate which variables are related to which. It isn't absolutely necessary to construct such a diagram, but it is often useful in understanding the model.

Note that there are two dashed lines across Figure 1–3. The only variable above the top line is the performance measure, PROFIT. The boxes below the bottom line contain either decision variables or exogenous variables, the inputs to the model. The variables and relationships in the middle make up the model.

We can now begin defining the relationships between the variables. We start with the physical relationships (those involving physical as opposed to dollar variables).

Physical Relationships

CAPACITY = 9200 + ADDITIONAL CAPACITY

The initial capacity of the mill is 9,200 MSF per quarter. To this is added any additional capacity that is leased.

PLYWOOD PRODUCTION = MINIMUM (CAPACITY, DEMAND)

Recall that plywood production in any quarter equals sales—the policy of no inventory requires this. If demand is higher than capacity, the firm will produce (and sell) all it can up to its capacity. That is, production is limited by capacity in this case. On the other hand, if demand is below capacity, then demand will limit production (and sales). Thus, production is limited by the smaller (i.e., minimum) of capacity or demand.

LOGS REQUIRED = .52 * PLYWOOD PRODUCTION

This relationship says that .52 MBF of logs are required for each MSF of plywood that is produced. The .52 is a constant that depends on the efficiency with which plywood can be manufactured from its raw material, logs. The asterisk * means "multiplied by." It is the standard symbol used in computer spreadsheets, and will be used as such throughout this chapter.

A short detour is needed here to explain constants. In building a model, there are numerical values, such as the .52 coefficient above, that are often estimated from cost or other data in the firm. Although these could be considered exogenous variables, they are of lesser importance and are assumed instead to be constants. They are expected to remain fixed (i.e., constant) for the analyses performed on the model.

LABOR HOURS = PLYWOOD PRODUCTION/LABOR PRODUCTIVITY

The total hours required for labor depends on the plywood production and on how productive labor is.

Financial Relationships

The remaining relationships in the model are financial. The following are simple accounting definitions and are self-explanatory. Division by 1,000 is necessary in some equations to convert to thousands of dollars.

PROFIT = REVENUE - OPERATING EXPENSE - OTHER EXPENSE
REVENUE = (PLYWOOD PRODUCTION * PLYWOOD PRICE)/1000
OPERATING EXPENSE = SUPPLIES EXPENSE + RAW MATERIAL EXPENSE + LABOR EXPENSE
OTHER EXPENSE = SALES EXPENSE + EQUIPMENT EXPENSE + FIXED EXPENSE
LABOR EXPENSE = (LABOR RATE * LABOR HOURS)/1000
RAW MATERIAL EXPENSE = (LOGS REQUIRED * LOG COST)/1000

A few relationships do need some explanation:

SUPPLIES EXPENSE = (28 * PLYWOOD PRODUCTION)/1000

Each MSF of plywood uses $28 in supplies in the production process. The $28 is another constant in the model.

SALES EXPENSE = .10 * REVENUE

Sales expense is 10 percent of sales revenue.

FIXED EXPENSE = 20

Fixed expense is $20,000 per quarter.

EQUIPMENT EXPENSE = (11 * CAPACITY)/1000

Recall that the mill equipment is leased. The fees for this lease are $11 per MSF of installed capacity per quarter.

Summary

Model building involves first simplifying a decision problem by selecting for study only the most important variables. These variables include decision variables (over which the decision maker has control), exogenous variables, performance measures, policies or constraints, and intermediate variables. The second step of model building is identifying the relationships among variables; that is, determining how the variables depend on one another. The model itself is the set of all these relationships.

Analysis Using the Model

The model for the plywood mill is now complete. We turn to management's use of the model. The first step is to make estimates for the exogenous variables. Let us suppose the estimates in Table 1–2 are prepared.

Note that these are predictions, based on informed judgment of the management, but they may turn out to be incorrect. One purpose of the model is to learn how errors in these estimates may affect the mill operations.

The decision variables are ADDITIONAL CAPACITY to be added and the LABOR RATE negotiated with the union. Suppose we assume for an initial base case that no additions to capacity will be made and that the labor rate is the same as last year at $9 per hour.

This allows us to complete the calculations for the model, and these are shown in Table 1–3. Note that the base case results in profit of $387,000 for the year.

You should pause at this point and carefully examine Table 1–3. Work through some of the numbers, using the relationships developed earlier. As an example, LOGS REQUIRED in the first quarter is 4,784, calculated as .52 * PLYWOOD PRODUCTION, one of the physical relationships described earlier. Note that PLYWOOD PRODUCTION is limited by capacity in the first, second, and fourth quarters, and by demand in the third.

Implementing the Model on a Computer

The calculations involved in Table 1–3 could, of course, be done by hand, and they would take perhaps 20 or 30 minutes, if you made no mistakes in arithmetic. This would be satisfactory if only one case or scenario were to be examined. However, we want to examine a whole series of cases, so a better approach would be to develop

Table 1–2 Estimates for Exogenous Variables

Variable	*Unit*	*First Quarter*	*Second Quarter*	*Third Quarter*	*Fourth Quarter*
Plywood price	$/MSF	125	125	130	130
Plywood demand	MSF	10,000	10,800	8,000	10,000
Log cost	$/MBF	75	75	75	80
Labor productivity	MSF/hour	0.4	0.4	0.4	0.4

TABLE 1–3 Plywood Mill Model Base Case

	Units	First Quarter	Second Quarter	Third Quarter	Fourth Quarter	Year Total
Decision Variables						
Additional Capacity	MSF	0	0	0	0	
Labor Rate	$/hour	9.00	9.00	9.00	9.00	
Exogenous Variables						
Plywood Price	$/MSF	125	125	130	130	
Plywood Demand	MSF	10,000	10,800	8,000	10,000	
Log Cost	$/MBF	75	75	75	80	
Labor Productivity	MSF/hour	0.4	0.4	0.4	0.4	
Physical Factors						
Actual Capacity	MSF	9,200	9,200	9,200	9,200	36,800
Plywood Production	MSF	9,200	9,200	8,000	9,200	35,600
Logs Required	MBF	4,784	4,784	4,160	4,784	18,512
Labor Hours Required	hours	23,000	23,000	20,000	23,000	89,000
Financial Factors						
Revenue	M$	1,150	1,150	1,040	1,196	4,536
Raw Material Expense	M$	359	359	312	383	1,413
Supplies Expense	M$	258	258	224	258	997
Labor Expense	M$	207	207	180	207	801
Total Operating Expense	M$	824	824	716	847	3,211
Sales Expense	M$	115	115	104	120	454
Fixed Expense	M$	20	20	20	20	80
Equipment Expense	M$	101	101	101	101	404
Total Other Expense	M$	236	236	225	241	938
Profit	M$	90	90	99	108	387

Note: Discrepancies in totals are due to rounding.

a computer version of the model. There are several ways this could be done. The model could be written in a general-purpose computer language such as BASIC, FORTRAN, Pascal, or C++; or it could be implemented on one of the spreadsheet programs such as Lotus 1-2-3, Excel, or Quattro that are available on personal computers. We shall illustrate this latter approach, since spreadsheet programs have become widely available, are easy to use, and are ideal for analysis of this type of problem.

A typical spreadsheet contains rows and columns, as shown in Figure 1–4. The rows are numbered starting at 1. The columns are indicated by letters, starting at A. A *cell* is at the intersection of each row and column and is indicated by its column and row designation. Thus, cell B3 is the cell in column B and row 3.

A cell can contain alphanumeric information such as the label "Decision Variables"; it can contain a number such as 9.00 for the Labor Rate; and it can also

FIGURE 1–4
Layout of Spreadsheet

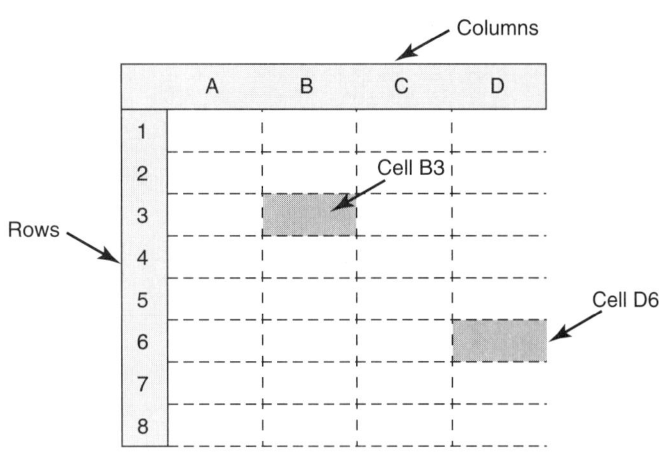

contain a formula. Formulas include the cell designations as variables. For example, if the cell D3 contained the following formula:[3]

=B3+C3

this would imply that the contents of cells B3 and C3 were to be added and the total stored in the D3 cell.

Table 1–4 shows the spreadsheet formulas for the first period (quarter) of our model. The first column in Table 1–4, column A, contains only the labels for the various variables in the model. The second column contains the units of measurement, which are also alphabetic information. The first several rows in the C column contain numeric values for the decision variables and the exogenous variables. The formulas are in column C starting at row 14.

The first formula, in cell C14, is:

=9200+C4

Since cell C4 contains Additional Capacity, this formula computes the actual capacity as the initial capacity of 9,200 MSF plus any additions. It is the spreadsheet equivalent of the relationship:

CAPACITY = 9200 + ADDITIONAL CAPACITY

developed on page 13.

Similarly, cell C15 contains:

=MIN(C9,C14)

[3]Commercial spreadsheet programs differ very slightly in how formulas are represented. We shall be using the Excel representation, which has an equals sign before each formula (versus a plus sign for Lotus 1-2-3 and Quattro). Excel does not include the sign @ as a part of a function name, as is done in other spreadsheets.

TABLE 1–4
Formulas as Entered on a Spreadsheet

	A	B	C
1			First
2		Units	Quarter
3	Decision Variables		
4	Additional Capacity	MSF	0
5	Labor Rate	$/hour	9
6			
7	Exogenous Variables		
8	Plywood Price	$/MSF	125
9	Plywood Demand	MSF	10000
10	Log Cost	$/MSF	75
11	Labor Productivity	MSF/hour	0.4
12			
13	Physical Factors		
14	Actual Capacity	MSF	=9200+C4
15	Plywood Production	MSF	=MIN(C9,C14)
16	Logs Required	MSF	=0.52*C15
17	Labor Hours Required	hours	=C15/C11
18			
19	Financial Factors		
20			
21	Revenue	M$	=(C15*C8)/1000
22			
23	Raw Material Expense	M$	=(C16*C10)/1000
24	Supplies Expense	M$	=(28*C15)/1000
25	Labor Expense	M$	=(C5*C17)/1000
26			
27	Total Operating Expense	M$	=C23+C24+C25
28			
29	Sales Expense	M$	=0.1*C21
30	Fixed Expense	M$	20
31	Equipment Expense	M$	=(11*C14)/1000
32			
33	Total Other Expense	M$	=C29+C30+C31
34			
35	Profit	M$	=C21-C27-C33

This is equivalent to the relationship:

PLYWOOD PRODUCTION = MINIMUM (DEMAND, CAPACITY)

Note that cell C9 is Plywood Demand, and cell C14 is Actual Capacity.

You should examine the remaining formulas in Table 1–4 to be sure you understand them.

Formulas for Other Quarters

The formulas for the other quarters of the year are similar, except they would be in columns D, E, and F of the spreadsheet. There is a procedure within the spreadsheet programs that allows one to copy or replicate the formulas to other columns when they are similar, as is the case here.[4] The totals for the year are sums of the items for the four quarters.

This section is not intended to be a detailed treatment of spreadsheet packages. They have many more features than we have space to illustrate here. Our purpose, rather, is to demonstrate how a case model can be set up in the spreadsheet format.

The analysis, using the spreadsheet program, is also quite straightforward. We simply make a change in one or more of the decision or exogenous variables, and the results appear on the computer screen almost immediately. It is also possible to modify the model by changing the relationships, or by adding new variables, or by extending the model over more time periods. Spreadsheet packages have the ability to create tables of results and to plot the results in various types of charts.

Examples of Analysis Using the Model

In the beginning of this chapter, we described the type of model we have built as a **case model.** This name comes from the type of analysis, which involves examining a number of cases or scenarios using the model. Each case uses different assumptions about the various variables in the model. Let us give some examples of how the managers at the plywood mill might examine a few such cases and thus use the model just developed to answer some management issues and to obtain insight into the decision problems they face.

Recall that the plywood mill management is facing negotiations with the union about the labor rate for the next year. The managers could use the model to analyze the effect of different labor rates on profitability. The current rate is $9 per hour; an increase to $10 could be entered in the model (by changing the values in the row labeled "Labor Rate" in Table 1–3). This results in a profit of $298,000 for the year, a reduction of $89,000. An even more interesting question is, "How much could the labor rate increase before the mill became unprofitable?" Eight different values for LABOR RATE are used in the model, first at $9 per hour, then $10, and so on through $16 per hour. Figure 1–5 shows a plot of the results. As can be seen, the break-even point (where profit is zero) occurs between $13 and $14 per hour, about $13.35.

[4]Cell C14 is the one exception to the statement that the formulas can be copied to the other columns. Cell D14 should be (=C14 + D4). That is, CAPACITY (in the second period) = CAPACITY (in the first period) plus second period ADDITIONAL CAPACITY. This formula should be entered in cell D14, and then it could be copied (replicated) to the third and fourth periods.

FIGURE 1–5
Break-Even Analysis for Labor Rate

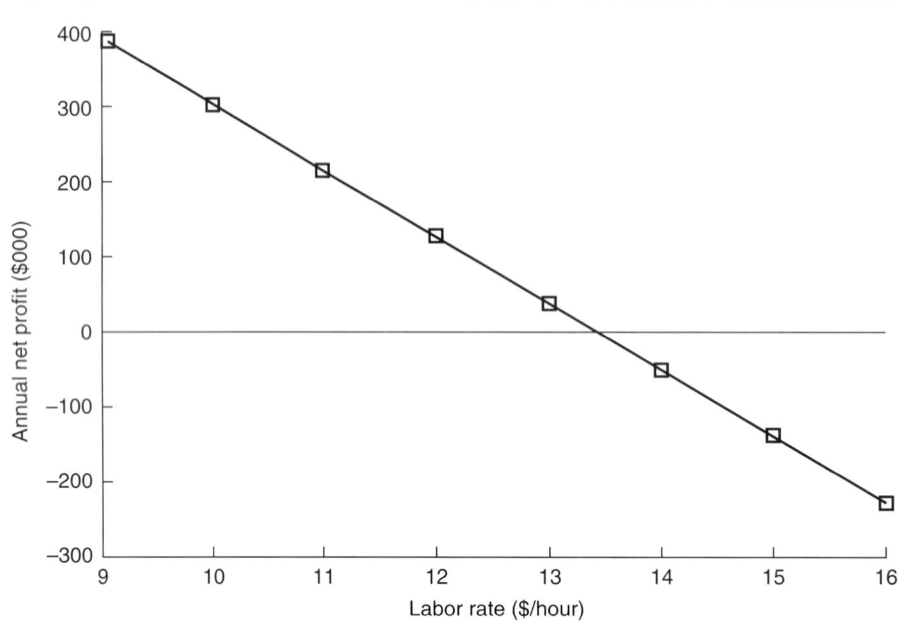

Suppose that as a part of the negotiations, management is asking the union to change some work rules that would increase the productivity of the workers. Suppose that these changes would increase LABOR PRODUCTIVITY from 0.4 MSF per hour to 0.5 MSF per hour. If the union were to agree to these work rule changes in exchange for an increase in the labor rate to $11 per hour, what would be the combined effect? This is shown in Table 1–5, which is the same as Table 1–3 except for these two changes (LABOR RATE is 11 and LABOR PRODUCTIVITY is 0.5). As you can see, there is a net increase in annual profit (from $387,000 to $405,000).

Another decision is whether or not additional capacity should be added to the mill. We can start with the base case and add different amounts of capacity in the first quarter. Table 1–6 presents the results of four cases, each with a different amount of added capacity. From this, it would appear that adding about 1,000 MSF of capacity would be best, although the differences are not very large.

Management might also ask how this capacity decision would change if the forecasts for plywood demand were incorrect. In other words, how sensitive is this capacity decision to demand? To examine this, let us suppose that the pattern of demand remains the same over the four quarters (second quarter high, third low), but that we consider one case in which the actual total demand turns out to be as little as half (50 percent) of the forecast demand, another case in which it is 60 percent of forecast, and so on up to 150 percent of forecast. At 100 percent, the actual and forecast are the same. Also, we consider the installation of 1,000 MSF, or 2,000 MSF, or 3,000 MSF additional capacity. This requires entering a large number of different combinations in the model and recording the results. Actually, some spreadsheet programs have procedures to do this kind of analysis in a few simple steps. The results are plotted in Figure 1–6 (some spreadsheets can even create plots like this).

TABLE 1–5 Plywood Mill Model Case with Increases in Labor Productivity and Labor Rate

	Units	First Quarter	Second Quarter	Third Quarter	Fourth Quarter	Year Total
Decision Variables						
Additional Capacity	MSF	0	0	0	0	
Labor Rate	$/hour	11.00	11.00	11.00	11.00	
Exogenous Variables						
Plywood Price	$/MSF	125	125	130	130	
Plywood Demand	MSF	10,000	10,800	8,000	10,000	
Log Cost	$/MBF	75	75	75	80	
Labor Productivity	MSF/hour	0.5	0.5	0.5	0.5	
Physical Factors						
Actual Capacity	MSF	9,200	9,200	9,200	9,200	36,800
Plywood Production	MSF	9,200	9,200	8,000	9,200	35,600
Logs Required	MBF	4,784	4,784	4,160	4,784	18,512
Labor Hours Required	hours	18,400	18,400	16,000	18,400	71,200
Financial Factors						
Revenue	M$	1,150	1,150	1,040	1,196	4,536
Raw Material Expense	M$	359	359	312	383	1,412
Supplies Expense	M$	258	258	224	258	997
Labor Expense	M$	202	202	176	202	783
Total Operating Expense	M$	819	819	712	843	3,192
Sales Expense	M$	115	115	104	120	454
Fixed Expense	M$	20	20	20	20	80
Equipment Expense	M$	101	101	101	101	405
Total Other Expense	M$	236	236	225	241	938
Profit	M$	95	95	103	112	405

Note: Discrepancies in totals are due to rounding.

TABLE 1–6 Results of Additional Capacity Added to Base Case in First Quarter

Additional Capacity (MSF)	*Annual Profit (M$)*
0*	387
1,000	405
2,000	374
3,000	330

*Base case.

Before commenting on the results of this analysis, we should point out that investments in new capacity would generally be evaluated over a long period of time. We have restricted the model to one year to keep it simple. Thus, our conclusions below are limited.

Figure 1–6
Effects of Errors in Demand Estimates and Additions to Capacity

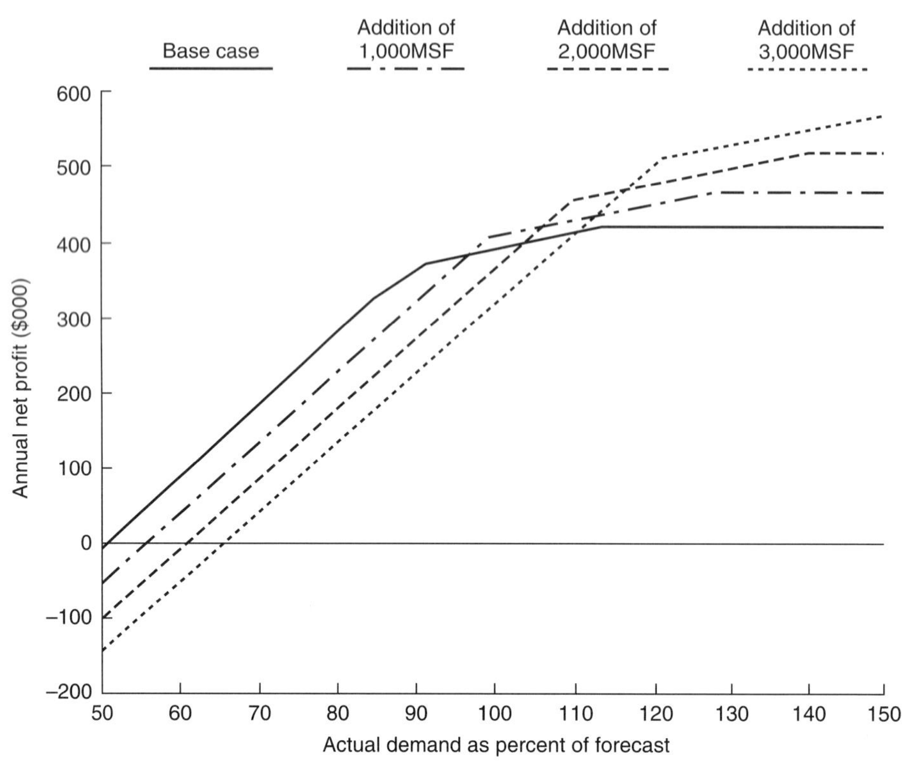

Note in Figure 1–6 that the decision about adding capacity does not significantly affect annual profit as long as the actual demand is close to forecast or only slightly above forecast. That is, the lines in Figure 1–6 are quite close together when actual demand is between about 100 percent and 110 percent of forecast. If management is reasonably confident about the demand forecast, then the capacity decision is not a critical one—the alternatives are about equally good. The cost of adding capacity is about equal to the additional profit the capacity creates. On the other hand, if management thinks that there is a good chance that actual demand might be substantially more or substantially less than forecast, then the capacity decision is indeed critical, since there are big differences between the best and worst alternatives. The top and bottom lines in Figure 1–6 at, say, the 70 percent and 130 percent points differ by over $100,000.

This analysis does not tell management what decision to make, only whether or not a problem exists. If indeed there is a substantial uncertainty about the accuracy of the forecasts, management could use decision analysis techniques as described in Chapter 6.

One of the major benefits of spreadsheet programs is that the manager gets to see instantly how *all* the variables included in the model are affected by changes in the data. This frees the manager, to some extent, from total dependence on a single performance measure. In the discussion above, we emphasized profit. Management would also be interested in the effects of the various plans being considered on other factors: for example, how many labor hours are required (and hence how many workers need to be hired) and how much raw material is needed (MBF of logs). As can be seen in Tables 1–4 and 1–5, this information is readily available and can be taken into account by management in making its decisions.

Sensitivity Analysis

The analysis above is an example of "what if" or sensitivity analysis. This type of analysis shows what happens if this or that change is made in one of the decision or exogenous variables. The aim is to see how the performance measure (profit) is affected; that is, how sensitive profit is to the change. This approach helps managers better understand the problem they face. Rather than producing "the answer," it is an aid to insight.

We can carry this analysis further by looking at the sensitivity of profit to each of the exogenous variables. This is done by considering cases for which each of the variables is 10 percent above and 10 percent below the base case values. The variables are varied one at a time, with the others set at the base case levels. The results are shown in Figure 1–7. This is called a **spider diagram** because of its resemblance to a spider web.

The steepness of a line in the spider diagram indicates how sensitive profit is to changes in that variable. Note that the line for plywood price is very steep; even small changes in the price have a big impact on profitability. A 10 percent reduction, for example, lowers profit to zero. On the other hand, the effect of changes in demand is more modest, particularly increases in demand (production is limited by capacity in this case). Again, note that these are one-at-a-time analyses, and they assume that all other factors are at base case levels. If desired, changes other than 10 percent can also be used.

FIGURE 1–7
Plywood Mill Model Sensitivity Analysis (Spider Diagram)

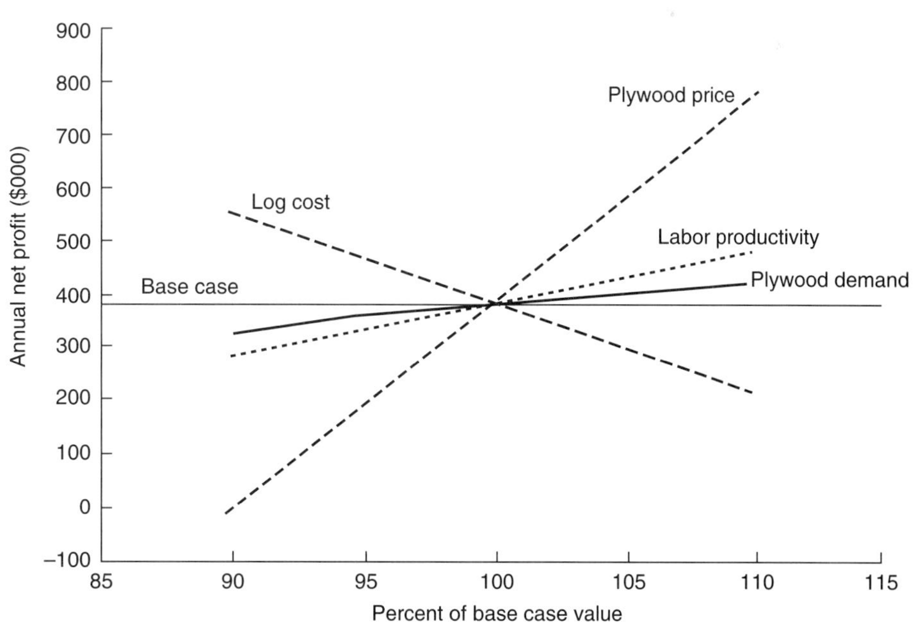

FIGURE 1–8 *The New York Times* **Model**

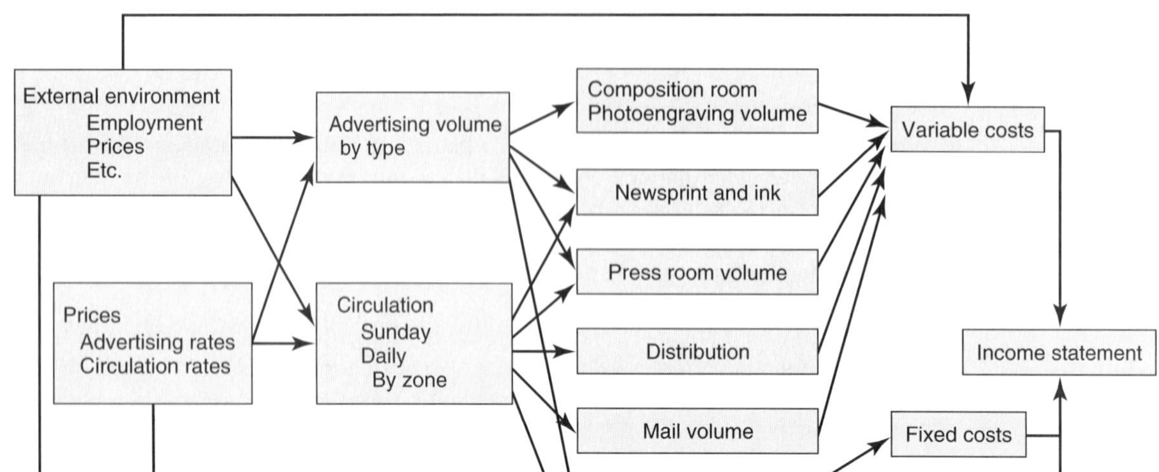

An Example: *The New York Times* Model

Figure 1–8 shows the outline of a model developed for *The New York Times* newspaper.[5] Exogenous variables such as employment, prices, and gross national product are used to forecast the levels of advertising by type (e.g., auto ads, department store ads, and so forth) and the circulation for the daily and Sunday papers by geographic zones. The advertising and circulation volumes are then converted into volumes for the various operating departments of the composition room and the press room and into requirements for newsprint and ink. Also, volumes of distribution and mail are estimated. Estimates of costs, including an allowance for inflation, are combined with these volume estimates to produce variable cost estimates. Fixed costs and revenues are also included and combined into a projected income statement.

The actual model contains about 400 equations and provides detailed estimates for revenues and costs. The model has been in use for a number of years and is integrated with the budgeting and planning processes at the *Times.* The model has been used to analyze new products such as special regional editions and to plan operations generally.

Summary

A model is a set of relationships among variables. This chapter illustrated a type of model called a case model. The method of analysis is to try out many different

[5]Leonard Foreman, "*The New York Times* Newspaper Planning Model," in *Corporate Planning Models,* ed. Thomas H. Naylor (Reading, Mass.: Addison-Wesley Publishing, 1979.)

examples or cases. In particular, sensitivity analysis examines the effect on the performance measures (e.g., profit) of changes in the decision and exogenous variables. The aim of sensitivity analysis is to increase the decision maker's understanding of the problem and the effect of different assumptions.

APPENDIX
PRESENT VALUE AND THE TIME VALUE OF MONEY

Case models of the type described in this chapter often involve cash flows over several years. Most major capital investments, for example, generate cash flows that last for several years. The time period in which money is received is an important aspect of its value. You should not be indifferent to receiving \$1,000 now as opposed to \$1,000 in five years. Even if you had no immediate need for the \$1,000 now, you could invest it and have substantially more than \$1,000 in five years.

A general approach to problems involving cash flows over time is to convert all such flows to present-value equivalents using a discount or interest rate and compound interest calculations.[6] The present value of \$1,000 received five years from now using a discount rate of 6 percent is:

$$\frac{1{,}000}{(1 + 0.06)^5} = 747.26$$

If you put \$747.26 in a bank account at an interest rate of 6 percent (compounded annually), you would have \$1,000 at the end of five years. In general, the present vale of any amount A, with discount rate r, received in n years is:

$$\frac{A}{(1 + r)^n}$$

If there is a stream of cash flows over a number of years, then the present value of the stream is the sum of the present values of each cash flow. Thus, the present value of \$10 received at the end of year 1, plus \$20 received at the end of year 2, is:

$$\frac{10}{(1 + 0.06)^1} + \frac{20}{(1 + 0.06)^2} = 27.23$$

Most of the spreadsheet programs have functions available to perform these present-value calculations. For example, many programs use the function @NPV (net present value) for this purpose.

Bibliography

Bodily, S. *Modern Decision Making: A Guide to Modeling with Decision Support Systems.* New York: McGraw-Hill, 1985.

Bonini, C. P. *Computer Models for Decision Analysis.* Palo Alto, CA: Scientific Press, 1980.

[6]For more detail on these procedures and for other techniques for evaluating cash flows over time, see H. Bierman and S. Smidt, *The Capital Budgeting Decision,* 7th ed. (New York: Macmillan, 1988).

Naylor, T. H. *Corporate Planning Models*. Reading, MA: Addison-Wesley Publishing, 1979.

Plane, D. R. *Management Science: A Spreadsheet Approach for Windows*. Danvers, MA: Boyd and Frazer Publishing, 1996.

Practice Problems[7]

1–1. Refer to the government contract example in this chapter. Suppose there was a 40 percent loss in yield due to tighter product specifications.

a. How many units would have to enter the production process in order to obtain 1,000 "good" units?

b. What is the total cost of obtaining 1,000 "good" units?

c. Should the contract be accepted? Why or why not?

1–2. The XYZ Appliance Company is considering replacing a metal gear with a plastic one. The plastic gear will save \$0.50 per unit but will require an expenditure of \$20,000 for a special mold to produce the gear. The special mold will last for one year. Annual sales are 80,000 units.

a. Should the company convert to the plastic gear? Why or why not?

b. Suppose now that the plastic gear is associated with a slightly higher first-year failure rate; specifically, for every 1,000 units sold, there will be an average of two additional failures from the plastic gear as compared with the metal gear. Failures cost the company \$40 (representing warranty repair costs and ill will). Now should the company convert to the plastic gear? Why or why not?

1–3. You have just founded MYOWN Company with the intention of manufacturing and marketing your invention—KARMA, a personal computer for turned-on people. Despite the rosy picture you paint of the company's future, the people at the bank insist on "some numbers." In particular, they want a statement showing your projected income, expenses, and profits for the first year.

The details of your planned operations are: A tentative decision has been made to set the selling price at \$1,600 for each KARMA. Manufacturing costs are expected to be \$300 per unit plus fixed costs of \$80,000 per year. Marketing costs are projected to be 10 percent of dollar sales plus \$10,000 in fixed costs. A preliminary estimate of first-year sales is 100 units.

a. Identify the decision variable(s), exogenous variable(s), performance measure, intermediate variable(s), and any policies or constraints for this problem.

b. Define the relationships between the variables identified in (*a*) above.

c. If you have access to a computer with a spreadsheet program, implement the model on the computer. The model format should look as shown here. You need to fill in the xxxxx spaces with numbers or formulas, as appropriate.

Unit Sales	xxxxx
Price	xxxxx
Variable Cost Unit	xxxxx
Projected Income Statement MYOWN COMPANY, 1997	
Sales (dollars)	xxxxx
Manufacturing Cost	xxxxx
Gross Margin	xxxxx
Marketing Cost	xxxxx
Profit Before Tax	xxxxx

d. Use the model to answer the following questions. (Note: Even if you don't have access to a spreadsheet, you can answer this part using a hand calculator, since the computations are not extensive.)

(1) What is the break-even number of units sold? The break-even point is the unit sales volume at which profit is zero. Make an approximate estimate.

(2) Suppose you could lower your price to \$1,400, and you believe this would increase unit sales to 130 units; or you could lower your price even further to \$1,200, and unit sales would be 150 units. Which of these (the two alternatives here plus the original) would you prefer?

Problems

1–4. Profit maximization has sometimes been described as the prime criterion to be applied in business decision making. If you were a business manager, what additional criteria would you employ in your decision making?

1–5. Consider some business or personal decision with which you are familiar. Describe this decision in terms of:

[7]Solutions for these problems are at the end of this chapter.

a. The alternatives that are available.
b. The criterion that you would use to select among the alternatives.
c. The important variables that should go into a model to aid in making this decision. To what extent can you quantify these variables?
d. To what extent can you quantify the relationships among the variables suggested in (*c*)?

1–6. Refer to Problem 1–3, the MYOWN Company. Suppose that you wish to extend the model to show profit for each year for five years. The initial sales price is set at $1,600, and the sales estimate for the first year is 100 units, as in Problem 1–3. Manufacturing cost is $300 per unit plus fixed costs of $80,000 per year for each year (again, as in Problem 1–3). However, suppose marketing costs are 10 percent of dollar sales (as in Problem 1–3) but fixed costs are $70,000 per year. Further, assume that unit sales increase 50 percent per year. That is, 1998 sales are 150 percent of 1997, 1999 are 150 percent of 1998, and so on.
a. Develop a model for this problem.
b. Implement the model on a spreadsheet program.
c. Use the model to answer the following questions:
(1) At the current sales estimate of 1997 sales of 100 units (growing 50 percent per year), how long will it be before your company shows a positive profit?
(2) Assuming the 50 percent growth rate continues to hold, how many units would you have to sell in the first year to just break even in the second year? How many units would you have to sell in the first year to break even in that year?
(3) Suppose that you could design KARMA to be more easily expandable as new devices come along. This would increase the unit manufacturing cost to $500 per unit. However, the sales growth rate should be 100 percent per year (i.e., unit sales would double each year). Is this alternative preferable?

1–7. Refer to Problems 1–3 and 1–6. Now add some additional complications. Assume that a market study has estimated the relationship between the price for KARMA and the first-year sales as:

$$\text{Unit sales} = 300 - .125 \cdot \text{Price}$$

for prices ranging from $500 to $2,000. You can set the price, but unit sales in the first year are determined by this function. As before, unit sales will increase 50 percent per year after the first year.

Suppose, further, that when unit sales exceed 200 units, you will introduce automated equipment that will cut the unit manufacturing cost from $300 per unit to $250 per unit. However, the fixed manufacturing cost will increase from $80,000 to $90,000 per year. (You should try to build this into the model so that it happens automatically when unit sales increase above 200 units. This can be done using the spreadsheet MIN or IF functions.)
a. Incorporate the changes into your spreadsheet model for the MYOWN Company.
b. Use the model to find the price that produces the largest total profit (sum over the five years). (Optional: If you are familiar with the concept of net present value, you can calculate the NPV of profits for the five years [use a 15 percent discount rate] and find the price that maximizes this value.)

1–8. The city manager of Suburbia is evaluating various levels of expenditures for police protection. She has found that the average response time (in minutes) to emergency calls is inversely related to the annual budget for Suburbia's police department. The specific relationship is:

$$R = \frac{50}{C}$$

where R = Average response time in minutes and C = Annual police budget in millions of dollars.

Each citizen of Suburbia evaluates the benefit of an emergency policy response as follows:

$$B = \$100 - \$10R$$

where B = Benefit in dollars. Thus, a response time of 10 minutes produces zero benefit, and a longer time produces a negative benefit.

There are 500,000 emergency calls annually in Suburbia.
a. Develop a spreadsheet model for this problem, assuming the performance measure is total benefit minus total cost. Evaluate alternative police budgets of $5 million, $10 million, $15 million, and $20 million. Which of these is preferred?
b. Now suppose the criterion is the ratio of total benefit divided by total cost. For the same possible budgets, which is most preferred?

More Challenging Problems

1–9. An executive is in the process of deciding on the price for a new product. His goal is to maximize profit. The alternatives are different possible prices from $2 per unit to $10 per unit. The model to be used is described below.

Let:
x = Number of units produced (and sold)
$C(x)$ = Total cost of producing x units
p = Price to be charged
NP = Total net profit (to be maximized)

Cost relationship: $C(x) = 800 + 1.25x$
Sales relationship: $x = -100 + 2{,}000/p$
Profit: $NP = p \cdot x - C(x)$

a. Comment on the model chosen by the executive in terms of the reasonableness of the relationships, the variables that were chosen (and ones left out), and the value of the model.

b. Find an approximate solution to the model by trial and error (i.e., try several values of price between \$2 and \$10, and try to find a price that gives a good profit).

1–10. An airport is considering installation of a sophisticated landing assistance device. The annual equivalent cost of this device (including all costs) is \$800,000 a year, which will not be recoverable from the airlines. The device will reduce the expected number of fatal crashes per year at the airport from 1.8 to 1.7.

The average flight into the airport carries 40 people (including crew), and the airplane has a resale value of \$2 million.

a. If the device is rejected, what implicit value is being placed on the value of the lives of occupants of the plane?

b. How much would you be willing to pay for the device?

1–11. The product manager of Crunchy Cereal is trying to determine the advertising budget for next year. She has the following information available: selling price is \$5 per case; variable cost of manufacture is \$2 per case; and the fixed costs for producing Crunchy Cereal totals \$100,000 per year. The manager has estimated the following relationship between sales of Crunchy Cereal (called X and measured in thousands of cases) and dollars spent for advertising (called Z and measured in thousands of dollars):

$$X = 50 + 1.2Z - 0.006Z^2$$

For:

$$0 \leq Z \leq 100$$

a. Formulate a model for net profit for Crunchy Cereal. That is, identify all variables and relationships necessary to determine profit.

b. Find an approximate optimal solution to the model by trial and error (that is, try a few values for advertising between \$0 and \$100,000, and find a good profit solution).

1–12. A computer company is considering introducing a new product, model B. Some of its sales would come at the expense of model A, a best-seller for the company. The economics are as follows:

	Model A	*Model B*
Fixed cost	\$10 million	\$20 million
Variable cost per unit	\$500	\$300
Wholesale selling price	\$1,500	\$1000

The fixed costs of model A have already been incurred, but not those for model B. Current sales of model A are 500,000 units annually. Introduction of model B would generate 600,000 units of B sold annually, but reduce A's sales to 300,000 units. The remaining product life for both products is one year; after that, they will be obsolete. Thus, a one-year analysis is appropriate.

a. Formulate a model to decide whether or not to introduce model B at this time. What decision would you recommend?

b. Suppose model A had not been previously introduced (and its fixed cost had not yet been incurred). Formulate a model for this situation and decide which product(s) should be introduced.

c. What other considerations would apply to the situation in (*a*)?

1–13. You are considering the purchase of an apartment building. The building contains 25 units and is for sale for \$300,000. You plan to keep the building for three years and then sell it.

You ascertain that the property taxes on the property are \$6,000 per year and that it will cost about \$300 per unit per year to administer and maintain the apartments. The taxes are expected to grow at a rate of 2 percent per year, and the maintenance costs are estimated to grow at a 15 percent per year rate.

You have not decided on the rent. Currently, the rent is \$300 per unit per month, but there is substantial turnover, and the occupancy rate is only 75 percent. That is, on average, 75 percent of the units are rented at any time. You estimate that if you lowered the rent to \$220 per unit per month, you would have 100 percent occupancy. Intermediate rental rates would produce intermediate occupancy rates (assume a linear relationship: Occupancy rate = 168.75 − .3125 · Rental rate). For example, a \$260 rental rate would have an 87.5 percent occupancy rate. You decide to fix the rental rate for the first year and increase it 10 percent per year for years 2 and 3. Whatever occupancy rate occurs in the first year will hold for years 2 and 3 also. For example, if you decide on the \$220 rate for year 1, the occupancy will be 100 percent all three years.

At the end of three years, you will sell the apartment building. The amount you expect to receive will be

TABLE 1–7
Spreadsheet Program

	Year 0	Year 1	Year 2	Year 3
Purchase Cost	xxxx			
Initial Rental Rate	xxxx			
Occupancy Rate	xxxx			
Maintenance Cost/Unit	xxxx			
Taxes	xxxx			
Sale Multiple	xxxx			
	Year 0	Year 1	Year 2	Year 3
Rental Rate		xxxx	xxxx	xxxx
Rental Income		xxxx	xxxx	xxxx
Expenses:				
Maintenance		xxxx	xxxx	xxxx
Taxes		xxxx	xxxx	xxxx
Total		xxxx	xxxx	xxxx
Operating Cash Flow		xxxx	xxxx	xxxx
Purchase Cost	xxxx			
Sale Receipt				xxxx
Net Cash Flow	xxxx	xxxx	xxxx	xxxx
Total Cash Flow				xxxx
(Present Value)				[xxxx]

some multiple of the rental income (before expenses) at that time. Your estimate is that this multiple will be 5.0. That is, if the rental income in year 3 is $75,000, then the sale price will be $375,000.

Your objective is to achieve the highest total cash flow over the three-year period. Cash flow in each year is the difference between rental income and expenses. Total cash flow includes that for each year plus the cash from the sale of the property minus its purchase cost. (Optional: Use net present value as the objective, with a discount rate of 15 percent.) *Note:* For the purpose of this exercise, ignore depreciation and other issues related to taxes.

a. Identify the decision variables, the exogenous variables, the performance measure, the intermediate variables, and the policies and constraints in this problem.

b. Construct the model by defining the relationships between the variables identified in (*a*).

c. Implement the model on a spreadsheet program. You may wish to use the format suggested in Table 1–7. The x's indicate that a number or formula is in that location. The last line is appropriate only if you use present value as the objective.

d. Use the model to find the initial rental rate that achieves the highest total cash flow (or highest net present value).

e. Study the sensitivity of total cash flow (or present value) to the following variables: maintenance cost per unit, annual taxes, and sale multiple. Do this by developing cases in which each of these factors is varied one at a time by 10 percent above and below the base case amounts given in the description above. Use the rental rate found in (*d*) for this analysis. Plot these results in a spider diagram. To which factor is total cash flow (or present value) most sensitive?

CASE 1–14

PATAWA DEVELOPMENT COMPANY

Alice and John Philips have founded the Patawa Development Company to build "spec" houses—that is, houses built on the speculation that a suitable buyer will be found. They are currently considering the purchase of an available lot in Sedona, Arizona, and they have made some preliminary plans about the size and type of house that could be built. The lot is not large, but it has a very scenic view of some of the famous Sedona rock formations.

Although the Philips have built spec houses before, none has been in the price range of the one in Sedona. Sedona is a fast-growing resort community, and the housing market is very uncertain.

The price of the lot is yet to be negotiated; the Philips think they can buy it for $160,000 dollars. They plan to build a 3,000-square-foot house on the lot, and they estimate the construction cost at $50 per square foot. Because the lot is sloped, there is some uncertainty about this cost. In addition, construction will require some earthmoving and drainage work; the amount of this is uncertain, although they have received an estimate of $50,000.

The major uncertainty is the sale price of the home. Based on a study of the Sedona realty market, the Philips expect to set a list price of $480,000 for the house (net of selling costs). However, they are quite unsure of this amount. If a buyer is found who really likes the house, the full list price can be obtained. In ordinary circumstances, they would expect to sell it for 10 percent less than list price; if the market is bad, an even lower price may be necessary. A related factor is how long it will take to sell the house. If a house sits on the market for some time, its list price tends to decline. One study estimated this decline at 2 percent per month.

The time taken to sell the house has another negative effect. The cost of developing the house will be financed by a bank loan. This includes the lot purchase cost, the construction cost, and the lot development cost. The cost of interest on this loan is .01 per month.[8]

The decision facing the Philips is whether or not to purchase the lot and proceed with building the house.

The Philips are concerned with the uncertainty in this decision problem. As a first step, they constructed high and low estimates for the various uncertain factors. These were not meant to be extreme cases but had the characteristic of "if things go well," "if things go as expected," and "if things go poorly." Table 1–8 summarizes these estimates.

a. Build a simple model using a spreadsheet to determine the profit the Philips can expect from this venture. Index months from month 1 to month 10. Assuming the "best guess" estimates, what decision is indicated?

b. Determine the sensitivity of your estimated profit to each of the factors listed in Table 1–8. Which factors potentially could change the decision?

TABLE 1–8
Uncertain Factors

Factor	*Best Guess Estimate*	*Low Estimate*	*High Estimate*
Lot cost	$160,000	−15%	+15%
Construction cost	$50 per square foot	−10%	+15%
Lot development cost	$50,000	−10%	+20%
Time to sell	2 months	1 month	10 months
Discount off list price	10%	25%	0%

Note: The list price of $480,000 is the initial offering. The list price declines by 2% per month, or $9,600 per month. Thus, the listing price for a sale in month 2 is $460,800 and that for month 10 is $384,000.

[8]For purposes of simplicity, ignore compounding in calculating interest cost. In other words, a loan for 6 months would have a total cost of 6 percent.

Case 1–15

Super Spuds, Inc.

Super Spuds, Inc., (SSI) purchases potatoes from growers and dehydrates them into potato flakes for sale to a large food processor. In the spring of the year, the company faces two decisions. The first involves how much of its potato requirements to purchase from the growers under a preseason contract. Such a contract in effect buys the potatoes before they are planted and guarantees the grower a specified price—in this case, $2 per hundredweight (cwt.). The remaining potatoes are purchased in the fall on the open potato market at whatever happens to be the market price at that time.

The second decision involves what price to charge the processor to whom SSI sells its potato flakes. This decision is actually reached in negotiations with the processor and also involves the quantity of potato flakes that the processor will order for that next year. In preparing for these negotiations, SSI has estimated that if it insists on last year's price of $33 per cwt. for flakes, the processor will likely order 800,000 cwt. It is possible to negotiate a price above or below this $33 price, but the effect will be that the processor will buy less (if higher price) or more (if lower price) than the 800,000 cwt. Members of SSI management have expressed their judgment about the relationship between the negotiated price and the flakes ordered as:

FLAKES ORDERED (Thous. cwt.) = 7400 - 200 * FLAKES PRICE

It takes six pounds of potatoes to make one pound of potato flakes. The variable cost for dehydrating the potatoes is $13 per cwt. of potato flakes up to 750,000 cwt., and $16 per cwt. above 750,000 cwt. Fixed costs are $4 million per year.

The cost of raw materials (process grade potatoes) depends, of course, on the decision about how much to buy using preseason contracts. However, management at SSI is considering changing this and could buy more or less of its requirements by preseason contract. The cost of potatoes using preseason contracts is $2 per cwt. The cost of purchasing potatoes on the open market is unknown. Management thinks that it might be anywhere from $1 per cwt. to $3 per cwt.

The profit for SSI is the revenue it gets from selling the potato flakes to the processor minus the costs of dehydrating the potatoes, the cost of purchasing the potatoes (preseason and open market), and the fixed costs.

a. Develop a model for SSI to aid in making the two decisions indicated. Identify the decision variables, exogenous variables, performance measure(s), intermediate variables, and policies and constraints. Then define the relationships between the variables.

b. Implement the model on a computer using a spreadsheet program.

c. Assume that SSI management is going to continue its policy of preseason contracting for one-half its potato requirements and that the forecast for the open market price for potatoes is $2 per cwt. (the same price as for the preseason contract). Calculate the SSI profit for a series of cases in which the price of potato flakes is varied from $31 to $34 in increments of $0.50 (that is, $31, $31.50, $32, $32.50, etc.). At what price is the profit the highest? How sensitive is the profit to differences in price between $32 and $33?

d. Assume a potato flakes price of $33 per cwt. Complete Table 1–9 by running a series of cases and calculating the profit for the different values of open market potato price and the different policies on what fraction of the potato requirements are obtained by preseason contracting that are shown. Which of these alternatives is most "conservative"?

TABLE 1–9

Percentage of Potatoes Obtained by Preseason Contract	**Open Market Price for Potatoes**		
	$1 per cwt.	*$2 per cwt.*	*$3 per cwt.*
25%	xxxx	xxxx	xxxx
50	xxxx	xxxx	xxxx
75	xxxx	xxxx	xxxx

CASE 1–16

CHASE MANUFACTURING[9]

Chase Manufacturing is a maker of small appliances and household gadgets, with a plant in Decatur, Indiana, and sales offices in Chicago. The products are sold under a variety of brand names through manufacturers' representatives who call on retail appliance dealers, hardware stores, and housewares specialty shops.

The research department at Chase has developed a new product—a wine bottle opener with distinctive features. The product is expected to have appeal as an inexpensive gift, especially during the Christmas season.

The executive committee at Chase is meeting to consider the new product. Jane Boxer, the marketing manager, opens the discussion.

> *Boxer:* I think this new wine bottle opener will be a winner for us. Although there are scads of openers on the market, ours is just unique enough to be a hit in the Christmas market. It is an ideal gift for the person who has everything.
>
> We plan to sell it through our normal channels and push it hard this year. By next year the novelty will have worn off, and we will probably drop it from the line.
>
> My plan calls for pricing the opener at $8 and for spending about $50,000 on advertising and promotion to inform and sell our customers on the product. As you know, our customers are primarily buyers for chain stores, specialty shops, and hardware stores. All our sales efforts are aimed at them. We estimate a total market potential of 104,000 units at the $8 price; and with the $50,000 advertising and promotion, we should reach about 65 percent penetration (i.e., sell 65 percent of 104,000, or about 68,000 units).
>
> I obtained estimates from accounting and manufacturing and prepared the projected income statement you have. (See Table 1–10.)

Jack Croxton, the controller, follows:

> *Croxton:* The estimates you used seem pretty reasonable to me, except for the general and administrative costs. Where did you get that 15 percent of sales calculation? Most of our general and administrative costs are in salaries and other fixed costs, and I would think this project would add at most $40,000 to these costs.
>
> *Boxer:* Our total corporate G&A expense was 15 percent of sales last year, and I simply used that same percentage. We will need to add a project manager and incur some other administrative costs, which I agree probably won't add more than $40,000. But shouldn't we use the same percent as total corporate G&A?

Mr. J. L. Chase, the president, interrupts.

> *Chase:* I agree that, on first blush, the project looks favorable. But why did you choose the $8 price and the level of $50,000 for advertising and promotion? Why not

[9]Source: Reprinted with permission of Stanford University Graduate School of Business. © 1985 by the Board of Trustees of the Leland Stanford Junior University.

TABLE 1–10

CASE MANUFACTURING COMPANY *New Wine Bottle Opener* *Pro Forma Analysis* *($000s)**	
Sales	$540.8
Manufacturing costs	282.8
Marketing costs	104.1
General and administrative costs	81.1
Total costs	468.0
Profit before tax	72.8

*Assumptions:
- Selling price, net of discounts—$8 per unit.
- Total market potential—104,000 units.
- Market penetration—65 percent.
- Unit sales (65 percent of 104,000)—67,600 units.
- Manufacturing costs—$80,000 plus $3 per unit.
- Marketing costs—10 percent of sales (sales commissions) plus $50,000 for advertising and promotion.
- General and administrative costs—15 percent of sales.

push the price down to $5? I'll guess there's a potential market of 200,000 units at that price. And perhaps we should spend more than $50,000 on advertising to ensure that we capture a good part of that potential.

Croxton: I worry, J. L., that if we cut the price, the margin will be too low to make any profit.

Manuel Olivera, the production manager, adds.

Olivera: Besides, we have limited production capacity. If we were to produce anything over 75,000 units, we would need to use overtime and do some subcontracting. This would push our variable costs up to $4 per unit for the units over 75,000. In addition, for volumes above 75,000 we would need some machinery, adding about $10,000 to the $80,000 that Jane has budgeted.

Croxton: If anything, I think we ought to consider a higher price, say $10 per unit. I realize that this would cut down on the market potential, but we would be making a healthy margin on those we sell.

Boxer: At a price of $10, I think our market potential would be only about 40,000 units.

Discussion continues for a few minutes, with no consensus about what price should be set.

Chase: Jane, I don't understand your points about market potential and how the $50,000 advertising will allow us to capture 65 percent of the market potential. Would you explain more?

Boxer: Well, J. L., you remember that research project that we have been conducting with our ad agency. This is our first chance to apply the results. Based upon interviews with a sample of customers, we have been able to assess the effectiveness of our past advertising. The result projected for this product is shown in Figure 1–9. We estimated our penetration of total market potential at three levels of advertising.

FIGURE 1–9
Chase Manufacturing Market Penetration versus Advertising Expenditures

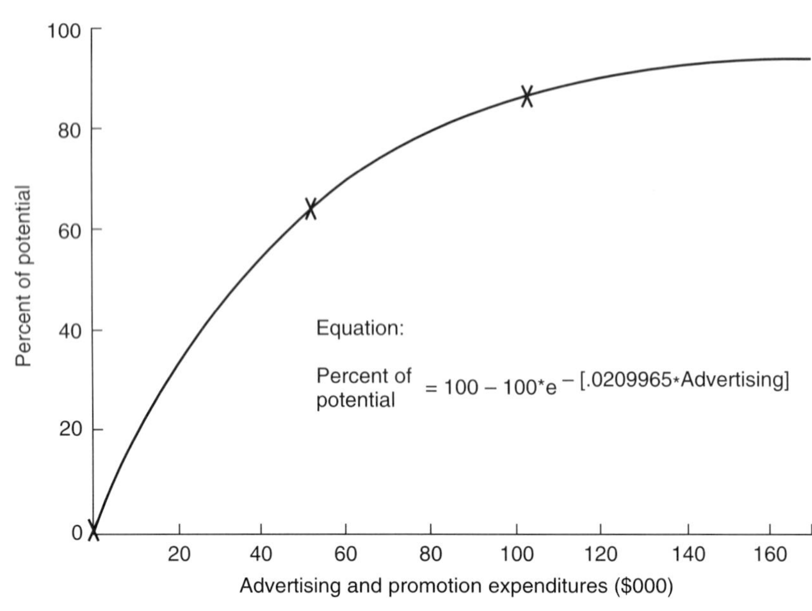

Obviously, if we spend nothing at all on promotion and advertising, our customers won't even know about our product and hence can't buy it. This is the point shown at the origin in Figure 1–9. We then carefully considered how we would spend a budget of $50,000 (what ads we would use, what special deals, and so on), and estimated that we would reach about 65 percent of the market potential. That is, we would reach 65 percent of all those who would be inclined to buy. Similarly, we estimated about 88 percent penetration of the total potential with an expenditure of $100,000. One of my assistants, who has a mathematical bent, fit the mathematical function shown to the three points. The curve makes sense to us.

Chase: But how did you settle on the $50,000 for advertising and promotion?

Boxer: Actually, it is tentative. We plan to do some more thinking about what expenditure would be optimal.

a. Build a model to aid the Chase executive committee in deciding about price and advertising for the new wine bottle opener.

As a help in this process, consider Figure 1–10. This chart shows three points relating price to total market potential. The point with a price of $8 and market potential of 104,000 units was given in the Boxer plan of Table 1–10. The point with a price of $5 and market potential of 200,000 units was suggested by Chase. The point with a price of $10 and market potential of 40,000 units was also given by Boxer.

Suppose it is reasonable to connect these points by a straight line, as shown in Figure 1–10. Economists call this a demand function. The equation of a straight line is:

$$\text{Market potential} = m \cdot \text{Price} + b$$

where m and b are constants to be determined. The constant m is called the slope of the line. See if you can determine the values of m and b by trial and error. If, after a while, you don't succeed, consult footnote 10.[10]

[10]The equation is: Market potential (thousand units) $= 360 - 32 \cdot$ Price

FIGURE 1–10
Chase Manufacturing Market Potential versus Price

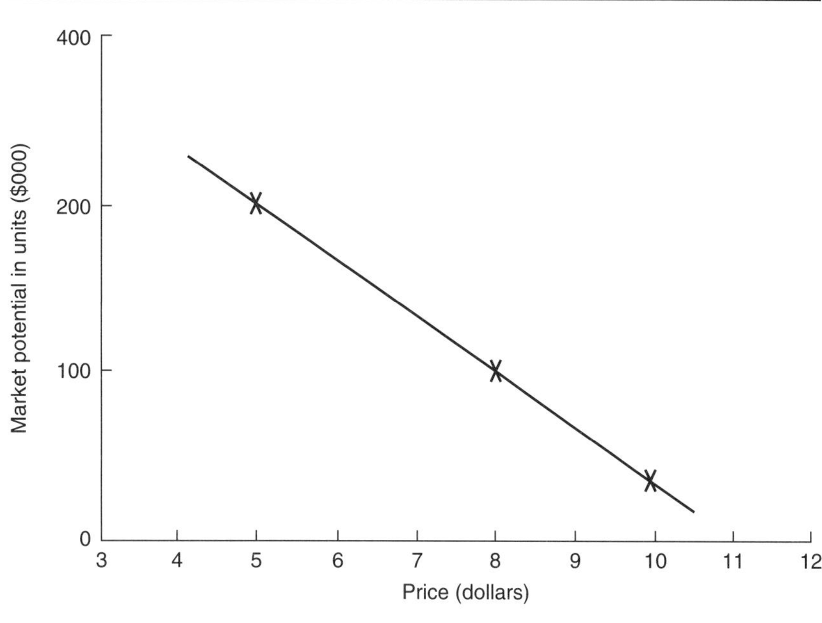

b. You should then define the other relationships in the Chase model.

c. Finally, use your model to calculate the profit for the following case:[11]

Price = $7 per unit
Advertising = $100,000

d. Implement your model using a spreadsheet program. Then, using trial and error, find the values for price and advertising that achieve the most profit.

e. Determine the values for profit if advertising is $70,000 and for prices from $7 to $9 (at $0.10 intervals). Plot this as a curve showing the relationship between price and profit. Repeat this for advertising of $90,000, and draw the curve on the same chart. Repeat again for advertising values of $100,000, $110,000, and $130,000. (All this can be done in a couple of steps with some spreadsheet programs.)

Based on these curves, what can you say about the best price and advertising?

CASE 1–17

GOTHAM CITY TIMES[12]

The executive committee of the *Gotham City Times* newspaper is meeting to consider proposals from the promotion department and from the operations manager. You, as assistant to the publisher, have been asked to study the financial effects of these proposals.

Operations of the *Times*. Most newspapers, including the *Times,* receive revenues from two sources: (1) circulation—that is, sales of newspapers to the reading public, and (2) sales

[11]In case you do not have a calculator that computes powers of *e,* the value of $e^{-(.0209965)(100)} =$ .122.

[12]Source: Reprinted with permission of Stanford University Graduate School of Business, © 1981 by the Board of Trustees of the Leland Stanford Junior University.

of advertising space. Costs are related to (1) the distribution system (getting the newspaper to customers); (2) editorial and news coverage; (3) composition; that is, setting type, photo-engraving layout, and artwork; (4) pressroom—that is, running the presses to produce the paper; and (5) newsprint (paper) and ink.

The circulation and advertising are interdependent for the *Times.* A larger circulation should lead to more advertising revenue, since the advertising would be reaching a larger audience, and advertisers would find this favorable. Similarly, readers buy a newspaper, in part, for the advertising.

The Revenues and Costs. For purposes of planning, a month is considered as a unit, and average monthly values for circulation, advertising, and news are used. The current average daily circulation is 1 million (or 30 million total per month). The average revenue is $0.15 per paper per day.

Advertising is measured in column inches. Currently, the paper contains 225,000 column inches of advertising per month, and this generates revenue of $20 per column inch. Editorial features and news make up the rest of the newspaper and are running currently at 135,000 column inches per month. No change in the space devoted to this category is contemplated. A newspaper page at the *Times* contains 200 column inches.

The variable costs of composition are shown in Table 1–11. The variable costs for the pressroom are shown in Table 1–12. A sheet is one copy of the page of the newspaper. For example, if a given edition contains 50 pages for the 1 million circulation of the *Times,* this results in 50 million sheets for that day. Note that the regular-time capacity of the pressroom is 1,500 million sheets per month.

Variable distribution costs depend upon the circulation and size, and they average $40 per ton of newspaper delivered. The fixed costs for editorial, composition, pressroom, and distribution are shown in Table 1–13. The cost of newsprint is $120 per ton and is entirely

TABLE 1–11
Cost of Composition

Type of Copy	*Variable Cost (per column inch)*
Advertising copy	$4
News, editorial, and feature copy	$6

TABLE 1–12
Pressroom Costs and Capacity

	Variable Cost (per million sheets printed)	*Capacity (in million sheets per month)*
Regular time	$ 800	1,500
Overtime	$1,200	Unlimited

TABLE 1–13
Fixed Costs

Department	*Fixed Cost ($000s per month)*
Editorial, news, and features	$1,000
Composition	90
Pressroom	300
Distribution	700
	$2,090

variable. A ton of newsprint is sufficient for printing 90,000 sheets. Because of strikes in some pulp mills, no more than 20,000 tons of newsprint will be available to the *Times* through regular suppliers each month. Newsprint in excess of 20,000 tons can be obtained only at a cost of $160 per ton.

The Proposals. The promotion department is considering a series of alternatives to increase circulation (trial subscriptions at reduced price, for example). Two of these proposals are shown as alternatives B and C in Table 1–14 indicating both the increased circulation and the cost of obtaining this increase. The cost is incurred in the first month, and the increase in circulation generally lasts about three months.

Also shown in Table 1–14 are the advertising volumes at the current rate of $20 per column inch, and the volume if the rate were to be increased to $22. Thus, proposals for changes in this rate could be evaluated at different possible levels of circulation. Advertising also has seasonal swings, above or below the normal levels given in Table 1–14. In particular, next month should be at normal, the following month at 15 percent above normal, and the third month at 10 percent below normal.

In addition, the operations manager wants to contract out the printing of various sections of the Sunday paper, with the aim of reducing or eliminating overtime in the pressroom. (*Note:* Various sections of the Sunday paper are printed all during the week, so this outside printing would have an even effect on the pressroom schedule.) The operations manager has a quote from a local printer to do the printing *and* supply the newsprint for $2,600 per million sheets printed. The outside printer, however, insists on a three-month contract with the same amount of work each month.

a. Indicate the general objective(s) for the model and the specific performance measure(s) that you would use.

b. Indicate in general terms the decisions to be made, and then define the specific decision variables to be used.

c. Identify other important variables (exogenous and intermediate) needed in the model. Be specific, and define the variables that should be used and the units of measurement.

d. Indicate what policies limit or constrain the decisions.

e. Indicate the relationships that must be identified in building the model. Be specific; that is, show the equations.

Consider as the base case one with the following values for the decision variables:

Initial circulation = 1 million per day
Price of advertising = $20 per inch
Initial quantity of advertising = 225,000 inches
Sheets printed outside = 0

TABLE 1–14
Promotion Alternatives and Effects on Circulation at Different Advertising Rates

Alternative	*Circulation (average daily)*	*Cost of Obtaining Additional Circulation ($000s)*	*Advertising Volume (thousands of column inches) at $20 rate*	*Advertising Volume (thousands of column inches) at $22 rate*
A (Base Case)	1,000,000*	0	225*	200
B (+10%)	1,100,000	400	235	225
C (+20%)	1,200,000	800	240	230

*Current levels.

TABLE 1–15

Parameter	Range		
	Low	*Base Case*	*High*
Newsstand price	.14	.15	.18
Pressroom capacity	1,400	1,500	1,700
Amount of editorial material	120	135	150
Initial quantity of advertising	200	225	240
Cost of purchasing newsprint (in excess of 20,000 tons)	120	160	180

f. Examine the proposal to have sheets printed outside as suggested by the operations manager. Should this be done? If so, for about how many million sheets per month should the contract be made?

g. If initial circulation could be increased by 1 percent with everything else remaining the same, what would be the effect on total profit for the quarter? Does this seem strange? How would you explain it?

h. At what level of circulation would quarterly profit be at $1 million?

i. How much would the initial quantity of advertising have to drop before quarterly profit became negative?

j. Papers in some cities have recently raised the newsstand price of the paper. Suppose *Gotham City Times* were to raise its price (other things remaining the same). Would this have a major or minor effect on profitability?

k. There are six possible combinations described in Table 1–14—alternatives A, B, and C, each with an advertising rate of either $20 or $22. With each of these, there are variations depending on how many (if any) sheets are printed outside. Pick two or three plans that you think might be presented to senior management for further consideration.

l. Consider each of the five parameters in Table 1–15. Each is given a range over which it might vary. How sensitive is the total profit to these variations? To which is profit most sensitive? Draw a spider diagram.

Solutions to Practice Problems

1–1. *a.* Set 1,000 = (1 − .40)*X*, and solve for *X*: *X* = 1000/.60 = 1,667 units.

b. Total cost = $5,000 + $30(1,667) = $5,000 + $50,000 = $55,000

c. Since revenue is only $50,000, under these circumstances the contract should be rejected (a loss of $5,000 would result if the contract were accepted).

1–2 *a.* The annual saving from the plastic gear is (50¢) (80,000 units) = $40,000. Since the annual cost of conversion is only $20,000, the company should convert to the plastic gear.

b. Additional annual costs of the plastic gear due to higher failures are ($40) (2/1000)(80,000) = $6,400. Thus, total costs are $20,000 + $6,400 = $26,400. This is still less than the saving of $40,000, so the company should still convert to plastic.

1–3 *a.* Decision variable: Price.
Exogenous variables: Unit Sales, Fixed Costs (both manufacturing and marketing), Variable Cost/Unit.
Performance measure: Profit
Intermediate variables: Sales (dollars), Manufacturing Cost, Marketing Cost, Gross Margin (optional).
Policies/constraints: None.

b. Relationships:
Sales (dollars) = Unit Sales * Price
Manufacturing Cost = 80,000 + 300 * Unit Sales
Gross Margin = Sales (dollars) − Manufacturing Cost
Marketing Cost = 10,000 + .10 * Sales (dollars)
Profit = Gross Margin − Marketing Cost
(If variable Gross Margin is not used, then Profit = Sales (dollars) − Manufacturing Cost − Marketing Cost.)

c. Using the format given in the problem, and assuming the labels are in column A and numbers and formulas in column B, we have:

	A	B
1	Unit Sales	100
2	Price	1600
3	Variable Cost/Unit	300
4		
5	Projected Income Statement	
6	MYOWN COMPANY, 1997	
7		
8	Sales (dollars)	= B1*B2
9	Manufacturing Cost	= (80000 + (B3*B1))
10		
11	Gross Margin	= B8-B9
12		
13	Marketing Cost	= (10000 + (.10*B8))
14		
15	Profit Before Tax	=B11-B13

d. (1) The break-even point occurs at a unit sales of about 79.

(2) The three alternatives and their profits are:

Base case: Price = 1,600; Unit sales = 100;
Profit = $24,000
Price = 1,400; Unit sales = 130;
Profit = $34,800
Price = 1,200; Unit sales = 150;
Profit = $27,000

Looking only at profit, the $1,400 price is best.

Motivating Example

Tata Iron and Steel Company—India

Tata Iron and Steel is India's largest producer of iron and steel, and, with annual production of 2.4 million tons, it is also one of the world's larger producers.[1] A simplified schemata of the Tata steel-making process is shown below. Iron ore is converted into hot iron metal in a blast furnace and then made into steel in one of three types of furnaces. The steel emerges from the furnaces as hot ingots, which are rolled into various semifinished products (slabs, billets, bars, etc.) in rolling mills.[2] The intermediate products can be sold to outside firms for finishing. Alternatively, Tata can finish them on its own finishing mills into various types of plate, tube, strips, structural steel, and other products.

In recent years, Tata faced a major problem. The various furnaces and mills required substantial electric power to operate. Although Tata supplied part of its power needs from its own generating plants, much of the power was supplied by governmental agencies. These agencies were suffering major power shortages, which were passed on to Tata. When a power shortage occurred, it forced Tata to shut down a part of its operations. This turned a profitable operation when power was available to one losing money when there were shortages.

A debate emerged within Tata management about what operations should be shut down when a power shortage occurred. The conventional wisdom indicated that the mill should maximize tonnage produced, and hence the finishing mills should be shut down since they were not adding tonnage but only finishing tonnage already produced. This implied a product mix with more emphasis on semifinished products and less of finished products.

Tata built a linear programming model of the steel-making process, taking into account the contribution of all the products, the capacities of the various stages of production, and the electric power required. (The details of this model will be discussed in a few pages.) The results indicated that a very different strategy was optimal—in particular, a balance of semifinished and finished products generated more profit (even though it resulted in less tonnage). In fact, using the new strategy resulted in an increase in profit of one-half million dollars per day when there was a power shortage. Over the course of one year, the company estimated that it had additional profits of $73 million because of the use of the linear programming model.

In addition to its use in helping determine the optimal product mix under reduced resource availability, the model has also been used by Tata to examine the profitability of building more electrical generating capacity of its own, to determine the price of scrap metal that might be used in the operations, and for other decisions.

[1] This example is based on Sinha *et al.*, "Strategic and Operational Management with Optimization at Tata Steel," *Interfaces* 25, no. 1 (January–February 1995). The paper was a winner of the Edelman award, given for outstanding applications of Management Science.

[2] There is also a continuous casting process for directly converting molten steel into products.

Example of Linear Programming Model

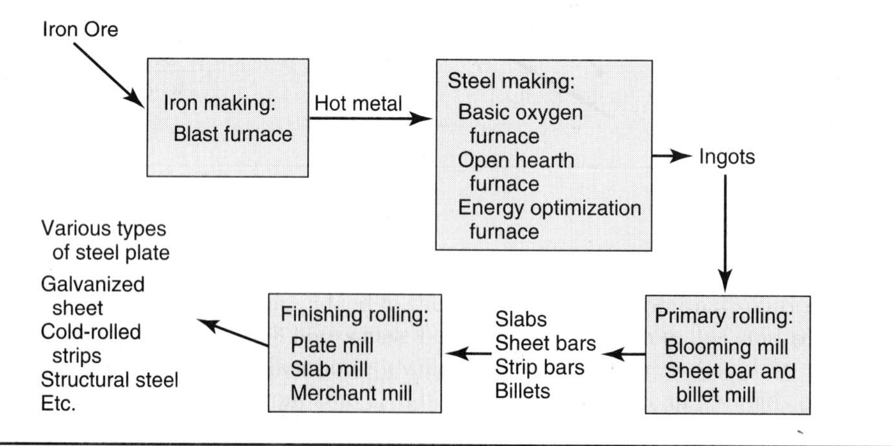

CHAPTER

2 Introduction to Linear Programming

Managers use models to aid in solving and understanding business decision problems. In general, a manager is trying to achieve some objective such as maximizing profit or minimizing cost. There are a set of factors under the control of the manager, called the decision variables. There are also a number of factors that limit or constrain what can be done. These may include, for example, capacities of plant and equipment, limits on market demands, or processing and delivery requirements.

A mathematical model is a simplified representation of the decision problem in which the decision variables, objective, and constraints are represented by mathematical symbols and equations. A linear programming model, or LP model, is a particular type of mathematical model in which the relationships involving the variables are linear, and in which there is a single performance measure or objective. An advantage of this type of model is that there exists a mathematical technique, called **linear programming,** that can determine the best or optimal decision even when there are thousands of variables and relationships. This chapter considers the formulation of linear programming models. The solution and interpretation of the results are treated in following chapters.

Since its discovery in the late 1950s, linear programming has been applied to a wide variety of decision problems in business and the public sector. The Tata Steel example is one current illustration. The formulations in this chapter and the problems and cases at the end are designed to give an appreciation for the diversity of problems to which linear programming can be applied and its value as a management tool.

In the linear programming model, there is a set of **decision variables** X_1, X_2, . . . , X_N. The linear programming model is designed to maximize (or minimize) an **objective function** of the form:

$$f = C_1X_1 + C_2X_2 + \ldots + C_NX_N$$

where f is some economic objective such as profits, production, costs, workweeks, or tons shipped. More profits are generally preferred to less profits, lower costs are preferred to higher costs, and so on. The manager wishes to select values for the decision variables to achieve the most profit, or least cost, or most production, and so forth. All of the coefficients C_1, C_2, . . . , C_N are constants, and all of the Xs are of the first power (no squares or cubes, for example). Thus, the function f is a **linear** function.

Generally, the manager cannot arbitrarily determine the values for the decision variables, the *X*s. Rather, the choice is limited by a set of relationships or constraints. These relationships involving the *X*s are also linear in form and are **linear inequalities** or **linear equalities:**

$$A_1X_1 + A_2X_2 + \ldots + A_NX_N \leq B_1$$

The *A* coefficients are constants. The constant B_1 restricts *f*, the objective function, as a result of restricting the decision variables, $X_1, X_2, \ldots, X_N$ (instead of $\leq$, we could have $\geq$ or an equality). The solution provided by linear programming is the set of values of the decision variables that achieves the desired maximum (or minimum) within the various constraints.

Linear programming does not allow for uncertainty in any of the relationships; there cannot be any probabilities or any random variables. Thus, the problem of maximizing the objective function subject to the various constraints is conceptually simple. Where there are only a few variables, common sense and some arithmetic will yield a solution, and decision makers have solved such problems for generations. However, as is often the case, intuition is of little use when the problem is more complex; when the number of decision variables is increased from three or four to hundreds or thousands, the problem defies rule-of-thumb procedures. Linear programming has made it possible to handle problems with large numbers of constraints in an orderly way.

This technique has exceptional power and generality. It is applicable to a variety of problems in a modern business organization and may be handled in a routine way with the aid of modern computers. It is one of the quantitative techniques that has provided management with a remarkable leverage on a set of problems that defied efficient solutions a relatively few years ago.

As a simple example, consider the following problem, which can be solved by the use of common sense or marginal analysis. Assume the incremental profit of product A is \$5 per unit, the profit of product B is \$2 per unit, and we can sell all we make of both products; further, either product may be produced with the same equipment. We can compute which product we should produce once we find out the capacity of our facilities in terms of A and B (see Table 2–1). The equipment can produce 100 units of A per day, or 600 units of B per day.

In this simple example, product B is obviously a more desirable product than A, since \$1,200 of profits per day is better than \$500. Now assume a more complicated problem where the plant is capable of making 20 different products in 15 different departments, and each product requires different production time in each department. If the difficulty of this problem is not impressive, assume that each department contains 10 processes, and each product requires different production time in each process. How do we determine the optimum product mix? A problem of this type is best solved by linear programming. The term **linear** is appropriate, since all profit

TABLE 2–1

Product	*Capacity (units per day)*	*Per Unit Profit*	*Total Incremental Profit per Day*
A	100	\$5	\$ 500
B	600	2	1,200

and production relationships are assumed to be proportional or linear; that is, the highest degree of any variable is 1, and no variables are multiplied by any other variable.

Because linear programming methods are generally used to solve complex problems involving many variables and constraints (often hundreds or thousands), a computer is necessary. The simplex method is the most common procedure and is widely available; it is included on many current spreadsheet packages for personal computers. Details of this method are treated in later chapters. Simple problems can sometimes be solved by graphic methods, and the next chapter introduces these methods primarily for the insight they provide about the problem solution.

In some of the examples to follow, the answers will be obvious; this is because the examples were constructed to be as simple as possible. In other examples, more complicated problems are treated, and some of the exercises are quite complex. The reader should keep in mind that we are attempting to illustrate a technique that may be applied to extremely complex problems. We apply it to simple situations for expository purposes. In practice, the computations in complex linear programming problems would be done on a computer.

Formulation of Linear Programming Problems

Before going into the details of learning how to solve linear programming problems, it is important to learn how to define the variables and equations—generally, how to set up a business problem in the form of maximizing (or minimizing) a linear function f, subject to linear constraints. We shall use the term **formulation** to mean translating a real-world problem into a format of mathematical equations. Formulation is often the most challenging part of analyzing a business problem.

We shall study several different problems, offering some experience in formulation and introducing some of the wide variety of problems that can be analyzed by linear programming.

Example 1: A Product-Mix Problem

A manufacturing firm produces two products, A and B. Each of these products must be processed through two different machines. One machine has 24 hours of available capacity, and the second machine has 16 hours. Each unit of product A requires two hours of time on both machines. Each unit of product B requires three hours of time on the first machine and one hour on the second machine. The incremental profit is \$6 per unit of product A and \$7 per unit of product B, and the firm can sell as many units of each product as it can manufacture.

The objective of the firm is to maximize profits. The problem is to determine how many units of product A and product B should be produced within the limits of available machine capacities.

Formulation. Let:

X_1 = Number of units of product A to be produced

X_2 = Number of units of product B to be produced

P = Total incremental profit to the firm

The objective function is:

$$\text{Maximize:} \quad P = 6X_1 + 7X_2$$

This equation states that the firm's total profit is made up of the profit from product A (\$6 times the number sold) plus the profit from product B (\$7 times the number sold).

The first constraint relates to the availability of time on the first machine. This can be expressed as:

$$2X_1 + 3X_2 \leq 24$$

Each unit of product A uses two hours of this machine, and each unit of product B uses three hours. Hence, the total hours used is expressed by the left-hand side of the expression above. This must be equal to or less than the total hours available on the first machine (24).

For the second machine, a similar constraint is:

$$2X_1 + 1X_2 \leq 16$$

In addition, implicit in any linear programming formulation are the constraints that restrict X_1 and X_2 to be non-negative. In terms of the problem, this means that the firm can produce only zero or positive amounts.

The total formulation is:

$$\begin{aligned} \text{Maximize:} \quad & P = 6X_1 + 7X_2 \\ \text{Subject to:} \quad & 2X_1 + 3X_2 \leq 24 \\ & 2X_1 + X_2 \leq 16 \\ & X_1, X_2 \geq 0 \end{aligned}$$

This example is simple, and one would not need linear programming to solve it. However, problems involving dozens of products and many different constraints cannot be solved intuitively, and linear programming has proved valuable in these cases.

Example 2: A Transportation Problem

A manufacturer of soap and detergents has three plants located in Cincinnati, Denver, and Atlanta. Major warehouses are located at New York, Boston, Chicago, Los Angeles, and Dallas. Sales requirements for the next year at each warehouse are given in Table 2–2.

There is some concern in the company about which factory should supply each warehouse. Factory capacity at each location is limited. Cincinnati has an annual

TABLE 2–2
Warehouse Requirements

Warehouse Location	*Annual Sales (000s of cases)*
New York	50
Boston	10
Chicago	60
Los Angeles	30
Dallas	20
Total	170

TABLE 2–3
Cost of Shipping 1,000 Cases of Soap

From \ To	New York	Boston	Chicago	Los Angeles	Dallas
Cincinnati	$240	$300	$160	$500	$360
Denver	420	440	300	200	220
Atlanta	300	340	300	480	400

capacity of 100,000 cases. Denver has a capacity of 60,000 cases, and Atlanta has a capacity of 50,000 cases.

The cost of shipping soap from each factory to each warehouse is given in Table 2–3. The company wishes to determine a shipping schedule that will minimize overall company transportation costs (denoted by C).

Formulation. Let:

X_{11} = Number of cases shipped from first factory (Cincinnati) to first warehouse (New York), in thousands of cases

Similarly:

$X_{12}, X_{13}, X_{14}, X_{15}$ = Number of cases shipped from first factory (Cincinnati) to second, third, and so on, warehouses (Boston, Chicago, and so on)
$X_{21}, X_{22}, X_{23}, X_{24}, X_{25}$ = Number of cases shipped from second factory (Denver) to first, second, and so on, warehouses
$X_{31}, X_{32}, X_{33}, X_{34}, X_{35}$ = Number of cases shipped from third factory (Atlanta) to first, second, and so on, warehouses

Then the objective is to:

$$\begin{aligned}\text{Minimize:}\quad C = {} & 240X_{11} + 300X_{12} + 160X_{13} + 500X_{14} + 360X_{15} \\ & + 420X_{21} + 440X_{22} + 300X_{23} + 200X_{24} + 220X_{25} \\ & + 300X_{31} + 340X_{32} + 300X_{33} + 480X_{34} + 400X_{35}\end{aligned}$$

The total cost is the sum of the products for each possible shipping route (from factory to warehouse) of the shipping cost from Table 2–3 times the number of thousands of cases shipped.

There are two sets of constraints for this problem. The first set guarantees that the warehouse needs will be met. Thus, for New York:

$$X_{11} + X_{21} + X_{31} = 50$$

This states that the sum of the cases shipped to New York from the first (Cincinnati), second (Denver), and third (Atlanta) factories must be 50,000 cases, the sales requirement for New York. For the other warehouses, we have:

$$\begin{aligned}\text{Boston:}\quad & X_{12} + X_{22} + X_{32} = 10 \\ \text{Chicago:}\quad & X_{13} + X_{23} + X_{33} = 60 \\ \text{Los Angeles:}\quad & X_{14} + X_{24} + X_{34} = 30 \\ \text{Dallas:}\quad & X_{15} + X_{25} + X_{35} = 20\end{aligned}$$

The second set of constraints guarantees that the factories do not exceed their capacities. Thus, for the Cincinnati factory:

$$X_{11} + X_{12} + X_{13} + X_{14} + X_{15} \leq 100$$

This expression indicates that the amount shipped from the first factory to the first, second, third, and so on, warehouses must not exceed the factory's capacity of 100,000 cases.

Similarly, for:

Denver: $X_{21} + X_{22} + X_{23} + X_{24} + X_{25} \leq 60$
Atlanta: $X_{31} + X_{32} + X_{33} + X_{34} + X_{35} \leq 50$

Finally, all the Xs must be greater than or equal to zero.

The solution of this linear programming problem will give the optimum (i.e., least-cost) shipping schedule for the company. This is an example of a special type of problem known, naturally enough, as the **transportation problem.**

In summary, the complete formulation of the problem is:

$$\text{Minimize:} \quad C = 240X_{11} + 300X_{12} + 160X_{13} + 500X_{14} + 360X_{15} + 420X_{21} + 440X_{22} + 300X_{23} + 200X_{24} + 220X_{25} + 300X_{31} + 340X_{32} + 300X_{33} + 480X_{34} + 400X_{35}$$

Subject to:

$$\left.\begin{aligned} X_{11} + X_{21} + X_{31} &= 50 \\ X_{12} + X_{22} + X_{32} &= 10 \\ X_{13} + X_{23} + X_{33} &= 60 \\ X_{14} + X_{24} + X_{34} &= 30 \\ X_{15} + X_{25} + X_{35} &= 20 \end{aligned}\right\} \text{Warehouse requirement constraints}$$

$$\left.\begin{aligned} X_{11} + X_{12} + X_{13} + X_{14} + X_{15} &\leq 100 \\ X_{21} + X_{22} + X_{23} + X_{24} + X_{25} &\leq 60 \\ X_{31} + X_{32} + X_{33} + X_{34} + X_{35} &\leq 50 \end{aligned}\right\} \text{Factory capacity constraints}$$

$$X_{11}, X_{12}, \ldots, X_{35} \geq 0$$

Example 3: A Blending Problem

Various grades of gasoline are obtained by blending together certain blending gasolines that are the direct output of the refinery operations. In an actual refining operation, there are many blending gasolines, many final-product gasolines (e.g., various grades of aviation and motor gasoline), and many characteristics that are considered important in the chemical composition of the various grades of gasoline (including, for example, octane rating, vapor pressure, sulfur content, and gum content). In this simplified example, we assume that a refinery has available only two types of blending gasoline, whose characteristics are shown in Table 2–4.

TABLE 2–4
Characteristics of Blending Gasolines

Available Blends	*Octane Rating*	*Vapor Pressure*	*Amount Available*
Blending gasoline, type 1	104	5	30,000 barrels
Blending gasoline, type 2	94	9	70,000 barrels

TABLE 2–5
Characteristics of Final-Product Gasolines

Final Products	*Minimum Octane Rating*	*Maximum Vapor Pressure*	*Maximum Sales*	*Selling Price (per barrel)*
Aviation gasoline	102	6	20,000 barrels	\$45.10
Motor gasoline	96	8	Any amount	32.40

These blending gasolines may be mixed to produce two final products, aviation gasoline and motor gasoline. The required characteristics of these final products are shown in Table 2–5.

When gasolines are mixed together, the resulting mixture has an octane and a vapor pressure in proportion to the volume of each gasoline mixed. For example, if 1,000 barrels of blending gasoline 1 were mixed with 1,000 barrels of blending gasoline 2, the resultant gasoline would have an octane rating of 99:

$$\frac{1{,}000 \cdot 104 + 1{,}000 \cdot 94}{2{,}000} = 99$$

and a vapor pressure of 7:

$$\frac{1{,}000 \cdot 5 + 1{,}000 \cdot 9}{2{,}000} = 7$$

The firm wishes to maximize revenue from the sale of final product gasoline.

Formulation. Let:

X_1 = Number of barrels of blending gasoline 1 used in aviation gasoline
X_2 = Number of barrels of blending gasoline 2 used in aviation gasoline
X_3 = Number of barrels of blending gasoline 1 used in motor gasoline
X_4 = Number of barrels of blending gasoline 2 used in motor gasoline

The objective function is then to maximize R = Total Revenue:

$$\text{Maximize:} \quad R = 45.10(X_1 + X_2) + 32.40(X_3 + X_4)$$
$$= 45.10X_1 + 45.10X_2 + 32.40X_3 + 32.40X_4$$

Note that $X_1 + X_2$ is the total amount of aviation gasoline mixed (in barrels), and since it sells at \$45.10 per barrel, the revenue from this product is $45.10(X_1 + X_2)$. Similarly, the revenue from motor gasoline is $32.40(X_3 + X_4)$, and the sum of these terms is the total revenue, R.

There are several kinds of constraints that affect how the refinery will blend its gasoline. The first is on the sales or demand side—the fact that no more than 20,000 barrels of aviation gasoline can be sold (see Table 2–5). This may be represented by the following expression:

$$X_1 + X_2 \leq 20{,}000$$

A second set of constraints related to available amounts of blending gasolines (see Table 2–4). Thus, we have:

$$X_1 + X_3 \leq 30{,}000$$

Note that $X_1 + X_3$ represents the total amount of blending gasoline 1 (the sum of the amount used in aviation gasoline, X_1, and the amount used in motor gasoline, X_3). The equation above states that the amount of blending gasoline 1 used must not exceed the amount available—30,000 barrels. A similar constraint for blending gasoline 2 is:

$$X_2 + X_4 \leq 70{,}000$$

Another set of constraints relates to the octane ratings of the final-product gasolines. Recall that the total amount of aviation gasoline is $X_1 + X_2$. Its octane rating will be determined by the relative amounts of $X_1 + X_2$ according to the following formula:

$$\text{Octane rating of aviation gasoline} = \frac{104 \cdot X_1 + 94 \cdot X_2}{X_1 + X_2}$$

The numbers 104 and 94 are from Table 2–4 and are the octane ratings of blending gasoline 1 and blending gasoline 2, respectively. From Table 2–5, we note that the octane rating of aviation gasoline must be at least 102. So we have the following constraint:

$$\frac{104X_1 + 94X_2}{X_1 + X_2} \geq 102$$

Rearranging this expression in order to make it a linear constraint, we have:

$$104X_1 + 94X_2 \geq 102X_1 + 102X_2$$

or

$$(104X_1 - 102X_1) + (94X_2 - 102X_2) \geq 0$$

or

$$2X_1 - 8X_2 \geq 0$$

Similarly, for the octane rating for motor gasoline, we have:

$$104X_3 + 94X_4 \geq 96(X_3 + X_4)$$

or

$$8X_3 - 2X_4 \geq 0$$

A final set of constraints is related to the vapor pressure requirements of the final-product gasolines. For aviation gasoline, we have:

$$5X_1 + 9X_2 \leq 6(X_1 + X_2)$$

or

$$-X_1 + 3X_2 \leq 0$$

and the vapor pressure requirement of motor gasoline is:

$$5X_3 + 9X_4 \leq 8(X_3 + X_4)$$

or

$$-3X_3 + X_4 \leq 0$$

In summary, the total formulation of the linear programming model is:

$$\text{Maximize:} \quad R = 45.10X_1 + 45.10X_2 + 32.40X_3 + 32.40X_4$$

$$\text{Subject to:} \quad X_1 + X_2 \leq 20{,}000 \quad \text{Demand constraint}$$

$$\left.\begin{array}{l} X_1 + X_3 \leq 30{,}000 \\ X_2 + X_4 \leq 70{,}000 \end{array}\right\} \text{Availability of blending gasoline constraints}$$

$$\left.\begin{array}{l} 2X_1 - 8X_2 \geq 0 \\ 8X_3 - 2X_4 \geq 0 \end{array}\right\} \text{Octane rating constraints}$$

$$\left.\begin{array}{l} -X_1 + 3X_2 \leq 0 \\ -3X_3 + X_4 \leq 0 \end{array}\right\} \text{Vapor pressure constraints}$$

$$X_1, X_2, X_3, X_4 \geq 0$$

Gasoline blending was one of the very first applications of linear programming to business problems. Our example here is, of course, very much of an oversimplification of the real problem, but it captures the essential elements. The problem, as formulated above, is called the **blending problem.** Blending problems turn up in many contexts. One example of such a problem is in the production of feeds for animals. A feed mix for chickens, for example, may be made up of several different kinds of grains, and so forth. The feed mix manufacturer would like to use the cheapest grains available. However, the manufacturer is constrained by the fact that the feed mix must satisfy certain nutritional requirements (similar to the constraints on vapor pressure and octane rating in our gasoline example). In fact, certain aesthetic constraints also have to be added—the chickens will not eat the mixes determined solely by nutritional constraints.

The three examples so far have dealt with problems in one time period—often called **static** problems. Linear programming has also been applied to **dynamic** problems; that is, those extending over several time periods. Consider the following example.

Example 4: A Scheduling Problem

A company faces a firm schedule of delivery commitments for a product over the next six months. The production cost varies by month due to anticipated changes in materials costs. The company's production capacity is 100 units per month on regular time and up to an additional 15 units per month on overtime.

Table 2–6 contains delivery requirements and production costs by month.

The cost of carrying an unsold unit in stock is $2 per month. The problem for the company is to determine the number of units to produce in regular time and

TABLE 2–6
Requirements and Costs

	Month					
	1	*2*	*3*	*4*	*5*	*6*
Delivery commitments (units)	95	85	110	115	90	105
Cost per unit in regular time	$30	30	32	32	31	32
Cost per unit in overtime	$35	35	37	37	36	37

overtime each month to meet requirements at minimum cost. The firm has no units on hand at the beginning of month 1 and wishes to have no units on hand at the end of month 6.

Formulation. Let:

$X_1, X_2, X_3, X_4, X_5, X_6$ = Number of units produced in regular time each month

$Y_1, Y_2, Y_3, Y_4, Y_5, Y_6$ = Number of units produced in overtime each month

$I_1, I_2, I_3, I_4, I_5, I_6$ = Number of units in stock (unsold) at the end of each month

Then the objective is to:

$$\text{Minimize: } C = 30X_1 + 30X_2 + 32X_3 + 32X_4 + 31X_5 + 32X_6 + 35Y_1 + 35Y_2 + 37Y_3 + 37Y_4 + 36Y_5 + 37Y_6 + 2I_1 + 2I_2 + 2I_3 + 2I_4 + 2I_5 + 2I_6$$

The first part of its expression is the regular-time production costs (from Table 2–6) times the amounts produced in regular time each month. The second part represents the overtime production costs times the amounts produced in overtime each month. The third part is the cost of carrying unsold units in stock times the number of unsold units each month.

The constraints on regular-time production are:

$$X_1 \leq 100$$
$$X_2 \leq 100$$
$$X_3 \leq 100$$
$$X_4 \leq 100$$
$$X_5 \leq 100$$
$$X_6 \leq 100$$

The constraints on overtime production are:

$$Y_1 \leq 15$$
$$Y_2 \leq 15$$
$$Y_3 \leq 15$$
$$Y_4 \leq 15$$
$$Y_5 \leq 15$$
$$Y_6 \leq 15$$

Finally, a group of *linking constraints* or balance constraints are needed to link the time periods together and ensure that delivery commitments are met. These constraints are of the form:

$$(\text{Sources of units}) = (\text{Uses of units})$$

or

$$\begin{pmatrix}\text{Opening}\\\text{inventory}\end{pmatrix} + \begin{pmatrix}\text{Regular-time}\\\text{production}\end{pmatrix} + \begin{pmatrix}\text{Overtime}\\\text{production}\end{pmatrix} = \begin{pmatrix}\text{Delivery}\\\text{commitments}\end{pmatrix} + \begin{pmatrix}\text{Ending}\\\text{inventory}\end{pmatrix}$$

For month 1, this becomes:

$$0 + X_1 + Y_1 = 95 + I_1$$

since there is no initial inventory. Rearranging gives:

$$X_1 + Y_1 - I_1 = 95$$

Similarly, for month 2:

$$I_1 + X_2 + Y_2 = 85 + I_2$$

or

$$I_1 + X_2 + Y_2 - I_2 = 85$$

For the remaining months:

$$\begin{aligned} &\text{Month 3:} \quad I_2 + X_3 + Y_3 - I_3 = 110 \\ &\text{Month 4:} \quad I_3 + X_4 + Y_4 - I_4 = 115 \\ &\text{Month 5:} \quad I_4 + X_5 + Y_5 - I_5 = 90 \\ &\text{Month 6:} \quad I_5 + X_6 + Y_6 - I_6 = 105 \end{aligned}$$

Since ending inventory should be zero, a final constraint is:

$$I_6 = 0$$

In summary, the formulation is:

Minimize: $C = 30X_1 + 30X_2 + 32X_3 + 32X_4 + 31X_5 + 32X_6 + 35Y_1 + 35Y_2 + 37Y_3 + 37Y_4 + 36Y_5 + 37Y_6 + 2I_1 + 2I_2 + 2I_3 + 2I_4 + 2I_5 + 2I_6$

Subject to:

$$\left.\begin{aligned} X_1 + Y_1 - I_1 &= 95 \\ I_1 + X_2 + Y_2 - I_2 &= 85 \\ I_2 + X_3 + Y_3 - I_3 &= 110 \\ I_3 + X_4 + Y_4 - I_4 &= 115 \\ I_4 + X_5 + Y_5 - I_5 &= 90 \\ I_5 + X_6 + Y_6 - I_6 &= 105 \end{aligned}\right\} \text{Inventory balance constraints}$$

$$\left.\begin{aligned} X_1 &\le 100 \\ X_2 &\le 100 \\ X_3 &\le 100 \\ X_4 &\le 100 \\ X_5 &\le 100 \\ X_6 &\le 100 \end{aligned}\right\} \text{Regular-time production constraints} \qquad \left.\begin{aligned} Y_1 &\le 15 \\ Y_2 &\le 15 \\ Y_3 &\le 15 \\ Y_4 &\le 15 \\ Y_5 &\le 15 \\ Y_6 &\le 15 \end{aligned}\right\} \text{Overtime production constraints}$$

$$I_6 = 0 \quad \text{Ending inventory constraint}$$

$$X_1, X_2, X_3, X_4, X_5, X_6, Y_1, Y_2, Y_3, Y_4, Y_5, Y_6 \ge 0$$
$$I_1, I_2, I_3, I_4, I_5, I_6 \ge 0$$

Example 5: An Integrated Corporate Planning Model

This example deals with the formulation of a large-scale or system model, designed primarily for planning the integrated activities of a business firm. The example, diagrammed in Figure 2–1, is oversimplified and includes only two species of trees, two lumber and plywood products, and very few of the technological constraints involved in the production of lumber and plywood (see Table 2–7). The objective function is not shown in Table 2–7. It would be obtained by taking the prices of the

TABLE 2–7 Constraints for Wood Products Firm

	Availability of Lumber	*Shipments of Lumber*	*Mill Constraints*	*Production Technology*	*Shipments to Markets*	*Market Demand*
Fir	$X_1 \le A_1$	$X_7 + X_9 = X_1 + X_3 - X_5$	$X_7 + X_8 \le A_3$ $a_1X_7 + a_2X_8 \le A_4$ etc.	$X_{11} = a_5X_7 + a_6X_8$ $X_{12} = a_7X_7 + a_8X_8$	$X_{11} + X_{12} = X_{15} + X_{16}$ $X_{13} + X_{14} = X_{17} + X_{18}$	$X_{15} \le D_1$ $X_{16} \le D_2$ $X_{17} \le D_3$ $X_{18} \le D_4$
Pine	$X_2 \le A_2$	$X_8 + X_{10} = X_2 + X_4 - X_6$	$X_9 + X_{10} \le A_5$ $a_3X_9 + a_4X_{10} \le A_6$ etc.	$X_{13} = a_9X_9 + a_{10}X_{10}$ $X_{14} = a_{11}X_9 + a_{12}X_{10}$		

Symbols (MBF stands for 000s of board feet):

X_1 = MBF of fir cut
X_2 = MBF of pine cut
X_3 = MBF of fir purchased from outside
X_4 = MBF of pine purchased from outside
X_5 = MBF of fir sold to outside
X_6 = MBF of pine sold to outside
X_7 = MBF of fir to sawmill
X_8 = MBF of pine to sawmill
X_9 = MBF of fir to plywood mill
X_{10} = MBF of pine to plywood mill
X_{11}, X_{12} = Production in MBF of two types of lumber (e.g., 2 × 4s and 2 × 6s)
X_{13}, X_{14} = Production in panels of two types of plywood (e.g., ½ inch and ⅜ inch)
X_{15} = Lumber sold to captive distributors
X_{16} = Lumber sold to outside market
X_{17} = Plywood sold to captive distributors
X_{18} = Plywood sold to outside markets
A_1 = MBF of fir available to cut
A_2 = MBF of pine available to cut
A_3 = Overall sawmill capacity
A_4 = Capacity of a particular part of sawmill (e.g., headrig saw)
A_5 = Overall plywood mill capacity
A_6 = Capacity of some particular part of plywood mill (e.g., lathe)
$a_1, a_2, \ldots, a_{12}$ = Technological coefficients
D_1, D_2, D_3, D_4 = Market demand limits

FIGURE 2–1 **Simplified Model of Wood Products Firm**

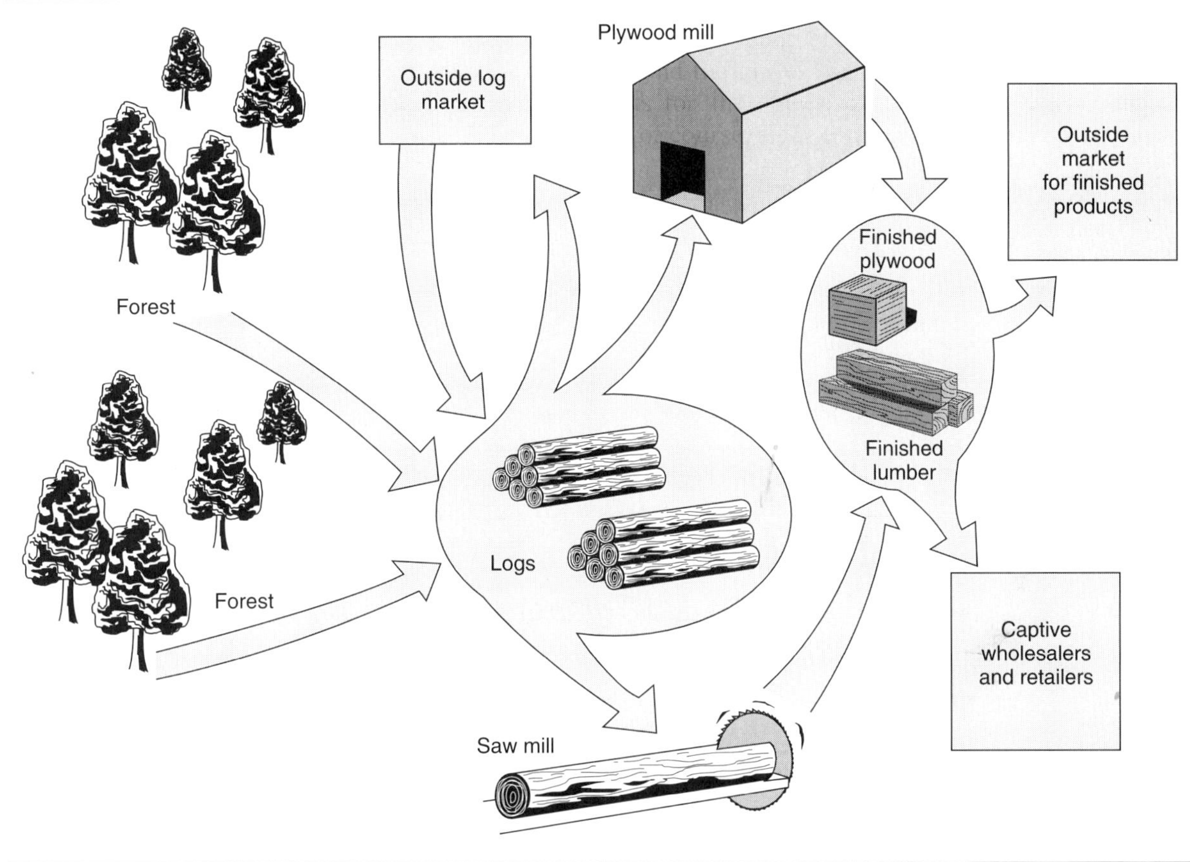

finished products times the output of these products and subtracting the variable operating costs throughout the whole system.

The Art of Formulating Linear Programming Models

Formulating any quantitative model means selecting out the important elements from the problem and defining how these are related. For real-world problems this is not an easy task and involves judgment and trial and error. In fact, it is more of an art than a systematic procedure. However, there are some steps that have been found useful in formulating linear programming models. These are:

1. Define in verbal terms the objective that you are trying to achieve in solving the problem. Select only one objective. For example, it might be "reduce cost" or "increase contribution to profit."
2. List verbally the decisions that are to be made as specifically as you can.
3. List verbally the constraining factors that affect these decisions. Try to be precise and complete. There are several general types of constraints listed below. See

if your problem has any of these conditions. Note that there may be other types of constraints as well. Any given problem will generally not have all of the types of constraints.

- *Capacity constraints.* These are limits because of the amount of equipment, space, or staff available. The constraint relating to the time available on the machine in Example 1 is an illustration.
- *Market constraints.* These are limits (either lower or upper limits or both) on how much product can be sold or used. See the limit on sales of aviation gasoline in Example 3.
- *Availability constraints.* These are limits because of scarcity of raw materials, labor, funds, or other resources. See the constraints relating to the availability of blending gasoline in Example 3.
- *Quality or blending constraints.* These are constraints that put limits on mixes of ingredients, usually defining the quality of output products. See the blending constraints for octane and vapor pressure in Example 3.
- *Production technology or material balance constraints.* These are constraints that define the output of some process as a function of the inputs, often with a loss for scrap. See the constraints in Example 5 relating production of plywood panels to inputs of fir and pine lumber used.
- *Definitional constraints.* These are constraints that define a given variable. Often, such constraints come from accounting definitions. See the inventory balance constraint in Example 4.

4. Define specifically the decision variables. This is often the hardest step. What is needed is a list of variables; that is, the *X*s and their definitions, including specification of units of measurement. In some problems, there may be more than one way of defining the variables. One approach is to start by trying to define specific variables that fit with the list of decisions in step 2. For example, if your decision is to "decide on a product mix," then a likely set of variables might be:

X_1 for units of first product
X_2 for units of second product.

And so on for all the products. Note that specifying values for all the *X*s in effect defines the product mix.

Another approach that sometimes helps in defining the decision variables is to draw a flow diagram showing how the various parts of the problem are related. See Figure 2–1 as an example. Then variables are defined to represent flows of goods, materials, and so on between the various parts. Note how the variables in Table 2–7 are associated with the arrows in Figure 2–1. For example, one arrow shows logs flowing to the plywood mill. Variables X_9 (MBF of fir to plywood mill) and X_{10} (MBF of pine to plywood mill) are the decision variables corresponding to this flow of timber.

5. Specifically define the constraints, using the decision variables. Take the list of constraints defined in verbal terms in step 3 and use the decision variables from step 4 to produce detailed constraints. The result is a set of constraints such as those illustrated in all five examples in this chapter.

6. Define the objective function in detail. For each decision variable from step 4, a cost or profit coefficient must be defined. It is important to include only costs

Tata Iron and Steel Company—India (continued)

The Tata Iron and Steel case introduced at the beginning of this chapter is another example of an integrated model—in Tata's terms, a "Works Planning Model." More of the detail is presented here to give a better understanding of the model.

The decision variables are the amount of each product produced at each stage of production. For example, one variable is the amount of molten iron with certain specifications emerging from a blast furnace. Another variable would be the amount of a certain type of slab produced on a blooming mill; another the amount of galvanized sheet of a certain type produced on a finishing rolling mill. There are many of these variables, since there are many types of steel and many different processes in manufacturing.

The objective function is to maximize the sum of the contribution for the set of products produced. For each product that is salable, contribution is the difference between the sale price and the variable cost of producing the product. For intermediate products that are not sold (e.g., molten steel), the contribution is negative and is simply the variable cost for that stage of production.

There are several types of constraints. One set reflects the capacity of each process. A given type of blooming mill, for example, has only so many hours available to operate. Each unit processed through that mill uses up time. So there is a constraint indicating that the total amount of time used must be no greater than that available. Similar constraints exist for each process.

Another set of constraints relates to material flow through a process. A blooming mill rolls steel ingots into blooms and slabs. An equation is necessary to indicate that the amount of output of blooms and slabs (plus any scrap) in tons equals the amount of input of ingots, in tons. Similar balance equations are needed for each process in the steel works.

Another set of equations defines the limits on the demand for salable steel products. For each product there are maximum amounts that can be sold, and there may also be a minimum amount to be produced if there are contracts requiring delivery.

A most important set of equations relates to the amount of electric power used. A critical part of building this model for Tata was a careful estimate of the variable amount of power used to produce each product in each process. There are also fixed power requirements. The total power requirement was then the sum of the fixed requirements and the variable needs that depended on the mix of products produced. This total amount of power was severely restricted during certain periods—the cause of the immediate crisis at Tata.[3]

The total model had about 770 variables and 680 constraint equations. Given today's technology, models of this size are easily solved—even on personal computers.

As indicated, the use of this model drastically changed the product mix during periods of power shortage, with significant increase in profitability for Tata. The model continues to be used for evaluating changes in the steel works.

[3]There is another set of constraints and variables relating to oxygen usage that has been omitted from this discussion. It involves the use of integer variables—entirely shut down an oxygen process or not. Such constraints can be handled by linear integer programming, discussed in a later chapter.

or profits that vary with the decisions under consideration. Fixed costs should always be excluded.

For example, labor cost per unit might seem a reasonable cost to include in a linear programming formulation defining what product mix a firm should produce. However, if the firm has a policy of paying employees for full-time work regardless of the actual time spent, then labor cost is really fixed. It does not vary with the product-mix decision and should be excluded from the objective function.

Although these six steps give a general outline for formulating linear models, there is no substitute for practice and experience. You should try several of the exercises at the end of the chapter to increase your ability to formulate models.

Additional Applications of Linear Programming

As indicated throughout the chapter, linear programming is a widely used tool for analyzing complex decision problems. The Tata Steel example and the formulations presented should give some appreciation for the great variety of problems that LP can solve.

The cases and problems at the end of this chapter should be scanned to gain some additional appreciation for the variety of problems to which LP has been applied. The great majority of these problems and cases are based on published applications or applications known to the authors. Of course, they have been greatly simplified—real problems often involve hundreds or thousands of variables and constraints. However, the essence of the problem has been preserved.

Many of the problems and cases are in production/operations, since this area continues to be a major area of application. But note that there are problems in finance (2 and 29), marketing (6), distribution (11 and 13), farming and mining (5, 17, 28, and 30), and service operations (15, 20, 24, and 26—Airlines and Rent-a-Car). There are also applications in the government/public sector (9, 12, and 22), including an environmental application concerning conservation of oysters (31).

Summary

A linear programming (LP) model is one in which a linear objective function is to be maximized or minimized subject to a set of linear constraints. All decision variables are non-negative. Formulating an LP model means translating a business decision problem into LP terminology by defining variables, specifying an objective function, and writing all constraints as equalities or inequalities. The examples and steps given above are designed to help you formulate LP problems.

Limitations of Linear Programming

Although linear programming has proven to be a valuable tool in solving large and complex problems in business and the public sector, there are limitations.

First, there is no guarantee that linear programming will give integer-valued solutions. For example, a solution may call for 8.241 trucks. The manager can buy or lease only 8 or 9 trucks—not 8.241. In many instances, rounding would give reasonably good solutions. In other situations, such answers may be poor. For example, in a decision about opening a new plant (a variable that can take on values of 0 or 1 only), a fractional answer would be useless. Fortunately, there are methods called *integer programming techniques* that can handle such problems. A later chapter discusses some of these techniques.

A second major limitation of linear programming is that uncertainty is not allowed. The model assumes known values for costs, constraint requirements, and so on, when in reality such factors may be unknown. Again, there are some approaches to dealing with this problem with techniques known as *linear programming under uncertainty* or *chance constrained programming.* Some of the advanced references in the chapter bibliography discuss these topics.

The third limitation is the assumption of linearity. Sometimes the objective or the constraints in real business problems are not linearly related to the variables.

Again, advanced techniques under the title of *nonlinear programming* are available for dealing with problems of this type.

These limitations indicate that linear programming cannot be applied to all business problems. However, for those problems for which it is applicable, it has proven to be a useful and powerful tool.

Summary

Linear programming is not useful for problems that require integer solutions, that involve uncertainty, or that have a nonlinear objective function or constraints, but it is applicable to a wide range of business decisions.

Bibliography

Bradley, S. P.; A. C. Hax; and T. L. Magnanti. *Applied Mathematical Programming.* Reading, MA: Addison-Wesley Publishing, 1977.

Charnes, A., and W. W. Cooper. *Management Models and Industrial Applications of Linear Programming.* 2 vols. New York: John Wiley & Sons, 1963.

Dantzig, G. B. *Linear Programming and Extensions.* Princeton, NJ: Princeton University Press, 1963.

Eppen, G. D.; F. J. Gould; and C. Schmidt. *Quantitative Concepts for Management.* 4th ed. Englewood Cliffs, NJ: Prentice Hall, 1993.

Geoffrion, Arthur M. "Better Distribution Planning with Computer Models." *Harvard Business Review.* July–August 1976.

Hillier, F., and G. J. Lieberman. *Introduction to Operations Research.* 6th ed. New York: McGraw-Hill, 1995.

Savage, S. L. *What's Best.* Oakland, CA: Holden-Day, 1986.

Schrage, L. *Linear, Integer and Quadratic Programming with LINDO.* 4th ed. Palo Alto, CA: Scientific Press, 1989.

Shapiro, R. O. *Optimization for Planning and Allocation: Text and Cases in Mathematical Programming.* New York: John Wiley & Sons, 1984.

Wagner, H. *Principles of Operations Research,* 2nd ed. Englewood Cliffs, NJ: Prentice Hall, 1975.

Practice Problems[4]

2–1. A firm produces four products: A, B, C, and D. Each unit of product A requires two hours of milling, one hour of assembly, and $10 worth of in-process inventory. Each unit of product B requires one hour of milling, three hours of assembly, and $5 worth of in-process inventory. Each unit of C requires 2½ hours of milling, 2½ hours of assembly, and $2 worth of in-process inventory Finally, each unit of product D requires five hours of milling, no assembly, and $12 of in-process inventory.

The firm has 120 thousand hours of milling time and 160 thousand hours of assembly time available. In addition, not more than $1 million may be tied up in in-process inventory.

Each unit of product A returns a profit of $40; each unit of B returns a profit of $24; each unit of product C returns a profit of $36; and each unit of product D returns a profit of $23. Not more than 20,000 units of product A can be sold; not more than 16,000 units of product C can be sold; and any number of units of products B and D may be sold. However, at least 10,000 units of product D must be produced and sold to satisfy a contract requirement.

Formulate the above as a linear programming problem. The objective of the firm is to maximize the profit resulting from the sale of the four products. Do not attempt to solve this problem.

[4]Solutions for these problems are at the end of this chapter.

2–2. The U-Save Loan Company is planning its operations for the next year. The company makes five types of loans, listed below, together with the annual return (in percent) to the company.

Type of Loan	*Annual Return (percent)*
Signature loans	15
Furniture loans	12
Automobile loans	9
Second home mortgage	10
First home mortgage	7

Legal requirements and company policy place the following limits on the amounts of the various types of loans.

Signature loans cannot exceed 10 percent of the total amount of loans. The amount of signature and furniture loans together cannot exceed 20 percent of the total amount of loans. First mortgages must be at least 40 percent of the total mortgages and at least 20 percent of the total amount of loans. Second mortgages may not exceed 25 percent of the total amount of loans.

The company wishes to maximize the revenue from loan interest, subject to the above restrictions. The firm can lend a maximum of $1.5 million.

Formulate this problem as a linear programming problem. Do not solve it.

2–3. A company sells two different products, A and B. The selling price and incremental cost information is as follows:

	Product A	*Product B*
Selling price	$60	$40
Incremental cost	30	10
Incremental profit	$30	$30

The two products are produced in a common production process and are sold in two different markets. The production process has a capacity of 30,000 labor-hours. It takes three hours to produce a unit of A and one hour to produce a unit of B. The market has been surveyed, and company officials feel that the maximum number of units of A that can be sold is 8,000; the maximum for B is 12,000 units. Subject to these limitations, the products can be sold in any combination.

Formulate the above problem as a linear programming problem; that is, write the appropriate equations.

2–4. Mangus Electric Products Co. (MEPCO) produces large electric transformers for the electrical industry. The company has orders (Table 2–8) for the next six months. The cost of manufacturing a transformer is expected to vary somewhat over the next few months due to expected changes in materials costs and in labor rates. The company can produce up to 50 units per month on regular time and up to an additional 20 units per month using overtime. The costs for both regular and overtime production are shown in Table 2–8.

The cost of carrying an unsold transformer in stock is $500 per month. The company has 15 transformers in stock on January 1, and wishes to have no less than 5 in stock on June 30.

Formulate a linear programming problem to determine the optimal production schedule for MEPCO.

2–5. The Transvaal Diamond Company mined diamonds in three locations in South Africa. The three mines differed in terms of capacities, number, weight of stones mined, and costs. These are shown in Table 2–9.

Due to marketing considerations, a monthly production of exactly 148,000 stones was required. A similar requirement called for at least 130,000 carats. (The average stone size was thus at least 130/148 = 0.88 carats.)

The problem for the company manager was to meet the marketing requirements at the least cost.

Formulate a linear programming model to determine how much should be mined at each location. Do not solve.

TABLE 2–8

	Month					
	Jan.	*Feb.*	*Mar.*	*April*	*May*	*June*
Orders (units)	58	36	34	69	72	43
Cost per unit at regular time (in $000s)	$18.0	17.0	17.0	18.5	19.0	19.0
Cost per unit at overtime (in $000s)	$20.0	19.0	19.0	21.0	22.0	22.0

TABLE 2–9

Mine	*Capacity (M^3 of earth processed)**	*Treatment† Costs (rand per M^3)*	*Grade (carats per M^3)*	*Stone Count (number of stones per M^3)*
Plant 1	83,000	R0.60	0.36	0.58
Plant 2	310,000	R0.36	0.22	0.26
Plant 3	190,000	R0.50	0.263	0.21

*M^3 is cubic meters. Rand is the South African currency.
†Mining costs are excluded from these figures. Assume that they are the same at each mine.

Problems

2–6. We want to select an advertising strategy to reach two types of customers: homemakers in families with over $25,000 annual income and homemakers in families with under $25,000 income.[5] We feel that people in the first group will purchase twice as much of our product as people in the second, and our goal is to maximize purchases. We may advertise either on TV or in a magazine; one unit of TV advertising costs $40,000 and reaches approximately 20,000 people in the first group and 80,000 in the second. One unit of advertising in the magazine costs $24,000 and reaches 60,000 people in the first group and 30,000 in the second.[6] We require that at least 6 units of TV advertising be used and that no more than 12 units of magazine advertising be used, for policy reasons. The advertising budget is $360,000.

Formulate this problem as a linear programming problem, defining all variables used.

2–7. The Super Sausage Company (SSC) has recently experienced drastic changes in raw material prices, and the manager has directed an analyst to reexamine the proportions in which SSC mixes ingredients to manufacture sausage.

Sausage manufacture involves meeting two key product requirements. The percentage of protein, by weight, must be at least 15 percent; and the percentage of fat, by weight, cannot exceed 30 percent (remaining weight is filler). SSC has the following four raw materials available for mixing, with the following characteristics:

Ingredient	*Percent Protein*	*Percent Fat*	*Cost per Pound*
A	40%	10%	$1.80
B	20	15	0.75
C	10	35	0.40
D	5	40	0.15

Formulate an LP model that would aid SSC in determining its most desirable mixing schedule. (Do not solve this problem.)

2–8. Refer to Example 1 in this chapter. Suppose the firm has a third product, product C, which can be produced on either the first or the second machine. Producing it on the first machine requires one hour of time; producing it on the second machine requires two hours of time. Product C has an incremental profit of $9 per unit.

Modify the formulation of Example 1 to include product C.

2–9. The American Safety Council must allocate its national budget for the next fiscal year. Irrevocable decisions have already been made concerning various "program areas" and their total funding; for example, a total of $110,000 has been allocated to prevention of automobile fatalities and reduction of property damage. However, detailed allocation decisions must be made concerning specific *projects* designed to contribute to the program missions. In the case of automobile fatality prevention and reduction of property damage, Table 2–10 contains the projects recommended by council analysts, together with appropriate data. The decision makers of the council want you to help them make their budget allocation (or project choice and magnitude) decisions. In response to a question

[5]This problem is adapted from F. M. Bass and R. T. Lonsdale, "An Exploration of Linear Programming in Media Selection," *Journal of Marketing Research* 3 (1966).

[6]In this problem, it is assumed that the magazine's audience has no overlap with the TV audience.

TABLE 2–10

Project	Upper Limit of Expenditure on Project (measured in $)	Expected Fatalities Prevented per $1,000 Expended	Expected Reduction in Property Damage per $1,000 Expended
1. Seat belt advertising	$ 80,000	0.33	$ 0
2. Research on improved highway design	20,000	0.25	20,000
3. Research on improved automobile design	75,000	0.15	30,000
4. Dollars spent lobbying for tougher state "drunk driving" penalties	100,000	0.27	10,000

concerning which of their two specific missions is more important, they said: "That's a tough question! On the one hand, human life is sacred and cannot be purchased for any amount of money. On the other hand, if there are two competing ways to save the *same number of lives,* we would naturally prefer the project that also results in the lower amount of property damage."

When asked specifically what "trade-off" between lives saved and property damage would make them be indifferent, they said: "That's really a tough question! However, we are aware that a certain government agency has, for internal resource allocation purposes, an implicit dollar value for human life saved of $300,000 (we think another agency also uses this number in making decisions about building additional safety into their equipment)."

Formulate an LP model whose solution would represent an optimal allocation of the budgeted $110,000, based on all the information above. Be sure to define all variables used. You need *not* solve the formulation.

2–10. The Empire Abrasive Company (EAC) produces aluminum-oxide grit for use in grinding wheels and coated abrasives. There are two types of finished product: coarse grit and fine grit. There are also two types of input material, called Surinam Crude and Chinese Crude (for the country of origin of the bauxite from which the crude is processed). Finally, there are two processing modes, called *fast* and *slow,* which can be used with either input material to produce varying percentages of the finished products. Table 2–11 describes the percentages of each finished product resulting from the possible combinations of input material and processing mode.

Surinam Crude costs $300 per ton, and Chinese Crude costs $350. *Fast* processing costs $50 per ton, and *slow* processing costs $40. Coarse grit is sold at a price of $500 per ton, and fine grit is sold for $325 per ton. EAC's plant can process 1,000 input tons of crude per week. There are no volume limits on amounts of finished product that can be sold.

Formulate a linear programming model of this problem that will indicate how EAC can obtain the most profitable situation. *Note:* EAC can use both types of crude and both types of processing modes; that is, fractional solutions are a distinct possibility.

2–11. The Consolidated Company has in the past contracted out the shipment of its products from its factory to its warehouses. The volume of deliveries is measured in ton-miles (the tons of product times the number of miles over which it is to be delivered).

TABLE 2–11 Output Percentages for Coarse and Fine Grit

	Surinam Crude Input		Chinese Crude Input	
	Fast Process	*Slow Process*	*Fast Process*	*Slow Process*
Percent coarse grit	45	25	35	20
Percent fine grit	50	70	60	80
Loss in yield	5	5	5	0

TABLE 2–12

Type	*Purchase Cost*	*Operating Cost (per ton-mile)*	*Capacity (ton-miles per month)*
Trailer	$30,000	$0.56	10,000
Medium	16,000	0.64	8,000
Pickup	10,000	0.80	6,000

Consolidated has 400,000 ton-miles to be delivered each month.

Currently, Consolidated is paying Speedie Trucking Company $1 per ton-mile to deliver the product. Consolidated is considering purchasing a fleet of trucks to take over part or all of this delivery service.

Three types of trucks are under consideration: large trailer-trucks, medium-sized trucks, and pickup trucks. Details of each are given in Table 2–12.

Speedie Trucking has indicated that it would be willing to continue to deliver any excess not delivered by Consolidated's own trucks at the rate of $1 per ton-mile.

Capital equipment funds are in short supply in Consolidated, and only $760,000 is available to purchase the equipment.

In addition to the budget limitation, there are other restrictions on the types of trucks purchased. The first involves dock loading space. Because of parking space and dock limitations, not more than 28 truck spaces are available. A trailer or medium truck would use one space. Two pickup trucks use one space.

Also, because of the types and sizes of deliveries, at least two-thirds of the trucks purchased would have to be either trailers or medium trucks.

Formulate this as a linear programming problem. Do not solve. Be careful to specify the objective and define the variables.

2–12. The Gotham City School system has three high schools that serve the needs of five neighborhood areas. The capacities of the various schools are:

School	*Capacity (maximum enrollment)*
A	4,000
B	3,000
C	2,000
Total	9,000

The size (number of high school students) and ethnic mix of each neighborhood are as shown:

Neighborhood	*Number of Students*	*Percent Minority Students*
1	2,100	30
2	2,400	80
3	1,300	20
4	800	10
5	1,600	20
Total	8,200	

The distances (in miles) from each neighborhood to each school are as shown:

	Neighborhood				
School	*1*	*2*	*3*	*4*	*5*
A	1.2	0.4	2.6	1.4	2.4
B	0.8	2.0	0.5	0.7	3.0
C	1.3	2.2	1.6	2.0	0.2

A federal judge has ruled that no high school in the city can have more than 50 percent nor less than 30 percent minority enrollment. Assume that students bused from each neighborhood have the same ethnic mix as the whole neighborhood. You wish to devise a busing plan that will minimize the total number of student-miles bused while meeting the judge's integration requirements, and at the same time guarantee that no student is bused more than 2.5 miles.

Formulate a linear programming model to solve this problem.

2–13. A manufacturer produces a product at three plants and distributes it through four market-service warehouses. The following data have been provided:

Warehouse	Selling Price (per unit)	Annual Demand (units)
1	$1.00	40,000
2	1.10	10,000
3	1.00	20,000
4	0.60	25,000

Plant	Unit Variable Production Cost	Annual Capacity (units)
A	$0.40	40,000
B	0.35	30,000
C	0.45	45,000

From \ To		Warehouse			
		1	2	3	4
Plant	A	$0.20	$0.20	$0.30	$0.30
	B	0.20	0.10	0.35	0.40
	C	0.45	0.30	0.20	0.20

a. Suppose the *marketing* manager wishes to *meet all demands at minimum cost.* Write out a linear programming formulation of this problem that would produce optimal production and shipping decisions. Let X_{A2} be the amount produced at factory A for shipment to warehouse 2, and so on. *Do not solve* the problem.

b. Suppose the group vice president wishes to meet only those demands that are incrementally profitable. That is, the group vice president wishes to maximize profits, or revenues less production and transportation costs. Modify your linear programming formulation of (*a*) to solve this problem optimally. Do not solve the problem.

2–14. The Acme Skateboard Company manufactures three different models of skateboards: Regular, Super, and Deluxe. Data on costs, selling prices, and other information for each model are presented in Table 2–13.

Acme has a work force of five *salaried* individuals working up to 40 hours per week and paid $520 per week each (including fringe benefits) whether they work a full 40 hours or not. Acme desires to find the optimal weekly production plan that will maximize profit and contribution to fixed labor cost.

Formulate an LP model that will maximize profit plus contribution to fixed costs.

2–15. The operations manager of Hervis Rent-A-Car Company thinks some type of mathematical model might be useful in weekly decisions on how to relocate rental cars from cities that have a surplus to cities where there is a deficit. Once a week, the manager collects data on the numbers of cars at each city; a comparison with a predetermined "target" number of cars for that city indicates the amount of surplus or deficit. (For example, if the Chicago Airport office has 67 cars currently, and its target is 80 cars, then it has a deficit of 13 cars.)

Each week the manager must determine how to relocate cars from the surplus cities to the deficit cities. Even though the target numbers do not change from week to week, the actual problem is different each week, due to more-or-less random aggregate patterns of rental clients. (For example, one week Chicago may have a deficit of 13 cars, as above; the next week, it may have 88 cars, or a surplus of 8 cars.)

TABLE 2–13

Model	Regular	Super	Deluxe
Selling price per unit	$7	$15	$25
Raw material cost per unit	$3	$ 6	$10
Labor-hours required for assembly, finishing, and packaging per unit*	0.1	0.2	0.5
Demand upper limit on weekly sales	1,000	800	300

*For example, 10 Regular skateboards can be produced in one labor-hour; alternatively, five Super models can be produced, or two Deluxe models.

The present approach to the problem is to start with the West Coast, and meet deficits using the *closest* cities having surpluses, if the manager hasn't already precommitted those surplus cars for a different city. Nevertheless, the manager thinks there should be a more systematic way to attack the problem. At the beginning of each week,the status of each city (number of cars surplus or deficit) is known; the manager also knows the cost of relocating a car from city i to city j, denoted by C_{ij}. Hervis services 100 cities coast to coast, with a total fleet of 10,000 cars. The sum of all target quantities is also 10,000 cars, so deficits are precisely balanced by surpluses.

a. Formulate an LP model to solve this problem.

b. The operations manager of Allegory Airlines (AA) has a problem similar to the Hervis car relocation problem. Each evening, each of AA's DC–9 aircraft terminates passenger flight operations at various cities; each morning, DC–9s are required at various cities to fly the next day's routes. Unfortunately, some cities end up with a DC–9 in the evening but don't need it in the morning, while the reverse occurs at other cities. AA's flight schedule remains unchanged for the seven days of the week, and in fact usually remains unchanged for three or four months. Thus, the problem faced by AA is *identical* every evening; for example, if Chicago has a surplus of two DC–9s tonight, it will have a surplus of two DC–9s every night until the next major schedule change.

AA has determined the cost to fly a plane from city i to city j, including such complexities as the cost to ferry the plane's crew and cabin attendants from city j back to their originating city (likely to be still a different city); this cost is denoted by C_{ij}.

Can your LP formulation for (*a*) of this question be used to solve AA's plane-relocation problem? (If yes, indicate changes in definitions of variables and any other required changes; if no, explain why not.)

More Challenging Problems

2–16. The Emory Aluminum Company rolls and sells aluminum foil in several widths. Customers can order rolls of foil 24 inches, 20 inches, 12 inches, or 8 inches wide. The foil is manufactured in a standard width of 54 inches, and the smaller widths are slit (cut) from the standard roll. There are many ways the smaller widths can be cut, as shown in Table 2–14.

For example, using method 3, one roll 24 inches wide, one roll 12 inches wide, and two rolls 8 inches wide are cut from the standard roll. This leaves 2 inches of scrap [54 − 24 − 12 − 2(8) = 2]. Because some scrap is generated by the slitting process, it is not possible to cut certain combinations (not shown). All rolls for cutting are a standard 54-inch width, and all orders are for the standard widths in the table. Furthermore, all orders are for a standard length (the length of a full roll).

Emory has received the following orders for the month of July:

Width	*Rolls Ordered*
24 inches	330
20 inches	120
12 inches	480
8 inches	160

Table 2–14

	Cutting Method												
Width	*1*	*2*	*3*	*4*	*5*	*6*	*7*	*8*	*9*	*10*	*11*	*12*	*13*
24 inches	2	1	1	1	1								
20 inches		1				2	2	1	1	1			
12 inches			1	2		1		2	1		4	2	
8 inches		1	2		3		1	1	2	4		3	6
Scrap (inches)	6	2	2	6	6	2	6	2	6	2	6	6	6

How should Emory cut rolls to fill these orders? Formulate a linear programming model for the problem but do not solve it.

2–17. A rancher has 1,000 acres on which to grow corn or barley, or feed cattle. Information on the two crops under consideration is given below:

Item	*Corn*	*Barley*
Seed and other cash costs per acre	$100	$120
Labor-hours required per acre	10	8
Yield (bushel per acre)	120	100
Selling price ($ per bushel)	$ 4.25	$ 5.25
Purchase price ($ per bushel)	$ 4.50	—

The rancher can plant the land in any mix of the two crops; or the land can be used to raise young steers and feed them for a year. The steers cost $150 each and are sold for $800 after feeding. Each steer requires 20 hours of labor, one-half acre of land, and 80 bushels of corn. The corn for the steers can be that grown on the ranch if enough is available, or it can be purchased.

The rancher can use either inexperienced labor, which costs $6 per hour, or experienced labor at a rate of $10 per hour. Each hour of inexperienced labor requires 0.15 hours of supervision, and each hour of experienced labor requires 0.05 hours of supervision. There are 2,000 hours of supervision available.

The rancher is limited to funds totaling $200,000 for buying seed and other cash costs for crops, for purchasing steers, and for paying labor.

Formulate as a linear programming model.

2–18. A manufacturer has contracted to produce 2,000 units of a particular product over the next eight months. Deliveries are scheduled as follows:

Month	*Units*
January	100
February	200
March	300
April	400
May	100
June	100
July	500
August	300
Total	2,000

The manufacturer has estimated that it costs her $1 to store one unit of product for one month. She has a warehouse capacity of 300 units.

The manufacturer can produce any number of units in a given month, since the units can be produced mostly with part-time labor, which can be easily obtained. However, there are costs of training new personnel and costs associated with laying off personnel who have been hired. The manufacturer has estimated that it costs approximately 75 cents per unit to increase the production level from one month to the next (e.g., if production in January is 200 and is increased to 300 in February, the cost is $75 for training the additional people required to produce at the 300-unit level). Similarly, it costs 50 cents per unit to reduce production from one month to the next. (At the end of eight months, all employees will be laid off, with the corresponding production-reduction costs.) Assume the production level before January is zero.

a. Formulate the above as a linear programming problem.

b. Suppose there is a limit on production of 300 units per month. Formulate the linear programming problem with this additional constraint.

2–19. A manufacturer of laptop computers has four models, two with color LCD (liquid crystal display) screens (the Sport model and the Superba model) and two models with black-and-white LCD screens (the Standard model and the Excel model). Each model requires assembly and test time and the requirements are shown in Table 2–15, together with the amount of time available for assembly and testing in the next month.

The LCD screens are purchased from an outside supplier and, because of an earthquake in Kobe, Japan (where many LCD screens are produced), they are in short supply. The outside supplier indicates that not more than 900 LCD screens in total could be supplied in the next month, and of these, not more than 500 could be color LCDs.

It is possible for the manufacturer to make available additional hours of test time by adding a third shift at the manufacturing facility and paying overtime wages. Up to 500 additional hours are available using this approach, but the premium cost is $10 per hour over that for regular time.

The manufacturer can sell all the laptops of any model that can be produced.

Assume that the manufacturer is interested in maximizing the contribution from laptop computers (less any overtime costs) for the next month. How many of each model should be produced? Formulate this problem as a linear programming model.

TABLE 2–15

	Standard Model	*Excel Model*	*Sport Model*	*Superba Model*	*Total Available*
Assembly time (hours)	8	10	12	15	10,000
Test time (hours)	2	3	4	6	2,500
Profit contribution (dollars per unit)	$120	$180	$240	$300	

2–20. The director of passenger services for Ace Air Lines was trying to decide how many new flight attendants to hire and train over the next six months. The requirements in number of flight attendant flight-hours needed were:

Month	*Hours Needed*
January	8,000
February	7,000
March	8,000
April	10,000
May	9,000
June	12,000

The problem was complicated by two factors. It took one month to train flight attendants before they could be used on regular flights. Hence, hiring had to be done a month before the need arose. Secondly, training of new flight attendants required the time of already trained attendants. It took approximately 100 hours of regular attendant time for each trainee during the month training period. In other words, the number of hours available for flight service by regular attendants was cut by 100 hours for each trainee.

The director of passenger services was not worried about January, because there were 60 attendants available. Company rules required that an attendant could not work more than 150 hours in any month. This meant that the director had a maximum of 9,000 hours available for January, 1,000 in excess of needs. (Attendants were not laid off in such cases; each merely worked fewer hours.)

Company records showed that 10 percent of the attendants quit their jobs each month for various reasons.

The cost to Ace Air Lines for a regular flight attendant was $1,500 per month for salary and fringe benefits, regardless of how many hours worked (of course, one could not work more than 150 hours). The cost of a trainee was $700 per month for salary and fringe benefits.

Formulate the above as a linear programming problem designed to solve the problem of the director of passenger services at minimum cost. Do not attempt to solve the programming problem. Be sure to identify all the symbols you use.

2–21. The land of Milkandhoney produced only three products—machinery, steel, and automobiles. All other goods were imported. The minister of the economy held the responsibility for economic planning, and he thought the welfare of the country could be served by maximizing the net dollar value of exports (that is, the value of the exports less the cost of the materials imported to produce those exports). Milkandhoney could sell all the steel, automobiles, or machinery it could produce on the world market at prices of $500 per unit for steel, $1,500 per unit for automobiles, and $2,500 per unit for machinery.

In order to produce 1 unit of steel, it took 0.05 units of machinery, 0.01 units of automobiles, 2 units of ore purchased on the world market for $100 per unit, and other imported materials costing $50. In addition, it took one-half worker-year of labor to produce each unit of steel. Milkandhoney's steel mills had a rated capacity of 100,000 units per year.

To produce 1 unit of automobiles, it took 1 unit of steel, 0.1 units of machinery, and 1 worker-year of labor. In addition, it took $300 worth of imported materials to produce each unit of automobiles. Automobile capacity was 700,000 units per year.

To produce 1 unit of machinery required 0.01 units of automobiles, 0.5 unit of steel, and 2 worker-years of labor, in addition to $100 for items imported from outside. The capacity of the machinery plants was 50,000 units per year.

The total personnel available for labor in Milkandhoney was 800,000 persons per year.

a. Assuming that no steel, automobiles, or machinery can be imported, formulate a linear programming model to determine the production mix that will maximize net exports (dollars). Be careful to define all variables and to state exactly all relationships among variables.

b. How would you formulate the linear programming problem if there were no restrictions on importation of any or all of the automobiles, steel, or machinery at the prices given? Can you see an obvious solution to the problem thus formulated?

2–22. The Stateside Electric Company is planning construction of new facilities in its area for the next 10 years.[7] It is possible to construct four types of electric power facilities—steam plants using coal for energy, hydroelectric plants with no reservoir, hydroelectric plants with small reservoirs (enough water storage capacity to meet daily fluctuations), and hydroelectric plants with large reservoirs (with enough water storage to meet seasonal fluctuations in power demand and water flow).

Consumption of electricity is based on three characteristics. The first is the total annual usage—the requirement in the area is estimated to be 4,000 billion kilowatt-hours by the 10th year. The second characteristic is the peak usage of power—usually on a hot summer day at about 4 PM. Any plan should provide enough peaking capacity to meet a projected peak need of 3,000 million kilowatts in the 10th year. The third characteristic is guaranteed power output—measured as the average daylight output in midwinter when the consumption is high and water levels for hydroelectric power are low. The 10-year requirement is for 2,000 million kilowatts of guaranteed power.

The various possible power plants vary in terms of how they can satisfy these characteristics. For example, hydroelectric plants with reservoirs are able to provide substantial peaking capacity, whereas steam plants and hydroelectric plants with no reservoirs are poor in this respect.

The characteristics of the various types of plants are shown in Table 2–16. Each is measured in terms of a unit of capacity. The unit of capacity is defined to be the capacity to produce 1 billion kilowatt-hours per year. Note that the types of plants vary substantially in their investment costs. The annual operating costs of the various types of plants also vary considerably. For example, the cost of coal makes the annual costs of the steam plants quite high, whereas the annual costs of operating the hydroelectric plants are relatively less. The final column in the table shows the discounted total costs, including both the investment cost and the discounted annual operating costs.

The company wants to develop a 10-year plan that would detail how much capacity of each type of plant to build. The objective is to minimize the total discounted cost. However, there is a restriction that no more than $350 million can be used for investment in plants over the 10 years.

Formulate this problem as a linear programming model.

2–23. In linear programming models, demand for a product is usually assumed known for certain. In reality, demand is often uncertain. This uncertain demand can sometimes be built into an LP model, as this exercise is designed to illustrate.

Refer to Problem 2–1 and its solution (given at the end of this chapter). Consider product A, which is assumed in the problem to have an upper limit on demand of 20 units. Suppose instead that the upper demand limit for product A is uncertain, but you assess a 0.4 probability that at most 10 can be sold, and a 0.6 chance that the upper limit is 20. Suppose, further, that if you produce more than 10 units and the upper limit of demand turns out to be only 10 units, you can sell the excess at a reduced price that would give you a profit of only $10 per unit. Your objective is to maximize expected profit. How would you modify the formulation for Problem 2–1 to accomplish this?

Hint: Define a new variable as the excess production of product A over 10 units, and consider the expected revenue to be received from the sale of any of these units.

[7] This problem is based on the article "Application of Linear Programming to Investments in the Electric Power Industry," P. Masse and R. Gibrat, *Management Science,* January 1957.

TABLE 2–16
Characteristics of Electric Plants per Unit (1 billion kilowatt-hours) of Annual Output

Type	*Guaranteed Output (millions of kilowatts)*	*Peak Output (millions of kilowatts)*	*Investment Cost ($000s)*	*Discounted Total Cost ($000s)*
Steam	0.15	0.20	$30	$ 65
Hydroelectric—no reservoir	0.10	0.10	40	42
Hydroelectric—small reservoir	0.10	0.40	60	64
Hydroelectric—large reservoir	0.80	0.90	100	110

TABLE 2–17

	Oct.	*Nov.*	*Dec.*	*Jan.*	*Feb.*	*Mar.*
Cars needed	380	360	300	360	330	340

TABLE 2–18

	Type of Lease		
	Three Months	*Four Months*	*Five Months*
Total lease cost	$1,140	$1,360	$1,500
Cost per month	380	340	300

2–24. The Premier Rent-a-Car Company operates a fleet of rental cars in a large western city. The company has forecast its demand for rental cars for the next six months, as shown in Table 2–17.

The company obtains its cars by leasing them from an automobile manufacturer. Three leasing plans are available, involving leases of three, four, or five months' duration. Cars are leased beginning on the first day of a month, and are returned to the manufacturer on the last day of the month at the end of the lease period. The costs for the three types of leases are shown in Table 2–18.

These costs include lease payments to the manufacturer and standard maintenance and repair expenses. A lease may be taken out in any month. The manufacturer has certain restrictions: At least 60 percent of the cars leased must be on the five-month lease, and no more than 20 percent can be on the three-month lease.

On September 30, the fleet consists of 300 cars. For 100 of these, the lease expires at the end of October; the lease on an additional 100 expires at the end of November; and the lease for the remaining 100 expires at the end of December. Premier would like to have between 300 and 350 cars remaining in the fleet at the end of March (after returning leased cars that are due to be returned that month).

Premier would like to minimize its leasing costs. Formulate a linear programming problem to solve this fleet-planning problem.

2–25. The Precision Pencil Company (PPC) produces wood pencils and the "lead" (actually graphite) that goes into the pencils. There are two major product classes: *regular* and *drafting* pencils. The production of lead for the two classes of product involves the same facilities, but for the higher-quality drafting lead, the various operations in the lead department require almost twice as much time per pound of lead produced as for the less demanding regular lead. The fabrication department is highly automated, and in this phase of manufacture, the rate of fabrication for each product class is identical. The accompanying table summarizes the maximum production rates in output per hour for each department (lead and fabrication) *when the department is used only for one class of product.*

	Product Class	
Department	*Regular (per hour)*	*Drafting (per hour)*
Lead	500 pounds	300 pounds
Pencil fabrication	30 gross*	30 gross*

*One gross is 144 pencils.

Regular pencils use 10 pounds of regular lead per gross, and drafting pencils use 15 pounds of drafting lead per gross.

Demand for the drafting pencils is constant at 6,500 gross per quarter. Demand for the regular pencils is constant at 7,800 gross per quarter for the first quarter of the year, then jumps to 10,400 gross per quarter for the second and third quarters (due to back-to-school orders), and then drops back to 7,800 gross per quarter for the fourth quarter.

TABLE 2–19 Fuel Requirements and Limits (1,000 gallons unless specified otherwise)

City Number	*Flight Sequence*	*Minimum Fuel Required*	*Maximum Fuel Allowed*	*Regular Fuel Consumption if Minimum Fuel Boarded*	*Additional Fuel Burned per Gallon of Tankered Fuel (i.e., fuel above minimum—in gallons)*	*Price per Gallon (cents)*
1	Los Angeles to Miami	23	33	12.1	0.040	82
2	Miami to Tampa	8	19	2.0	0.005	75
3	Tampa to La Guardia	19	33	9.5	0.025	77
4	La Guardia to Los Angeles	25	33	13.0	0.045	89
1	Los Angeles to Miami (etc.)					

Each department (lead and fabrication) has available 520 hours per quarter of regular-time production. In addition, up to 78 hours per quarter of overtime production are available. Inventories of both finished pencils and finished lead may be carried over from one quarter to the next.

The variable cost to manufacture a pound of lead is \$0.10 for the regular lead and \$0.15 for the drafting lead on regular-time production. The variable cost for a gross of pencils (including the lead cost) is \$4 for the regular pencils and \$4.50 for the drafting pencils on regular-time production. These costs are increased by 10 percent for overtime production. The total cost of holding inventory is 20 percent of the variable cost per year.

Formulate a linear programming model whose solution would indicate a production plan for PPC for the four quarters of the year. Do not attempt to solve it.

2–26. Nationwide Airlines,[8] faced with a sharply escalating cost of jet fuel, is interested in optimizing its purchases of jet fuel at its various locations around the country. Typically, there is some choice concerning the amount of fuel that can be placed on board any aircraft for any flight segment, as long as minimum and maximum limits are not violated. The flight schedule is considered as a chain of flight segments, or legs, that each aircraft follows. The schedule ultimately returns the aircraft to its starting point, resulting in a "rotation." Consider the following rotation:

Los Angeles–Miami–Tampa–
La Guardia–Los Angeles

The fuel for any one of these flight segments may be bought at its departure city, or it may be purchased at a previous city in the sequence and "tankered" for the flight. Of course, it takes fuel to carry fuel, and thus an economic trade-off between purchasing fuel at the lowest-cost location and tankering it all around the country must be made.

The data in Table 2–19 have been obtained. The column labeled "Regular fuel consumption" takes into account fuel consumption if the minimum amount of fuel is on board, and the column labeled "Additional fuel burned" indicates the additional fuel burned in each flight segment per gallon of "tankered" fuel carried; tankered fuel refers to fuel *above* the minimum amount.

Note that fuel originally carried into Los Angeles should equal fuel carried into Los Angeles on the next rotation, in order for the system to be in equilibrium.

An analyst has begun to formulate this as an LP problem. The following unknowns have been defined:

I_i = Leftover fuel inventory coming into city i (1,000 gallons)
X_i = Amount of fuel purchased at city i (1,000 gallons)

Thus, $(I_i + X_i)$ is the amount of fuel on board the aircraft when it departs city i.

Formulate as a linear programming problem.

[8]This problem has been adapted from D. Wayne Darnell and Carolyn Loflin, "National Airlines Fuel Management and Allocation Model," *Interfaces,* February 1977, pp. 1–16.

2–27. Acme Injectors (AI) produces fuel injectors for automobiles.[9] The tolerance between a needle and an injector body is critical; and even the most modern machinery cannot grind needles and bodies to exactly this tolerance. AI produces groups of needles and bodies and then sorts them into 1 of 10 classes such that matching a needle of class i with a body of class i will meet the required tolerance.

Suppose that the grinding machines can be set at any class from 1 to 10 for both needles and bodies, and suppose that for each of these settings, the percentage of product output in all classes is known and specified by P_{ijN} and P_{ijB}; that is, P_{ijN} represents the percentage of needles produced in class j when the needle-grinding machine is set at class i, and similarly for bodies. Classes $j = 0$ and $j = 11$ record defects (needles and bodies that are unusable). The grinding machines can be set to different values during different parts of a production run.

a. Formulate an LP model to determine grinding machine settings that maximize the percentage of needles and bodies that can be assembled into good injectors. Assume the production quantities are sufficiently large so that the output exactly matches the P_{ijN} and P_{ijB} percentages.

b. Now consider a highly simplified version of this problem, where needle grinding can be done perfectly; that is, $P_{ijN} = 1$ if $j = i$ and 0 if $j \neq i$. Also, for body grinding, assume $P_{i,i-1\ B} = 0.25$; $P_{i,i\ B} = 0.50$; and $P_{i,i+1\ B} = 0.25$ (all other values of P_{ijB} are zero). Can you solve this problem by inspection?

[9] This problem is taken from G. J. Gutierrez, W. H. Hausman, and H. L. Lee, "Dynamic Control of Imperfect Component Production for Assembly Operations," *IIE Transactions* 27 (1995), pp. 669–78.

Case 2–28

Impala Gold Company

The Impala Gold Company operated a gold mine in the Orange Free State, South Africa. The mining operation consisted of mining underground, at a depth of 4,000 feet, gold-bearing rock. The rock was transported up the mine shafts to a mill that crushed the rock and extracted the gold.

The Impala mine had three shafts. Information on these shafts is given in Table 2–20. Note that the rock mined in each shaft area has a different gold content as well as different costs.

Rock mined from all three shafts was sent to the mill to be crushed and refined. The mill capacity depended on how fine the rock was ground. If the rock was ground fine, mill capacity was 240,000 tons per month, and 95 percent of the gold was recovered in the operation. Rock from each shaft could be ground separately. The cost of milling a ton of rock ground fine was 1.12 rand per ton. If the rock was ground coarse, mill capacity was 250,000 tons per month, but gold recovery dropped to 90 percent. The cost of milling a ton of rock ground coarse was 0.85 rand. The mine could sell all the gold it produced at a price of 0.80 rand per gram.

The mine manager was concerned about how much rock he should mine in each shaft area. He noted that the mill capacity was not sufficient to handle all three shafts operating at full capacity. The problem was further complicated by the legal requirements that a mine could not mine "above the average grade" of the ore reserves. In the Impala mine, this

Table 2–20

	Shaft 1	*Shaft 2*	*Shaft 3*
Hoist capacity of shaft (tons per month)	85,000	90,000	95,000
Ore grade (grams of gold per ton of rock)	25	20	15
Variable cost of mining rock (rands per ton)	6	5	4

average grade was 20 grams per ton. Thus, there was the legal restriction that the mix of rock from the three shafts could not exceed an average of 20 grams per ton in ore grade.

Formulate a linear programming model to maximize profit from operating the mine.

Case 2–29

Racy's Department Store[10]

The treasurer of Racy's department store is performing her financial planning for the next six months, September through February. Because of the Christmas season, Racy's needs large amounts of cash, particularly in the months of November and December; and a large cash inflow occurs in January and February when customers pay their Christmas bills. These requirements are summarized in Table 2–21 (in $000s).

The treasurer has three sources of short-term funds to meet Racy's needs. These are:

1. Pledge Accounts Receivable. A local bank will lend Racy's funds on a month-by-month basis against a pledge on the accounts receivable balance at the beginning of a given month. The maximum loan is 75 percent of the receivables in a given month. The cost of this loan is 1.5 percent per month of the amount borrowed.

2. Stretch Payment of Purchases. Payment of the purchases can be delayed one month. Thus, for example, the $100,000 planned for payments for November could be delayed until December, and Racy's could use the funds to meet November needs. When purchase payments are thus stretched, Racy's loses the 3 percent discount it normally receives for prompt payment.

3. Use Short-Term Loan. A bank is willing to lend Racy's any amount from $40,000 to $100,000 on a six-month basis. The loan would be taken out in full in the beginning of September for a fixed amount and paid back in full at the end of February. It would not be possible to add to the loan or to pay off part of the loan during the period. The cost of the loan would be 1 percent per month, payable each month.

In any period, if the firm has excess funds, they can be invested in short-term government securities that return 0.5 percent per month.

The objective of the treasurer is to minimize the net interest cost to Racy's while meeting the firm's cash needs.

Table 2–21

	Sept.	*Oct.*	*Nov.*	*Dec.*	*Jan.*	*Feb.*
Accounts receivable balance (at beginning of month)	$70	$50	$70	$120	$100	$ 50
Planned payments of purchases (on assumption that discount is taken)	80	90	100	60	40	50
Cash needs for operations	—	30	60	90	—	—
Cash surplus from operations	20	—	—	—	30	150

[10]This case is based on A. A. Robichek, D. Teichroew, and J. M. Jones, "Optimal Short-Term Financing Decisions," *Management Science,* September 1965.

Formulate the above short-term financing decision as a linear programming problem. Be sure to label all variables and to explain the relationships between variables.

Case 2–30

Daguscahonda Mines Corporation

Daguscahonda Mines Corporation (DMC) operates a strip coal–mining operation in western Pennsylvania. Three mine sites (A, B, and C) currently are used, each producing coal of somewhat different sulfur and ash content. Coal from these sites is transported to a common crusher that grinds the coal into a finer mix. The coal is then "washed" to remove some of the sulfur and ash. In the washing process, the crushed coal is fed into a large tank containing a fluid. The cleaner coal floats and is removed for sale. Coal containing a heavier concentration of impurities sinks to the bottom and is discarded.

By using washing fluids of different densities (that is, having differing specific gravities), the amount of impurities removed can be controlled. Three fluids are currently in use, called here Light, Medium, and Heavy. With the Heavy fluid, a greater percentage of the coal is recovered (i.e., floats), but a smaller percentage of the impurities is removed. Refer to Table 2–22.

For example, if the coal from mine A is washed using Light fluid, only 40 percent of the coal is recovered for sale. This recovered coal contains 0.62 percent sulfur and 1.6 percent ash. On the other hand, the use of Heavy fluid increases the yield to 55 percent, but the recovered coal contains 1.04 percent sulfur and 2.1 percent ash.

The crushing and washing operation is set up so that any combination of coal from the mines can be used in conjunction with any of the fluids. After the washing operation, all the recovered coal is mixed to make one blend, sold by DMC. Environmental requirements limit the blend to a maximum of 0.5 percent sulfur and 2.0 percent ash.

There are some other restrictions. The equipment available limits the amount that can be produced in each mine. See Table 2–23. The crusher can handle a maximum of 8,000 tons per week of unwashed coal on regular time, but can be worked overtime up to an additional 4,000 tons. The cost of the crushing operation is $5 per ton of *unwashed coal* on regular time and $7.50 per ton on overtime. The washing tank can handle up to 6,000 tons of *recovered coal* on regular time and an additional 3,000 tons on overtime. The cost of washing is $10 per ton of *recovered coal* on regular time and $15 on overtime.

Table 2–22
Effects of Different Fluids on Coal Recovery and Impurities Remaining

Mine Source and Fluid Type	*Tons of Coal Recovered per Ton Input*	*Percent Sulfur Content of Recovered Coal*	*Percent Ash Content of Recovered Coal*
Mine A			
Light	0.40	0.62%	1.6%
Medium	0.50	0.91	1.9
Heavy	0.55	1.04	2.1
Mine B			
Light	0.70	0.22	1.9
Medium	0.90	0.35	2.3
Heavy	0.95	0.47	2.5
Mine C			
Light	0.62	0.42	1.5
Medium	0.75	0.50	1.8
Heavy	0.82	0.78	2.2

TABLE 2–23
Costs and Capacities of DMC Mines

Mine	*Capacity (maximum tons mined per week)*	*Cost ($ per ton mined)*
A	6,000	$25
B	2,300	45
C	5,000	40

The variable costs of operating each mine are also shown in Table 2–23. In addition, it costs $2 per ton of unwashed coal for Light fluid, $4 per ton of unwashed coal for Medium fluid, and $6 per ton of unwashed coal for Heavy fluid. DMC sells its coal blend for $100 per ton.

Formulate as a linear programming model.

CASE 2–31

MARYLAND DEPARTMENT OF NATURAL RESOURCES[11]

In recent years, the number of oysters in Chesapeake Bay has declined dramatically because of overfishing, bay pollution, and the spread of certain oyster diseases. The Maryland Department of Natural Resources (MDNR) has undertaken a program to increase oyster harvests. Oyster larvae, called *spat,* need to attach themselves to clean substrate to survive and grow. Old oyster shells provide an ideal environment for this attachment. The MDNR program involves dredging up old oyster shells, cleaning them, and "planting" them in areas oysters are known to grow, called oyster bars. The MDNR wants its program to be as effective as possible, within the budget available and within the limited time window when such planting is feasible.

The oyster shells are dredged and cleaned at one central location. From there they are transported to the oyster bars on a barge towed by a tug. They are then planted at the bar, and the tug and barge return for another load. There are many different oyster bars in the bay.

Because of the need to match this program with the timing of the oyster spawning and not disturb the breeding patterns of other marine life, there is only a short period when planting of shells is possible. There are also political considerations. Certain counties want what they consider at least a "fair share" of the oyster plantings.

Although there are many oyster bars to be planted across several counties, we shall consider only five bars for this case. Example data are shown in Table 2–24.

The oyster bars to be planted are various distances from the site where the oyster shells are dredged and cleaned. The first row in Table 2–24 indicates this distance by showing how many barge loads per day can be delivered to a given bar. Bar 1 is quite far, and it takes two days to deliver a barge load of shells and return (thus, a rate of 0.5 per day). Bar 4, on the other hand, is quite close, and two round trips per day can be made to that site. A barge contains 40,000 bushels of cleaned shells. Because there are only 25 days in total available to plant shells,[12] this distance is a limiting factor in how many shells can be planted at each

[11] This case is based on Qiwen Wang, Bruce Golden, Edward Wasil, and Sridhar Bashyam, "An Operational Analysis of Shell Planting Strategies for Improving the Survival of Oyster Larvae in the Chesapeake Bay," working paper, University of Maryland and American University, December 1993.

[12] There were actually about 45 days available. We have modified some of the numbers in the actual situation to fit this simplified case.

TABLE 2–24

	Bar 1	*Bar 2*	*Bar 3*	*Bar 4*	*Bar 5*
Barge loads per day	0.50	0.70	1.00	2.00	0.60
Cost per bushel planted	\$0.35	\$0.28	\$0.24	\$0.15	\$0.30
Relative attractiveness	0.9	0.8	0.5	0.4	0.6
Maximum bushels (thousands)	700	300	700	400	700
Minimum fraction of total	0.2	0.1	0.1	0.05	0.2

site. The contract with the tug and barge company specifies a total of only 70 barge-tug days available in total for all bars during the whole season.

There is also a total cost budget of \$500,000 available. The numbers in the second row of Table 2–24 indicate the cost of planting a bushel of shells at each location. The major differences relate to the barge-tug time needed to haul to the site.

The third row in Table 2–24 indicates the relative attractiveness of planting a bushel at each site. These estimates were based on historical data. This is the measure used to evaluate the overall effectiveness of the planting program.

The fourth row in Table 2–24 indicates the maximum number of bushels that can be effectively planted at each bar. The maximum number of bushels that can be dredged and cleaned over the period is 2 million. Finally, the fifth row in Table 2–24 is a political factor. The county in which each bar is located expects at least that fraction of the total shells to be planted at that site. For example, the county containing Bar 1 expects 20 percent of the total shells to be planted there.

Formulate as a linear programming model. The objective is to maximize the bushels planted weighted by relative attractiveness. The constraints relate to budget, barge-tugs available in total and days for each site, maximum shells at each bar, total shells available, and political considerations. Note: Although the number of barge-tug loads would generally be integer valued, ignore this for this formulation.

Solutions to Practice Problems

2–1. Let (all units are in thousands):

X_1 = Thousands of units of product A produced
X_2 = Thousands of units of product B produced
X_3 = Thousands of units of product C produced
X_4 = Thousands of units of product D produced

Maximize: $P = 40X_1 + 24X_2 + 36X_3 + 23X_4$
Subject to:

$2X_1 + 1X_2 + 2.5X_3 + 5X_4 \leq 120$ (milling constraint)
$1X_1 + 3X_2 + 2.5X_3 + 0X_4 \leq 160$ (assembly constraint)
$10X_1 + 5X_2 + 2X_3 + 12X_4 \leq 1{,}000$ (in-process inventory constraint)
$X_1 \leq 20$ (demand on product A)
$X_3 \leq 16$ (demand on product C)
$X_4 \geq 10$ (contract requirement on product D)
All $X_i \geq 0$

Solution: $X_1 = 10$; $X_2 = 50$; $X_3 = 0$; $X_4 = 10$; $P =$ \$1,830 thousand

2–2. Let (all units are in \$ millions):

X_1 = Funds in signature loans
X_2 = Funds in furniture loans
X_3 = Funds in automobile loans
X_4 = Funds in second home mortgages
X_5 = Funds in first home mortgages

Maximize: $P = 0.15X_1 + 0.12X_2 + 0.09X_3 + 0.10X_4 + 0.07X_5$
Subject to:

$X_1 + X_2 + X_3 + X_4 + X_5 \leq 1.5$ (total funds available)
$X_1 \leq 0.10(X_1 + X_2 + X_3 + X_4 + X_5)$
or
$0.9X_1 - 0.1X_2 - 0.1X_3 - 0.1X_4 - 0.1X_5 \leq 0$

$X_1 + X_2 \le 0.20(X_1 + X_2 + X_3 + X_4 + X_5)$ or
$0.8X_1 + 0.8X_2 - 0.2X_3 - 0.2X_4 - 0.2X_5 \le 0$
$X_5 \ge 0.40(X_4 + X_5)$ or $-0.4X_4 + 0.6X_5 \ge 0$
$X_5 \ge 0.20(X_1 + X_2 + X_3 + X_4 + X_5)$ or
$-0.2X_1 - 0.2X_2 - 0.2X_3 - 0.2X_4 + 0.8X_5 \ge 0$
$X_4 \le 0.25(X_1 + X_2 + X_3 + X_4 + X_5)$ or
$-0.25X_1 - 0.25X_2 - 0.25X_3 + 0.75X_4 - 0.25X_5 \le 0$
All $X_i \ge 0$

Solution: $X_1 = 0.15$; $X_2 = 0.15$; $X_3 = 0.525$;
$X_4 = 0.375$; $X_5 = 0.30$; $P = 0.146$

2–3. Maximize: $P = 30A + 30B$
Subject to:
$3A + 1B \le 30{,}000$
$A \le 8{,}000$
$B \le 12{,}000$

2–4. Let:

$X_1, X_2, \ldots, X_6$ = Number of transformers produced in regular time each month
$Y_1, Y_2, \ldots, Y_6$ = Number produced on overtime each month
$I_1, I_2, \ldots, I_6$ = Number of transformers in stock at the *end* of each month

Constraints:
Capacity:

$X_i \le 50$ for $i = 1, 2, \ldots 6$
$Y_i \le 20$ for $i = 1, 2, \ldots 6$

Inventory definition:

$I_1 = 15 + X_1 + Y_1 - 58$ for January
$I_i = I_{i-1} + X_i + Y_i - \text{Orders}_i$ For $i = 2, 3, \ldots 6$

Final inventory:

$I_6 \ge 5$

Objective function:

Minimize: $18X_1 + 17X_2 + 17X_3 + 18.5X_4 + 19X_5 + 19X_6 + 20Y_1 + 19Y_2 + 19Y_3 + 21Y_4 + 22Y_5 + 22Y_6 + 0.5I_1 + 0.5I_2 + 0.5I_3 + 0.5I_4 + 0.5I_5 + 0.5I_6$

Solution:

Month	*Regular Production*	*Overtime Production*	*Inventory*
January	43	0	0
February	50	0	14
March	50	11	41
April	50	0	22
May	50	0	0
June	48	0	5

Total cost is \$5,511 (thousand).

An alternative basic solution exists that involves regular production of 50 in January, and only 4 produced on overtime in March, with appropriate modifications in ending inventories in January (7) and February (21).

2–5. Let:

$X_1 = M^3$ of earth processed at plant 1
$X_2 = M^3$ at plant 2
$X_3 = M^3$ at plant 3

Minimize $C = 0.60X_1 + 0.36X_2 + 0.50X_3$
Subject to:
$0.58X_1 + 0.26X_2 + 0.21X_3 = 148{,}000$ (stone count requirement)
$0.36X_1 + 0.22X_2 + 0.263X_3 \ge 130{,}000$ (carat requirement)

$X_1 \le 83{,}000$
$X_2 \le 310{,}000$ (capacity requirement)
$X_3 \le 190{,}000$

Solution: $X_1 = 61{,}700$; $X_2 = 310{,}000$; $X_3 = 150{,}500$
Minimum cost = C = 223,880 rand

Motivating Example

Optimal Leases at GE Capital[1]

GE Capital, a part of GE's financial service business, arranges and structures leases for various large capital investments. These include ships, trucks, railcars, aircraft, construction and production equipment, and other products. For example, rather than purchase outright a piece of equipment such as a railroad tankcar, a shipper may enter into an arrangement in which GE Capital buys the tankcar and leases it to the shipper for a period of time. GE Capital is the lessor and the shipper is the lessee in this arrangement. A part of the funds for the purchase is generally provided by a third party, a financial institution.

GE Capital wants to structure the lease so that the schedule of payments meets the financial needs of the lessee. It also has to satisfy the loan repayment requirements of the financial institution making the loan. In addition, because there are important tax implications, the Internal Revenue Service has a very detailed set of rules about the payments and other arrangements of the lease.

This problem has been formulated as a linear programming problem. The decision variables represent the amount and timing of the lease payments. The requirements in the previous paragraph form the constraints for the problem. There are two possible objective functions. The first is the profitability of the lease payments to GE Capital. The second is the cost to the lessee, represented by the net present value of the lease payments. Depending on the circumstances, one of these is optimized and the other treated as a constraint. For example, in a very competitive market for a lease, an analyst using the linear programming model may define the minimum acceptable profitability for GE Capital as a constraint. Then, in order to provide the most competitive lease arrangement, the model may be solved by minimizing the cost to the lessee. In other circumstances, the cost to the lessee may be set as a constraint and the profitability to GE Capital maximized.

The lease structuring package is a part of a decision support and accounting-service system for use by approximately 300 GE Capital analysts. The mathematical programming approach has been demonstrated to be significantly better than the heuristic search process used previously. The linear programming model was originally built into the mainframe computing system, but recently it has been adapted so that it can be used on personal computers.

[1]This example is based on Charles J. Litty, "Optimal Lease Structuring at GE Capital," *Interfaces*, May–June 1994, pp. 34–45.

CHAPTER

3 SOLUTION OF LINEAR PROGRAMMING PROBLEMS

This chapter addresses the solution to linear programming problems. Since actual linear problems may be large and complex, sophisticated computer methods are used to solve them. One purpose of this chapter is to introduce solution packages that are available on personal computers. But for a manager facing a decision problem, the model solution is only a part of the answer. Analysis using models aims to get a better understanding of the problem, and the effect of various constraints and "what if" questions—in short, **sensitivity analysis.** The insight gained is often more valuable than the specific numerical answer. One of the advantages of linear programming is that it is very rich in providing such sensitivity information as a direct part of the solution. In order to understand this sensitivity analysis, it is necessary to have some understanding of the solution process. Hence, the first part of this chapter focuses on the graphical method for solving LP problems—not because this is used in practice, but because it provides such understanding. Next, the algebraic solution method is addressed, and finally the solution using the Solver spreadsheet package.

Graphic Solution

It is usually not possible to solve linear programming problems graphically because of our inability to visualize more than three spatial dimensions. However, it is useful to see how a simple problem can be solved graphically, since higher dimension problems have analogous solutions.

Situation. A firm manufactures two products, A and B. Each of these requires time on two machines. The first machine has 24 hours available, and the second has 16 hours available. Each unit of product A requires two hours of time on both machines. Each unit of product B requires three hours of time on the first machine and one hour on the second machine. The incremental profit is $6 per unit of A and $7 per unit of B, and the firm can sell as many of either product as it can manufacture.

Problem. Assuming the objective is to maximize profit, how many units of product A and product B should be produced?

Formulation. Let:

X_1 = Number of units of product A to be produced
X_2 = Number of units of product B to be produced
P = Incremental profit

We can express the situation and the objective (to maximize profit) using the equations below:

$$\begin{aligned} \text{Maximize:} \quad & P = 6X_1 + 7X_2 \\ \text{Subject to:} \quad & 2X_1 + 3X_2 \leq 24 \\ & 2X_1 + X_2 \leq 16 \\ & X_1, X_2 \geq 0 \end{aligned}$$

Solution. In Figure 3–1, the two constraining equations are shown. The equation:

$$2X_1 + 3X_2 \leq 24$$

is the constraint imposed by limitation of hours available (24) on the first machine, and all points to the left and below the line are possible (feasible) combinations of X_1 and X_2. Similarly:

$$2X_1 + X_2 \leq 16$$

is the constraint associated with the second machine, and the points to the left and below are feasible. We also have constraints $X_1 \geq 0$ and $X_2 \geq 0$, since we cannot have negative output.

Consider the point marked F inside the shaded region in Figure 3–1 involving production of five units of product A and four units of product B. This requires $2 \times 5 + 3 \times 4 = 22$ hours of time on the first machine. Since this is less than the

FIGURE 3–1
LP Constraints and Feasible Region

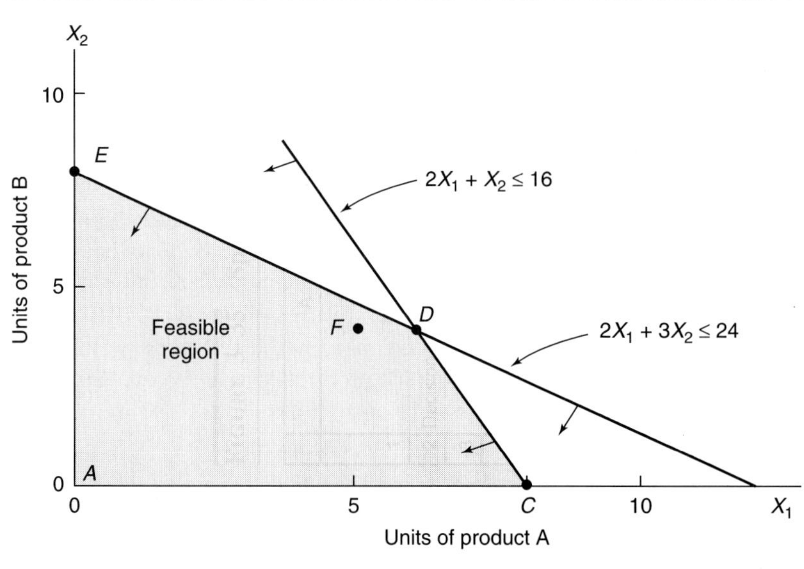

24 hours available, it satisfies the first machine constraint. Similarly, $2 \times 5 + 1 \times 4 = 14$ hours of time on the second machine are required, again less than the 16 available hours. Finally, both X_1 and X_2 are positive, satisfying the non-negativity constraints. Since the solution represented by point F does not violate any constraint, it is a **feasible** point. The shaded region $ACDE$ in Figure 3–1 is the set of points that are feasible under all constraints, and it is called the **feasible region.**

Our aim is to find the point or points in the feasible region $ACDE$ that maximizes profit. We now show that *the optimum point will always be at a corner point of the feasible region*. The four corner points in $ACDE$ are the points A, C, D, and E. One of these points must be an optimum solution to the linear programming problem.[2]

To see intuitively why the optimum solution will always be at a corner point of the feasible region, we plot a set of profit functions. A *profit function* is a line containing all combinations of X_1 and X_2 that represent a constant amount of profit. In Figure 3–2, a series of profit functions for different profit levels are shown as dashed lines.

Consider the profit function for which $P = 42$. The equation of this line is:

$$P = 42 = 6X_1 + 7X_2$$

This line contains many feasible points (points within $ACDE$), all of which would give \$42 in profit. But the line $P = 54$ is better than $P = 42$, since it contains feasible points with profit of \$54. Note that the profit line $P = 54$ is parallel to the line $P = 42$; in LP problems, all profit lines will be parallel to one another. We continue considering lines parallel to line $P = 42$ until we reach the line $P = 64$. Here, there

FIGURE 3–2
Profit Functions
$P = 6X_1 + 7X_2$

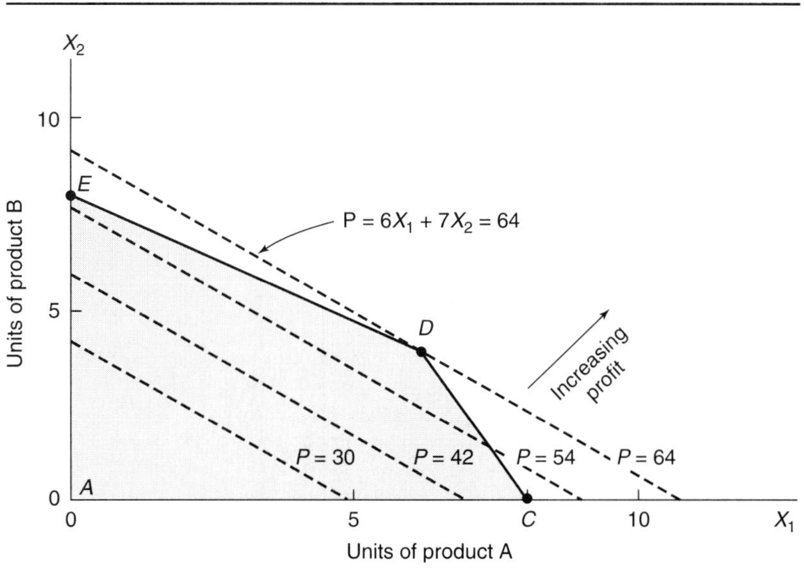

[2]We shall show shortly that two or more adjacent corner points can be alternative optimal solutions.

is only one point in the *ACDE* region—namely, *D* itself, and *D* (which is $X_1 = 6$, $X_2 = 4$) is the optimal solution. For larger values of *P*, there are no points in the *ACDE* region.

The particular corner point that is the optimum solution depends on the slope of the profit function: that is, on the relative profitability of products A and B. If, for example, product A were much more profitable per unit than B—say, \$8 per unit for A versus \$2 per unit for B—then the objective function would be:

$$P = 8X_1 + 2X_2$$

The profit functions for this alternative case are shown in Figure 3–3. Note that point *C* now is the optimum solution. Similarly, if product B were much more profitable than A, and the objective function were, say:

$$P = 2X_1 + 8X_2$$

then point *E* would be the optimum. If the firm lost money on both products A and B, then point *A*, the origin with no production of either, would be the optimum.

Alternative Optimal Solutions. It is possible for the profit functions to have exactly the same slope as one of the constraint equations. For example, if the objective function were $P = 8X_1 + 4X_2$, it would represent a series of lines parallel to *CD*, as in Figure 3–4. In this case, there are multiple optimal solutions. Corner points *C* and *D* both are optimum points with profit of \$64. But so are all the points lying on the line *CD* in Figure 3–4.

More Dimensions. Visualize extending the LP problem to three dimensions, as shown in Figure 3–5. The constraints represent planes in three-dimensional space,

FIGURE 3–3
Alternative Profit Functions
$P = 8X_1 + 2X_2$

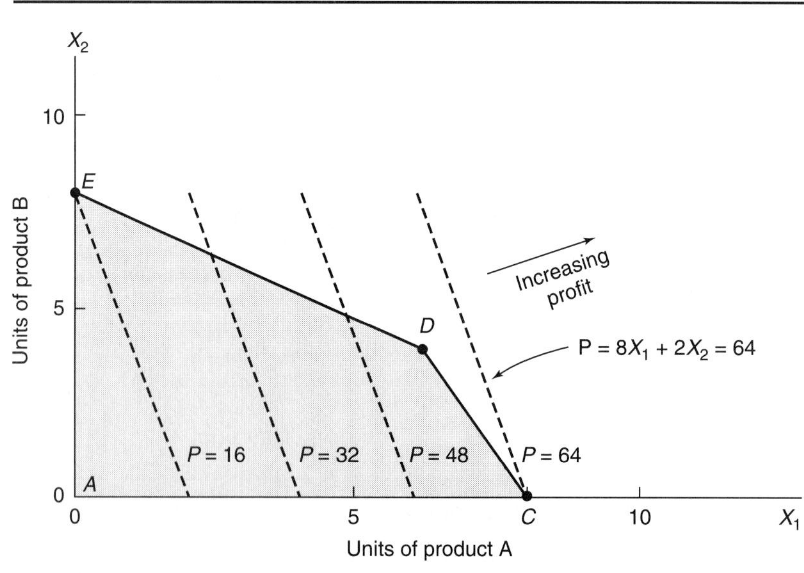

and the feasible region is a three-dimensional area bounded by these planes. The corner points *A, B, . . . O* represent places where these constraint planes intersect. The profit functions (not shown) are also planes. As in the two-dimensional case, the optimal solution must be at one of the feasible corner points.

While we cannot visualize what a four- (or more) dimensional problem would look like, the basic ideas can be extended to problems with many variables using algebraic methods.

FIGURE 3–4
Multiple Optimal Solutions
$P = 8X_1 + 4X_2$

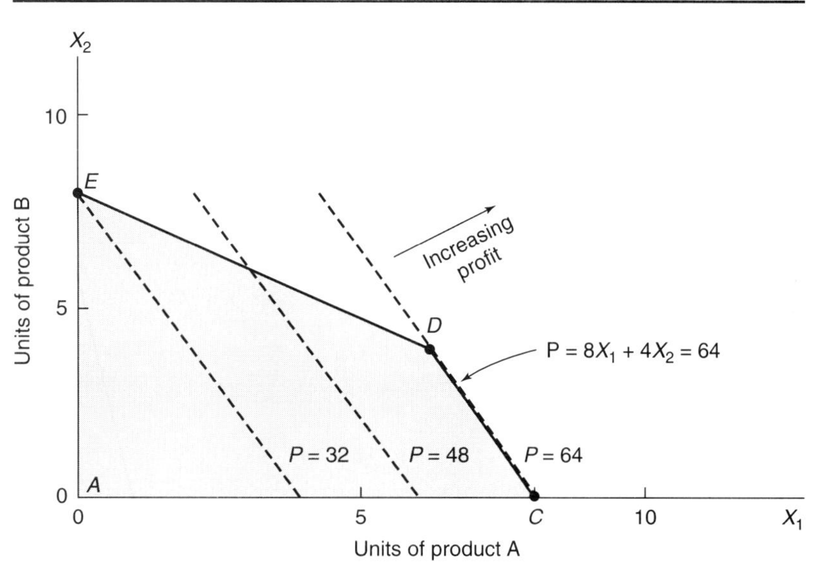

FIGURE 3–5
Feasible Region in Three Dimensions

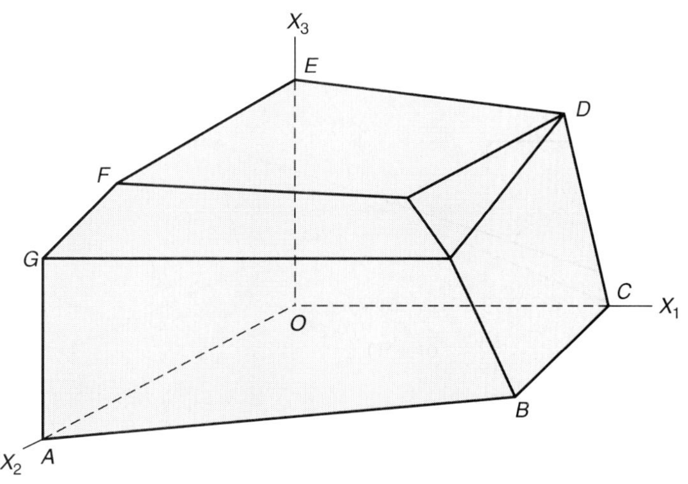

Summary

The optimal solutions to a linear programming problem always lie at a corner point of the feasible region. There may be alternative optimal solutions, involving adjacent corner points (and points on the line connecting them).

Sensitivity Analysis on the Constraints

Finding the solution to a decision model is only the first step in analysis. It is also important for the manager to understand how sensitive that solution is to changes in assumptions and exogenous factors. This is true also for linear programming models, and one of the very nice features of LP models is that much of this sensitivity analysis comes directly from the solution to the problem. We shall address these ideas first graphically, and later in the chapter by interpreting the output of computer programs used to solve LP problems.

Let us expand slightly the problem we have been using as our example. Suppose that there is a market limit of six units on the number of units of product B that can be sold. The formulation now becomes:

$$\begin{aligned} \text{Maximize:} \quad & P = 6X_1 + 7X_2 \\ \text{Subject to:} \quad & 2X_1 + 3X_2 \leq 24 \\ & 2X_1 + X_2 \leq 16 \\ & X_2 \leq 6 \\ & X_1, X_2 \geq 0 \end{aligned}$$

and is graphed in Figure 3–6.

FIGURE 3–6
Feasible Region for Revised Problem

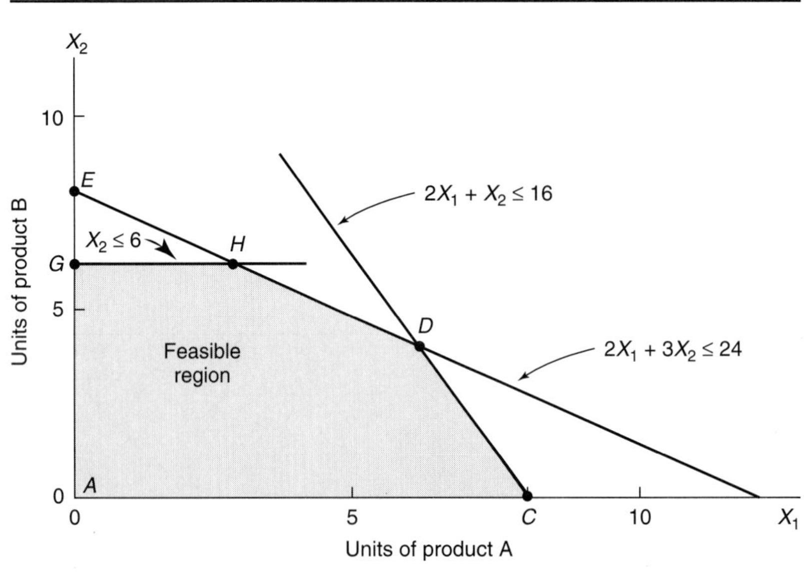

Shadow Prices

Consider the constraint equation for machine 1, specifying that a maximum of 24 hours could be made available. In LP terminology, this capacity limit is often called the **right-hand side** (or simply **RHS**) value, since it is on the right-hand side of the inequality sign. Suppose an extra hour could be made available so that the constraint now becomes:

$$2X_1 + 3X_2 \leq 25$$

What happens to the solution?

This case is shown graphically in Figure 3–7. The new optimal solution moves to the point D', which has $X_1 = 5.75$ and $X_2 = 4.5$.[3] Since the old solution called for $X_1 = 6$ and $X_2 = 4$, an additional hour of time on machine 1 results in a reduction

FIGURE 3–7 Sensitivity Analysis for Machine 1 Constraint

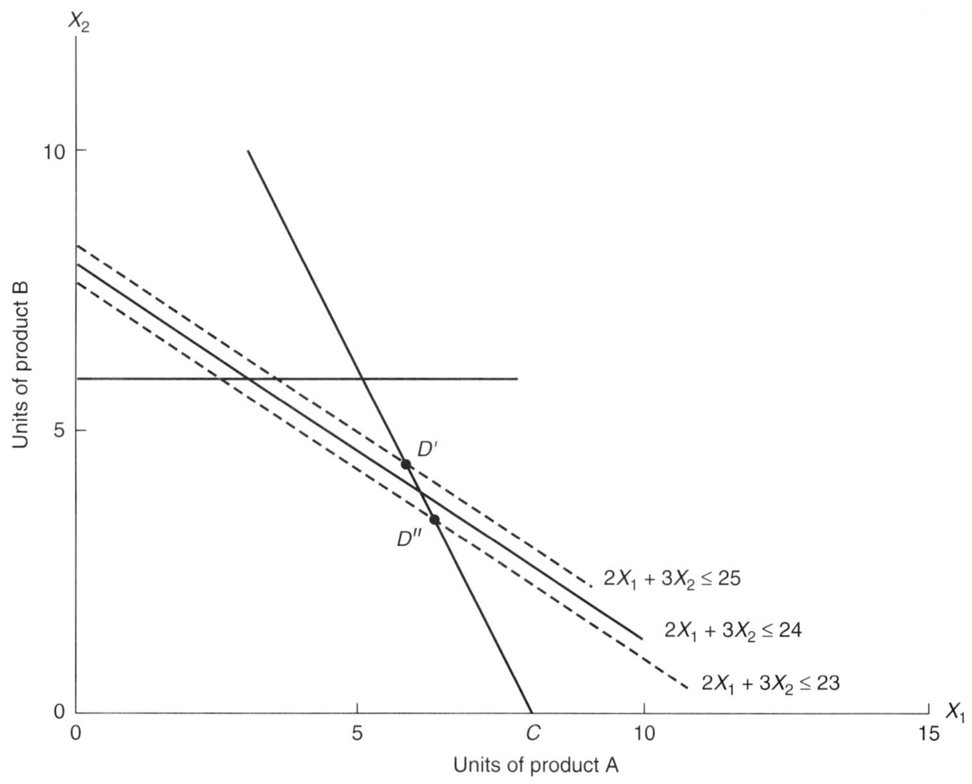

[3]This solution can be found by simultaneously solving the two equations $2X_1 + X_2 = 16$ and $2X_1 + 3X_2 = 25$. Note that this is not an integer solution, but the *X*s could be interpreted as rates of production.

of 0.25 units of product A and an increase of 0.5 units of product B. The net change in the objective function P is thus:

$$-(0.25)\$6 + (0.50)\$7 = \$2$$

or an increase of \$2 in profit.[4] This is called the **shadow price,** *marginal value,* or *dual price.* It is the incremental change in profit per unit change in the RHS of a constraint.

Note that the shadow price also holds for a decrease in the RHS value. For example, if only 23 hours were available on machine 1, the point D'' in Figure 3–7 would be the optimal solution ($X_1 = 6.25$ and $X_2 = 3.5$), with a *decrease* in profit of \$2. *Thus, the shadow price, dual price, or marginal value represents the incremental increase in profit when a constraint is relaxed by one unit, and the decrease in profit when a constraint is tightened by one unit.*

Exactly the same analysis can be applied to the constraint on machine 2. This is shown in Figure 3–8. When that constraint is relaxed by adding an additional hour, the constraint becomes:

$$2X_1 + X_2 \leq 17$$

FIGURE 3–8 Sensitivity Analysis for Machine 2 Constraint

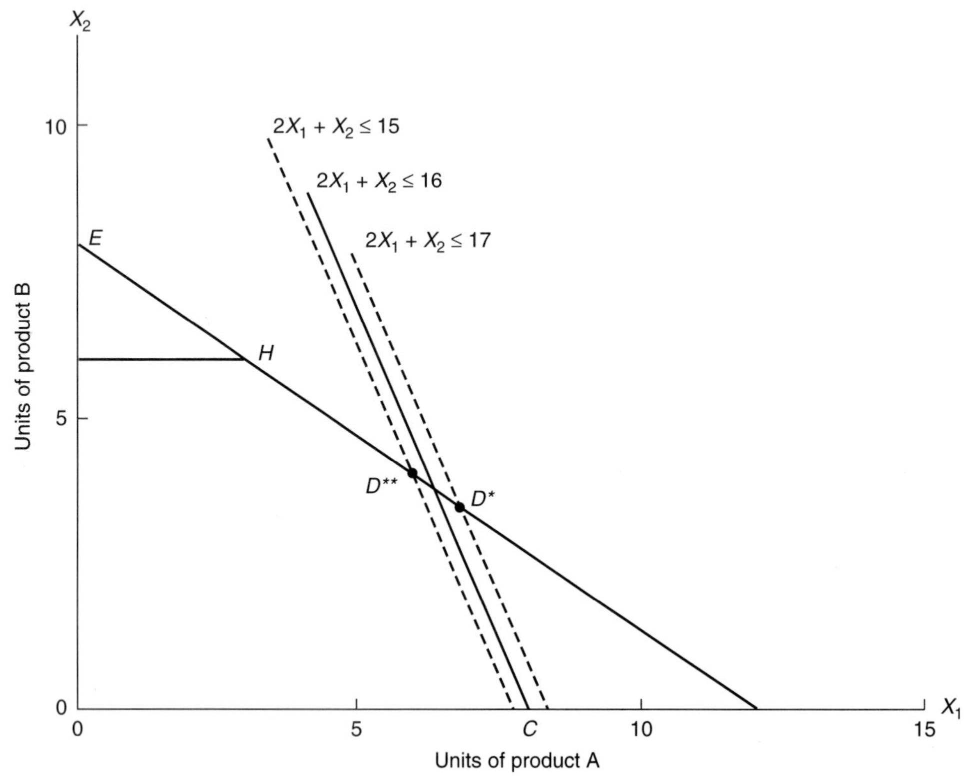

[4]Another way to see this is to put the new values into the objective function $6X_1 + 7X_2$, giving a profit of \$66, versus \$64 previously, for an increase of \$2.

and the optimum point is D^* with $X_1 = 6.75$ and $X_2 = 3.5$. This represents an increase of 0.75 in the units of product A and a decrease of 0.5 units of product B. The net effect on profit is:

$$+(0.75)\$6 - (0.5)\$7 = \$1$$

A similar reduction in the RHS (i.e., in the hours available) of constraint 2 results in a solution of $X_1 = 5.25$ and $X_2 = 4.5$ and a decrease in profit of \$1. Thus, the shadow price associated with the machine 2 constraint is \$1.

Consider the third constraint, the limit on demand for product B:

$$X_2 \leq 6$$

A one-unit increase in this limit to $X_2 \leq 7$ and a one-unit decrease to $X_2 \leq 5$ are shown graphed in Figure 3–9. Note that neither change affects the solution at all because the constraint $X_2 \leq 6$ is not binding. The optimal solution called for only four units of product B, and so the market limit of six units doesn't matter. Thus, the shadow price is zero. In fact, *the shadow price of any nonbinding constraint is always zero.*

Reduced Costs—Shadow Prices for Non-Negativity Constraints. It is also possible to determine the marginal values associated with forcing at least one unit of a

FIGURE 3–9 Sensitivity Analysis on Market Demand for Product B

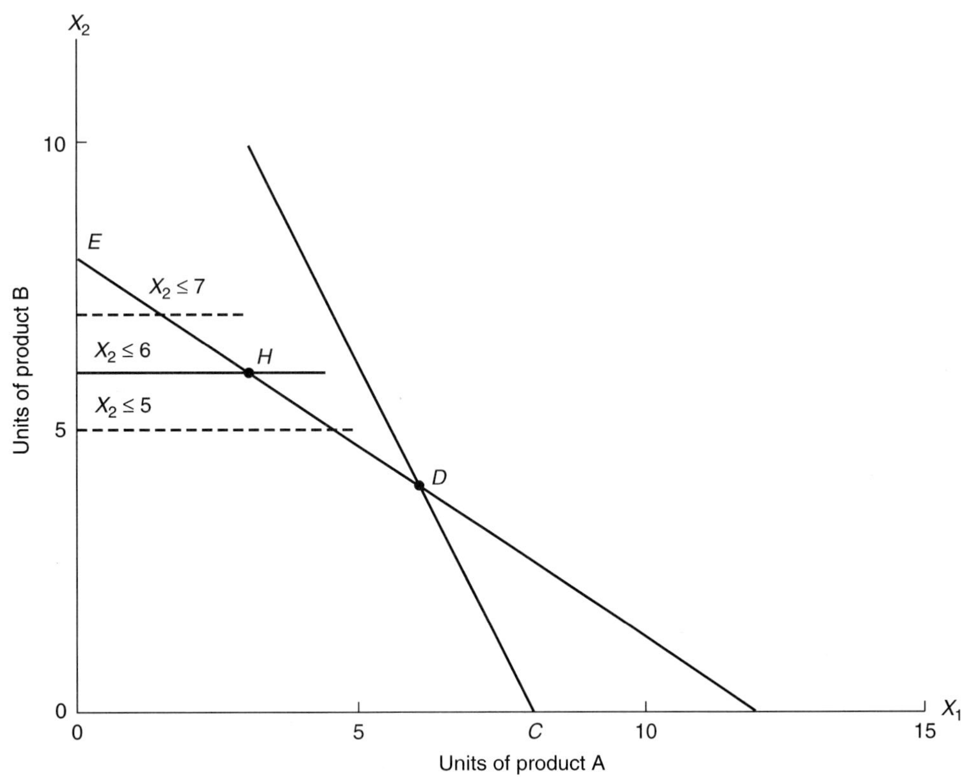

decision variable into the solution. Recall that the non-negativity constraints are $X_1 \geq 0$, $X_2 \geq 0$. Forcing one unit into the solution can be thought of as changing a non-negativity constraint to $X_1 \geq 1$ or $X_2 \geq 1$. The marginal values for doing this are called **reduced costs.**

Consider again our basic problem as graphed in Figure 3–9. The optimal solution calls for $X_1 = 6$ and $X_2 = 4$. Both of these are positive values, and hence, neither of the non-negativity constraints is binding. Thus, the marginal value (i.e., the reduced cost) associated with changing them is zero, just as for other non-binding constraints.

However, suppose the objective function were $P = 10X_1 + 3X_2$, as shown in Figure 3–10. Then point C is the optimum solution, with $X_1 = 8$ and $X_2 = 0$, producing profit of \$80. Note that since $X_2 = 0$, the non-negativity constraint $X_2 \geq 0$ is binding. Now suppose we must produce at least one unit of product B because of a commitment to a long-time customer, so that we change the constraint to $X_2 \geq 1$. This changes the optimum solution in Figure 3–10 to C', with $X_1 = 7.5$, $X_2 = 1$, and a profit of \$78, a reduction of \$2 from the previous level. Thus, in this case, the reduced cost or marginal value associated with the non-negativity constraint on X_2 is \$2, the cost of keeping the goodwill of our customer.

Use of Shadow Prices. These shadow prices have important managerial uses. Although constraints and limits exist in the world, most of them are not absolute. For example, the manager who formulated the example LP problem determined the hours available on each machine under ordinary circumstances. But it may be possible to obtain additional hours by working overtime, by buying additional equipment, or by rescheduling other uses. The shadow prices tell how much this is worth, at the margin, and thus help to identify key bottlenecks. In our example, the manager knows that it is twice as valuable (\$2 versus \$1) to obtain additional hours for machine 1 as it is for machine 2.

FIGURE 3–10
Sensitivity Analysis for Non-Negativity Constraint $X_2 \geq 0$

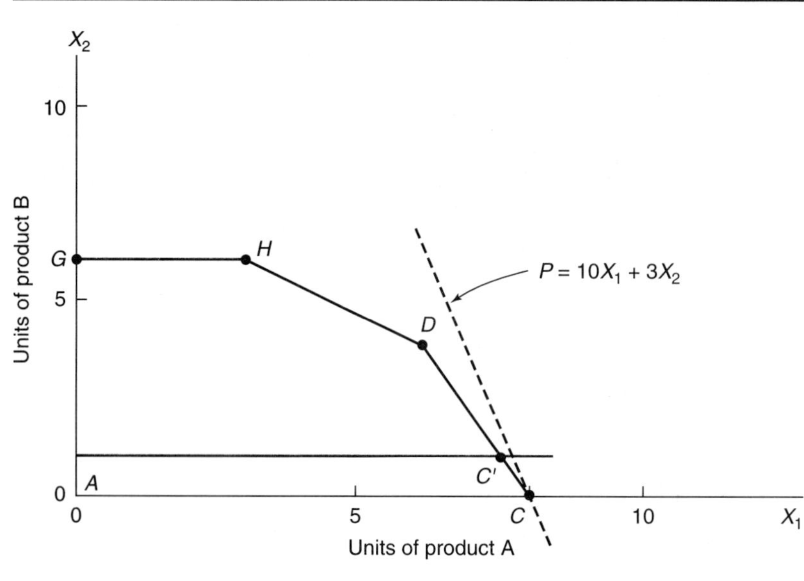

The value of carefully examining constraints or bottlenecks has been highlighted in a recent managerial approach called the Theory of Constraints.[5] This has led to cost accounting systems detailing the costs of these constraints.[6] Overall, the idea is to focus management attention on managing the bottlenecks or constraints in a system. The shadow prices obtained from a linear programming model can be quite useful in this process.

Summary

A shadow price or dual price represents the marginal value associated with a unit change in the RHS of a constraint. A reduced cost similarly represents the marginal value of forcing one unit of a decision variable into the solution. Reduced costs can be thought of as shadow prices on the non-negativity constraints. If a constraint is not binding, its shadow price is zero.

Right-Hand Side (RHS) Ranges

While the shadow prices give the marginal value of making a small change in a constraint limit (i.e., in the RHS value), it would be a mistake to believe that these values would hold if capacity were changed arbitrarily. At some point, additional capacity becomes excess and has no value. Hence, there are limits on the range of capacity over which the marginal values hold.

Consider again the constraint of 24 hours for the time available for machine 1. Figure 3–11 shows what happens as additional hours are made available. Recall from the initial discussion of shadow prices that each additional hour resulted in a reduction of 0.25 units of product A and an increase of 0.5 units of product B. The shadow price associated with each incremental hour was $2. With 28 hours available, the optimal solution has moved from *D* to *J*. At *J*, the solution is $X_1 = 5$ and $X_2 = 6$. Beyond this point, additional hours on machine 1 will have no effect, since the constraint $X_2 \leq 6$ now becomes binding. Given the other constraints in the problem, 28 hours of time on machine 1 is the maximum that can be profitably used. Thus, this increase of 4 hours up to 28 hours available represents the upper limit on the range over which the shadow price of $2 is valid.

Similarly, as hours of machine 1 time are reduced, the optimal solution moves down to point *C* in Figure 3–11, in which 16 hours of machine time are used. As hours are reduced, the decrease in profit comes from increasing units of product A and reducing units of product B. But at point *C*, no units of product B are being produced, so this substitution process is no longer possible. Thus, the lower limit on the range of the shadow price of $2 for machine 1 time is a reduction of 8 hours (from 24 to 16).

---

[5] E. Goldratt, *The Theory of Constraints* (New York: North River Press, 1990).

[6] See C. Horngren, G. Foster, and S. Datar, *Cost Accounting, A Managerial Approach,* 8th ed. (Englewood Cliffs, NJ: Prentice Hall, 1994), pp. 816–20.

FIGURE 3–11
Range on Machine 1 Constraint

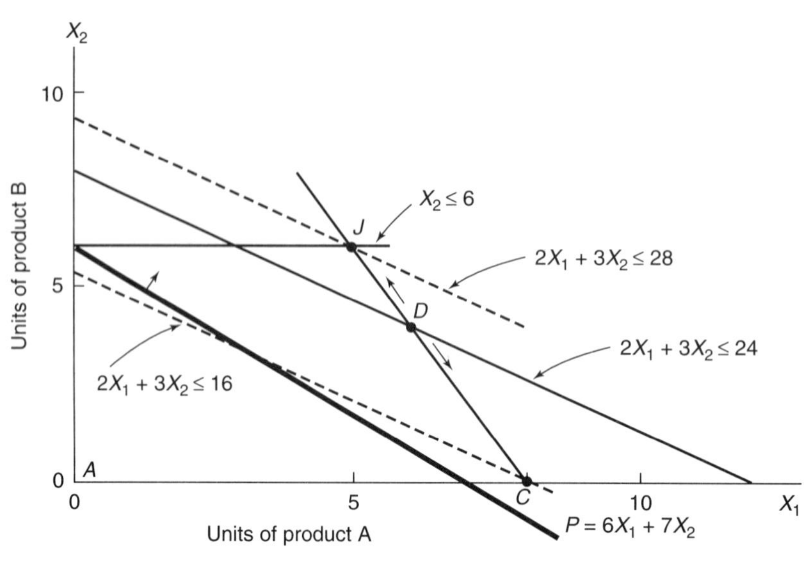

FIGURE 3–12
Range on Machine 2 Constraint

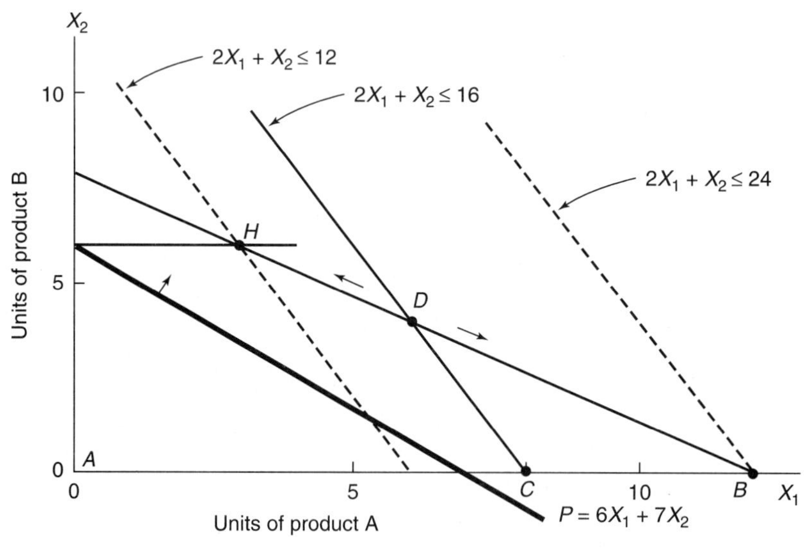

For machine 2, a similar analysis can be performed. Figure 3–12 shows the limits. As hours are added to the 16 available, the optimal solution moves from *D* to *B*. At this point , 8 hours have been added (from 16 to 24), and additional hours will add no value. When hours available are reduced by 4 (from 16 to 12), the optimal solution moves from *D* to *H*. Thus, the shadow price of \$1 holds over the range from 12 to 24 hours of time available on machine 2.

The constraint on market demand for product B, $X_2 \leq 6$, is somewhat different. Recall that this constraint is not binding and has a shadow price of zero. The optimal solution calls for only four units of product B. Hence, the current demand limit could be increased indefinitely without any effect; if the constraint were $X_2 \leq 10$ or $X_2 \leq 100$, it would not matter. On the other hand, if the demand limit were to fall to four units so that the constraint were $X_2 \leq 4$, it would become binding. Any reduction below this four-unit limit would reduce profit. Hence, the range on the demand limit (i.e., the RHS) for the third constraint is from four units to infinity, and within this range the zero shadow price holds.

For the three constraints, sensitivity analysis has produced the following ranges for the RHS values:

Constraint	*Current Limit*	*Shadow Price*	*Allowable Increase*	*Allowable Decrease*
Machine 1 hours	24	\$2	4	8
Machine 2 hours	16	\$1	8	4
Demand for product B	6	0	Infinite	2

Summary

The shadow prices express the marginal value for changing the RHS of a constraint, but these values hold only over limited ranges.

Sensitivity Analysis—New Product Evaluation

Shadow prices can be useful in identifying bottlenecks or constraints that are costly and might be profitably changed. Shadow prices can also be useful in evaluating new products. Consider an extension of our example. The company's research and development department has created a new product, product C. It is very profitable, \$10 per unit, but it requires four hours of time on machine 1 and three hours on machine 2. Should the company produce any units of product C?

Of course, we could reformulate the whole LP problem to add this new product. But a quick answer can be obtained by using the shadow prices. Producing any of product C will require reducing the amounts of the other two products, since all products compete for time available on the two machines. Recall that the shadow prices imply that an hour of time on machine 1 has a value of \$2 and for machine 2, a value of \$1. One unit of product C requires four hours and three hours on the two machines, respectively. Hence, the **opportunity cost** for a unit of product C is:

[(Shadow price on machine 1 hours) × (Hours required on machine 1)] +
[(Shadow price on machine 2 hours) × (Hours required on machine 2)]

or

$$\$2 \times 4 + \$1 \times 3 = \$11$$

This represents the cost of the lost opportunity to produce products A and B. Since the unit profit for product C is only \$10, it should not be produced, since the opportunity cost exceeds the unit profit.

Another Example

The same firm has another new item, product D, which requires one hour of time on each machine. It has a per unit profit of \$5. Should any be produced?

The opportunity cost for this product is:

$$\$2 \times 1 + \$1 \times 1 = \$3$$

Since the per unit profit of \$5 exceeds the opportunity cost of \$3, some of product D should be produced.

This analysis does not tell us exactly how many units of product D to make—only that we should include it in the product mix. The manager would reformulate the LP problem to include a new decision variable for product D, and re-solve the LP problem.

Summary

The opportunity cost for a new product is calculated as the sum of the:

$$(\text{Shadow price}) \cdot (\text{Units required})$$

for all constraints affected. If the opportunity cost is less than the unit profit for the new product, then it is profitable and at least some of it should be included in the optimal solution. If the opportunity cost is greater than the unit profit, then the product should not be produced.

Sensitivity Analysis—Objective Function Coefficients

A manager may be interested in what happens to the solution of an LP problem if one of the coefficients of the objective function changes due to, for example, an increase in the price of a key raw material. We can do a graphical analysis similar to what was done for changes in RHS coefficients.

Suppose the per unit profit for product A is indeed fixed at \$6 per unit, but the unit profit for B, while expected to be \$7, might change. Figure 3–13 shows the profit functions as the unit profit of product B increases to \$8, then \$9, and then \$10. When the objective function coefficient for X_2 is \$8 (i.e., unit profit of \$8 for product B), the profit function is $P = 6X_1 + 8X_2$ and point D is still the optimal solution. When the coefficient of X_2 increases to \$9, the profit function slope is identical to that of the machine 1 constraint and lies exactly on that constraint line. Hence, there are alternative optimal solutions and both D and H are optimal corner points. Suppose the coefficient of X_2 increases more—say, to \$10 per unit—so that the profit function is $P = 6X_1 + 10X_2$, as shown in Figure 3–13. Note that there are points above this line (i.e., with higher profit) in the feasible region and hence the point D is no longer optimal. Point H now becomes the unique optimal solution. That is, when the coefficient of X_2 exceeds \$9, the optimum jumps from point D to point H.

FIGURE 3–13
Sensitivity Analysis: Increasing the per Unit Profit of Product B

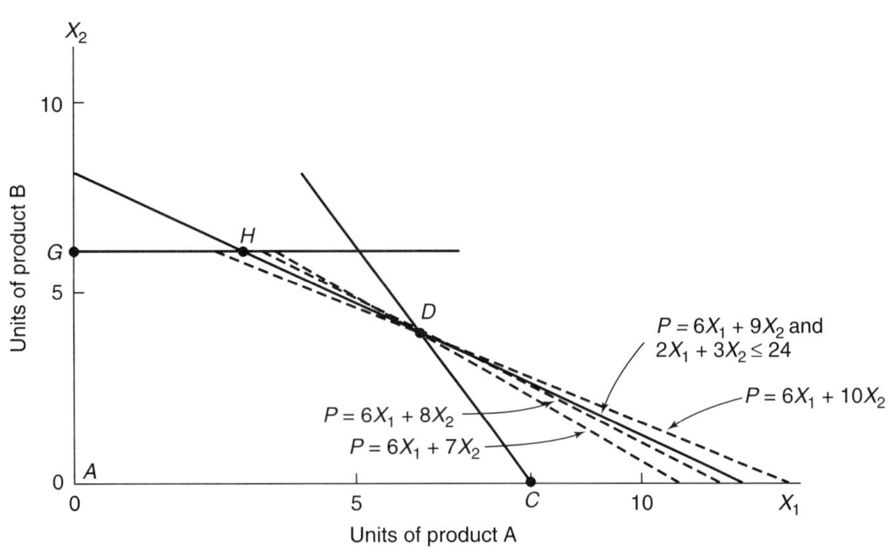

FIGURE 3–14
Sensitivity Analysis: Decreasing the per Unit Profit of Product B

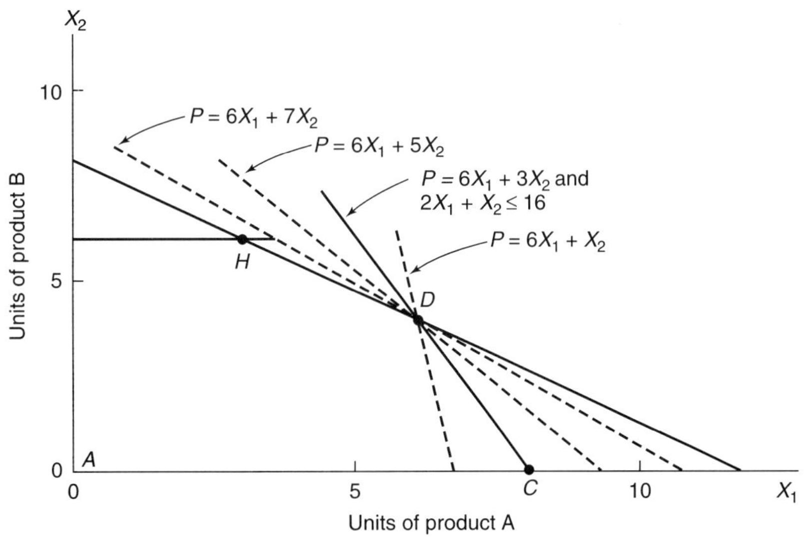

A similar analysis holds if the coefficient of X_2 falls. Figure 3–14 shows the profit function for values \$5, \$3, and \$1 for the coefficient of X_2. For a coefficient of 3, the profit function is $P = 6X_1 + 3X_2$; now, the profit function lies exactly on the constraint for machine 2 and points D and C are both optimal. When the coefficient falls further—say, to 1—the optimal point moves to C.

The same analysis can be done for the profit of A, holding the coefficient of X_2 constant and varying that for X_1. Although the graphical analysis is not shown, the results indicate that the coefficient for X_1 can fall from 6 to 4.67 before the optimal point shifts to H. Similarly, the coefficient can increase from 6 to 14 before the optimal point jumps to C.[7] These results can be summarized as follows:

Objective Function Coefficient Ranges
Range in Which the Solution Remains Unchanged

Variable	*Current Coefficient*	*Allowable Increase*	*Allowable Decrease*
Product A	6	8	1.33
Product B	7	2	4

RHS Ranges versus Objective Coefficient Ranges. The sensitivity analysis ranges for the objective coefficients developed above and those for the RHS coefficients are similar in concept. However, there are also some important differences.

Within the range specified for the objective coefficient ranges, the optimal solution remains exactly the same—that is, the firm should produce six units of product A and four units of product B. Beyond the range, the optimal solution *jumps abruptly* to another corner point. The total profit, of course, varies with changes in the coefficients, but, to repeat, the solution stays fixed within the ranges.

In contrast, within the RHS ranges, the solution changes as the optimal point moves along one of the constraint lines. In our example, different amounts of products A and B are produced as the optimal point moves. At the limit of the range, a new corner point becomes the optimal solution.[8]

Summary

The ranges, both for the RHS coefficients and for the objective function coefficients, provide important information in interpreting the LP solution. The RHS ranges determine the limits within which the shadow price holds for each constraint. The objective coefficient ranges determine limits within which the solution remains the same.

Minimization

So far, our example has involved maximization of the objective function. Minimization is similar, as the following example shows.

[7]Actually, the analysis for X_1 is unnecessary, since all that matters i the slope of the profit function. This is determined by the ratio of the two coefficients. When the ratio (coefficient of X_1)/(coefficient of X_2) is between ⅔ and 2.0, the optimal point is D. When the ratio is below ⅔, the optimal shifts to H; above 2.0, it shifts to C.

[8]In the terms of the algebraic formulation to be discussed shortly, the basic variables remain the same within the range. At the limit, the set of basic variables changes.

Example

A company has two mills. The decision variables are the number of hours per week that each operates. The first mill can operate a maximum of 40 hours, and the second a maximum of 60 hours per week. Each hour of operation at the first mill results in 3 tons of finished product; each hour at the second mill produces 4 tons of product. The company has commitments to customers for at least 175 tons of finished product. It costs \$20,000 for each hour of operation of the first mill and \$40,000 per hour for the second; the company wishes to keep costs as low as possible. For policy reasons, the company wishes to operate at least as many hours at the second mill as at the first.

The LP formulation is:

Let: X_1 = Weekly hours at the first mill
X_2 = Weekly hours at the second mill

Objective function:

Minimize:	$C = 20X_1 + 40X_2$	(thousands of \$)
Subject to:	$X_1 \leq 40$	(mill maximum)
	$X_2 \leq 60$	(mill maximum)
	$3X_1 + 4X_2 \geq 175$	(customer requirements—tons)
	$X_2 \geq X_1$ or $-X_1 + X_2 \geq 0$	(policy requirement)
	$X_1 \geq 0, X_2 \geq 0$	(non-negativity constraints)

The solution is graphed in Figure 3–15 with the feasible region shaded. The cost functions are dashed lines. Since we seek a minimum value, the preferred lines (with smaller cost) are below. The optimum corner point occurs at $X_1 = 25$, $X_2 = 25$ with each mill operating at 25 hours per week, with a cost of \$1,500 (thousand).

FIGURE 3–15
Graphic Analysis for Minimization Problem

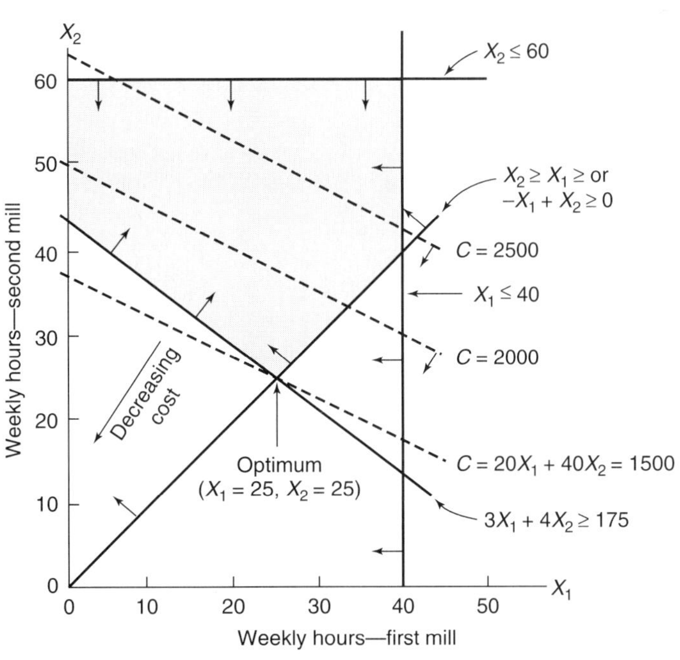

Note that the basic concepts of feasible region, corner points, and optimal solution are the same as in the maximization case. The basic ideas of sensitivity analysis and ranges are also similar and will be presented for this example later in the chapter in the section on interpretation of computer output.

Algebraic Approach

Up to now, we have considered only the formulation of linear programming problems in algebraic terms. In this section, we shall extend the algebraic approach to demonstrate some important LP concepts.

Consider the original maximization problem that was solved at the beginning of this chapter. Recall that we had:

$$\begin{aligned} \text{Maximize:} \quad & P = 6X_1 + 7X_2 \\ \text{Subject to:} \quad & 2X_1 + 3X_2 \leq 24 \\ & 2X_1 + X_2 \leq 16 \\ & X_1, X_2 \geq 0 \end{aligned}$$

The first step in our algebraic procedure is to convert the inequality expressions in the problem to equalities. This is done by adding two new variables, X_3 and X_4, called **slack variables.** The slack variables represent *unused capacity* in the first and second constraint, respectively. Thus, X_3 is the number of unused hours of capacity on machine 1 and X_4 is the number of unused hours on machine 2. It is always possible to convert the inequalities to equalities since there must be some amount—the unused capacity X_3—that, when added to $(2X_1 + 3X_2)$, will equal 24 (X_3 may be equal to or greater than zero).

The constraints of the problem are now rewritten as:

$$\begin{aligned} 2X_1 + 3X_2 + X_3 &= 24 \\ 2X_1 + X_2 + X_4 &= 16 \\ X_1, X_2, X_3, X_4 &\geq 0 \end{aligned}$$

The objective function now becomes:

$$\text{Maximize: } P = 6X_1 + 7X_2 + 0X_3 + 0X_4$$

The slack variables introduce no profit, so their coefficients in the profit equation are zero.

Any values for X_1, X_2, X_3, and X_4 that satisfy the constraint equations are a feasible solution to the linear programming problem. The shaded area in Figure 3–16 contains all the feasible solutions, as was discussed earlier in the chapter.

In the general linear programming problem, there are m constraint equations. After the slack variables have been added, there are more than m variables. You may recall from a course in algebra that one can find a single unique solution to a set of m linear equations if there are exactly m unknown variables. But with more than m variables, as in the LP case, there is no unique solution.

However, suppose we arbitrarily select any m variables and set the rest equal to zero, then solve the m equations for the selected m variables to obtain a solution. Such a solution is called a **basic solution.** The selected variables are called the **basic solution variables** or simply the **basis.** The variables set equal to zero are the **outside variables** or nonbasic variables.

FIGURE 3–16
Basic Solutions

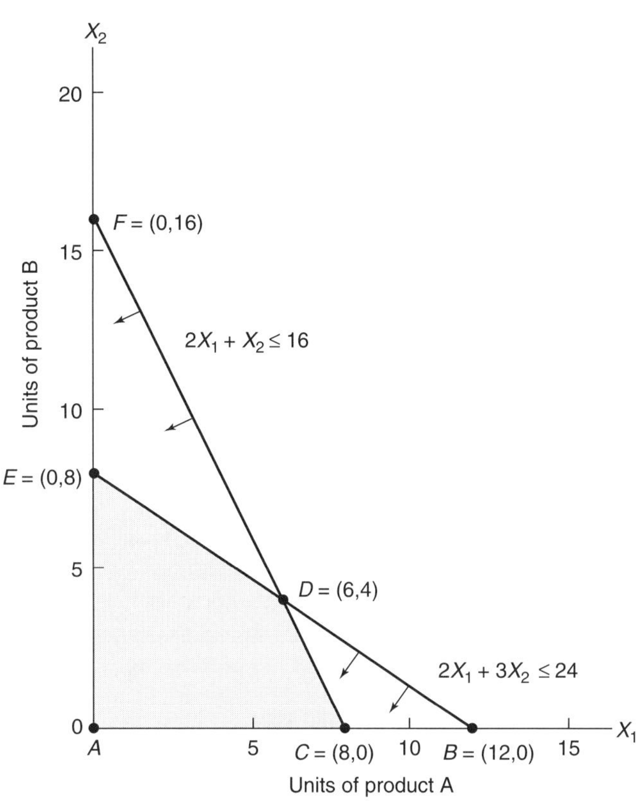

In the example above, there are four unknown variables and two constraint equations.[9] To find a basic solution, we select any two variables and set the remaining two equal to zero. Suppose we arbitrarily select X_1 and X_3 as basic variables and set $X_2 = X_4 = 0$. The equations become:

$$2X_1 + 3(0) + X_3 = 24$$
$$2X_1 + 1(0) + 1(0) = 16$$

or

$$2X_1 + X_3 = 24$$
$$2X_1 = 16$$

The solution is $X_1 = 8$, $X_3 = 8$ (and recall that $X_2 = X_4 = 0$). This is one basic solution to the linear programming example. The other basic solutions can be obtained in a similar fashion and are given in Table 3–1. Note that some of the solutions call for negative values for one of the variables. These basic solutions are infeasible, since an LP problem does not allow negative values for any variables.

Each basic solution corresponds to an intersection of pairs of lines in Figure 3–16. Points *A, C, D,* and *E* correspond to the corner points of the feasible region. Points *B* and *F* are infeasible solutions. Thus, the *basic feasible* solutions

[9]For this purpose, we do not count the non-negativity constraints.

TABLE 3–1
Basic Solutions

Outside Variables (set equal to zero)	*Solution Variables*	*Profit*	*Label in Figure 3–16*
X_1 and X_2	$X_3 = 24,\ X_4 = 16$	0	*A*
X_1 and X_3	$X_2 = 8,\ X_4 = 8$	56	*E*
X_1 and X_4	$X_2 = 16,\ X_3 = -24$	Infeasible	*F*
X_2 and X_3	$X_1 = 12,\ X_4 = -8$	Infeasible	*B*
X_2 and X_4	$X_1 = 8,\ X_3 = 8$	48	*C*
X_3 and X_4	$X_1 = 6,\ X_2 = 4$	64	*D*

correspond exactly with the corner points of the feasible region. Earlier in this chapter, we showed that the optimum solution to a linear programming problem must be a corner point. By the same token, *the optimum solution must be a basic feasible solution.*

In this simple problem, the optimum solution can be found by enumerating all the basic solutions, eliminating the infeasible ones, calculating the profit for each, and selecting the best, as is done in Table 3–1. However, a reasonably sized business problem may have thousands or millions of basic feasible solutions, and this procedure would not be efficient. Instead, we rely on the simplex method.

The algebraic approach presented here is the foundation for the output presented in computer programs for solving LP problems. There are two important points to reiterate. The first is that slack variables are added to the formulation to represent unused capacity of some resource. If a constraint is of the greater-than-or-equal type, such as the one used to represent customer requirements in the minimization example discussed earlier:

$$3X_1 + 4X_2 \geq 175$$

then a **surplus** variable is added—say, X_3—so that:

$$3X_1 + 4X_2 = 175 + X_3$$

or

$$3X_1 + 4X_2 - X_3 = 175$$

where X_3 represents the amount (in tons) by which the customer requirement is exceeded. These slack and surplus variables are important in interpreting linear programming solutions.

A second point is that *the number of variables in a basic solution (and hence in the optimal solution) is equal to the number of constraints in the LP problem* (not counting the non-negativity constraints).

Computer Solution of Linear Programming Problems

Computer software is widely available for the solution of linear programming problems, not only on large computers but even on personal computers. A very large problem involving thousands of variables and constraints requires the power of a large computer. However, such problems as the exercises in this book and moderate-sized real problems can be effectively solved on personal computers.

The method generally used for solving linear programming problems is called the *simplex method.* It was originally developed in 1957 by George Dantzig. Briefly, the simplex method starts with a basic solution from the algebraic approach discussed earlier in the chapter. It then modifies this basic solution by adding and dropping a variable, always increasing profit (or reducing cost) until an optimal solution is found. It is a search process, but it turns out to be amazingly efficient in solving very big problems. Modifications and refinements have been added to the basic simplex approach to make the computer programs more accurate and efficient. In 1984, Dr. N. Karmarkar invented an approach that solves linear programming problems using a method different from the simplex method. While this method has been shown to be efficient in solving extremely large LP problems, it is not yet known how widespread this new method will become.

There are many software packages available for solving linear programming problems on personal computers. One such package is the LINDO program.[10] (LINDO stands for Linear INteractive Discrete Optimizer.) Appendix B to this chapter describes the use of LINDO for LP problems. *What's Best* is another linear programming package that is an add-in to spreadsheets.[11]

The most widely available package for optimization, including linear programming, is Solver, which comes packaged with the Excel and Quattro Pro spreadsheets. Several examples using the Excel Solver package will be illustrated.

Consider the problem presented in the first part of this chapter—a firm with two products, constraints on the time available on the two machines used to produce the product, and a market demand limit on product B (see Figure 3–6). The formulation of this problem on an Excel spreadsheet is given in Figure 3–17. The top part of the figure shows the numbers, while the middle part shows the spreadsheet formulas. The values for the two decision variables, number of units of product A and B, respectively, are placed in cells B2 and C2, respectively. A solution showing a production schedule of one unit of each is given—clearly, not the optimum.

The coefficients for the objective function are in cells B4 and C4, and the objective function itself is in cell F4. The coefficients for the constraints on machine time and product B market limit are in cells B7 through C9, and the total usage is given in the D column. For example, cell D7 contains the total amount of machine 1 time used by this production plan (5 hours). The slack or unused capacity is shown in column G.

You should review this spreadsheet formulation carefully to make sure you understand it. This is not the only way to set up the problem on a spreadsheet, but it has certain conveniences.

A first step in solving the problem is to invoke the Solver program, which is found on the Excel Tools menu. That is, click on the Tools heading, and then on the Solver choice. The dialogue box shown in Figure 3–18 will appear on the screen. The Target Cell is the cell containing the objective function—in this case, cell F4. It is added to the dialogue box cell either by typing it in or clicking on the appropriate cell in the spreadsheet. One can either maximize or minimize by choosing the appropriate category to mark. The Changing Cells are Excel terminology for the decision variables. Click on that cell in the dialogue box, and either type in "B2:C2" or highlight those decision variable cells on the spreadsheets.

---

[10]Linus Schrage, *LINDO, An Optimization Modeling System,* 4th ed. (Palo Alto, CA: Scientific Press, 1991).

[11]Sam L. Savage, *Fast QM* (New York: McGraw-Hill, 1993).

FIGURE 3–17 Spreadsheet Model and Solution for the First Example

Model as Formulated on the Spreadsheet

	A	B	C	D	E	F	G
1		Product A	Product B				
2	Decision Variables	1	1				
3						Total Profit	
4	Objective Function:	6	7			13	
5							
6	Constraints:						Slack
7	Machine 1 time (hours)	2	3	5	<=	24	19
8	Machine 2 time (hours)	2	1	3	<=	16	13
9	Product B market limit		1	1	<=	6	5

Spreadsheet Showing the Model Equations

	A	B	C	D	E	F	G
1		Product A	Product B				
2	Decision Variables	1	1				
3						Total Profit	
4	Objective Function:	6	7			=B4*B2+C4*C2	
5							
6	Constraints:						Slack
7	Machine 1 time (hours)	2	3	=B7*B2+C7*C2	<=	24	=F7-D7
8	Machine 2 time (hours)	2	1	=B8*B2+C8*C2	<=	16	=F8-D8
9	Product B market limit		1	=B9*B2+C9*C2	<=	6	=F9-D9

Model Showing Optimal Solution

	A	B	C	D	E	F	G
1		Product A	Product B				
2	Decision Variables	6	4				
3						Total Profit	
4	Objective Function:	6	7			64	
5							
6	Constraints:						Slack
7	Machine 1 time (hours)	2	3	24	<=	24	0
8	Machine 2 time (hours)	2	1	16	<=	16	0
9	Product B market limit		1	4	<=	6	2

FIGURE 3–18
Solver Parameters Dialogue Box

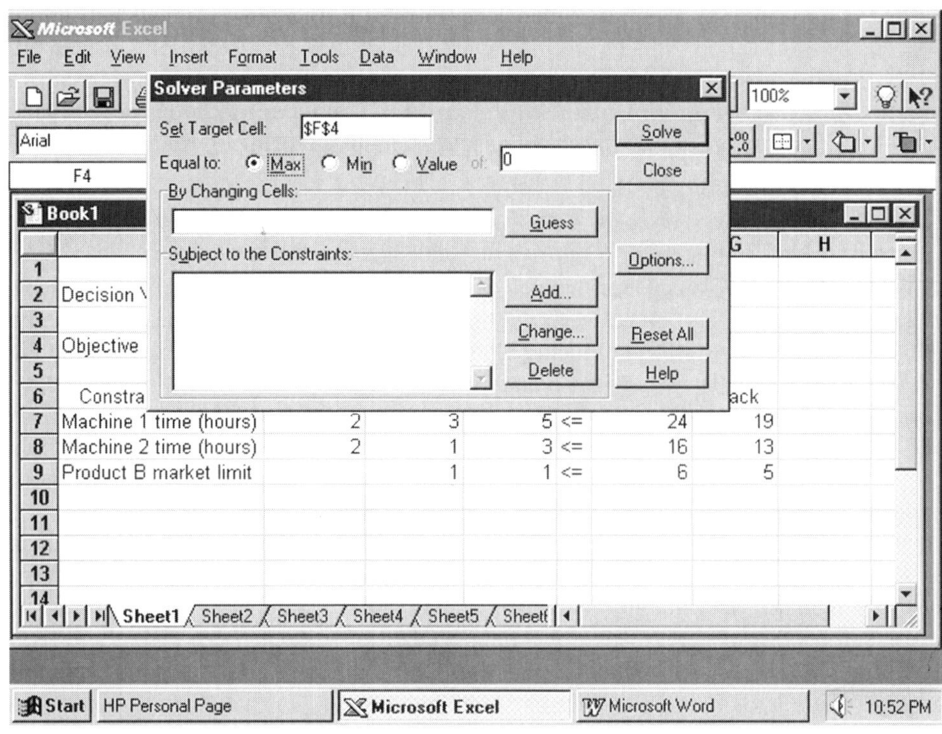

We next must add the constraints. Click on the box that says Add . . . , and an Add Constraint dialogue box, as in Figure 3–19, will appear.

We first add the constraint that all the decision variables must be greater than zero. It is important to do this since Solver does not otherwise assume non-negative values. Fill in the cells "B2:C2" in the Cell Reference box either by typing them in or highlighting them in the spreadsheet; type in "0" in the right-hand box; and click on the down arrow to select the ">=" symbol. Then click the Add button.

A second Add Constraint dialogue box appears, as shown in the middle part of Figure 3–19. In the Cell Reference box, highlight or type in cells "D7:D9". These cells contain the total amount of machine time used, and the total amount of Product B, the factors that are constrained. In the right-hand box, highlight or type cells "F7:F9". These are the right-hand side values giving the constraint values. Next, click on the OK button to indicate that all constraints have been entered. The Solver Parameters dialogue box, as shown at the bottom of Figure 3–19, should appear, showing the complete setup of the linear programming problem.

One final step remains—telling Solver that this is indeed a linear programming problem. To do this, click on the Options button. In the dialogue box that appears, make sure there is an "*X*" in the box next to Assume Linear Model; if not, click on the box. Then click on the OK button, to return to the Solver Parameters dialogue box. You are now finally ready to solve the model, so click on the Solve button.

After some computation, a Solver Results dialogue box appears, indicating that a solution was found. Check the option to Keep the Solver Solution and highlight the reports you wish to save. The solution is transferred to the spreadsheet—see the bottom panel of Figure 3–17. Also, reports are saved on separate pages in the

FIGURE 3–19 Defining the Constraints in Solver

First Add Constraint dialogue box

Add Constraint
Cell Reference: $B$2:$C$2
Constraint: >= =0
OK Cancel Add Help

Second Add Constraint dialogue box

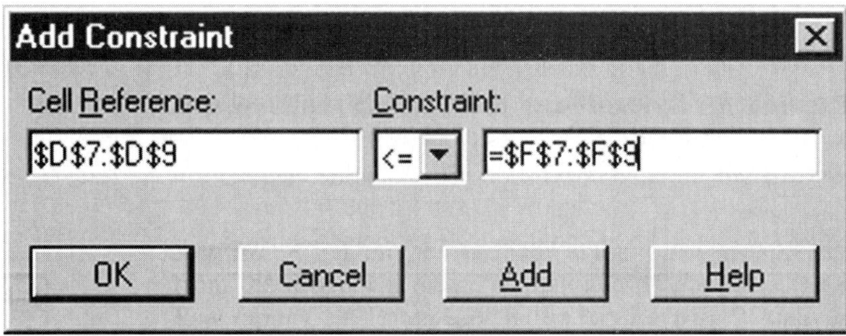

Solver Parameters dialogue box complete

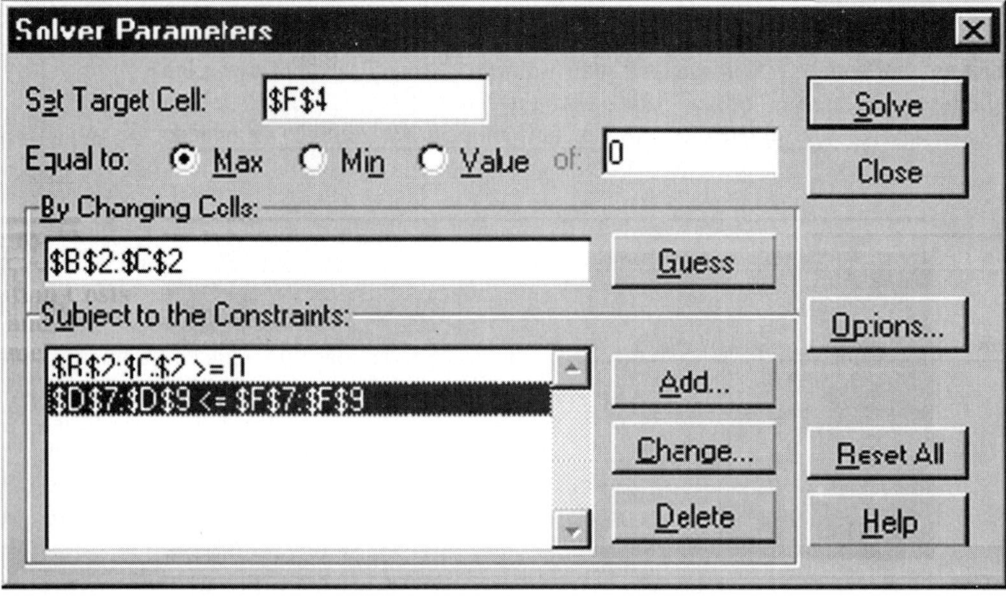

spreadsheet. The Answer and Sensitivity reports are shown in Figure 3–20. (The Limits Report is of less value and is not discussed.) The Answer Report is self-explanatory except to note that Solver uses row and column headings as names for variables and constraints. The Sensitivity Report shown in Figure 3–20 provides the shadow prices for the constraints and the ranges over which these prices are valid. It also provides the reduced costs for the objective function coefficients and the ranges on the coefficients. These, of course, are the values we obtained earlier using the graphic approach.

FIGURE 3–20 Solver Reports

Solver Answer Report

Target Cell (Max)

Cell	Name	Original Value	Final Value
$F$4	Objective Function: Total Profit	13	64

Adjustable Cells

Cell	Name	Original Value	Final Value
$B$2	Decision Variables Product A	1	6
$C$2	Decision Variables Product B	1	4

Constraints

Cell	Name	Cell Value	Formula	Status	Slack
$D$7	Machine 1 time (hours)	24	$D$7<=$F$7	Binding	0
$D$8	Machine 2 time (hours)	16	$D$8<=$F$8	Binding	0
$D$9	Product B market limit	4	$D$9<=$F$9	Not Binding	2
$B$2	Decision Variables Product A	6	$B$2>=0	Not Binding	6
$C$2	Decision Variables Product B	4	$C$2>=0	Not Binding	4

Solver Sensitivity Analysis Report

Changing Cells

Cell	Name	Final Value	Reduced Cost	Objective Coefficient	Allowable Increase	Allowable Decrease
$B$2	Decision Variables Product A	6	0	6	8	1.333333333
$C$2	Decision Variables Product B	4	0	7	2	4

Constraints

Cell	Name	Final Value	Shadow Price	Constraint R.H. Side	Allowable Increase	Allowable Decrease
$D$7	Machine 1 time (hours)	24	2	24	4	8
$D$8	Machine 2 time (hours)	16	1	16	8	4
$D$9	Product B market limit	4	0	6	1E+30	2

Another Example—Minimization

Consider the example used in Figure 3–15 involving a company that wished to minimize the cost of operating two mills. The company must meet customer requirements and wishes to satisfy a policy constraint that the second mill should operate at least as many hours as the first. Review the formulation given earlier in this chapter. Figure 3–21 shows the implementation of this formulation on the spreadsheet, including the model equations. A box at the bottom of Figure 3–21 shows the values to be specified in the Solver Parameters dialogue box. Finally, the Solver Answer and Sensitivity Analysis Reports are given in Figure 3–22.

The solution calls for operating each mill at 25 hours per week, resulting in a total cost of $1,500 per week. The constraint shown in row 9 (Customer Requirements) is binding and the shadow price on this constraint is $8.57, indicating that each additional ton would cost $8.57; and this marginal value would hold for an addition of 105 tons. Note also that the policy constraint is binding—it is costing the company money to use this policy. The reason, of course, is that Mill 2 is more expensive to operate per ton produced. Note from the Sensitivity Report that if Mill 2 could reduce its per day cost by $13.33, the solution would change. This is the relative inefficiency for Mill 2.

Many additional examples of formulating and solving linear programming models using Solver are given in the problems at the end of this chapter. They are worth reviewing, since some problems can be organized very differently and effectively on spreadsheets. This is particularly true of problems that are of the transportation format (shipping from factories to warehouses, for example—see Problem 3–9) or have a time dimension (production scheduling over time, for example—see Problem 3–11).

There are also two appendixes to this chapter. Appendix A gives some hints and cautions in using Solver in Excel. You should review this carefully before using Solver. Appendix B illustrates the solution of linear programming problems using the LINDO package for personal computers.

Interpreting Alternate Solutions and Degeneracy

Recall from the algebraic formulation in this chapter that, in an LP problem with m constraints, a basic solution will have exactly m basic variables. We can determine the basic variables in solver output by simply identifying the decision variables or slack or surplus variables that are nonzero. Sometimes it happens that there are less than m nonzero variables in the optimal solution. This means that one or more of the basic variables just happens to turn out to be exactly zero. This is called *degeneracy.*

Generally, degeneracy is not a problem, except that care is needed in interpreting some of the shadow prices. In particular, when examining the right-hand side ranges, a particular shadow price may have a zero allowable increase, a zero allowable decrease, or both. In other words, the shadow price may hold only over a limited range, or no range at all. As long as this is recognized in interpreting LP output, degeneracy need not be a particular problem.

Sometimes an LP problem can have more than one optimal solution (see the example in Figure 3–4). When the solution is not degenerate, this case is easy

FIGURE 3–21 Spreadsheet Model for Minimization Example

Optimum Solution

	A	B	C	D	E	F	G	H
1		Mill 1	Mill 2					
2	Weekly Hours	25	25					
3						Total		
4	Cost	20	40			1500		
5								
6	Constraints:						Slack	Surplus
7	Available Hours Mill 1	1		25	<=	40	15	
8	Available Hours Mill 2		1	25	<=	60	35	
9	Customer Requirements (tons)	3	4	175	>=	175		0
10	Policy Requirement	-1	1	0	>=	0		0

Model Equations

	A	B	C	D	E	F	G	H
1		Mill 1	Mill 2					
2		0	0					
3						Total		
4		20	40			=B4*B2+C4*C2		
5								
6							Slack	Surplus
7		1		=B7*$B$2+C7*$C$2	<=	40	=F7-D7	
8			1	=B8*$B$2+C8*$C$2	<=	60	=F8-D8	
9		3	4	=B9*$B$2+C9*$C$2	>=	175		=D9-F9
10		-1	1	=B10*$B$2+C10*$C$2	>=	0		=D10-F10
11								
12				(See above for labels				
13				in column A)				

Dialogue Box Values

Solver Parameters

Target cell (objective function)		**F4**
Objective:		**Minimize**
Changing cells (decision variables)		**B2:C2**
Constraints	**D7:D8<=F7:F8**	Mill hours available
	D9:D10>=F9:F10	Customer requirement and policy constraint
	B2:C2>=0	Non-negative decision variables

FIGURE 3–22 Solver Reports for Minimization Example

Solver Answer Report

Target Cell (Min)

Cell	Name	Original Value	Final Value
$F$4	Cost Total	0	1500

Adjustable Cells

Cell	Name	Original Value	Final Value
$B$2	Weekly Hours Mill 1	0	25
$C$2	Weekly Hours Mill 2	0	25

Constraints

Cell	Name	Cell Value	Formula	Status	Slack
$D$7	Available Hours Mill 1	25	$D$7<=$F$7	Not Binding	15
$D$8	Available Hours Mill 2	25	$D$8<=$F$8	Not Binding	35
$D$9	Customer Requirements (tons)	175	$D$9>=$F$9	Binding	0
$D$10	Policy Requirement	0	$D$10>=$F$10	Binding	0
$B$2	Weekly Hours Mill 1	25	$B$2>=0	Not Binding	25
$C$2	Weekly Hours Mill 2	25	$C$2>=0	Not Binding	25

Solver Sensitivity Analysis Report

Changing Cells

Cell	Name	Final Value	Reduced Cost	Objective Coefficient	Allowable Increase	Allowable Decrease
$B$2	Weekly Hours Mill 1	25	0	20	10	60
$C$2	Weekly Hours Mill 2	25	0	40	1E+30	13.33333333

Constraints

Cell	Name	Final Value	Shadow Price	Constraint R.H. Side	Allowable Increase	Allowable Decrease
$D$7	Available Hours Mill 1	25	0	40	1E+30	15
$D$8	Available Hours Mill 2	25	0	60	1E+30	35
$D$9	Customer Requirements (tons)	175	8.571428571	175	105	175
$D$10	Policy Requirement	0	5.714285714	0	43.75	26.25

to identify in Solver output. If there is a decision variable that has a zero value and also a zero reduced cost, it indicates an alternate optimum. Similarly, a constraint with zero slack (or surplus) and a zero shadow price also indicates an alternate optimum.

Actually finding the alternate optimum, or determining if there are alternate solutions when degeneracy exists, is not easily done using the Solver output and is not discussed here.

Summary

This chapter presented the basic ideas in the solution of linear programming problems, first in the form of graphic solutions, and then in the output from computer software.

The optimal solution of an LP problem is a *corner point* of the feasible region. This corresponds, in algebraic terms, to a *basic feasible solution,* containing m basic variables (where m is the number of constraints).

Sensitivity analysis on the constraints involves first finding the *shadow price,* the marginal value for a unit change in the right-hand side value of the constraint, and secondly, finding the range of values over which the shadow price holds (the *RHS ranges*).

The *reduced cost* is a similar marginal value associated with introducing a unit of a decision variable into the optimal solution.

The *objective function coefficient ranges* provide additional sensitivity analyses. These ranges indicate the changes in the objective function coefficients within which the optimal solution remains the same.

Computer software is widely available for solving LP problems. The Solver program, which is available for the Excel and other spreadsheets, is illustrated, including the formulation of spreadsheet models, optimizing, and interpreting the sensitivity output. The output of other LP software is similar, including that for LINDO, which is described in Appendix B.

Appendix A
Suggestions for Using Excel Solver

Solver, as implemented in Excel and other spreadsheets, is a general optimizing tool. This means that it can be used to solve problems that involve integer variables and nonlinear functions, as well as linear ones. Nonlinear and integer problems are much more difficult to solve. Thus, there are many features of Solver that are not necessary for standard linear programming formulated problems. Also, because it is so flexible, Solver can be quite tricky at times. These suggestions are designed to introduce you to Solver with minimal difficulty.

Suggestion 1. Look at the descriptions for using Solver that are in the *Excel Users Guide* or use the Help function in Excel. This latter help, of course, is available within the Excel program itself, so you can access it if you encounter difficulties in setting up a problem. Before using Solver, you should at least review these sources of information.

Excel also contains some excellent examples of linear programming models set up in Solver.[12] These are contained in the following:

Windows		**Macintosh**	
Workbook:	SOLVSAMP.XLS in	Workbook:	Solver Samples in
Directory:	Excel\Examples\Solver	Folder:	Solver Examples

[12]These examples are also described in the Solver chapter in the *Excel Users Guide.*

The second (Shipping Routes), and fourth (Maximizing Income) examples are excellent linear programming cases. The third example (Staff Scheduling) is also a linear model, but it involves integer variables. The first (product mix) has a non-linear objective function.

Suggestion 1 includes at least a quick look at the second and fourth examples.

Suggestion 2. Use the Standard Model Format in setting up the Excel spreadsheet model. All linear programming models can be formulated in a standard model format as follows:

Decision variables: $X_1, X_2, X_3 \cdots X_N$

Objective: Maximize (or minimize) $C_1X_1 + C_2X_2 + C_3X_3 + \cdots + C_NX_N$

Subject to:

$$\begin{aligned} a_{11}X_1 + a_{12}X_2 + a_{13}X_3 + \cdots + a_{1N}X_N &\leq b_1 \\ a_{21}X_1 + a_{22}X_2 + a_{23}X_3 + \cdots + a_{2N}X_N &\leq b_2 \\ &\vdots \\ a_{k1}X_1 + a_{k2}X_2 + a_{k3}X_3 + \cdots + a_{kN}X_N &\leq b_k \end{aligned}$$

Non-negative decision variables: $X_1, X_2, X_3 \cdots X_N \geq 0$

The values for the C_i and a_{ij} are constants. The b_j values are also constants and are called the right-hand side (or RHS) values. These are the constraining values. The constraints are shown above as less than or equal ($\leq$), but they can alternatively be equalities ($=$), or greater than or equal ($\geq$).

All of the examples used in this chapter were formulated in this standard format, so you may wish to review them to see concrete examples.

Once a linear programming problem has been formulated in the standard format, it can be implemented on the spreadsheet, as shown in Figure 3–23. As indicated, each decision variable is assigned a column, with the variable name at the top. One row is reserved for the decision variable values themselves (i.e., the solution to the problem). The constants in the linear program are entered in three blocks. The objective function coefficients (the C_is) are in a row (row 4 in Figure 3–23); the constraint coefficients (the a_{ij}s) are in an array in the middle of the table; and the right-hand side (RHS) constants (the b_js) are in a column on the right side of the spreadsheet (column Q in Figure 3–23). Each constraint is given a name to identify it in column A.

The actual constraint equations themselves are in a column beside the set of constraint coefficients (Column O). These cells contain formulas referring to the decision variable cells and the cells containing the constraint coefficients. They are called the left-hand side (LHS) of the inequalities (or equalities), and display how much of a given constraint resource is actually used in the solution. The difference between this amount and the capacity limits (RHS values) is shown in column R, labeled Slack or Surplus.

Finally, the objective function is shown in cell Q4. It also is a formula involving the decision variables and the objective function coefficient constants.

There are several advantages of using this format. Formulating the linear programming problem in the standard format is a useful discipline to ensure correct formulation. Secondly, it is easy to implement, particularly if the SUMPRODUCT function to be discussed shortly is used. Thirdly, the Excel Solver Answer and Sensitivity Reports come out properly labeled, and hence are easier to understand.

FIGURE 3–23 Spreadsheet for Standard Format Linear Programming Problem

	A	B	C	D	E	...	N	O	P	Q	R
1		Name for Decision Variable 1	Name for Decision Variable 2	Name for Decision Variable 3	Name for Decision Variable 4	...	Name for Decision Variable N				
2	Decision Variables	Values for Decision Variables $X_1, X_2, \ldots$									
3										Total	
4	Objective Function	Objective Function Coefficients $C_1, C_2, \ldots$								Obj. Fun. Total	
5											Slack or Surplus
6											
7									<=		
8	Name for each constraint	Value for the constraint coefficients a_{ij}						Constraint Equations (Left Hand Side)		Constraint Limits (Right Hand Side) b_j	Difference between RHS and LHS
9									or		
10											
11									=		
12											
13									or		
14											
...									.=		
25											

FIGURE 3–24 Illustration of the SUMPRODUCT Function

	A	B	C	D	E	F	G
1		Product A	Product B	Product C			
2	Decision Variables	1	2	3			
3							Total
4	Objective Function	10	20	25			
5							
6	Machine Time	3	5	2	19	<=	100
7							

Formula: = B2*B6+C2*C6+D2*D6

Alternate Formula: =SUMPRODUCT (B2:D2,B6:D6)

Suggestion 3. Use the SUMPRODUCT function. This is a spreadsheet function that makes formulation of LP problems on spreadsheets much easier. Consider the part of the spreadsheet shown in Figure 3–24. The decision variables are in cells B2 through D2. The coefficients for the constraint on Machine Time (row 6) indicate that it takes 3 hours for Product A, 5 hours for Product B, and 2 hours for

Product C. The constraint equation, indicating how much machine time is used, would ordinarily be written in the spreadsheet as:

=B2*B+C2*C+D2*D

Note that the group of cells B2, C2, and D2 form an *array*, and this is written as B2:D2 (an *array* is a rectangular group of cells). The constraint cells also form an array: B:D.

The SUMPRODUCT function takes the form:[13]

SUMPRODUCT(array 1, array 2)

or, for our example:

SUMPRODUCT(B2:D2,B:D).

This multiplies the individual elements in the first array by the corresponding ones in the second, then sums these products. In other words, it produces exactly the same result as the detailed formula above. With just three variables, this does not seem particularly helpful. However, consider what the regular formula would look like with 20 or 50 variables, whereas the SUMPRODUCT function would be about the same.

The SUMPRODUCT function can be used for each of the constraint equations. After the first is set up, it can be copied down to the other cells.[14] The objective function can also use the SUMPRODUCT function.

Several problems at the end of this chapter have LP models formulated using the SUMPRODUCT function. In particular, consider Problems 9, 10, and 11 and the answer to Problem 3 at the end of this chapter.

Suggestion 4. Before invoking Solver to obtain a solution to the linear programming model, check out your spreadsheet formulation carefully. It is very frustrating to have Solver tell you that it can't find a solution, only to discover some "bug" in your spreadsheet. Check the equations you have entered. Also, try out different values for the decision variables and look at the results. Are they correct, and do they make sense?

Suggestion 5. Make sure you do not have any nonlinearities in your model. The use of spreadsheet functions, in particular, can sometimes cause problems. The functions SUM and SUMPRODUCT are linear functions, and are useful. However, financial functions such as IRR (internal rate or return) and NPV (net present value), math functions such as LOG (logarithm), and logical functions such as IF are nonlinear and may cause problems.

Suggestion 6. Make sure that the Assume Linear Model box in the Solver Options dialogue box is checked. This guarantees that the efficient linear programming procedure is used rather than a general search process.

---

[13]The SUMPRODUCT function will take from 2 to 30 arrays, but for our purposes we want only 2 arrays. An array can contain more than one row or column, and this is useful in some formulations that do not follow the standard format.

[14]For copying, remember to set the reference to the decision variable cells as absolute references. Thus, the first function would be: =SUMPRODUCT($B$2:$D$2, B:D).

Suggestion 7. Use proper scaling. All computer programs do calculations with a limited number of digits of accuracy. If you have one set of constants in the model with values like 245,732 and others with values like 0.00006731, Solver may give an incorrect answer or fail to find an optimal solution. Simply rescale—instead of dollars, use thousands or millions of dollars; instead of pounds, use cwt. (hundred-weight) or tons. The idea is to get the coefficients somewhat of the same order of magnitude.

Suggestion 8. This suggestion concerns defining the constraints in the Solver Add Constraint dialogue box. *On the right-hand side of the constraints in this box, place only constants (such as 0) or references to cells that contain constants. In particular, do* ***not*** *place references to cells that vary as the solution changes.* Solver can have difficulties if variables cells are on the right-hand side. If you use the standard format of Suggestion 2, this caution is, of course, unnecessary.

Appendix B
Use of LINDO for Linear Programming Problems

LINDO (which stands for Linear INteractive Discrete Optimizer)[15] is a popular software package for solving linear programming problems on personal computers. It is a standalone package—not packaged with a spreadsheet.

As a first step, the problem is formulated in algebraic terms, just as was done earlier in this chapter. However, the decision variables can be given short names—here, they are PRODA and PRODB, for units of products A and B, respectively. The problem is entered into the computer in this formulation format. See Table 3–2 for the problem that was used throughout the chapter. The solution and comments are also provided in the table. Note that the output includes not only the solution but also the reduced cost for each variable, the shadow prices (LINDO calls them *dual* prices) for the constraints, and the ranges for both the objective coefficients and the right-hand side values.

Another Example

Consider the example used in Figure 3–15, involving a company that is trying to minimize the cost of operating two mills while meeting customer requirements. The LINDO formulation is shown in Table 3–3 exactly as it is entered into the computer, and the solution is also given. Variables MILL1 and MILL2 refer to the weekly hours at the first and second mills, respectively. Note that the solution calls for operating each mill for 25 hours. The third constraint refers to the customer requirements of 175 tons. The dual price or shadow price for this constraint is \$8.57, indicating that each additional ton would cost \$8.57; this marginal value would hold for an addition of 105 tons.

[15] Linus Schrage, *LINDO: An Optimization Modeling System*, 4th ed. (Palo Alto: Scientific Press, 1991).

Table 3–2 LINDO Computer Solution

LINDO output	Comments
```MAX 6 PRODA + 7 PRODB``` SUBJECT TO 2) 2 PRODA + 3 PRODB <= 24 3) 2 PRODA + PRODB <= 16 4) PRODB <= 6 END	Formulation: PRODA and PRODB are decision variables 2) is a constraint on machine 1. 3) is a constraint on machine 2. 4) is a market demand constraint.
LP OPTIMUM FOUND AT STEP 2	LP optimum found after examining two corner points.
OBJECTIVE FUNCTION VALUE 1) 64.0000000	Optimum profit is $64.
VARIABLE / VALUE / REDUCED COST PRODA 6.000000 .000000 PRODB 4.000000 .000000	Optimal solution is 6 units of product A and 4 units of product B; reduced costs are both zero since some of each is produced.
ROW / SLACK OR SURPLUS / DUAL PRICES 2) .000000 2.000000 3) .000000 1.000000 4) 2.000000 .000000	No slack in constraints 2) and 3). Slack in constraint 4) implies unused demand for product B. Dual prices (shadow prices) are shown.

NO. ITERATIONS= 2

RANGES IN WHICH THE BASIS IS UNCHANGED:

OBJ COEFFICIENT RANGES

VARIABLE	CURRENT COEF	ALLOWABLE INCREASE	ALLOWABLE DECREASE
PRODA	6.000000	8.000000	1.333333
PRODB	7.000000	2.000000	4.000000

Ranges in which the optimal solution remains the same.

RIGHTHAND SIDE RANGES

ROW	CURRENT RHS	ALLOWABLE INCREASE	ALLOWABLE DECREASE
2	24.000000	4.000000	8.000000
3	16.000000	8.000000	4.000000
4	6.000000	INFINITY	2.000000

Ranges in which the set of variables in the basic solution remains the same.

TABLE 3–3
LINDO Output for Second Example

```
MIN        20 MILL1+ 40 MILL2
SUBJECT TO
        2)  MILL1 <=    40
        3)  MILL2 <=    60
        4)  3 MILL1 + 4 MILL2 >=      175
        5) - MILL1 + MILL2 > = 0

LP OPTIMUM FOUND AT STEP   2

        OBJECTIVE FUNCTION VALUE

        1)        1500.00000

VARIABLE             VALUE          REDUCED COST
   MILL1          25.000000              .000000
   MILL2          25.000000              .000000

     ROW   SLACK OR SURPLUS          DUAL PRICES
      2)          15.000000              .000000
      3)          35.000000              .000000
      4)            .000000            -8.571428
      5)            .000000            -5.714285

NO. ITERATIONS = 2

RANGES IN WHICH THE BASIS IS UNCHANGED:

                                OBJ COEFFICIENT RANGES
VARIABLE               CURRENT          ALLOWABLE          ALLOWABLE
                          COEF           INCREASE           DECREASE
   MILL1             20.000000           9.999999          60.000000
   MILL2             40.000000           INFINITY          13.333330

                                RIGHTHAND SIDE RANGES
     ROW               CURRENT          ALLOWABLE          ALLOWABLE
                           RHS           INCREASE           DECREASE
       2             40.000000           INFINITY          15.000000
       3             60.000000           INFINITY          35.000000
       4            175.000000         105.000000         175.000000
       5               .000000          43.750000          26.250000
```

Bibliography

Eppen, G. D.; F. J. Gould; and C. Schmidt. *Introduction to Management Science.* 4th ed. Englewood Cliffs, NJ: Prentice Hall, 1993.

Hillier, F., and G. J. Lieberman. *Introduction to Operations Research.* 6th ed. New York: McGraw-Hill, 1995.

Rubin, D., and H. Wagner. "Shadow Prices: Tips and Traps for Managers and Instructors." *Interfaces,* July–August 1990, pp. 150–57.

Savage, Sam. *Fast QM.* New York: McGraw-Hill, 1993.

Schrage, Linus. *LINDO: An Optimization Modeling System.* 4th ed. Palo Alto: Scientific Press, 1991.

Users Guide: Microsoft Excel. Microsoft Corp. 1994.

Practice Problems[16]

3–1. Solve the following problem graphically:

$$\begin{aligned} \text{Maximize:}\quad & P = 2X_1 + 5X_2 \\ \text{Subject to:}\quad & X_1 + 3X_2 \leq 16 \\ & 4X_1 + X_2 \leq 20 \\ & X_2 \leq 4 \\ & X_1, X_2 \geq 0 \end{aligned}$$

3–2. A company sells two different products, A and B. The selling price and incremental cost information is as follows:

	Product A	*Product B*
Selling price	$60	$40
Incremental cost	30	10
Incremental profit	$30	$30

The two products are produced in a common production process and are sold in two different markets. The production process has a capacity of 30,000 labor-hours. It takes three hours to produce a unit of A and one hour to produce a unit of B. The market has been surveyed, and company officials feel that the maximum number of units of A that can be sold is 8,000; the maximum for B is 12,000 units. Subject to these limitations, the products can be sold in any combination.

a. Solve the problem graphically to find the optimal product mix.

For (*b*) through (*d*) of this problem, consider each case separately. Also, convert all units to thousands. Solve graphically.

b. Suppose the maximum number of units of product A that can be sold is actually 9,000 units (rather than 8,000, as in the base case). What effect does this have on the solution? What is the effect on the profit? What is the shadow price for the constraint on the sales limit for product A?

c. Suppose the maximum number of units of product B that can be sold is actually 13,000 units (rather than 12,000 as in the base case). What effect does this have on the solution? What is the effect on the profit? What is the shadow price for the constraint on the sales limit for product B?

d. Suppose there are 31,000 labor-hours available, rather than 30,000, as in the base case. What effect does this have on the solution? What is the effect on the profit? What is the shadow price for the constraint on the number of labor-hours?

e. Refer to (*b*), (*c*), and (*d*) above. Determine by graphic means the right-hand side ranges over which the shadow prices hold for each of the three constraints.

3–3. A firm produces four products: A, B, C, and D. Each unit of product A requires two hours of milling, one hour of assembly, and $10 worth of in-process inventory. Each unit of product B requires one hour of milling, three hours of assembly, and $5 worth of in-process inventory. Each unit of C requires 2½ hours of milling, 2½ hours of assembly, and $2 worth of in-process inventory. Finally, each unit of product D requires five hours of milling, no assembly, and $12 of in-process inventory.

The firm has 1,200 hours of milling time and 1,600 hours of assembly time available. In addition, not more than $10,000 may be tied up in in-process inventory. Each unit of product A returns a profit of $40; each unit of B returns a profit of $24; each unit of product C returns a profit of $36; and each unit of product D returns a profit of $23. Not more than 200 of product A can be sold; not more than 160 units of product C can be sold; and any number of units of products B and D may be sold. However, at least 100 units of product D must be produced and sold to satisfy a contract requirement. The objective of the firm is to maximize the profit resulting from the sale of the four products.

Formulate and solve this problem using the spreadsheet Solver package. If you do not have the package available or were unable to solve it, refer to the Solver output given in the answers at the end of this chapter. Then answer the following questions:

a. What is the solution to the problem? How many units of each product are produced, and in which constraints is there slack or surplus? What is the optimum profit?

b. What is the value of an additional hour of milling time? An additional hour of assembly time? An additional $1 in working capital for in-process inventory?

c. Suppose the company could spend money on advertising that would have the effect of increasing the limit on demand for either product A or product C. How much should the company be willing to spend to increase the demand for product A by one unit? How much to increase the demand for product C by one unit?

[16]Solutions for these problems are at the end of this chapter.

d. Suppose that the contract for product D required 130 units (rather than 100). What effect would this have on the profit?

e. Suppose the profit per unit for product C were actually \$46 (rather than \$36). How would the solution change (i.e., how much of each product would be produced)? How much would the profit change?

f. A new product, product E, is under consideration. It requires 2 hours of milling time, 5 hours of assembly, and \$20 in working capital. The profit per unit is \$50. Should any units of product E be produced?

3–4. The U-Save Loan Company is planning its operations for the next year. The company makes five types of loans, listed below, together with the annual return (in percent) to the company.

Type of Loan	*Annual Return (percent)*
Signature loans	15%
Furniture loans	12
Automobile loans	9
Second home mortgage	10
First home mortgage	7

Legal requirements and company policy place the following limits on the amounts of the various types of loans.

Signature loans cannot exceed 10 percent of the total amount of loans. The amount of signature and furniture loans together cannot exceed 20 percent of the total amount of loans. First mortgages must be at least 40 percent of the total mortgages and at least 20 percent of the total amount of loans. Second mortgages may not exceed 25 percent of the total amount of loans.

The company wishes to maximize the revenue from loan interest, subject to the above restrictions. The firm can lend a maximum of \$1.5 million.

Formulate this problem as a linear programming model. If you have access to a computer and the Solver program, find the optimal solution. If not, refer to the spreadsheet formulation and the Solver output in the answers at the end of this chapter. Then answer the following questions:

a. What is the solution to the problem? How much of each type of loan should the company have? What is the total return expected from this plan?

b. If the company could raise additional funds beyond the \$1.5 million currently available to lend, what would be the return on each additional dollar? Over what range would this value hold?

c. Suppose the annual return for second home mortgages were to increase from 10 to 12 percent. What effect would this have on the solution to the problem (i.e., on the loan portfolio)? What effect would it have on the total return? Suppose the rate for second mortgages went to 14 percent. What effect would this have? How high would the rate for second mortgages have to go before it had an effect on the loan portfolio?

Problems

3–5. Solve the following minimization problem graphically.

$$\begin{aligned} \text{Minimize:}\quad & C = 4X_1 + 2X_2 \\ \text{Subject to:}\quad & X_1 \geq 6 \\ & X_1 + X_2 \geq 10 \\ & X_1, X_2 \geq 0 \end{aligned}$$

3–6. We want to select an advertising strategy to reach two types of customers; homemakers in families with over \$25,000 annual income and homemakers in families with under \$25,000 income.[17] We feel that people in the first group will purchase twice as much of our product as people in the second, and our goal is to maximize purchases. We may advertise either on TV or in a magazine; one unit of TV advertising costs \$40,000 and reaches approximately 20,000 people in the first group and 80,000 in the second. One unit of advertising in the magazine costs \$24,000 and reaches 60,000 people in the first group and 30,000 in the second. (It is assumed, for this problem, that the magazine's audience has no overlap with the TV audience.) We require at least 6 units of TV advertising be used and that no more than 12 units of magazine advertising be used, for policy reasons. The advertising budget is \$360,000.

Solve the problem graphically to find the optimal solution.

[17]This problem is adapted from F. M. Bass and R. T. Lonsdale, "An Exploration of Linear Programming in Media Selection," *Journal of Marketing Research* 3 (1966).

3–7. The Delight Dairy Company (DD) produces a broad line of dairy products. For production planning purposes, the products have been aggregated into two major classes: Ice Cream (many flavors, many package sizes) and Specialties (ice-cream sticks, ice-cream sandwiches, prepackaged ice-cream cones, etc.). Each class has its own distinct packaging equipment, but the two classes use a common, single ice-cream manufacturing machine; they also use the same pool of experienced labor to produce and package each class of product.

The Ice Cream class requires two hours of the ice-cream manufacturing machine, one hour on its own packaging line, and three labor-hours to produce 1,000 gallons of finished product.

The Specialties class requires one hour of the ice-cream manufacturing machine, one hour on its own packaging line, and six labor-hours to produce the equivalent of 1,000 gallons of finished product. One thousand gallons of Ice Cream can be sold by DD for $900, and the equivalent of 1,000 gallons of Specialties can be sold for $1,500. (Raw material costs are approximately equal for 1,000 gallons of the two classes of product.)

The company currently works a one-shift operation (40 shop-hours per week) and currently employs three full-time employees and one ¾-time employee for a total of 120 + 30 = 150 labor-hours per week.

a. Formulate a linear programming model for production planning for Delight Dairy and solve the problem graphically.

b. Suppose that 10 additional labor-hours could be made available (by converting the ¾-time position to full time). What does this do to the solution? Show the result graphically. Calculate the shadow price for an additional labor-hour.

c. How many additional labor-hours can be added before the shadow price calculated in (*b*) changes? Show the result graphically.

d. Refer to the base case described in (*a*). Suppose competition has forced the price of Ice Cream down from $900 to $600 for 1,000 gallons. Would this change the production plan for DD? If so, what would be the new plan?

3–8. Refer to Problem 3–7 (Delight Dairy). Formulate the problem on a spreadsheet and solve it using the Solver package. Then answer parts (*b*) through (*d*) as in Problem 3–7.

FIGURE 3–25 Spreadsheet Formulation of Soap Manufacturer's Transportation Problem

	A	B	C	D	E	F	G	H	I
1			**Cost of Shipping 1,000 Cases of Soap**						
2	To From	New York	Boston	Chicago	Los Angeles	Dallas			
3	Cincinnati	240	300	160	500	360			
4	Denver	420	440	300	200	220			
5	Atlanta	300	340	300	480	400			**Total Cost**
6									36,000
7			**Shipment Amounts**						
8	To From	New York	Boston	Chicago	Los Angeles	Dallas	Total Shipped		Factory Capacity
9	Cincinnati	40	0	60	0	0	100	<=	100
10	Denver	0	0	0	30	20	50	<=	60
11	Atlanta	10	10	0	0	0	20	<=	50
12									
13	Total Received	50	10	60	30	20			
14		>=	>=	>=	>=	>=			
15	Warehouse Need	50	10	60	30	20			

3–9. A manufacturer of soap and detergents has three plants, located in Cincinnati, Denver, and Atlanta. Warehouses are located in New York, Boston, Chicago, Los Angeles, and Dallas. The decision problem is which factories should supply each warehouse. The model has been formulated on the spreadsheet shown as Figure 3–25.

The costs of shipping 1,000 cases from each factory to each warehouse are shown in cells B3 through F5 in the upper part of the spreadsheet. The decision variables (the amounts to be shipped over each route) are shown in cells B9 through F11 in the lower part of the figure. The optimal shipping schedule is shown. The constraints relate to the capacities of the factories (shown in column I) and the amounts needed at each warehouse (shown in row 15).

Figure 3–26 shows the model equations. Note that the objective function in cell I6 is the SUMPRODUCT function for the shipping costs and shipping amounts. It multiplies each amount shipped by its cost, then sums them up. The sums of the rows are in column G (amounts shipped) and the sums of the columns in row 13 (amount received at each warehouse). Finally, Figure 3–27 shows the contents of the Solver Parameter dialogue box. Examine these spreadsheets carefully to be sure you understand the formulation.

Figure 3–28 gives the Solver Answer Report and Figure 3–29 gives the Solver Sensitivity Report for this problem. Answer the following questions by referring to the spreadsheet and Solver reports.

a. Put in words the optimal production and shipping plan for this manufacturer.

b. Suppose, for policy reasons, the company wanted to ship at least 1,000 cases from Cincinnati to Dallas. Would this increase the cost? By how much?

c. Suppose the company was considering a marketing program to increase the sales in the warehouse regions. If all else is equal (except shipping costs), which warehouse region would yield the most profit? Which would give the least profit?

d. Suppose the capacity of the Cincinnati plant can be increased by 10 percent by using overtime. The cost of this would be $1,000. Should this be done? Why or why not?

e. In the optimal plan, the Cincinnati plant is not shipping any soap to the Dallas warehouse. Suppose that the shipping department was able to negotiate a very favorable rate of $180 per 1,000 cases for the Cincinnati–Dallas route. Would this change the optimal shipping plan? How do you know?

FIGURE 3–26 Spreadsheet Showing Model Equations

	A	B	C	D	E	F	G	H	I
1									
2	To From	New York	Boston	Chicago	Los Angeles	Dallas			
3	Cincinnati	240	300	160	500	180			
4	Denver	420	440	300	200	220			
5	Atlanta	300	340	300	480	400			**Total Cost**
6									=SUMPRODUCT(B3:F5,B9:F11)
7									
8	To From	New York	Boston	Chicago	Los Angeles	Dallas	Total Shipped		Factory Capacity
9	Cincinnati	40	0	60	0	0	=SUM(B9:F9)	<=	100
10	Denver	0	0	0	30	20	=SUM(B10:F10)	<=	60
11	Atlanta	10	10	0	0	0	=SUM(B11:F11)	<=	50
12									
13	Total Received	=SUM(B9:B11)	=SUM(C9:C11)	=SUM9(D9:D11)	=SUM(E9:E11)	=SUM(F9:F11)			
14		>=	>=	>=	>=	>=			
15	Warehouse	50	10	60	30	20			

FIGURE 3–27
Information for Solver Parameters Dialogue Box

Solver Parameters		
Target cell (objective function)		**I6**
Objective:		**Minimize**
Changing cells (decision variables)		**B9:F11**
Constraints:	**B9:F11 >= 0**	Non-negative decision variables
	G9:G11 <= I9:I11	Factory capacity constraints
	B13:F13 >= B15:F15	Warehouse needs must be met

FIGURE 3–28
Excel Solver Answer Report for Transportation Problem

Target Cell (Min)

Cell	Name	Original Value	Final Value
$I$6	Cost Total	-	36,000

Adjustable Cells

Cell	Name	Original Value	Final Value
$B$9	Cincinnati New York	0	40
$C$9	Cincinnati Boston	0	0
$D$9	Cincinnati Chicago	0	60
$E$9	Cincinnati Los Angeles	0	0
$F$9	Cincinnati Dallas	0	0
$B$10	Denver New York	0	0
$C$10	Denver Boston	0	0
$D$10	Denver Chicago	0	0
$E$10	Denver Los Angeles	0	30
$F$10	Denver Dallas	0	20
$B$11	Atlanta New York	0	10
$C$11	Atlanta Boston	0	10
$D$11	Atlanta Chicago	0	0
$E$11	Atlanta Los Angeles	0	0
$F$11	Atlanta Dallas	0	0

(continued)

FIGURE 3–28
(concluded)

Constraints

Cell	Name	Cell Value	Formula	Status	Slack
\$B\$13	Total Received New York	50	\$B\$13>=\$B\$15	Binding	0
\$C\$13	Total Received Boston	10	\$C\$13>=\$C\$15	Binding	0
\$D\$13	Total Received Chicago	60	\$D\$13>=\$D\$15	Binding	0
\$E\$13	Total Received Los Angeles	30	\$E\$13>=\$E\$15	Binding	0
\$F\$13	Total Received Dallas	20	\$F\$13>=\$F\$15	Binding	0
\$G\$9	Cincinnati Total Shipped	100	\$G\$9<=\$I\$9	Binding	0
\$G\$10	Denver Total Shipped	50	\$G\$10<=\$I\$10	Not Binding	10
\$G\$11	Atlanta Total Shipped	20	\$G\$11<=\$I\$11	Not Binding	30
\$B\$9	Cincinnati New York	40	\$B\$9>=0	Not Binding	40
\$C\$9	Cincinnati Boston	0	\$C\$9>=0	Binding	0
\$D\$9	Cincinnati Chicago	60	\$D\$9>=0	Not Binding	60
\$E\$9	Cincinnati Los Angeles	0	\$E\$9>=0	Binding	0
\$F\$9	Cincinnati Dallas	0	\$F\$9>=0	Binding	0
\$B\$10	Denver New York	0	\$B\$10>=0	Binding	0
\$C\$10	Denver Boston	0	\$C\$10>=0	Binding	0
\$D\$10	Denver Chicago	0	\$D\$10>=0	Binding	0
\$E\$10	Denver Los Angeles	30	\$E\$10>=0	Not Binding	30
\$F\$10	Denver Dallas	20	\$F\$10>=0	Not Binding	20
\$B\$11	Atlanta New York	10	\$B\$11>=0	Not Binding	10
\$C\$11	Atlanta Boston	10	\$C\$11>=0	Not Binding	10
\$D\$11	Atlanta Chicago	0	\$D\$11>=0	Binding	0
\$E\$11	Atlanta Los Angeles	0	\$E\$11>=0	Binding	0
\$F\$11	Atlanta Dallas	0	\$F\$11>=0	Binding	0

FIGURE 3–29 Excel Solver Sensitivity Report for Transportation Problem

Changing Cells

Cell	Name	Final Value	Reduced Cost	Objective Coefficient	Allowable Increase	Allowable Decrease
$B$9	Cincinnati New York	40	0	240	20	80
$C$9	Cincinnati Boston	0	20	300	1E+30	20
$D$9	Cincinnati Chicago	60	0	160	80	220
$E$9	Cincinnati Los Angeles	0	360	500	1E+30	360
$F$9	Cincinnati Dallas	0	200	360	1E+30	200
$B$10	Denver New York	0	120	420	1E+30	120
$C$10	Denver Boston	0	100	440	1E+30	100
$D$10	Denver Chicago	0	80	300	1E+30	80
$E$10	Denver Los Angeles	30	0	200	280	200
$F$10	Denver Dallas	20	0	220	180	220
$B$11	Atlanta New York	10	0	300	80	20
$C$11	Atlanta Boston	10	0	340	20	340
$D$11	Atlanta Chicago	0	80	300	1E+30	80
$E$11	Atlanta Los Angeles	0	280	480	1E+30	280
$F$11	Atlanta Dallas	0	180	400	1E+30	180

Constraints

Cell	Name	Final Value	Shadow Price	Constraint R.H. Side	Allowable Increase	Allowable Decrease
$B$13	Total Received New York	50	300	50	30	10
$C$13	Total Received Boston	10	340	10	30	10
$D$13	Total Received Chicago	60	220	60	30	10
$E$13	Total Received Los Angeles	30	200	30	10	30
$F$13	Total Received Dallas	20	220	20	10	20
$G$9	Cincinnati Total Shipped	100	-60	100	10	30
$G$10	Denver Total Shipped	50	0	60	1E+30	10
$G$11	Atlanta Total Shipped	20	0	50	1E+30	30

Note: 1E + 30 indicates a very large (unlimited) value.

3–10. A manufacturer of television sets makes four models: (1) a portable black-and-white set called the Sport, (2) a regular black-and-white set called the Standard, (3) a portable color set called the Traveler, and (4) a regular color set called the Super. Each set requires time to assemble and test. The assembly and testing requirements for each model are shown in Table 3–4, together with the amount of time available for assembly and testing. In addition, due to a strike, there is a shortage of picture tubes. The supplier of picture tubes indicates that he will not be able to supply more than a total of 180 picture tubes in the next month; and of these, not more than 100 can be color picture tubes.

The problem is formulated on a spreadsheet and the optimal solution is shown in Figure 3–30. The Solver Sensitivity Report is also given. Answer the following questions using the information in Figure 3–30.

a. What is the optimum production schedule for the television manufacturer? Are there any alternative optimum schedules?
b. What is the marginal value of an additional hour of assembly time? Over what range of assembly time is this marginal value valid?
c. Suppose that 80 additional hours of test time could be obtained on the outside for $4 per hour. Should this be done? What will be the increase in profit?
d. What is the marginal value of an additional hour of test time? Over what range is this value valid?
e. Suppose that a price change is instituted that changes the marginal profit of the Sport model from $40 to $45. Would this change the optimum production plan? Suppose that the price of the Sport model changed from $40 to $55. In this case, would there be a change in the production plan?
f. How much would the price of the Standard model have to change before there would be a change in the production schedule?
g. Suppose that additional picture tubes can be obtained from another supplier, but at a cost of $2 more than the regular supplier's price for black and white and $5 more for color. Should any of these be purchased? How many?
h. Management is considering the introduction of a new color model called the Mate. The Mate model would require only 10 hours of assembly and 3 hours of test. The marginal profit from this new model would be $70. Should the new model be produced? If so, what will be the marginal value of producing one unit of the Mate model?

TABLE 3–4

	Sport Model	*Standard Model*	*Traveler Model*	*Super Model*	*Total Available*
Assembly time (hours)	8	10	12	15	2,000
Test time (hours)	2	2	4	5	500
Marginal profit (dollars)	40	60	80	100	

FIGURE 3–30 Spreadsheet and Solver Sensitivity Report

Optimal Solution

	A	B	C	D	E	F	G	H	I
1		Sport Model units	Standard Model units	Traveler Model units	Super Model units				
2	Units Produced	0	125	0	50				
3								Total	
4	Marginal Profit per unit	40	60	80	100			$12,500	
5						Amount used		Available	Slack
6	Assembly Time	8	10	12	15	2,000	<=	2,000	0
7	Testing Time	2	2	4	5	500	<=	500	0
8	Total Picture tubes	1	1	1	1	175	<=	180	5
9	Color Picture tubes			1	1	50	<=	100	50

Model Equations

	A	B	C	D	E	F	G	H	I
1		Sport Model units	Standard Model units	Traveler Model units	Super Model units				
2		0	125	0	50				
3								Total	
4		40	60	80	100			=SUMPRODUCT($B$2:$E$2,B4:E4)	
5						Amount used		Available	slack
6		8	10	12	15	=SUMPRODUCT($B$2:$E$2,B6:E6)	<=	2000	=H6-F6
7		2	2	4	5	=SUMPRODUCT($B$2:$E$2,B7:E7)	<=	500	=H7-F7
8		1	1	1	1	=SUMPRODUCT($B$2:$E$2,B8:E8)	<=	180	=H8-F8
9				1	1	=SUMPRODUCT($B$2:$E$2,B9:E9)	<=	100	=H9-F9

Solver Sensitivity Report

Changing Cells

Cell	Name	Final Value	Reduced Cost	Objective Coefficient	Allowable Increase	Allowable Decrease
$B$2	Units produced Sport Model units	0	-10	40	10	1E+30
$C$2	Units produced Standard Model units	125	0	60	6.666666667	20
$D$2	Units produced Traveler Model units	0	-5.55112E-16	80	5.55112E-16	1E+30
$E$2	Units produced Super Model units	50	0	100	50	6.93889E-16

Constraints

Cell	Name	Final Value	Shadow Price	Constraint R.H. Side	Allowable Increase	Allowable Decrease
$F$6	Assembly Time	2000	5	2000	33.33333333	500
$F$7	Testing Time	500	5	500	100	20
$F$8	Total Picture tubes	175	0	180	1E+30	5
$F$9	Color Picture tubes	50	0	100	1E+30	50

Note: Values such as −5.55112E − 16 and 6.93889 E-16 are equivalent to zero.

More Challenging Problems

3–11. A company faces a firm schedule of delivery commitments for a product over the next six months. The production cost varies by month due to anticipated changes in materials costs. The company's production capacity is 100 units per month on regular time and up to an additional 15 units per month on overtime.

The spreadsheet formulation for this problem is shown as Figure 3–31. The regular and overtime costs for each month are shown in the top part of the figure. The cost of carrying an unsold unit in inventory is $2 per month, and this also is shown in the spreadsheet. The number of units that must be shipped each month is shown in the last row of Figure 3–31. The firm has no units on hand at the beginning of January, and wishes to have none on hand at the end of June.

The decision variables are the number of units produced on regular time, number on overtime, and ending inventory for each month; these are in the box in the middle of Figure 3–31. The objective is to meet the shipping requirements at minimum cost.

The bottom part of the Figure 3–31 gives the set of equations relating production, inventory, and shipments. The equation is:

$$\text{Beginning inventory} + \text{Production} - \text{Shipments} = \text{Ending inventory}$$

This can be restated as:

$$\begin{matrix}\text{Beginning} \\ \text{inventory}\end{matrix} + \text{Production} - \begin{matrix}\text{Ending} \\ \text{inventory}\end{matrix} = \text{Shipments}$$

It is these shipments that must exactly match the shipping requirements on the bottom line of the spreadsheet. Also, of course, Beginning Inventory of one period is the Ending Inventory of the previous period.

The spreadsheet with equations is shown in Figure 3–32. Note that the objective function—the Total Cost in cell I9—uses the SUMPRODUCT function. This multiplies the unit costs (for regular time, overtime, and inventory) times the scheduled value for each month and sums across the months. Examine the equations in the spreadsheet to be sure you understand the formulation.

Figure 3–33 shows the Solver Parameters dialogue box values. The first set of constraints relates to the capacity limit on Regular-Time production. The second relates to the Overtime capacity limit. The third set equates the amount available for shipment (see above) to the shipping requirements. The fourth indicates that there is to be no inventory in June. And the last set constrains the decision variables to be non-negative.

FIGURE 3–31 Spreadsheet Formulation of Production Scheduling Problem

	A	B	C	D	E	F	G	H	I
1			Costs						
2		January	February	March	April	May	June		
3	Regular Time Cost	30	30	32	32	31	32		
4	Overtime Cost	35	35	37	37	36	37		
5	Inventory Cost	2	2	2	2	2	2		
6			Decision Variables						
7		January	February	March	April	May	June		Total
8	Regular Time Production	100	100	100	100	95	100		Cost
9	Overtime Production	0	0	0	5	0	0		$18,810
10	Ending Inventory	5	20	10	0	5	0		
11			Production/Shipments/Inventory Constraints						
12	Beginning Inventory	0	5	20	10	0	5		
13	Plus Amount Produced	100	100	100	105	95	100		
14	Less Ending Inventory	5	20	10	0	5	0		
15	Available for Shipment	95	85	110	115	90	105		
16	Shipping Requirements	95	85	110	115	90	105		

FIGURE 3–32 Production Scheduling Spreadsheet Showing Model Equations

	A	B	C	D	E	F	G	H	I
1			Costs						
2		January	February	March	April	May	June		
3	Regular Time Cost	30	30	32	32	31	32		
4	Overtime Cost	35	35	37	37	36	37		
5	Inventory Cost	2	2	2	2	2	2		
6									
7		January	February	March	April	May	June		Total
8	Regular Time Production	100	100	100	100	95	100		Cost
9	Overtime Production	0	0	0	5	0	0		=SUMPRODUCT(B3:G5,B8:G10)
10	Ending Inventory	5	20	10	0	5	0		
11									
12	Beginning Inventory	0	=B14	=C14	=D14	=E14	=F14		
13	Plus Amount Produced	=B8+B9	=C8+C9	=D8+D9	=E8+E9	=F8+F9	=G8+G9		
14	Less Ending Inventory	=B10	=C10	=D10	=E10	=F10	=G10		
15	Available for Shipment	=B12+B13-B14	=C12+C13-C14	=D12+D13-D14	=E12+E13-E14	=F12+F13-F14	=G12+G13-G14		
16	Shipping Requirements	95	85	110	115	90	105		

FIGURE 3–33

Information for Solver Parameters Dialogue Box

Solver Parameters		
Target cell (objective function)		**I9**
Objective:		**Minimize**
Changing cells (decision variables)		**B8:G10**
Constraints:	**B8:G8 <= 100**	Capacity limit on regular time
	B9:G9 <= 15	Capacity limit on overtime
	B15:G15 = B16:G16	Shipments = Beginning inventory plus Production minus Ending inventory
	G10 = 0	No June ending inventory
	B8:G10 >= 0	Non-negative decision variables

Figure 3–34 shows the Solver Sensitivity Report for this solution (the Solver Answer report is not shown—the solution values are given in the spreadsheet in Figure 3–31).

Refer to these figures in answering the following questions:

a. What is the solution to the problem? That is, what should be the company's production schedule for the next six months? What is the cost of this plan?

b. After completing the production plan shown in Figure 3–31, the company received an additional order for five units for January (increasing the commitments for that month from 95 to 100). The production manager argues that the marginal cost of producing these five units is $35 each (the overtime cost) since the plant is already scheduled to operate at full regular-time capacity. The sales manager argues that the marginal cost should only be $30 per unit, since previously only 95 units were the delivery commitment for January. What do you think will be the incremental cost of producing these five additional units? Why?

c. Suppose the company could temporarily increase the regular-time capacity for the month of April by 10 units. This would increase the cost of these extra 10 units from the regular-time cost of $32 per unit to $34 per unit. The cost of overtime units would continue to be $37 per unit. Should this change be made? How do you know?

d. Suppose that your accountant just informed you that a mistake had been made in estimating the regular-time per unit cost for the month of April. Instead of the $32 used in the analysis, the correct cost per unit should be $36. Would this change the production plan? Would it change the estimated total cost? By how much? (Assume nothing else changes.)

3–12. Co-Op Farm owns 1,000 acres of land on which it grows crops for sale to members of its grocery chain. Current plans call for the farm to grow corn and wheat on the land. Seed and other cultivation costs per acre are $100 for corn and $120 for wheat. Corn requires 10 labor-hours per acre, while wheat requires 8 labor-hours per acre. The yield at year-end in bushels per acre is 120 for corn and 100 for wheat. The farm can plant the land in any mix of the two crops. The farm receives $4.25 per bushel for corn sold and $5.25 per bushel for wheat sold to the grocery chain. The grocery chain can buy at most 100,000 bushels of corn and 175,000 bushels of wheat.

The farm is considering the possible raising of up to 2,000 steer cattle to sell beef to the grocery chain. To accomplish this, some of the land planned for corn or wheat can be dedicated as pasture to raise the young steers and feed them for one year. The steers cost $150 to purchase and are sold for $800 after feeding for one year. Each steer requires 20 hours of labor, one-half acre of land, and consumes 80 bushels of corn during its final fattening. The corn for the steers can be grown on the farm, if enough is available, or it can be purchased. If corn is purchased to feed the steers, it costs $4.50 per bushel.

The farm can use student labor, which costs $6 per hour, or experienced farmhands can be hired for $10 per hour. Each hour of student labor requires nine minutes (.15 hours) of supervision, and each hour of experienced farmhand labor requires three minutes (.05 hours) of supervision. There are 2,000 hours of supervision available.

The farm has $200,000 available to fund its farming operation. To efficiently operate the farm, the farm modeled its options as a linear program.

This problem is formulated on a spreadsheet and the optimal solution is shown in Figure 3–35. The Solver

FIGURE 3–34 Excel Solver Sensitivity Report for Production Scheduling Example

Changing Cells

Cell	Name	Final Value	Reduced Cost	Objective Coefficient	Allowable Increase	Allowable Decrease
$B$8	Regular Time Production January	100	0	30	1	1E+30
$C$8	Regular Time Production February	100	0	30	3	1E+30
$D$8	Regular Time Production March	100	0	32	3	1E+30
$E$8	Regular Time Production April	100	0	32	5	1E+30
$F$8	Regular Time Production May	95	0	31	4	1
$G$8	Regular Time Production June	100	0	32	1	1E+30
$B$9	Overtime Production January	0	4	35	1E+30	4
$C$9	Overtime Production February	0	2	35	1E+30	2
$D$9	Overtime Production March	0	2	37	1E+30	2
$E$9	Overtime Production April	5	0	37	2	1
$F$9	Overtime Production May	0	5	36	1E+30	5
$G$9	Overtime Production June	0	4	37	1E+30	4
$B$10	Ending Inventory January	5	0	2	1	4
$C$10	Ending Inventory February	20	0	2	1	2
$D$10	Ending Inventory March	10	0	2	1	2
$E$10	Ending Inventory April	0	8	2	1E+30	8
$F$10	Ending Inventory May	5	0	2	4	1
$G$10	Ending Inventory June	0	0	2	1E+30	1E+30

Constraints

Cell	Name	Final Value	Shadow Price	Constraint R.H. Side	Allowable Increase	Allowable Decrease
$B$15	Available for Shipment January	95	31	95	5	5
$C$15	Available for Shipment February	85	33	85	10	5
$D$15	Available for Shipment March	110	35	110	10	5
$E$15	Available for Shipment April	115	37	115	10	5
$F$15	Available for Shipment May	90	31	90	5	95
$G$15	Available for Shipment June	105	33	105	5	5
$G$10	Ending Inventory June	0	35	0	5	0
$B$8	Regular Time Production January	100	-1	100	5	5
$C$8	Regular Time Production February	100	-3	100	5	10
$D$8	Regular Time Production March	100	-3	100	5	10
$E$8	Regular Time Production April	100	-5	100	5	10
$F$8	Regular Time Production May	95	0	100	1E+30	5
$G$8	Regular Time Production June	100	-1	100	5	5
$B$9	Overtime Production January	0	0	15	1E+30	15
$C$9	Overtime Production February	0	0	15	1E+30	15
$D$9	Overtime Production March	0	0	15	1E+30	15
$E$9	Overtime Production April	5	0	15	1E+30	10
$F$9	Overtime Production May	0	0	15	1E+30	15
$G$9	Overtime Production June	0	0	15	1E+30	15

FIGURE 3–35 Spreadsheet and Solver Sensitivity Report (for Problem 3–12)

	A	B	C	D	E	F	G	H	I	J	K	L	M	N
1		Acres planted in corn	Acres planted in wheat	Steers purchased and sold	Student labor-hours	Experienced labor-hours	Purchased corn fed to steers	Grown corn fed to steers	Bushels of corn sold	Bushels of wheat sold				
2	Decision Variables	118.0812	793.3579	177.1218	11070.00	0	0	14169.74	0	79335.79				
3													Total profit	
4	Profit contribution (dollars)	-100	-120	650	-6	-10	-4.50	0	4.25	5.25			$358,210	
5	Constraints:												Constraint limit	slack
6	Acreage limit	1	1	0.5							1,000.00	<=	1,000	0
7	Maximum number of steers			1							177./12	<=	2,000	1,822.88
8	Upper limit on wheat sold									1	79,336	<=	175,0000	95,664
9	Upper limit on corn sold								1		0	<=	100,000	100,000
10	Upper limit supervision hours				0.15	0.05					1,661	<=	2,000	339
11	Budget limit	100	120	150	6	10	4.5				200,000	<=	200,000	0
12	Labor required	10	8	20	-1	-1					0	=	0	0
13	Required corn feed for steers			-80			1	1			0	=	0	0
14	Total production/usage of corn	120							-1		0	=	0	0
15	Wheat production/sale		100							-1	0	=	0	0

Changing Cells

Cell	Name	Final Value	Reduced Cost	Objective Coefficient	Allowable Increase	Allowable Decrease
$B$2	Decision Variables Acres planted in corn	118.0811808	0	-100	6.505376344	10.25
$C$2	Decision Variables Acres planted in wheat	793.3579336	0	-120	5.857142857	6.368421053
$D$2	Decision Variables Steers purchased and sold	177.1217712	0	650	151.25	6.833333333
$E$2	Decision Variables Student labor-hours	11070.1107	0	-6	2.42	0.394230769
$F$2	Decision Variables Experienced labor-hours	0	-4.151291513	-10	4.151291513	1E+30
$G$2	Decision Variables Purchased corn fed to steers	0	-0.364391144	-4.5	0.364391144	1E+30
$H$2	Decision Variables Grown corn fed to steers	14169.7417	0	0	1.890625	0.085416667
$I$2	Decision Variables Bushels of corn sold	0	-0.055811808	4.25	0.055811808	1E+30
$J$2	Decision Variables Bushels of wheat sold	79335.79336	0	5.25	0.058571429	0.063684211

Constraints

Cell	Name	Final Value	Shadow Price	Constraint R.H. Side	Allowable Increase	Allowable Decrease
$K$6	Acreage limit	1000	350.6457565	1000	190.4761905	278.7878788
$K$7	Maximum number of steers	177.1217712	0	2000	1E+30	1822.878229
$K$8	Upper limit on wheat sold	79335.79336	0	175000	1E+30	95664.20664
$K$9	Upper limit on corn sold	0	0	100000	1E+30	100000
$K$10	Upper limit supervision hours	1660.516605	0	2000	1E+30	339.4833948
$K$11	Budget limit	200000	0.037822878	200000	23589.74359	32000
$K$12	Labor required	-1.81899E-12	6.226937269	0	20476.19048	5333.333333
$K$13	Required corn feed for steers	-3.63798E-12	-4.305811808	0	09526.31579	13763.44086
$K$14	Total production/usage of corn	-9.09495E-12	-4.305811808	0	09526.31579	13763.44086
$K$15	Wheat production/sale	0	-5.25	0	79335.79336	95664.20664

Sensitivity Report is also given. Answer each of the following questions independently, using the information in Figure 3–35.

a. What is the optimal farming schedule (i.e., the solution to the problem)? What is the total dollar payoff?

b. By how much would the price of corn sold have to change and in which direction (increase or decrease) for the farm to consider selling any corn to the Co-Op groceries?

c. What is the value of an additional hour of labor to the farm?

d. If the farm could borrow an additional $15,000 to help finance the farm's operation, what is the maximum interest rate (simple annual interest), if any, that the farm would be willing to pay?

e. A neighboring ranch has offered to lease 200 acres of land to Co-Op Farm for a fixed fee of $65,000, to be paid out of profits at year-end after crops and steers have been sold. Should the farm accept the offer?

f. By how much would the cost of "seed and other cultivation costs" of wheat have to increase before the farm would change the amount of acreage devoted to growing wheat?

g. The farm is contemplating the growing of tomatoes. Tomato plants can be acquired for $50 per acre. Tomatoes require 15 hours of labor per acre. An acre of tomatoes produces 40 bushels of salable tomatoes. Assuming tomatoes can be sold for $12 per bushel, should the farm devote any acreage to the growing of tomatoes?

h. For a fixed cost of $10,000, the farm can apply fertilizer to the land at the beginning of the planting season. The fertilizer is applied to all the land and increases the yield of corn to 130 bushels per acre and the yield of wheat to 110 bushels per acre. Would the farm find it profitable to apply the fertilizer?

i. The Co-Op would like to have some experienced farm labor on the farm. What would be the rate of change in payoff as experienced farmhand labor-hours were added?

j. The shadow price on constraint 3 (demand for labor) is 6.23. Yet the farm can hire unlimited student labor at $6.00 per hour. Explain this apparent contradiction.

3–13. The Ajax Nut Company sells mixed nuts of two quality levels. The more expensive mix has a higher proportion of cashews, whereas the cheaper mix contains more peanuts.

The prices for nuts purchased by Ajax are cashews, 50 cents a pound, and peanuts, 20 cents a pound. The two mixes sold by Ajax and their prices are mixture A, 80 cents a pound, and mixture B, 40 cents a pound. Ajax can sell any amount of each of these mixtures but, due to a shortage of nuts, can obtain no more than 200 pounds of cashews and 400 pounds of peanuts.

Management has decided that mixture A should not contain more than 25 percent peanuts nor less than 40 percent cashews. Mixture B should have no more than 60 percent peanuts and no less than 20 percent cashews.

How should Ajax mix its nuts? That is, how many pounds of mixture A should be produced (and what should be its composition), and how many pounds of mixture B (and its composition)? Formulate the linear programming model and find the optimal solution using the Solver package.

3–14. The Paul Bunyan Lumber Company produces pine and fir saw lumber and two types of plywood. The company has a profit contribution of 4 cents a board foot (bf) for pine and 6 cents a bf for fir. Type 1 plywood contributes $1.20 per panel, and type 2 earns $1.50 per panel.

For the month of December, the company has 2,580 thousand bf (MBF) of pine available for either saw lumber or plywood. Similarly, 2,040 MBF of fir are available. One panel of type 1 plywood requires 16 bf of pine and 8 bf of fir. One panel of type 2 plywood requires 12 bf of each species.

Saw lumber is restricted only by the capacity of the headrig saw. The saw can handle 400 MBF per month of any species.

The plywood mill can be restricted by either the peeler or the dryer. During the month, no more than 250,000 panels of lumber may be peeled, and there are 920,000 minutes of dryer time available. Each type 1 panel requires four minutes of dryer time, and each type 2 panel requires six minutes of dryer time.

Market conditions limit the number of type 1 panels sold to no more than 120,000 and the number of type 2 panels to no more than 100,000. Any amounts of saw lumber can be sold. The company formulated a linear programming model of its operations as follows:
Let:

P = Profit contribution in thousands of dollars
X_1 = MBF of pine saw lumber sold
X_2 = MBF of fir saw lumber sold
X_3 = Thousands of panels of type 1 plywood sold
X_4 = Thousands of panels of type 2 plywood sold

Maximize:
$P = 0.04X_1 + 0.06X_2 + 1.20X_3 + 1.50X_4$

Subject to:

$$X_1 + 16X_3 + 12X_4 \leq 2{,}580 \text{ (availability of pine)}$$
$$X_2 + 8X_3 + 12X_4 \leq 2{,}040 \text{ (availabilty of fir)}$$
$$X_1 + X_2 \leq 400 \text{ (sawmill capacity)}$$
$$X_3 + X_4 \leq 250 \text{ (peeler capacity)}$$
$$4X_3 + 6X_4 \leq 920 \text{ (dryer capacity)}$$
$$X_3 \leq 120 \text{ (market demand, type 1 plywood)}$$
$$X_4 \leq 100 \text{ (market demand, type 2 plywood)}$$

Find the optimal solution using the Solver package.

Solutions to Practice Problems

3–1. See Figure 3–36. The solution is $X_1 = 4$, $X_2 = 4$, and $P = 28$.

Figure 3–36
(for Problem 3–1)

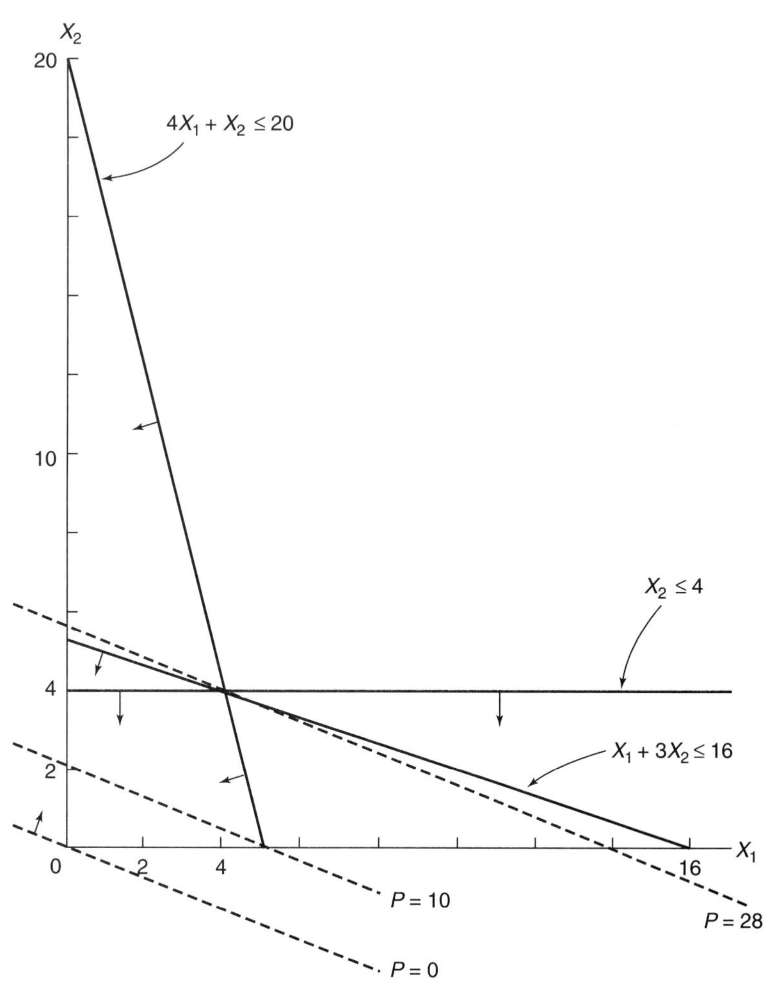

3–2. Maximize P = 30A + 30B
Subject to:
3A + 1B ≤ 30,000
A ≤ 8,000
B ≤ 12,000
A, B, ≥ 0

a. See Figure 3–37. The optimal solution is 6 thousand units of product A and 12 thousand units of B, with profit of $540 thousand.

b. See Figure 3–38. Note that the constraint $A \leq 8$ is not binding since $A = 6$ in the optimal solution. Hence, increasing the limit on A will have no effect on the solution or on the profit. The *shadow price* is zero.

c. See Figure 3–39. Note that the optimum solution shifts to $A = 5.67$, $B = 13$, with profit of $560 thousand. This represents an increase in profit of $20 thousand from the base case ($560 − 540 = $20). Hence, the shadow price is $20. That is, each unit increase in the limit on production of product B will increase profit by $20.

d. See Figure 3–40. Note that the optimum solution shifts to $A = 6.33$, $B = 12$, with profit $P = \$550$. This is an increase in $10 from the base case. Hence, the shadow price for labor hours is $10.

FIGURE 3–37
(for Problem 3–2*a*)

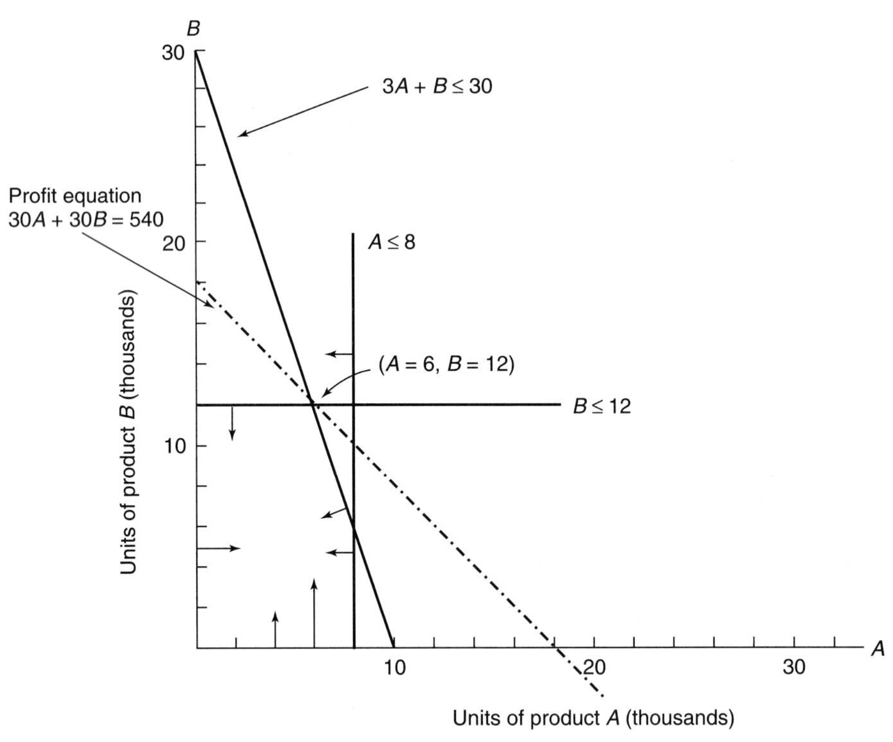

FIGURE 3–38
(for Problems 3–2*b* and 3–2*e*)

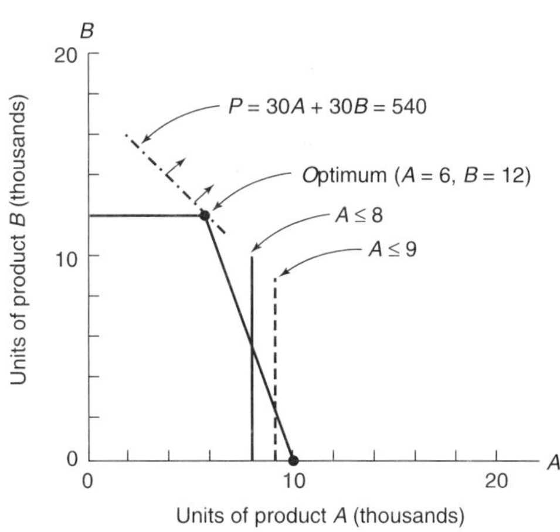

FIGURE 3–39
(for Problem 3–2*c*)

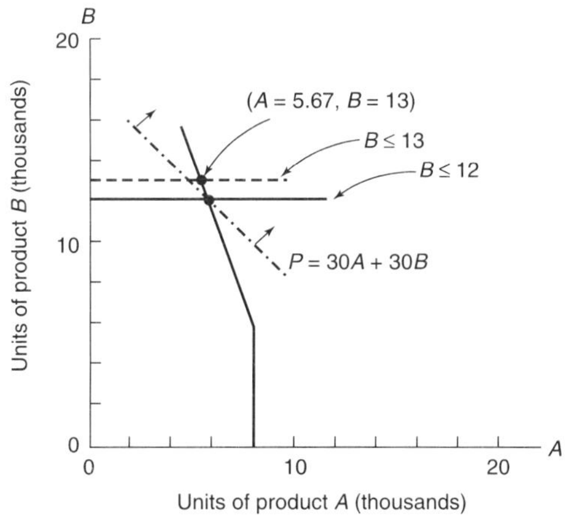

FIGURE 3–40
(for Problem 3–2*d*)

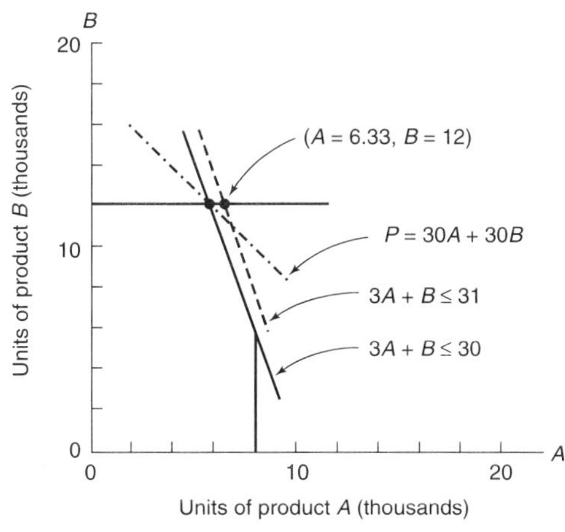

3–2. *(continued)*

e. *Sales limit on product A:* Refer to Figure 3–38. The shadow price on this constraint is zero. Note that increasing the limit on product A will have no effect at all; hence, there is no upper limit. The optimal solution includes six thousand units of product A. A reduction in the sales limit below this will affect the solution. Hence, the range is from six thousand upward (with no upper limit) and this is the range within which the shadow price of zero holds.

Sales limit on product B: Refer to Figure 3–41. Note that as additional units of B can be produced, the optimum moves up to the point ($A = 0$, $B = 30$). Beyond this point, additional sales of B cannot be made because of the labor hours. Hence, the upper limit is 30 thousand units. As the sales limit of B is reduced down to six thousand units, the corner point ($A = 8$, $B = 6$) is reached. Beyond this, the solution changes. Hence, six thousand units is the lower limit. In summary, the shadow price of \$20 per unit of B holds over the range 6 to 30 thousand in the sales limit for product B.

Limit on labor hours: The second graph for this problem is shown in Figure 3–42. When labor hours increase up to 36 thousand (i.e., to the constraint $3A + B \leq 36$), a new corner point ($A = 8$, $B = 12$) is reached. As hours are decreased, the corner point ($A = 0$, $B = 12$) is reached when 12 thousand hours are available. Hence, the range on labor hours is from 12 thousand hours to 36 thousand hours, and within this range, the shadow price of \$10 holds.

FIGURE 3–41
(for Problem 3–2*e*)

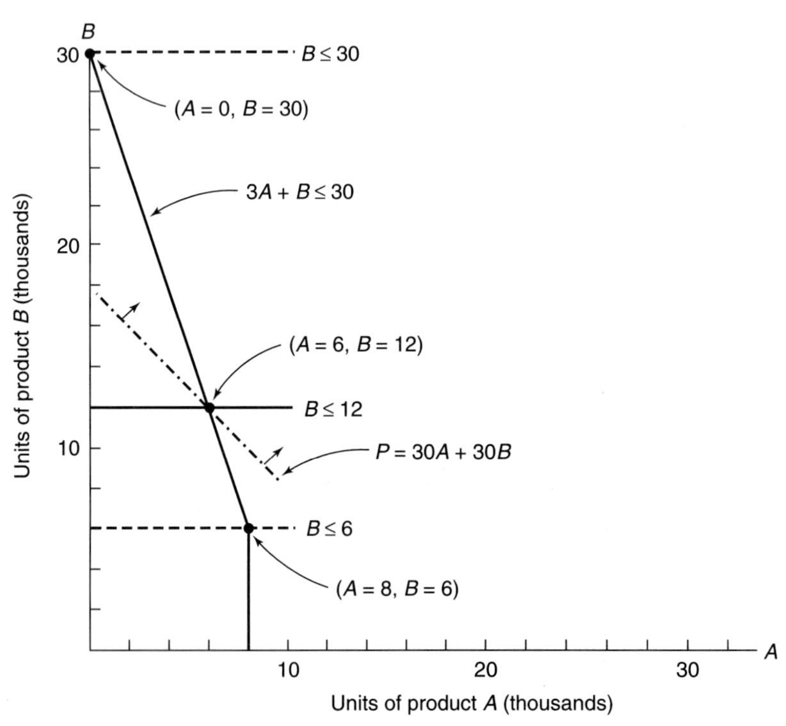

FIGURE 3–42
(for Problem 3–2*e*)

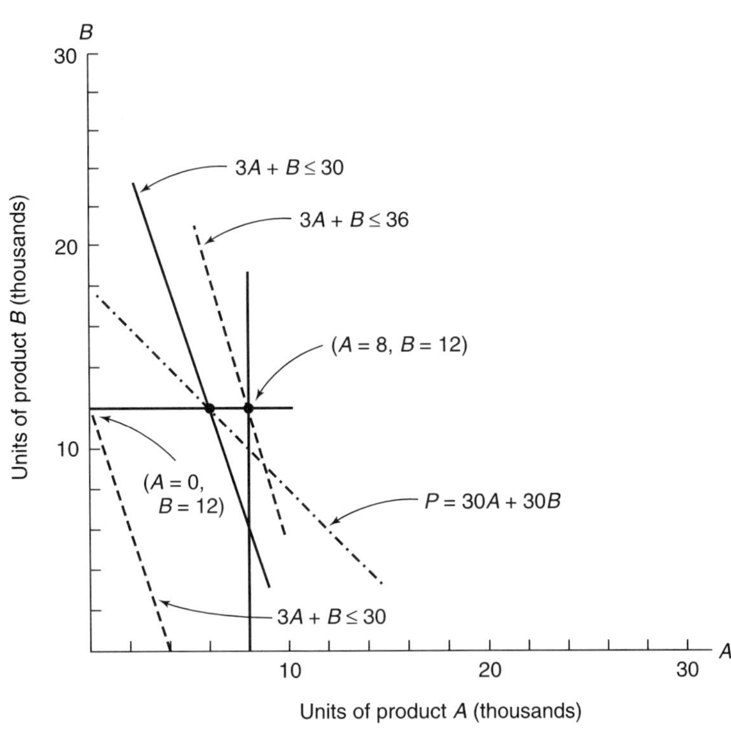

3–3. The formulation is:
Let A, B, C, D be the units of each product produced. Then

Maximize: P = 40A + 24B + 36C + 23D

Subject to:

$2A + 1B + 2.5C + 5D \leq 1{,}200$ (milling capacity)

$1A + 3B + 2.5C \leq 1{,}600$ (assembly capacity)

$10A + 5B + 2C + 12D \leq 10{,}000$ (inventory limit)

$A \leq 200$ (demand for product A)

$C \leq 160$ (demand for product C)

$D \geq 100$ (contract minimum for product D)

$A, B, C, D, \geq 0$

The Excel model is shown in Figure 3–43, both as it appears on the spreadsheet, and as the equations underlying it. (In this latter form, the first columns have been collapsed so that the formulas fit across the page). The final solution is shown in the spreadsheet and in the Answer Report from Solver. The Solver Sensitivity Analysis report is also shown (Figure 3–44).

a. The solution calls for 100 units of product A, 500 units of product B, no product C, and 100 units of product D, with a profit of $18,300. Also note that there is $5,300 of unused working capital, 100 units of unused demand for product A, and 160 units of unused demand for product B.

3–3. *(continued)*

b. Look at the shadow prices in the Solver Sensitivity Analysis report (Figure 3–44). The values are $19.20 for an additional hour of milling capacity, $1.60 for an additional hour of assembly capacity. Since all working capital for inventory is not used, the shadow price for that resource is 0.

c. Neither of these constraints is binding (all available demand is not being satisfied) and the shadow prices are zero. Hence the company should not spend anything to increase demand.

d. Note that this constraint is binding with a shadow price of −$73.00. A change in the constraint to require 130 units means an increase of 30 units. This is within the allowable increase limit in the Solver Sensitivity Analysis report. Hence a change in the requirement would *reduce* profit by (30)(73) = $2,190.

e. Examine the allowable increase for Product C on the top part of the Sensitivity Analysis report. The increase limit is 16. Hence a price increase of $10 on product C would not change the solution mix. And since no units of product C are being produced, the profit also would not change.

f. The opportunity cost for one unit of Product E can be calculated as:

Resource	*Usage*	*Opportunity Cost*	*Total*
Milling	2	19.2	38.4
Assembly	5	1.6	8.0
Inventory	20	0	0
Total			46.4

Since the profit per unit of $50 is greater than the opportunity cost of $46.40, at least some of this new product should be produced. The problem would need to be reformulated and re-solved with this new product to determine the exact number.

FIGURE 3–43 Solver Model (with optimal solution) (for Problem 3–3)

	A	B	C	D	E	F	G	H	I	J
1		Product A	Product B	Product C	Product D					
2										
3	Decision Variables	100	500	0	100					
4										
5								Total		
6	Objective Function	40	24	36	23			$18,300		
7										
8	Constraints:					Total Usage		Constraint Limit	Slack	Surplus
9	Milling Capacity	2	1	2.5	5	1200	<=	1200	0	
10	Assembly Capacity	1	3	2.5	0	1600	<=	1600	0	
11	Inventory Limit	10	5	2	12	4700	<=	10000	5300	
12	Demand Product A	1				100	<=	200	100	
13	Demand Product C			1		0	<=	160	160	
14	Contract Min. Prod. D				1	100	>=	100		0

(continued)

FIGURE 3–43 *(concluded)*

Equations for Solver Model

	A	B	C	D	E	F	G	H	I	J
1		Prod	Prod	Prod	Prod					
2										
3	Decis	100	500	0	100					
4										
5								Total		
6	Objec	40	24	36	23			=SUMPRODUCT($B$3:$E$3,B6:E6)		
7										
8	Const					Total Usage		Constraint Limit	Slack	Surplus
9	Milling	2	1	2.5	5	=SUMPRODUCT($B$3:$E$3,B9:E9)	<=	1200	=H9-F9	
10	Asse	1	3	2.5	0	=SUMPRODUCT($B$3:$E$3,B10:E10)	<=	1600	=H10-F10	
11	Invent	10	5	2	12	=SUMPRODUCT($B$3:$E$3,B11:E11)	<=	10000	=H11-F11	
12	Dema	1				=SUMPRODUCT($B$3:$E$3,B12:E12)	<=	200	=H12-F12	
13	Dema			1		=SUMPRODUCT($B$3:$E$3,B13:E13)	<=	160	=H13-F13	
14	Contr				1	=SUMPRODUCT($B$3:$E$3,B14:E14)	<=	100		=F14-H14

FIGURE 3–44 Solver Answer and Solver Sensitivity Reports (for Problem 3–3)

Solver Answer Report

Target Cell (Max)

Cell	Name	Original Value	Final Value
$H$6	Objective Function Total Profit	0	18300

Adjustable Cells

Cell	Name	Original Value	Final Value
$B$3	Decision Variables Product A	0	100
$C$3	Decision Variables Product B	0	500
$D$3	Decision Variables Product C	0	0
$E$3	Decision Variables Product D	0	100

Constraints

Cell	Name	Cell Value	Formula	Status	Slack
$F$14	Contract Min. Prod. D Total Usage	100	$F$14>=$H$14	Binding	0
$F$9	Milling Capacity Total Usage	1200	$F$9<=$H$9	Binding	0
$F$10	Assembly Capacity Total Usage	1600	$F$10<=$H$10	Binding	0
$F$11	Inventory Limit Total Usage	4700	$F$11<=$H$11	Not Binding	5300
$F$12	Demand Product A Total Usage	100	$F$12<=$H$12	Not Binding	100
$F$13	Demand Product C Total Usage	0	$F$13<=$H$13	Not Binding	160
$B$3	Decision Variables Product A	100	$B$3>=0	Not Binding	100
$C$3	Decision Variables Product B	500	$C$3>=0	Not Binding	500
$D$3	Decision Variables Product C	0	$D$3>=0	Binding	0
$E$3	Decision Variables Product D	100	$E$3>=0	Not Binding	100

Solver Sensitivity Report

Changing Cells

Cell	Name	Final Value	Reduced Cost	Objective Coefficient	Allowable Increase	Allowable Decrease
$B$3	Decision Variables Product A	100	0	40	8	16
$C$3	Decision Variables Product B	500	0	24	73	4
$D$3	Decision Variables Product C	0	-16	36	16	1E+30
$E$3	Decision Variables Product D	100	0	23	73	1E+30

Constraints

Cell	Name	Final Value	Shadow Price	Constraint R.H. Side	Allowable Increase	Allowable Decrease
$F$14	Contract Min. Prod. D Total Usage	100	-73	100	33.33333333	33.33333333
$F$9	Milling Capacity Total Usage	1200	19.2	1200	166.6666667	166.6666667
$F$10	Assembly Capacity Total Usage	1600	1.6	1600	500	500
$F$11	Inventory Limit Total Usage	4700	0	10000	1E+30	5300
$F$12	Demand Product A Total Usage	100	0	200	1E+30	100
$F$13	Demand Product C Total Usage	0	0	160	1E+30	160

3–4. The algebraic formulation is given below followed by Figure 3–45, the Solver formulation and solution including the Solver Sensitivity report. Let:

X_1 = Funds in signature loans (thous \$)
X_2 = Funds in furniture loans (thous \$)
X_3 = Funds in automobile loans (thous \$)
X_4 = Funds in second home mortgages (thous \$)
X_5 = Funds in first home mortgages (thous \$)

Maximize: $P = 0.15X_1 + 0.12X_2 + 0.09X_3 + 0.10X_4 + 0.07X_5$

Subject to: $X_1 + X_2 + X_3 + X_4 + X_5 \leq 1{,}500$ (total funds available)

$X_1 \leq 0.10(X_1 + X_2 + X_3 + X_4 + X_5)$ or $0.9X_1 - 0.1X_2 - 0.1X_3 - 0.1X_4 - 0.1X_5 \leq 0$

$X_1 + X_2 \leq 0.20(X_1 + X_2 + X_3 + X_4 + X_5)$ or $0.8X_1 + 0.8X_2 - 0.2X_3 - 0.2X_4 - 0.2X_5 \leq 0$

$X_5 \geq 0.40(X_4 + X_5)$ or $-0.4X_4 + 0.6X_5 \geq 0$

$X_5 \geq 0.20(X_1 + X_2 + X_3 + X_4 + X_5)$ or $-0.2X_1 - 0.2X_2 - 0.2X_3 - 0.2X_4 + 0.8X_5 \geq 0$

$X_4 \leq 0.25(X_1 + X_2 + X_3 + X_4 + X_5)$ or $-0.25X_1 - 0.25X_2 - 0.25X_3 + 0.75X_4 - 0.25X_5 \leq 0$

All $X_i > 0$

a. The solution calls for \$150 thousand in signature loans, \$150 thousand in furniture loans, \$525 thousand in auto loans, \$375 thousand in second mortgages, and \$300 in first mortgages. The total return is \$146,250.

b. Look at the Solver Sensitivity Report and the shadow price on the Total Funds Available constraint, which is 0.0975. This is the return for each additional dollar (i.e. 9.75%). There is no limit on the increase (1E+30 is Excel's way of saying "infinity".) The limit on the decrease is \$1500 (the total amount of the funds available). This means that the incremental return is 9.75% from zero on up without limit. At first this may seem strange, but notice that all the constraints, except that on total funds available, are relative and limit the percentages in the portfolio. Hence, once the optimal mix is obtained, the return it generates is limited only by the total funds available.

c. Refer to the upper part of the Solver Sensitivity Report for Second Mortgages. There is no limit on the increase (the 1E+30 value again). Hence, an increase from 10% to 12% would not affect the solution at all (in terms of the mix). However, the total return would increase by (.02)(375) = \$75 thousand. That is, the \$375 thousand in second mortgages would earn 2 percent more.

FIGURE 3–45 Solver Formulation (including optimal solution) (for Problem 3–4)

	A	B	C	D	E	F	G	H	I	J	K
1		Signature Loans	Furniture Loans	Automobile Loans	Second Mortgages	First Mortgages					
2	Decision Variables: Amount (thous $)	150	150	525	375	300					
3									Total Return (thous $)		
4	Annual Return (%)	0.15	0.12	0.09	0.1	0.07			146.25	Slack	Surplus
5	Constraints:										
6	Total Funds Available	1	1	1	1	1	1500	≤	1500	0	
7	Signature Loans Limit	0.9	-0.1	-0.1	-0.1	-0.1	0	≤	0	0	
8	Signature + Furniture Limit	0.8	0.8	-0.2	-0.2	-0.2	0	≤	0	0	
9	Second Mortgage Limit	-0.25	-0.25	-0.25	0.75	-0.25	0	≤	0	0	
10	Firsts to Total Mortgages Minimum				-0.4	0.6	30	≥	0		30
11	Firsts to Total Loans Minimum	-0.2	-0.2	-0.2	-0.2	0.8	0	≥	0		0

Solver Equations

	A	B	C	D	E	F	G	H	I	J	K
1											
2		150	150	525	375	300					
3									Total Return (thous $)		
4		0.15	0.12	0.09	0.1	0.07			=SUMPRODUCT($B$2:$F$2,B4:F4)		
5										Slack	Surplus
6		1	1	1	1	1	=SUMPRODUCT($B$2:$F$2,B6:F6)	<=	1500	=I6-G8	
7		0.9	-0.1	-0.1	-0.1	-0.1	=SUMPRODUCT($B$2:$F$2,B7:F7)	<=	0	=I7-G7	
8		0.8	0.8	-0.2	-0.2	-0.2	=SUMPRODUCT($B$2:$F$2,B8:F8)	<=	0	=I8-G8	
9		-0.25	-0.25	-0.25	0.75	-0.25	=SUMPRODUCT($B$2:$F$2,B9:F9)	<=	0	=I9-G9	
10					-0.4	0.6	=SUMPRODUCT($B$2:$F$2,B10:F10)	>=	0		=G10-I10
11		-0.2	-0.2	-0.2	-0.2	0.8	=SUMPRODUCT($B$2:$F$2,B11:F11)	>=	0		=G11-I11
12											
13			Note: Columns A to F have been compressed to show equations.								
14											

Solver Sensitivity Report

Changing Cells

Cell	Name	Final Value	Reduced Cost	Objective Coefficient	Allowable Increase	Allowable Decrease
$B$2	Decision Variables: Amount (thous $) Signature Loans	150	0	0.15	1E+30	0.03
$C$2	Decision Variables: Amount (thous $) Furniture Loans	150	0	0.12	0.03	0.03
$D$2	Decision Variables: Amount (thous $) Automobile Loans	525	0	0.09	0.01	0.02
$E$2	Decision Variables: Amount (thous $) Second Mortgages	375	0	0.1	1E+30	0.01
$F$2	Decision Variables: Amount (thous $) First Mortgages	300	0	0.07	0.02	0.4875

Constraints

Cell	Name	Final Value	Shadow Price	Constraint R.H. Side	Allowable Increase	Allowable Decrease
$G$6	Total Funds Available	1500	0.0975	1500	1E++30	1500
$G$7	Signature Loans Limit	0	0.03	0	150	150
$G$8	Signature + Furniture Limit	0	0.03	0	525	150
$G$9	Second Mortgage Limit	0	0.01	0	75	375
$G$10	Firsts to Total Mortgages Minimum	30	0	0	30	1E+30
$G$11	First to Total Loans Minimum	0	-0.02	0	525	50

Motivating Example

Fleet Scheduling at Delta Airlines[1]

Put yourself in the position of the group that schedules the aircraft for Delta Airlines. In the United States, there are over 2,500 flights each day. There are 450 aircraft available, but they aren't all the same—in fact, there are 10 different types that vary by size, speed, amount of noise created, and so on. On top of this, a maintenance schedule for the aircraft must be included. And allowance must be made for the pilot crews—pilots are limited in the types of aircraft they are certified to fly. Also, crews must be scheduled so that they can obtain the proper amount of rest each day. Some cities restrict the types of aircraft that can operate at certain times of day (because of noise restrictions, for example). And there are other constraints, such as that the same aircraft must be used for certain continuing flights.

This is a very complex task even to get a feasible schedule, but it is critical to Delta also to get an economical one. Operating a fleet of aircraft is very expensive, including personnel costs, fuel costs, and maintenance costs. But there is also a cost called *spill.* Spill is the number of passengers that are not carried because capacity is insufficient. For example, if a small plane is scheduled for a given flight segment but the number of people who want to fly on that segment could fill a jumbo jet, the airline loses a lot of revenue.

Delta Airlines uses a very large mathematical programming model to solve this fleet-scheduling problem. The objective is to minimize the cost (operating cost plus spill cost) subject to the restrictions described above. It is a mixed integer programming model. There are approximately 20,000 binary integer variables (variables that have values of 0 or 1), and these variables assign individual fleet aircraft to specific flight segments. There are about 40,000 other integer variables. And the model has about 40,000 constraints in all. A large computer is used to solve this program.

The result of this effort is significantly improved fleet scheduling. Delta estimates that the model should save an estimated $300 million over three years.

Delta is not the only airline using integer programming for fleet and crew scheduling. American Airlines also reports substantial savings with similar models.[2]

[1]This example is based on R. Subramanian, R. P. Scheff, Jr., J. D. Quillinan, D. S. Wiper, and R. E. Marsten, "Coldstart: Fleet Assignment at Delta Air Lines," *Interfaces,* January–February 1994, pp. 104–120.

[2]J. Abara, "Applying Integer Linear Programming to the Fleet Assignment Problem," *Interfaces,* July–August 1989, pp. 20–28; and R. Anbil, E. Gelman, B. Patty, and R. Tanga, "Recent Advances in Crew-Pairing Optimization at American Airlines," *Interfaces,* January–February 1991, pp. 62–74.

CHAPTER

4 Special Topics in Mathematical Programming

The category of mathematical programming includes a wide variety of techniques used to solve optimization problems. The decision maker is trying to maximize or minimize some objective, subject to a set of constraints. The most widely used technique in this category, of course, is simple linear programming. This has been discussed in detail in other chapters.

This chapter extends that discussion in several directions. First is integer programming, which allows some or all of the decision variables to be integer valued while keeping linear relationships in the objective function and constraints. The formulation of these problems is presented, and then the solution using the Solver package. Next, optimization, which includes nonlinear functions, is discussed. Finally, the case in which the decision maker has not one but multiple objectives is considered.

Integer Programming

Many business problems could be suitably formulated and solved by linear programming, except for one drawback—they require solutions that are integers. For example, a variable X in a linear programming model may refer to whether or not a new plant is built. If $X = 1$, the plant is to be built; $X = 0$ means no plant; and a value of X anywhere in between ($X = 0.56$, for instance) makes no sense. There is no guarantee that the standard solution procedures for linear programming will give an integer solution.[3]

To deal with this problem, a set of techniques has been developed called **integer programming.** Some problems may require that all variables in the problem be integers—the **all-integer solution.** A special case of the all-integer solution occurs when all the variables can take on values of only 0 or 1. The most general case of integer programming is that in which some variables are required to be integers, but others can take on any values. This is called the **mixed-integer programming** problem.

[3]An important exception to this is the solution of network problems by LP, which do give integer solutions. The transportation problem and critical-path problem are examples of such network problems.

Work Crew Scheduling at McDonald's[4]

It might seem that only large companies with big computers make use of mathematical programming techniques. Here is an example of a program on an inexpensive personal computer used by managers of a set of McDonald's restaurants to schedule the work force.

The need for workers varies significantly at different times of the day. And workers have different skills, different lengths of shifts, and personal requirements that limit their availability. Student employees, for example, may need to fit their work schedules in with their class schedules. The manager of a fast-food restaurant may have 150 or so employees to schedule over a week, a task that, when done by hand, generally took eight hours each week. A computer program was developed that had a mathematical programming model at the core but also involved a simple interface for the user for data entry and use.

The benefits of this program included not only reducing the staffing costs for the restaurant but also relieving the manager of a tedious and time-consuming task.

[4]Based on R. R. Love, Jr., and J. M. Hoey, "Management Science Improves Fast-Food Operations," *Interfaces,* March–April 1990, pp. 21–29.

The first part of this chapter will illustrate how integer programming formulations can represent a number of important management problems. The solution of these problems using the Solver program for the Excel spreadsheet will be demonstrated. One technique used to solve integer programs, called the branch and bound procedure, is explained in the appendix to this chapter. Before proceeding, we will first illustrate a simple two-variable integer programming problem.

Example

Consider the following integer programming problem:

$$\begin{aligned} \text{Maximize:} \quad & P = 4X_1 + 5X_2 \\ \text{Subject to:} \quad & \tfrac{2}{3}X_1 + X_2 \leq 1 \\ & X_1 \leq 1 \\ & X_1, X_2 \geq 0 \\ & X_1, X_2 \text{ integer} \end{aligned}$$

The constraints and the objective function are plotted in Figure 4–1. Possible integer solutions are noted by small dots.

If we attempt to solve this problem ignoring the integer restrictions, the optimal linear programming solution is $X_1 = 1$, $X_2 = \tfrac{1}{3}$, denoted as A, producing a profit of \$5.67. However, this solution is not an integer solution, since $X_2 = \tfrac{1}{3}$. We might try to round the LP solution to the closest integer solution; in Figure 4–1, the closest integer solution to point A is $X_1 = 1$, $X_2 = 0$, producing a profit of \$4. However, such rounding can sometimes produce a solution that is infeasible; for example, if our second constraint were $X_1 \leq 0.95$ instead of $X_1 \leq 1$, then the solution $X_1 = 1$, $X_2 = 0$ would not satisfy the constraints.

More important, the rounded solution may not be optimal. In our example, consider the solution $X_1 = 0$, $X_2 = 1$; this solution is feasible and produces a larger profit (\$5), although it is not the "closest" integer solution to the answer found using ordinary LP. As more dimensions are added to the problem, the rounding approach

FIGURE 4–1

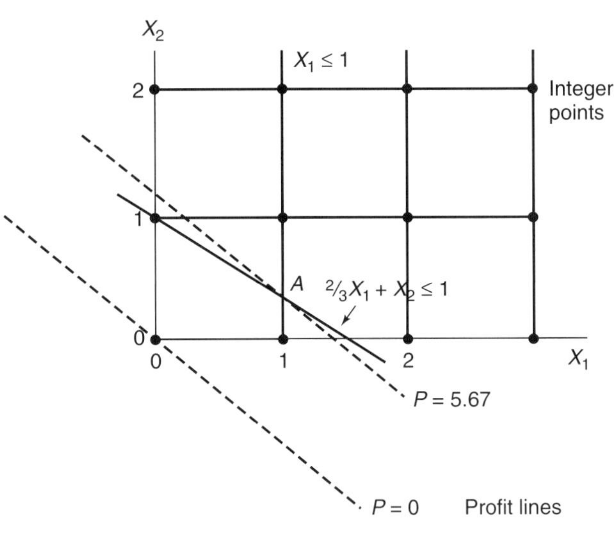

to solution becomes less and less desirable, and a systematic approach to finding a solution is necessary.

Before we describe ways of solving integer linear programming problems, we will first illustrate a variety of problems that can be formulated in this manner.

Formulation of Integer Programming Problems

In general, integer programming problems are formulated in much the same way as the standard linear programming problems discussed in earlier chapters, with the added proviso that one or more variables must assume integer values. That is, we establish a linear objective function that is maximized or minimized subject to linear constraints. However, there are some uses of zero/one variables that are unique to integer programming. A **zero/one** or **binary** variable is one that can take on only values of 0 or 1. The value 1 can be used to indicate the presence of something (a factory, for example); 0 indicates its absence. The use of binary variables is illustrated below.

The Fixed-Charge Problem

Suppose a given product, if it is produced, contributes \$50 per unit to profit. However, a one-time expense of \$1,000 is incurred in setting up the machinery for a production run. This cost is zero if no units are produced.

Let X be the number of units produced. Then we could formulate the problem so that:

$$\text{Contribution} = \begin{cases} 50X - 1{,}000 & \text{if } X > 0 \\ 0 & \text{if } X = 0 \end{cases}$$

However, Contribution is not a linear function of X in this formulation.

To rewrite the formulation in a linear form, we introduce a new variable Y, which takes on only the integer values of 0 or 1. Then we maximize $(50X - 1{,}000Y)$ subject to whatever other constraints we have plus the following two:

$$Y \leq 1 \qquad \text{and } Y \text{ is an integer}$$
$$\text{and } X \leq MY \qquad \text{where } M \text{ is some very large number}$$

Note that when $Y = 0$, the second constraint forces X to be 0 and the contribution $(50X - 1{,}000Y)$ is 0 also; when $Y = 1$, there is no practical limit on X; moreover, the fixed-charge amount \$1,000 is deducted from the profit. Hence, the use of the zero/one or binary integer variable Y allows us to formulate this type of problem with linear constraints.

The fixed-charge type of problem is common in business. There is an investment cost to build a new plant before any production can occur. There are usually fixed costs that have to be incurred if a second shift is undertaken or a new warehouse is opened.

Note in the above example that the objective function value and constraints are *linear*. That is, they involve only a constant times a variable (no squares or products of variables). One mistake that is sometimes made in integer programming formulations is to use nonlinear functions. For example, the fixed-charge problem could be formulated by maximizing $50XY - 1{,}000Y$ with Y a zero/one variable as above. Note that this satisfies the requirements, since there is no profit or cost if $Y = 0$, and the profit is $50X - 1{,}000$ if $Y = 1$. However, the term $50XY$ is nonlinear because it involves the product of the two variables X and Y. Hence, this formulation would not be a valid integer linear programming problem.

Another approach to formulating this fixed-charge cost might be to use a spreadsheet "IF" function. Suppose, for example, the number of units produced (the X value) were in cell D2 on the spreadsheet. Then the total cost might be written as:

=IF(D2>0, 50*D2−1,000, 0)

While this is a logically correct formulation, it also is *not* a linear function, and would *not* be appropriate for a linear model.

Batch Size Problem

A similar problem is one in which some minimum level is required before an activity is undertaken. For example, a firm may have to buy a minimum quantity of at least 50 units of a certain product. Let X be the number of units bought. Then either $X = 0$ or $X \geq 50$.

This situation can be formulated with a zero/one integer variable Y by using constraints as follows:

$$X \leq MY \quad (M \text{ is a very large number})$$
$$X \geq 50Y$$

Note that if $Y = 0$, then, by the first constraint, X must be 0. If $Y = 1$, then, by the second constraint, X must be at least 50.

Either-Or Constraints

Sometimes, in a decision situation, either one or another constraint must hold, but not both. For example:

Either: $5X_1 + 2X_2 \leq 10$
Or: $3X_1 - 4X_2 \leq 24$
But not both

We can handle this in integer programming with the use of a zero/one Y variable by using both of the following modified constraints:

$$5X_1 + 2X_2 \leq 10 + MY$$
$$3X_1 - 4X_2 \leq 24 + M(1 - Y)$$

Note that when $Y = 0$, the first constraint is binding, but the right-hand side of the second becomes very large and hence is not binding. And conversely, when $Y = 1$, the second constraint binds but the first does not because MY is very large.

Examples of Integer Formulations

A Capital Budgeting Problem

Suppose that a firm has N projects ($i = 1, 2 \ldots N$) in which to invest capital. For each project i, let:

P_i = Net present value (the return of project i above cost, expressed in dollars of present value)[5]
C_i = Capital outlay at time zero for project i
R_{1i} = Cash flow in year 1 for project i
R_{2i} = Cash flow in year 2 for project i
.
.
.
R_{ti} = Cash flow in year t for project i

where each of the P, C, and R values is a known constant.

The firm wishes to select a *set* of projects to maximize net present value. A project is either undertaken in total, or rejected; that is, the firm cannot select some fraction of the project. The constraints may be of several kinds. For example:

1. A limited amount of funds available for investment at time zero—call this amount K.
2. Minimum required positive cash flows in future years 1, 2, . . . Call these requirements F_t.

For each project, we define a zero/one integer variable Y_i, where $Y_i = 1$ if the ith project is to be undertaken, and $Y_i = 0$ if not. We can then formulate this capital budgeting illustration as an integer programming problem as follows:

Maximize total net present value achieved:

$$P_1Y_1 + P_2Y_2 + P_3Y_3 + \ldots + P_NY_N$$

[5]To calculate the net present value, funds received in the future are discounted at an appropriate interest rate.

Subject to:
Capital available to invest:

$$C_1Y_1 + C_2Y_2 + \ldots + C_NY_N \leq K$$

Cash flow required in first period:

$$R_{11}Y_1 + R_{12}Y_2 + \ldots + R_{1N}Y_N \geq F_1$$

Cash flow required in second period:

$$R_{21}Y_1 + R_{22}Y_2 + \ldots + R_{2N}Y_N \geq F_2$$

In general, cash flow required in t^{th} period:

$$R_{t1}Y_1 + R_{t2}Y_2 + \ldots + R_{tN}Y_N \geq F_t$$

In addition to these constraints, there may be restrictions on specific combinations of projects. For example, projects 3 and 4 may be mutually exclusive alternatives so that the firm would want either project 3 or 4 (or possibly neither) *but not* both included in the set of projects. The following constraint can be added that would achieve this:

$$Y_3 + Y_4 \leq 1$$

Note that this constraint would allow project 3 ($Y_3 = 1$) or project 4 ($Y_4 = 1$) but not both.[6] If exactly one of the two projects were required, there would be an equality:

$$Y_3 + Y_4 = 1$$

However, if the projects were such that at least one must be included (and possibly both), the constraint would become:

$$Y_3 + Y_4 \geq 1$$

As another example, suppose projects 5 and 6 were such that project 5 must be included if project 6 is included, but not necessarily the reverse. For example, project 5 might be building a factory in New England. Project 6 might be adding a second production line to this new factory. Obviously, the second line cannot be added if there is no factory, but the factory can be built without adding the second line. The following constraint will satisfy these requirements:

$$Y_6 \leq Y_5$$

Note that Y_5 can take on values of 0 or 1; however, Y_6 can be 1 only if Y_5 is also 1. Thus, the requirements are met.

The solution to this integer programming problem would result in a subset of Y variables, each equal to 1. The projects associated with these Y variables are selected for the capital budget. They satisfy all the constraints and maximize the objective function (highest total present value). The other Y variables would have values of 0; these are the rejected projects. This is an example in which all variables are binary (0 or 1).

---

[6]A brief word of caution is in order. These types of constraints often seem to be formulated easily by such expressions as $Y_3 \cdot Y_4 = 0$, which would require $Y_3 = 0$ or $Y_4 = 0$ or both. However, such a constraint is nonlinear because it involves the product of two variables. Integer linear programming requires linear constraints and a linear objective function.

The maximum net present value of the problem should be compared to the solution that would result with a relaxation of one or more of the constraints so that the cost of the constraints can be estimated. If desired, the model can be modified to include investments of future years and their cash flows. Keep in mind that expanding the scope of the model also expands the amount of inputs that are required, and the reliability of these inputs is apt to be low.

A Capacity Expansion Problem

Many firms having products with growing demand are faced with the decision of when to add new production capacity and how much to add. Consider, as an example, an electric utility that has estimated the demand for power in its region over the next nine years. Let D_t be the projected demand for the tth year ($t = 1, 2, \ldots 9$) above the current level. Let us suppose that three different size electric generating plants can be built with designation i ($i = 1, 2, 3$). Let K_i be the capacity and C_i the construction cost of the ith size of facility.

The utility wishes to minimize the discounted cost of new facilities, subject to having sufficient capacity to meet demands. Let α_t be the present value factor for year t (α_t is a number, less than 1, from a present value table). Let Y_{it} be a zero/one variable that has a value of 1 if a size i facility is built in year t. Thus, $Y_{25} = 1$ implies that a size 2 facility is to be added in year 5. Then our objective function is:

Minimize:

$$\alpha_1[C_1Y_{11} + C_2Y_{21} + C_3Y_{31}] + \alpha_2[C_1Y_{12} + C_2Y_{22} + C_3Y_{32}] + \alpha_3[C_1Y_{13} + C_2Y_{23} + C_3Y_{33}] + \ldots + \alpha_9[C_1Y_{19} + C_2Y_{29} + C_3Y_{39}]$$

The first term in brackets represents the cost of any facility added in the first year, the second term is the same for the second year, and so on. The constraints require that sufficient capacity be added to meet expected additional demand. For the first year:

$$K_1Y_{11} + K_2Y_{21} + K_3Y_{31} \geq D_1$$

For the second year, any capacity added in the first year (above) plus that added in the second year is available to satisfy second-year demand D_2:

$$[K_1Y_{11} + K_2Y_{21} + K_3Y_{31}] + [K_1Y_{12} + K_2Y_{22} + K_3Y_{32}] \geq D_2$$

Similarly, for the third year:

$$[K_1Y_{11} + K_2Y_{21} + K_3Y_{31}] + [K_1Y_{12} + K_2Y_{22} + K_3Y_{32}] + [K_1Y_{13} + K_2Y_{23} + K_3Y_{33}] \geq D_3$$

and so on for each year.

Note that each of the above constraints requires that the *accumulated* capacity equals or exceeds demand for a given year.

There may be additional constraints on the number of different sizes of facilities based on technical or other considerations. For example, if no more than four of the first size of facility can be built, a constraint can be added as follows:

$$Y_{11} + Y_{12} + Y_{13} + \ldots + Y_{19} \leq 4$$

Factory Size and Location

Suppose a firm is introducing a new product and must decide on the location and size of the factories to manufacture the product. The firm wishes to minimize the costs of manufacturing and distribution, as well as the costs for construction and operation of the facilities.

Three sites are available. Either a small or a large factory can be built on each site. At one of the sites, it is also possible to construct an extra large (huge) factory. Table 4–1 shows the costs and capacities for these alternatives. The annual cost in Table 4–1 includes the overhead for the facility as well as an annualized cost for the construction.

The firm must supply product to four regions. The distribution cost from each factory site to each region and the requirements for the regions are shown in Table 4–2.

The firm's problem is to decide which sites to use, how large a factory to build on the sites selected, and how much each factory should ship to each region.

The variables can be defined as:

A1 = Shipments (in 000s of units) from site A to region 1
A2 = Shipments (in 000s of units) from site A to region 2
.
.
.
C4 = Shipments (in 000s of units) from site C to region 4

TABLE 4–1
Costs and Capacities

Location	*Size*	*Annual Cost ($000s)*	*Capacity (000s of units)*	*Manufacturing Costs ($/Unit)*
A	Small	1,000	600	5.00
	Large	1,500	1,200	4.00
B	Small	1,200	600	5.00
	Large	1,600	1,200	4.00
	Huge	2,000	2,000	3.50
C	Small	900	600	6.00
	Large	1,400	1,200	5.00

TABLE 4–2
Distribution Costs ($/unit) and Requirements

From Factory Site / *To*	*Region 1*	*Region 2*	*Region 3*	*Region 4*
A	1	2	3	4
B	2	3	2	3
C	4	3	2	1
Requirements at Region (000s of units)	500	200	700	800

PAS = Production (in 000s of units) at Small plant at site A
PAL = Production (in 000s of units) at Large plant at site A
.
.
.
PCL = Production (in 000s of units) at Large plant at site C

YAS = Integer zero/one variable that is 1 if a Small plant is to be constructed on site A, and 0 otherwise.
YAL = Integer zero/one variable that is 1 if a Large plant is to be constructed on site A, and 0 otherwise.
.
.
.
YCL = Integer zero/one variable that is 1 if a Large plant is to be constructed on site C, and 0 otherwise.

The formulation of this model is shown in Figure 4–2. The solution will be illustrated shortly.

The objective function to be minimized contains the distribution costs times the units shipped on a given route (for example, 2 A2); the manufacturing cost times the units manufactured by site and factory size (for example, 5 PAS); and the annual cost times the zero/one variables (for example, 1,000 YAS).

FIGURE 4–2
Formulation of Factory Size and Location Model

Minimize: A1 + 2 A2 + 3 A3 + 4 A4 + 2 B1 + 3 B2
+ 2 B3 + 3 B4 + 4 C1 + 3 C2 + 2 C3 + C4
+ 5 PAS + 4 PAL + 5 PBS + 4PBL + 3.5 PBH + 6 PCS + 5 PCL
+ 1,000 YAS + 1,500 YAL + 1,200 YBS + 1,600 YBL + 2,000 YBH
+ 900 YCS + 1,400 YCL

Subject to:

Region 1 Requirements:	A1 + B1 + C1 ≥ 500
Region 2 Requirements:	A2 + B2 + C2 ≥ 200
Region 3 Requirements:	A3 + B3 + C3 ≥ 700
Region 4 Requirements:	A4 + B4 + C4 ≥ 800
Production at A:	A1 + A2 + A3 + A4 − PAS − PAL ≤ 0
Production at B:	B1 + B2 + B3 + B4 − PBS − PBL − PBH ≤ 0
Production at C:	C1 + C2 + C3 + C4 − PCS − PCL ≤ 0
Capacity at Small A:	PAS − 600 YAS ≤ 0
Capacity at Large A:	PAL − 1,200 YAL ≤ 0
Capacity at Small B:	PBS − 600 YBS ≤ 0
Capacity at Large B:	PBL − 1,200 YBL ≤ 0
Capacity at Huge B:	PBH − 2,000 YBH ≤ 0
Capacity at Small C:	PCS − 600 YCS ≤ 0
Capacity at Large C:	PCL − 1,200 YCL ≤ 0
At most one plant at A:	YAS + YAL ≤ 1
At most one plant at B:	YBS + YBL + YBH ≤ 1
At most one plant at C:	YCS + YCL ≤ 1
	All Variables ≥ 0
	YAS, YAL, YBS, YBL, YBH, YCS, YCL are binary integer variables

The first set of constraints in Figure 4–2 guarantees that the regional requirements are met. For example:

$$A1 + B1 + C1 \geq 500$$

requires that shipments to region 1 from sites A, B, and C are at least as great as the region's requirements of 500 units. (An equality sign could also have been used here.) The next set of constraints are production balance constraints. For example, the Production at (site) A equation is:

$$A1 + A2 + A3 + A4 \leq PAS + PAL$$

which can be rewritten as:

$$A1 + A2 + A3 + A4 - PAS - PAL \leq 0$$

This restricts the shipments from site A (i.e., A1 + A2 + A3 + A4) to be no greater than the production in a small (PAS) plus large (PAL) factory. Similar constraints hold for the B and C sites.

The next set of constraints limit the production capacity. For example, the Capacity at Small A is:

$$PAS \leq 600\ YAS \quad \text{or} \quad PAS - 600\ YAS \leq 0$$

This guarantees that the production at site A with a small factory does not exceed 600 units if YAS = 1 (i.e., if a small factory is constructed at site A) and is 0 if YAS = 0. Similar capacity constraints represent the other size factories and sites.

The final set of constraints limits each site to only one facility. For example:

$$YBS + YBL + YBH \leq 1$$

requires that at most one of the three variables can be 1. That is, either a small plant, a large plant, a huge plant, or none at all can be built at site B.

Summary

An integer linear programming model is a linear programming model with the additional requirement that some or all of the variables must be integers. Formulating an integer linear programming model is similar to formulation of LP models, except that the integer restriction allows one to include fixed charges, either-or constraints, and related concepts.

Solution of Integer Programming Problems

Ordinary linear programming problems are solved by the simplex method, which very efficiently produces optimal solutions even for large problems. However, these solutions are not necessarily integer. Sometimes, of course, a noninteger LP solution can be rounded off appropriately to give an integer solution. If the rounded solution is feasible and has a profit close to that obtained for the noninteger problem, the rounding procedure is likely to be adequate. However, for many important problems, this procedure will not work. In particular, if the problem contains zero/one variables of the type illustrated in the formulations earlier in this chapter, rounding will generally give infeasible solutions or ones that are not close to optimal, as was illustrated in Figure 4–1. Hence, a solution procedure designed for integer problems is required.

When a problem is required to have an integer solution, it means that there are a finite number of possible solution points. One approach is to use **complete enumeration** and evaluate every possible solution to find the optimum. If there are only a few integer variables, enumeration may be feasible and an efficient procedure. However, for most realistic problems, the number of possible solutions is very large and complete enumeration is not computationally realistic.

Complete enumeration might not be necessary if we could find ways of eliminating whole groups of solutions from consideration. The **branch and bound technique** is a method for doing this. Basically, the potential solutions are organized in a tree or hierarchy. A method is used to find a bound for a subset of these solutions. A bound is an upper limit (in the case of profit maximizing) or lower limit (for cost minimization). If a feasible solution can be found that is better than the bound for the subset, the entire subset can be eliminated. The process continues until the optimum is found—the solution that is better than the bounds on all the subsets. More details of this procedure are included in the appendix to this chapter.

Another technique is called the **cutting-plane** method. It is a variant of the simplex method, and in fact starts with the simplex solution to the linear programming problem, ignoring the integer requirements. Then new constraints (*cutting planes,* or simply *cuts*) are added to the problem that make infeasible the previous noninteger optimal solution but do not exclude any feasible integer solutions. A new LP solution is obtained and the process repeated (i.e., new cuts added) until an integer solution is found. This method is less widely used than the branch and bound method.

Using Solver for Integer Programming Problems

Solver is a package incorporated in the Excel and Quattro spreadsheets. Its use in solving ordinary linear programming problems has been illustrated in earlier chapters. Solver also has the ability to solve integer programming problems. One simply has to identify which variables are to be integer valued. The use of Solver is illustrated for the factory size and location problem formulated earlier.

Figure 4–3 shows the spreadsheet model for this example, with the optimal solution exhibited (there is also an alternative optimum involving a small factory at site C). Figure 4–4 displays the contents of cells AB6 through AF26, which contain the equations for the model. And Figure 4–5 shows the values entered in the Solver Parameters dialogue box. A few words of explanation about the constraints in Figure 4–5: The first (B6:AA6 $\geq$ 0) requires that all the decision variables be non-negative. The second (AB10:AB13 $\geq$ AD10:AD13) requires that the region needs be met (or exceeded). The third (AB14:AB26 $\leq$ AD14:AD26) includes the balance constraints, the capacity constraints, and the only-one-factory-per-site constraints. The last two constraint sets relate only to the zero/one integer variables. The constraint U6:AA6 $\leq$ 1 restricts the values to be less than or equal to 1, and the last constraint requires that they be integer valued. Since they must be greater than or equal 0, and less than or equal 1, and integer, they must be either 0 or 1.

In addition, after clicking the options button, the box indicating linear model must be marked.

FIGURE 4–3 Spreadsheet Model Showing Optimal Solution

	A	B	C	D	E	F	G	H	I	J	K	L	M	N	O	P	Q	R	S	T	U	V	W	X	Y	Z	AA	AB	AC	AD	AE	AE
1											Factory Location Problem																					
2																																
3		Shipments from Location A to				Shipments from Location B to				Shipments from Location C to				Amount Produced A		Amount Produced B			Amount Produced C		Production at A??		Production at B??			Production at C??						
4		Region 1	Region 2	Region 3	Region 4	Region 1	Region 2	Region 3	Region 4	Region 1	Region 2	Region 3	Region 4	Small Plant	Large Plant	Small Plant	Large Plant	Huge Plant	Small Plant	Large Plant	Small Plant	Large Plant	Small Plant	Large Plant	Huge Plant	Small Plant	Large Plant					
5		A1	A2	A3	A1	B1	B2	B3	B4	C1	C2	C3	C4	PAS	PAL	PBS	PBL	PBH	PCS	PCL	YAS	YAL	YBS	YBL	YBH	YCS	YCL					
6	Decision Variables	0	0	0	0	500	200	700	0	0	0	0	800	0	0	0	0	1400	0	800	0	0	0	0	1	0	1					
7																														Total		
8	Cost	1	2	3	4	2	3	2	3	4	3	2	1	5	4	5	4	3.5	6	5	1000	1500	1200	1600	2000	900	1400			$16,100		
9																															Slack	Surplus
10	Region 1 requirements	1				1				1																		500	≥	500		0
11	Region 2 requirements		1				1				1																	200	≥	200		0
12	Region 3 requirements			1				1				1																700	≥	700		0
13	Region 4 requirements				1				1				1															800	≥	800		0
14	Production at Location A	1	1	1	1									–1	–1													0	≤	0	0	
15	Production at Location A					1	1	1	1							–1	–1	–1										0	≤	0	0	
16	Production at Location A									1	1	1	1						–1	–1								0	≤	0	0	
17	Capacity at Small A													1							–600							0	≤	0	0	
18	Capacity at Large A														1							–1200						0	≤	0	0	
19	Capacity at Small B															1							–600					0	≤	0	0	
20	Capacity at Large B																1							–1200				0	≤	0	0	
21	Capacity at Huge B																	1							2000			–600	≤	0	600	
22	Capacity at Small C																		1							–600		0	≤	0	0	
23	Capacity at Large C																			1							–1200	–400	≤	0	400	
24	Only one Plant at A																				1	1						0	≤	1	1	
25	Only one Plant at B																						1	1	1			1	≤	1	0	
26	Only one Plant at C																									1	1	1	≤	1	0	
27																																
28					Optimal Integer Solution																											

FIGURE 4–4 Equations from Spreadsheet Model

	AB	AC	AD	AE	AF
6					
7			Total		
8			=SUMPRODUCT($B$6:$AA$6,B8:AA8)		
9				slack	surplus
10	=SUMPRODUCT($B$6:$AA$6,B10:AA10)	≥	500		=AB10-AD10
11	=SUMPRODUCT($B$6:$AA$6,B11:AA11)	≥	200		=AB11-AD11
12	=SUMPRODUCT($B$6:$AA$6,B12:AA12)	≥	700		=AB12-AD12
13	=SUMPRODUCT($B$6:$AA$6,B13:AA13)	≥	800		=AB13-AD13
14	=SUMPRODUCT($B$6:$AA$6,B14:AA14)	≤	0	=AD14-AB14	
15	=SUMPRODUCT($B$6:$AA$6,B15:AA15)	≤	0	=AD15-AB15	
16	=SUMPRODUCT($B$6:$AA$6,B16:AA16)	≤	0	=AD16-AB16	
17	=SUMPRODUCT($B$6:$AA$6,B17:AA17)	≤	0	=AD17-AB17	
18	=SUMPRODUCT($B$6:$AA$6,B18:AA18)	≤	0	=AD18-AB18	
19	=SUMPRODUCT($B$6:$AA$6,B19:AA19)	≤	0	=AD19-AB19	
20	=SUMPRODUCT($B$6:$AA$6,B20:AA20)	≤	0	=AD20-AB20	
21	=SUMPRODUCT($B$6:$AA$6,B21:AA21)	≤	0	=AD21-AB21	
22	=SUMPRODUCT($B$6:$AA$6,B22:AA22)	≤	0	=AD22-AB22	
23	=SUMPRODUCT($B$6:$AA$6,B23:AA23)	≤	0	=AD23-AB23	
24	=SUMPRODUCT($B$6:$AA$6,B24:AA24)	≤	1	=AD24-AB24	
25	=SUMPRODUCT($B$6:$AA$6,B25:AA25)	≤	1	=AD25-AB25	
26	=SUMPRODUCT($B$6:$AA$6,B26:AA26)	≤	1	=AD26-AB26	

FIGURE 4–5 Solver Parameters Dialogue Box Information

Target Cell (Objective)	**AD8**
Objective	**Minimize**
Changing cells (decision variables)	**B6:AA6**
Constraints	**B6:AA6 ≥ 0** **AB10:AB13 ≥ AD10:AD13** **AB14:AB26 ≤ AD14:AD26** **U6:AA6 ≤ 1** **U6:AA6 integer**

(Check linear model in options dialogue box.)

Because it uses the branch and bound procedure that involves solving a sequence of linear programming problems, using Solver for integer problems takes much longer than it does for ordinary LP problems. Also, the Solver Reports are not of value as they are in ordinary LP. There is no Sensitivity Report, and the Answer Report merely gives the same information as displayed on the spreadsheet.

Summary

The solution to integer programming problems involves much more complicated procedures than the simplex method. The branch and bound and cutting-plane methods are two such methods. Solution procedures for integer problems have been incorporated into software for personal computers, including the Solver program for spreadsheets.

General Optimization

The solution techniques discussed so far assume that the problem can be formulated as a linear model with both a linear objective function and linear constraints. But many important management problems involve nonlinear functions. An important example is the management of investment portfolios in finance, where the objective might be to minimize the risk for a given expected return. Risk is measured as the variance of the portfolio, and the variance is a square (nonlinear) measure. In marketing models, the effect on sales of different amounts spent on advertising is generally a nonlinear function. Hence, linear programming cannot be used for these problems.

Fortunately, there are generalized optimization techniques that can be used to solve many of these types of problems. One approach is to use **mathematical analysis** or **calculus.** Using calculus, one can optimize a function by taking the derivative, setting it equal to zero, and then solving. If there are constraints, a technique called Lagrangian multipliers is used. This approach is limited to relatively small problems with rather simple functions. There are also a wide variety of procedures developed for specific nonlinear models. For example, **quadratic programming** is a technique for solving problems with linear constraints but a quadratic objective function.

General Search Procedures

In recent years, computer software has been developed that solves general optimization problems using search and trial and error procedures. In explaining how these algorithms work, it is helpful to use an analogy. Suppose you are trying to find the highest peak in a range of uncharted mountains. And suppose it is very hazy, so that you cannot see very far in any direction. The search procedure would have you start out at some location and examine the terrain around you to find the steepest uphill direction. You then go in that direction for some distance (say, 500 yards), and stop. You again examine the surrounding terrain, pick the steepest uphill direction, and go the indicated distance in that new direction. You continue this process until you reach a point where all directions are downhill. This is the end of your search—you have reached a peak (but not necessarily the highest peak).

The computer algorithms work similarly. The steps are:

1. Start with a trial solution and evaluate it.
2. Evaluate the "ground" around the trial solution by testing several "close-by" points. Methods differ on how these points are chosen and on how many to choose.

3. Choose a "direction" to go based on the trial points. Again, methods vary on how this is done. The direction depends on whether it is a maximization or minimization problem.
4. Take a "step" of a specified size in the direction found in step (3). This leads to a new trial solution. The size of the step taken may vary over the search.
5. Repeat steps (1) through (4), but:
6. Stop when, in evaluating the "close-by" points, there is no direction that improves the solution. That is, all directions lead downhill if maximizing, or uphill if minimizing.

There are many general optimization programs available even on personal computers.[7] In fact, the Solver program also can solve general optimization problems. This will be illustrated shortly.

Recently, some even more exotic optimization procedures have been developed.[8] **Genetic search** uses a process similar to the way generations of a species might evolve. It starts with a set of trial solutions to the problem. The values of the variables for each trial solution are mapped into a set equivalent to biological hereditary genes. The trial solutions are evaluated, and the better ones are selected. These better solutions are then "mated" with each other, producing the next generation of offspring. That is, the new solutions have "genes" that are genetic combinations of their parents. This second generation of solutions is then evaluated, the better ones selected to be mated for the third-generation offspring. There is an occasional "mutation" of genes (creating a diverse solution). The process is repeated until there is no significant improvement in the best solution. A related search process is called **simulated annealing,** which generates new solutions similar to the process used in annealing glass or metal.

An Example Using Solver

Tanglin Software Products has just developed a new software product designed to make business presentations more colorful and effective. The company is developing the marketing plan for the product. The two decision variables are the price to charge and the amount to spend on advertising. Based on the sales of similar products, the company has carefully estimated the expected effects of different levels of price and advertising on unit sales. The cost of developing the product has already been incurred, so it is not relevant, but there are costs of actually producing the product (making the CD disks and manuals and packaging the product) and costs of supporting the product with call-in and Internet on-line support.

The model for this decision is shown on the spreadsheet in Figure 4–6. The equation for QUANTITY sold (in cell E9) has three components. The first is a negative price effect (higher price implies lower unit sales). The second is an advertising effect that has both linear and square terms, reflecting a positive but diminishing effect of advertising. The third term reflects an interaction between price and

[7]Examples are GINO (see J. Liebman, L. Lasdon, A. Waren, and L. Schrage, *Modeling and Optimization with GINO* [Danvers, MA: Boyd & Frazer, 1986], and MINOS (published by Stanford Business Software, Mountain View, CA).

[8]An example of this type of program is a product called *Evolver* (developed by Axcelis software company of Seattle, WA), which works as an add-in to spreadsheet programs.

FIGURE 4–6 Spreadsheet for Non-Linear Model Example

	A	B	C	D	E	F	G	H	I	J
1		**Tanglin Software Products**								
2						Upper				
3		Decision Variables				Limit				
4			Price ($)	145.6375		250				
5			Advertising (M$)	295.399		300				
6										
7		Projected Income Statement (thous. $)								
8										
9			Unit Sales (M)		112.5063					
10			Dollar Sales (M$)		$16,385					
11			Costs:							
12			Advertising		$ 295					
13			Production		$ 1,688					
14			Support		$ 3,000	3,000				
15			Total Costs		$ 4,983					
16										
17			Net Contribution		$11,402					
18										
19										
20		**Model Documentation:**								
21			**Cell names**	**Cell**						
22			PRICE	D4						
23			ADVERTISING	D5						
24			QUANTITY	E9						
25										
26		**Cell**	**Cell equation**							
27		E9	QUANTITY=100-0.6*PRICE+1.1*ADVERTISING-0.0011*ADVERTISING^2							
28			-.003*ADVERTISING*PRICE							
29		E10	= QUANTITY*PRICE							
30		E12	= ADVERTISING							
31		E13	=15*QUANTITY							
32		E14	=200+25*QUANTITY-.001*QUANTITY^2							
33		E15	=E12+E13+E14							
34		E17	=E10-E15							
35										
36		Solver Dialogue Box Information								
37										
38		Target cell (objective function)				**E17**				
39		Objective				**Maximize**				
40		Changing cells (decision variables)				**D4:D5**				
41										
42		Constraints:								
43			**D4:D5≥0**							
44			**D4:D5≤F4:F5**							
45			**E14≤F14**							
46										

advertising: Advertising has a bigger effect at a low price than it does at a higher price. Cell E10 contains the Dollar Sales (QUANTITY times PRICE). Cell E13 is the production cost ($15 per unit). Cell E14 is the support costs, which is a quadratic function reflecting some economies of scale.

The information entered into the Solver dialogue box is similar to that entered for linear problems. The objective to be maximized is in cell E17, and the decision variables are in cells D4 and D5. The constraints require that the decision variables be non-negative, and less than limits established as reasonable by management. The third constraint limits the support costs to be less than or equal to $3 million. This reflects management judgment that, because of a shortage of technically trained personnel, the firm should not commit to more unit sales than could be supported by the expenditure of $3 million.

Note that this problem is nonlinear, both in the objective function and in one of the constraints. Hence, linear programming cannot be used to solve it. Thus, we would *not* check the Assume Linear Model box in the Solver options menu. However, Solver can use its general search procedure to find the optimal solution, and this is shown in the spreadsheet—a price of about $145 and advertising of $295,000.

Solver produces a Sensitivity Report for nonlinear problems somewhat similar to that for linear problems. The one for our software example is shown in Figure 4–7. The interpretation of the Lagrange Multipliers is similar to that of shadow prices in linear programming. In particular, because the constraints on upper limits on Price and Advertising were not binding, the Lagrange Multipliers for these constraints are zero. However, the constraint on Support costs is binding, with the Lagrange multiplier of $1.22. This implies that, at the margin, each additional dollar of support costs will increase total net contribution by $1.22 (and each reduction of $1 will reduce contribution by $1.22). The Reduced Gradient values for the decision variables (or changing cells) have a similar interpretation to the Reduced Cost for linear programming solutions. In contrast to linear programming models, these marginal values (Lagrange multipliers and reduced gradients) hold only at the optimal solution and not over a range. However, they may still produce valuable information for the decision maker.

Cautions in the Use of Nonlinear Programs

While nonlinear programming methods are powerful solution procedures, the user should be aware of some limitations. The most important is that the procedure may

FIGURE 4–7
Solver Sensitivity Report for Tanglin Software Example

Changing Cells

Cell	Name	Final Value	Reduced Gradient
$D$4	PRICE	145.637467	0
$D$5	ADVERTISING	295.3989567	0

Constraints

Cell	Name	Final Value	Lagrange Multiplier
$D$4	PRICE	145.637467	0
$D$5	ADVERTISING	295.3989567	0
$E$14	Support	$ 3,000	$1.22

produce a *local optimum* rather than the *global optimum*. Think of the mountain climbing analogy used above. The program may arrive at the top of a small hill (with all local directions pointing downhill) and hence proclaim an optimum. But there might be a very large mountain just out of sight, with a much higher peak. There is no guarantee in general nonlinear programming that the highest peak (global optimum) will be found.[9] This is an important concern. One approach is to solve the problem several times, each time starting from a very different initial solution. This will increase the chance that the global optimum will be found.

A second problem that is sometimes encountered is that no solution may be found. This can occur because of the way the search process works (to continue the mountain climbing analogy, the process may take a step that goes over a cliff and cannot recover). In spreadsheet models such as Solver, a trial solution may cause trouble with some of the functions or equations in the model—trying to divide by zero or trying to take the logarithm of a negative number. Such problems will cause the solution process to stop without reaching an optimum. Finally, scaling may cause a problem in model solution. All computer codes compute with a certain degree of accuracy. If a model has coefficients that vary greatly in magnitude (e.g., one number being .00000023 and another 123,345,210), computational difficulties may occur. This can be handled by rescaling the values—convert to millions or billions, for example, for one or several variables.

Summary

Models that contain nonlinear objectives or constraints (or both) may be solved by general optimization methods. These usually involve a search process generating a sequence of trial solutions. Some newer methods create successive "generations" of trial solutions. Computer programs are widely available for solving these problems, including ones for personal computers. The Solver program for spreadsheets is illustrated. Some caution in the use of general optimization methods is necessary.

Multiple Objectives and Goal Programming

In linear programming, a single objective is maximized or minimized subject to constraints. In many important problems, particularly in the public sector, there are several objectives that the decision maker is trying to achieve. We now consider incorporating these multiple objectives in linear programming.

Consider, as an example, the manager of a state forest. State law may specify that the forest manager must manage the forest so as to enhance timber growth, increase cover and food for forest animals, and—of course—do this at as low a cost as possible.

Suppose our manager has two activities that can be undertaken—thinning the forest (cutting out undergrowth) and cutting fire lanes. Let:

X_1 = Acres of land thinned
X_2 = Kilometers of fire lanes cut

[9]In contrast, when the model is linear (i.e., linear programming), there is a single optimum value (with possible alternate optima), and this problem of local optima does not exist.

TABLE 4–3
Costs and Benefits for Forest Activities

	Activity	
	Thinning (variable X_1, per acre)	*Fire Lanes (variable X_2, per kilometer)*
Costs:		
Cost (dollars)	\$500	\$500
Labor required (hours)	150	50
Benefits:		
Timber growth (units)	10	−5
Animal cover (units)	−10	60

Each of these activities has a cost and requires labor. In addition, each produces benefits (possibly negative) in terms of timber growth and animal cover.

As shown in Table 4–3, thinning costs \$500 per acre, requires 150 labor-hours per acre, and results in timber growth of 10 units, but reduces animal cover by 10 units for each acre thinned. Cutting fire lanes costs \$500 per kilometer cut, requires 50 labor-hours per kilometer cut, reduces timber growth by 5 units per kilometer cut, and increases animal cover by 60 units per kilometer cut.

The decision problem for the forest manager is to determine X_1 and X_2; that is, how many acres to thin and how many kilometers of fire lanes to cut. The manager has available only 90,000 hours of labor. In addition, forest conditions limit the cutting of fire lanes to no more than 300 kilometers. The manager has a budget of \$350,000.

The constraints for the problem can be expressed as:

$$
\begin{aligned}
150X_1 + 50X_2 &\leq 90{,}000 && \text{(labor-hours)}\\
X_2 &\leq 300 && \text{(limit on fire lanes)}\\
500X_1 + 500X_2 &\leq 350{,}000 && \text{(budget)}
\end{aligned}
$$

Three goals are to be satisfied simultaneously. The manager should achieve as much timber growth as possible, should provide as much animal cover as possible, and should reduce costs below budget as much as possible. There are several approaches for incorporating all these multiple objectives; we describe each in turn.

Approach 1: Single Objective with Others as Constraints

The manager may decide that one objective is of such importance that it overrides the others. The other objectives may be built in as constraints at some minimal level. The problem then becomes an ordinary linear programming problem of maximizing an objective function subject to constraints.

For example, our manager may decide that timber growth is most important. The objective then becomes:

$$\text{Maximize:} \quad 10X_1 - 5X_2$$

where the coefficients 10 and −5 from Table 4–3 are the effects on timber growth of thinning and cutting fire lanes, respectively. The constraints on labor-hours, fire lanes, and budget, as shown above, would apply. The manager may also specify that there must be at least a minimal level of 1,000 units of animal cover with the additional constraint:

$$-10X_1 + 60X_2 \geq 1{,}000$$

where the coefficients of -10 and 60 represent the effects of thinning and cutting fire lanes on animal cover (see Table 4–3).

Figure 4–8 graphs this problem. The shaded region is the feasible region satisfying all the constraints, including that on animal cover. The objective of maximizing timber growth is obtained at the point $X_1 = 563$ and $X_2 = 111$, with 5,080 units of timber growth (see point *A* in Figure 4–8).

It would have been possible for the manager to choose to maximize animal cover, while setting a minimum level for timber growth as a constraint. Or minimal levels for both animal cover and timber growth could be specified, and cost minimized. A major difficulty with this approach is that it does not involve any balancing or *trade-offs* of the various objectives. The manager might be more satisfied with more animal cover and less timber, but there is no direct way to achieve this. The manager could try different sets of constraints until a satisfactory solution emerges, but this is an awkward approach.

Approach 2: Define Trade-Offs among Objectives

One approach to multiobjective problems is to specify the trade-offs among the objectives. In the present example, one would specify how much a unit of timber growth was worth, and how much a unit of animal cover was worth, both in dollar

FIGURE 4–8 Solution to Example Problem with Maximization of Timber Growth Objective

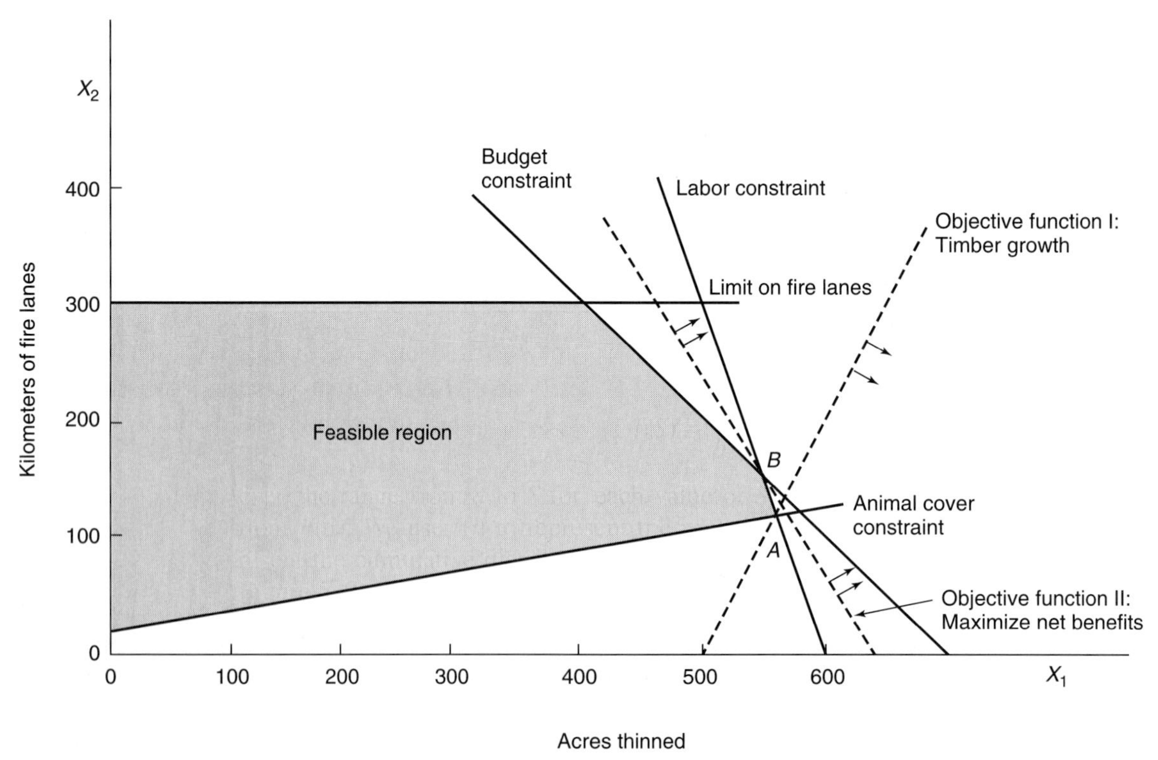

terms. Then these objectives could be traded off with each other and with dollars of cost. By this process, the total net benefits in dollars could be maximized.

For example, suppose the manager decided that a unit of timber growth was worth $600 and a unit of animal cover was worth $100. This implies that the manager would be indifferent between obtaining an additional unit of timber growth or six units of animal cover, or $600 savings.

Given these values, we can compute the net benefit for each of the decision variables X_1 and X_2. Recall that each unit of X_1 (acres thinned) produces 10 units of timber (worth $600 each), removes 10 units of animal cover (at $100 each), and costs $500. Hence, the net benefit of a unit of X_1 is:

$$10(\$600) - 10(\$100) - \$500 = \$4,500$$

Similarly, the net benefit of a kilometer of fire lanes is computed as $-5(\$600) + 60(\$100) - \$500 = \$2,500$. Then the linear programming problem to maximize net benefits is:

$$\begin{aligned} \text{Maximize:} \quad & 4,500X_1 + 2,500X_2 \\ \text{Subject to:} \quad & 150X_1 + 50X_2 \leq 90,000 \\ & X_2 \leq 300 \\ & 500X_1 + 500X_2 \leq 350,000 \end{aligned}$$

The optimal solution to this linear programming problem results in values of $X_1 = 550$ and $X_2 = 150$ (see point B in Figure 4–8). This can be converted into units of timber and animal cover, resulting in 3,750 units of timber and 3,500 units of animal cover.

The success of using this approach lies in being able to define the necessary trade-offs. This is not an easy task. Our manager may find it very difficult to attach a dollar value to a unit of animal cover. Some people would balk at even trying to provide such a value.

Approach 3: Goal Programming

A third approach is that of *goal programming*. The decision maker specifies desirable goals for each objective. Then the problem is formulated so as to minimize the shortfall related to obtaining these goals. The goals are usually specified at desirable (high) levels, so that it is not possible to satisfy all simultaneously.

Suppose the manager in our example set as desirable goals the production of 5,000 units of timber and 6,000 units of animal cover. The constraints then become:

$$\begin{aligned} \text{Timber:} \quad & 10X_1 - 5X_2 + U_1 - E_1 = 5,000 \\ \text{Animal Cover:} \quad & -10X_1 + 60X_2 + U_2 - E_2 = 6,000 \\ \text{Cost:} \quad & 500X_1 + 500X_2 + U_3 - E_3 = 350,000 \\ \text{Labor:} \quad & 150X_1 + 50X_2 \leq 90,000 \\ \text{Fire lanes:} \quad & X_2 \leq 300 \end{aligned} \tag{4–1}$$

The variables U_1, U_2 represent the amounts by which the plan fails to achieve the timber goal of 5,000 units and the animal cover goal of 6,000 units. Thus, these can be described as the shortfall or *underage*. The variable U_3 is the savings in dollars below the budget level.

The variables E_1, E_2, and E_3 represent the amounts by which the specified goals are *exceeded*—that is, the *overage*.

One method of forming the objective function in goal programming is to minimize the shortfall. Thus, the objective might be to minimize $(U_1 + U_2 - U_3)$. This would minimize the amounts by which timber growth and animal cover fell below the goals and maximize the cost underage (by minimizing the negative of U_3) subject to the constraints above. The simplicity of this approach is appealing. But there is a major assumption, that one unit savings in dollars has the same value as a unit shortfall in timber and a unit shortfall in animal cover. The objective function has given equal weight to each.

A better approach is to define specifically the trade-offs among the various objectives. Suppose our manager decides that one unit in shortfall for timber is worth 600 times as much as a dollar savings and that a unit shortfall in animal cover is worth 100 times a dollar savings. Then the objective function would be:

$$\text{Minimize:} \quad 600U_1 + 100U_2 - U_3$$

again subject to the constraints (4–1).

This objective function attaches zero value to exceeding any of the goals of timber growth or animal cover. The manager might decide that there is some value to these overages and attach weights to the E variables also. For example, exceeding the timber goal may have value of \$50 per unit, and exceeding the animal cover value may be worth \$25 per unit. Also, each dollar over the cost budget (E_3) may be five times as important as a dollar saved (U_3). Then the objective function becomes:

$$\text{Minimize:} \quad 600U_1 + 100U_2 - U_3 - 50E_1 - 25E_2 + 5E_3$$

Minimizing the negative values for U_3, E_1, and E_2 is equivalent to maximizing.

One optimum solution to this linear programming problem requires thinning 550 acres and cutting 150 kilometers of fire lanes. The budget is met exactly. There are shortfalls of 250 units for the timber goal and 2,500 units for the animal cover goal. There is an alternative optimum basic solution, requiring 537 acres thinned, 189 kilometers of fire lanes cut, and 579 unit shortfall on timber but no shortfall on animal cover. However, this requires exceeding the budget by \$13,160.

We can now observe that goal programming differs from Approach 2 (directly defining the trade-offs) in two respects:

1. Specific goals are incorporated and a different value is attached to the shortfall and excess of the goal. In Approach 2, a single weight was attached to each objective, and this applied over the entire range of possible values.
2. The objective function is defined in terms of the objectives themselves. In Approach 2, the net benefits for each activity had to be calculated, and these net benefits were then included in the objective function. The goal programming approach makes it easier to see the relative value attached to each of the multiple objectives.

Approach 4: Priority Programming

Suppose the manager in our example balks at assigning specific trade-offs among the various multiple objectives but is willing to assign priorities to each, indicating the order in which each is to be satisfied. For example, suppose the goal constraints are specified as:

Timber:	$10X_1 - 5X_2 + U_1 - E_1 = 3{,}000$
Animal Cover:	$-10X_1 + 60X_2 + U_2 - E_2 = 1{,}000$
Cost:	$500X_1 + 500X_2 + U_3 - E_3 = 350{,}000$

The manager lists priorities as:

1. Minimize the shortfall of timber growth (U_1).
2. Minimize the shortfall of animal cover (U_2).
3. Minimize budget excess (E_3).
4. Maximize excess timber growth (E_1).
5. Maximize excess animal cover (E_2).
6. Maximize budget savings (U_3).

The priority programming approach is to attempt to achieve each objective *sequentially,* rather than *simultaneously.* We will illustrate the approach graphically.

Consider Figure 4–9. Panel A shows the feasible region, considering only the constraints on labor and the limit on fire lanes. The manager's first priority is to

FIGURE 4–9 Steps in Priority Programming Example

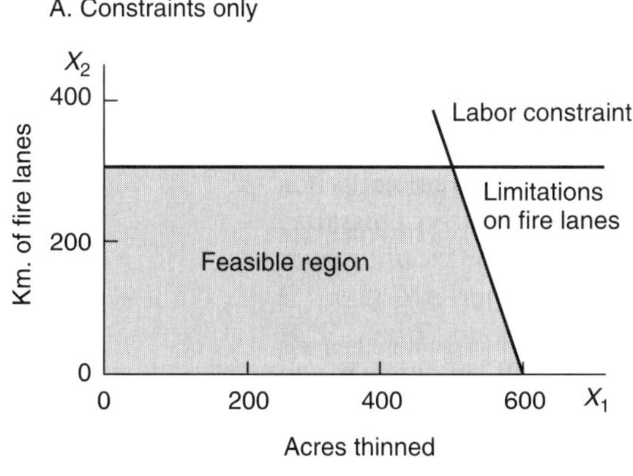

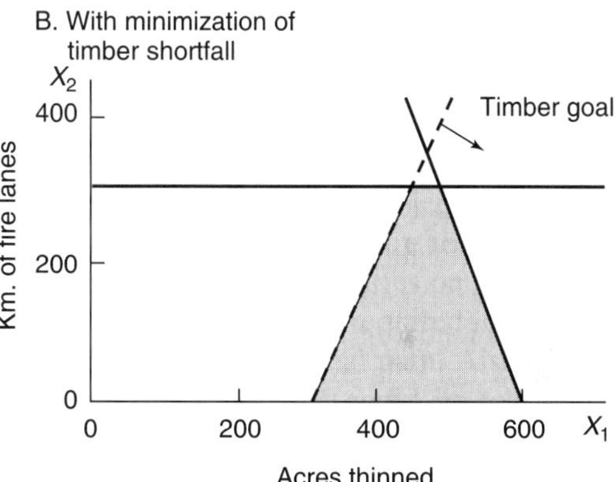

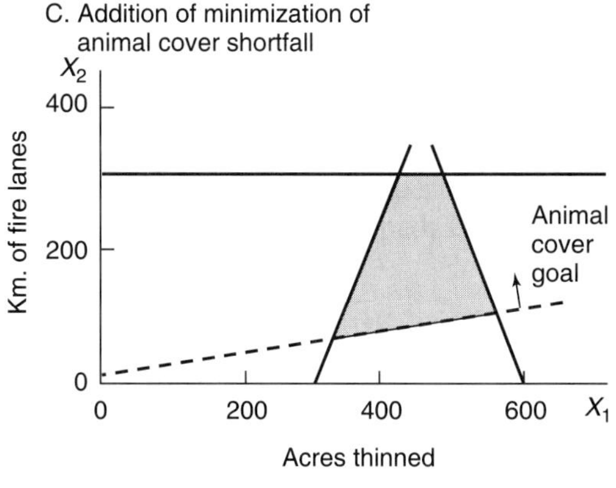

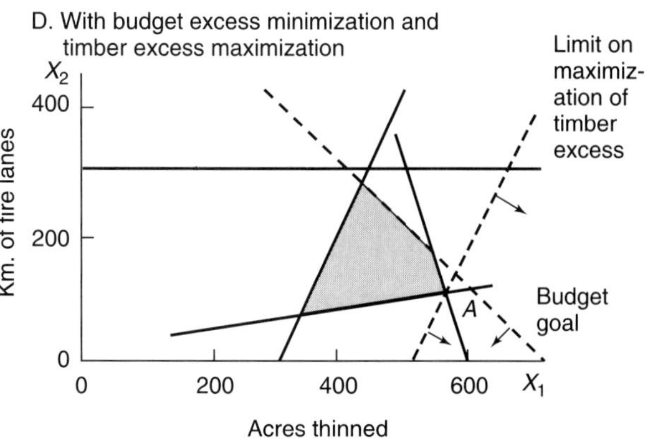

minimize the shortfall in timber growth. In Panel B, this is minimized until there is no shortfall, and the remaining feasible region is shown as the shaded area. If there were no feasible region remaining, the priority programming process would stop, having achieved only as much as possible of the highest priority goal.

Since there is some feasible region left, the next highest priority is considered—namely, minimization of shortfall in animal cover. This is shown in Panel C, and this can also be minimized until there is no shortfall, with the remaining feasible region shown in gray.

The third priority goal of minimizing budget excess is shown in Panel D. This also may be achieved in total. Finally, the fourth-order priority goal of maximization of excess timber growth is invoked. This results in the solution, shown as point *A* in Panel D, of 563 acres thinned (X_1) and 111 kilometers of fire lanes cut (X_2). Since there is no feasible region remaining, it is not possible to proceed to the fifth- and sixth-order priority goals.

Special computer programs have been developed for priority programming. For a two-variable problem, of course, the solution can be obtained graphically, as we have illustrated. But more realistic problems involve many dimensions, and graphic solutions are not possible. The reader who is interested in the priority programming algorithm is referred to the references given at the end of this chapter.

Summary

There are several methods of incorporating multiple objectives in linear programming problems. Simple approaches involve converting to a single-objective function by weighting the objectives or by incorporating the secondary objectives as constraints. Goal programming involves defining goals and including variables for deviations from these goals (either shortfalls or excesses). The objective function is defined to minimize the (possibly weighted) deviations. Priority programming defines goal constraints similarly, but involves satisfying the goals in sequential order, rather than simultaneously.

Appendix
The Branch and Bound Algorithm

As discussed in this chapter, integer programming problems can be solved by the branch and bound procedure. Actually, it is a general solution process that can be applied to many types of problems, and it is of interest in its own right. We shall first consider its application to integer problems.

When a problem is required to have an integer solution, it means that there are a finite number of possible solution points. While it may be theoretically possible to completely enumerate every possible solution, this is generally not computationally feasible. However, if we could find ways of eliminating whole groups of solutions from consideration, complete enumeration might be feasible. The branch and bound technique is a method for doing this.

The Tree of Solution Possibilities

With integer problems, there are a finite number of possible solutions, and it is possible to represent them by a **tree diagram.** This can best be shown by an example. Consider the following integer programming problem:

$$
\begin{array}{llr}
\text{Maximize:} & P = 6X_1 + 3X_2 + X_3 + 2X_4 & \\
\text{Subject to:} & X_1 + X_2 + X_3 + X_4 \leq 8 & \\
& 2X_1 + X_2 + 3X_3 \leq 12 & \\
& 5X_2 + X_3 + 3X_4 \leq 6 & \\
& X_1 \leq 1 & \\
& X_2 \leq 1 & \\
& X_3 \leq 4 & \\
& X_4 \leq 2 & \\
& X_1, X_2, X_3, X_4 \text{ all integers} &
\end{array}
$$

Note that the constraints $X_1 \leq 1$ and $X_2 \leq 1$ in effect mean that X_1 and X_2 are zero/one integer variables. Variable X_3 can take on five values (0, 1, 2, 3, 4), and variable X_4 can have three values. Hence, considering only the last four constraints, there are $2 \cdot 2 \cdot 5 \cdot 3 = 60$ possible solutions. The enumeration of these 60 possible solutions is shown graphically in the tree in Figure 4–10. The order of variables in the tree is arbitrary, but the end of the tree must have 60 branches, one for each possible solution. Note that many of these solutions are infeasible; that is, they do not satisfy the first three constraints.

For such a small problem as this one, a computer could evaluate all 60 possibilities very quickly. However, as the problems grow in size, a complete evaluation becomes impractical.[10]

The **branch and bound** approach is designed to reduce the search by chopping off whole branches or limbs of this tree of possibilities and hence limiting the number of possibilities investigated. The key idea in eliminating branches is:

A branch can be eliminated if it can be shown to contain no feasible solution better than one already obtained.

The effective use of the branch and bound procedure requires a procedure to *bound* or find an *upper limit* for all the possible solutions in a given branch (a *lower limit* is needed when minimizing). The solution to the equivalent ordinary linear programming problem provides one convenient bound.

Consider our problem above, and solve it as a linear programming problem using the simplex method (that is, ignore the integer requirements). The solution is:

$$X_1 = 1, X_2 = 0, X_3 = 3.33, X_4 = 0.89$$

which is not an integer solution.[11] The profit is $P = 11.11$. This is the maximum profit that can be obtained, given the first three constraints. We know that there is

[10]To see this, consider a problem with 10 integer variables, each of which can take on five integer values (0, 1, 2, 3, or 4). The number of possible solutions is $5^{10} = 9{,}765{,}625$. Enumeration and evaluation of this many possible solutions would be a long and cumbersome way to proceed.

[11]Thus, we need a way of limiting the search to some smaller set of possible solutions. The ordinary LP problem has "relaxed" or omitted the integer constraints; this is sometimes called the *LP relaxation* of the integer programming problem.

FIGURE 4–10
Tree Showing All Possible Integer Solutions for $X_1 \leq 1, X_2 \leq 1, X_3 \leq 4, X_4 \leq 2$

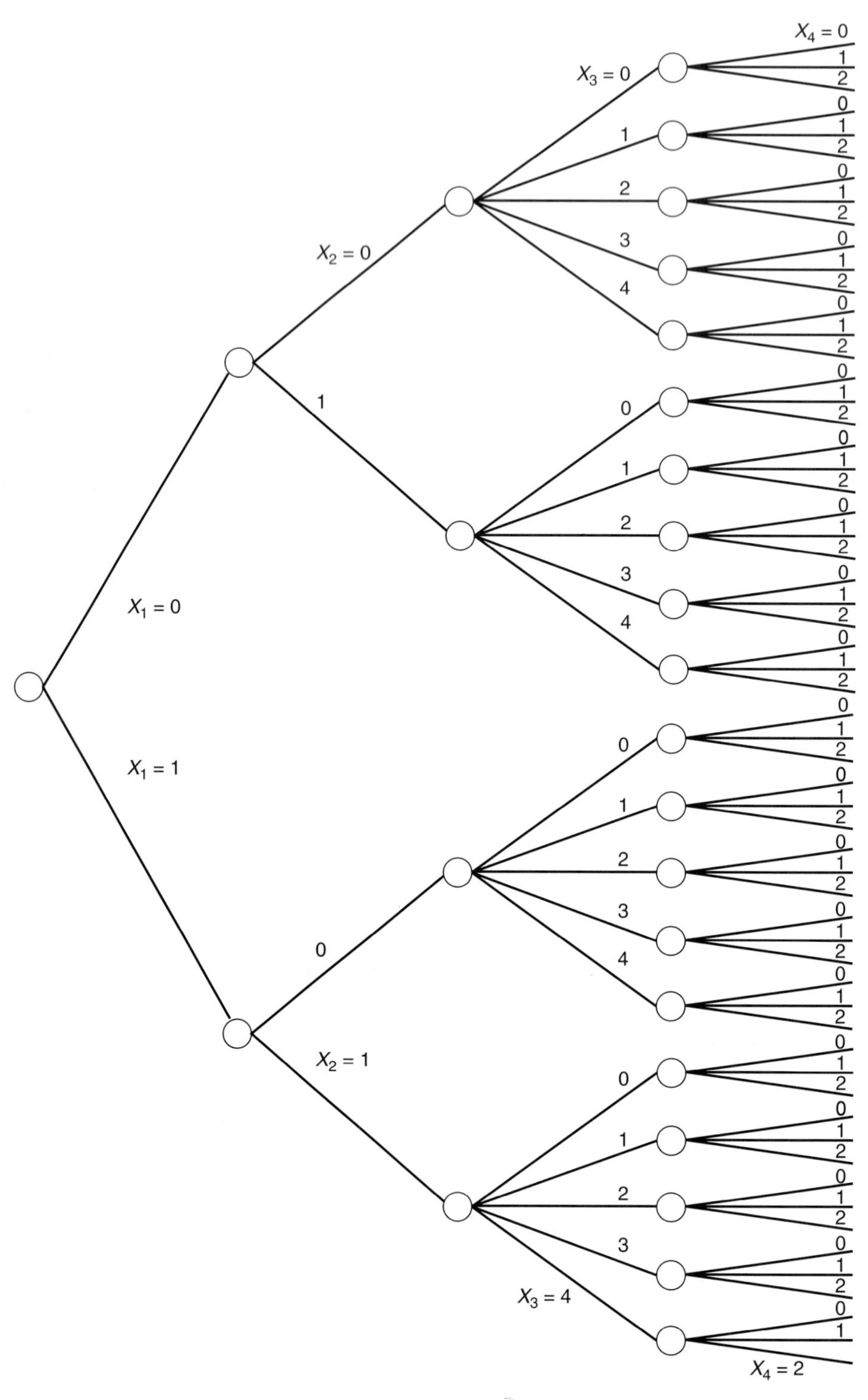

FIGURE 4–11 Summary of Steps in Solution of First Example Problem

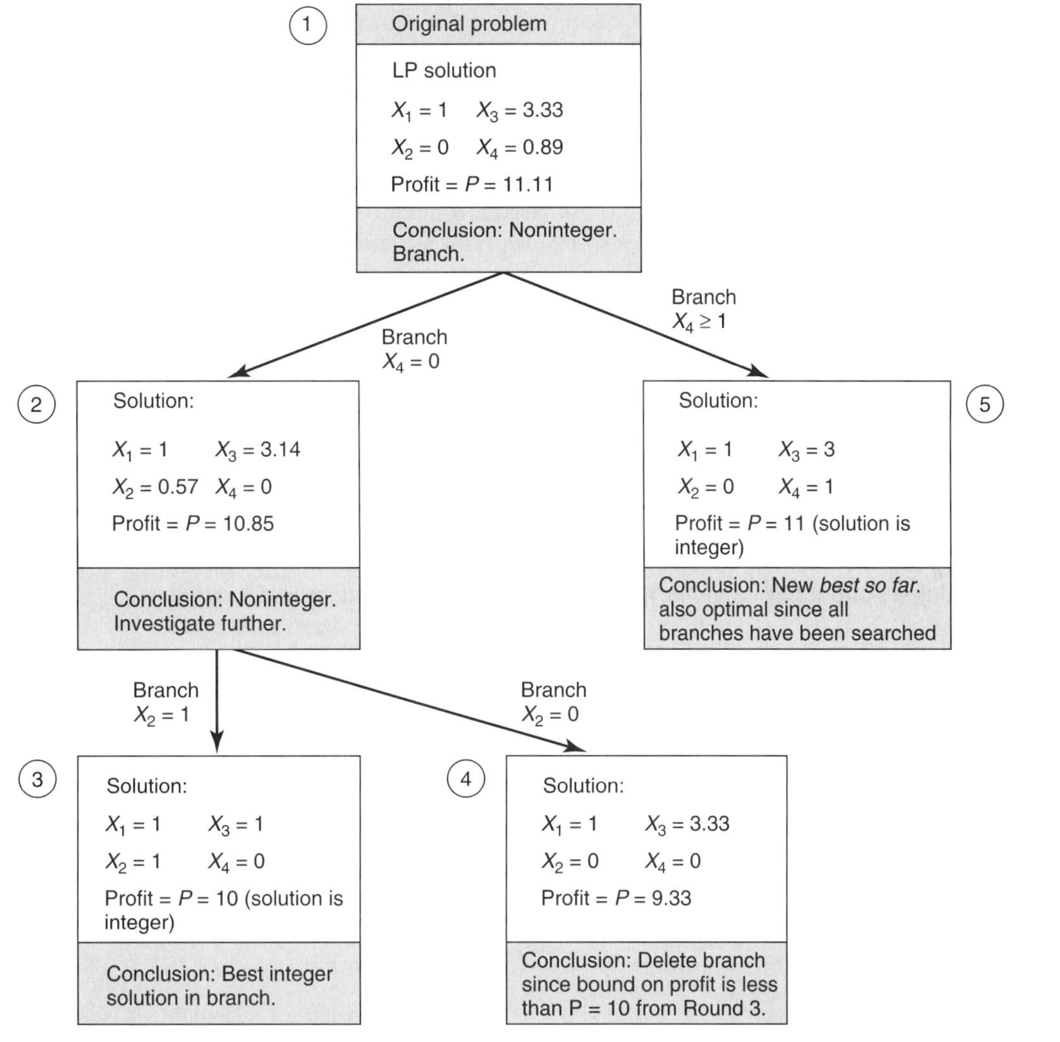

no solution, and hence no integer solution, that can have a profit higher than 11.11. Thus, the value 11.11 is a *bound* on all the solutions in the problem. For any branch, we can find a bound (upper limit) in exactly the same way.

The steps in the branch and bound procedure are illustrated in Figure 4–11 for the example problem. The numbers in circles indicate the sequence of rounds for the development of the tree and for the branch and bound procedure.

Branch and Bound Solution of Example

Round 1. The first step is to solve the problem as an ordinary linear programming problem. If we are very lucky, the solution may turn out to be integer, but even when it is not, the initial LP solution is a good place to start. The LP solution to our example is $X_1 = 1, X_2 = 0, X_3 = 3.33, X_4 = 0.89$, and the profit is $P = 11.11$. This is not an integer solution, so we must proceed further.

Before proceeding, note that there is one obvious integer solution, $X_1 = X_2 = X_3 = X_4 = 0$, with profit $P = 0$. It is unlikely that this is the optimal solution, but it gives an initial "best so far" solution.

Round 2

Step 1. Begin. The initial feasible integer solution is $X_1 = X_2 = X_3 = X_4 = 0$, with profit $P = 0$.

Step 2. Branch. We must now select a variable and construct *branches.* The variable to be selected is arbitrary. A procedure that seems to work well is to branch on variables that are noninteger at the current stage. From round 1, both X_3 and X_4 are noninteger; let us arbitrarily select X_4 for branching. The previous solution has $X_4 = 0.89$. Hence, a sensible pair of branches would require either $X_4 = 0$ or $X_4 \geq 1$. Note that this branching divides all the possible solutions into *two groups,* those for which $X_4 = 0$, and those for which $X_4 \geq 1$. Since X_4 must be an integer, it is not possible for X_4 to be between 0 and 1. This procedure defines the first pair of branches shown in Figure 4–11. Let us arbitrarily select the branch $X_4 = 0$ for initial investigation. To represent this branch, we replace the last constraint ($X_4 \leq 4$) in the example problem by the constraint $X_4 = 0$. Then the problem becomes:

$$
\begin{array}{ll}
\text{Maximize:} & P = 6X_1 + 3X_2 + X_3 + 2X_4 \\
\text{Subject to:} & X_1 + X_2 + X_3 + X_4 \leq 8 \\
& 2X_1 + X_2 + 3X_3 \leq 12 \\
& 5X_2 + X_3 + 3X_4 \leq 6 \\
& X_1 \leq 1 \\
& X_2 \leq 1 \\
& X_3 \leq 4 \\
& X_4 = \mathbf{0}
\end{array}
$$

Step 3. Bound. The LP solution to this problem is $X_1 = 1, X_2 = 0.57, X_3 = 3.14, X_4 = 0$. The profit is $P = 10.85$ and this profit value is a *bound* on all the solutions on the branch $X_4 = 0$ (that is, for all the solutions for which $X_4 = 0$).

Step 4. Compare. Compare the best solution so far to the bound just generated. The best integer solution so far has profit $P = 0$, while the bound is $P = 10.85$; thus, we cannot yet eliminate this branch, and we investigate further down the branch.

Round 3

Step 2. Branch. Select a new variable to branch—say, X_2 (see Figure 4–11). Note that X_2 is noninteger in the LP solution above. Variable X_2 can only take on values of 0 or 1, so there are only two possible branches: $X_2 = 0$ or $X_2 = 1$. That is, we subdivide the possible solutions into two groups, those that have $X_2 = 0$, and those with $X_2 = 1$. (Recall that we are still working under the branch $X_4 = 0$, so that we are also dealing only with the possible solutions for which $X_4 = 0$.)

We arbitrarily select the branch $X_2 = 1$ and substitute this constraint in the problem above in place of $X_2 \leq 1$. The new problem is:

$$\begin{array}{ll} \text{Maximize:} & P = 6X_1 + 3X_2 + X_3 + 2X_4 \\ \text{Subject to:} & X_1 + X_2 + X_3 + X_4 \leq 8 \\ & 2X_1 + X_2 + 3X_3 \leq 12 \\ & 5X_2 + X_3 + 3X_4 \leq 6 \\ & X_1 \leq 1 \\ & X_2 = \mathbf{1} \\ & X_3 \leq 4 \\ & X_4 = \mathbf{0} \end{array}$$

Step 3. Bound. The LP solution to this problem is: $X_1 = 1, X_2 = 1, X_3 = 1, X_4 = 0$, with a profit $P = 10$. Note that the solution happens to be integer.

Step 4. Compare. This integer solution is better than our *best solution so far* ($P = 0$). It becomes the new "best so far" solution. Also, we do not have to investigate further down in this branch, as we have the optimum for this branch. That is, for the set of possible solutions for which $X_4 = 0$ and $X_2 = 1$, there is none better than the one just obtained. However, there are other branches to review.

Round 4

Step 2. Branch. Move back to the branch $X_2 = 0$ (see Figure 4–11), and select it for investigation. That is, we now consider the set of possible solutions for which $X_2 = 0$ (still within the set for which $X_4 = 0$). The problem to solve is the same as above (Round 3, Step 2) with the constraint $X_2 = 0$ replacing $X_2 = 1$.

Step 3. Bound. The LP solution to this problem is: $X_1 = 1, X_2 = 0, X_3 = 3.33, X_4 = 0$, with profit $P = 9.33$.

Step 4. Compare. This bound is *less than* the previous best so far ($P = 10$ from Round 3, Step 3). Hence, we can eliminate this branch from further consideration. It cannot contain an integer solution with profit greater than 10, since the best unrestricted solution has a profit of only 9.33.

Round 5

Step 2. Branch. Move back up the tree to the branch $X_4 \geq 1$, which we created in Round 2, Step 2 (see Figure 4–11).

Step 3. Bound. We solve the same LP problem as in Step 2 of Round 2 with the constraint $X_4 \geq 1$ replacing $X_4 = 0$. The solution is $X_1 = 1, X_2 = 0, X_3 = 3, X_4 = 1$, and the profit $P = 11$. Again, note that this is an integer solution.

Step 4. Compare. The solution above is integer and is better than the previous best solution. It thus becomes the new *best so far*. It is a bound on all solutions below the branch ($X_4 \geq 1$), so we do not need to investigate further down that branch.

Step 5. Completion. All branches have been investigated, and hence, the best so far solution obtained in Step 3 of Round 5 is the optimal integer solution, with profit $P = 11$.

We have completed the example problem. Since all branches have been investigated, the optimum solution is our current *best so far:*

$X_1 = 1$
$X_2 = 0$
$X_3 = 3$
$X_4 = 1$
$P = 11$

The summary of the procedures is given in Figure 4–11. Note that we did not have to investigate many branches—in fact, only five—to obtain the best solution from the 60 possibilities given in Figure 4–10.

The general series of steps for the branch and bound solution procedure is given in the Summary below.

Summary

1. *Begin.* Find an *initial feasible integer* solution. (If it is difficult to find an initial solution, this step may be omitted.)
2. *Branch.* Select a variable and divide the possible solutions into two groups. Select one branch—that is, one of the groups—to investigate.
3. *Bound.* Find a *bound* for the problem defined by the branch selected. In our case, we use the LP solution to the integer problem as the bound. Note that the bound represents the upper limit for all possible solutions in a given branch.
4. *Compare.* Compare the bound obtained for the branch being considered with the *best solution so far* for the previous branches examined. If the bound is less than the best so far, delete the whole new branch. Then go on to branches not yet examined.

   If the bound of this new branch is greater than the best solution so far, and if the solution is *integer,* then it becomes the new *best solution so far;* next, go on to examine other branches not yet considered.

   If the bound of the new branch is greater than the best solution so far, but the solution is *not integer,* there may be better solutions further down in the tree. Therefore, move one level down in the tree and branch (that is, go to Step 2).
5. *Completion.* When all branches have been examined, the *best solution so far* is the optimal solution.

Another Example

Figure 4–12 shows the solution tree for the factory size and location example discussed in this chapter (see Figure 4–3). In this case, there are seven binary variables, so there are 128 possible integer cases, each involving the solution of an LP problem with 19 other variables. A summary of the steps from Figure 4–12 follows:

Steps 0 through 5. Continue branching until a feasible integer solution is found at step 5. This solution becomes the best so far.

FIGURE 4–12 Steps in Solution of Factory Size and Location Example

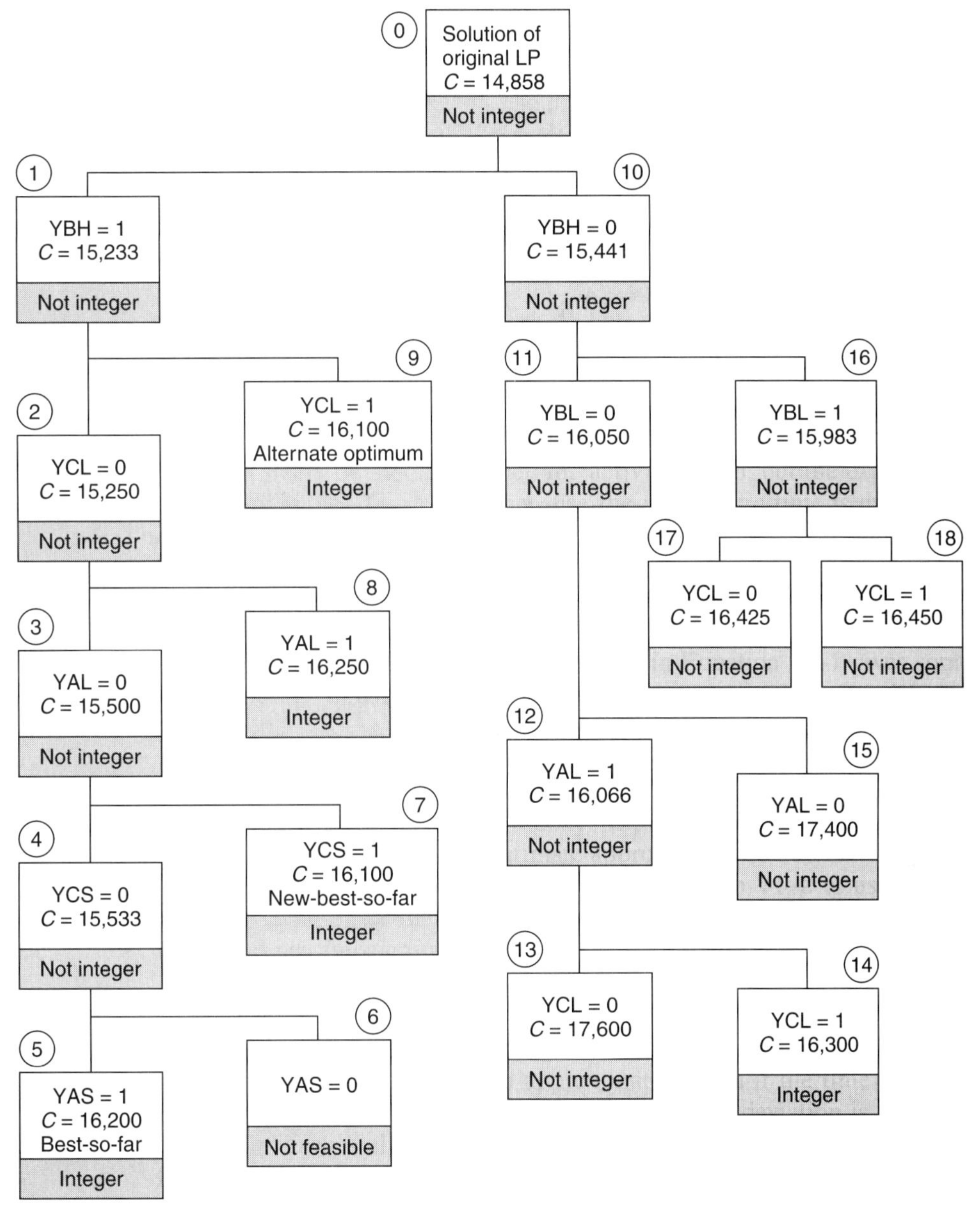

Step 6. Solution not feasible. Cut off branch.

Step 7. Integer solution, new best-so-far solution with cost of $16,100.

Step 8. Integer but more costly than current best-so-far. Cut off branch.

Step 9. Integer solution and equal to best-so-far.

Steps 10 through 12. Noninteger solutions, but bounds are better (less cost) than current best-so-far solution. Continue branching.

Step 13. Bound is worse than best-so-far. Cut off branch.

Step 14. Integer, but bound is worse than best-so-far. Cut off branch.

Steps 15 through 18. Bounds are worse than best-so-far. Cut off branches.

All branches have been considered, and the alternate best-so-far solutions (steps 7 and 9) are the optimum solutions. The solution of step 9 is the one given in Figure 4–3. The alternate involves a small factory at site C, and a different shipping pattern.

Discussion

It is necessary in the branch and bound procedure to create the equivalent of the tree structure, such as given in Figures 4–11 and 4–12. Computer programs that are in use on real problems have complex *heuristics* (rules of thumb) about how to develop the tree and which branches to investigate first.[12]

The branch and bound procedure is a general approach to problem solution. In the examples in this chapter, we have used the solution of an ordinary linear programming problem as the way to obtain a bound. But there are problems where a bound may be obtained by a different, much simpler process. An example is the *assignment* problem. Suppose a firm has five factories and five sales regions, and each factory is assigned to uniquely supply one of the regions. This can be formulated as an integer programming problem and solved as we have above. However, there are ways of obtaining bounds on the cost for this assignment problem that are much easier to obtain than solving a linear programming problem. Thus, this bounding procedure can be used within the branch and bound process to solve the problem.

Bibliography

Bazaraa, M. S.; H. D. Sherali; and C. M. Shetty. *Nonlinear Programming: Theory and Algorithms.* 2nd ed. New York: Wiley, 1993.

Bradley, S. P.; A. C. Hax; and T. L. Magnanti. *Applied Mathematical Programming.* Reading, Mass: Addison Wesley Publishing, 1977.

Hillier, F. and G. J. Lieberman. *Introduction to Operations Research.* 6th ed. New York: McGraw-Hill, 1995.

Lee, S. M. *Goal Programming for Decision Analysis.* New York: Van Nostrand Reinhold, 1973.

Nemhauser, G. L. and L. A. Wolsey. *Integer and Combinatorial Optimization.* New York: Wiley, 1988.

Winston, Wayne L. *Operations Research Applications and Algorithms.* Englewood Cliffs, N.J.: Prentice Hall, 1994.

Practice Problems[13]

4–1. A major movie studio plans to produce five specific movies over the next three years. Define a variable Y_{it} in which the subscript i refers to the particular movie (i = 1, 2, 3, 4, 5) and the subscript t refers to the year (t = 1, 2, 3). Y_{it} is a zero/one variable that has value 1 if the ith movie is produced in the tth

[12]You can see the steps Solver takes by checking the box Show Iteration Results in the Solver Options dialogue box.

[13]Solutions for these problems are at the end of this chapter.

year, and has value 0 otherwise. Consider each situation below separately, and formulate one or more linear integer constraints that satisfy the stated condition.

a. No more than one movie may be produced in the first year.
b. Movie 2 cannot be produced before movie 3. They may be produced in the same year, however.
c. At least one movie must be produced each year.
d. Movie 4 must be produced no later than year 2.
e. Movies 1 and 5 cannot be produced in the same year.

4–2. A research administrator in the Federal Science Foundation is trying to decide which projects to fund for the coming year. She has received the eight proposals listed below. After careful study, she has made a subjective estimate of the value of each project on a scale of 0 to 100. The research administrator wants to find a mix of projects having the greatest total value. However, there are several limitations. First, she has a budget of $320,000. Second, she must either accept or turn down a project (i.e., no partial funding). Third, certain projects are related. She does not wish to fund both projects G and H. Project D should not be funded unless A is also funded (but A can be funded without D).

a. Formulate the administrator's problem as a linear (integer) programming problem.
b. Solve the problem using the Solver program.

Proposal	*Cost ($000s)*	*Value*
A	$ 80	40
B	15	10
C	120	80
D	65	50
E	20	20
F	10	5
G	60	80
H	100	100

4–3. The Bendigo company manufactures three products, ANZAs, BOZOs, and KARMAs. Bendigo has partially formulated its weekly product mix problem as a linear programming problem as follows:

Maximize: $100A + 120B$

Subject to:

$$3A + 7B + 2K \leq 1{,}000$$
(machine time available)
$$A + 1.5B + 2K \leq 300$$
(labor-hours available)
$$23A + 18B + 25K = \text{RMUSED}$$
(raw material used)

where *A*, *B*, and *K* refer to the number of ANZAs, BOZOs, and KARMAs produced per week. At this point, Bendigo ran into trouble and turned to you to help complete the formulation.

For each of the parts below, add to or modify the formulation to incorporate the situation described. Formulate as a linear integer problem, using integer (including binary) variables as required. In each case, define any new variables, any new or modified constraints, and any additions or modifications to the objective function. Treat each part independently.

a. KARMAs are stamped on a special machine that is leased from the manufacturer. Up to 200 KARMAs can be stamped in a week. The lease specifies a fixed fee of $800 per week if any KARMAs are produced. However, there is no charge if the machine is not used in any week.
b. The cost of raw material is 25 cents per unit if less than 1,000 units are purchased. If 1,000 or more units are purchased, the cost is 20 cents per unit for all units purchased. An unlimited amount of raw material is available in any week, but it cannot be stored from one week to the next.
c. The sales revenue for a KARMA depends on the amount purchased. Bendigo receives $100 each for the first 20 units produced, $150 each for the next 50 units produced, and $120 each for any additional units up to a maximum of 200 total units produced.
d. The sales department estimates that the maximum sales are 100 units for ANZAs and 120 units for BOZOs. However, a selling campaign might be undertaken, at a cost of $5,000, on either product. The selling campaign would increase the demand by 50 units for the selected product. Because of the limited sales force, the campaign could be done for either ANZAs or BOZOs but not both.

4–4. A firm produces two products, A and B. The profit contribution and resource usages for a unit of each product are shown below.

	Product A	*Product B*
Profit contribution ($ per unit)	15	10
Resource usages:		
Machine time (hours per unit)	4	5
Raw material (tons per unit)	5	4
Skilled labor (hours per unit)	1	5
Unskilled labor (hours per unit)	2	0

The firm has available a maximum of 100 hours of machine time and 30 hours of unskilled labor.

There is a shortage of raw material. The firm has received an allocation of 100 tons from its headquarters, with instructions to use as little as possible, returning any excess for use in other divisions. More than the 100 tons allocated could be obtained, but only if "absolutely necessary."

The firm has a skilled labor force with 75 hours available on regular time. These skilled workers are reluctant to work overtime but will if necessary. Management wants to utilize the skilled workers during regular time as fully as possible.

The firm has a $300 profit goal, which it hopes to meet or exceed.

a. Define the decision variables, and define the constraints on machine time and unskilled labor.

b. Formulate the goal constraints on skilled labor, raw material, and profit. Allow for both underages and excesses in these constraints.

c. Assume that management attaches costs of $15 per ton to using raw material in excess of the allocation, $10 per hour to overtime for skilled workers, and $5 per hour to idle time for skilled workers. In addition, raw material unused (below the allocation) has a value of $5 per ton. A dollar of profit has the same value, regardless of whether or not the profit goal is exceeded.

Formulate the goal programming objective function.

d. Before going on with this part, check to see that your formulation is correct (by looking at the answers at the end of the book).

Now graph the decision problem. First, include the constraints on unskilled labor and machine time. Next, draw in the lines representing the skilled labor and raw material goals. Finally, include the profit goal.

e. Evaluate the following possible solution points. Find each point on your graph. For each one, substitute in each of the goal equations to determine the underage or excess. Then substitute these values in the objective functions of (*c*). Find the optimal solution (with lowest value). The points are:

(1) Product A = 8.33 units; product B = 13.33 units.

(2) Product A = 11.11 units; product B = 11.11 units.

(3) Product A = 15 units; product B = 8 units.

(4) Product A = 15 units; product B = 6.25 units.

Problems

4–5. The chief of the Punxsutawney Police Department was trying to make up her budget request for the following year. A key element was the number of police personnel she would need for patrol duty. She had just received a study (see the accompanying table) that estimated how many patrols should be on the Punxsutawney streets during each four-hour period.

These estimates were based partly on past experience for requests for aid and for investigation of crimes, and partly on requirements for a new program of crime prevention. The new program stressed the visibility of patrol units on the streets during high potential crime times.

The chief's problem rose because she had to schedule police personnel on eight-hour shifts and not just for the four-hour segments shown in the table. The department was operating with the six staggered eight-hour shifts shown in the following table, and the chief wanted to keep this policy.

Estimated Requirements for Police Patrols on Weekdays, by Time of Day

Time Period	*Patrols Needed*
10 PM to 2 AM	13
2 AM to 6 AM	1
6 AM to 10 AM	7
10 AM to 2 PM	6
2 PM to 6 PM	6
6 PM to 10 PM	17
Total	50

Punxsutawney Police—Staggered Shifts

Shift	*Beginning Time*	*Ending Time*
1	10 PM	6 AM
2	2 AM	10 AM
3	6 AM	2 PM
4	10 AM	6 PM
5	2 PM	10 PM
6	6 PM	2 AM

The chief's problem was to decide on the minimum number of personnel needed to meet the requirements. Assume that each patrol involved a single patrolperson. Also consider only the problem for weekdays. Formulate a linear integer programming problem to solve the chief's problem.

4–6. The dean of a business school is planning enrollment in the school's two major programs, an undergraduate course leading to a BBA degree, and a graduate program leading to the MBA. The dean has available 36 senior faculty and 42 junior faculty. To teach the courses for each BBA candidate, .02 senior faculty and .03 junior faculty are required. In other words, for every 100 BBAs, the school needs two senior faculty and three junior faculty. For every 100 MBAs, six senior faculty and four junior faculty are required.

The dean's problem is to determine the number of MBA and BBA students to enroll. Tuition for an MBA is $15,000 per year and $12,000 per year for a BBA. The university provost has decreed that the enrollment in the MBA program is limited to no more than half the enrollment in the BBA program.

The dean has three objectives. The first is tuition income and the dean has set a goal of $15 million. A second objective is to satisfy the needs of local business for BBAs, and a goal of an enrollment level of 1,000 BBAs has been set. The third objective is to satisfy the demand for MBAs, and the goal of 400 MBAs has been set. Assume that the dean wishes to meet the demand for BBAs and MBAs as closely as possible, with excesses and underages both to be avoided, if possible. Also, the dean wishes to obtain as much tuition income as possible.

a. Formulate the constraints for the dean's problem as a goal-programming problem. Allow both underages and excesses for the goal constraints.

b. Formulate the objective function, assuming the following weights for each underage or excess.

Weight ($ equivalents)	*Objective*
15	Tuition underage
30,000	Shortfall in meeting BBA demand
24,000	Shortfall in meeting MBA demand
3	Tuition excess
9,000	BBA goal excess
6,000	MBA goal excess

c. Graph the problem. First, graph only the nongoal constraints. Then draw in the goal equations. Find the solution that is optimal. You may need to try several points to find which one is optimal. Consider points that are intersections of the various constraints and goal equations.

d. Assume that the dean wishes to assign priorities to the various goals in the order shown under (*b*). That is, minimizing tuition underage is the highest priority, minimizing the shortfall in BBA demand is next, and so on. Use the priority programming approach, and graphically solve the problem.

4–7. (***Note:*** this problem requires knowledge of the material in the appendix to this chapter.) Use the branch and bound procedure to solve the following problem:

$$\begin{aligned} \text{Maximize:} \quad & 3X_1 + 6X_2 + X_3 \\ \text{Subject to:} \quad & X_1 + X_2 + X_3 \le 7 \\ & 5X_1 + X_2 + X_3 \le 15 \\ & X_1 + 4X_2 \le 9 \\ & X_1 \le 3;\ X_2 \le 3;\ X_3 \le 3 \end{aligned}$$

All variables are integers.

4–8 Refer to the illustration of the factory size and location problem in this chapter. The formulation given allows each region's requirements to be met partially from each of two or more factory sites. Suppose we wish to require that a region be supplied entirely from only one factory site. How would you formulate this problem?

4–9. The Snohomish Extrusion Company is planning its production schedule for the next quarter. Snohomish makes three products: alphas, betas, and gammas. The major factors used in manufacturing these products are labor-hours, raw material, and electric power. The requirements for each are as follows:

	Alphas	*Betas*	*Gammas*
Labor (hrs.)	5	2	1
Raw material (lbs.)	10	13	8
Power (kwh.)	300	180	120
Contribution per unit ($) excluding cost of labor, raw material, and power	170	240	120

Snohomish has up to 4,000 labor-hours available on its first-shift operations (for the quarter), and the labor contract allows up to this amount at the rate of $10 per hour. Raw materials (regular resin) cost $2 per pound, and up to 20,000 pounds can be purchased. Power costs 3 cents per kwh., and any amount can be purchased.

Snohomish has formulated the linear programming problem as follows:

Maximize:

$$170A + 240B + 120C - 10FSH - 2RMR - 0.03PA$$

Subject to:

$$5A + 2B + 1C = FSH$$
$$FSH \leq 4{,}000 \text{ (labor requirements)}$$
$$10A + 13B + 8C = RMR$$
$$RMR \leq 20{,}000 \text{ (raw material requirements)}$$
$$300A + 180B + 120C = PA \text{ (power requirement)}$$

where:

A = Number of alphas produced
B = Number of betas produced
C = Number of gammas produced
FSH = Number of labor-hours used on first-shift operations
RMR = Pounds of raw material (regular resin) used
PA = Kwh. of power used at $0.03 price

Parts (*a*) through (*c*) below propose modifications of the above linear program. You should define whatever new variables are needed, including integer or binary integer (zero/one) variables. Also, show how you would modify any constraint and the objective function. Treat each case independently.

a. A second-shift operation is possible. This shift would allow an additional 2,000 labor-hours. Labor would cost $12 per hour on the second-shift operations. In addition, if the second shift is to operate, there will be fixed costs of $900 incurred (for supervision, overhead, and so on).

b. The price of power to Snohomish really depends on the amount used. The cost is $0.03 per kwh. for the first 30,000 kwh. The cost of additional power beyond this amount is $0.02 per kwh.

c. A new raw material, a special resin, has just been announced. This special raw material costs $4 per pound but would require considerably less per unit (only two pounds per unit for each of the three products). The use of this new raw material would require the lease of special-purpose equipment costing $8,000. In addition, there is a minimum order quantity of 2,000 pounds (and a maximum order quantity of 10,000 pounds) of this special raw material. Snohomish must decide which of the two raw materials to use. That is, Snohomish can use either the regular or the special resin, but not both.

4–10. Amazing Airlines (AA) is about to add two new cities to its route schedule. In particular, daily service is being inaugurated from Chicago to Seattle and return, and from Chicago to Denver and return. AA's decision problem involves what aircraft to assign to each of these two routes. AA has six planes available, with characteristics as shown in Table 4–4. A given aircraft will fly from Chicago to its destination and back daily. Any combination of aircraft types may be assigned to each route.

TABLE 4–4
Planes Available for New Routes

			Operating Costs ($000s)	
Plane Type	*Number Available*	*Seating Capacity*	*Chicago to Seattle and Return*	*Chicago to Denver and Return*
A	1	320	108	101
B	2	250	90	88
C	3	130	66	62

Amazing Airlines' market research department has done a careful study of demand on these routes, and the results are shown in the table below. These demand estimates are the maximum that AA would carry, assuming there was adequate seat capacity assigned to the given route.

Estimated Demand on New Routes

Route Leg	*Estimated Daily Demand*	*One-Way Fare*
Chicago to Seattle	310	$410
Seattle to Chicago	240	410
Chicago to Denver	290	350
Denver to Chicago	265	350

Formulate this problem as a linear integer programming problem.

4–11. The Rowbottom Sand and Gravel Company has the following amounts of materials to deliver to six customers:

Customer	*Amount (tons)*
A	¼
B	½
C	1½
D	½
E	¾
F	1

There are five trucks that can be used to make these deliveries. With the use of dividers, a truck can deliver a mix of loads up to its capacity. However, a customer's order cannot be split between trucks. Trucks available and their capacities are:

Truck	*Capacity (tons)*
1	1
2	2
3	1
4	2
5	1½

The costs associated with each truck delivering to the customer is given in the following table:

Costs of Delivering Orders to Customers ($)

Truck \ *Customer*	*A*	*B*	*C*	*D*	*E*	*F*
1	17	19	21	20	20	21
2	15	18	20	18	19	23
3	18	19	22	22	21	22
4	15	16	19	18	18	20
5	16	15	20	22	19	20

In addition to these costs, there is a fixed cost of $10 on trucks 1, 3, and 5 and $15 on trucks 2 and 4. These costs are incurred if the truck is used at all.

Finally, there is the restriction that the same truck cannot deliver to both customers A and B.

Formulate this as an integer programming problem.

4–12. ***Note:*** This problem requires knowledge of the material in the appendix to this chapter.

Use the branch and bound procedure to solve the following problem:

Maximize:

$$15X_1 + 3X_2 + 8X_3 - 10Y_1 - 10Y_2 - 2Y_3$$

Subject to:

$$\begin{aligned} 3X_1 + 2X_2 + X_3 - 10Y_1 &\leq 5 \\ 4X_1 - X_2 + 5X_3 - 12Y_2 &\leq 6 \\ X_1 + X_2 + X_3 - 4Y_3 &\leq 0 \end{aligned}$$

where the variables X_1, X_2, X_3 are not required to be integer, but Y_1 and Y_2 are zero/one variables, and $Y_3 \leq 3$ is also integer.

More Challenging Problems

4–13. The San Francisco office of the MBA Consulting Group is trying to schedule its consultants for the next four weeks. MBA has accepted four consulting jobs that must be completed during this time. The jobs, the required number of consultants, and the time requirements are as shown below. MBA has a policy that once a consultant is assigned to a job, that person stays with the job until finished. Furthermore, once a job is begun, it is carried through to completion without interruption.

The San Francisco office has a permanent staff of four consultants. It was immediately obvious to the branch manager that the requirements could not be met with this staff. Additional consultants could be obtained from the national office in New York. However, the national office only assigns consultants on a monthly (i.e., four-week) basis. Hence, any consultants added must be added for all four weeks. Since the branch is charged for these national office consultants, the branch manager wants to minimize the number used while still meeting the job requirements.

a. Formulate this problem as an integer linear problem. (*Hint:* Let Y_{it} be a zero/one variable that is 1 if the ith job is started in period t, and 0 otherwise.)

Job	*Weeks Required for Job*	*Consultants Required Each Week*
1	3	2
2	2	3
3	1	5
4	1	4

b. Solve the problem using the Solver program.

4–14. A very important problem in finance is that of portfolio selection. Suppose you are considering investing in three mutual funds, one devoted to international stocks, one to domestic stocks, and one fund that includes only bonds. You would like to have a portfolio (i.e., a mix) of these funds. So the decision is what relative portion of your available funds to invest in each.

You would like to achieve as high a return as possible and, based on historical data, you have estimated the expected return for each fund. These returns are shown in Table 4–5. However, the funds differ greatly in variability of returns from year to year. The measure of this variability is the variance of returns for each fund. Also, the returns are not independent of each other—there is some correlation in the returns of the three funds. A measure of this is the covariance between two funds, a measure of how the two move together. For example, the covariance between the International stock fund and the Domestic stock fund is negative, indicating a (slight) tendency for the funds to move in opposite directions.

Let R_i be the return for investing in the ith mutual fund, and X_i be the fraction of our portfolio invested in that fund; then the expected return for the whole portfolio is:

$$\text{Expected portfolio return} = \Sigma\, X_i \cdot R_i$$

The variance of the portfolio is a measure of risk or variability. Let σ_i^2 be the variance of returns for the ith fund. Also, let cov_{ij} be the covariance between the ith and j^{th} funds. The variance of the entire portfolio is given (for our three-fund example) by:

$$\begin{aligned}&\text{Portfolio Variance} = \\ &X_1^2 \cdot \sigma_1^2 + X_2^2 \cdot \sigma_2^2 + X_3^2 \cdot \sigma_3^2 \\ &+ 2X_1X_2\text{cov}_{12} + 2X_1X_3\text{cov}_{13} \\ &+ 2X_2X_3\text{cov}_{23}\end{aligned}$$

a. Develop a spreadsheet model for this problem. Your objective is to maximize portfolio return, subject to a constraint on the variance of the portfolio (i.e., on

TABLE 4–5 Expected Returns, Variances, and Covariances

Fund	*Expected Return*	*Variance of Return*	*Covariances*	*Domestic Stock Fund*	*Bond Fund*
International stocks	0.12	0.0083	International stocks	−0.00059	0.00073
Domestic stocks	0.10	0.0042	Domestic stocks		0.00219
Bonds	0.07	0.0016			

the riskiness of the portfolio). To start, assume that this limit is a variance of .0025 for the portfolio. Note that, while the objective is a linear function, the constraint on risk is not. Use Solver to find the solution.

b. Now assume that your objective is to minimize risk, subject to a constraint that the overall portfolio return is at least 10.5 percent. Use Solver to find the solution.

c. Identify the "efficient frontier"—the trade-offs between risk and return by trying various values for the constraint on returns, optimizing, and noting the portfolio variance.

4–15. A firm makes four products, labeled A, B, C, and D. The executive committee is meeting to decide on the product mix. The controller wants the mix that achieves the most profit; the sales manager wants to obtain the largest market share; and the production manager wants to balance the production facility. The president must mediate these potentially conflicting objectives.

The information on the four products is shown in Table 4–6, which shows the hours required per unit for each product in assembly, test, and machine time, as well as time in departments 1 and 2.

The profit per unit for each product is also shown in Table 4–6. The controller thinks the firm should emphasize products B and C, since they produce the most profit per unit. The controller would like to see the firm have a profit of $10,000.

The marketing manager views each product as a sale and, hence, counting as one point in market share. A point in market share is a 0.01 percent share. The goal for the marketing manager is 800 share points (that is, 8 percent of the total market).

The production manager notes that the firm has 3,000 hours of assembly time available, 1,000 hours of test time available, and 7,500 hours of machine time available. There are no limits on hours for departments 1 and 2. However, it is the balancing of the hours worked in these departments that is of concern. The production manager would like the hours worked in each of departments 1 and 2 to be as nearly equal as possible.

The president has decided that a weighting must be given to each objective. A dollar profit is worth the same, regardless of whether above or below the controller's goal of $10,000. A point of market share is worth $10 below the 800 goal, but worth only $5 above it. A one-hour imbalance in production departments has a cost of $10.

Formulate this as a goal-programming problem. Solve on a computer, if possible.

4–16. The Franchise Food Products Company operates two chains of ready-food stores, the Piazo Pizza chain and the Fisher Fish and Chips chain. The firm is expanding operations into Santa Clara County and is looking for sites to open new stores. Ten sites have been identified as potential sites, and the net revenue (in present-value terms) of each has been estimated for use either as a Piazo Pizza parlor or a Fisher Fish and Chips restaurant. Let P_j ($j = 1, 2, \ldots, 10$) be the net revenue for use of site j as a pizza parlor and F_j ($j = 1, 2, \ldots, 10$) be the net revenue for the same site if it is used as a fish restaurant.

The company operates both chains of restaurants by franchising out the rights in a given region. According to the terms of the agreement with any Pizza franchise, franchisees have the exclusive rights within a two-mile radius of their restaurants. This means any sites selected

TABLE 4–6

	Product			
	A	*B*	*C*	*D*
Resources:				
Assembly time (hours)	4	15	5	2
Test time (hours)	2	2	2	1
Machine time (hours)	6	2	10	12
Department 1 (hours)	1	2	1	*
Department 2 (hours)	½	1	2	*
Goals:				
Profit ($)	10	50	20	5
Market share (points)	1	1	1	1

*Product D requires two hours of time, but this can be done either in department 1 or department 2, or split between them as desired.

TABLE 4–7 Distance (miles) between Potential Restaurant Sites

From \ To	2	3	4	5	6	7	8	9	10
1	3.7	2.2	3.2	6.4	7.3	8.6	8.8	13.0	10.2
2		2.6	5.7	3.3	6.6	9.6	10.3	13.1	7.5
3			3.2	4.5	5.3	7.4	7.7	11.4	8.2
4				7.5	5.7	5.6	5.7	10.4	10.3
5					5.2	9.4	10.1	11.5	4.4
6						4.8	5.6	6.6	5.5
7							1.2	5.2	10.2
8								5.9	11.4
9									10.2

for Pizza parlors must be at least four miles apart. A similar agreement exists in contracts with Fisher Fish franchises, but the exclusive rights are guaranteed within 2.5 miles; that is, the restaurants must be at least five miles apart. There are no restrictions on locations between the two chains (a Pizza parlor could be right next to a Fisher Fish restaurant, for example). Table 4–7 shows the distances between sites.

Each of the 10 potential sites may be developed as either a Pizza parlor or a Fish restaurant, but not both. Of course, it need not be developed at all.

Formulate the above as an integer programming problem to maximize the net revenue to Franchise Foods Products Company.

4–17. The Ininob Manufacturing Company produces three products: widgets, yamis, and zots. The company is trying to determine its production schedule for these products for the next month. The company sells widgets for $50 each, and zots for $40 each. At these prices, up to 200 widgets and 30 zots can be sold. The price for yamis has not yet been decided. Two prices are under consideration—$50 and $60. At the $50 price, up to 100 can be sold. At the $60 price, up to 60 can be sold.

Ininob purchases the raw material from which all three products are produced from a single firm. Widgets require 0.1 tons of raw material for each one produced. Yamis require 0.2 tons each; and zots require 0.3 tons each. Because of a shortage, there are only 50 tons of raw material available for production of all three products. The cost of the raw material is $20 per ton.

The first step in the production process for all three products is a molding and heating operation. This requires a special-purpose machine. A maximum of 400 hours are available on this machine. No additional hours can be obtained, since the machine is already operating three shifts. The variable cost of operating this machine is $8 per hour. Each widget requires one hour on the machine; each yami requires two hours; and each zot requires one-half hour.

After the molding and heating operation described above, each product is finished. Zots are finished on a zotting machine. It costs $500 to set up this machine and $10 per zot finished. If no zots are produced, there is, of course, no setup cost.

Widgets and yamis are finished on a widgeting machine. There is a cost of $1,000 to set up this machine. However, once set up, the machine can finish either widgets or yamis or both. If neither yamis nor widgets are to be produced, the setup cost is not incurred. The variable cost of operating this machine is $10 per unit for either yamis or widgets.

Ininob has to decide its production schedule for all three products at the beginning of the month, and also to decide on the price of yamis.

Formulate the problem as an integer linear programming problem.

4–18. A firm has three factories that supply five sales regions. The transportation costs and sales requirements are shown in Table 4–8.

Each factory can operate at either one-shift or two-shift operations. The costs and capacities are shown in Table 4–9.

Note that the fixed costs for the first shift are large because the general overhead of the factory is included, whereas the fixed costs of the second shift include only those fixed costs associated with operating the second shift.

Management is considering adding an additional 400 units of capacity to factory 3 (200 units to each shift). The variable cost would be $1 per unit on the first shift and $1.50 per unit on the second shift. Additional fixed charges would be $300 on the first shift and $50 on the

TABLE 4–8
Shipping Costs from Factories to Sales Regions

Factories \ *Sales Regions*	*1*	*2*	*3*	*4*	*5*	*Total Sales Requirements*
1	\$1	\$1	\$6	\$3	\$5	
2	2	1	4	1	6	
3	4	3	1	3	4	
Sale Requirements (units)	100	200	200	400	100	1,000

TABLE 4–9
Factory Operating Costs and Capacities

	First Shift			**Second Shift**		
	Variable Cost (per unit)	*Fixed Cost*	*Capacity (units)*	*Variable Cost (per unit)*	*Fixed Cost*	*Capacity (units)*
Factory 1	\$3.00	\$200	100	\$4.50	\$50	100
Factory 2	1.50	500	300	2.00	70	300
Factory 3	1.00	400	200	1.50	70	200

second shift. (These amounts would include the required return on investment.)

It is company policy not to operate any second shift below 40 percent of capacity nor any first shift below 60 percent of capacity (i.e., a shift either operates at zero or above these limits).

The company wants to determine the optimum shipping schedule (factories to warehouses). In addition, it wishes to find out whether or not the additional capacity should be added to factory 3 and which, if any, shifts should be shut down in the various factories. (Note that the closing down of both shifts means closing down the factory.)

Formulate the problem as a mixed-integer linear programming problem. (One caution—be sure your formulation guarantees that the second shift doesn't operate without a first shift.) To make the formulation easier to write down, you may use symbols instead of the numbers given in Tables 4–8 and 4–9.

4–19. The city of Shamut has called for bids for construction of its new town hall. The call for bids lists five parts of the total job:

F — Foundation
S — Structure
P — Plumbing and heating
E — Electrical
I — Interior

The bid procedure specified that bids could be made on different parts or combinations of parts of the job, and multiple bids were allowed.

Five area contractors, each considered reliable by Shamut, have submitted various bids. The bids for the five contractors—Able, Baker, Charley, Dog, and Easy—are shown in Table 4–10.

In addition, Easy specified in its bid that it would give a discount of 10 percent from the stated single-part bid amounts if it received the contract for four or more parts of the job.

Your task as city manager is to award contracts in such a way as to minimize the cost to Shamut of getting the whole job done.

One complicating factor is that contractors Able and Baker are feuding with each other, and each has specified in the bids that they will not accept the contract for any part if the other does any part of the job.

Formulate an integer linear programming model to help the city manager decide on what bids to accept. Use no more than 25 decision variables. Make your formulation general; that is, do not arbitrarily delete bids just because you can see that they are not going to be accepted. Your formulation should be general enough so that it would hold up with different bid prices (of course, with changes in these numbers in the model).

TABLE 4–10

Contractor	Bid Number	Job Parts in Bid	Bid Amount ($000s)
Able	1	*F* only	$ 700
	2	$F + S$	3,800
	3	$F + S + P$	4,500
Baker	1	$P + E$	1,100
	2	$P + E + I$	1,900
	3	Whole job	5,800
Charley	1	*P* only	700
	2	*E* only	600
	3	*I* only	1,000
	4	$P + E$	1,200
Dog	1	$S + P$	3,600
	2	$S + P + E$	4,100
	3	$F + S + P + E$	4,600
Easy	1	*F* only	900
	2	*S* only	3,200
	3	*P* only	800
	4	*E* only	500
	5	*I* only	1,200

4–20. The Wintel Company is building a new semiconductor processing plant. It must determine the capacity of the plant (annual Volume in millions of units of chips produced) and the number of different varieties of chips to be manufactured in the plant (Variety). There are economies of scale in plant volume, but diseconomies of scale as more variety is offered. However, increasing Variety produces higher revenues per chip. After careful study, company management has estimated that the following relationships determine plant construction cost, unit variable cost per chip, and unit revenue per chip:

Construction cost (millions of \$) $= 30 + 2*\text{Volume} - .004*\text{Volume}^2 + 0.1*\text{Variety}$

Unit variable cost (\$ per chip) $= 30 - 0.2*\text{Volume}^2 + 0.0003*\text{Variety}^2$

Unit revenue (\$ per chip) $= 42 + 0.05*\text{Variety}$

The upper limit on Volume is 5.0 million units per year; the upper limit on Variety is 100 different chip types. Due to rapidly changing technology, Wintel will write off the entire plant investment in two years. The company can sell all the chips the plant can make.

a. Formulate this problem as a general nonlinear programming problem and use Solver to solve it.

b. How sensitive is the net contribution to changes in Variety? Perform a "what if" analysis using different values of Variety.

CASE 4–21

THE ALLEN COMPANY

The Allen Company is involved in the development of residential property. Figure 4–13 shows a map of a new development in the planning stages.

The access roads are shown in the map and are broken into segments labeled *A* through *F*. In addition, the area is broken into five subsections (labeled I through V on the map). Allen plans to develop this entire subdivision over an 18-month period.

FIGURE 4–13
Map of Wuthering Heights Development

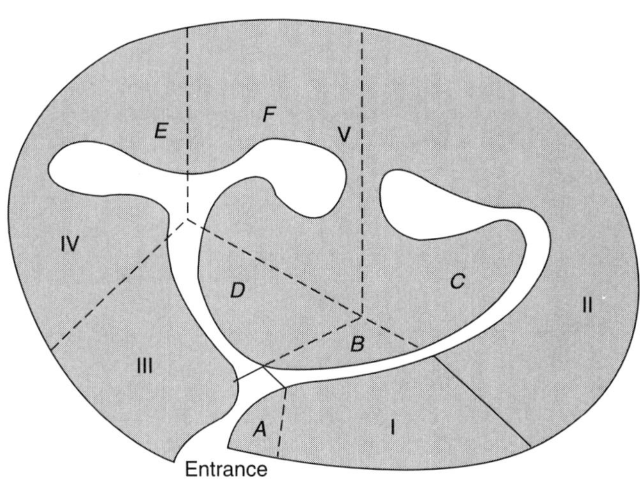

The planning problem involves determining the order in which the roads and subsections are to be built. For planning purposes, the time is broken into three half-year periods. In any period (half year), any number of road segments can be constructed (subject to financial constraints described below). The only restriction is that a segment cannot be constructed before the roads leading to it. (For example, segment *C* could not be constructed before segment *B*. However, they could be constructed simultaneously.)

Houses can be constructed in any subsection no sooner than *one period after* the access roads to that section are completed. The table below gives the access roads that must be finished at least one period before the various subsections can be developed:

Subsection	*Roads Required*
I	A, B
II	A, B, C
III	A, D
IV	A, D, E
V	A, D, F

Any number of subsections can be developed in any period, and they can be completed in one period. The only restrictions on subsection development are road construction (discussed above) and financial (see below).

Suppose the cost of constructing the various road segments are: K_A, K_B, . . . , K_F. Designate the cost of constructing the housing subsections as: C_I, C_{II}, . . . , C_V. These costs represent the net amount funded by the Allen Company over and above the construction mortgages available from the bank. These costs are incurred in the period when a subsection is developed.

Designate the profit received from selling a subsection as P_I, P_{II}, . . . , P_V. Again, these are net of the repayment of the mortgages on construction. The profits are received *one period after* development (that is, a one-period lag).

To finance this project, the Allen Company has available its own capital of $500,000. It also has the option of borrowing money from the bank (in addition to mortgage money).

However, the bank insists on lending the full amount of the loan over the whole period of the project. That is, if an amount L is to be borrowed, it is obtained at the beginning of the project and paid back in full (with interest) at the end of two years. The two-year period is necessary so that profits from sales of property in the third period (and received in the fourth half year) can be used to repay the loan. The minimum loan is $1 million (that is, either zero or at least $1 million must be borrowed). The interest rate is 10 percent per year.

Formulate this problem as a mixed-integer linear programming problem. Assume that if a subsection is to be developed in any period, it will be fully finished (that is, no partial completions). The objective is to minimize the amount of interest on the bank loan.

Case 4–22

Rodney Development Company[14]

Jane Rodney, president of the Rodney Development Company, was trying to decide what types of stores to include in her new shopping center at Puyallup Mall. She had already contracted for a supermarket, a drug store, and a few other stores that she considered essential. However, she had available an additional 16,000 square feet of floor space yet to allocate. She drew up a list of the 15 types of stores she might consider (Table 4–11), including the floor space required by each. Rodney did not think she would have any trouble finding occupants for any type of store.

The lease agreements Rodney used in her developments included two types of payment. The store had to pay a certain annual rent, depending on the size and type of store. In

Table 4–11
Characteristics of Possible Lessees, Puyallup Mall Shopping Center

Type of Store	*Size of Store (000s of sq. ft.)*	*Annual Rent ($000s)*	*Present Value ($000s)*	*Construction Cost ($000s)*
Clothing				
1. Men's	1.0	$ 4.4	$ 28.1	$ 24.6
2. Women's	1.6	6.1	34.6	32.0
3. Variety (both)	2.0	8.3	50.0	41.4
Restaurants				
4. Fancy restaurant	3.2	24.0	160.0	124.4
5. Lunch room	1.8	19.2	77.8	64.8
6. Cocktail lounge	2.1	20.7	100.4	79.8
7. Candy and ice-cream shop	1.2	7.7	45.2	38.6
Hardgoods				
8. Hardware shop	2.4	19.4	80.2	66.8
9. Cutlery and variety	1.6	11.7	51.4	45.1
10. Luggage and leather	2.0	15.2	62.5	54.3
Miscellaneous				
11. Travel agency	0.6	3.9	18.0	15.0
12. Tobacco shop	0.5	3.2	11.6	13.4
13. Camera store	1.4	11.3	50.4	42.0
14. Toys	2.0	16.0	73.6	63.7
15. Beauty parlor	1.0	9.6	51.2	40.0

[14]For an example of this type of problem, see J. C. Bean, C. E. Noon, S. M. Ryan, and G. J. Salton, "Selecting Tenants in a Shopping Mall," *Interfaces,* March–April 1988.

addition, Rodney was to receive a small percentage of the store's sales if the sales exceeded a specified minimum amount. The amount of annual rent from each store is shown in the second column of Table 4–11. In order to estimate the profitability of each type of store, Rodney calculated the present value of all future rent and sales percentage payments. These are given in the third column. Rodney wants to achieve the highest total *present value* over the set of stores she selects. However, she could not simply pick those stores with the highest present values, for there were several restrictions. The first, of course, was that she has available only 16,000 square feet.

In addition, a condition on the financing of the project required that the total annual rent should be at least as much as the annual fixed cost (taxes, management fees, debt service, and so forth). These annual costs were \$130,000 for this part of the project. Finally, the total funds available for construction of this part of the project were \$700,000, and each type of store required different construction costs depending on the size and type of store (fourth column in the table).

In addition, Rodney had certain requirements in terms of the mix of stores that she considered best. She wanted at least one store from each of the Clothing, Hardgoods, and Miscellaneous groups, and at least two from the Restaurant category. She wanted no more than two from the Clothing group. Furthermore, the number of stores in the Miscellaneous group should not exceed the total number of stores in the Clothing and Hardgoods groups combined.

Formulate Rodney's problem as an integer linear programming problem.

Solutions to Practice Problems

4–1. *a.* $Y_{11} + Y_{21} + Y_{31} + Y_{41} + Y_{51} \leq 1$

b. $Y_{21} \leq Y_{31}$; $Y_{22} \leq Y_{31} + Y_{32}$
$Y_{23} \leq Y_{31} + Y_{32} + Y_{33}$

c. $Y_{11} + Y_{21} + Y_{31} + Y_{41} + Y_{51} \geq 1$
$Y_{12} + Y_{22} + Y_{32} + Y_{42} + Y_{52} \geq 1$
$Y_{13} + Y_{23} + Y_{33} + Y_{43} + Y_{53} \geq 1$

d. $Y_{41} + Y_{42} = 1$

e. $Y_{11} + Y_{51} \leq 1$; $Y_{12} + Y_{52} \leq 1$; $Y_{13} + Y_{53} \leq 1$

4–2. Let X_1 through X_8 be zero/one variables that have a value 1 if a project is funded, and value 0 if not. Then:

Maximize: $40X_1 + 10X_2 + 80X_3 + 50X_4 + 20X_5 + 5X_6 + 80X_7 + 100X_8$
Subject to: $80X_1 + 15X_2 + 120X_3 + 65X_4 + 20X_5 + 10X_6 + 60X_7 + 100X_8 \leq 320$ (funds constraint); $X_7 + X_8 \leq 1$ (not both projects G and H); $X_4 \leq X_1$ (no project D unless also A).

The solution calls for funding A, C, E, and H. Total value is 240 units, and the total funds of \$320,000 are all utilized. The Excel Solver model and solution are shown in Figure 4–14.

4–3. *a.* Let Y_1 be a binary variable, with $Y_1 = 1$ if the stamping machine is used and 0 otherwise. An additional constraint $K \leq 200\ Y_1$ is added; and $-800Y_1$ is added to the objective function.

b. Let Y_2 be a binary variable, with $Y_2 = 1$ if 1,000 or more units are purchased, and 0 otherwise. Let R_1 be raw material purchased at the \$.25 price, and R_2 be units of raw material purchased at the \$.20 price. The following constraints are added: RMUSED $\leq R_1 + R_2$; $R_2 \geq 1{,}000\ Y_2$; and $R_2 \leq MY_2$, where M is a very large number. Add to the objective function: $-0.25R_1 - 0.20R_2$. The constraint $R_1 \leq 1{,}000\ (1 - Y_2)$ could also be added, but it is not necessary.

c. Let K_1 be the number of KARMAs sold at the \$100 price, K_2 be the number sold at the \$150 price, and K_3 be the number sold at the \$120 price. Let Z_1 be a binary variable with value of 1 if 20 or less units are produced; Z_2 is also a binary variable with value of 1 if production is between 20 and 70 units; and Z_3 is a binary variable with value of 1 if production exceeds 70 units.

New constraints: $K = K_1 + K_2 + K_3$; $K_1 \leq 20Z_1$; $K_2 \leq 50Z_2$; $K_3 \leq 130Z_3$; $K_1 \geq 20Z_2$; $K_2 \geq 50Z_3$; and $Z_1 \geq Z_2$ and $Z_2 \geq Z_3$. (Actually, the last constraint isn't necessary.) Add to the objective function: $100K_1 + 150K_2 + 120K_3$.

d. Let W_1 be a binary variable that takes on a value of 1 if the campaign is to be undertaken for ANZAs and 0 otherwise; similarly, $W_2 = 1$ if the campaign is done for BOZOs. Then, the following constraints are added: $A \leq 100 + 50W_1$; $B \leq 120 + 50W_2$; $W_1 + W_2 \leq 1$. Add to the objective function: $-5{,}000W_1 - 5{,}000W_2$.

FIGURE 4–14 Solver Solution for Problem 4–2.

	A	B	C	D	E	F	G	H	I	J	K	L
1					Projects							
2		A	B	C	D	E	F	G	H			
3	Objective: Value	40	10	80	50	20	5	80	100			
4												Total Value
5	Decision (fund/no)	1	0	1	0	1	0	0	1			240
6	Constraints:											
7	Cost	80	15	120	65	20	10	60	100	320	≤	320
8	Not both G & H							1	1	1	≤	1
9	No D unless A	-1			1					-1	≤	0
10												
11				Equations:								
12				Cell	Equation							
13				J7	=SUMPRODUCT(B7:I7,$B$5:$I$5)							
14				J8	=SUMPRODUCT(B8:I8,$B$5:$I$5)							
15				J9	=SUMPRODUCT(B9:I9,$B$5:$I$5)							
16				L5	=SUMPRODUCT(B3:I3,$B$5:$I$5)							
17												
18				Solver Parameters Box Values								
19												
20				Iarget Cell (maximlze)				**L5**				
21				Changing Cells:			**B5:15**					
22				Constraints:			**J7:J9 ≤ L7:L9**					
23							**B5:I5 ≤ 1**					
24							**B5:I5 ≥ 0**					
25							**B5:15 integer**					

4–4. *a.* X_1 = Units of product A; X_2 = Units of product B;
$2X_1 \le 30$ (unskilled labor); $4X_1 + 5X_2 \le 100$ (machine time)

b. Skilled labor: $X_1 + 5X_2 + U_1 - E_1 = 75$
Raw material: $5X_1 + 4X_2 + U_2 - E_2 = 100$
Profit: $15X_1 + 10X_2 + U_3 - E_3 = 300$

c. Minimize $5U_1 + 10E_1 - 5U_2 + 15E_2 + U_3 - E_3$

d. See the graph in Figure 4–15.

e. (1) $U_1 = E_1 = E_2 = E_3 = 0$; $U_2 = 5$; $U_3 = 41.7$;
Objective function = 16.7

(2) $E_1 = U_2 = E_2 = E_3 = 0$; $U_1 = 8.3$; $U_3 = 22.3$;
Objective function = 63.6

(3) $E_1 = U_2 = U_3 = 0$; $U_1 = 20$; $E_2 = 7$; $E_3 = 5$;
Objective function = 200

(4) $E_1 = U_2 = E_2 = E_3 = 0$; $U_1 = 28.75$; $U_3 = 12.5$;
Objective function = 156.3

Alternative 1 is the lowest. Note that this plan actually is under the profit goal by \$41.7, but it has a value of \$25 for returning five units of raw material.

Figure 4–15

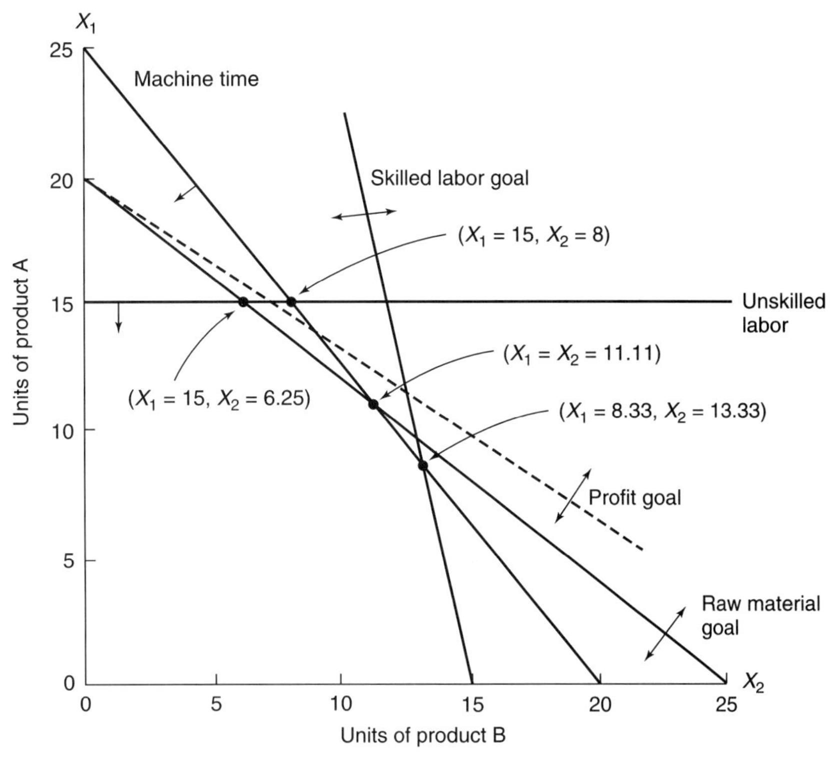

X_1
25
20
15
10
5
0
Units of product A
Machine time
Skilled labor goal
$(X_1 = 15, X_2 = 8)$
Unskilled labor
$(X_1 = X_2 = 11.11)$
$(X_1 = 15, X_2 = 6.25)$
$(X_1 = 8.33, X_2 = 13.33)$
Profit goal
Raw material goal
X_2
0
5
10
15
20
25
Units of product B

PART

II Decision Analysis

Motivating Example

Modeling Space Shuttle Tiles[1]

The Space Shuttle has about 25,000 black tiles on its underside to protect the shuttle from the extreme heat that occurs on its reentry into the Earth's atmosphere prior to landing. After each flight, some of these tiles are repaired and others have to be replaced. In seeking a systematic way to assess the risk of shuttle failure (loss of vehicle or crew) due to tile failure, Pate-Cornell and Fischbeck applied a technique called probabilistic risk analysis to this situation.

On a typical shuttle flight, a few hundred of the 25,000 tiles are damaged, mostly by debris or debonding (separation). Tile loss per se will not cause the loss of the vehicle, but the increased heating or burn-through of the aluminum skin can lead to failure of critical components. Among all 25,000 tiles, some have higher probabilities of being damaged by debris, some are subject to higher head load during reentry, and some protect critical flight controls and other critical systems.

The researchers divided all 25,000 tiles into 33 "zones" based on the following probabilities:

1. How susceptible they were to damage.
2. The vulnerability of adjacent tiles once one was lost.
3. The probability of burn-through.
4. The probability of loss of a critical subsystem following a burn-through.

Assessing these probabilities required the use of both historical data on debris and debonding and expert assessments of the probability of losing the shuttle given that a particular subsystem was exposed to high temperatures. The analysis enabled NASA managers to rank the tiles on a risk-criticality index and set priorities for maintenance operations.

The study showed that focusing on improved methods for securing the insulation on parts of the shuttle (in particular, the external tank and the solid rocket boosters) had a large payoff in reducing the likelihood of debris-caused failure. Also, external inspection of the most risk-critical tiles for weak bonding had a similarly large payoff. In sum, the recommended improvements could reduce the probability of a shuttle accident attributable to tile failure by about 70 percent.

[1]See M.-Elisabeth Paté-Cornell and Paul S. Fischbeck, "Risk Management for the Tiles of the Space Shuttle," *Interfaces,* January–February 1994, pp. 64–86.

CHAPTER

5 INTRODUCTION TO PROBABILITY

If all business decisions could be made under conditions of certainty, the only valid justification for a poor decision would be failure to consider all the pertinent facts. With *certainty,* one can make a *perfect* forecast of the future. Unfortunately, however, the manager rarely if ever operates in a world of certainty. Usually, the manager is forced to make decisions when there is uncertainty as to what will happen after the decisions are made. In this latter situation, the mathematical theory of probability furnishes a tool that can be of great help to the decision maker.

In this chapter, we shall present some of the notation and basic relationships of probability theory that the reader will apply in later chapters. Although the mathematics of probability is well defined, it will soon become obvious to the person attempting to apply the models of this book that there is a great deal of uncertainty concerning the informational inputs that are required. Also, many of the models abstract from the complexities of the real world.

Objective and Subjective Probabilities

Most of us are familiar with the laws of chance regarding coin flipping. If someone asks about the probability of a head on one toss of a coin, the answer will be one-half, or 0.50. This answer is based on common experience with coins, and assumes that the coin is a *fair* coin and that it is "fairly" tossed. This is an example of **objective probability.** There are two interpretations of objective probability. The first relies on the **symmetry of outcomes** and implies that outcomes that are identical in essential aspects should have the same probability. A *fair* coin is defined to be one that is evenly balanced and has two sides that are identical (except for minor differences in the image). Hence, each side should have equal probability of one-half (ignoring the possibility of the coin landing on its edge). If the coin were bent, weighted, or two-tailed, the answer would be different. As another example, suppose we have a box containing three red and seven black balls (that are the same size, have the same feel, and are otherwise identical except for color), and the balls are thoroughly mixed. The symmetry of outcome interpretation would assign a 0.10 probability to each ball, and hence a 0.30 chance of drawing a red ball.

The **relative frequency** interpretation of objective probability relies on historical experience in identical situations. Thus, if a coin has been flipped 10,000 times with 4,998 heads, we would conclude that the probability was 0.50 (i.e., 4,998/10,000 rounded) for a head the next time the coin was flipped in the same manner as before.

A **subjective interpretation** of probabilities is often useful for business decision making. In the case of objective probability, definitive historical information, common experience (objective evidence), or rigorous analysis lie behind the probability assignment. In the case of subjective interpretation, quantitative historical information may not be available; and instead of objective evidence, personal experience becomes the basis of the probability assignment. For managerial decision-making purposes, the subjective interpretation is frequently required, since reliable objective evidence may not be available.

In contrast to the coin flipping situation, assume a manager is trying to decide whether or not to build a new factory, and the success of the factory depends largely on whether or not there is a recession in the next five years. A probability assigned to the occurrence of a recession would be a subjective weight. A long history and common experience that can be projected into the future with confidence are not directly available, as in the coin or ball examples. However, it may be appropriate, and indeed necessary, to consider the event "occurrence of a recession"; and after gathering evidence and using business judgment, the manager may be able to assign a probability to that event that could be used for decision-making purposes. There would certainly be less agreement on this probability than there would be on the probabilities of drawing a red ball, or of a fair coin coming up heads. Since we are primarily concerned in this book with management decisions, we shall often assign subjective probabilities to events that have a critical bearing on the management decision. This procedure aims to ensure consistency between a decision maker's judgment about the likelihood of the possible states of nature and the decision that is made.

One important objective of the suggested decision process is to allow the decision maker to think in terms of the possible events that may occur after a decision, the consequences of these events, and the probabilities of these events and consequences, rather than having the manager jump immediately to the question of whether or not the decision is desirable.

Basic Statements of Probability

Two fundamental statements about probabilities are:

1. Probabilities of all the various possible outcomes of a trial must sum to one.
2. Probabilities are always greater than or equal to zero (i.e., probabilities are never negative) and are less than or equal to one. The smaller the probability, the less likely the event.

The first statement indicates that if A and B are the only candidates for an office, the probability that A will win plus the probability that B will win must sum to one (assuming a tie is not possible).

The second statement results in the following interpretations. If an event has a positive probability, it may possibly occur; the event may be impossible, in which case it has a zero probability; or the event may be certain to occur, in which case the

Table 5–1

Event: Elect	*Probability*
Democratic candidate A	0.18
Democratic candidate B	0.42
Republican candidate C	0.26
Republican candidate D	0.14
	1.00

probability is equal to one. Regardless of whether probabilities are interpreted as objective probabilities or as subjective weights, it is useful to think in terms of a weighting scale running from zero to one. If someone tosses a coin of unknown characteristics 500 times to obtain an estimate of objective probabilities and the results are 225 heads and 275 tails, the range of possible results may be converted to a zero-to-one scale by dividing by 500. The actual results are 225/500 = 0.45 heads and 275/500 = 0.55 tails. Hence, if we wish to derive probabilities, we shall manipulate the data so as to adhere to the zero-to-one scale. The 0.45 and the 0.55 may be used as estimators of the true probabilities of heads and tails (the true probabilities are unknown).

Mutually Exclusive Events

Two or more events are **mutually exclusive** if only one of the events can occur on any one trial. The probabilities of mutually exclusive events can be added to obtain the probability that one of a given collection of the events will occur.

Example
The probabilities shown in Table 5–1 reflect the subjective estimate of a newspaper editor regarding the relative chances of four candidates for a public office (assume a tie is not possible).

These events are mutually exclusive, since in one election (or in one trial) only one event may occur; therefore the probabilities are additive. The probability of a Democratic victory is 0.60; of a Republican victory, 0.40; or of either B or C winning, 0.68. The probability of both B and C winning is zero, since only one of the mutually exclusive events can occur on any one trial.

Independent Events

Events may be either independent or dependent. If two events are (statistically) **independent,** the occurrence of one event will not affect the probability of the occurrence of the second event.[2]

[2]Statistical independence or dependence is to be distinguished from causal independence or dependence. Simply because two events are statistically dependent on each other does not imply that one is caused by the other. Whenever we use the terms *dependence* or *independence,* we mean statistical dependence or independence.

When two (or more) events are independent, the probability of both events (or more than two events) occurring is equal to the product of the probabilities of the individual events. That is:

$$P(A \text{ and } B) = P(A) \cdot P(B) \quad \text{if } A,B \text{ independent} \tag{5–1}$$

where

$P(A \text{ and } B)$ = Probability of events A and B both occurring
$P(A)$ = Probability of event A
$P(B)$ = Probability of event B

Equation 5–1 indicates that the probability of A and B both occurring is equal to the probability of A times the probability of B, if A and B are independent. If A is the probability of a head on the first toss of the coin, and B is the probability of a head on the second toss of the coin, then:

$$P(A) = \tfrac{1}{2}$$
$$P(B) = \tfrac{1}{2}$$
$$P(A \text{ and } B) = \tfrac{1}{2} \cdot \tfrac{1}{2} = \tfrac{1}{4}$$

The probability of A and then B occurring (two heads) is one-fourth. $P(A \text{ and } B)$ is the **joint probability** of events A and B. Where appropriate, the word *and* can be omitted to simplify the notation, and the joint probability can be written simply as $P(AB)$.

To define independence mathematically, we need the symbol $P(B|A)$. The symbol $P(B|A)$ is read "the probability of event B, given that event A has occurred." $P(B|A)$ is the **conditional probability** of event B, given that event A has taken place. Note that $P(B|A)$ does not mean the probability of event B divided by A—the vertical line followed by A means "given that event A has occurred."

With independent events:

$$P(B|A) = P(B) \quad \text{if } A,B \text{ independent} \tag{5–2}$$

That is, the probability of event B, given that event A has occurred, is equal to the probability of event B if the two events are independent. With two independent events, the occurrence of the one event does not affect the probability of the occurrence of the second [in like manner, $P(A|B) = P(A)$]. Equations 5–1 and 5–2 are the basic definitions of independence between two events.

Dependent Events

Two events are **dependent** if the occurrence of one of the events affects the probability of the occurrence of the second event.

Example: Dependent Events

Flip a fair coin and determine whether the result is heads or tails. If heads, flip the same coin again. If tails, flip an unfair coin that has a three-fourths probability of heads and a one-fourth probability of tails. Is the probability of heads on the second toss in any way affected by the result of the first toss? The answer here is yes, since the result of the first toss affects which coin (fair or unfair) is to be tossed the second time.

Another example of dependent events involves mutually exclusive events. If events A and B are mutually exclusive, they are dependent. Given that event A has occurred, the conditional probability of *B* occurring must be zero, since the two events are mutually exclusive. That is, $P(B|A) = 0$ if events *A* and *B* are mutually exclusive.

Summary

A probability is a number between zero and one representing the likelihood of the occurrence of some event. Probabilities may be objective, if based on symmetry or a large amount of experience, or subjective, if based on the judgment of the decision maker. The probability of the occurrence of one of two or more mutually exclusive events is the sum of the probabilities of the events. Two events are independent if the occurrence of one does not affect the probability of occurrence of the other.

Conditional, Marginal, and Joint Probabilities

We now introduce a very important probability relationship:

$$P(B|A) = \frac{P(A \text{ and } B)}{P(A)} \quad \text{if } P(A) \neq 0 \tag{5–3}$$

The conditional probability of event *B*, given that event *A* has occurred, is equal to the joint probability of *A* and *B*, divided by the probability of event *A*.

We can multiply both sides of the equation by $P(A)$ and rewrite Equation 5–3 as:

$$P(A \text{ and } B) = P(B|A) \cdot P(A) \tag{5–4}$$

That is, the joint probability of *A* and *B* is equal to the conditional probability of *B* given *A* times the probability of *A*.

Let us look at these formulas assuming independent events. By Equation 5–3:

$$P(B|A) = \frac{P(A \text{ and } B)}{P(A)}$$

But by Equation 5–1:

$$P(A \text{ and } B) = P(A) \cdot P(B)$$

for independent events. Substituting $P(A) \cdot P(B)$ for $P(A \text{ and } B)$ in Equation 5–3 gives:

$$P(B|A) = \frac{P(A) \cdot P(B)}{P(A)} = P(B) \tag{5–2}$$

This is the mathematical definition of independence given earlier in Equation 5–2.

We shall next make use of two examples to illustrate:

1. Unconditional (marginal) probabilities. The term **marginal** refers to the fact that the probabilities are found in the margins of a joint probability table (see Table 5–3, a little later in this chapter); they sum to one. A marginal probability refers to the probability of the occurrence of an event not

conditional on the occurrence of another event. $P(A)$ and $P(B)$ are examples of unconditional or marginal probabilities.

2. Conditional probabilities, such as $P(A|B)$ and $P(B|A)$.
3. Joint probabilities, such as $P(A \text{ and } B)$ or $P(AB)$.

Example 1

Assume we have three boxes, which contain red and black balls as follows:

Box 1: 3 red and 7 black
Box 2: 6 red and 4 black
Box 3: 8 red and 2 black

Suppose we draw a ball from box 1; if it is red, we draw a ball from box 2. If the ball drawn from box 1 is black, we draw a ball from box 3. The diagram in Figure 5–1 illustrates the game. Consider the following probability questions about this game:

1. What is the probability of drawing a red ball from box 1? This probability is an *unconditional* or *marginal* probability; it is 0.30. (The marginal probability of getting a black is 0.70.)
2. Suppose we draw a ball from box 1, and it is red; what is the probability of another red ball when we draw from box 2 on the second draw? The answer is 0.60. This is an example of a *conditional probability.* That is, the probability of a red ball on the second draw if the draw from box 1 is red is a conditional probability.
3. Suppose our first draw from box 1 was black; what is the *conditional* probability of our second draw (from box 3 this time) being red? The probability is 0.80. The draw from box 1 (the conditioning event) is very important in determining the probabilities of red (or black) on the second draw.
4. Suppose, before we draw any balls, we ask the question: What is the probability of drawing two red balls? This would be a *joint* probability; the event would be a red ball on both draws. The computation of this joint probability is a little more complicated than the above questions, and some analysis will be of value. Computations are as follows:

$$P(A \text{ and } B) = P(B|A) \cdot P(A) \tag{5–4}$$

FIGURE 5–1

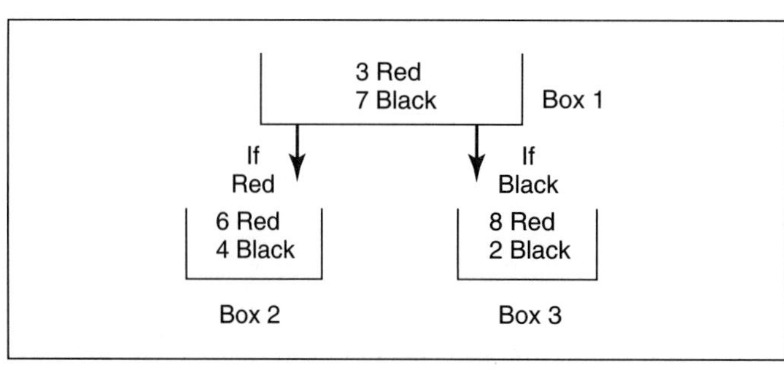

Table 5–2 and Figure 5–2 show the joint probability of two red balls as 0.18 [i.e., $P(R$ and $R)$ or more simply $P(RR)$, the top branch of the tree]. The joint probabilities may be summarized as follows:

Two red balls	$P(RR) = 0.18$
A red ball on first draw and a black ball on second draw	$P(RB) = 0.12$
A black ball on first draw and a red ball on second draw	$P(BR) = 0.56$
Two black balls	$P(BB) = 0.14$
	1.00

TABLE 5–2

	Marginal	•	Conditional	=	Joint
Event	$P(A)$	·	$P(B\|A)$	=	$P(A \text{ and } B)$
RR	$P(R) = 0.30$		$P(R\|R) = 0.60$		$P(RR) = 0.18$
RB	$P(R) = 0.30$		$P(B\|R) = 0.40$		$P(RB) = 0.12$
BR	$P(B) = 0.70$		$P(R\|B) = 0.80$		$P(BR) = 0.56$
BB	$P(B) = 0.70$		$P(B\|B) = 0.20$		$P(BB) = 0.14$

FIGURE 5–2
Tree Diagram

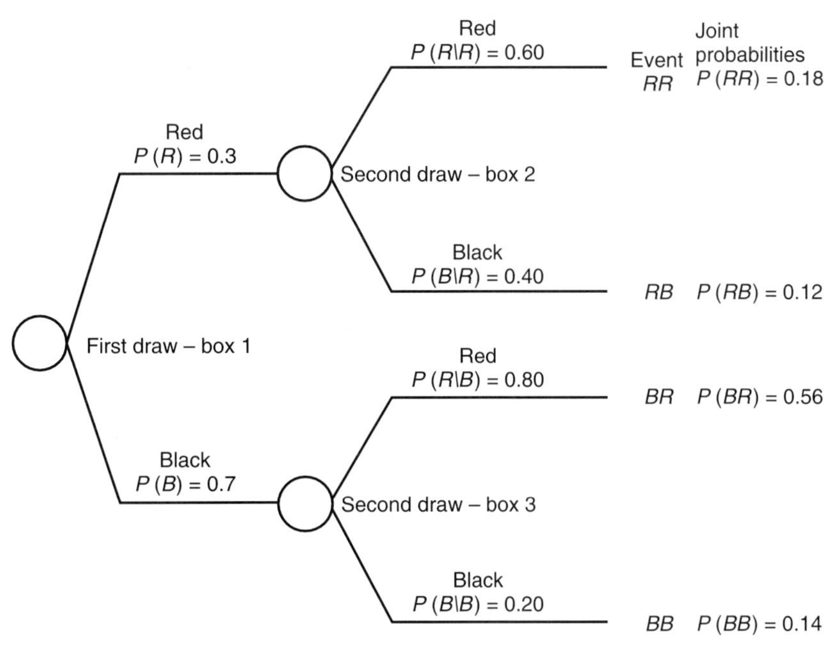

Figure 5–2 is called a **tree diagram.** This is a very useful device for illustrating uncertain situations. The first fork shows that either a red or a black may be drawn, and the probabilities of these events are given. If a red is drawn, we go to box 2, where again a red or black may be drawn, but with probabilities determined by the fact that the draw will take place in box 2. For the second forks, we have conditional probabilities (the probabilities depend on whether a red or a black ball was chosen on the first draw). At the end of each path are the joint probabilities of following that path. The joint probabilities are obtained by multiplying the marginal (unconditional) probabilities of the first branch by the conditional probabilities of the second branch.

Table 5–3 presents these results in a joint probability table; the intersections of the rows and columns are *joint* probabilities. The column on the right gives the unconditional probabilities (*marginals*) of the outcome of the first draw; the bottom row gives the *unconditional* or *marginal* probabilities of the outcomes of the second draw. Table 5–3 effectively summarizes the tree diagram.

Now, let us compute some additional probabilities:

1. Probability of one red and one black ball, regardless of order: $= 0.56 + 0.12 = 0.68$
2. Probability of a black ball on draw 2: $= 0.26$

   Explanatory calculation:

   Probability of red–black $= 0.12$

   Probability of black–black $= 0.14$

   Probability of black on draw 2 $= 0.26$
3. Probability of second draw being red *if* first draw is red: $= 0.60$

   If first draw is red, we are in the *R* row of Table 5–3, which totals 0.30. The question is, what proportion is 0.18 of 0.30? The answer is 0.60; or in terms of the appropriate formula:

$$P(R_2|R_1) = \frac{P(R_2 \text{ and } R_1)}{P(R_1)} = \frac{0.18}{0.30} = 0.60$$

TABLE 5–3
Joint Probability Table

First Draw \ Second Draw	*R*	*B*	*Marginal Probability of Outcome on First Draw*
R	*P*(*RR*) 0.18	*P*(*RB*) 0.12	0.30
B	*P*(*BR*) 0.56	*P*(*BB*) 0.14	0.70
Marginal Probability of Outcome on Second Draw	0.74	0.26	1.00

TABLE 5–4

Event	Probability	Formula
HH	$P(HH) = \frac{1}{2} \cdot \frac{1}{2} = \frac{1}{4}$	$P(H) \cdot P(H)$
HT	$P(HT) = \frac{1}{2} \cdot \frac{1}{2} = \frac{1}{4}$	$P(H) \cdot P(T)$
TH	$P(TH) = \frac{1}{2} \cdot \frac{1}{2} = \frac{1}{4}$	$P(T) \cdot P(H)$
TT	$P(TT) = \frac{1}{2} \cdot \frac{1}{2} = \frac{1}{4}$	$P(T) \cdot P(T)$

Example 2

Suppose a fair coin is flipped twice and we ask for the following probabilities:

1. Probability of two heads.
2. Probability of one head and one tail in two flips.
3. Probability of the second toss being a head.
4. Probability of the second toss being a head, given that the first toss is a tail.

Table 5–4 gives all possible outcomes from two tosses and their probabilities. Now, using the table, we can determine the four requested probabilities:

1. $P(HH) = \frac{1}{4}$
2. $P(HT + TH) = \frac{1}{2}$
3. $P(HH + TH) = \frac{1}{2}$
4. $P(H|T) = \dfrac{P(TH)}{P(T)} = \dfrac{\frac{1}{4}}{\frac{1}{2}} = \frac{1}{2}$

One important feature of the above example is that it illustrates *independence.* Note that the last two probabilities computed are the same; the probability of a head on the second toss is one-half, regardless of the outcome of the first toss. The two events are said to be *independent,* since the probability of heads on the second toss is not affected by the outcome of the first toss. That was not the case in Example 1, where the probability of a red ball on the second draw was affected by the outcome of the first draw. To summarize this result:

Dependence (Example 1)

$$\text{Conditional probability of red on second draw, given red on first draw} = \frac{\text{Joint probability of } RR\ (0.18)}{\text{Marginal probability of red on first draw } (0.30)} = 0.60$$

General formula:

$$P(B|A) = \frac{P(A \text{ and } B)}{P(A)} \tag{5–3}$$

Independence (Example 2)

$$\text{Conditional probability of a head on second toss, given a tail on first toss} = \frac{\text{Joint probability of } TH(\frac{1}{4})}{\text{Marginal probability of tail on first toss } (\frac{1}{2})} = \text{0.50, marginal probability of tossing a head}$$

TABLE 5–5
Survey of 100 Families, Classified by Income and Buying Behavior

	Low Income (family income below $30,000)	*High Income (family income of $30,000 or more)*	*Total Number of Families*
Family is:			
Buyer of specialty food products	18	20	38
Nonbuyer	42	20	62
Total number of families	60	40	100

General formula:

$$P(B|A) = P(B) \tag{5–2}$$

if B is independent of A.

Example 3
We give a further illustration of the basic probability definitions. A survey is taken of 100 families; information is obtained about family income and about whether the family purchases a specialty food product. The results are shown in Table 5–5.

Suppose a family is to be selected at random from this group.

1. What is the probability that the family selected will be a buyer? Since 38 of the 100 families overall are buyers, the probability is 0.38. Note that this is a *marginal* or *unconditional* probability.
2. What is the probability that the selected family is both a buyer and with high income? Note that this is a *joint* probability. P(Buyer and High income) = 20/100 = 0.20.
3. Suppose that a family is selected at random and you are informed that it has high income. What is the probability that this family is a buyer? Note that this asks for the *conditional* probability P(Buyer|High income). Of the 40 families with High income, 20 are Buyers. Hence, the probability is 20/40 = 0.50.
4. Are the events Buyer and High income independent for this group of families? Note from question 1 that P(Buyer) = 0.38; from question 3, P(Buyer|High income) = 0.50. These are not the same. Hence, the two events are *dependent.* Knowing that the family has high income affects the probability that it is a buyer. Another way of expressing this dependence is to say that the percentage of buyers is not the same for the high- and low-income families.

Revision or Probabilities

Having discussed joint and conditional probabilities, let us investigate how probabilities are revised to take account of new information.

Suppose we do not know whether a particular coin is fair or unfair. If the coin is fair, the probability of a tail is 0.50; but if the coin is unfair, the probability of a tail is 0.10. Assume we assign a prior probability to the coin being fair of 0.80 and

FIGURE 5–3

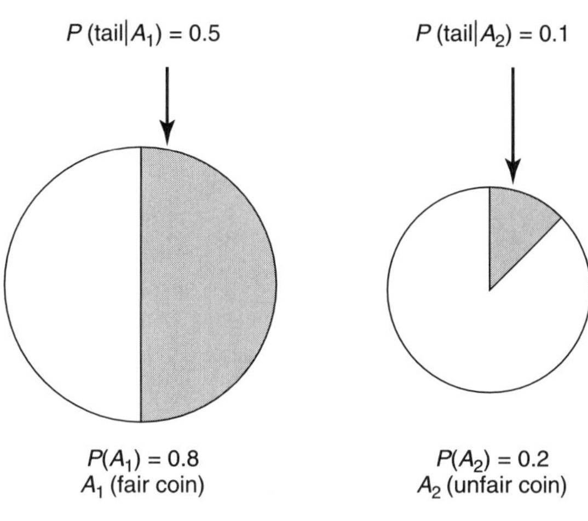

a probability of 0.20 to the coin being unfair. The event "fair coin" will be designated A_1, and the event "unfair coin" will be designated A_2. We toss the coin once; say, a tail is the result. What is the probability that the coin is fair?

Figure 5–3 shows that the conditional probability of a tail, given that the coin is fair, is 0.50; that is, $P(\text{tail}|A_1) = 0.50$. If the coin is unfair, the probability of a tail is 0.10; $P(\text{tail}|A_2) = 0.10$.

Let us compute the joint probability $P(\text{tail and } A_1)$. There is an initial 0.80 probability that A_1 is the true state; and if A_1 is the true state, there is a 0.50 conditional probability that a tail will result. The joint probability of state A_1 being true and obtaining a tail is $(0.80 \cdot 0.50) = 0.40$. Thus:

$$P(\text{tail and } A_1) = P(A_1) \cdot P(\text{tail}|A_1) = 0.80 \cdot 0.50 = 0.40$$

The joint probability of a tail *and* A_2 is equal to:

$$P(\text{tail and } A_2) = P(A_2) \cdot P(\text{tail}|A_2) = 0.20 \cdot 0.10 = 0.02$$

A tail can occur in combination with the state "fair coin" or in combination with the state "unfair coin." The probability of the former combination is 0.40; of the latter, 0.02. The sum of the probabilities gives the unconditional probability of a tail on the first toss; that is, $P(\text{tail}) = 0.40 + 0.02 = 0.42$:

$$\begin{aligned} P(\text{tail and } A_2) &= 0.02 \\ P(\text{tail and } A_1) &= \underline{0.40} \\ P(\text{tail}) &= 0.42 \end{aligned}$$

If a tail occurs, and if we do not know the true state, the conditional probability of state A_1 being the true state is, using Equation 5–3:

$$P(A_1|\text{tail}) = \frac{P(\text{tail and } A_1)}{P(\text{tail})} = \frac{0.40}{0.42} = 0.95$$

Thus, 0.95 is the **revised** or **posterior probability** of A_1, given that a tail has occurred on the first toss.

Similarly:

$$P(A_2|\text{tail}) = \frac{P(\text{tail and } A_2)}{P(\text{tail})} = \frac{0.02}{0.42} = 0.05$$

In more general symbols:

$$P(A_i|B) = \frac{P(A_i \text{ and } B)}{P(B)}$$

Conditional probability expressed in this form is known as **Bayes theorem.** It has many important applications in evaluating the worth of additional information in decision problems.

In this example, the *revised probabilities* for the coin are 0.95 that it is fair and 0.05 that it is unfair (the probabilities were initially 0.80 and 0.20). These revised probabilities exist after one toss when the toss results in a tail. It is reasonable that the probability that the coin is unfair has decreased, since a tail appeared on the first toss, and the unfair coin has only a 0.10 probability of a tail.

Example 4: The Monty Hall Puzzle

For over 25 years, there was a very popular program on television called "Let's Make a Deal," hosted by Monty Hall. As a part of the show, contestants were presented with three doors. Behind one was a big prize—a fancy new automobile. Behind the other two were nonprizes—a goat or something similar. The contestant picks a door, but before it is opened, Monty may open one of the other doors to reveal a goat. Monty then offers the contestant the choice of keeping his original choice or of switching to the other unopened door. Should the contestant switch or not?

This is the question posed and answered by columnist Marilyn vos Savant (billed as having the highest IQ in the world). This column generated thousands and thousands of letters, many disagreeing with Ms. vos Savant's conclusion.

One assumption needs to be made explicit before attacking this puzzle. Assume that Monty always opens one of the other doors after the contestant has picked, and that he only opens the door with a goat. (Monty knows where the goats are.) Before reading on, you might think about whether the contestant should switch. Some think that, because Monty only opens a door with a goat, there is no new information and the probabilities do not change. Some argue that the odds are 50–50 for the prize being in the other door. Ms. vos Savant argued that the contestant should switch. What is your answer?

The analysis of this problem is an application of the revision of probabilities. Let us assume that our contestant chooses door 2—the analysis for any other choice is similar. Table 5–6 shows the conditional probabilities about which door is opened by Monty, given which door has the Big Prize. This is a description of Monty's behavior. If the prize is behind door 1, then he will open door 3 (remember, the contestant has chosen door 2). If the prize is actually behind door 2, then Monty can choose either door 1 or 3 with equal chance. And finally, if the prize is behind door 3, he opens door 1.

Initially, there is an equal chance (i.e., ⅓) that the big prize is behind any door. So we can compute the joint probability table as shown in Table 5–7. These values are obtained by using the rule $P(A \text{ and } B) = B(A|B)\, P(B)$.

TABLE 5–6
Conditional Probability Table
Prob(Door Opened by Monty|Door with Big Prize)

Big Prize Is Behind	*Monty Opens Door*		
	Door 1	*Door 2*	*Door 3*
Door 1	0	0	1
Door 2	½	0	½
Door 3	1	0	0

TABLE 5–7
Joint Probability Table
Prob(Big Prize Door *and* Door Opened by Monty)

Big Prize Is Behind	*Monty Opens Door*			*Marginal Probability*
	Door 1	*Door 2*	*Door 3*	
Door 1	0	0	⅓	⅓
Door 2	⅙	0	⅙	⅓
Door 3	⅓	0	0	⅓
Marginal Probability	½	0	½	

Now suppose, as indicated earlier, our contestant initially chooses door 2, and then Monty opens door 1. Should the contestant switch? We can calculate the probability of winning the big prize for the two strategies, switch and stay:

Switch

Prob(Door 3 has Big Prize|Monty opens door 1) =

P(Big Prize is door 3 and Monty opens door 1)/P(Monty opens door 1) =

(1/3)/(1/2) = 2/3

Stay

Prob(Door 2 has Big Prize|Monty opens door 1) =

P(Big Prize is door 2 and Monty opens door 1)/P(Monty opens door 1) =

(1/6)/(1/2) = 1/3

The contestant should switch—the odds are two-thirds that the prize is behind the other door. If Monty had opened door 3, the analysis would be exactly the same and the contestant should switch to door 1. Similarly, if the contestant initially had chosen some door other than door 2, the same analysis would be done.

Another view of the problem is presented in the tree diagram in Figure 5–4. Here, the initial probability of the contestant choosing a door with a goat behind it is ⅔. Under that circumstance, when Monty reveals the second goat, then switching would guarantee the prize (see upper branch of Figure 5–4). On the other hand, if the original door chosen contained the prize, then switching would lead to a goat.

FIGURE 5–4
Monty Hall Puzzle

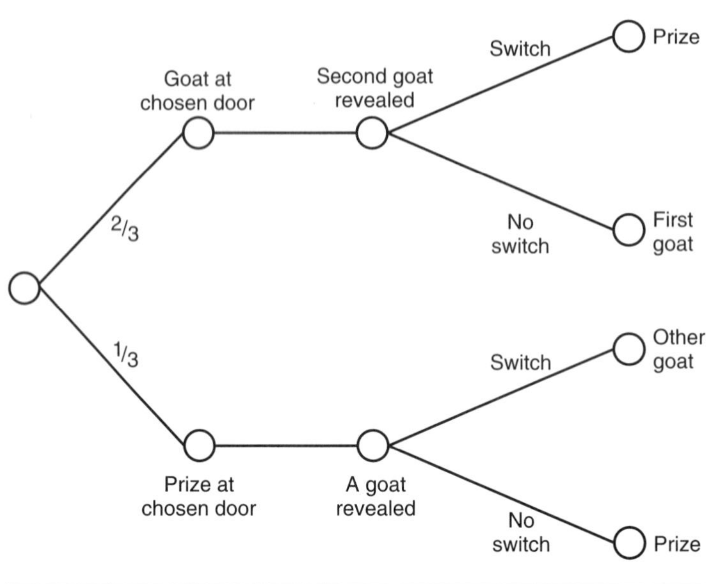

Weighting these outcomes according to the initial ⅔ and ⅓ probabilities leads to the same result.

This result was surprising to many of Ms. vos Savant's readers, including many who were mathematicians and statisticians.

The result depends very critically on the assumption about Monty's behavior. If Monty does not have to open a door (as was sometimes the case in the game show), then this analysis would not hold.

Summary

A joint probability is the probability of the occurrence of two or more events. A conditional probability is the probability of occurrence of an event, given that some other event is known to have occurred. A marginal probability is the unconditional probability of the occurrence of some event.

A prior probability of the occurrence of an event may be revised using Bayes theorem to produce a revised or posterior probability.

Random Variables and Probability Distributions

A **probability function** is a rule that assigns probabilities to each element of a set of events that may occur. If, in turn, we can assign a specific numerical value to each element of the set of events, a function that assigns these numerical values is termed a **random variable.** The **value** of a random variable is the general outcome of a random (or probability) experiment. It is useful to distinguish between the random variable itself and the values that it can take on. The value of a random variable is unknown until the event occurs (i.e., until the random experiment has been performed). However, the probability that the random variable will be any specific value is known in advance. The probability of each value of the random variable is equal to the sum of the probabilities of the events assigned to that value of the random variable.

For example, suppose we define the random variable Z to be the number of heads in two tosses of a fair coin. Then the possible values of Z, and the corresponding probabilities, are:

Possible Values of Z	*Probability of Each Value*
0	¼
1	½
2	¼

Random variables can be grouped into **probability distributions,** which can be either discrete or continuous. **Discrete** probability distributions are those in which the random variable can take on only specific values. The table above is an example of such a distribution since the random variable Z can be only 0, 1, or 2. A **continuous** probability distribution is one in which the value of the random variable can be any number within some given range of values—say, between zero and infinity. For example, if the random variable was the height of members of a population, a person could be 5.3 feet, 5.324 feet, 5.32431 feet, and so on, depending on the ability of instruments to measure. Some additional examples of random variables are shown in the Table 5–8.

A discrete probability distribution is sometimes called a **probability mass function** (p.m.f.) and a continuous one is called a **probability density function** (p.d.f.). Graphs of the two types of distributions are shown in Figures 5–5 and 5–6.

For a discrete distribution, the height of each line represents the probability for that value of the random variable. For example, 0.30 is the probability that tomorrow's demand will be 0.2 tons in Figure 5–5. For a continuous random variable, the height of the probability density function is *not* the probability for an event. Rather, the *area under the curve* over any interval on the horizontal axis represents the probability of taking on a value in that interval. For example, the shaded area on the left in Figure 5–6 represents the probability that tomorrow's demand will be in the *interval* between 0.1 and 0.2 tons.

TABLE 5–8

Random Variable (denoted by a capital letter)	*Description of the Values of the Random Variable*	*Discrete or Continuous*	*Values of the Random Variable*
U	Possible outcomes from throwing a pair of dice	Discrete	2, 3, . . . , 12
X	Possible number of heads, tossing a coin five times	Discrete	0, 1, 2, 3, 4, 5
Y	Possible daily sales of a newspaper, where S represents the inventory available	Discrete	0, 1, 2, . . . , S
T	Time between arrivals of calls at 911 Emergency Call Center	Continuous	0 to ∞
L	Life of an electronic component of a computer	Continuous	0 to ∞

FIGURE 5–5
Discrete Probability Distribution (probability mass function or p.m.f.)

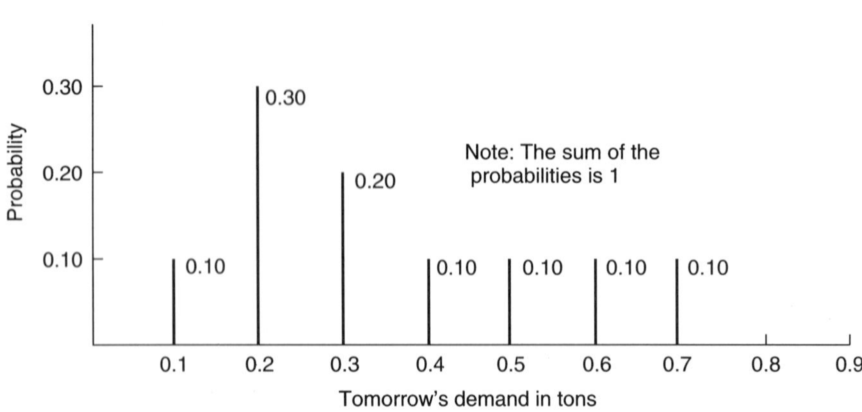

FIGURE 5–6
Continuous Probability Distribution (probability density function or p.d.f.)

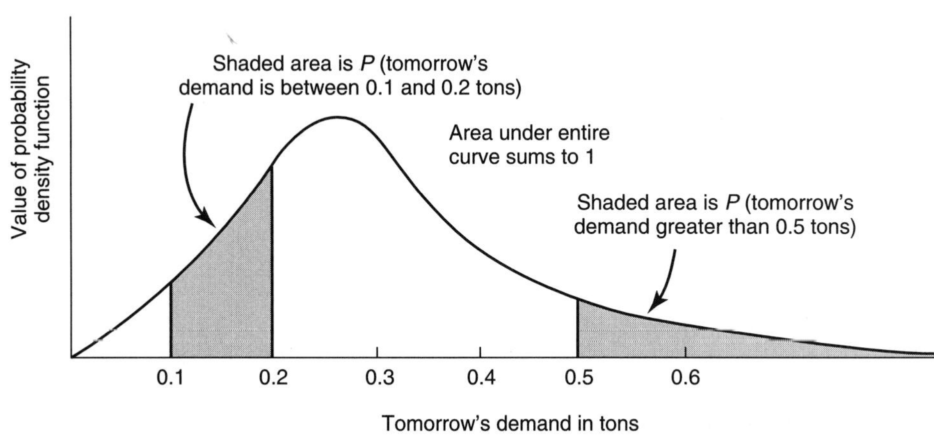

Cumulative Mass Functions

Associated with probability mass functions are cumulative mass functions. A cumulative mass function shows cumulative probability. For example, consider the random variable S with the discrete probability mass function shown in Table 5–9.

In addition to being interested in the probability of S being equal to 2 [i.e., $P(S = 2) = 0.40$], we may wish to know the probability of S being equal to or less than 2 [i.e., $P(S \leq 2) = 0.60$]. The function giving values of this nature is called the *cumulative* mass function. The probability mass function and cumulative mass function of a "less than or equal to" type for the example in Table 5–9 are shown in Table 5–10 and Figure 5–7.

We may also wish to know the probability of S being greater than 2:

$$P(S > 2) = 1 - P(S \leq 2) = 1 - 0.60 = 0.40$$

Given the probability mass function, we can obtain the cumulative mass function and such variations as $P(S \geq 2)$ or $P(2 \leq S \leq 4)$.

TABLE 5–9
Probability Mass Function Example

s	$P(S = s)$
0	0.00
1	0.20
2	0.40
3	0.30
4	0.10
	1.00

TABLE 5–10
Cumulative Mass Function Example

s	$P(S = s)$	$P(S \leq s)$
0	0.00	0.00
1	0.20	0.20
2	0.40	0.60
3	0.30	0.90
4	0.10	1.00

FIGURE 5–7
Plot of Probability Mass Function and Cumulative Mass Function

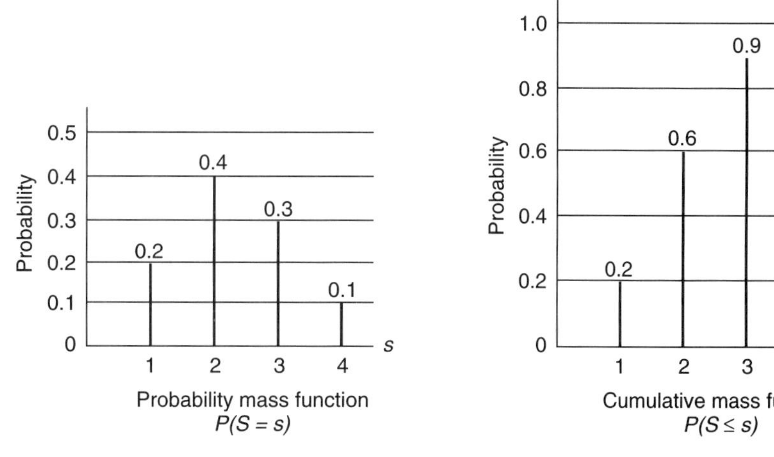

Cumulative Distribution Functions

Cumulative distribution functions are associated with continuous probability density functions just as cumulative mass functions are associated with discrete probability mass functions.

We shall illustrate the cumulative distribution function using a rectangular or uniform probability distribution (refer to Figure 5–8). If S is between a and b ($a \leq S \leq b$), then the value of the probability density function is $1/(b - a)$, and zero otherwise. If we sum the area under the probability density function:

FIGURE 5–8
Probability Density Function $f(S) = \dfrac{1}{b-a}$, $a \le S \le b$; $f(S) = 0$ **Otherwise**

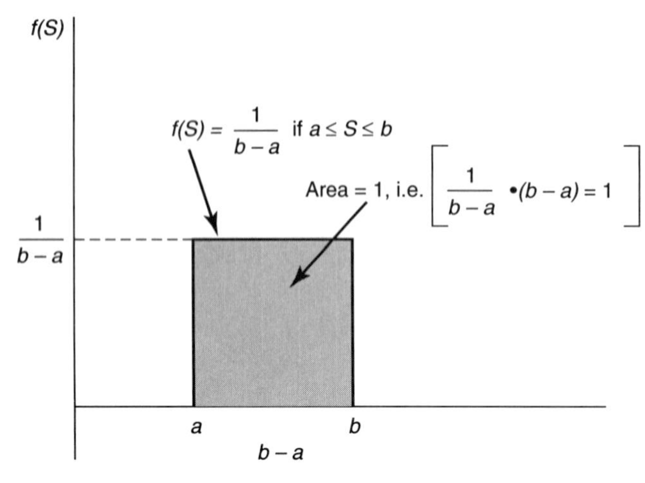

FIGURE 5–9
$F(S)$, Cumulative Distribution Function for $f(S) = \dfrac{1}{b-a}$

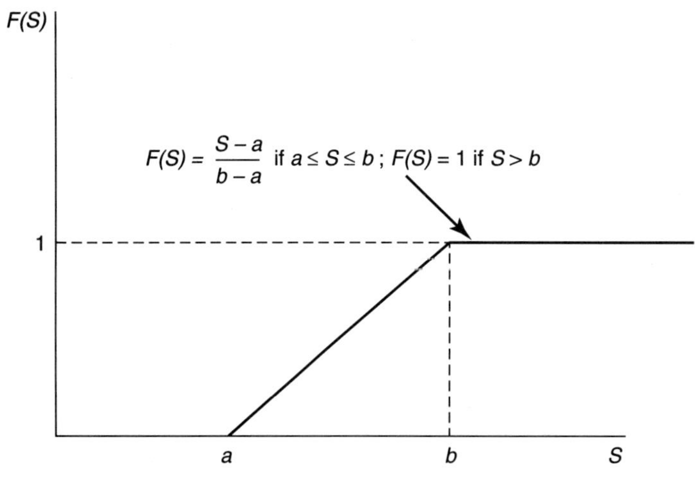

$$f(S) = \frac{1}{b-a}$$

over the range from a to S for each value of S, we obtain the cumulative distribution, $F(S)$. We use $f(\cdot)$ to represent the probability density function and $F(\cdot)$ to represent the cumulative distribution function of the "less than or equal to" type (see Figure 5–9).

The Expected Value of a Random Variable

The **expected value** or **expectation** of a random variable is the sum of the values of the random variable weighted by the probability that the random variable will take

TABLE 5–11
Computation of the Expected Value

Values of the Random Variable, X (tomorrow's demand)	*Probability of X_i $P(X_i)$*	*Probability Weighted Demand, $X_iP(X_i)$*
$X_1 = 25$ units	$P(X_1) = 0.05$	1.25
$X_2 = 26$ units	$P(X_2) = 0.10$	2.60
$X_3 = 27$ units	$P(X_3) = 0.15$	4.05
$X_4 = 28$ units	$P(X_4) = 0.30$	8.40
$X_5 = 29$ units	$P(X_5) = 0.20$	5.80
$X_6 = 30$ units	$P(X_6) = 0.20$	6.00
	1.00	$E(X) = 28.10$

on that value. The expected value is thus the mean or weighted average value. Consider the example of Table 5–11.

In this case, 28.10 is the *expected* or *mean* demand. This is written as:

$$E(X) = 28.10$$

The expected value is calculated, as in Table 5–11, by weighting each value of the random variable by its probability, then summing. The mathematical definition of the mean, in symbols, is:

$$E(X) = \sum_{i=1}^{n} X_iP(X_i) \tag{5–5}$$

X_i is the ith value of the random variable; $P(X_i)$ is the probability of the ith value; and $\sum_{i=1}^{n}$ is the symbol meaning summation of all items for $i = 1$ to $i = \text{n}$, inclusive. The symbol Σ is read as "sigma." In our example, $n = 6$, since there are six possible values of the random variable. Hence:

$$E(X) = \sum_{i=1}^{6} X_iP(X_i) = X_1P(X_1) + X_2P(X_2) + \cdots + X_6P(X_6)$$

Substituting the specific values:

$$\begin{aligned} E(X) = \sum_{i=1}^{6} X_iP(X_i) &= 25(0.05) + 26(0.10) + 27(0.15) + 28(0.30) \\ &\quad + 29(0.20) + 30(0.20) \\ &= 28.10 \end{aligned}$$

The calculation of the expected value of a continuous random variable requires the use of more sophisticated mathematics (calculus).[3] However, the expected value has exactly the same interpretation as that for the discrete case.

[3]The expected value of random variable X with probability distribution function $f(X)$ is:

$$E(X) = \int_{all\ X} X \cdot f(X)dX.$$

TABLE 5–12
Computation of the Variance

Value of the Random Variable, X_i	Probability, $P(X_i)$	Squared Deviation from the Mean of 28.1 $[X_i - E(X)]^2$	Squared Deviation Weighted by the Probability $[X_i - E(X)]^2P(X_i)$
$X_1 = 25$	0.05	$(25 - 28.1)^2 = 9.61$	0.4805
$X_2 = 26$	0.10	$(26 - 28.1)^2 = 4.41$	0.4410
$X_3 = 27$	0.15	$(27 - 28.1)^2 = 1.21$	0.1815
$X_4 = 28$	0.30	$(28 - 28.1)^2 = 0.01$	0.0030
$X_5 = 29$	0.20	$(29 - 28.1)^2 = 0.81$	0.1620
$X_6 = 30$	0.20	$(30 - 28.1)^2 = 3.61$	0.7220
	1.00		1.9900

$$Var(X) = \left[\sum_{i=1}^{6} (X_i - 28.1)^2 P(X)_i\right] = 1.9900$$

The Variance and Standard Deviation of a Random Variable

Frequently, we want to know how the values of the random variable are dispersed about the mean. The variance and the standard deviation provide measures of this dispersion.

The **variance** is defined as the sum of *squared* deviations of the values of the random variable from its mean, weighted by the probability of the deviation. The mathematical statement is as follows:

$$Var(X) = \sum_{i=1}^{n} [X_i - E(X)]^2 P(X_i) \tag{5–6}$$

$E(X)$ is the mean; X_i, the ith value of the random variable; and $P(X_i)$, its probability. Note that the larger the dispersion of all X_is for $i = 1$ to $i = n$, inclusive, the larger the values of $[X_i - E(X)]^2$ and the larger the variance.

Table 5–12 shows the calculation of the variance for the random variable demand for the example in Table 5–11.

The **standard deviation** is the square root of the variance, and in our example, the standard deviation is $\sqrt{1.99}$, or about 1.41. The standard deviation is usually designated by σ (a small sigma), and the variance is frequently written as σ^2. Excel's functions = VARIANCE.

The variance of a continuous random variable has the same interpretation as that for the discrete case, although the mathematical formula is more complex and involves calculus.[4]

Example

This example shows how we obtain information about a random variable using the probability rules developed earlier. Suppose you have a product you are trying to sell to two customers. For Big Stores, you assess that there is a 20 percent chance that you will sell 200 cases, a 40 percent chance of a 100-case sale, and a 40 percent

[4]The variance of a random variable X with probability distribution function $f(X)$ is:

$$\sigma^2 = Var(X) = \int_{all\ X} [X - E(X)]^2 f(X)dx = E[X - E(X)]^2$$

FIGURE 5–10

Sales to Little Markets (cases)	*Sales to Big Stores (cases)*			*Marginal Probability*
	200	*100*	*0*	
100	0.5 / 0.1			0.4
0			0.5 / 0.2	0.6
Marginal Probability	0.2	0.4	0.4	1.0

chance of no sale. For Little Markets, you think the chances are 40 percent for a 100-case order and 60 percent for no order. Further, you think that the sales to the two markets are dependent. If Big Stores were to buy 200 cases, the chances would be 50 percent that Little would make the 100-case order (and, of course, 50 percent chance for no order). And if Big Stores were to buy zero cases, the chances would be 50–50 that Little would also not order.

Suppose you are interested in the random variable *X*, the total sales to both customers. Let us develop the probability distribution for this random variable. We begin by constructing Figure 5–10, the joint probability table, and include the information we have.

Note that the overall probabilities of sales of 200, 100, and 0 cases to Big Stores are shown along the bottom margin of Figure 5–10. Similarly, the marginal probabilities of sales to Little Markets are shown in the right-hand column. We also know that $P(\text{Little sales} = 100|\text{Big sales} = 200) = 0.5$. This conditional probability is shown in the upper corner of the upper left box. We also know $P(\text{Little sales} = 0|\text{Big sales} = 0) = 0.5$, and this is similarly shown in the upper corner of the lower right box in Figure 5–10.

Using:

$$P(AB) = P(A|B)P(B)$$

we can calculate the joint probability:

$$P(\text{Little} = 100 \text{ and Big} = 200) = P(\text{Little} = 100|\text{Big} = 200) \cdot P(\text{Big} = 200)$$
$$= (0.5)(0.2) = 0.1$$

Similarly,

$$P(\text{Little} = 0 \text{ and Big} = 0) = P(\text{Little} = 0|\text{Big} = 0) \cdot P(\text{Big} = 0)$$
$$= (0.5)(0.4) = 0.2$$

These joint probabilities are shown in the appropriate boxes in Figure 5–10.

It is now possible to fill in the rest of Figure 5–10 using the fact that the totals of the joint probabilities in any row or column must equal the marginal probabilities. The completed table is shown as Figure 5–11.

The lower right-hand corners of the boxes in Figure 5–11 contain the values for the random variable *X*, the total sales, equal to the sum of the sales to Big Stores and

FIGURE 5–11

Sales to Little Markets (cases)	*Sales to Big Stores (cases)* 200	100	0	*Marginal Probability*
100	0.1 / 300	0.1 / 200	0.2 / 100	0.4
0	0.1 / 200	0.3 / 100	0.2 / 0	0.6
Marginal Probability	0.2	0.4	0.4	1.0

TABLE 5–13
Probability Distribution for Total Sales

(1) Sales in Cases X_i	*(2)* Probability $P(X_i)$	*(3)* $X_i \cdot P(X_i)$	*(4)* Squared Deviation from the Mean of 120 $[X_i - E(X)]^2$	*(5)* Squared Deviation Weighted by the Probability $[X_i - E(X)]^2P(X_i)$
0	0.2	0	$(0 - 120)^2 = 14{,}400$	2,880
100	0.5	50	$(100 - 120)^2 = 400$	200
200	0.2	40	$(200 - 120)^2 = 6{,}400$	1,280
300	0.1	30	$(300 - 120)^2 = 32{,}400$	3,240
	1.0	$E(X) = 120$		$Var(X) = 7{,}600$

Little Markets. The probability distribution for X is shown in columns 1 and 2 of Table 5–13.

The calculation of the expected value of this distribution is shown in column (3) of Table 5–13. That is, $E(X) = 120$ cases. The variance for total sales is also calculated; see columns (4) and (5): $Var(X) = 7{,}600$.

Multivariate Probability Distributions

A **multivariate probability distribution** is a function expressing the joint probabilities for two or more random variables. This is similar to the joint probability tables earlier in the chapter (see Table 5–3, for example). Consider the case of two random variables X and Y. The expected values [$E(X)$ and $E(Y)$] and variances [$Var(X)$ and $Var(Y)$] for the variables individually are much the same as defined above. However, there is an additional measure of variability called the covariance, which measures the degree to which the two variables tend to be related. The covariance is:

$$Cov(X,Y) = E[(X - E(X)) \cdot (Y - E(Y))]$$

As an example, consider the joint distribution of the height and weight of individuals (let X be the height and Y be the weight). The covariance measures the extent to which there is a relationship between height and weight. Since, generally, taller people tend to weigh more than average, and shorter people weigh less than average, the covariance is positive.

If the covariance term is negative, it indicates that high values of one variable tend to be associated with low values of the other, and vice versa. For example, consider the joint distribution of average family income and crime rate in various districts of a city. Generally, districts with higher than average family income tend to have lower than average crime rates, and lower-income areas have higher crime rates. The covariance in this case is negative.

If two variables are independent, the covariance is zero.

A related measure of the degree of relationship between two variables is the **correlation coefficient,** defined as:

$$\rho = \frac{Cov(X,Y)}{\sqrt{Var(X) \cdot Var(Y)}}$$

The correlation coefficient can take on values of $+1$ if the two variables are perfectly (linearly) positively related, -1 if they are perfectly negatively related, 0 if they are independent, and values in between depending of the degree of association of the variables.

General multivariate distributions can involve any number of variables. The covariance and correlation coefficient can be defined as above for any pair of variables.

Sums of Random Variables

The expectation of a sum of random variables is the sum of the expectations of those random variables. Thus, the mean of the random variable $(X + Y + Z)$ is:

$$E(X + Y + Z) = E(X) + E(Y) + E(Z)$$

The variance of a sum of random variables involves the sum of the variances and covariances as follows:

For two variables X and Y: $Var(X + Y) = Var(X) + Var(Y) + 2Cov(X,Y)$
For three variables, X, Y, and Z, the variance of the sum is:
$Var(X + Y + Z) = Var(X) + Var(Y) + Var(Z) + 2Cov(X,Y) + 2Cov(X,Z) + 2Cov(Y,Z)$

The pattern for more than three variables is similar. If the variables are independent, the covariance terms in the above formulas are zero. That is, *the variance of a sum of random variables is the sum of the variances, if the variables are independent.* So, for independent variables:

$$Var(X + Y + Z) = Var(X) + Var(Y) + Var(Z) \quad \text{if } X, Y, Z \text{ are independent}$$

A Constant Times a Random Variable

The expectation of a constant (c) times a random variable is the constant times the expectation of the random variable. That is:

$$E(cX) = cE(X)$$

The variance of a constant times a random variable is the constant squared times the variance of the random variable. That is:

$$Var(cX) = c^2Var(X)$$

Finally, suppose that there is a random variable X multiplied by a constant c, and a second random variable Y multiplied by a constant d; then the variance of the sum of these terms is given by:

$$Var(cX + dY) = c^2Var(X) + d^2Var(Y) + 2cdCov(X,Y)$$

Example

An important application of this theory of sums of random variables is in finance. Suppose you were considering investing a sum of money—say, $100,000—in two possible stocks, Moon Computers, and the Fickle Pickle Company. You consider the returns each might make over the next year as a random variable. Based on historical data modified by your judgment, you estimate the expected value and variance of return for each stock. For Moon Computers, you expect a return of 0.12 (i.e., 12 percent) and a variance on return for that stock of .008. For Fickle Pickle, your expected value of return is .10 (i.e., 10 percent) and the variance on return is .003. Furthermore, you have estimated the covariance between the returns of the two stocks as −0.0006. There is a very slight tendency for the stock returns to be inversely related.

You are considering investing in either or both of these stocks. You would like to have a high return on your money, and in this regard, Moon Computer looks better since its expected return is 12 percent (versus 10 percent for Fickle Pickle). On the other hand, the variance is a measure of the variability of return, and hence a measure of risk, and Moon Computers also has higher variance (0.008 versus 0.003 for Fickle Pickle). So you will need to make some trade-off of expected return and risk.

Suppose you consider a *portfolio* or mix of these stocks. Your return on this portfolio is also a random variable and is given by the following expression:

$$\text{Portfolio return} = Z = cX + (1 - c)Y$$

where

X is the random variable for the return on Moon Computers
Y is the random variable for the return on Fickle Pickle
Z is the random variable for the portfolio return
c is a constant representing the fraction of the $100,000 invested in Moon Computers
$(1 - c)$ is also a constant representing the remaining fraction—which is invested in Fickle Pickle

The expected value and variance for your portfolio return can be calculated from the above formulas for sums of random variables:

$$\begin{array}{c}\text{Expected}\\\text{portfolio return}\end{array} = E(Z) = cE(X) + (1 - c)E(Y)$$

$$\begin{array}{c}\text{Variance of}\\\text{portfolio return}\end{array} = Var(Z) = c^2Var(X) + (1 - c)^2Var(Y) + 2c(1 - c)Cov(X,Y)$$

Table 5–14 shows the results of these calculations for different portfolio mixes ranging from 100 percent Moon Computers to 100 percent Fickle Pickle. Of course, when the portfolio is 100 percent Moon Computers, the expected value and variance for return are exactly the same as for that stock. Similarly, when 100 percent is in Fickle Pickle (i.e., 0 percent in Moon Computers in Table 5–13), the expected value and variance are those of Fickle Pickle. But consider a portfolio that is 50 percent of each. The expected return is halfway between the two individual returns. But note the variance for that case, a value of 0.0024, which is less than the value of a portfolio entirely of Fickle Pickle. That is, the mixed portfolio was able to reduce the risk (i.e., the variance) even below that of the least risky stock and get a better expected return. This is a simple illustration of the diversification benefit in portfolio investing in finance.

This simple example considered only two stocks. Actual investment portfolios may have many stocks and may even be a portfolio of mutual funds of stocks and bonds or other assets. The idea is to achieve as low risk as possible for a given expected return, or alternatively, to achieve as high return as possible for fixed risk.

Another Example

Let us return to the example used earlier of sales to two stores, Little Markets and Big Stores. Refer to Figure 5–11, which contained the joint probabilities for the random variables sales to Big Stores (variable B) and Little Markets (variable L). Consider the random variable X, which is total sales: $X = B + L$. In that example, the expected value and variance were calculated by enumerating all the possibilities. Let us return to that example and calculate the expected value and variance for the variable X using the formulas for sums of random variables.

First, the expected value and variance for each variable is calculated as shown in Tables 5–15 and 5–16. Also, the covariance is calculated in Table 5–17.

TABLE 5–14

	Fraction of Portfolio in Moon Computers				
Value of c	1.0	0.75	0.50	0.25	0.0
Expected return for portfolio	0.120	0.115	0.110	0.105	0.100
Variance of return for portfolio	0.0080	0.0045	0.0024	0.0020	0.0030

TABLE 5–15 Calculation of Mean and Variance for Big Stores

Sales to Big Stores	*Probability*			
B_i	$P(B_i)$	$B_i \cdot P(B_i)$	$[B_i - E(B_i)]^2$	$[B_i - E(B_i)]^2\,P(B_i)$
0	0.4	0	6,400	2,560
100	0.4	40	400	160
200	0.2	40	14,400	2,880
		$E(B) = 80$		$Var(B) = 5{,}600$

TABLE 5–16
Calculation of Mean and Variance for Little Markets

Sales to Little Markets	Probability			
L_i	$P(L_i)$	$L_i \cdot P(L_i)$	$[L_i - E(L_i)]^2$	$[L_i - E(L_i)]^2\ P(L_i)$
0	0.6	0	1,600	960
100	0.4	40	3,600	1,440
		$E(L) = 40$		$Var(L) = 2,400$

TABLE 5–17
Calculation of Covariance of Sales

Sales to Little Markets	Sales to Big Stores	Joint Probability		
L_i	B_j	$P(L_i,B_j)$	$[L_i - E(L_i)][B_j - E(B_j)]$	$P(L_i,B_j)[L_i - E(L_i)][B_j - E(B_j)]$
0	0	0.2	$(-40)(-80) = 3,200$	640
0	100	0.3	$(-40)(20) = -800$	−240
0	200	0.1	$(-40)(120) = -4,800$	−480
100	0	0.2	$(60)(-80) = -4,800$	−960
100	100	0.1	$(60)(20) = 1,200$	120
100	200	0.1	$(60)(120) = 7,200$	720
				$Cov(L,B) = -200$

The expected value of the random variable X is the sum of the expected values:

$$E(X) = E(B) + E(L) = 80 + 40 = 120.$$

The variance of the random variable X is:

$$Var(X) = Var(B) + Var(L) + 2Cov(B,L) = 5,600 + 2,400 + 2(-200) = 7,600$$

These results, of course, are the same as calculated earlier.

Summary

A random variable attaches a numerical value to various outcomes of a random process. Probabilities for random variables can be displayed in a probability distribution. The expected value is the weighted average of the values of a random variable, the weights being the probabilities of occurrence. The variance and standard deviation are measures of dispersion of a random variable.

A multivariate probability distribution expesses the joint probabilities for two or more random variables. The covariance is a measure of the degree of relationship between two variables.

The expected value of a sum of random variables is the sum of the expected values. The variance of a sum of random variables is the sum of the variances if the variables are independent. Otherwise, the variance of the sum must also include the sum of two times the covariances.

The Bernoulli Process and the Binomial Distribution

A **Bernoulli process** may be described as follows:

1. The outcomes or results of each trial in the process are characterized as one of *two types* of possible outcomes, such as:
   a. Success, failure.
   b. Yes, no.
   c. Heads, tails.
   d. Zero, one.
2. The probability of the outcome of any trial is "stable" and does not change throughout the process. For example, the probability of heads, given a fair coin, is 0.50 and does not change, regardless of the number of times the coin is tossed.
3. The outcome of any trial is *independent* of the outcome of any previous trial. In other words, the past history of the process would not change the probability assigned to the next trial. In our coin example, we would assign a probability of 0.50 to the next toss coming up heads, even if we had recorded heads on the last 10 trials (we assume the coin is fair).
4. The number of trials is discrete and can be represented by an integer such as 1, 2, 3, and so on.

Given a process, we may know that it is Bernoulli, but we may or may not know the stable probability characteristic of the process. With a fair coin, we may know the process is Bernoulli, with probability 0.50 of a success (say heads) and probability 0.50 of a failure (tails). However, if we are given a coin and told it is not fair, the process (flipping the coin) may still be Bernoulli, but we do not know the probability characteristic. Hence, we may have a Bernoulli process with a known or unknown probability characteristic.

Many business processes can be characterized as Bernoulli for analytical purposes, even though they are not true Bernoulli in every respect. If the "fit" is close enough, we may assume that the Bernoulli process is a reasonable characterization. Let us discuss some examples.

Example 1
Suppose we are concerned with a production process where a certain part (or product) is produced on a machine. We may be interested in classifying the parts as "good" or "defective," in which case the process may be Bernoulli. If the machine is not subject to fast wear—that is, if a setting will last for a long run of parts—the probability of good parts may be sufficiently stable for the process to qualify as Bernoulli. If, on the other hand, more defectives occur as the end of the run approaches, the process is not Bernoulli. In many such processes, the occurrence of good and defective parts is sufficiently stable (no pattern over time is observable) to call the process Bernoulli. The probability of good and defective parts may remain stable through a production run, but it may vary from run to run (because of machine setting, for example). Here, the process could still be considered Bernoulli, but the probability of a success (or failure) will change from run to run.

Example 2
A different example of a Bernoulli process is a survey to determine whether or not consumers prefer liquid to powdered soaps. The outcome of a survey interview

could be characterized as "yes" (success) or "no" (failure) answers to the question. If the sample of consumers was sufficiently randomized (no pattern to the way in which the yes or no answers occur), Bernoulli (with an unknown probability) may be a useful description of the process.

Note that if the probability of a success in a Bernoulli process is 0.50, the probability of a failure is also 0.50 (since the probabilities of the event happening and the event not happening add to one). If the probability of a success is p, the probability of a failure is $(1 - p)$.

The Binomial Probability Distribution

In order to answer probability questions about a Bernoulli process, we need to know what the probability parameter of the process is, such as the 0.50 value in the fair coin example. In addition, we need to know the number of trials we are going to use. Hence, to analyze a Bernoulli process, we need to know (1) the process probability characteristic, p, and (2) the number of trials, n.

The symbols and relationships given in Table 5–18 are useful.

TABLE 5–18

Relationship or Symbol	*Interpretation*
$P(R = r \mid p, n)$	The probability that the unknown number of successes, R (the random variable), is *equal to* some specific number, r (say, 10), given a specific number of trials, n (say, 20) and some specific probability, p, of a success on each trial.
$P(R \geq r \mid p, n)$	The probability that the number of successes is *greater than or equal to* a specific number, r, given values for p and n. This is called a *cumulative* probability. Table C (in the Appendix at the end of the text) contains values of cumulative probabilities.
$P(R > r \mid p, n)$	The probability that the number of successes is *greater than* a specific number. This inequality is exclusive; that is: $$P(R > 10)$$ excludes 10, and includes 11 and up.
$P(R \leq r \mid p, n)$	The probability that the number of successes is *less than or equal to* a specific number (say, 10).
$P(R < r \mid p, n)$	The probability that the number of successes is *less than* a specific number.
$P(R = 10) = P(R \geq 10) - P(R \geq 11)$	The probability of exactly 10 successes can be read from Appendix Table C by subtracting two cumulative probabilities. If: $$P(R \geq 11)$$ is subtracted from $P(R \geq 10)$, the result is the probability of *exactly* 10 successes.
$P(R < 10) = 1 - P(R \geq 10)$	Since the probabilities add to 1, if the probability of 10 or more successes is subtracted from 1, the result is the probability of less than 10 successes.
$P(R \leq 10) = 1 - P(R \geq 11)$	Since *less than or equal to* 10 includes 10, subtract the probability of 11 or more successes from 1.
$P(R > 10) = P(R \geq 11)$	To read a strict inequality from Appendix Table C, add 1 to the number desired. The $$P(R > 10)$$ excludes 10, so this probability is the same as $P(R \geq 11)$, which includes 11 but excludes 10.

The Binomial Probability Function

If the assumptions of the Bernoulli process are satisfied and if the probability of a success on one trial is p, then the probability distribution of the number of successes, R, in n trials, is a **binomial distribution.** The binomial probability distribution function is:

$$P(R|n, p) = \frac{n!}{R!(n-R)!} p^R (1-p)^{n-R} \tag{5–7}$$

where $n!$ (called n-factorial) equals $n(n-1)(n-2) \ldots (2)(1)$ and $0!$ is defined to be equal to 1.

Performing computations using Equation 5–7 can be tedious if the number of trials is large. For this reason, tables of the cumulative binomial distribution have been provided at the end of the book in Table C. Table 5–17 illustrates a wide range of probability definitions and indicates how to use Table C in the appendix.

Binomial Probabilities on Spreadsheets

The Excel and Quattro spreadsheet programs have a function that can be used for evaluating binomial probabilities, both individual terms and cumulative probabilities. The form of the function is:

=BINOMDIST(*R*,*n*,*p*,0 or 1)

where R is the number of successes, n is the number of trials, and p is the probability of success on each trial. The last term is either a zero or one;[5] if a zero is entered, the individual binomial term is given; if a one is used, the cumulative value (of the $\leq$ type) is given. Suppose, for example, we want the probability of exactly three successes in five trials, with a probability of success of $p = 0.4$—$P(R = 3|n = 5, p = 0.4)$. This is:

=BINOMDIST(3,5,0.4,0), which equals 0.2304

For the probability of 3 or fewer successes in five trials, with $p = 0.4$—$P(R \leq 3|n = 5, p = 0.4)$

=BINOMDIST(3,5,0.4,1), which equals 0.9130

Note that this is the reverse cumulative from that given in Table C. (Table C has *greater than or equal* values; the spreadsheet function has *less than or equal* values.)

Example 1
Suppose we plan to toss a fair coin three times and would like to compute the following probabilities:

a. The probability of three heads in three tosses.
b. The probability of two or more heads in three tosses.
c. The probability of fewer than two heads in three tosses.

[5]More precisely, the fourth term can be any logical value that, if it evaluates to FALSE, the function gives the individual binomial term; and if it evaluates to TRUE, the function gives the cumulative term.

TABLE 5–19

Possible Outcomes	Probability of Each Outcome
HHH	1/8
HHT	1/8
HTH	1/8
THH	1/8
TTH	1/8
THT	1/8
HTT	1/8
TTT	1/8
	1

In this example, the Bernoulli process p is 0.50, and a head constitutes a success. The number of trials (n) is three.

The first probability is the probability of three heads (successes) in three tosses (three trials), given that the probability of a head on any one toss is 0.50. This probability can be written as follows:

$$P(R = 3|p = 0.50, n = 3) = ?$$

where P = Probability, R = Number of successes, n = Number of trials, and p = Probability of a success on any one trial. The left side of the equation should be read "the probability of three successes, given a process probability of 0.50 and three trials."

In answering the probability questions, let us first list all the possible outcomes of the three trials and compute the probabilities (see Table 5–19).

Probabilities	Interpretation
a. $P(R = 3\|p = 0.50, n = 3) = 1/8$	The probability of three heads in three trials is one-eighth. This is the probability of *HHH*. See Table 5–19.
b. $P(R \geq 2\|p = 0.50, n = 3) = 4/8$	The probability of two or more heads is four-eighths. This is the probability of two heads plus the probability of three heads and is calculated by summing the probabilities of the following combinations: *HHH, HHT, HTH, THH.*
c. $P(R < 2\|p = 0.50, n = 3) = 4/8$	The probability of less than two heads is the probability of either zero or one head and is calculated by summing the probabilities of the following combinations: *TTH, THT, HTT, TTT.*

The above probabilities can also be calculated using Equation 5–7. This is illustrated for Problem *a*.

$$P(R = 3|p = 0.5, n = 3) = \frac{3!}{3!(0!)}(0.5)^3(0.5)^0 = 0.1250$$

Finally, the probabilities can also be obtained from Appendix Table C, or the spreadsheet BINOMDIST function.

Calculations	*Explanation*
a. $P(R = 3 \mid p = 0.50, n = 3) = 0.1250$	Look in Appendix Table C under $n = 3$, $p = 0.50$; read down the column to $$P(R \geq 3) = 0.1250$$ and subtract from this: $$P(R \geq 4) = 0$$ (four successes in three trials is impossible). The answer is 0.1250, or one-eighth. Alternatively, use the spreadsheet function: =BINOMDIST(3,3,0.5,0) = 0.125
b. $P(R \geq 2 \mid p = 0.50, n = 3) = 0.5000$	Look in Table C under $n = 3$, $p = 0.50$, and read $R \geq 2$; the answer is 0.50. For the spreadsheet version, note that: $P(R \geq 2 \mid n = 3, p = 0.5) = 1 - P(R \leq 1 \mid n = 3, p = 0.5)$ = 1 − BINOMDIST(1,3,0.5,1) = 1 − 0.5 = 0.5. If we wanted $P(R = 2)$, we would compute this as follows: $P(R \geq 2 \mid 0.50, 3) = 0.5000$; Less: $P(R \geq 3 \mid 0.50, 3) = 0.1250$; $P(R = 2 \mid 0.50, 3) = 0.3750$. In the spreadsheet, this is: =BINOMDIST(2,3,0.5,0) = 0.375
c. $P(R < 2 \mid p = 0.50, n = 3) = 0.5000$	This probability is equal to: $$1 - P(R \geq 2) = 1 - 0.50 = 0.50$$

Example 2

A very large lot of manufactured goods is to be sampled as a check on its quality.[6] Suppose it is assumed that 10 percent of the items in the lot are defective and that a sample of 20 items is drawn from the lot. What are the following probabilities:

1. Probability of exactly zero defectives in the sample?
2. Probability of more than one defective in the sample?
3. Probability of fewer than two defectives in the sample?

We can answer as follows. Let $p = 0.10$ and $n = 20$. Then:

$$a.\quad P(R = 0 \mid p = 0.10, n = 20) = P(R \geq 0) - P(R \geq 1) = 1.0 - 0.8784 = 0.1216$$

[6]Strictly speaking, if the lot is of finite size, the sampled items are not independent and hence the Bernoulli assumptions are not exactly satisfied; a different distribution called the *hypergeometric distribution* should be employed. However, if the lot size is large relative to the sample, the use of the Bernoulli assumption introduces little error.

The probability of zero or more defectives is 1.0, and $P(R \geq 1)$ is read directly from Table C.

b. $P(R > 1) = P(R \geq 2) = 0.6083$ from Table C.

c. $P(R < 2) = 1.0 - P(R \geq 2) = 1.0 - 0.6083 = 0.3917$

Summary

A Bernoulli process involves a specific number of trials, each with two possible outcomes; the probability of each outcome remains the same; and the trials are independent.

The binomial probability distribution gives the probabilities for each possible number of successes in a given number of trials of a Bernoulli process. Binomial probabilities can be determined using Table C in the appendix or by the BINOMDIST function in a spreadsheet.

The Normal Probability Distribution

The **normal distribution,** sometimes called the **Gaussian distribution,** is an extremely important distribution. It is easier to manipulate mathematically than many other distributions and is a good approximation for several of the others. In many cases, the normal distribution is a reasonable approximation for a prior probability distribution for business decision purposes; and in the following chapters, we shall use the normal distribution in many of the applications. Despite its general application, it should not be assumed that every process can be described as having a normal distribution.

The normal distribution has a probability density function that is a smooth, symmetric, continuous, bell-shaped curve, as pictured in Figure 5–12. The area under the curve over any interval on the horizontal axis represents the probability of the random variable, *X,* taking on a value in that interval. As with any continuous probability density function, the area under the curve sums to 1.

A normal distribution is completely determined by its expected value or mean (denoted by μ) and standard deviation (σ); that is, once we know the mean and

FIGURE 5–12

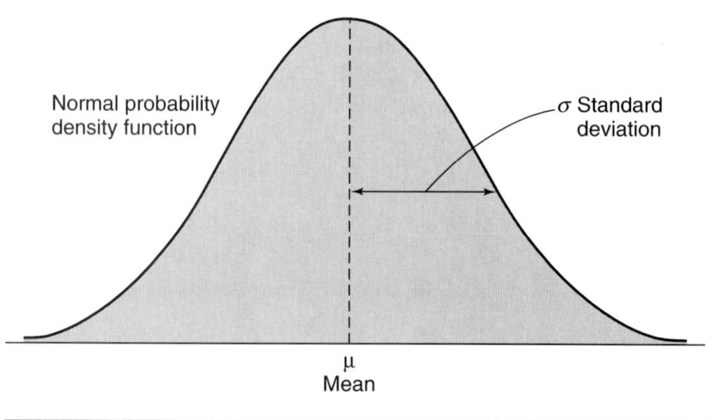

standard deviation, the shape and location of the distribution is set. The curve reaches a maximum at the mean of the distribution. One half of the area lies on either side of the mean. The greater the value of σ, the standard deviation, the more spread out the curve.[7] This is illustrated in Figure 5–13.

With any normal distribution, approximately 0.50 of the area lies within ± 0.67 standard deviations from the mean; about 0.68 of the area lies within ± 1.0 standard deviations; and 0.95 of the area lies with ± 1.96 standard deviations. See Figure 5–14.

Since the normal probability function is continuous (a probability density function), probability cannot be read directly from the graphs. We must consider the probability of the value of a random variable being in an interval (see Figure 5–15).

FIGURE 5–13

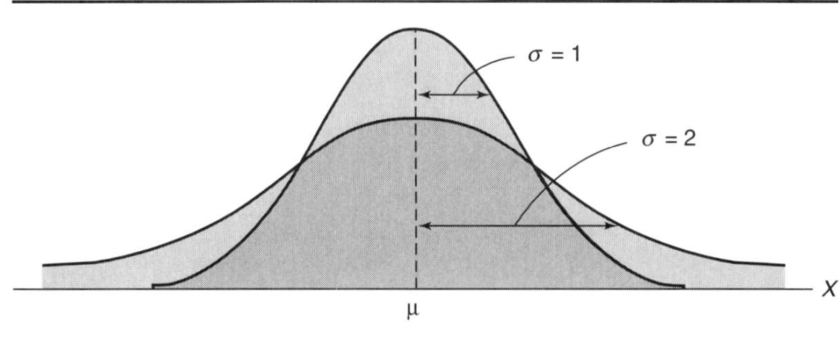

FIGURE 5–14

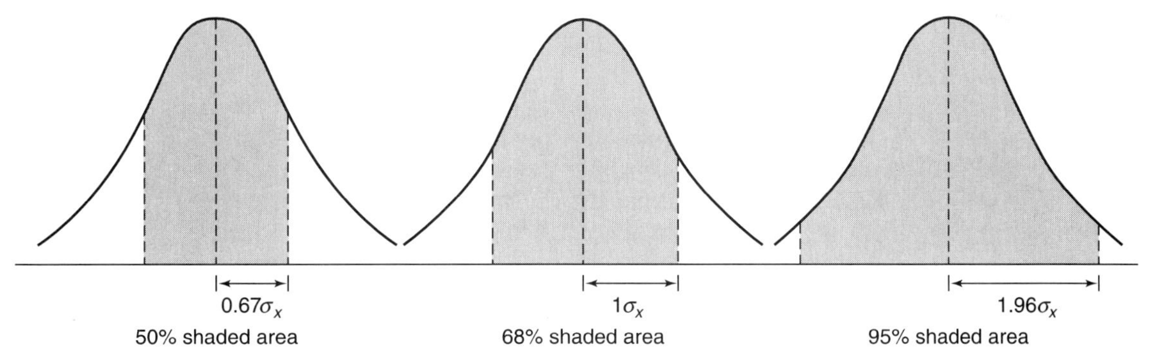

[7]The normal probability density function with parameters μ and σ is:

$$f_N(x) = \frac{1}{\sigma(2\pi)^{1/2}} e^{-(x-\mu)^2/2\sigma^2}, \quad -\infty < x < \infty$$

The normal cumulative distribution function is:

$$F_N(x) = \int_{-\infty}^{x} f_N(y)dy$$

FIGURE 5–15

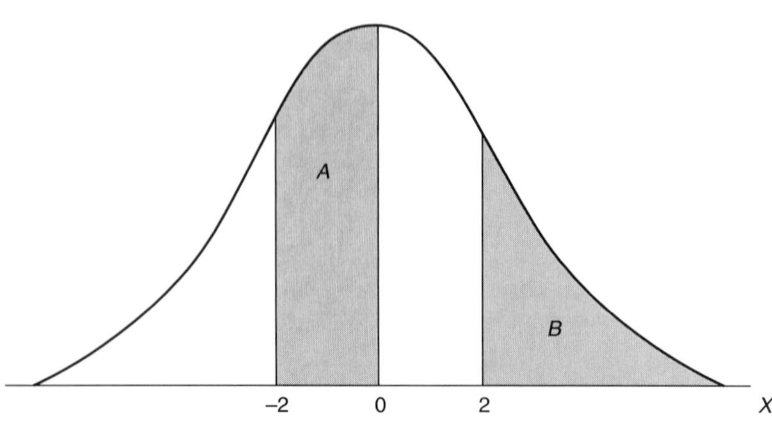

In Figure 5–15:

$$P(-2 \le X \le 0) = \text{Shaded area } A$$

$$P(X \ge 2) = \text{Shaded area } B$$

$P(0 \le X \le 2) =$ Area between A and B (also equal to the shaded area A because of the symmetry of the normal curve)

Right and Left Tails

The symbol F_N is used to represent a cumulative distribution function of a normal probability distribution. It is the area under the *left* tail of a normal probability density function. In Figure 5–16, the shaded area is the left tail of a normal curve; that is, $F_N(b)$. $F_N(b)$ is the probability of X being equal to or less than b; that is:

$$F_N(b) = P(X \le b) \tag{5–8}$$

We now introduce a new symbol, G_N, which we define as the area under the *right* tail of a normal probability density function. In Figure 5–16, the unshaded area is the right tail of a normal curve; that is, $G_N(b)$.

$G_N(b)$ is the probability of X being greater than b; that is:

$$G_N(b) = P(X > b)$$

From Figure 5–16, it can be seen that $F_N(b)$ and $G_N(b)$ are related:[8]

$$G_N(b) = 1 - F_N(b) \tag{5–9}$$

since the total area under the probability density function sums to 1 by definition.

[8]The basic mathematical relationships may be stated as:

$$F_N(b) = \int_{-\infty}^{b} f_N(X)dX$$

and

$$G_N(b) = \int_{b}^{\infty} f_N(X)dX$$

FIGURE 5–16

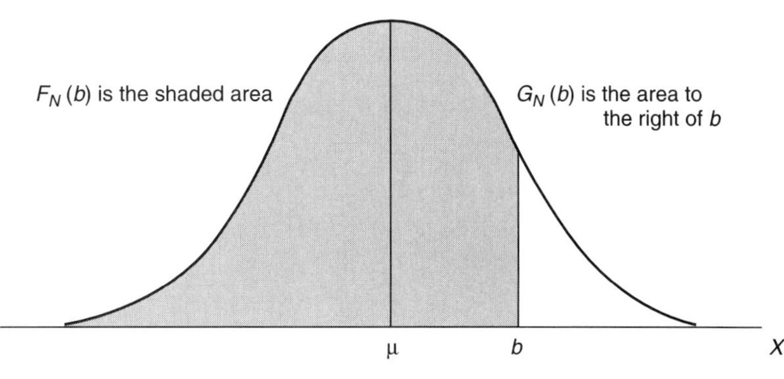

The Standardized Normal Variable and Normal Probability Tables

A normal distribution with $\mu = 0$ (mean of 0) and $\sigma = 1$ (standard deviation of 1) is said to be a **standard normal distribution.** If a normal distribution has a mean other than 0 or a standard deviation other than 1, we may standardize the distribution. The ability to standardize normal distributions is one of the useful features of the distribution and allows us to look up normal probabilities in a relatively short table.

To standardize a normal random variable, we shall define a new **standardized normal variable,** *Z*, as follows:

$$Z = \frac{X - \mu}{\sigma} \tag{5–10}$$

where X is the nonstandardized normal random variable we are concerned with, μ is the mean of this random variable, and σ is its standard deviation. In the above expression, Z is the distance of X from its mean, μ, measured in units of standard deviations. For example, if $Z = 4$, then:

$$4 = \frac{X - \mu}{\sigma}$$

so that:

$$4\sigma = X - \mu$$
$$X = \mu + 4\sigma$$

Thus, $Z = 4$ corresponds to a value of X that is four standard deviations larger than its mean. As a result of this operation, Z is a standardized, normally distributed random variable, which has a mean of 0 and a standard deviation of 1. Since we look up the probabilities in terms of Z, and all Zs have a mean of 0 and a standard deviation of 1, we need only one table of probabilities. Table A (in the appendix at the end of the text) is a table of cumulative normal probabilities. It should be noted that in Equation 5–10, we are transforming a value from one normal distribution into a value of a standard normal distribution. The value being transformed must come from a normal distribution.

Assume we are concerned with a normally distributed random variable, X, with mean $\mu = 8$ and standard deviation $\sigma = 3$. Let us find the following probabilities:

1. $P(X \le 10)$.
2. $P(X > 10)$.
3. $P(10 < X \le 15)$.

Example 1
We first standardize the random variable X for the value $X = 10$:

$$Z = \frac{X - \mu}{\sigma} = \frac{10 - 8}{3} = \frac{2}{3} = 0.67$$

We then look up the probability $P(Z \le 0.67)$ in Table A and find it equals 0.7486. The probability of X being less than 10 is 0.7486. [Note that $P(X \le 10)$ is the same as $P(X < 10)$, since the probability of being exactly 10 is defined to be zero if the probability distribution is continuous.]

Example 2
From Example 1, we know that for $X = 10$, $Z = 0.67$, and:

$$P(X \le 10) = P(Z \le 0.67) = 0.7486$$

Then:

$$P(X > 10) = 1 - P(X \le 10) = 0.2514$$

If the probability of X being less than 10 is 0.75, the probability of X being greater than 10 is 0.25. In terms of areas, if the area to the left of 10 is 0.75, and the total area under the density function is 1, then the area to the right of 10 is (1 − 0.75), or 0.25.

Example 3
We want to determine area C of Figure 5–17. The area $C + D$ is $P(X > 10)$. Area D is $P(X > 15)$. The first step is to know $P(X > 10) = 0.2514$ from Example 2. To calculate area D or $P(X > 15)$, the first step is to compute Z for a value of $X = 15$.

$$Z = \frac{15 - 8}{3} = \frac{7}{3} = 2.33$$

FIGURE 5–17

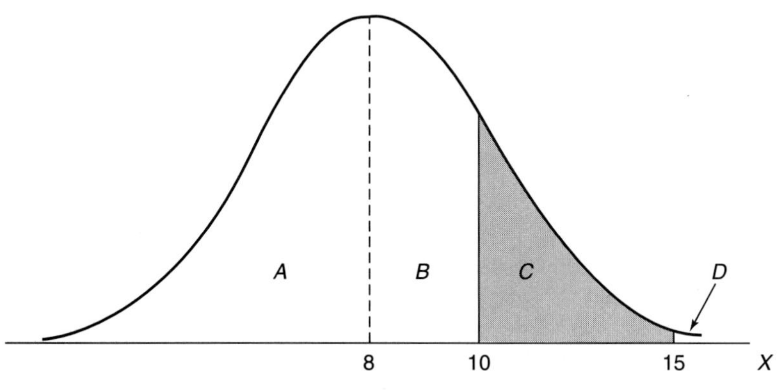

In Table A (in the appendix at the end of the text), we find:

$$P(Z \leq 2.33) = 0.99010$$

We can now calculate area *D:*

$$P(X > 15) = P(Z > 2.33) = 1 - P(Z \leq 2.33)$$
$$= 1 - 0.99010 = 0.00990$$

The probability of X being larger than 10 and less than 15 (or equivalently, Z being larger than 0.67 and less than 2.33) is area $C + D$ minus area D:

$$P(10 < X \leq 15) = P(X > 10) - P(X > 15)$$
$$= P(Z > 0.67) - P(Z > 2.33)$$
$$= 0.2514 - 0.0099 = 0.2415$$

Normal Probabilities on Spreadsheets

The Excel and Quattro spreadsheet function NORMSDIST provides exactly the same values as in Table A in the Appendix.[9] That is, for any value of the standardized value of Z, it provides the left tail cumulative normal probability. For example, for $P(Z \leq 0.67)$, use:

=NORMSDIST(0.67) = 0.7486

Summary

Discrete probability distributions have random variables that take on only specific values. The random variable for continuous distributions may be any value within a range. For a continuous probability distribution, probability is given by an area under the density function.

The normal distribution is a symmetric bell-shaped distribution that can be characterized by its mean and standard deviation. Normal probabilities are obtained by using the standardized normal variable Z and Appendix Table A or the NORMSDIST spreadsheet function.

Bibliography

Drake, A. W. *Fundamentals of Applied Probability Theory.* New York: McGraw-Hill, 1967.

Devore, J. L. *Probability and Statistics for Engineering and the Sciences.* 2nd ed. Monterey, CA: Brooks/Cole Publishing, 1987.

Pitman, J. *Probability.* New York: Springer-Verlag, 1993.

Ross, S. M. *A First Course in Probability.* 4th ed. New York: Macmillan, 1994.

[9]The function NORMSINV is the inverse, giving the appropriate value of Z for a given cumulative probability. Functions NORMDIST and NORMINV also provide normal probabilities using the values of X, μ, *and* σ.

Practice Problems[10]

5–1. Compute the following probabilities, which pertain to flipping a fair coin three times:
a. *P* (three heads).
b. *P* (two or more heads in three tosses).
c. *P* (one or more tails in three tosses).
d. *P* (the last toss being a head).

5–2. Assume three urns:

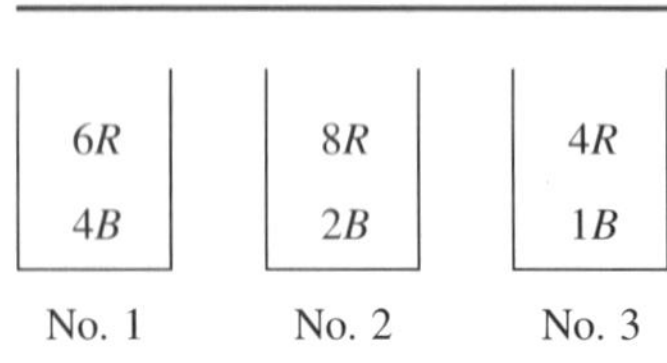

Draw a ball from no. 1: if red, go to no. 2; if black, go to no. 3.
a. What is *P* (red on second draw, given red on draw 1)?
b. What is *P* (black on second draw, given red on draw 1)?
c. What is *P* (red on second draw, given black on draw 1)?
d. What is *P* (black on second draw, given black on draw 1)?
e. What is *P* (black on second draw)?
f. Answer (*a*)–(*e*) if urn no. 3 was as follows:

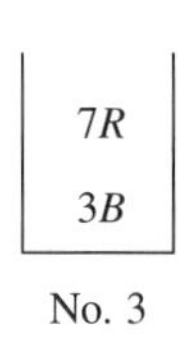

5–3. Assume an unfair coin has a 0.60 probability of a tail and a 0.40 probability of a head.
Determine the following:
a. In two tosses, the probability of:
(1) Two heads.
(2) Two tails.
(3) One head.
(4) One or more heads.
(5) One or more tails.
(6) One tail or less.
b. In three tosses, the probability of:
(1) Three heads.
(2) Two heads.
(3) One head.
(4) One or more heads.

5–4. Assume a normal distribution with mean of 12 and standard deviation of 4. Compute the following:
a. $P(X \geq 15)$.
b. $P(X < 10)$.
c. $P(10 < X \leq 15)$.
d. $P(X > 17)$.
e. $P(15 < X \leq 17)$.

5–5. Using the binomial tables, look up the following probabilities:
a. $P(R = 4|0.50,10)$
b. $P(R > 4|0.50,10)$
c. $P(R \geq 4|0.40,8)$
d. $P(R < 4|0.20,10)$
e. $P(R = 0|0.30,10)$
f. $P(R \geq 5|0.60,10)$
For (*f*), see the note at the bottom of the first page of Table C in the appendix.

5–6. Given a random variable *X* normally distributed with mean of 15 and standard deviation of 3, determine the value of *x* in each case.
a. $P(x \leq X) = 0.8413$.
b. $P(X > x) = 0.2946$.
c. $P(X > x) = 0.02275$.

5–7. Thirty chief executive officers in a certain industry are classified by age and by their previous functional position as shown in the table below:

Previous Functional Position	**Age**		
	Under 55	*55 and Older*	*Total*
Finance	4	14	18
Marketing	1	5	6
Other	4	2	6
Total	9	21	30

Suppose an executive is selected at random from this group.
a. What is the probability that the executive chosen is under 55? What type (marginal, conditional, joint) of probability is this?
b. What is the probability that an executive chosen at random is 55 or older and with Marketing as the previous functional position? What type of probability is this?
c. Suppose an executive is selected, and you are told that the previous position was in Finance. What is

[10]Solutions for these problems are at the end of this chapter.

the probability that the executive is under 55? What kind of probability is this?

d. Are age and previous functional position independent factors for this group of executives?

5–8. The following probabilities are assigned to the possible values of the fraction defective in a manufacturing process. Compute the expected value, the variance, and the standard deviation of the random variable, fraction defective.

Event	*Probability of Event*
0.01 defective	0.10
0.02 defective	0.15
0.03 defective	0.20
0.04 defective	0.30
0.05 defective	0.20
0.10 defective	0.03
0.15 defective	0.02
	1.00

5–9. Assume that the probability of a salesperson making a sale at a randomly selected house is 0.1. If a salesperson makes 20 calls a day, determine the following:

a. The probability of no sales.

b. The probability of one sale.

c. The probability of four or more sales.

d. The probability of more than four sales.

e. The probability of four sales.

5–10. Refer to the example in the chapter relating to Figure 5–3. Suppose a head occurs on the first toss. Calculate the revised (posterior) probabilities for the fair and unfair coin in this case.

5–11. Daily sales of a certain product are known to have a normal distribution of 20 per day, with a standard deviation of 6 per day.

a. What is the probability of selling fewer than 16 on a given day?

b. What is the probability of selling between 15 and 25 units on a given day?

c. How many units would have to be on hand at the start of a day in order to have less than a 10 percent chance of running out?

Problems

5–12. Which of the following frequency distributions would be "objective" and which "subjective"?

a. Number of heads in 100,000 tosses of a fair coin.

b. Number of heads in the next 100,000 tosses of an untested coin.

c. Number of "prosperous" years in the next 10 years.

d. The earnings of the Ford Motor Company in the next five years (number of "profitable" and number of "loss" years).

e. The probability of drawing the name of a male randomly from the student directory of Cornell University.

5–13. Discuss the following statements:

a. "There is a 1.5 probability that the next president will be ________."

b. "The probability of the sun not rising tomorrow is −1.0."

c. "There is a 0.40 probability that I'll pass and a 0.70 probability that I'll flunk the examination."

5–14. Discuss whether the following events are dependent or independent:

a. (1) The Giants winning the World Series.
(2) The Giants winning the pennant of the National League.

b. (1) The savings from using a machine in year 2.
(2) The savings from using the same machine in year 1.

c. (1) The successful marketing of a high-priced car.
(2) The successful marketing of a low-priced clothing line.

5–15. Consider two urns:

	Urn 1	*Urn 2*
Red balls	7	4
Black balls	3	6

$P(R_1) = P$ of red on first draw
$P(R_2) = P$ of red on second draw
$P(B_1) = P$ of black on first draw
$P(B_2) = P$ of black on second draw

a. Take a ball from urn 1, replace it, and take a second ball. What is the probability of:
(1) Two reds being drawn?
(2) A red on the second draw if a red is drawn on the first draw?

(3) A red on the second draw if a black is drawn on the first draw?

b. Take a ball from urn 1; replace it. Take a ball from urn 2 if the first ball was black; otherwise, draw a ball from urn 1. What is the probability of:

(1) Two reds being drawn?

(2) A red on the second draw if a red is drawn on the first draw?

(3) A red on the second draw if a black is drawn on the first draw?

5–16. Draw a tree diagram for Problem 5–15*a*.

5–17. Draw a tree diagram for Problem 5–15*b*.

5–18. Prepare a joint probability table for Problem 5–15*a*.

5–19. Prepare a joint probability table for Problem 5–15*b*.

5–20. *a.* What is the probability of eight heads in eight tosses of a fair coin?

b. Suppose a fair coin is flipped seven times and all the tosses are heads. What is the probability of the eighth toss being a head? Explain.

5–21. Assume that we have a box containing six red balls and four black balls. We draw two balls, one at a time, without replacing the first ball. For this experiment:

a. Draw a tree diagram showing the process.

b. Prepare a joint probability table.

c. Compute the following probabilities:

$$P(B_2|B_1)$$

$$P(R_2|B_1)$$

$$P(R_2|R_1)$$

5–22. Assume there are two urns:

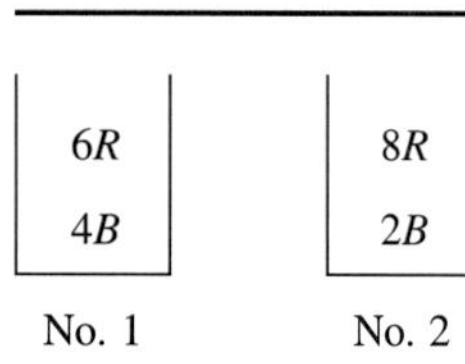

There is equal probability of choosing each urn. You take an urn, draw one ball, and find it is red. You want to know which urn you have. You cannot look inside the urn.

a. What is the probability that you drew the ball from urn 1? From urn 2?

b. If the ball is black, what is the probability that the ball is from urn 1?

5–23. For the probability distribution of sales given below, write out the required probability functions:

Sales(s) (in units)	*Probability*
1	0.10
2	0.15
3	0.20
4	0.30
5	0.20
10	0.03
15	0.02
	1.00

Required probability functions:

$$P(S \geq s)$$

$$P(S > s)$$

$$P(S < s)$$

$$P(S \leq s)$$

5–24. Find the following probabilities for a normally distributed random variable, *X:*

a. Mean of 0, standard deviation of 1:

$$P(X > 0.8)$$

$$P(X \leq 0.8)$$

$$P(X \geq -0.8)$$

$$P(-0.8 \leq X \leq 1.2)$$

b. Mean of 6, standard deviation of 2:

$$P(X > 8)$$

$$P(X \leq 8)$$

$$P(X \geq -8)$$

$$P(-8 \leq X \leq 12)$$

c. Mean of 6, standard deviation of 1:

$$P(X > 8)$$

$$P(X \leq 8)$$

$$P(X \geq 4)$$

$$P(4 \leq X \leq 12)$$

5–25. Find the value of the following normally distributed random variables, given each set of conditions:

a. *X* is normal; mean, 0; standard deviation, 1.

$$P(X > x) = 0.02068$$

What is *x*?

b. X is normal; mean, 8; standard deviation, 3.

$$P(Z > z) = 0.1587$$

What is x? (Z and z are the standardized values of X and x.)

c. X is normal; mean, 8; standard deviation, 3.

$$P(Z \leq z) = 0.7224$$

What is x?

d. X is normal; mean, 10; standard deviation, 2.

$$P(Z > z) = 0.2327$$

What is x?

5–26. Demand for a product is known to be normally distributed with mean of 240 units per week and standard deviation of 40 units. How many units should a retailer have in stock to ensure a 5 percent or less chance of running out during the week?

5–27. On a midterm exam, the scores were distributed normally with mean of 72 and standard deviation of 10. Student Wright scored in the top 10 percent of the class on the midterm.

a. Wright's midterm score was at least how much?

b. The final exam also had a normal distribution, but with mean of 150 and standard deviation of 15. At least what score should Wright get in order to keep the same ranking (i.e.,top 10 percent)?

5–28. An investor wishes to invest in one of two projects. The returns for both projects are uncertain, and the probability distribution for returns can be expressed by a normal distribution in each case. Project A has a mean return of $240,000 with a standard deviation of $20,000. Project B has a mean return of $250,000 and a standard deviation of $40,000.

a. Consider a return of $280,000. Which project has a higher chance of returning this much or more?

b. Consider a return of $220,000. Which project has a higher chance of returning this much or more?

5–29. A survey was conducted among the readers of a certain magazine. The results showed that 60 percent of the readers were homeowners and had incomes in excess of $25,000 per year; 20 percent were homeowners but had incomes of less than $25,000; 10 percent had incomes in excess of $25,000 but were not homeowners; and the remaining 10 percent were neither homeowners nor had incomes in excess of $25,000.

a. Suppose a reader of this magazine is selected at random and you are told that the person is a homeowner. What is the probability that the person has income in excess of $25,000?

b. Are home ownership and income (measured only as above or below $25,000) independent factors for this group?

5–30. A survey was conducted of families in an urban and the surrounding suburban area. The families were classified according to whether or not they customarily watch two TV programs. The data are shown in Table 5–20 in percentages of the total.

a. If a family is selected from this group at random, what is the probability that it views both programs?

b. If the family selected views program A, what is the probability that it also views program B?

c. Are the events (views program A) and (views program B) independent events?

d. Is the event (views program B) independent of the event (urban)?

e. Consider the event (view either program A or B or both). Is this event independent of the event (urban)?

5–31. A sales manager lists the following probabilities for various sales levels for a new product:

Probability	*Sales (in units)*
0.10	50
0.30	100
0.30	150
0.15	200
0.10	250
0.05	300

Calculate the mean, the variance, and the standard deviation for the random variable sales. (*Hint:* One way

TABLE 5–20

	Watch Program A				
	Yes		*No*		
Watch Program B	*Urban*	*Suburban*	*Urban*	*Suburban*	*Total*
Yes	10%	14%	5%	1%	30%
No	15	21	20	14	70
Total	25%	35%	25%	15%	100%

to make the computations easier is to treat blocks of 50 as one unit. Thus, 200 is four, 250 is five, etc.).

5–32. A manager is making a plan for her division for next year. Profit (P) is judged to be a linear function of units sales (X) and fixed costs (Y) as follows:

$$P = \$20X - Y$$

Suppose that the manager is uncertain about the unit sales and fixed costs, but is willing to represent them as independent random variables with expected values and standard deviations as follows:

$$E(X) = 10{,}000 \text{ units} \qquad \sigma_X = 2{,}000 \text{ units}$$

$$E(Y) = 150{,}000 \text{ dollars} \qquad \sigma_Y = 50{,}000 \text{ dollars}$$

What is the expected value and standard deviation of the random variable P?

5–33. Specify which of the following are Bernoulli processes:

a. A house-to-house salesperson making sales calls.
b. Placing coins in a slot machine that has two payoffs—zero or jackpot.
c. Purchase of shares of common stock.
d. Inspection of a wire coil for defects as it is being manufactured.
e. Inspection of castings as they come off the production line.

Give brief explanations for your answers.

5–34. A feeder airline flies a 14-seat plane. The airline allows up to 16 confirmed reservations to be accepted for a flight. Historical experience has shown that there is a 30 percent chance that each passenger may be a "no-show." What is the probability that one or more people will be "bumped" from the flight if 16 reservations are confirmed?

5–35. Bruce Jones has applied to five schools that indicate to the applicant in January one of three classifications: "likely," "possible," or "unlikely." Bruce has received notification that he is "possible" in all five of the schools. Past results indicate the following probabilities for each school:

Likely: 0.98 probability of being accepted

Possible: 0.30 probability of being accepted

Unlikely: 0.005 probability of being accepted

a. What is the probability of Bruce being accepted by one or more of the schools? (Assume independence.)
b. What is the probability of Bruce being accepted by all five schools?

5–36. An accountant is about to audit 24 accounts of a firm. Sixteen of these accounts are high-volume customers. If the accountant selects four of the accounts at random, what is the probability that at least one is a high-volume account?

Hint: First, find the probability that none of the selected accounts are high volume.

5–37. Two athletic teams have met 10 times, and the Big Red has won 6 of the contests. It is felt that the past experience is indicative of future outcomes. Now the two teams are going to play in an elimination tournament. Assume the outcome of each game is independent of other games.

a. If the teams play one game, what is the probability that the Big Red will win?
b. If the teams play a two-out-of-three series, what is the probability that the Big Red will win?
c. If the teams play four out of seven, what is the probability that the Big Red will win?

5–38. The president of a large electric utility has to decide whether to purchase one large generator (Big Jim) or four smaller generators (Little Arnies) to attain a given amount of electric generating capacity. On any given summer day, the probability of a generator being in service is 0.95 (the generators are equally reliable). Equivalently, there is a 0.05 probability of a failure.

a. What is the probability of Big Jim being out of service on a given day?
b. What is the probability of either zero or one of the four Arnies being out?
c. If five Little Arnies are purchased, what is the probability of at least four operating?
d. If six Little Arnies are purchased, what is the probability of at least four operating?

5–39. Suppose you flip a coin until four heads have been obtained. What is the probability that it will take exactly seven flips to obtain the four heads?

Hint: The seventh flip must be a head, and three of the first six flips must be heads to obtain the required condition.

5–40. Newspaper articles frequently cite the fact that in any one year, a small percentage (say, 10 percent) of all drivers are responsible for all automobile accidents. The conclusion is often reached that if only we could single out these accident-prone drivers and either retrain them or remove them from the roads, we could drastically reduce auto accidents. You are told that of 100,000 drivers who were involved in one or more accidents in one year, 11,000 of them were involved in one or more accidents in the next year.

a. Given the above information, complete the entries in the joint probability table in Table 5–21.
b. Do you think searching for accident-prone drivers is an effective way to reduce auto accidents? Why?

TABLE 5–21

First Year \ *Second Year*	*Accident*	*No Accident*	*Marginal Probability of Event in First Year*
Accident			0.10
No Accident			0.90
Marginal Probability of Event in Second Year	0.10	0.90	1.00

5–41. This classical probability problem is similar to the Monty Hall puzzle. Three prisoners (Joval, Reginald, and Mordrid) are in jail in medieval times. The king has decreed that one of them, chosen at random, is to be executed on the following morning. One of the prisoners, Joval, has a friendly chat with the prison guard and finds out that the guard knows who is to be executed. Joval begs the guard to tell him if he is to be the one. The guard replies that he is sworn not to tell. Finally, after much prompting, the guard tells Joval, "I cannot tell you who is to be executed, but I will tell you that Reginald is **not** the one." Joval is disturbed by this news. "Why did you tell me that? Now I know that there is a one in two chance for my execution, whereas before it was one in three."

Was Joval's probability calculation correct?

More Challenging Problems

5–42. A safety commissioner for a certain city performed a study of the pedestrian fatalities at intersections. He noted that only 6 of the 19 fatalities were pedestrians who were crossing the intersection against the light (i.e., in disregard of the proper signal), whereas the remaining 13 were crossing *with* the light. He was puzzled because the figures seemed to show that it was roughly twice as safe for a pedestrian to cross against the light as with it. Can you explain this apparent contradiction to the commissioner?

5–43. Suppose a new test is available to test for drug addiction. The test is 95 percent accurate "each way"; that is, if the person *is* an addict, there is a 95 percent chance the test will indicate "yes"; if the person is *not* an addict, then 95 percent of the time the test will indicate "no." Suppose it is known that the incidence of drug addiction in urban populations is about 1 out of 1,000. Given a positive (yes) test result, what are the chances that the person being tested is addicted?

5–44. A satellite is being launched to gather data on atmospheric conditions on a distant planet. The satellite contains two power cells, and each is estimated to have a 90 percent chance of functioning correctly. The two cells are located in different parts of the satellite so that the failure of either cell is not likely to be related to the other (that is, they are independent).

There are two measuring instruments on the satellite, the primary instrument and a backup instrument. Because they are located together, the reliability of these instruments is not considered to be independent. The probabilities of failure and success are given as follows:

Primary Instrument \ *Backup Instrument*	*Good*	*Fail*
Good	0.6	0.2
Fail	0.1	0.1

The primary instrument requires only one power cell to function, but the backup instrument requires both power cells to operate. If either instrument works, the mission of the satellite is a success. What is the probability of a successful mission?

5–45. This is a classical probability problem. Try out your intuition before solving it systematically.

Assume there are three boxes and each box has two drawers. There is either a gold or silver coin in each drawer. One box has two gold, one box two silver, and one box one gold and one silver coin. A box is chosen at random, and one of the two drawers is opened. A gold coin is observed.

G	G	S
G	S	S

What is the probability of opening the second drawer in the same box and observing a gold coin?

5–46. Assume you can choose between two different gambles. In one gamble, you know that 50 red and 50 black balls are in a jar, and one ball is to be chosen perfectly randomly. You will receive a prize if you guess what the color of the ball drawn will be. In the second gamble, there is an undisclosed number of red and black balls in a jar, and again you are to guess the color of the draw for an identical prize.

Which gamble would you choose to participate in? Why?

5–47. A restaurant seats 100 people. The owner recently decided to provide a free birthday cake to any person having a birthday on the day he or she dined at the restaurant. Assuming $p = 1/365 = 0.003$ and $n = 100$, the owner found the following entry in an extensive binomial table:

$$P(R \geq 6|n = 100, p = 0.01) = 0.0005$$

The owner felt that, since his p was smaller than 0.01, this probability should be an upper limit on the probability of six or more birthday cakes being requested each night. He therefore ordered five cakes each night. After 10 evenings, he had "run out" of cakes three times! What do you suppose went wrong with his analysis?

5–48 The Acme Company has two warehouses located in different cities. Demand for the product is independent in each warehouse district. However, both warehouses have identical probability distributions for demand as follows:

Demand (units)	*Probability*
0	0.10
1	0.50
2	0.30
3	0.10
	1.00

Assume that each warehouse normally stocks two units.

a. What is the probability that one or the other of the warehouses (not both) will have more demand than stock?

b. What is the probability that both warehouses will be out of stock?

5–49. Refer to Problem 5–48. Suppose the Acme Company consolidated the two warehouses into a single one serving both cities. The consolidated warehouse would carry a stock of four units.

a. Determine the probability distribution of demand at the consolidated warehouse.

b. What is the probability that the consolidated warehouse would be out of stock by one unit? By two units? Compare these to the answers obtained in Problem 5–48.

5–50. Professor Smullyan describes an island, the inhabitants of which are either knights or knaves.[11] Knights never lie, and knaves never tell the truth. Suppose that you know that 80 percent of the inhabitants (both knights and knaves) are in favor of electing Professor Smullyan as king of the island. The island is made up of 60 percent knights and 40 percent knaves, but you cannot tell which is which. Suppose you take a sample of 10 inhabitants at random and ask, "Do you favor Smullyan as king?" What is the probability that you will get six or more "yes" answers?

5–51. It has been found that when a malfunction occurs in an electrical system, the following parts have probabilities of causing the malfunction as indicated:

Part	*Probability of Causing Malfunction*
A	0.40
B	0.10
C	0.30
D	0.20
	1.00

[11] Raymond Smullyan, *What Is the Name of This Book* (Englewood Cliffs, NJ: Prentice Hall, 1978).

a. Assuming it is equally fast to check each of the four parts, in what order would you suggest the parts be checked? Why?

b. Now suppose that the time involved in checking the parts is as follows (assume parts must be checked one at a time):

Part	*Time to Check (hours)*
A	2
B	1
C	¾
D	⅓

Under these conditions, in what order would you suggest the parts be checked if the malfunction is to be found in the shortest time, on average? Why?

5–52. You are interested in the price of potatoes next year. Three factors affect this price: acreage planted in winter wheat, acreage planted in potatoes, and weather conditions. A combination of large potato acreage and favorable weather conditions will result in a price of $2 per cwt. (hundred lbs). Medium potato acreage and favorable weather will result in a $4 per cwt. price. Small potato acreage and favorable weather will result in a $6 price. Unfavorable weather will increase the price in each case by $2 per cwt. You assess a 0.8 chance for favorable weather and a 0.2 chance for unfavorable weather. Weather is independent of acreage planted.

The acreage planted in potatoes depends to some extent on the acreage planted in winter wheat. Based on past experience, you assess a 30 percent chance for heavy planting of winter wheat, and 70 percent for light planting of winter wheat. If there is heavy planting of winter wheat, the chance for large potato acreage is zero, the chance for medium potato acreage is ⅔, and the chance for small potato acreage is ⅓. If there is light planting of winter wheat, the chances for large, medium, and small potato acreage are 2/7, 3/7, and 2/7, respectively.

Consider the price of potatoes as the random variable. Determine the probability distribution for this random variable. What is the expected price?

5–53. John McEnroe has been known to exhibit anger during a tennis match. A statistician noted that John won more points than he lost immediately after he became angry. From this it was concluded that John benefited from his outbursts. Evaluate the conclusion.

5–54.[12] There are 15 blue cabs and 85 green cabs. A witness reported that a blue cab caused an accident and then drove off. However, there is evidence that witnesses are wrong 20 percent of the time (and right 80 percent of the time). What is the probability that the cab was blue?

5–55. Suppose that the midterm exam that you took for this course last week had two questions, the first worth 60 points and the second worth 40 points. The instructor has announced that the distribution of scores on each question is normally distributed, with means and standard deviations as follows:

Question	*Mean*	*Standard Deviation*
1	40	10
2	30	5

However, other than indicating that the total scores were normally distributed, the instructor did not give any additional information about the total scores.

a. What is the mean (expected value) score for the overall exam?

b. Given only the information above, can you calculate the variance or standard deviation for the overall scores? What additional assumption could you make that would allow you to do so? Would it be a reasonable assumption in this case?

c. Suppose that the instructor also announced that the correlation between scores on the first question and that on the second was 0.60. Given this, calculate the variance and standard deviation for total scores.

d. Suppose your score was 85. In what percentile does that place you? In other words, what percent of the class scored lower than you?

5–56. You have an endowment—say, $100,000—that you are considering investing in three mutual funds. The International fund invests in a variety of international stocks. The U.S. stocks fund invests in American stocks, and the U.S. Bonds fund invests in high-grade corporate bonds. Based on past experience, you have estimated the expected returns, variances, and covariances for these funds as follows:

[12]This question is based on S. C. Salop, "Evaluating Uncertain Evidence with Sir Thomas Bayes: A Note for Teachers," *The Journal of Economics Perspectives,* Summer 1987, pp. 155–59.

Fund	Expected Return (%)
International	10%
U.S. stocks	12
U.S. bonds	7

The variance/covariance matrix is:

	International	U.S. Stocks	U.S. Bonds
International	0.0090		
U.S. Stocks	−0.00114	0.0036	
U.S. Bonds	0.000323	−.000102	0.0003

The values on the diagonal are the variances. That is, 0.0090 is the variance of returns for the International stock fund. The covariances are the off-diagonal elements. For example, the covariance between the International fund returns and those of the U.S. Stock fund is −0.00114.

You are considering two options:

a. Investing 20 percent of your portfolio in the International fund, 60 percent in the U.S. Stock fund, and the remaining 20 percent in the U.S. Bond fund, or:

b. Investing 50 percent in the International fund, and 25 percent in each of the U.S. Stock and Bond funds.

Which of these options is better? Why?

Solutions to Practice Problems

5–1. The possible outcomes are: (Outcomes are independent.)

HHH	1/8	THH	1/8
HHT	1/8	TTH	1/8
HTT	1/8	THT	1/8
HTH	1/8	TTT	1/8

Total = 8/8 = 1

a. $P(\text{three heads}) = 1/8$ or $P(\text{three heads}) = P(H) \cdot P(H) \cdot P(H) = 1/2 \cdot 1/2 \cdot 1/2 = 1/8$.

b. $P(\text{two or more heads})$:

HHH	1/8
HHT	1/8
HTH	1/8
THH	1/8
	1/2

c. $P(\text{one or more tails})$:

HHT	1/8
HTT	1/8
HTH	1/8
THH	1/8
TTH	1/8
THT	1/8
TTT	1/8
	7/8

or $1 - P(\text{HHH}) = 1 - 1/8 = 7/8$

d. $P(\text{the last toss being a head})$:

HHH	1/8
HTH	1/8
THH	1/8
TTH	1/8
	1/2

Note: Since outcomes are independent, this is $P(\text{heads})$ on one toss of fair coin, which is 1/2.

5–2.

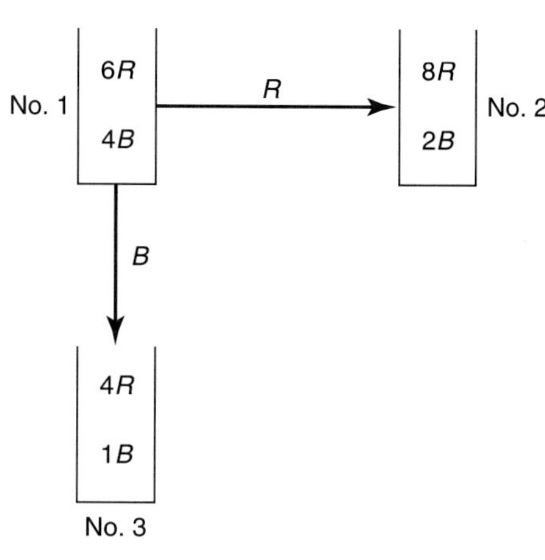

a. $P(\text{red on second}|\text{red on first}) = 8/10 = 4/5$

b. $P(\text{black on second}|\text{red on first}) = 2/10 = 1/5$

c. $P(\text{red on second}|\text{black on first}) = 4/5$

d. $P(\text{black on second}|\text{black on first}) = 1/5$

e. $P(\text{black on second})$

$= P(B_2|R_1) \cdot P(R_1) + P(B_2|B_1) \cdot P(B_1)$

$= \frac{1}{5} \cdot \frac{3}{5} + \frac{1}{5} \cdot \frac{2}{5} = \frac{1}{5}$

f.

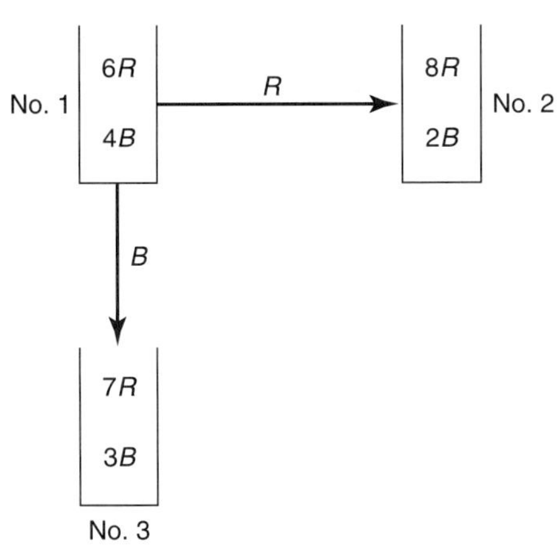

a. $P(\text{red on second}|\text{red on first}) = 8/10 = 4/5$
b. $P(\text{black on second}|\text{red on first}) = 2/10 = 1/5$
c. $P(\text{red on second}|\text{black on first}) = 7/10$
d. $P(\text{black on second}|\text{black on first}) = 3/10$
e. $P(B_2) = P(B_2|R_1) \cdot P(R_1) + P(B_2|B_1) \cdot P(B_1)$
$$= \frac{1}{5} \cdot \frac{3}{5} + \frac{3}{10} \cdot \frac{2}{5} = .24$$
In the first instance, the conditioning event was not important because the proportions of reds and blacks in urns nos. 2 and 3 are the same. Thus, independence exists. In the second case, the proportions are not the same, so the conditioning event is important.

5–3. *a.* $n = 2$ $P(\text{heads}) = .4$ $P(\text{tails}) = .6$
(1) $P(2 \text{ heads}) = .16$
(2) $P(2 \text{ tails}) = .36$
(3) $P(1 \text{ head}) = .48$
(4) $P(1 \text{ head}) + P(2 \text{ heads}) = .48 + .16 = .64$
(5) $P(1 \text{ tail}) = .48$
$P(1 \text{ tail}) + P(2 \text{ tails}) = .48 + .36 = .84$
(6) $P(R \leq 1) = 1 - P(R > 1) = 1 - .36 = .64$
A partition of the event, two tosses, is:

				Probability
P(1 head) =	.48	or	HH =	.16
P(2 heads) =	.16		HT =	.24
P(2 tails) =	.36		TH =	.24
	1.00		TT =	.36
				1.00

b. $n = 3$
(1) $P(3 \text{ heads}) = .064$
(2) $P(2 \text{ heads}) = .288$
(3) $P(1 \text{ head}) = .432$
(4) $.064 + .288 + .432 = .784$

5–4. *a.* $Z = (15 - 12)/4 = .75$; $P(Z \geq .75) = 1 - .7734 = .2266$
b. $Z = (10 - 12)/4 = -.50$; $P(Z \leq -.50) = P(Z \geq .50) = 1 - .6915 = .3085$
c. $P(10 < X \leq 15) = 1 - P(X < 10) - P(X \geq 15) = 1 - .3085 - .2266 = .4649$
d. $Z = (17 - 12)/4 = 1.25$; $P(Z > 1.25) = 1 - .8944 = .1056$
e. $P(15 < X \leq 17) = P(X > 15) - P(X > 17) = .2266 - .1056 = .1210$

5–5. *a.* $P(R \geq 4|.5, 10) = .8281$
$P(R \geq 5|.5, 10) = .6230$
$P(R = 4|.5, 10) = .8281 - .6230 = .2051$
b. $P(R > 4|.5, 10) = P(R \geq 5|.5, 10) = .6230$
c. $P(R \geq 4|.4, 8) = .4059$
d. $P(R < 4|.2, 10) = 1 - P(R \geq 4|.2, 10) = 1 - .1209 = .8791$
e. $P(R = 0|.3, 10) = 1 - P(R \geq 1|.3, 10) = 1 - .9718 = .0282$
f. $P(R \geq 5|.6, 10) = 1 - P(R \geq 6|.4, 10) = 1 - .1662 = .8338$

5–6. *a.* From the table, $P(Z \leq 1.0) = .8413$; hence, $x = 15 - (1)(3) = 12$
b. $P(X > x) = 1 - P(x \leq X) = 1 - .2946 = .7054$; $P(Z \leq .54) = .7054$; hence, $x = 15 + (.54)(3) = 16.62$
c. $P(X \geq x) = 1 - P(x \leq X) = 1 - .02275 = .97725$ $P(Z \leq 2.0) = .97725$ from Table A; hence $x = 15 + 2(3) = 21.0$

5–7. *a.* $P(\text{under } 55) = 9/30 = .30$. This is a marginal or simple probability.
b. $P(55 \text{ or older, Marketing}) = 5/30 = .167$. Joint probability.
c. $P(\text{under } 55|\text{Finance}) = 4/18 = .222$. conditional probability.
d. No. Note that $P(\text{under } 55)$ does not equal $P(\text{under } 55|\text{Finance})$, which would be necessary for independence. Generally, the "Other" category executives are younger than their counterparts who were in Finance and Marketing.

5–8. See Table 5–22. Expected percent defective is 3.80. Variance of random variable is 5.360. Standard deviation of the random variable is $\sqrt{5.36} = 2.32$.

TABLE 5–22

Value of the Random Variable X_i (percent defective)	*$P(X_i)$ P(event)*	*$X_iP(X_i)$*	*Squared Deviations from the Mean of 3.8; $[X_i - E(X)]^2$*	*Squared Deviations Weighted by the Probability: $P(X_i) \cdot [X_i - E(X)]^2$*
1	.10	.10	$(-2.80)^2 = 7.84$	.784
2	.15	.30	$(-1.80)^2 = 3.24$	.486
3	.20	.60	$(-.80)^2 = .64$	.128
4	.30	1.20	$(.20)^2 = .04$	.012
5	.20	1.00	$(1.20)^2 = 1.44$	.288
10	.03	.30	$(6.20)^2 = 38.44$	1.153
15	.02	.30	$(11.20)^2 = 125.44$	2.509
	1.00	3.80 percent		5.360

5–9. *a.* $P(R = 0|p = .1, n = 20) = .1216$
b. $P(R = 1) = .2701$
c. $P(R \geq 4) = .1330$
d. $P(R > 4) = .0432$
e. $P(R = 4) = .0898$

5–10. $P(\text{head and } A_1) = (.8)(.5) = .40$
$P(\text{head and } A_2) = (.2)(.9) = .18$
$P(\text{head}) = .58$
$P(A_1|\text{head}) = .40/.58 = .690$
$P(A_2|\text{head}) = .18/.58 = .310$

5–11. Note: No correction is made in computations for the fact that only integral units could be sold. With this interpretation, it would be appropriate to write probability of sales less than 16 as $P(X \leq 15.5)$.
a. $P(X < 16) = P(Z < -2/3) = .2514$
b. $P(15 \leq X \leq 25) = P(-.83 \leq Z \leq .83) = .7967 - .2033 = .5934$
c. $P(X \geq x) = .10$. Solve for x. $P(Z \geq z) = .10$ for $z = 1.28$
$x = 20 + 1.28(6) = 27.7$ or 28 units

Motivating Example

Investment in a Major Transmission System

Oglethorpe Power Corporation (OPC) is a firm in Georgia that generates and distributes electrical power to consumer-owned cooperatives.[1] OPC learned that the Florida Power Corporation wanted to purchase additional power from Georgia. (Florida imports a significant part of its power needs from Georgia, Alabama, and South Carolina.) Transmission of the additional power would require the construction of a 500-kilovolt transmission line. The investment required was on the order of $100 million, with potential savings (revenues minus costs) of about $20 million per year.

The decision facing OPC management was whether or not to construct this transmission line; if so, whether or not to upgrade associated transmission facilities; and finally, what form of control over the system to negotiate with Florida Power. There were major uncertainties associated with the investment. In particular, the construction cost, the competitive situation in Florida, the long-run power demand in Florida, the share of that demand that OPC would get, and finally, the spot price for power all could have significant effects on the profitability of the venture.

Management decided to do a formal decision analysis of this decision problem. An analysis team, including outside consultants, worked with top management to define the problem using an influence diagram and then to diagram the problem in a decision tree format. Probabilities for the uncertain variables were obtained from groups within the firm that had expertise in those areas.

An analysis using expected monetary value (EMV) revealed the optimal decision, but it also showed that there was substantial risk associated with that policy. An analysis calculating the value of information about the major uncertainties revealed that obtaining information about the competitive situation before making the decision could have a big impact, and the firm undertook a study to do this. The analysis led to a strategy that substantially reduced the risk for the optimal EMV policy.

The analysis was done in a two-week period and identified a strategy quite different from, and significantly better than, that which would have been undertaken without the study.

[1]This is based on Adam Borison, "Oglethorpe Power Corporation Decides about Investing in a Major Transmission System," *Interfaces* 25, no. 2 (March–April 1995), pp. 25–36.

CHAPTER

6 DECISION MAKING UNDER UNCERTAINTY

In this chapter we consider the application of probability concepts to business decisions that must be made under conditions of uncertainty. We shall develop a means for making consistent decisions and for estimating the cost of uncertainty. We shall initially propose expected monetary value as an appropriate criterion for decision making. Later in the chapter, we will describe the limitations of expected monetary value and suggest modifications in the analysis.

We will also introduce the opportunity to experiment; that is, to gather additional information and revise probabilities before making the decision.

Conditional Value

Suppose a grocer is faced with a problem of how many cases of milk to stock to meet tomorrow's demand. Assume that any milk that remains unsold at the end of the day will represent a complete loss to the grocer. Also, any unsatisfied demand bears no cost except the cost of the lost sale; the disappointed customer will come back in the future. This example is highly simplified but illustrates the basic principles of conditional and expected value.

In our analysis of the grocer's problem, it would be helpful if we knew something about past sales, on the assumption that this experience may serve as a guide to what may be expected in the future. Suppose the grocer has maintained records such as those shown in Table 6–1.

TABLE 6–1 Historical Demand

Total Demand per Day	*Number of Days Each Demand Level Was Recorded*	*Probability of Each Event*
25 cases	20	0.10
26 cases	60	0.30
27 cases	100	0.50
28 cases	20	0.10
	200	1.00

With a purchase price (variable cost) of $8 per case and a selling price of $10 per case, the table of conditional values (Table 6–2) is a description of the problem facing the grocer. The possible actions (number of cases to buy) facing the grocer are listed across the top of the table. It is, of course, possible to buy 24 or 29 cases, and so on; but if, in the last 200 days, sales were in the range of 25–28 cases, the grocer might view a stock of greater than 28 or less than 25 as having zero probability of occurring. We shall make this assumption. The possible (conceivable) events—in this example, the possible sales—are listed in the far left column. If the grocer is willing to assign probabilities in accordance with the historical data, then events (sales) other than those listed will carry zero probabilities; they are considered impossible events.

Table 6–2 can be thought of as a **conditional value** or conditional profit table. Corresponding to each action the grocer takes, and each event that happens, there is a given conditional profit. These profits are conditional in the sense that a certain profit results from following a specific course of action (act) and having a specific demand (event) occur. All the possible combinations are shown in Table 6–2. For example, if 26 cases were stocked and the demand turned out to be 25 cases, the grocer would have a profit of $42 (that is, $25 \cdot 10 - 26 \cdot 8$). The best act for each possible event is indicated by an asterisk.

Looking at the act column "Stock 27," let us trace through the calculations of each dollar amount. This is done in Table 6–3. Similar computations have to be made for acts "Stock 25," "Stock 26," and "Stock 28."

The calculations of Table 6–3 reflect the fact that if 27 cases are stocked, only 27 can be sold, even if the demand turns out to be 28 cases. Hence, the profit reaches

TABLE 6–2 Conditional Values

	Possible Actions			
Event: Demand	*Stock 25*	*Stock 26*	*Stock 27*	*Stock 28*
25 cases	$50*	$42	$34	$26
26 cases	50	52*	44	36
27 cases	50	52	54*	46
28 cases	50	52	54	56*

*Best act for the event (the largest profit in each row).

TABLE 6–3 Conditional Profits of Act "Stock 27"

Event: Demand	*Selling Price*	*Total Revenue*	*Cost of 27 Cases (27 · $8)*	*Conditional Profit of Act "Stock 27"*
25 cases	$10	$250	$216	$34
26 cases	10	260	216	44
27 cases	10	270	216	54
28 cases	10	270	216	54

a maximum of $54 for the sale of 27 units and levels off at that figure even if 28 units are demanded.

The Loss Table

In addition to making a table showing conditional profits (Table 6–2), it is possible to construct a table showing conditional *opportunity losses* (Table 6–4). Consider the act "Stock 28." If the demand turns out to be 28, the grocer will make a profit of $56. This is the best that can be achieved with a demand of 28. With a demand of 28, if the grocer had stocked only 27, the profit would have been $54; this act would entail a $2 *opportunity loss* compared with the *best* action with a demand of 28. If the demand were 28 and the grocer stocked 26, there would be a $4 conditional opportunity loss ($56 − $52). **Opportunity loss** can be defined in general as the *amount of profit forgone by not choosing the best act for each event.* With this definition, the conditional opportunity loss table shown in Table 6–4 can be constructed.

It should be emphasized that a conditional profit (or loss) relates to a profit conditional on both:

1. An event happening.
2. A given action.

We do not know which event is going to occur; there is uncertainty. Therefore, the conditional profit for a decision is not one number but a table of profits (or losses) associated with possible events. Profit is $44 only on condition of both stocking 27 units and having an actual demand of 26 units. If the demand is different than 26 units, the actual profit will be different than $44.

TABLE 6–4 Conditional Opportunity Losses

	Act			
Event: Demand	*Stock 25*	*Stock 26*	*Stock 27*	*Stock 28*
25 cases	$0	$8	$16	$24
26 cases	2	0	8	16
27 cases	4	2	0	8
28 cases	6	4	2	0

Computations of Conditional Opportunity Losses

Event: Demand	*Optimum Act for Each Event*	*Profit of Optimum Act*	*Difference between Profit of Optimum Act and the Act of Stocking*			
			Stock 25	*Stock 26*	*Stock 27*	*Stock 28*
25	25	$50	$50 − $50 = $0	$50 − $42 = $8	$50 − $34 = $16	$50 − $26 = $24
26	26	52	52 − 50 = 2	52 − 52 = 0	52 − 44 = 8	52 − 36 = 16
27	27	54	54 − 50 = 4	54 − 52 = 2	54 − 54 = 0	54 − 46 = 8
28	28	56	56 − 50 = 6	56 − 52 = 4	56 − 54 = 2	56 − 56 = 0

Expected Monetary Value

Even though the conditional values and losses help characterize the problem facing the grocer, it is not yet possible to offer an optimum solution. The grocer could choose the best act with advance knowledge of tomorrow's demand, but this information is not available in our example. The problem facing the grocer is to assign probabilities to the possible events and then to analyze the action alternatives. If the probabilities are based on historical information (see Table 6–1), they will be as shown in Table 6–5. If the grocer believes that for some reason tomorrow's demand will vary somewhat from the observed pattern, the probability assignment should be modified.

The next step is to bring the assigned probabilities into the analysis. We accomplish this by *weighting the conditional values of each event in the conditional value table by the probability of the event occurring, and adding the products.* The resulting number is the **expected monetary value** for the act; the optimum act is the one with the highest expected monetary value. The calculations are given in Table 6–6 for the acts of stocking 26 and 27 units. The calculations for 25 and 28 units would be similar.

In Table 6–6, the expected monetary value (EMV) is calculated by multiplying each conditional value by its probability and then adding the weighted conditional values. Table 6–7 shows the expected monetary values for all four acts. For the act "Stock 26," the grocer calculates an expected monetary value of $51, the highest EMV. Therefore, based on expected monetary value, 26 cases should be stocked.

Note that the EMV OF $51 will not be the profit on any one day. It is the expected or average profit. If the decision were repeated for many days (with the same probabilities), the grocer would make an average of $51 per day by stocking

TABLE 6–5

Event: Demand	*Probability of Event*
25 cases	0.10
26 cases	0.30
27 cases	0.50
28 cases	0.10
	1.00

TABLE 6–6
Calculation of Expected Monetary Values

		Act: Stock 26		*Act: Stock 27*	
Event: Demand	*Probability of Event*	*Conditional Value (CV)*	*CV Weighted by Probability of Event*	*Conditional Value (CV)*	*CV Weighted by Probability of Event*
25 cases	0.10	$42	$ 4.20	$34	$ 3.40
26 cases	0.30	52	15.60	44	13.20
27 cases	0.50	52	26.00	54	27.00
28 cases	0.10	52	5.20	54	5.40
	1.00				
Expected monetary value			$51.00		$49.00

TABLE 6–7
Summary of Expected Monetary Values

Act	Expected Monetary Value	
Stock 25	$50	
Stock 26	51	(optimum act)
Stock 27	49	
Stock 28	42	

26 cases of milk. Even if the decision were not repeated, the action with the highest EMV is the best alternative that the decision maker has available.

To summarize, our plan for solving the grocer's problem is as follows:

1. Construct a payoff (conditional value) table listing the acts and events that are considered to be possibilities and listing the outcomes for each act and event. In listing the events, be sure that each event is mutually exclusive (i.e., make sure that no two or more events can occur simultaneously) and that all events considered together are exhaustive (i.e., that the events listed cover all the possibilities). This table includes the economics of the problem (costs, revenues, and profits) by presenting a conditional value (or loss) for each act and event combination.
2. Assign probabilities to the events.
3. Calculate an EMV for each act by weighting (multiplying) the conditional values by the assigned probabilities and adding the weighted conditional values to obtain the EMV of the act.
4. Choose the act with the largest EMV.

Expected Opportunity Loss

The grocer can also choose the best act by minimizing **expected opportunity loss (EOL).** The procedure is the same as just outlined except that instead of using the payoff table (conditional value table, Table 6–2) and conditional profits, we shall use the conditional opportunity loss table (Table 6–4) and conditional opportunity losses. The calculations for act "Stock 26" and act "Stock 27" are as given in Table 6–8.

TABLE 6–8
Calculation of Expected Opportunity Losses

		Act: Stock 26		Act: Stock 27	
Event: Demand	Probability of Event	Conditional Losses (CL)	CV Weighted by Probability of Event	Conditional Losses (CL)	CV Weighted by Probability of Event
25 cases	0.10	$8	$0.80	$16	$1.60
26 cases	0.30	0	0.00	8	2.40
27 cases	0.50	2	1.00	0	0.00
28 cases	0.10	4	0.40	2	0.20
	1.00				
Expected opportunity loss			$2.20		$4.20

TABLE 6–9 Summary of Expected Opportunity Losses

Act	*Expected Opportunity Losses*	*Comparison of Expected Opportunity Losses with Optimum*
Stock 25	$ 3.20	$1
Stock 26	2.20 (optimum act)	0
Stock 27	4.20	2
Stock 28	11.20	9

From Table 6–9, we find that the grocer should choose act "Stock 26," which has an expected loss of $2.20, the lowest of the four expected opportunity losses.

Summary

Let us summarize the various measures of profitability that have been introduced:

Conditional value. The actual profit that would result following a given action, conditional on a given event occurring.

Conditional opportunity loss. The relative loss (i.e., the profit not earned) following a given action, conditional on a given event occurring.

Expected monetary value. The conditional values weighted by the probability of the events occurring, and summed for each act.

Expected opportunity loss. The conditional opportunity losses weighted by the probability of the events occurring, and summed for each act.

The optimum act is the act with the greatest expected monetary value, and thus, the smallest expected opportunity loss.

Risk in Decision Making

Although expected monetary value may be a good guide to action in many cases, it may not be in others. This does not destroy the expected value model; it means we must modify the analysis when the situation warrants it. Let us consider a major difficulty with expected monetary value.

Suppose a manager has a chance to invest $500,000 in a speculative new product. Assume that if the product is successful, there will be net profits of $1 million. However, if the product is not successful, there will be a loss of the $500,000 spent to develop, produce, and sell the new product. Our manager's conditional value table is given in Table 6–10.

If, after gathering evidence, the manager assigns a subjective probability of 0.90 of success, the EMV of the act "Invest" would be $850,000 ($1,000,000 × 0.90 − $500,000 × 0.10 = $850,000), as compared with an EMV of zero for the act "Do not invest." Suppose, however, that the firm is in a very difficult financial position, and a $500,000 loss would result in certain bankruptcy. In such a case, EMV may be a poor guide to action. The manager may be unwilling to accept a 0.10 probabil-

TABLE 6–10
Conditional Value

Event	Act	
	Invest	*Do Not Invest*
Product successful	$1,000,000	0
Product not successful	−500,000	0

ity of losing $500,000 regardless of the size of the conditional profits or the EMV, because of the undesirable consequences of the loss. If so, the manager has a large disutility for such a loss, and this should be brought into the analysis. That is, in situations that involve a substantial amount of risk, EMV may not be the best decision criterion.

If the amounts of money involved in the payoff are not large, then EMV is a reasonable guide to action. Such is the case of the grocer's problem above. "Large" in this context, is, of course, relative. Decisions involving millions of dollars may not be large for a major oil company or a Wall Street currency trader, but certainly would be for most individuals. Whether a particular decision seems risky also depends on individual preferences. Some individuals are quite *risk averse,* and might be unwilling to take even moderate risks, while others may be *risk neutral* (indifferent to risk), or even *risk preferring.* There are formal methods for incorporating risk into the decision analysis called **utility theory.** This is covered in the detail in a later chapter.

Even when the decision involves substantial risk, the calculation and evaluation of the expected monetary value can provide useful information for the decision maker. The decision maker faced with the major potential loss in the example of Table 6–10 knows from the EMV calculation that the investment is "worth" $850,000. The decision maker knows how much he or she is giving up to avoid the possible loss. Alternatively, he or she may be able to find a partner willing to share in the venture; this could substantially reduce the downside risk.

Expected Profit with Perfect Predictions

Returning to our example of the grocer, let us raise the following question: "What profit could the grocer *expect* to make in the future if each day's demand could be *predicted with certainty* the day before the particular demand occurred?" To answer this question, let us construct a conditional value table that will show the conditional profit for the *best* act, given each event. Table 6–11 is constructed by choosing the best act and recording the highest profit figures for each event (this information can be obtained from Table 6–2). For example, if we knew tomorrow's demand would be 27, we would stock 27 cases, for a profit of $54. If we stocked 26, we would forgo the $2 profit on one unit; and if we stocked 28, we would have to scrap one unit at a loss of $8. Table 6–11 shows the profit resulting from the best action for each possible event.

Let us convert these conditional optimal profit figures to an expectation. This can be done by weighting the profit for each event by the probability of the event occurring. The calculation is shown in Table 6–12, where the **expected profit with**

TABLE 6–11
Conditional Value Table for Optimal Decisions with Perfect Prediction

	Act			
Event: Demand	*Stock 25*	*Stock 26*	*Stock 27*	*Stock 28*
25 cases	$50			
26 cases		$52		
27 cases			$54	
28 cases				$56

TABLE 6–12
Expected Profit with Perfect Prediction

Event: Demand	*Probability of Event*	*Conditional Profit (CP)*	*CP Weighted by Probability of Event*
25 cases	0.10	$50	$ 5.00
26 cases	0.30	52	15.60
27 cases	0.50	54	27.00
28 cases	0.10	56	5.60
Expected profit with perfect prediction			$53.20

perfect prediction ($53.20) is the profit the grocer could make on the average if each day's demand could be predicted in advance. Thus, the optimum amount would be ordered each day.

Before the perfect predictor is used, the grocer is still uncertain as to what the prediction will be, since any one of the four events may occur. Before the prediction, the profit is an *expectation,* since we do not know which event will occur. To decide whether or not to use the predictor, our grocer must assign a value to the perfect prediction and compare this value with the cost of the predictor. Remember that before buying the information, we do not know what the prediction will be.

Expected Value of Perfect Information

In many decision problems, the manager faces the question of whether to act immediately or delay action and seek more information. The important thing to the manager is to balance the *cost* of additional information against the *value* (additional profit) of the information. The cost part of this decision (cost of obtaining information) is usually easier to calculate than the value of the information. However, using the expected value model, we have a way of quantifying the value of additional information.

Referring again to our grocer example, we showed in Table 6–12 that the expected profit with perfect prediction is $53.20. Previously, in Table 6–7, we showed that the EMV of the best act under uncertainty, "Stock 26," is $51. The difference:

$$\$53.20 - \$51 = \$2.20$$

is the increase in expected profit from a free, perfect predictive device. Hence, $2.20 is the **expected value of perfect information (EVPI).** That is:

$$\text{EVPI} = \text{Expected profit with perfect prediction} - \text{EMV (of optimal act)}$$

TABLE 6–13

	Act			
	Stock 25	*Stock 26*	*Stock 27*	*Stock 28*
EMV (under uncertainty)	\$50.00	\$51.00	\$49.00	\$42.00
EOL	3.20	2.20	4.20	11.20
Expected profit (with perfect prediction)	\$53.20	\$53.20	\$53.20	\$53.20

Note from Table 6–9 that \$2.20 is also the *expected opportunity loss* of the optimum act. We might expect this result, since the perfect predictor should reduce the opportunity loss that exists under uncertainty to zero. Hence, the expected opportunity loss of the optimum act measures the EVPI. A useful check on computations is provided by the following identity:

$$\begin{matrix}\text{EMV (of any act)} \\ +\ \text{EOL (of the same act)}\end{matrix} = \begin{matrix}\text{Expected profit with} \\ \text{perfect prediction}\end{matrix}$$

This calculation is shown in Table 6–13.

It is important to note that it is the EOL of the *optimal act* that is equal to the EVPI. If the grocer chooses the act "Stock 28," there will be an EMV of \$42 and an EOL of \$11.20. The EVPI is *not* \$11.20, because the grocer can increase the EMV to \$51 by choosing a different act ("Stock 26"), and this requires *no* additional information. The value of additional information is measured starting from the assumption that the optimal action would be chosen, given the information already available.

Interpretation of EVPI

The EVPI can be thought of as a general measure of the economic impact of the uncertainty in the decision problem. As the name implies, it is the value of obtaining a perfect prediction. As such, it is an upper bound on what it would be worth to get additional information before acting. If the EVPI is small, additional information would not help much. If it is a large amount, then the decision maker should examine methods for obtaining information before acting. More on this later in the chapter!

But since it is also the expected opportunity loss, the EVPI is a measure of opportunities forgone. In this sense, if the EVPI is large, it should be a signal to the decision maker to seek alternatives that are not currently being considered. The EVPI in our grocer's problem was not very large (\$2.20 per day), but if it had been, it would be an indication to see if the stocking problem couldn't be solved in a different way. The grocer, for example, might arrange to have the dairy make two or more deliveries per day, with the amount on the subsequent deliveries dependent on sales—a "just-in-time" inventory system. These might have additional costs, which would need to be evaluated. The point is that EVPI can be a trigger to look for alternatives. Note that this is what happened in the Oglethorpe Power Transmission motivating example at the beginning of this chapter—the high EVPI about the competitive situation prompted consideration of alternative ways of structuring the deal with Florida Power.

Sensitivity Analysis of Subjective Probabilities

Estimating probabilities is one of the most difficult steps in applying the expected monetary value decision criterion. Sometimes it is possible to avoid this step, at least partially, by leaving the estimation of probabilities to the last. For each act, a range of probabilities can be found over which the given act is optimal. The decision maker then determines in which interval the probabilities lie.

We will illustrate this using a previous example. In Table 6–10, the conditional values for a new product decision were given ($1 million if the product is successful; −$500,000 if it fails; and zero if it is not introduced). Let p be the probability of success, and hence $(1 - p)$ is the probability of failure for the new product. Assuming the decision maker wishes to use the EMV criterion, the expected value of introducing the product is:

$$\begin{aligned} \text{EMV} &= p(1{,}000{,}000) + (1 - p)(-500{,}000) \\ &= -500{,}000 + 1{,}500{,}000p \end{aligned}$$

For the product to be introduced, EMV must be greater than zero. That is:

$$-500{,}000 + 1{,}500{,}000p > 0$$

or

$$p > \frac{500{,}000}{1{,}500{,}000} = \frac{1}{3}$$

Hence, if the decision maker feels that the chances are greater than one-third for success, the product should be introduced. Note that the decision maker does not have to specify an exact value for p in order to make the decision.

Example

To further clarify this concept, consider again the example of the grocer deciding how many cases of milk to stock. From Table 6–7, we determined that the optimum act was to stock 26 cases. This result was obtained using the probabilities in the first column in Table 6–14. You can check that the action "Stock 26" remains optimal for all the various sets of probabilities shown in Table 6–14.[2] Hence, the decision maker can see that the decision is not *sensitive* to the variations in the probabilities that are presented in Table 6–14. Other variations could cause a change in decision.

TABLE 6–14
Alternative Possible Sets of Probabilities

	Sets of Probabilities			
Event: Demand	*1*	*2*	*3*	*4*
25 cases	0.1	0.2	0.05	0.1
26 cases	0.3	0.3	0.15	0.1
27 cases	0.5	0.4	0.40	0.3
28 cases	0.1	0.1	0.40	0.5

[2]The act "Stock 26" remains optimal as long as $p(\text{demand} = .25) < 0.20$ and $p(\text{demand} \geq 27) < 0.80$. This model is developed in detail in a later chapter.

For example, if the probability attached to the event "demand of 25 cases" is greater than 0.20, then the optimal decision changes to ordering 25 cases.

The general approach suggested by this example is *sensitivity analysis.* The decision maker makes a preliminary set of estimates (for probabilities or for payoffs). Variations in these estimates are then made. If the variations do not change the optimal decision, one need go no further. If, on the other hand, the decision is sensitive to the changes, then the manager must refine the preliminary estimates in order to arrive at a decision.

Summary

The expected value of perfect information is the worth to the decision maker of a perfect forecast of an uncertain event. Sensitivity analysis examines the degree to which a decision depends on (is sensitive to) assumptions or estimates, particularly estimates of probabilities.

Decision Trees

The previous sections of this chapter developed the decision criterion of expected monetary value and analyzed simple decisions using conditional value tables. This section describes a general approach for more complex decisions that is useful both for *structuring* the decision problem and for finding a solution. The approach utilizes a **decision tree,** a graphic tool for describing the actions available to the decision maker, the events that can occur, and the relationship between these actions and events.

Decision Tree for Grocer's Problem

To illustrate the basic ideas, let us first develop the decision tree for the grocery problem of the last section. Recall that the decision involves how many cases of milk to order. The decision point is represented by a *square box* or *decision node* in Figure 6–1. The alternatives are represented as *branches* emanating from the decision node.

Suppose the grocer were to select some particular alternative—say, order 28 cases. There are several possible events that can happen, each event representing a number of cases of milk that customers might demand. These are shown in Figure 6–2 as branches emanating from a round node. (We are using the convention of a square box for a decision node and a circle for an event node.) Note that these branches represent uncertain events over which the decision maker has no control. However, probabilities can be assigned to each event and are entered under each branch in parentheses.

At the end of each branch is the conditional profit associated with the selected action and given event (the same values as in Table 6–2). The conditional profit thus represents the profit associated with the decisions and events along the path from the first part of the tree to the end. For example, the $26 in Figure 6–2 is the profit associated with ordering 28 cases of milk, and then experiencing a demand 25 cases.

FIGURE 6–1
Grocer's Alternatives

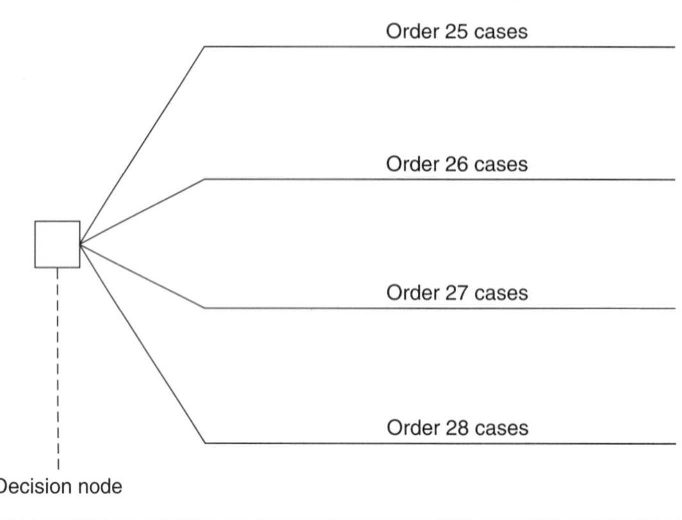

FIGURE 6–2
Events for Alternative "Order 28 Cases"

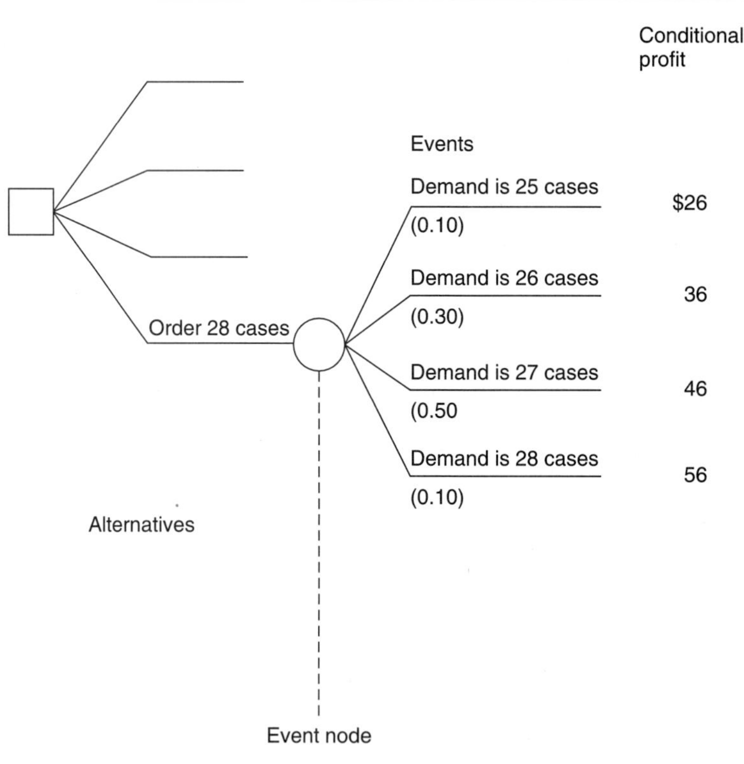

The expected monetary value (EMV) is calculated for each event node exactly as was done in the previous section (see Table 6–6). That is, probabilities are multiplied by conditional profits and summed. The EMV is placed in the event node to indicate that it is the expected value calculated over all branches emanating from that node.

FIGURE 6–3 Complete Decision Tree—Grocer's Problem

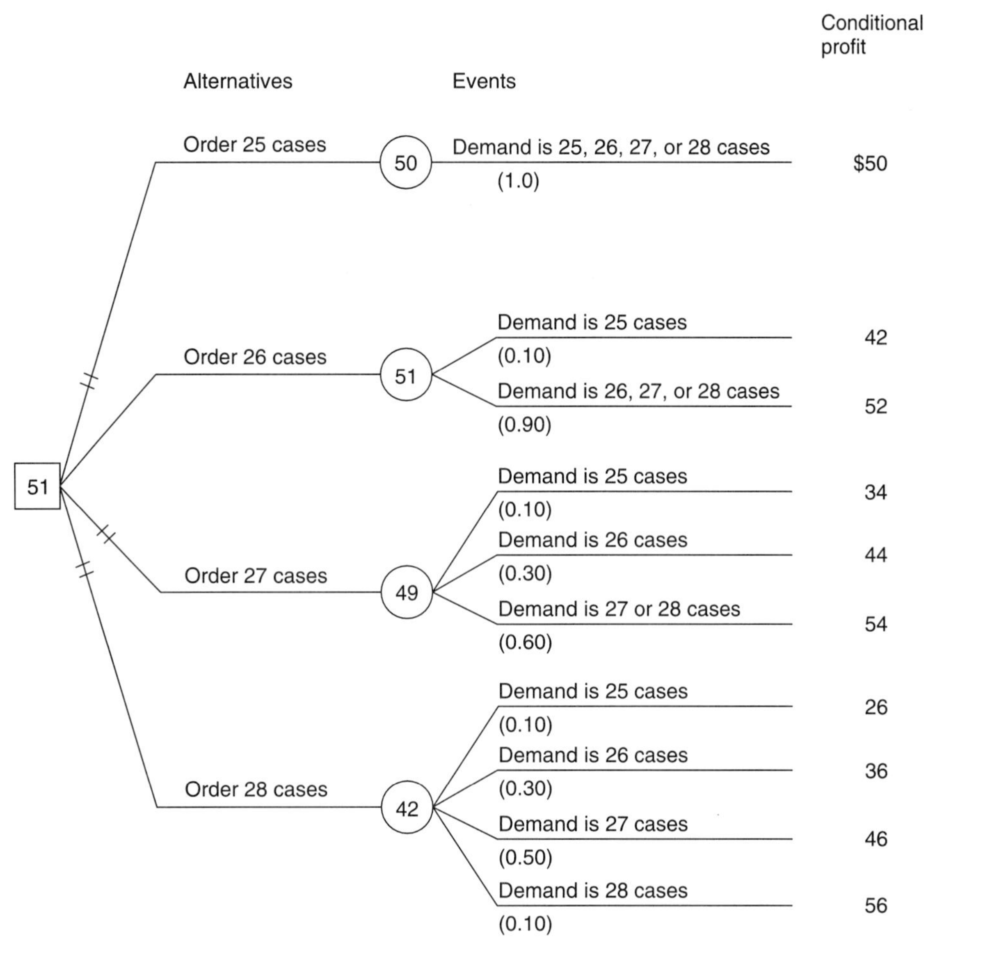

Figure 6–3 shows the complete decision tree for the grocer's problem. Note that it is not necessary to list every possible event separately for all decisions. Thus, when 26 cases are ordered, there are only two events that lead to different conditional profits: Demand is 25 cases with a profit of $42; and demand is 26 or more (that is, demand is 26, 27, or 28 cases) with a profit of $52. If the grocer orders 25 cases, there is only one outcome—namely, the sale of all 25 cases with conditional profit of $50.

In Figure 6–3, the expected monetary values are shown in the event nodes. The grocer must then choose which action to take, and this choice is to select the one with the highest EMV—namely, order 26 cases with EMV = $51. This is indicated in the tree by putting 51 in the decision node (square box) at the beginning of the tree. In addition, the mark || is drawn across the nonoptimal decision branches, indicating that they are not to be followed.

In summary, the decision tree uses the same idea of maximizing expected monetary value developed in the previous section. For the grocery example, the use of a table, such as Table 6–2, may seem easier. However, as the decision problem becomes more complex, the decision tree becomes more valuable in organizing the information needed to make the decision. This is especially true if the manager must make a *sequence* of decisions, rather than a single decision, as the next example will illustrate.

Decision Tree Example

Suppose the marketing manager of a firm is trying to decide whether or not to market a new product and at what price to sell it. The profit to be made depends on whether or not a competitor will introduce a similar product and on what price the competitor charges.

Note that there are two decisions: (1) introduce the product or not, and (2) the price to charge. Likewise, there are two events: (1) competition introduces a competitive product (or not), and (2) the competitor's price. The timing or sequence of these decisions and events is very important in this decision. If the marketing manager must act before knowing whether or not the competitor has a similar product, the price may be different than with such knowledge. A decision tree is particularly useful in this type of situation, since it displays the order in which decisions are made and events occur.

Suppose in our example that the firm must introduce or decide to scrap its new product shortly. However, the price decision can be made later. If the competitor is going to act, it will introduce its product within a month. In three months, our firm will establish and announce its price. After that, the competitor will announce its price. This can be diagrammed in the decision tree in Figure 6–4. Note that this is a sequential decision problem. Our firm must make a decision *now* about introduction and *subsequently* set price, *after* learning about the competitor's action.

The decision tree shows the structure of the decision problem. To complete the analysis, conditional profits must be estimated for every combination of actions and events (that is, for every path through the tree). Suppose our marketing manager has done this, and the profits are shown in Figure 6–4 at the ends of the tree. These profit values include the costs of introducing the product and the profits made from its sale. Negative values indicate that introduction costs exceeded subsequent profit from sales.

Also, the probabilities for each event must be assessed by the decision maker; for our example they are shown under the event branches in Figure 6–4. Note that these probabilities may depend on prior actions or events. Thus, the probabilities for the competitor's price behavior in Figure 6–4 are different when our price is high than when our price is low.

Influence Diagram

We can also represent the manager's problem using an *influence diagram.* See Figure 6–5. This influence diagram is quite simple, so it may not seem particularly helpful in structuring the decision problem and the decision tree. However, for more complex situations, it may be very useful to draw an influence diagram prior to developing the detailed decision tree; the influence diagram would be an excellent way to structure our assumptions about the important factors and relationships in the model. In general, we recommend using decision trees to solve problems of this type.

FIGURE 6–4 Decision Tree for Product Introduction Example

Events
(competitor's
price)
Conditional
profit
($000)
Alternatives
(our price)
Events
Alternatives
Introduce
product
Competitive
product introduced
(0.8)
Set high price
High
(0.3)
Medium
(0.5)
Low
(0.2)
$150
0
–200
Set medium price
High
(0.1)
Medium
(0.6)
Low
(0.3)
250
100
–50
Set low price
High
(0.1)
Medium
(0.2)
Low
(0.7)
100
50
–100
No competitive
product
(0.2)
Set high price
Set medium price
Set low price
500
300
100
Do not introduce product
0
First decision
point
Second decision
point

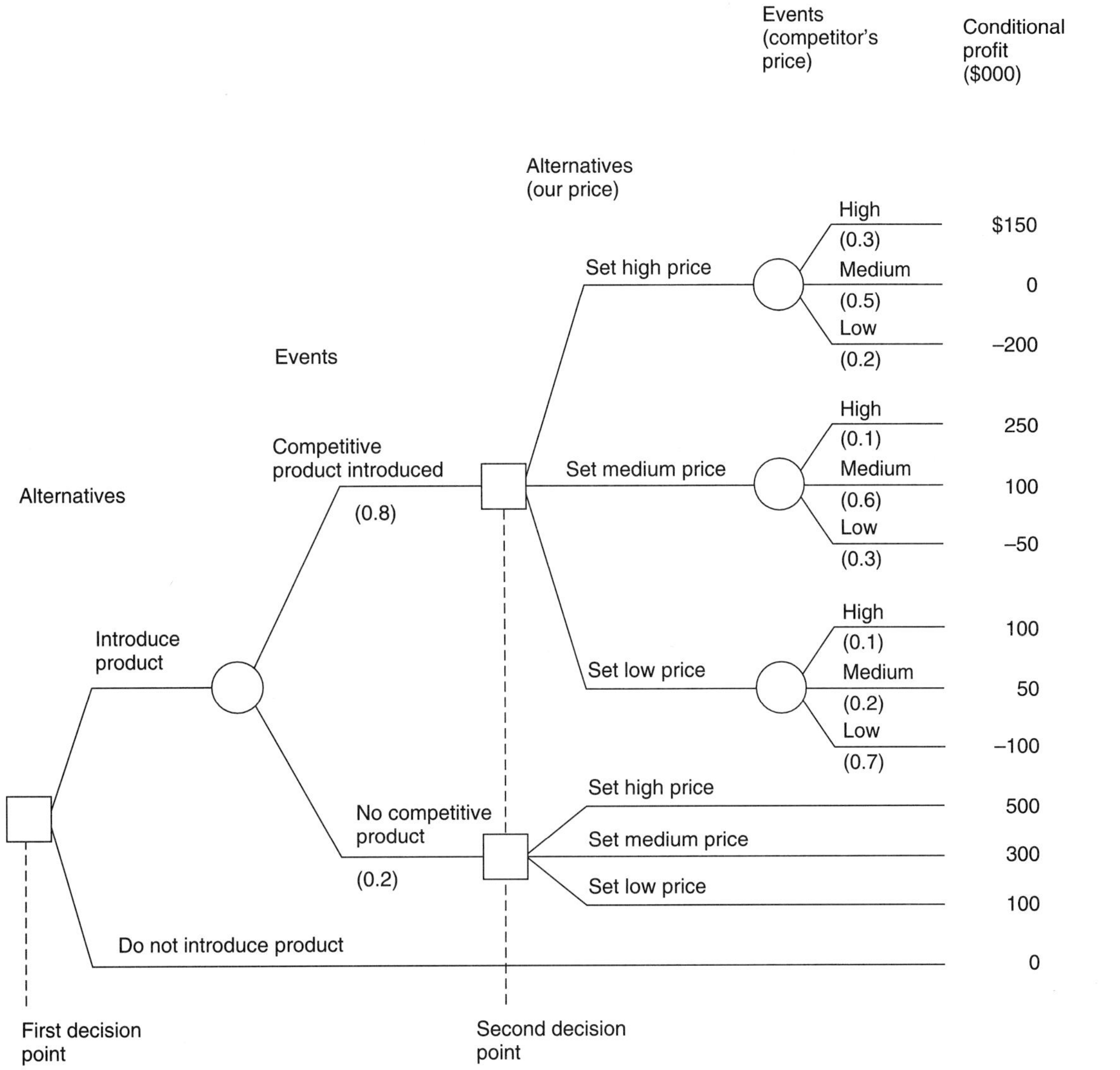

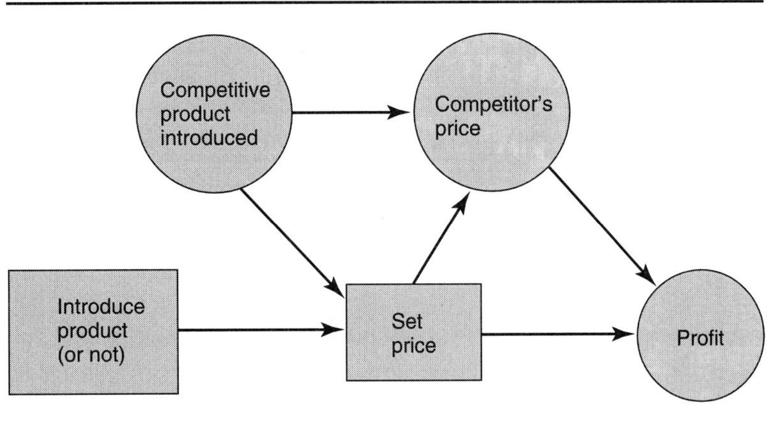

FIGURE 6–5 Influence Diagram for Product Introduction Example

Competitive
product
introduced
Competitor's
price
Introduce
product
(or not)
Set
price
Profit

Analysis of the Decision Problem

To analyze a decision tree, we begin at the end of the tree and work backwards. For each set of event branches, the EMV is calculated as illustrated, and for each set of decision branches, the one with the highest EMV is selected. This is illustrated in Figure 6–6 for our example. First, the EMVs are calculated for the event nodes associated with competitor's price. For example, the EMV of $5,000 in the topmost right circle in Figure 6–6 represents the sum of the product of probabilities for high, medium, and low prices times the respective conditional profits:

$$\text{EMV} = (0.3)(150) + (0.5)(0) + (0.2)(-200) = 5$$

The other values are computed similarly.

FIGURE 6–6 Completed Decision Tree for Product Introduction Example

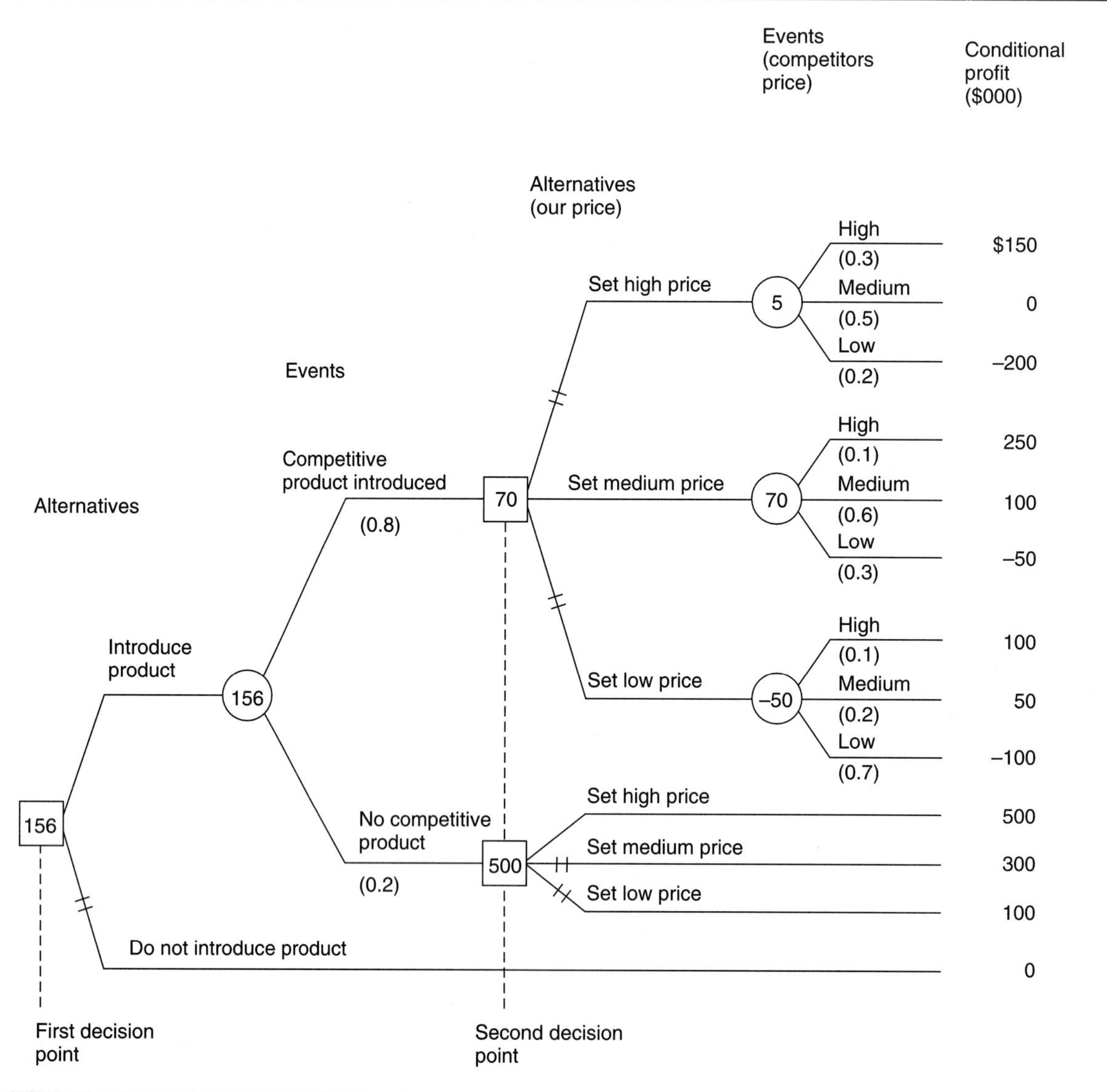

Now, if we move back on the decision tree to the second decision point, we are faced with two decision situations. The first—when a competitive product has been introduced—involves setting a high, medium, or low price with expected profits of \$5,000, \$70,000, and −\$50,000, respectively. Assume the choice is the one with highest expected profit—the medium price. A mark || is placed on the lines related to the other alternatives, indicating that they are nonoptimal, and the expected profit of \$70,000 is attached to the upper box of the second decision point.

When no competitive product is introduced, the best choice is a high price, with profit of \$500,000.

At the event point to the left, an expected value of \$156,000 is computed by multiplying the expected profit given a competitive product (\$70,000) by its probability, 0.8, and adding the profit given no competitive product (\$500,000) times its probability of 0.2. The EMV in thousands is:

$$\text{EMV} = (0.8)(70) + (0.2)(500) = 156$$

Finally, the decision to market the product is made, since the expected net profit of \$156,000 is greater than the zero profit from not marketing the product.

Note that the decision that results from an analysis of the decision tree is not a fixed decision, but rather it is a *strategy:* Introduce the product and charge a high price if there is no competitive entry; but charge a medium price if there is competition.

Developing the Decision Tree

The decision tree is a model of a decision situation, and like all models, it is an abstraction and simplification of the real problem. Only the important decisions and events are included; otherwise, the tree becomes too "bushy." And judgment is required, not only about what to include, but also to assess probabilities.

In drawing a decision tree, certain rules must be observed:

1. The branches emanating from any node must be all the same logical type, either events or alternatives, and never a mix of the two.
2. The events associated with branches from any event node must be mutually exclusive and all events included, so that the sum of the probabilities is one.
3. The alternatives associated with a decision node must include all the alternatives under consideration at that point.

It is generally helpful to develop the tree in chronological sequence, so that the proper order of decisions and events is maintained. However, some aspects of drawing the tree are arbitrary. For example, in the case above, suppose the firm must announce its decision about the new product and establish the price before any information about the competitor is known. The part of the tree relating to these decisions could be drawn in either of the two equivalent ways shown in Figure 6–7. Exactly the same options would be available for diagramming the events associated with the competitor's product introduction and the competitor's price, if they occurred without any intervening decision on our firm's part.

Recall from the discussion of risk earlier in the chapter that expected monetary value is not an appropriate decision criterion if the conditional profits or losses are

FIGURE 6–7
Alternative Ways of Diagramming Decision (revised example)

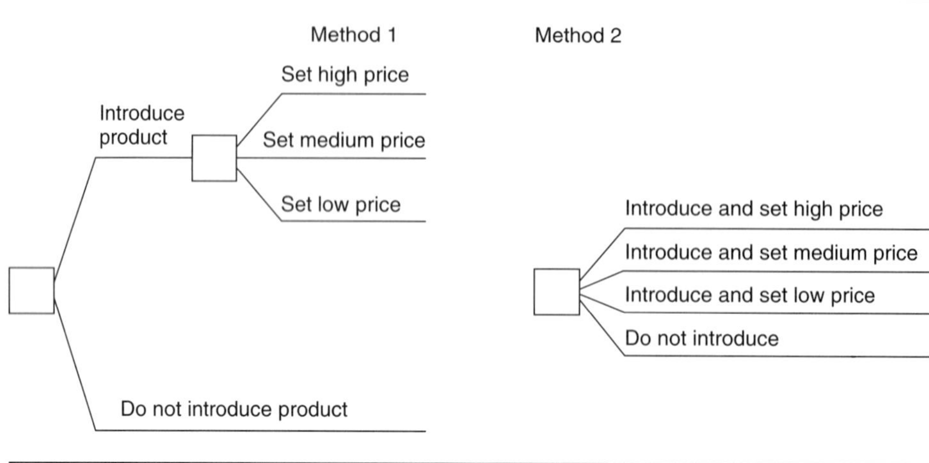

so large that the decision maker views the alternatives as having significantly different consequences. In such situations, utility values are used in the decision tree in place of conditional profits. This is considered in detail in a later chapter.

Summary

A decision tree is a graphic device for showing the sequence of decision alternatives and events involved in making a decision under uncertainty. A decision tree is analyzed by calculating the expected value for each event node and choosing the alternative with the highest profit for decision nodes, starting with the end of the tree and moving backward toward the origin.

Stock Options and Decision Analysis

In today's financial markets, there are a number of financial instruments or derivatives that take the form of an option. Their evaluation is a very important and practical application of the decision analysis ideas we have discussed, so we examine stock options briefly.

First, what is a *stock option?* There are many variations, but in the simplest form, a *call* option is the right to buy a stock at some future date at a given price. In an American option, the option can be exercised any time up to the expiration date; in a European option, it is exercised on the expiration date. How should an option be valued?

As a concrete example, suppose you are given (by a rich uncle) an option for 1,000 shares of Ventures, Inc. It is a European variety option and will expire in 90 days. The call price is $22 per share. The current price of a share of Ventures, Inc., is $20. What is the option's value? Clearly, the value depends on what the price will be in 90 days. If the price is at or below $22, the option has no value, since you would not buy a stock at an option price that is higher than what you would pay on the open market. On the other hand, if the stock price 90 days from now is, say, $26, you could exercise the option, buy the 1,000 shares for $22 per share, and immediately sell them on the market for $26, making a profit of $4 per share or $4,000 in total.

In order to evaluate the option, we must have some probability distribution for the stock price for Ventures, Inc., in 90 days. Although there are sophisticated models in finance for analyzing stock price movements, let us simply assume that the probabilities given in Table 6–15 have been estimated. Note that the expected price is $21.74, below the call striking price of $22.00.

The value of the option is calculated in Table 6–16. If the market price in 90 days is below the striking price of $22, the option is not exercised and there is zero value. When the price is above $22, a profit is realized by exercising the option and reselling the stock at the market price. The expected return is calculated at $1.14 per share. This is the value of the option. Note that the option has value even though the expected price of $21.74 (see Table 6–15) is below the striking price of $22.

Note that the process is the same as was done to calculate the value of perfect information in a decision situation. The value of an option allows one to act with perfect information—that is, after the actual market price is known. There are many other optionlike investment vehicles in finance, and elaborate models have been developed to evaluate them, all relying on the underlying concepts of decision analysis.

The option idea can also be applied to capital investments in business (see the box on how Merck uses options theory). Businesses make investments in research, in equipment, and in marketing, but the returns are often highly uncertain. To the extent that a firm can abandon a project at various stages and reduce its losses, the investment can be viewed as an option. For example, a firm may be able to do a preliminary market study of a new product before building the production facilities, only building the facilities if the market test proves positive enough. Specific

TABLE 6–15

Stock Price for Ventures, Inc. in 90 days ($ per share)	*Probability*
$16	0.05
18	0.15
20	0.25
22	0.20
24	0.20
26	0.10
28	0.03
30	0.02
$21.74 = Expected Value	1.00

TABLE 6–16

Stock Price for Ventures, Inc., in 90 days ($ per share)	*Decision: Exercise Option?*	*Option Value ($ per share)*	*Probability*	*Expected Value Calculation*
16	No	0	0.05	$0
18	No	0	0.15	0
20	No	0	0.25	0
22	Indifferent	0	0.20	0
24	Yes	2	0.20	0.40
26	Yes	4	0.10	0.40
28	Yes	6	0.03	0.18
30	Yes	8	0.02	0.16
				Total = $1.14

examples like this are considered in the next section. We wish merely to note the parallel to option theory.[3]

Revision of Probabilities

In this section, we introduce the opportunity to experiment; that is, to gather additional information and revise probabilities before making the decision.

We shall deal with the simplest of possible situations where there is only one unknown. For example, the decision may hinge on the demand for the product in the next year. Assume it has been decided to experiment. Demand is the only unknown. In this situation (which could be an inventory problem), the decision process is as follows:

1. Choose the decision criterion; we assume the expected value decision rule.
2. Describe the set of possible outcomes and possible decisions.
3. Assign probabilities to the possible outcomes (states of nature).
4. Determine a profit function (conditional profits).
5. Conduct an experiment.
6. Revise the assigned probabilities.
7. Compute the expected profit for each decision.
8. The optimum decision is the act with the highest expected profit.

The above process assumes that it has previously been determined that experimentation is desirable. We now investigate that question.

The Value of Imperfect Information

Here, we shall introduce a general method for evaluating the possibility of obtaining more information regarding a decision problem.

[3]See A. Dixit and R. Pindyck, *Investment under Uncertainty* (Princeton, NJ: Princeton University Press, 1994), where this parallel is developed in detail.

Capital Investment Decisions as Options

In a recent article in the *Harvard Business Review,* Judy Lewent, the chief financial officer at Merck—a leading firm in the pharmaceutical industry—was interviewed on how she and her staff evaluate the firm's major investments in drug research. It takes many years to bring a drug to market, and along the way are substantial investments in research, clinical trials, and production technology amounting in total to several hundred million dollars, and the returns are highly uncertain. Historically, 7 out of 10 products do not recover this investment. Judy Lewent indicated, "Option analysis, like the kind used to value stock options, provides a more flexible approach to valuing our research investments than traditional financial analysis because it allows us to evaluate those investments at successive stages of a project."[4]

This decision process can be considered as a decision tree with several decision points at which the firm can choose to continue to invest or abandon the project, events that determine the success or failure at various stages, and finally an event node with branches for the value realized when the product is brought to market. (See problem 6–31, Evergreen Pharmaceutical Company, for a concrete example.) Judy Lewent and her staff have developed sophisticated methods, based on Merck's experience, for evaluating the likelihood of success at various stages and the costs and ultimate value of a new drug in the market. They then use a technique called *Monte Carlo* analysis for evaluating the tree. (Monte Carlo analysis is covered in a later chapter. But the basic structure of the problem is the decision tree as developed in this chapter.)

[4] "Scientific Management at Merck: An Interview with CFO Judy Lewent," *Harvard Business Review,* January–February 1994.

The expected value of perfect information (EVPI) introduced earlier sets an upper limit on the value of additional information in a decision situation. Most information that we can obtain is **imperfect** in the sense that it will *not* tell us exactly which event will occur. Even so, imperfect information will still have value if it will improve the expected profit.

The term *experiment* is intended here to be very broad. An experiment may be a study by economists to predict national economic activity, a consumer survey by a market research firm, an opinion poll conducted on behalf of a political candidate, a sample of production line items taken by an engineer to check on quality, or a seismic test to give an oil well–drilling firm some indications of the presence of oil.

In general, we can evaluate the worth of a given experiment only if we can estimate the reliability of the resulting information. A market research study may be helpful in deciding whether or not to introduce a new product. However, the experiment can be given a specific economic value before the study only if the decision maker can say beforehand how closely the market research study can estimate the potential salcs.

An example will make this clear. Suppose the sales of a potential new product will be either large or small (the product will be either a success or a flop). The conditional value table for this decision is shown in Table 6–17. The conditional value of \$4 million is the net profit (present value) if the potential sales are large. The −\$2 million is the cost if the product sells poorly.

TABLE 6–17
Conditional Value Table for Decision on Introduction of New Product ($ millions)

		Actions	
Outcome	*Probabilities*	*Introduce Product*	*Do Not Introduce*
High sales	0.3	4.0	0
Low sales	0.7	−2.0	0
Expected monetary value		−0.2	0

Based on expected monetary value (EMV), the indicated action is not to introduce the product. However, the decision maker, being reluctant to give up a probability of 0.3 of making $4 million, may consider gathering more information before taking action. As a first step, let us calculate the expected value of perfect information (EVPI). Recall from earlier in this chapter that:

$$\text{EVPI} = \text{Expected profit with perfect predictor} - \text{EMV (optimal act)}$$

With a perfect predictor, the company would introduce the product if sales were high, and not introduce if sales were low, resulting in an expected value of $0.3 \times 4 + 0.7 \times 0 = 1.2$. The EMV of the optimal act (do not introduce) is zero. Hence:

$$\text{EVPI} = 1.2 - 0 = 1.2$$

Thus, there is an expected value of $1.2 million that can be obtained through perfect information. The value of imperfect information will be less.

The decision maker can perform an experiment in this situation. Suppose the experiment takes the form of a market survey conducted in two representative cities. The survey will cost $0.2 million.

There are three possible outcomes from the survey: (1) The survey may predict success (high sales) for the new product; (2) the survey may predict failure (low sales); or (3) the survey result may be inconclusive. In the past, surveys such as the one proposed often correctly predicted the success or failure of a new product, but sometimes success was predicted for a product that later failed, and vice versa.

If the marketing manager takes the survey before acting, the decision can be based on the survey predictions. Figure 6–8 shows the influence diagram for this problem. This problem can be expressed in terms of a decision tree, as shown in Figure 6–9. The upper part of the tree shows the decision process if no survey is taken. This is the same analysis as presented in Table 6–17, with probabilities of 0.3 and 0.7 for high and low sales, expected profit of −$0.2 million for introduction, and an indicated decision of no introduction with $0 profits.

FIGURE 6–8
Influence Diagram for Problem on Introduction of New Product

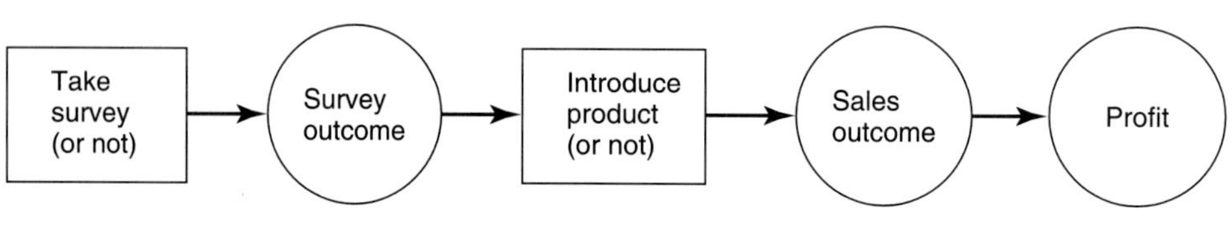

FIGURE 6–9 Decision Tree for Problem on Introduction of New Product

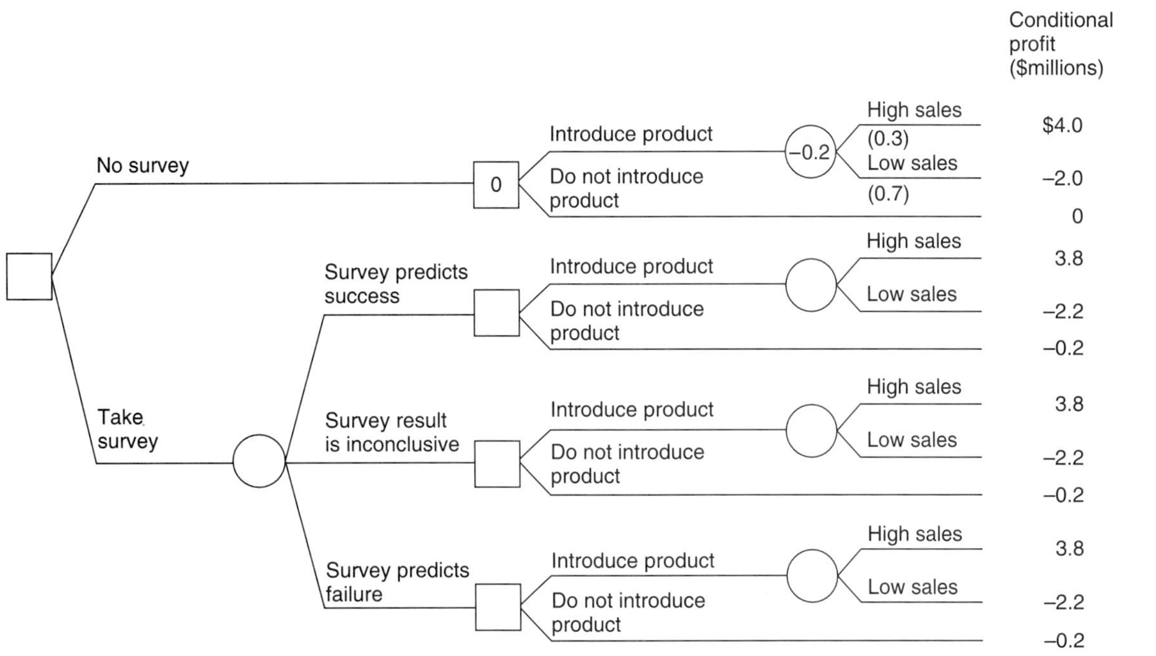

Conditional profit ($millions)

No survey — 0 — Introduce product — −0.2 — High sales (0.3) $4.0; Low sales (0.7) −2.0
Do not introduce product 0

Take survey —
Survey predicts success — Introduce product — High sales 3.8; Low sales −2.2; Do not introduce product −0.2
Survey result is inconclusive — Introduce product — High sales 3.8; Low sales −2.2; Do not introduce product −0.2
Survey predicts failure — Introduce product — High sales 3.8; Low sales −2.2; Do not introduce product −0.2

The lower part of the tree, following the branch "Take survey," displays the possible survey results and the subsequent decision possibilities. After each of the three possible survey outcomes, a decision about whether or not to introduce the product must be made. If the product is introduced, the sales will either be high with a profit of $3.8 million, or low with a loss of $2.2 million. Note that the cost of the survey ($0.2 million) has been included in these profit and loss amounts.

Determining Probabilities

In order to complete the analysis of Figure 6–9, we need the probabilities for the various events. Let us suppose that the marketing manager estimates the probabilities shown in Table 6–18. These are the conditional probabilities for the various survey results given the potential sales level of the product. For example, when a new product has high sales potential, the survey predicts success with probability 0.4; the survey predicts failure with probability 0.2; and the survey will be inconclusive with probability 0.4. Such probabilities would reflect past experience with surveys of this type, modified perhaps by the judgment of the marketing manager.

The probabilities shown in Table 6–18 express the reliability or accuracy of the experiment. With these estimates, the marketing manager can evaluate the economic

TABLE 6–18 Conditional Probabilities of Survey Predictions, Given Potential Sales

Experimental Results (survey prediction)	Potential Level of Sales: High Sales (H)	Low Sales (L)
Survey predicts success (S) (i.e., high sales)	0.4	0.1
Survey inconclusive (I)	0.4	0.5
Survey predicts failure (F) (i.e., low sales)	0.2	0.4
	1.0	1.0

TABLE 6–19 Joint Probability Table

Potential Level of Sales	Survey Prediction: Success (S)	Inconclusive (I)	Failure (F)	Marginal Probabilities of Sales Level
High (H)	P(S and H)	P(I and H)	P(F and H)	P(H)
Low (L)	P(S and L)	P(I and L)	P(F and L)	P(L)
Marginal Probabilities of Survey Prediction	P(S)	P(I)	P(F)	1.00

Potential Level of Sales	Survey Prediction: Success (S)	Inconclusive (I)	Failure (F)	Marginal Probabilities of Sales Level
High (H)	0.12	0.12	0.06	0.30
Low (L)	0.07	0.35	0.28	0.70
Marginal Probabilities of Survey Prediction	0.19	0.47	0.34	1.00

worth of the survey. Without these reliability estimates, no specific value can be attached to taking the survey.

The conditional probabilities of Table 6–18 are not directly useful in Figure 6–9. Rather, we need the *unconditional* probabilities of the various survey outcomes (all we have available are the survey probabilities conditional on sales level). We also need the conditional probabilities of a high and low sales level, given a survey prediction of success, and so on.

Table 6–19 is a joint probability table. The top part of the table shows the symbols, and the bottom displays the equivalent numerical values. In the right-hand column, we have the original probabilities assessed by the marketing manager: a 0.3 chance that the product will have high sales (*H*) and a 0.7 chance for low sales (*L*). From these, and from the conditional probabilities of Table 6–18, the joint probabilities of Table 6–19 can be calculated. Thus, the joint probability of both a prediction of "success" by the survey (*S*) and high level of actual sales (*H*) is calculated by multiplying the conditional probability of a successful prediction, given a high sales level (which is 0.4 from Table 6–18), by the probability of a high sales level:

$$P(S \text{ and } H) = P(S|H)P(H) = (0.4)(0.3) = 0.12$$

Similarly:

$$P(S \text{ and } L) = P(S|L)P(L) = (0.1)(0.7) = 0.07$$
$$P(I \text{ and } H) = P(I|H)P(H) = (0.4)(0.3) = 0.12$$

and so on.

The marginal probabilities of sales level in Table 6–19 (the right-hand column) are equal to the sum of the joint probabilities in each row. Note that these are precisely the original probabilities for high and low sales, and they are designated **prior probabilities** because they were assessed before any information from the survey was obtained. The marginal probabilities of the survey predictions are equal to the sum of the joint probabilities in each column.

To understand Table 6–19, it is useful to think of it as representing the results of 100 past situations identical to the one under consideration. The probabilities then represent the frequency with which the various outcomes occurred. For example, in 30 of the 100 cases, the actual sales for the product turned out to be high; and in these 30 high-sales cases, the survey predicted success in 12 instances [that is $P(H \text{ and } S) = 0.12$], was inconclusive in 12 instances, and predicted failure in 6 instances.

The marginal probabilities of survey prediction in the bottom row of Table 6–19 can then be interpreted as the relative frequency with which the survey predicted "success," "inconclusive," and "failure," respectively. For example, the survey predicted "success" 19 out of 100 times—12 of these times when sales actually were high and 7 times when sales were low.

These marginal probabilities of survey prediction are important to our analysis, for they give us the probabilities associated with the information received by the marketing manager before the decision to introduce the product is made. The marginal probabilities are entered beside the appropriate branches in Figure 6–10.

We still need to calculate the probabilities for the branches labeled "High sales" and "Low sales" in the lower part of Figure 6–10. We cannot use the values of 0.3 and 0.7 for these events as we did in the upper part of the tree because those probabilities were calculated independent of taking a survey. The marketing manager will have received information from a survey, and the probabilities should reflect this information. The required probabilities are the conditional probabilities for the various levels of sales given the survey result. For example, for the upper branch of the "Take survey" path, we need $P(H|S)$, the probability of high sales (H) given that the survey predicts success (S). This can be computed directly from the definition of conditional probability, using the data from Table 6–19:

$$P(H|S) = \frac{P(H \text{ and } S)}{P(S)} = \frac{0.12}{0.19} = 0.632$$

And the probability of low sales, given a survey prediction of success, is:

$$P(L|S) = \frac{P(L \text{ and } S)}{P(S)} = \frac{0.07}{0.19} = 0.368$$

These probabilities are called **posterior probabilities,** since they come after the inclusion of the information to be received from the survey. The survey has not been

FIGURE 6–10 Completed Decision Tree

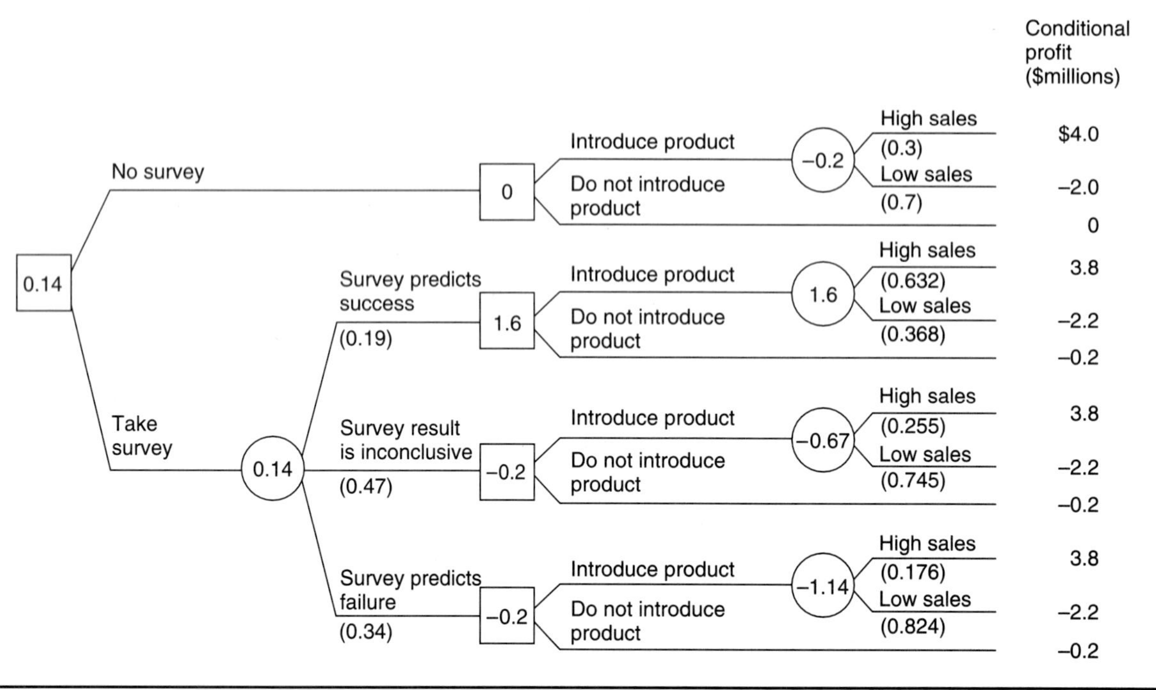

made yet, but the calculations are based on the possible survey results. To understand the meaning of the above calculations, think again of Table 6–19 as representing 100 past identical situations. Then, in 19 cases [since $P(S) = 0.19$], the survey predicted success. And of these 19 cases, 12 actually had high sales result. Hence, the posterior probability for high sales is, as calculated, $12/19 = 0.632$.

The posterior probabilities based on survey predictions of "inconclusive" and "failure" can be calculated similarly:

$$P(H|I) = \frac{0.12}{0.47} = 0.255$$

$$P(L|I) = \frac{0.35}{0.47} = 0.745$$

and

$$P(H|F) = \frac{0.06}{0.34} = 0.176$$

$$P(L|F) = \frac{0.28}{0.34} = 0.824$$

These values are also listed in Figure 6–10.

FIGURE 6–11
Reduced Part of Decision Tree

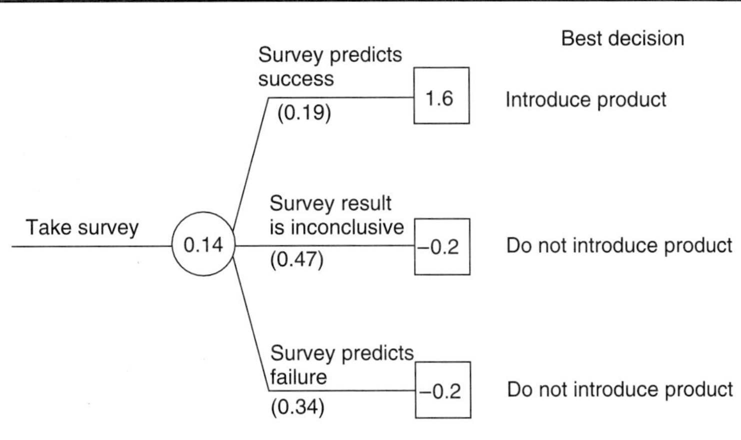

All the necessary information is now available, and Figure 6–10 can be analyzed—starting from the right and working backward. The expected values are shown in the circles. For example, follow out the branches "Take survey," "Survey predicts success," and "Introduce product." The expected value of 1.6 shown in the circle at the end of these branches is calculated as:

$$0.632 \times 3.8 + 0.368 \times (-2.2) = 1.6$$

Thus, the firm can expect a profit of \$1.6 million if the product is introduced after receiving a survey prediction of success. Since this is better than the −\$0.2 million associated with not introducing the product, the decision to introduce is taken, and the "Do not introduce product" branch is marked with || to indicate it is not optimal.

There are expected losses of \$0.67 and \$1.14 (including survey costs) if the survey gives inconclusive and failure predictions, respectively. In these cases, it is better *not* to introduce the product, and the "Introduce product" branches are marked with ||.

The part of the decision tree relating to taking the survey is now reduced to that shown in Figure 6–11. The expected value in the circle node is calculated as:

$$0.19 \times 1.6 + 0.47 \times (-0.2) + 0.34 \times (-0.2) = 0.14$$

Thus, if the survey is taken and the manager acts on the basis of the information received, the expected profit is \$0.14 million. Since this is better than the zero profit that would be obtained from not taking the survey, it should be taken. Note that the decision in this case is a *strategy* involving actually two decisions: a decision now to take the survey, and the subsequent decision to introduce the product if the survey predicts success, but not to introduce it otherwise.

The Value of the Survey Information

Taking the survey in the above example is a means of obtaining additional information. The information is not perfect because the survey cannot tell exactly whether the sales will be high or low. The net expected profit from taking the survey was \$0.14 million. This included the cost of the survey (\$0.2 million); and if we add back this amount, the expected value from the survey will be \$0.14 + \$0.2 or \$0.34 million. We can think of this as the expected profit from a costless survey. Hence, the **value of the imperfect information** obtained from the survey in this situation is \$0.34 million. The survey would be worth taking as long as its cost did not exceed this amount.

Recall that earlier in the chapter we calculated the expected value of perfect information (EVPI) as \$1.2 million. The value of the survey (imperfect information) is substantially below this, reflecting the fact that the survey can give inconclusive or incorrect information as indicated in Table 6–18.

Taking a sample represents a means of obtaining information. This information is imperfect, since the sample is not likely to represent exactly the population from which it is taken.

Summary

Decision theory involves the choice of a decision criterion (i.e., a goal)—say, maximize expected profit. If possible and feasible, an experiment is conducted. The prior probabilities of the states of nature are revised, based on the experimental result. The expected profit of each possible decision is computed, and the act with the highest expected profit is chosen as the optimum act.

Before undertaking an experiment, the decision maker must determine whether the expected profit associated with acting after receiving the result of the experiment is sufficiently large to offset the cost of the experiment. The analysis involves finding the optimum rule (which tells what decision to make as a function of the experimental result) and evaluating the expected profit using that rule.

Decision Analysis on Personal Computers

As illustrated in this chapter, there generally is only a modest amount of calculation involved in decision analysis problems. Nonetheless, there are many software packages available for personal computers that aid in drawing trees and influence diagrams, calculating expected values and EVPI, and with more advanced features. A recent survey listed 30 packages, many of which have student editions for reasonable prices.[5]

[5]See Dennis Buede, "Aiding Insight II," *OR/MS Today,* June 1994. Not all of these are general-purpose decision analysis packages; some do special analysis, such as risk analysis using Monte Carlo methods.

Conclusion

This chapter has covered the use of probabilities in making business decisions under conditions of uncertainty. The criterion of maximization of expected monetary value was developed, and the concept of the value of information was examined. Influence diagrams and decision trees and their uses have been introduced. The value of imperfect information has also been illustrated.

The ideas in this chapter are important for two related reasons. First, formal decision analysis can be used to effectively solve important business decision problems (see the Oglethorpe Power and Merck Pharmaceutical examples and the problems at the end of this chapter). But perhaps more important is the conceptual framework for thinking about decisions under uncertainty. Much of modern financial theory involving investment analysis is built on the basic ideas presented here. Inventory theory in operations is another area that uses these concepts.

The material in this chapter is extended in subsequent chapters. The next chapter introduces risk and other factors into the decision process. Other chapters treat inventory theory, simulation, and queuing theory that build on decision analysis.

Bibliography

Behn, R. D., and J. W. Vaupel. *Quick Analysis for Busy Decision Makers.* New York: Basic Books, 1982.

Bell, D. E., and A. Schleifer, Jr. *Decision Making under Uncertainty.* Cambridge, MA: Course Technology, Inc., 1995.

Brown, R. V.; A. S. Kahr; and C. Peterson. *Decision Analysis for the Manager.* New York: Holt, Rinehart & Winston, 1974.

Bunn, D. W. *Applied Decision Analysis.* New York: McGraw-Hill, 1984.

Holloway, C. *Decision Making under Uncertainty: Models and Choices.* Englewood Cliffs, NJ: Prentice Hall, 1979.

McNamee, P., and J. Celona. *Decision Analysis for the Professional with Supertree.* Palo Alto, CA: Scientific Press, 1987.

Pratt, J. W.; H. Raiffa; and R. Schlaifer. *Introduction to Statistical Decision Theory.* New York: McGraw-Hill, 1965.

Raiffa, H. *Decision Analysis.* Reading, MA: Addison-Wesley Publishing, 1968.

Samson, D. *Managerial Decision Analysis.* Burr Ridge, IL: Richard D. Irwin, 1988.

Schlaifer, R. *Analysis of Decisions under Uncertainty.* New York: McGraw-Hill, 1969.

Spetzler, C. S., and C. A. Stael von Holstein. "Probability Encoding in Decision Analysis," *Management Science,* November 1975, pp. 340–58.

SRI Decision Analysis Group. *Readings in Decision Analysis.* Menlo Park, CA: Stanford Research Institute, 1976.

Practice Problems[6]

6–1. Assume the following conditional value table applies to a decision:

		Conditional Monetary Value of		
Event	*Probability of Event*	*Act 1*	*Act 2*	*Act 3*
A	0.35	4	3	2
B	0.45	4	6	5
C	0.20	4	6	8

[6]Solutions for these problems are given at the end of this chapter.

a. Present a table of expected monetary values and determine the optimum act.
b. Present a table of expected opportunity losses.
c. Compute the conditional value table, assuming a perfect predicting device.
d. Compute the expected value assuming a perfect predicting device.
e. Compute the expected value of perfect information.

6–2. A newsstand operator assigns probabilities to the demand for *Fine* magazine:

Event: Demand	*Probability of Event*
10 copies	0.10
11 copies	0.15
12 copies	0.20
13 copies	0.25
14 copies	0.30
	1.00

Issues sell for 50 cents and cost 30 cents.
a. If the operator *can* return any unsold copies for full credit, how many should be ordered?
b. If the operator *cannot* return unsold copies, how many copies should be ordered?
c. What is the optimum expected profit in (*b*)?

6–3. A manufacturer of hair tonic is considering production of a new hairdressing. The incremental profit is $10 per unit (on a present value basis), and the necessary investment in equipment is $500,000. The estimate of demand is as follows:

Units of Demand	*Probability*
30,000	0.05
40.000	0.10
50,000	0.20
60,000	0.30
70,000	0.35
	1.00

a. Should the new product be produced? What is the expected profit?
b. What is the expected value of perfect information?
c. How would the expected value of perfect information change if the probability of 30,000 units was 0.10 and the probability of 70,000 units was 0.30?

6–4. The Cooper Cola Company (CCC) must decide which of three products to introduce. Because of a shortage of working capital, only one can be introduced. The marketing manager drew up the decision tree shown in Figure 6–12. Suppose you accept this tree as a reasonable representation of CCC's decision problem, and that CCC is willing to use EMV as the decision criterion.

What is the optimal strategy for CCC, and what is the expected profit of this strategy?

6–5. A company is trying to decide about the size of a new plant currently planned for Atlanta. At present, the company has only a minimal sales effort in the southern states. However, when the Atlanta plant is completed, a major promotion effort will be undertaken. Management is somewhat uncertain about how successful this effort will be. It is estimated that there is a 0.4 chance that the company will capture a *significant* share of the market and a 0.6 chance that only a *moderate* market share will result.

A *large* plant will be needed if a significant market share is realized. A *small* plant would suffice for the moderate case. The cost of the large plant is $8 million; the cost of the small plant, $5 million.

If a significant market share materializes, the estimated present value of resulting profits (excluding cost of the plant) is $13 million; if a moderate share materializes, the present value of the resulting profits (again excluding cost of the plant) is $8 million.

Management has one other alternative. This is to build a small plant, wait to see the result of the promotion effort, and then expand the plant if the situation warrants. It would cost an additional $4.5 million to expand the small plant to the capacity of a large one.
a. Draw a decision tree for this problem.
b. What decision should the company make, and what is the expected value?

6–6. You are charged with the inventory control job in the Volant Manufacturing Company. You think there is about a 0.4 chance of a recession next year. If there is a recession next year, you should sell the AE4 model now for the last-offer price of $1 million because you could get only $800,000 for it in a recession year. These amounts would be received in one year. However, you have a promise from the purchasing agent of a leading company to buy the AE4 for $1.3 million if there is no recession (amount payable one year hence). After some preliminary calculations, you are still undecided about selling and determine to gather evidence about the chances of a recession next year. You discover that bad debts have been rising recently. A little investigation indicates that for the last 10 recessions, bad debts

FIGURE 6–12 CCC Decision Tree (Problem 6–4)

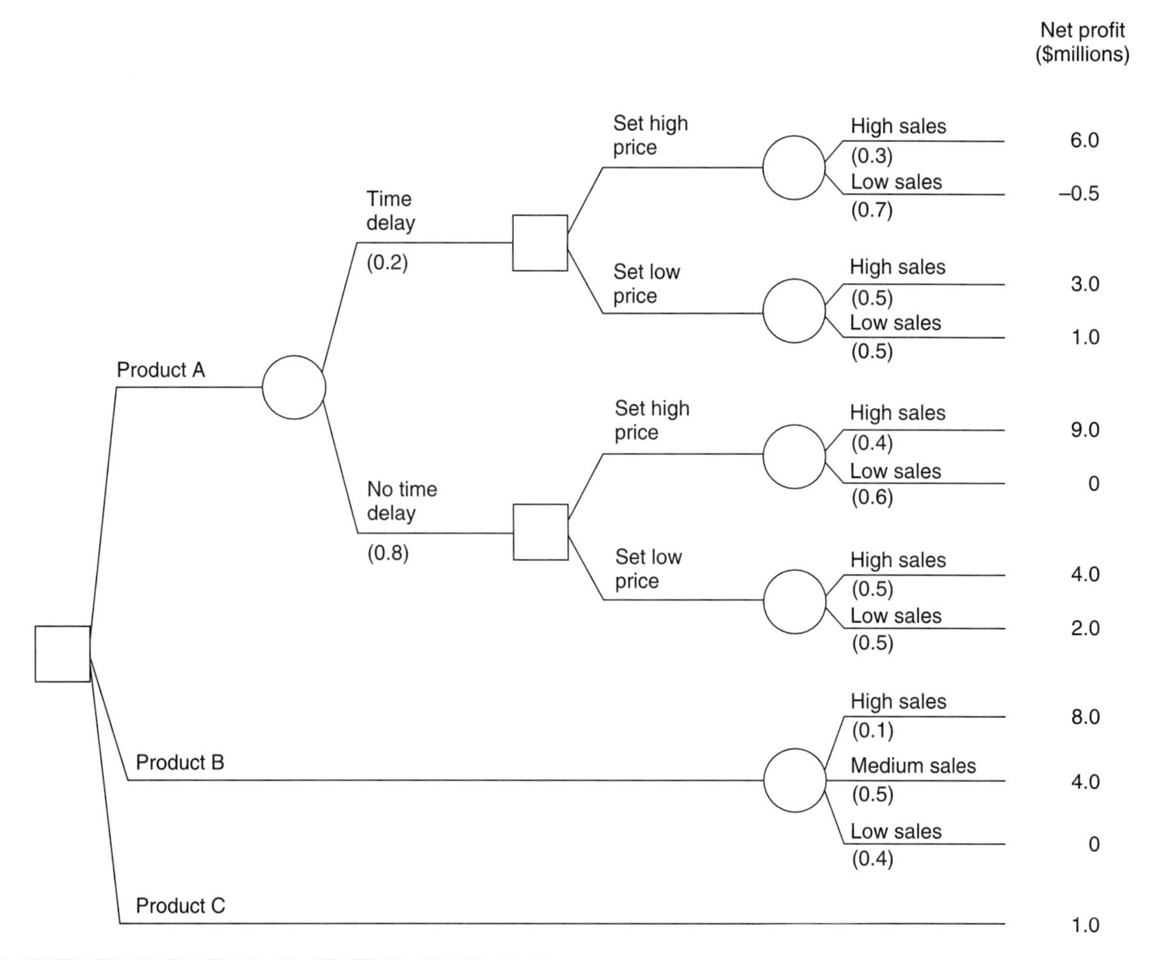

started to increase approximately a year early in eight instances. You are willing to accept 0.8 as an estimate of the probability of bad debts rising, given that a recession will occur a year later. In the same sense, you find that for 10 randomly selected normal years, the economy experienced rising bad debts the previous year in three instances. Thus, you take 0.3 as an estimate of:

$$P(\text{rising bad debts} \mid \text{recession next year})$$

If you revise your prior probabilities as shown in the chapter, what will you do about the AE4?

6–7. The probability of two dice, if they are fair dice, giving either a 7 or an 11, is $\frac{2}{9}$. If the dice are loaded in a certain fashion, the probability of a 7 or an 11 is $\frac{4}{9}$. An acquaintance asks you to play a game with him. If he throws a 7 or an 11, he will collect \$3 from you; if not, he will pay you \$1. Since the game would give you an advantage if the dice were fair, you have suspicions about your acquaintance. In particular, you feel that there is a 0.7 chance that he is using loaded dice with probability $\frac{4}{9}$ for 7 or 11. To allay your fears, your opponent offers to let you roll the dice twice. You do, and you do not get a 7 or an 11 in either of the two throws.

Should you play the game with your acquaintance? Show your calculations.

6–8. Refer to the example in the chapter as shown in Figure 6–9 and Table 6–18. Suppose the reliability of the market survey was described by the following conditional probabilities:

	Actual Level of Sales	
Survey Prediction	*High*	*Low*
Success	0.3	0.2
Inconclusive	0.5	0.5
Failure	0.2	0.3
	1.0	1.0

Assuming all the other information in the example is the same, should the survey be taken?

6–9. Refer to the example in the chapter as shown in Figure 6–10. Assume that the profits are as given in Table 6–17, and the conditional probabilities as given in Table 6–18. However, now assume that management's prior probabilities are 0.5 for high sales and 0.5 for low sales.

a. What is the optimum action before consideration of a survey? What is the expected value of this action?
b. What is the expected value of the survey information?

Problems

6–10. An analysis and forecast of next month's sales results in the following probability distribution:

Event: Demand	*Probability*
10 units	0.10
11 units	0.70
12 units	0.20
	1.00

The profit per unit is $5. The cost of the product sold is $6. If the product is not sold during the month, it is worthless (leftover units are of no value).

a. Compute the expected (mean) sales for the month.
b. Prepare a table of conditional values for the different possible acts.
c. Prepare a table of expected monetary values, and indicate the optimum act.

6–11. (Continuation of Problem 6–10)

a. Prepare a table of conditional opportunity losses.
b. Prepare a table of expected opportunity losses.
c. Indicate the optimum act.
d. Rank the acts. Show the differences between the expected opportunity losses of each act and the EOL of the optimum act.
e. Rank the acts, using expected values. Show the differences between the EMV of each act and the EMV of the optimum act. Compare these results with those of (*d*).

6–12. Refer to Problem 6–10.

a. Present the conditional value table, assuming a perfect predicting device.
b. Compute the expected value, assuming a perfect predicting device.
c. Compute the expected value of perfect information.

6–13. A manufacturer of sporting goods has the following demand and probability schedule for a yearly fishing guide magazine:

Event: Demand	*Probability of Event*
100,000	0.20
200,000	0.20
300,000	0.20
400,000	0.20
500,000	0.20
	1.00

The incremental costs of production are $400 per thousand, the selling price is $500 per thousand, and the salvage value of unsold magazines is zero.

a. The manufacturer reasons as follows: "Since there is equal chance of demand being less or greater than 300,000, I shall produce the most likely amount, 300,000." Do you agree? If not, why not?
b. What is the expected value of a perfect prediction?

6–14. A real estate investor owns a gasoline station she has leased to a major oil company for a rental fee based on a share of profits. If the station is successful, the present value of future rentals is estimated at $1 million. If the station is not successful, the present value of the rentals will be $200,000. The oil company has offered the investor $600,000 to buy the property outright. On an expected monetary value basis, what probability would need to be assigned to "success" for the investor to be indifferent between selling and not selling?

6–15. A bookstore owner can purchase 20,000 of a publisher's leftovers for $2.50 per copy. By making use of advertising in a nationally distributed newspaper, he hopes to be able to sell the books for $10 per copy. Leftover books can be sold at $1 per copy to other retailers. His estimate of demand is:

Demand	*Probability of Demand*
5,000	0.10
10,000	0.50
20,000	0.40
	1.00

The cost of advertising is $60,000, and incremental costs of shipping the books that are sold are $1.25 per copy.

a. Should the bookstore owner purchase the books?
b. What is the expected profit with a perfect predicting device?
c. What is the maximum amount the owner should pay for perfect information?

6–16. When a new shopping center is built, the electric company must assign a transformer to the location. Since this is done before the occupants of the shopping center are known, there is uncertainty about the amount of electricity to be used (for example, beauty salons use much more electricity than toy stores) and hence, uncertainty about the size of the transformer needed. A too small transformer would have to be replaced, and one too large would result in more expense than necessary. A table giving these costs is shown below:

Amount of Electricity Ultimately needed	*Size of Transformer Originally Installed*		
	Small	*Medium*	*Large*
Little	50	100	150
Medium	140	100	150
Much	190	190	150

Suppose, for a given shopping center, the following probabilities are assigned to the amount of electricity ultimately needed:

Need	*Probability*
Little	0.2
Medium	0.7
Much	0.1
	1.0

a. Draw up an opportunity loss table.
b. What decision should be made? Why?
c. What is the expected value of perfect information?

6–17. Artex Computers has contracted to deliver two model X-60 computer systems to a Japanese university. The terms call for the payment of 150 million Japanese yen to Artex on delivery of the computers in six months. The current exchange rate is 150 yen to the dollar. However, there is some concern in the financial markets about the future value of the yen. This is reflected in the currency future market in which yen "forward" six months can be bought or sold at the rate of 155 yen to the dollar. In particular, Artex can sell "short" the 150 million yen and receive $967,700 U.S. dollars now. The treasurer of Artex has assigned the following probabilities to the exchange rate for yen in six months:

Exchange Rate (yen per dollar)	*Probability*
140	0.1
150	0.6
160	0.2
170	0.1
	1.0

a. Assuming that Artex is willing to use EMV as the decision criterion, should it sell the yen short or wait until payment is received in six months?
b. Does EMV appear to be a reasonable criterion in this problem?

6–18. A company owns a lease granting it the right to explore for oil on certain property. It may sell the lease for $75,000, or it may drill for oil. The four possible drilling outcomes are listed below, together with probabilities of occurrence and dollar consequences:

Possible Outcome	Probability	Consequences ($ thousands)
Dry well	0.16	−$ 500
Gas well only	0.40	250
Oil and gas combination	0.24	500
Oil well	0.20	1,000

Draw a decision tree for this problem, and compute the expected monetary value for the act "drill." Should the company drill or sell the lease?

6–19. The ABC Promotion Company has the opportunity to put on a "sure fire" athletic contest. However, if it rains, the game cannot be played. If the game is played, the firm stands to net $2 million. If it rains, the firm stands to lose out of pocket (not opportunity cost) $1 million. There is a 0.2 probability of rain. It wants to know whether or not to buy insurance against rain.

Draw a decision tree. How much could the firm pay for insurance to cover the $1 million loss and be no worse off on an expected value basis than if it did not buy insurance? Should it buy insurance at that price?

6–20. The Plastic Production Company needs to expand its production capacity. This can be done in one of two ways: using overtime in its current plant or leasing another plant. Overtime has a cost penalty (above regular time) of $3 per case of product produced, and can only be used for up to 15,000 cases per year. Leasing another plant would entail an annual fixed leasing cost of $25,000; however, the work force of this plant would be paid on a regular-time basis and could produce any number of cases up to a maximum of 20,000 cases annually.

The company estimates that additional demand (beyond what can be produced in its current plant in regular time) may take on the following values, with corresponding probabilities:

Additional Demand (cases per year)	Probability
5,000	0.3
10,000	0.5
15,000	0.2

a. Draw a decision tree for this problem, and find the optimal decision to minimize expected costs.

b. Suppose a market research company offers to perform a survey to determine the exact quantity of additional demand that will be forthcoming. Should the company be willing to pay $1,000 for such a perfect survey? Why or why not? What is the expected opportunity loss (EOL) of the best decision in (*a*)?

6–21. The QPC Company is deciding whether to market product A or product B. The decision depends on the speed with which the distributors accept the product and the type of marketing strategy (promotion or advertising) employed by QPC. The company has diagrammed its decision problem as shown in Figure 6–13. The cash flows associated with the various decisions and events are shown at the end of the tree branches. Assume that QPC is willing to use EMV to make this decision.

a. What is the optimal strategy for QPC, and what is the expected cash flow for this strategy?

b. Suppose that QPC had to make a decision about the marketing strategy (promotion or advertising) *before* finding out about the speed of the distributors' acceptance. Would this matter, and would the optimal expected cash flow be reduced? Why? Answer without redrawing the tree.

6–22. A camera manufacturer produces two models (standard and deluxe). In preparation for the heavy Christmas selling season, production volumes must be determined. Variable cost of the standard camera is $10, and selling price is $20; variable cost of the deluxe model is $20, and selling price is $35. Demand is estimated as follows:

Standard Model		Deluxe Model	
Demand	Probability	Demand	Probability
6,000	0.30	2,000	0.20
8,000	0.70	4,000	0.80

Any cameras not sold during the Christmas season are sold at salvage price of $5 for the standard and $10 for the deluxe model. The manufacturer thinks that different segments of the market purchase the two different models; thus, the probabilities of sales given above are independent.

Suppose production capacity is unlimited. Then the two decision can be made independently. What are the optimal quantities of each model to produce? What are the two optimal EMVs?

FIGURE 6–13 QPC Decision Tree (Problem 6–21)

Introduce	Distributor acceptance	Marketing strategy	Product sales level	Cash flow ($ millions)
Product A	Quick (0.3)	Promotion	High (0.7)	9
			Low (0.3)	–1
		Advertising	High (0.8)	7
			Low (0.2)	–3
	(0.7) Slow	Promotion	High (0.4)	7
			Low (0.6)	–2
		Advertising	High (0.7)	5
			Low (0.3)	–4
Product B	Quick (0.5)	Promotion	High (0.7)	5
			Low (0.3)	1
		Advertising	High (0.8)	4
			Low (0.2)	0
	(0.5) Slow	Promotion	High (0.4)	4
			Low (0.6)	0
		Advertising	High (0.7)	3
			Low (0.3)	–1

6–23. (Continuation of Problem 6–22) Now suppose that, due to capacity constraints, total production is limited to 10,000 cameras. Construct a decision tree for this situation, and analyze it to obtain optimal production quantities in this case.

6–24. (Continuation of Problem 6–22) Now suppose that production is limited to a total of 10,000 cameras but that the manufacturer now thinks that the probabilities of demands are *no longer independent* for the two models. Specifically, the accompanying joint probability table describes the probabilities of demands.

Construct a decision tree for this situation, and find the optimal act and its EMV.

Joint Probability Table

Standard Demand \ *Deluxe Demand*	*2,000*	*4,000*	*Marginal Probability of Demand for Standard*
6,000	0.20	0.10	0.30
8,000	0	0.70	0.70
Marginal Probability of Demand for Deluxe	0.20	0.80	1.00

6–25. The Oxenol Company uses natural gas in its production-processing operations. Neighboring companies in its upstate New York area have successfully drilled for gas on their premises, and Oxenol is considering following suit. Their initial expenditure would be for drilling; this would cost \$40,000. If they struck gas, they would have to spend an additional \$30,000 to cap the well and provide for the necessary hardware and control equipment. At the current price of natural gas, if the well is successful it will have a value of \$150,000. However, if the price of gas rises to double its current value, a successful well will be worth \$300,000. The company thinks its chance of finding gas is 30 percent; it also believes that there is a 50 percent chance that the price of gas will double.

a. Draw a decision tree for this problem, filling in the probabilities and values.

b. Complete the tree by calculating EMVs. What should the company do?

6–26. You must bet on a toss of a coin of unknown physical characteristics. The coin is tossed by a machine. The decision you have to make is to bet heads or tails.

Assume that the payoffs are described by the table below:

	You Bet	
Actual Result	*Heads*	*Tails*
Heads	+100	−100
Tails	−400	+100

Your prior judgment indicates that you believe that there is a one-half chance that the coin to be tossed is fair (i.e., has a 0.5 probability of heads and a 0.5 probability of tails); further, you believe that there is a one-fourth chance that the coin is two-headed (no chance of tail); and finally, you believe that there is a one-fourth chance that the coin is two-tailed (no chance of head).

You are given the opportunity to experiment before you bet. The coin will be tossed twice. After observing the results, you will be required to bet either heads or tails on the next toss.

a. Suppose both experimental tosses came up heads. What decision would you make (i.e., what would you bet on the next toss)? What is the expected payoff?

b. Suppose the experimental tosses came out with one head and one tail? What would be your decision? What is the expected payoff?

c. Suppose two tails resulted? What would be your decision? What is the expected payoff?

d. Suppose you had a choice of playing or not playing in this game (before the experimental tosses are flipped). Would you play? What is the expected payoff of playing?

6–27. The UVW Music Company makes music boxes for a variety of toys and miscellaneous products. UVW has a guarantee on its music boxes against breakage for a one-year period.

The sales manager was concerned with the number of music boxes that were being returned under the guarantee. He thought an excessive number of music boxes that fail to last one year would damage the image of a quality product that UVW was trying to achieve. On checking, he found that approximately 5 percent of the music boxes were returned for repair within one year.

The production manager said that the trouble in almost every case was a break in a crucial spring mechanism within the music box. UVW was having trouble obtaining a spring that was entirely satisfactory. There was a special alloy that could be used in the spring and would guarantee virtually no breakage. A spring made of special alloy would cost $2 each as opposed to the cost of 20 cents for the spring currently used. The production manager did not feel the incidence of 1 failure out of 20 warranted using a part 10 times as expensive.

The production manager added that in the music boxes that were returned with a broken spring, the special-alloy spring was used for the repair, so that a second breakage was extremely unlikely. In addition, the cost of handling and repairing a box with a broken spring was $13 plus the $2 for the special-alloy spring.

The sales manager argued that the special-alloy spring should be used in each music box. He felt that in addition to the direct cost of repairing a broken music box, there was a goodwill cost of roughly $5 every time a customer's music box broke.

The decision was not a trivial one, since UVW had estimated sales of 20,000 music boxes over the next year.

a. Which alternative should UVW take?

b. What is the EVPI?

6–28. Refer to Problem 6–27. An alternative action is suggested by the UVW chief engineer. He has been approached by an instrument manufacturer with a test device that could measure the strength of the springs currently used and tell whether each was "strong" or "weak." An experimental program was introduced in which 100 springs were classified as either strong or weak and then put in UVW music boxes. The boxes were then put through a process designed to simulate about one year's wear. The results are shown below:

Results of Test of 100 Springs

Test Device Prediction	*Actual Behavior*		
	Good	*Defective*	*Total*
Strong	79	1	80
Weak	16	4	20
Total	95	5	100

The production manager did not think the test would be useful. He noted that four good springs were rejected for every bad one that was detected. Further, the test did not eliminate all defective springs.

The chief engineer thought the test would be economically feasible. He noted that the cost of the equipment and other costs associated with the test device would amount to about $4,000 for the next year.

The sales manager still preferred using all special-alloy springs but would accept using the test since, as he noted, it would reduce the number of defectives to about 1 percent.

Should UVW obtain the test device and use it to screen springs?

Hint: Five springs need to be tested to get four that test "strong." Hence, the cost of a test "strong" spring is $5/4 \times 20¢ = 25¢$.

6–29. Refer to Problem 6–18. Suppose a test can be made at a cost of $25,000 to determine the type of underground formation (types I, II, or III). The underground formation is related to the type of well, but the relation is imperfect; of 25 wells selected at random from sites near our well, the following table illustrates historical occurrences of well type and underground formation.

Historical Occurrences (25 wells)

Type of Well \ *Formation*	*I*	*II*	*III*	*Total*
Dry	4	0	0	4
Gas	1	9	0	10
Gas, oil combination	0	6	0	6
Oil	0	0	5	5
Total	5	15	5	25

If the test is made, and you subsequently decide not to drill, you can no longer sell the lease for $75,000; your prospective purchasers will conclude that since you decided not to drill, they should not also, so the lease will have zero value after a "test without drill" outcome.

Construct a decision tree for this problem. Should you sell the lease without testing, drill without testing, or test? If you decide to test, under what circumstances will you subsequently drill? What is the maximum EMV?

6–30. The credit card manager of a commercial bank must approve or reject applications for the bank's credit card. She currently uses a "scoring" procedure whereby a series of characteristics stated on an individual's credit card application are weighted by predetermined numerical weights. Based on the total weighted score, an applicant is classified either "good" or "bad" according to whether the score exceeds or falls below the predetermined cutoff score.

Recently, the manager has been considering an alternative procedure whereby an applicant would be rejected if the score fell below a new "low cutoff" score, accepted if the score fell above a new "high cutoff" score, and investigated further if it fell in between. "Further investigation" involves an extensive credit investigation at a cost of $50 each. Available data are as shown in the accompanying tables. (The "Very good" and "Very bad" groups are determined by scoring alone; the other two groups are determined after the credit bureau check.)

The bank has determined that the present value of future *profit* for an applicant who "pays" is $400, and the present value of the *losses* incurred by an applicant who "does not pay" is −$200.

a. Based on the above information, is the proposed system to be preferred to the current system? Why? For 1,000 applicants, what is the maximum EMV in present value terms?

b. In order to improve on the current system above, what additional information would you like to have? How might this information be obtained in actual practice?

Current System (results for 1,000 applicants)

Current Classification by Scoring Only \ *Actual Performance*	*Pays*	*Does Not Pay*	*Total*
Good	400	100	500
Bad	*	*	500
Total	*	*	1,000

*Cannot determine payment performance of those applicants whose applications were rejected.

Proposed System (estimated results for 1,000 applicants)

Proposed Classification by Scoring and Credit Check When Indicated \ *Actual Performance*	*Pays*	*Does Not Pay*	*Total*
Very good (scoring alone)	350	50	400
Good (scoring + check)	150	100	250
Bad (scoring + check)	*	*	50
Very bad (scoring alone)	*	*	300
Total	*	*	1,000

*Cannot determine payment performance of those applicants whose applications were rejected.

More Challenging Problems

6–31. Evergreen Pharmaceutical Company is contemplating an invitation to invest in Startup Biotech, a company engaged in research that may ultimately lead to a drug effective for reducing prostate problems in older men. Startup needs money now for R&D, more money in a few years for clinical trials, and finally money for processing equipment in six or seven years. In return, Evergreen would get part ownership of Startup.

Carol Evers is CFO at Evergreen and is responsible for evaluating these sorts of deals. She views them as if they were stock options. The details of the plan offered by Startup are as follows.

Evergreen would invest \$2 million now that would help fund the R&D activity for the new drug over the next three years. If the R&D were successful, Startup would need an additional \$2 million for clinical trials. Evergreen would have the option of providing this \$2 million or it could terminate its agreement with Startup. The clinical trial would last another two years and would either be completely successful, partially successful, or not successful. If the trials were completely successful, Startup would need \$4 million for processing equipment to produce and market the drug. If the trials were partially successful, Startup would need only \$2 million for processing equipment. And if the trials were not successful, the drug would not be marketed. Evergreen would have the option of providing this \$4 million (in the case of completely successful trial) or \$2 million (when the trial was partially successful), or it would have the option to terminate the agreement with Startup.

In return for its investments, Evergreen would get stock ownership in Startup. If the drug were developed and the clinical trials completely successful, this would be quite valuable, although there was considerable uncertainty about how valuable. At this time, Evergreen thought there was a 10 percent chance the value would be \$50 million, a 20 percent chance for \$30 million, a 30 percent chance for \$20 million, and a 40 percent chance for \$10 million. On the other hand, if the clinical trials were only partially successful, there was a 60 percent chance for only a \$5 million value, a 20 percent chance for a \$10 million value, and a 20 percent chance for \$20 million value. If the clinical trials were unsuccessful, the value would be zero.

Finally, based on experience with other similar firms, Evergreen thought that there was only a 50 percent chance that the R&D effort would be successful. If it reached the clinical trial stage, it assessed a 50 percent chance that it would be completely successful, 20 percent chance of partial success, and 30 percent chance of being unsuccessful.

Evergreen has the option of terminating its agreement with Startup at any time. However, if this is done, Evergreen receives nothing from Startup.

Diagram the problem facing Evergreen. Ignore any issues associated with discounting cash flows in this simplified problem. Enter the probabilities in the tree and net cash flows at the end of the tree. Roll back the tree and indicate what Evergreen should do. What is the EMV?

6–32. Football Concessions had the franchise to sell soft drinks, hot dogs, and so on at Wombat University home football games. This was a profitable operation, since crowds could be estimated reasonably accurately and the right amount of food purchased.

However, the November weekend Wombat was due to play its arch rival, Carbunkle U., posed a problem for the concessionaire. Both teams were undefeated, and the winner was sure to get a Bowl bid. Advance sales of tickets indicated that if the weather was nice, a crowd of more than 80,000 people could be expected. On the other hand, it was raining on Friday, and the weather prediction called for possible showers or rain on Saturday. If the rain was heavy, it was possible that a crowd of only 20,000 would show up for the game.

The concessionaire had to order his food on Friday. He generally ordered on the basis of \$.50 per person, and this had proven reasonably accurate in the past. He had a markup of 100 percent (i.e., selling price was double cost). He could generally save about 20 percent of the value (cost) of anything that he had left over.

The concessionaire assigned the following probabilities to the various possible crowd sizes. He generally felt that either it would clear up and a large crowd would result, or it would rain and a small crowd be present. The possibility of a medium-sized crowd, he believed, was less likely.

Crowd Size	*Probability*
20,000	0.30
40,000	0.20
60,000	0.10
80,000	0.40
	1.00

How much food should the concessionaire order?

6–33. Pocatello Potato Products (PPP) buys fresh Idaho potatoes and processes them into frozen french fries and other frozen potato products. PPP buys its potatoes in two ways, by preseason contract and by purchase on the open market. Under a preseason contract, entered into before the crop is planted, the processor (PPP) agrees to buy the crop of a potato grower at an agreed price per hundredweight (cwt.) of potatoes. For the current season, the preseason contract price is \$4 per cwt. Alternatively, PPP can wait until the potato crop has been harvested and buy its potato requirements on the open market at prevailing market prices. In the past few years, market prices of potatoes in Idaho have fluctuated considerably, ranging from \$2 to \$8 per cwt. Previously, PPP has preseason contracted for about half its needs, filling the other half with open market purchases.

The president of PPP is reconsidering this decision. She thinks the preseason contract price of \$4 is too high and that there are almost three chances out of four that the market price will be \$4 or less. In fact, she has carefully assessed a probability distribution for possible open-market prices of potatoes:

Open Market Price (\$ per cwt.)	*Probability*
\$2.50	0.02
3.00	0.10
3.50	0.40
4.00	0.20
4.50	0.12
5.00	0.06
5.50	0.04
6.00	0.03
6.50	0.02
7.00	0.01
	1.00

Because of other requirements (storage space, etc.), PPP does not wish to have less than 30 percent of its requirements preseason contracted, nor more than 70 percent. Next year, PPP will need 2 million cwt. of potatoes for processing. Assuming that PPP wishes to minimize the expected cost of potato purchases, how much should they preseason contract? What do you recommend to the president of PPP?

6–34. A chemical company is building a plant to market Agrixon, a new chemical used primarily in agriculture. The firm is uncertain about the demand for Agrixon during the initial year of sales. However, the following probability distribution was assessed.

Demand for Agrixon for Initial Year (kilograms)	*Probability*
800	0.2
1,000	0.4
1,200	0.3
1,400	0.1
	1.0

Agrixon is produced on a special-purpose machine. Each such machine has a yield of 200 kilograms of Agrixon per year. The fixed cost of purchasing and operating one machine is \$560,000 per year, which includes supervision, maintenance, and other fixed charges, plus annualized interest and equipment costs. Suppose the profit from one year's production of one machine (not including fixed costs) is \$1.3 million, assuming demand is sufficient to run the machine for the entire year.

The problem facing the chemical company is to decide how many machines to install in the plant for the first year. The second and subsequent years pose little problem, because the firm is able to buy additional machines if needed, and any unused capacity can be absorbed in future years as sales grow.

How many machines should the firm install to maximize expected net profit in the first year?

6–35. Little Electronics Company has initiated an antitrust and unfair trade practices lawsuit against Artex Computers, asking a settlement of \$10 million in damages. On November 4, Little receives an offer from Artex to settle the suit for a payment to Little of \$3.5 million.

The management at Little is trying to decide whether to accept the settlement or to proceed with the suit. The lawyers agree that the chances are about two in three that Little will win. They point out, however, that even if Little wins the suit, the chances are only about one in two that the judge will award the full \$10 million; the judge is equally likely to grant a partial settlement of \$5 million. The lawyers further estimate it will cost about \$200,000 in legal fees between November and June (when the case is scheduled to be heard), plus another \$100,000 in legal fees to try the case (which is expected to last three months).

In making the offer for the \$3.5 million settlement, Artex stressed that it was a "final offer," and that the offer would be good for only 30 days. However, Little management and lawyers agree that Artex will probably make a new offer in June, just before the trial begins. After some thought, it is decided that 0.60 is a good estimate of the probability of a new Artex offer in June. And if there is a new offer, the chances are 7 in 10 that it will be \$4.5 million and 3 in 10 for a \$5.5 million settlement.

If Artex makes no last minute offer in June, Little itself can initiate a settlement. In this case, Little will have to settle for \$2.5 million, because Artex will interpret the action as weakness in Little's case.

Diagram the decision problem facing Little Electronics. Assuming Little is willing to use EMV in making this decision, what strategy should be used?

6–36. In early January, Etta Laboratories received an order for 10,000 ounces of its new product, Calbonite, an ingredient used to manufacture a new variety of drugs. This was by far the largest order ever received for Calbonite—total production in the previous year had been only 1,200 ounces. The order called for 5,000 ounces to be delivered in June and the remainder in November.

The process now used to synthesize Calbonite was a long one, involving processing small batches of raw material through several stages. The company would have to invest $50,000 in new equipment to bring the production capacity up to the 1,000 ounces per month level needed to meet the order. (It would take the month of January to order and set up the equipment.) The variable manufacturing cost per ounce using this process was known to be $15.

One of the research chemists at Etta had just discovered a new process for synthesizing Calbonite. If the process could be made to work on a large scale, it would greatly simplify the production process, with potentially great savings in cost. Ordinarily, a discovery of this sort would be tested thoroughly in the laboratory and in a small pilot plant to be sure it worked and to estimate production costs. This would take about a year. However, because of the potential savings, management wondered if it should shorten this test period. The engineering department suggested a crash testing program lasting five months. At the end of this period, it would be known whether or not the process would work, and estimated production costs would be determined. This test would cost $20,000 more than the more extended test.

It was estimated that there was a 0.9 chance the new process would work. Further, given that the new process worked, the chances were 4 out of 10 that the production cost would be $2 per ounce, 4 out of 10 that it would be $10 per ounce, and 2 out of 10 that it would be $18 per ounce.

If a decision was made at this stage to use the new process, the month of June would be used to set up the new manufacturing process. Thus, if this testing program were utilized, the company would have to set up and run the first 5,000 ounces using the old process.

Also, note that only the incremental costs associated with crash testing the program need to be charged against that alternative. Since this company would test and buy the equipment for the new process if the tests were successful independent of this decision, the costs associated with these activities need not be considered in this decision.

a. Draw a decision tree for this problem.

b. What decisions should be made? What is the expected cost of filling this order?

6–37. Mary Lamb is trying to decide what to do about an apartment building she inherited from her great aunt in Walla Walla. If she were to sell it today, she could get $100,000. Since Mary doesn't need the money immediately, she is considering holding on to the property for sale later.

Suppose Mary can sell the building now, at the end of next year (year 1), or at the end of the following year (year 2). She has decided not to keep it more than two years.

For each year that Mary keeps the building, she receives $5,000 in rents (actually, rent less operating costs). Mary consults with the local Walla Walla real estate gurus and then assesses the following probabilities about increases or decreases in the value of the property: During each year (year 1 and year 2) there is a 20 percent chance that the value of the building will increase by $10,000 and an 80 percent chance that the value will decrease by $10,000 (things are a little unsettled in Walla Walla). These are the *overall* probabilities for *each* year.

However, what happens in the first year and the second are not independent. Mary believes that if the value increases in the first year, then there is a 60 percent chance that the value will also increase in the second year. Of course, if the value decreases in the first year, there are corresponding changes in the second-year probabilities, subject to the overall probabilities mentioned above.

As a first-cut analysis, Mary decides to consider only the amount received from selling the building (including the increases or decreases in value, if any) plus the amount received for rent. (Do not worry about discounting or taxes or other complications.)

a. Diagram the decision problem facing Mary. Include payoff values at the ends of the tree and probability values where appropriate.

b. What decision should Mary make?

c. (Optional.) Assume a discount rate of 15 percent. What decision should Mary make? (With a discount rate of 15 percent, cash flows received at the end of year 1 are worth $1/1.15 = 0.87$ present-value dollars; cash flows received at the end of year 2 are worth 0.76 present-value dollars.)

6–38. Artex Computers is going to purchase 10,000 units of a certain part that is to be assembled into the Artex products. The order is to be placed with the lowest bidder, with the 10,000 units to be delivered at a rate of 1,000 per month over the next 10 months.

The Frank Machine Shop (FMS) is considering bidding on this order. Two factors are puzzling Mr. Frank in his attempts to fix a bid price. The first factor deals with FMS's chances of winning the bid. Mr. Frank finally decides to consider only two bids—either $12 per unit or $13 per unit. He estimates that the chances are two-thirds of winning at the former price and one-third of winning at the latter price.

The second factor involved in the decision is the FMS unit manufacturing cost. Two production processes are available. The first, process A, is known to cost $10 per unit. The second, process B, is one that FMS has not used before. The chief supervisor says that there is a one-fourth chance that the per unit cost will be $9; a one-half chance that the cost will be $10; and a one-fourth chance that the cost will be $11, if process B is used.

The chief supervisor has suggested that she conduct an experiment with the new process (B). She could produce 10 or 15 units; and from the experience gained, she believes she could estimate unit cost "pretty well." The cost of this test would be $500. When asked to be more specific about how accurate the estimate of cost would be, the chief supervisor provided the table below.

Mr. Frank is not sure that this information is at all relevant to his problem. The controller has argued that the test suggested may be valuable but should be performed after the bid is awarded. Otherwise, he argues, the firm may spend $500 and then not win the contract. The supervisor believes the test should be done before the bid, since it may influence FMS's bid price.

What actions should FMS take? What is the expected profit?

Chances of Various Estimated Costs

Supervisor's Estimated Cost	Actual per Unit Cost $9	$10	$11
$ 9	0.8	0.1	0.1
10	0.1	0.8	0.1
11	0.1	0.1	0.8
	1.0	1.0	1.0

6–39. The Breezy Breakfast Foods Company is considering marketing a new breakfast cereal. If the new cereal is successful, it will mean a $10 million profit (present value) over the life of the product. If unsuccessful, a $2 million loss on investment will be incurred. Management currently thinks there is a 50–50 chance that the product will be successful.

Two market research firms have approached Breezy with proposals to obtain more information. Attitude Surveys collects data on consumer attitudes with respect to specific characteristics of a product, such as sweetness, caloric content, nutritive value, and so on, and produces a forecast of "success" or "fail." Of the 50 studies this company has performed on similar products recently, their experience has been as follows:

Attitude Surveys Experience

Forecast \ Actual Outcome	Success	Failure
Success	20	5
Failure	5	20

A second company, Market Competition Inc., performs analysis in an entirely different, independent manner. This company performs extensive analysis on competitive products, and produces a recommendation of "success" or "fail" based on the anticipated amount and quality of competitive products. Its experience with 50 studies has been as follows:

Market Competition Experience

Forecast \ Actual Outcome	Success	Failure
Success	22	3
Failure	0	25

Attitude Surveys charges $100,000 per survey, and Market Competition charges $150,000.

a. Consider only Attitude Surveys. Use a decision tree to decide whether or not Breezy should purchase this survey.

b. Consider only Market Competition, Inc. Use a decision tree to decide whether or not Breezy should purchase this survey.

6–40. The MBA Movie Studio is trying to decide how to distribute its new movie *Claws*. The movie has the potential of being a great financial success (a "smash"), but the executives are not sure because the subject is controversial. And they have seen some films heralded as "smashes" become "flops" with disastrous financial consequences.

The decision facing MBA is whether or not to put out the movie *Claws* on a limited first-run basis. This means that the movie will show only in a few select theaters during the first six months. After six months, it will be released generally. If the movie turns out to be a success, this is clearly the best approach because the studio makes considerable profit from these select theaters.

The other alternative is to release the film for wide distribution immediately.

The profits for the two alternatives are given in the accompanying table, and classified in terms of whether the film is a "Smash," "Medium" success, or "Flop."

Profits from Film *Claws*

		Actions	
Level of Success	*Probability*	*Limited Initial Release*	*Widespread Release*
Smash	0.3	$22 million	$12 million
Medium	0.4	8	8
Flop	0.3	−10	−2
	1.0		

There is considerable discussion in MBA about the potential of *Claws.* Management has finally agreed on the probabilities shown in the table, but which decision to make is still not clear. One possibility is to have a few sneak previews of the movie and get the audience's opinions. The cost of such a process would be about $50,000, and several executives in the company think it would be money wasted, since sneak preview audiences tend to rate a movie as good or outstanding even when it later turns out to be a flop. To support this, the following table was produced, describing the company's past experience with 40 sneak preview audience reactions.

Sneak Preview Audience Reaction

	Movie's Actual Success			
Audience Rating	*Smash*	*Medium*	*Flop*	*Totals*
Outstanding	9	12	3	24
Good	1	6	5	12
Poor	0	2	2	4
Totals	10	20	10	40

a. Draw the decision tree for this problem.

b. Calculate the posterior probabilities for "Smash," "Medium," and "Flop," given the various audience reactions.

c. Assume that MBA is willing to base its decision on expected monetary value. What decision should the MBA Movie Studio make about the movie *Claws?*

Case 6–41

Mailmart

Mailmart is a growing mail-order catalog company specializing in "toys for grown-up girls and boys." It features a specialty line of carpentry and gardening tools, games and puzzles, and craft supplies such as needlework. Mailmart produces and mails a catalog quarterly to a select mailing list made up mostly of past customers.

In order to expand, Mailmart occasionally rents a mailing list from an outside source such as another catalog company, a credit card company, or a magazine. Mailmart has just been offered the opportunity to rent a special mailing list from Carleton, Inc., a company that specializes in creating mailing lists. Carleton claims that this list has been specially created for Mailmart and contains only individuals who have the right customer profile (moderate to high income, older, home owners, past catalog buyers). The list, however, is expensive. Specifically, Carleton is asking $100,000 for the list of 100,000 names.

Tanya McDonald is the president of Mailmart and she is uncertain about whether or not to rent the list. In addition to the $100,000 cost of the list, it would cost Mailmart another $150,000 to print and mail catalogs. So the company would have to invest $250,000 before any sales resulted. And McDonald was quite uncertain about the sales that would result. To help make decisions such as these, Mailmart focuses on the average dollar sale from the customer's first order. Usually, the average first-order amount was only about $1 per name on the mailing list (note that 90 percent or more might order nothing), and McDonald judged that there was a .70 probability of this. However, she judged that there was some chance that the list from Carleton really was a special list and would result in average first-order sales of $4 per list name (with probability .20) or $7 per list name (with probability .10).

Based on past experience, Mailmart estimated that for each $1 of first order, the company made a discounted profit of $1.20. This takes into account the fact that a customer who orders once has a good chance of ordering again in the future and becoming a regular customer.

Taking this into account, McDonald has summarized the payoffs if she rents the list in the following table:

Event	*Probability*	*Discounted Payoff ($ thousands)*
Average order is $1	0.7	−$130
Average order is $4	0.2	$230
Average order is $7	0.1	$590

a. Assuming that she is an expected value decision maker, what decision should McDonald make, and what is the expected value?

b. What is the expected value of perfect information?

Before making a decision about the Carleton mailing list, McDonald has an idea. She called Carleton and asked if they would consider giving her a random sample of, say, 500 names from the list and Mailmart would use these as a test sample for the entire list. Carleton thought this was a good idea, but insisted that they charge for the sample list. A meeting was scheduled to negotiate this charge.

In preparation for this meeting, McDonald did some calculations based on past experience with the variability in order amounts and assuming a sample size of 500 names. That is, she calculated the amount of sampling error that might be expected in each of the cases mentioned above. These calculations resulted in the conditional probabilities—probabilities of various sample estimates, given the true potential of the mailing list—shown in Table 6–20.

c. Draw the decision tree for this extended problem. Fill in the probabilities on the tree and the payoffs at the end of the tree. For purposes of this analysis, ignore any

TABLE 6–20
Conditional Probabilities
Probability (Survey Estimate | True Potential)

*Survey Estimate** *(average dollar amount of first order in sample)*	**True Potential of Entire Mailing List Average**		
	First Sale = $1	*First Sale = $4*	*First Sale = $7*
Less than $2.50 per name	0.92	0.10	0.06
Between $2.50 and $5.50 per name	0.08	0.80	0.16
More than $5.50 per name	0	0.10	0.78
Total	1.00	1.00	1.00

*Average dollar amount of first order in sample.

costs for using the sample of names supplied by Carleton. What decision should be made?

d. What is the maximum amount that Mailmart would be willing to pay Carleton for the test list of names?

Case 6–42

Wabash Ski Area

Susan Parks, chief analyst for the state Department of Forests, is formulating a recommendation to the governor about the proposed Wabash Ski Area. The department had originally proposed a full-scale ski resort, but due to gasoline shortages, inflation, and other factors, the original estimates about the number of people using the resort have been questioned. Two other alternatives have also been proposed. One alternative is to build a smaller facility and expand it in two years if demand justifies it. The other alternative is to postpone the whole project for two years. Parks has collected estimates of costs, revenues, and probabilities concerning the various alternatives.

It will cost $15 million to build a full-sized facility all at one time. If a smaller facility is built and later expanded, it will cost $12 million to build the smaller initial part and $6 million to expand it later. Parks has decided to use three levels of potential demand for skiing at Wabash: high, medium, and low. The costs and revenues for these cases are shown in Table 6–21. The Department of Forests uses a measure of benefits in evaluating this type of project. The benefits measure includes revenues and costs in dollars, but it also includes a value for the recreation benefits provided by the facility (at a rate of $1 per visitor day).

After consulting with her colleagues, Parks estimates that there is a 0.10 chance that demand in the *next two years* will be high, 0.60 for medium demand, and 0.30 for low demand. Demand beyond the second year depends on what occurs during the first two years. These probabilities have also been assessed and are shown in Table 6–22.

Consider a 15-year period for evaluating this project, and calculate the total 15-year net benefits. Do not include any allowance for inflation, discounting, or growth in demand other than what is indicated in these tables. Assume that at the end of two years, the Department of Forests will be able to evaluate demand over the subsequent 13 years with certainty.

Table 6–21
Estimates of Visitor Days and Costs for Wabash Area

	Annual Visitor Days (000s)	*Annual Revenue from Leases and Concessions ($000s)*	*Fixed Costs ($000s)*	*Net Revenue ($000s)*	*Weighted Net Benefits* ($000s)*
Large-scale facility					
High demand	800	$2,400	$700	$1,700	$2,500
Medium demand	500	1,600	700	900	1,400
Low demand	200	600	700	−100	100
Smaller-scale facility					
High demand	500	$1,600	$400	$1,200	$1,700
Medium demand	400	1,000	400	600	1,000
Low demand	200	600	400	200	400

*Weighted net benefits includes both dollar revenue and visitor days valued at $1 per day.

TABLE 6–22
Probabilities for Demand at Wabash Facility beyond Year 2

Demand up to Year 2	*Demand beyond Year 2*	*Probability*
High	High	1.0
Medium	High	⅓
	Medium	½
	Low	⅙
Low	High	⅙
	Medium	⅓
	Low	½

Finally, assume that the department is willing to use expected net benefits as a criterion in making its recommendation to the governor.

a. Diagram this decision problem as a decision tree.
b. Fill in the probabilities and benefits in the tree.
c. What recommendation should be made to the governor?

CASE 6–43

PARTICULAR MOTORS

In June 1998, the managing director of Particular Motors, an Australian automobile manufacturer, is considering the future of the Torana model. Currently, the Torana is offered with a choice of an L4 engine (four cylinder imported from Germany), or an L6 or V8 engine, both manufactured in Australia. A major face-lift of this model is scheduled for release to the public in February 2001. A major decision involves whether or not Particular Motors should build its own L4 engine in Australia.

Australia, as elsewhere, is faced with an energy crisis. Under serious consideration by the government in Canberra is a law mandating a substantial increase in the price of gasoline. Such an increase in gasoline cost would lead to greater sales of the Torana with the smaller L4 engine, and reductions in sales of the Torana with the L6 and V8 engines. Three possible prices for gasoline may be set by the government—$1.10, $1.35, or $1.60 Australian dollars per liter. The sales department estimates sales of the three models over the three-year period 2001–4 as follows (after 2004, there will be a new face-lift for the Torana):

Gasoline Price	**Total Three-Years' Sales of Torana with**			
	L4 Engine	*L6 Engine*	*V8 Engine*	*Total*
$1.10	25,000	75,000	20,000	120,000
1.35	80,000	75,000	15,000	170,000
1.60	120,000	50,000	10,000	180,000

The contribution for each type of car is:

Model	*Profit Contribution per Car*
Torana with imported L4 engine	$100
Torana with Australian L4 engine	300
Torana with L6	350
Torana with V8	400

The public relations expert in Canberra is asked about the outlook for fuel prices. After serious consideration, the following probabilities are assessed:

Gasoline Price ($ per liter)	*Probability*
$1.10	0.10
1.35	0.50
1.60	0.40
	1.00

A complicating factor in the decision about building the L4 engine in Australia is the possibility of passage by the government of a Local Content Bill. This bill, if passed, would force Toyota and Nissan to increase the local content of their Australian-assembled cars, and this mans buying an Australian model L4 engine. There is a 60 percent chance this bill will pass, and Particular Motors would then negotiate a contract with Nissan and Toyota (assuming, of course, that it had decided to produce the L4 engine in Australia) to get the Japanese business of 100,000 L4 engines over the 2001–4 period. The contribution of each engine sold to the Japanese is expected to be $100.

In order to set up the manufacture of the Australian L4 engine, Particular Motors must commit $4 million in 1998 (before the fuel price or the Local Content Bill decision is known) to build the main transfer line for the engine block. The completion of the production facility will require an additional $14 million, but this can be postponed until after the government decides about the fuel price and on whether or not to pass the Local Content Bill.

To meet the requirements for the Japanese contracts, additional investment will be required. This can be done in one of two ways. A $1 million investment now will incorporate the necessary requirements into the production system, and an additional $1 million will be required when the production system is completed later. Alternatively, the production system can be modified later (after learning about fuel prices and the Local Content Bill), but to do it at that time would require $4 million. [Note: In this problem, all $ units are Australian dollars.]

a. Draw up the decision tree facing Particular Motors.

b. Include only the *incremental cash flows* associated with the L4 engine decision.

c. Include the probabilities on the tree.

d. Find the optimal strategy for Particular Motors. What is the expected incremental cash flow?

Hint: To simplify the tree slightly, note that the Japanese contract will be undertaken regardless of fuel price, if the Local Content Bill passes and if, of course, Particular decides to make an Australian L4 engine.

CASE 6–44

ABLE MEDICAL CLINIC

The Medical Policy Committee at Able Medical Clinic is considering adoption of a policy on screening for Blodget's disease.[7] A new, inexpensive test (called the Fox test) has just been announced and some members of the committee argue that Able should use the test to screen all of the clinic's patients. They point out that the test costs only $100 and is relatively reliable with a sensitivity and specificity each of 95 percent (that is, the false-positive and false-negative rates are only 5 percent). For a person with the disease, there is a 95 percent chance that the test will correctly give a positive result, and a 5 percent chance for a false-negative result. Similarly, for a person who does not have the disease, the test will correctly give a negative result 95 percent of the time and a false-positive result 5 percent. These proponents for mass screening argue that there is little danger of a misdiagnosis, since there is a second test—the Deer test—that can be administered. The Deer test is absolutely reliable, and costs $500. A person testing positive on the Fox test could be given the Deer test to confirm the diagnosis.

The proponents argue further that, if caught at an early stage, the treatment cost for Blodget's disease is about $3,000 per patient. At the later stage of development, the disease is relatively easy to detect, generally by an ordinary medical exam. However, the cost of treating the disease at this stage is substantially more—about $90,000—in part because, on some occasions, there are severe complications and a fatality in rare cases.

Another member of the committee expressed concern about the "human cost" of false positives. He pointed out that patients often get very upset when a test result is positive, despite assurances that it may be a false-positive. Even a 5 percent false-positive rate could cause a lot of anxiety if applied to a wide range of Able's patients.

The medical director was not sure how to incorporate all this information and analyze the problem. However, it was doubtful that any screening policy should be applied uniformly to all Able patients. Blodget's disease generally affected people in the 20 to 30 age range, especially men. The highest risk group appeared to be men, 20 to 30, who experienced certain types of stiffness and loss of mobility in shoulder and knee joints. About 1 in 10 such men had Blodget's disease. For people under 20 and over 50—the low risk group—only about 2 in 10,000 had Blodget's disease. For the remainder—the medium risk group—only about 1 in 100 had the disease.

a. Select one of the risk groups—say, the medium group (with 1 in 100 chance for the disease). Draw the decision tree for the problem that shows the various test results and the decisions that can be made using this information. Include the no-test case in your tree. Add the dollar payoffs and probabilities to the tree, and roll it back to determine the best decision.

b. Do the same analysis for the other two groups. What is the best alternative in each case? What policy would you recommend for the clinic?

---

[7]Blodget's disease is entirely fictional.

Case 6–45

Telco

It is 7 PM on Christmas Eve at the Emergency Control Center at Telco, the San Francisco Bay Area telephone company. Larry Nettles, the manager on duty, has received several reports from Operator Services that customers are having difficulty making calls out of their local dialing areas. Checking his diagnostic printouts from key switching offices, Larry confirms what he has dreaded most—the trouble is in one of the three marine cable routes crossing San Francisco Bay.

With marine cables, it is necessary to identify as quickly as possible which one is causing the trouble and to isolate the troubled location. Only after this is done can the calls be rerouted. The only way to identify which of the three cables is at fault (and where) is to dispatch a tugboat and crew to examine each cable at selected intervals and isolate the problem. This search process has to be done on a trial and error basis, one cable at a time.

Telco has prepared for such an emergency. A detailed study has been made of the three cables and how likely trouble might occur. The study took into account the length of the cable route, the age of the cable, and the number of shipping lanes crossed by the cable. Based on this data, Telco assessed the probabilities of cable troubles as follows (we will assume that the probabilities for two or three cables being in trouble simultaneously are zero):

Cable	*Location*	*Probability of Trouble*
Cable 1	San Francisco/Oakland	0.3
Cable 2	Sausalito/Oakland	0.5
Cable 3	Hayward/San Francisco	0.2

The above probabilities imply, for example, that if there is a cable in trouble, it is more than twice as likely that it is in cable 2 rather than in cable 3.

Studies are also available that indicate the number of calls over each cable and the revenue generated from these calls. Christmas Eve is, of course, a peak time for calls, and revenue losses will be significant if Telco fails to quickly isolate a troubled cable. These are estimated to be:

Cable	*Revenue Losses ($000s per hour)*
Cable 1	$ 28
Cable 2	90
Cable 3	120

To locate the malfunctioning cable, the Emergency Control Center has to dispatch a tugboat and crew, at a cost of $1,000 per hour. Only one tug is available. The crew has to examine each cable in turn until the faulty one is isolated. The Emergency Center's decision problem is to tell the crew in which order to search.

Past experience indicates that if a cable were defective, it would take the crew one hour to isolate the defective location, and rerouting procedures could begin immediately thereafter. However, if a cable were not defective, it would take the crew two hours to check it out completely before moving on to the next cable. For example, if cable 3 were actually the defective one, but the crew examined cable 1 first, then cable 2 before going on to cable 3, the total search time would be five hours (two hours to check out cable 1 as OK, two hours to check out cable 2 as OK, and one hour to isolate the trouble in cable 3).

a. Draw a decision tree that would help the Emergency Center manager decide about the order in which the tug crew should examine the cables. Include probabilities in your tree. (In the cases where a cable has been searched and found not defective, assume that the *relative* probabilities for the other two are not changed.) Include the evaluation units (payoffs) at the end of branches of your decision tree. Assume that Telco is willing to use the total cost (revenue lost plus tug and crew cost) as the relevant payoff measure.

b. What search strategy should Telco use?

Solutions to Practice Problems

6–1. *a.* Expected monetary value

Event	*P(Event)*	*Act 1*	*Act 2*	*Act 3*
A	.35	1.4	1.05	.70
B	.45	1.8	2.70	2.25
C	.20	.8	1.20	1.60
	EMV:	4.0	4.95*	4.55

*Optimum act.

b. Expected opportunity loss

Event	*Act 1*	*Act 2*	*Act 3*
A	0	.35	.70
B	.90	0	.45
C	.80	.40	0
EOL:	1.70	.75*	1.15

*Optimum act.

c.

Event	*Conditional Value under Certainty*
A	4
B	6
C	8

d.

Event	*P(Event)*		*Conditional Value*		*Expected Value under Certainty*
A	.35	·	4	=	1.40
B	.45	·	6	=	2.70
C	.20	·	8	=	1.60
				EMV:	5.70

e. Expected monetary value under certainty 5.70
Expected monetary value of optimum act 4.95
EVPI (also the EOL of the optimum act) .75

6–2. *a.* Since there is no penalty loss for unsold copies, the operator should order at least 14 or more copies to make certain all demand is satisfied.

b. See Table 6–23.

6–3. *a.* See Table 6–24.
Expected Profit is $80,000.
The best act is to introduce the product.

b. See Table 6–25.
The EVPI is 20,000; the EOL of the best act.

c. The EVPI would increase from 20,000 to 30,000 and the EV of the best act would decrease from 80,000 to 60,000. The profit under certainty would be 90,000 instead of 100,000. EVPI increases because the possible expected loss associated with introducing the product is more serious.

TABLE 6–23 Expected value table (Problem 6–2)

	Event	P(Event)	*Acts: Stock* 10 CV	10 EV	11 CV	11 EV	12 CV	12 EV	13 CV	13 EV	14 CV	14 EV
Demand	10	.10	2.00	.20	1.70	.17	1.40	.14	1.10	.11	.80	.08
	11	.15	2.00	.30	2.20	.33	1.90	.29	1.60	.24	1.30	.195
	12	.20	2.00	.40	2.20	.44	2.40	.48	2.10	.42	1.80	.36
	13	.25	2.00	.50	2.20	.55	2.40	.60	2.60	.65	2.30	.575
	14	.30	2.00	.60	2.20	.66	2.40	.72	2.60	.78	2.80	.84
	EMV:	1.00		2.00		2.15		2.23		2.20		2.050

The best act under conditions of zero salvage value is "Stock 12."

TABLE 6–24
Expected value table (Problem 6–3*a*)

Event	P(Event)	*Acts* — *Introduce* CV*	*Introduce* EV	*Do Not Introduce* CV	*Do Not Introduce* EV
30,000 demand	.05	(200,000)	(10,000)	0	0
40,000 demand	.10	(100,000)	(10,000)	0	0
50,000 demand	.20	0	0	0	0
60,000 demand	.30	100,000	30,000	0	0
70,000 demand	.35	200,000	70,000	0	0
	1.00	EMV:	80,000		0

*Calculation of CV:
30,000 · $10 − 500,000 = (200,000)
40,000 · $10 − 500,000 = (100,000)
50,000 · $10 − 500,000 = 0
60,000 · $10 − 500,000 = 100,000
70,000 · $10 − 500,000 = 200,000

TABLE 6–25
Expected loss table (Problem 6–3*b*)

Event	P(Event)	*Acts* — *Introduce* CL	*Introduce* EL	*Do Not Introduce* CL	*Do Not Introduce* EL
30,000 demand	.05	200,000	10,000	0	0
40,000 demand	.10	100,000	10,000	0	0
50,000 demand	.20	0	0	0	0
60,000 demand	.30	0	0	100,000	30,000
70,000 demand	.35	0	0	200,000	70,000
	1.00		20,000		100,000

FIGURE 6–14 (Problem 6–4)

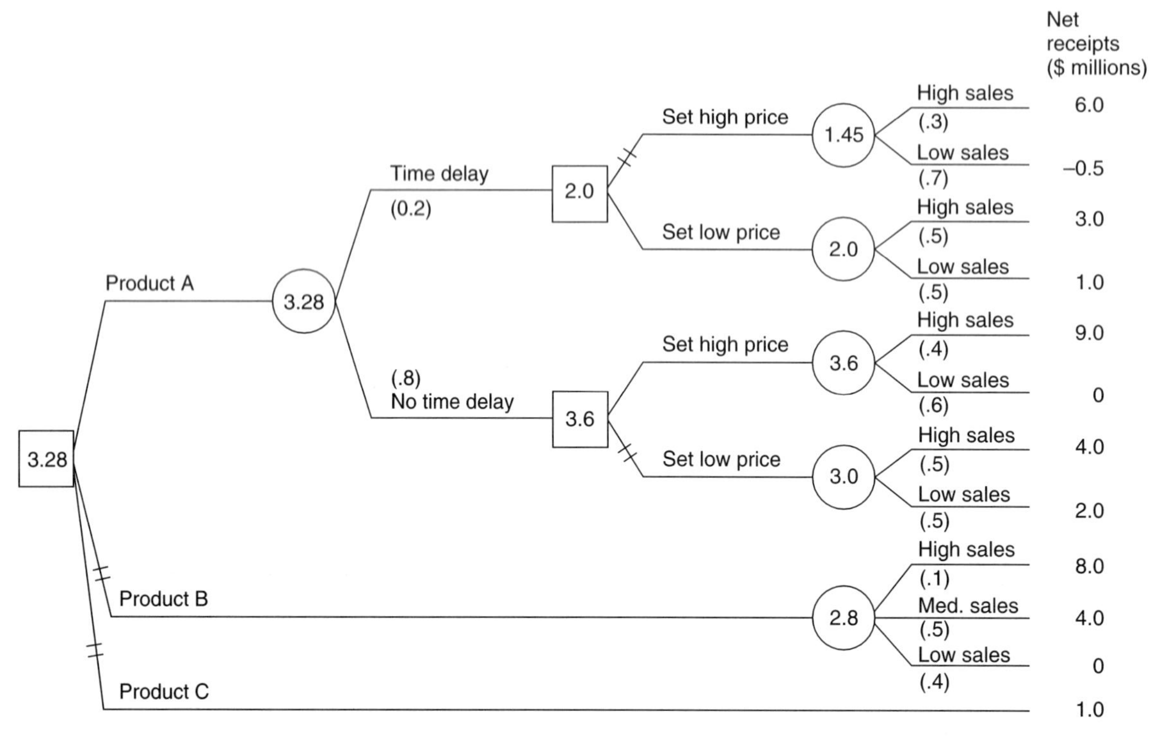

6–4. The optimal strategy is to introduce product A; set a low price if there is a time delay; set a high price if there is no time delay. The expected net profit is $3.28 million. The development of the tree is shown in Figure 6–14.

6–5. *a.* See Figure 6–15.

b. The firm should build the small plant and expand it if the promotion effort captures a significant share of the market. The expected net profit is $3.2 million.

6–6. With a prior probability of 0.4 for a recession, you would not sell. That is:

$$.4(\$.8 \text{ million}) + .6(\$1.3 \text{ million}) = \$1.10 \text{ million}$$

which is greater than $1.0 million.

To revise the prior probability: (let B = Bad debts rising)

State	*Prior (p)*	*P(B|p)*	*P(B, p)*	*Posterior P(p|B)*
Recession	.4	.8	.32	.64
Normal	.6	.3	.18	.36
			$p(B)$ = .50	

Now it would be wise to sell. That is:

$$.64(\$.8 \text{ million}) + .36(\$1.3 \text{ million}) = \$.98 \text{ million}$$

which is less than $1.0 million.

6–7. The probability of the test result (the two rolls with neither a 7 nor an 11) is $\frac{5}{9} \cdot \frac{5}{9}$ if the dice are

FIGURE 6–15 (Problem 6–5)

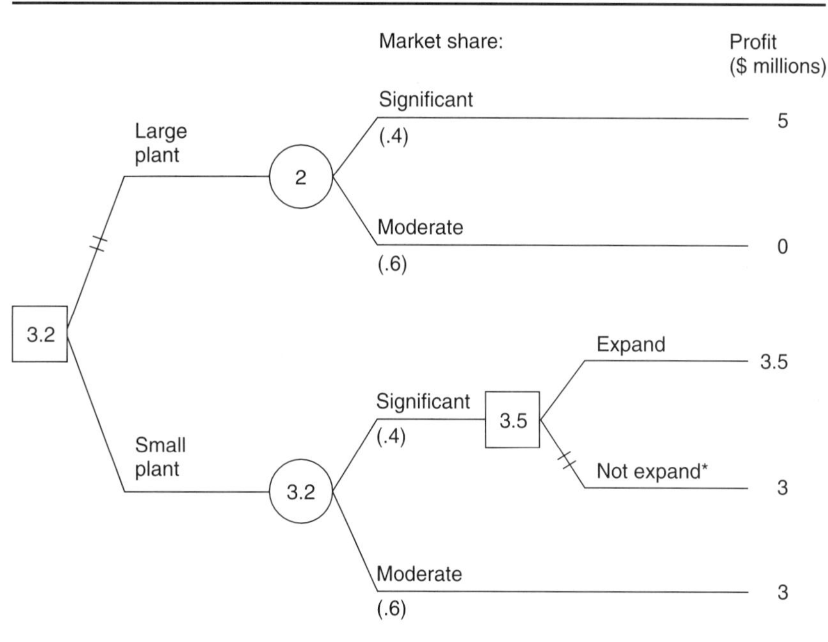

*The assumption here is that, without expansion, the firm can keep only the moderate market share.

loaded, and 7⁄9 · 7⁄9 if they are not. Call the test result S and the state (loaded or not) p. Then:

State (p)	*Prior*	*P(S|p)*	*P(S, p)*	*P(p|S)*
Loaded	.7	$\left(\frac{5}{9}\right)^2 = \frac{25}{81}$	$\frac{17.5}{81}$	.54
Unloaded	.3	$\left(\frac{7}{9}\right)^2 = \frac{49}{81}$	$\frac{14.7}{81}$	.46
		$P(S) =$	$\frac{32.2}{81}$	

If the dice are loaded, the expected payoff per play is $\frac{4}{9}(-\$3) + \frac{5}{9}(\$1) = \$-\frac{7}{9}$; if not $\frac{2}{9}(-\$3) + \frac{7}{9}(\$1) = \$\frac{1}{9}$

$$E(V) = .54\left(-\frac{7}{9}\right) + .46\left(\frac{1}{9}\right) = -\$.37. \text{ Don't play.}$$

6–8. See Table 6–26.
The posterior probabilities are:

$$P(H|S) = \frac{.09}{.23} = .39 \qquad P(L|S) = .61$$

$$P(H|I) = \frac{.15}{.50} = .30 \qquad P(L|I) = .70$$

$$P(H|F) = \frac{.06}{.27} = .22 \qquad P(L|F) = .78$$

TABLE 6–26 Joint Probability Table (Problem 6–8)

Level of Sales	*Survey Prediction*			*Marginal Probability*
	Success	*Inconclusive*	*Failure*	
High	.09	.15	.06	.30
Low	.14	.35	.21	.70
Marginal probability	.23	.50	.27	1.00

The decision tree is shown in Figure 6–16.

The survey should not be taken, since the net value is negative (−0.122). Thus, the cost of the survey of $0.2 million exceeds the expected value (which is 0.2 − 0.122 or $.078 million).

6–9. See Table 6–27.

The posterior probabilities are:

$P(H|S) = .20/.25 = 0.80 \quad P(L|S) = .05/.25 = 0.20$

$P(H|I) = .20/.45 = 0.44 \quad P(L|I) = .25/.45 = 0.56$

$P(H|F) = .10/.30 = 0.33 \quad P(L|F) = .20/.30 = 0.67$

The tree is shown in Figure 6–17.

a. See upper branches of tree. Without the survey, the product should be introduced. The expected profit is $1.0 million.

b. Zero. As can be seen, the survey never changes the decision to introduce the product (in the case of failure prediction, either action has the same expected value). Hence, the survey has no value. The company would be wasting the $.2 million cost.

FIGURE 6–16

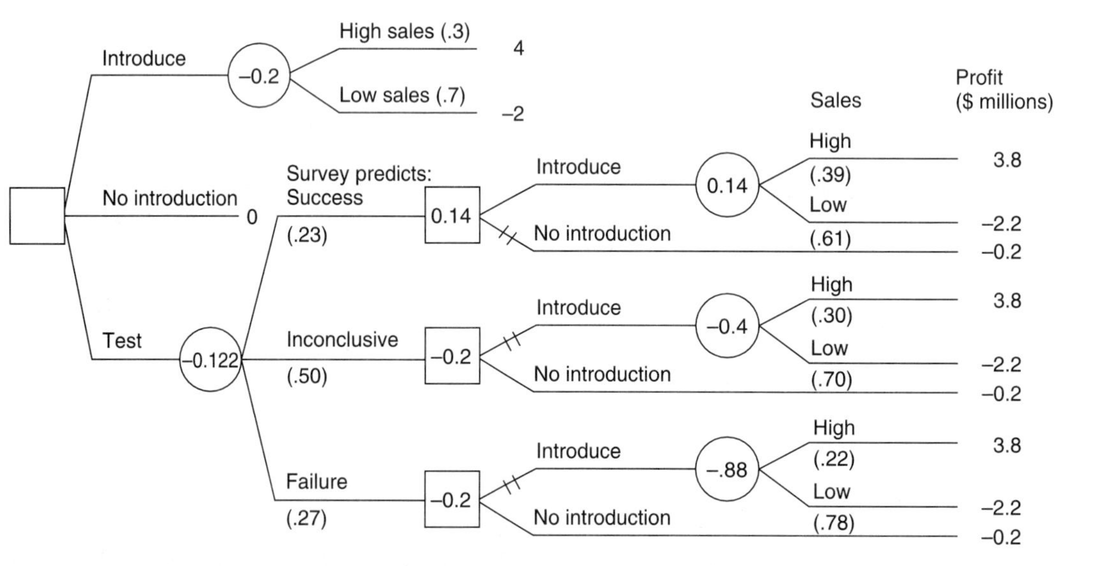

TABLE 6–27
Joint Probability Table (Problem 6–9)

Potential Level of Sales	*Survey Prediction*			*Marginal Probability*
	Success	*Inconclusive*	*Failure*	
High	0.20	0.20	0.10	0.5
Low	0.05	0.25	0.20	0.5
Marginal probability	0.25	0.45	0.30	

Figure 6–17 (Problem 6–9)

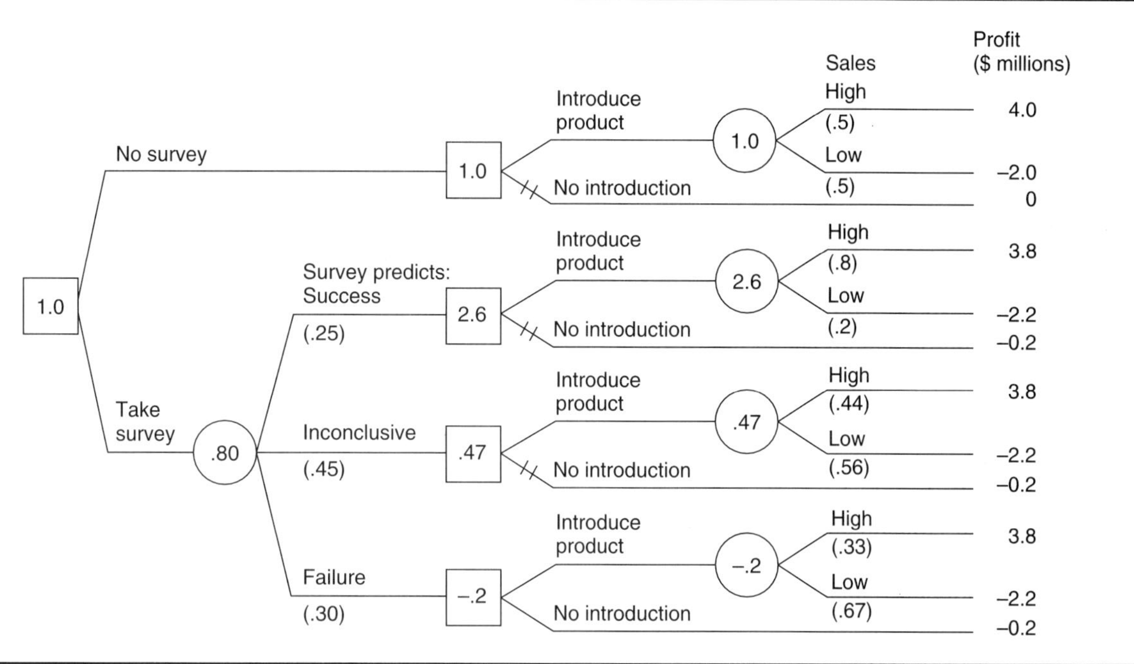

Motivating Example

Decision and Risk Analysis at Du Pont

Du Pont, one of the world's major producers of chemicals, is also involved in oil, medical, agricultural chemicals, and other products. Decision and risk analysis has been used routinely at Du Pont to evaluate strategic decisions for the various divisions and product or business groups.[1] The company reports one specific application for a business group that had a satisfactory but declining financial performance because of loss of market share and declining prices. A project team was formed that worked with management in various parts of the business. For reasons of confidentiality, specific details of the products are not available, but the products were manufactured in the United States, Europe, and Asia and distributed worldwide. The first step was to properly frame the problem and develop the alternatives. Two strategies (plus the base case *status quo*) were selected for study: a product differentiation strategy involving new product introduction, and a cost leadership strategy involving production efficiency to achieve lower prices. An influence diagram was developed to identify the important factors affecting profitability with these strategies, and the probabilities associated with the uncertainties were assessed using groups of experts within the company. These three alternatives were examined in detail. This involved calculating the cumulative probability distributions to assess the risk. Sensitivity analysis and value of information calculations were also performed to further understand the uncertainties affecting the decision. A strategy was chosen that is expected to increase this business unit's value by approximately $175 million when implemented.

[1]See F. V. Drumm and C. F. Rolle, "Management and Application of Decision and Risk Analysis in Du Pont," *Interfaces,* November–December 1992, pp. 84–93.

CHAPTER

7 Decision and Risk Analysis

The basic elements for decision making under uncertainty were introduced in the previous chapter. In particular, a decision maker has a set of **alternatives** under consideration, uncertain **events** can occur, and there is a **payoff** associated with each combination of alternative and event. Probabilities are assessed for events representing the **likelihood** of occurrence. If the decision involves a sequence of decisions or events, a **decision tree** can be drawn to structure the decision problem. Finally, the **expected monetary value (EMV)** decision criterion is used to select the decision with the highest expected value.

The EMV criterion is a sensible guideline in a great many decision situations. In particular, if the amounts of money involved are small or if the decision is a repetitive one, such as inventory stocking policy, then the expected value criterion is likely to be adequate. Of course, "small" in this context is relative—decisions involving tens or hundreds of thousands of dollars are small for a large corporation, but would not be small for most individuals. However, consider the following examples:

Example

Assume that you are given a choice in each of the following paired alternatives. You may select one of the *A* choices, one of the *B* choices, and one of the *C* choices. Make a note of the set of alternatives you choose.

A_1 =	The certainty of a \$100,000 gift, tax-free	*or* A_2 =	On the flip of a fair coin, nothing if it comes up heads, or a tax-exempt gift of \$250,000 if the coin turns up tails.
B_1 =	No gain or loss	*or* B_2 =	One chance out of 100 of incurring a \$9,000 debt, and a 99/100 chance of winning \$100.
C_1 =	A gift of \$10,000, tax-free.	*or* C_2 =	A payment of 2^N cents, where N is the number of times a fair coin is flipped until tails comes up. If tails appears on the first toss, you receive 2 cents; if the coin shows heads on the first toss and tails on the second, you receive 4 cents; two heads in a row followed by tails yields 8 cents; and so forth. However, you are allowed to participate only once; the sequence stops with the first showing of tails.

Most people would choose the set A_1, B_1, and C_1. However, the mathematical expectation (or expected monetary value) favors the alternatives A_2, B_2, and C_2. The expected value of alternative A_2 is one-half (the probability of the fair coin showing heads) times zero (the monetary value associated with heads) plus one-half (the probability of tails) times \$250,000, or \$125,000. Since this expected value is \$25,000 more than the expected value of choice A_1, you should have selected A_2 *if you wanted to maximize expected monetary value.*

Similarly, with B_2 the expected net gain is 99/100 (the appropriate probability) times \$100 (the amount of gain) less 1/100 times \$9,000. This amount is \$9, which is larger than the zero dollar gain associated with B_1. If you made decisions so as to maximize expected monetary gain, you would accept the very small chance of a large loss; but most of us would choose B_1.

The expected monetary value of the game described in C_2 is infinite. The chance of the first tail appearing on the first toss is ½; on the second toss, ¼; on the third, ⅛; on the fourth, 1/16; and so on. The related rewards would be 2 cents, 4 cents, 8 cents, 16 cents, and so on. The expected monetary value, by definition, is the sum of the monetary outcomes, weighted by the associated probabilities. In this case:

$$\begin{aligned} \text{EMV} &= \tfrac{1}{2}(2¢) + \tfrac{1}{4}(4¢) + \tfrac{1}{8}(8¢) + \tfrac{1}{16}(16¢) + \cdots \\ &= 1¢ + 1¢ + 1¢ + 1¢ + \cdots = \infty ¢ \end{aligned}$$

The fact that no prudent person would choose this game in preference to the certainty of \$10,000 or even of a more modest amount provides the essentials of the famous St. Petersburg paradox. This paradox led Daniel Bernoulli to the first investigations of utility rather than the expectation of monetary value as a basis of decision making.

Since most people would choose A_1, B_1, and C_1 rather than the three alternatives with greater monetary expectation, it seems reasonable to conclude that people do not always make decisions so as to maximize expected monetary value. What, then, is an alternative criterion for decision making?

We shall consider in this chapter two approaches that take risk into account in making a decision—namely the **dominance criterion** and **expected utility.**

Dominance

There are several methods by which a choice based on dominance can be made. The simplest case is called **outcome dominance,** in which the worst profit outcome from one act is at least as good as the best of some second act. As an example, consider acts d_1 and d_2 in Table 7–1.

The worst profit outcome for act d_1 is 0 (when q_3 occurs); the best profit for act d_2 is also 0 (when q_2 occurs). Hence, act d_1 dominates act d_2. One is assured of doing as well or better with d_1, regardless of what happens.

A second form of dominance is called **event dominance;** it occurs if one act has a profit equal to or better than that of a second act for each event. Consider acts d_1 and d_3 in Table 7–1. For each event (that is, each state of nature), the conditional profit for act d_1 is greater than that for act d_3. Hence, d_1 dominates d_3 by event dominance. Regardless of what event occurs, d_1 is better than d_3. Note that d_1 also dominates d_2 by event dominance.

TABLE 7–1
Conditional Profit Table

Event	Probability	Act d_1	d_2	d_3	d_4
q_1	0.3	2	−1	1	1
q_2	0.2	1	0	0	0
q_3	0.5	0	−1	−1	2

TABLE 7–2
Cumulative Probability Table

	Act			
	d_1		d_4	
Conditional Profit X	P(X)	P(X or more)	P(X)	P(X or more)
−1	0.0	1.0	0.0	1.0
0	0.5	1.0	0.2	1.0
1	0.2	0.5	0.3	0.8
2	0.3	0.3	0.5	0.5

A third form of dominance is called **probabilistic dominance.**[2] To demonstrate this, we need to reorganize the information in Table 7–1 into the form shown in Table 7–2. Here, the events are defined in terms of the conditional profit and are ordered from lowest (−1) to highest (2). The probabilities for each profit are shown in the $P(X)$ columns. The columns labeled $P(X$ or more) show the probability of obtaining a profit of X or more dollars. Consider act d_1: we are sure (probability is 1.0) of obtaining a profit of −1 or more and also 0 or more. The probability is 0.5 of obtaining 1 or more; and 0.3 of obtaining 2 or more. Such probabilities as $P(X$ or more) are called *cumulative probabilities.*

One act **probabilistically dominates** a second if $P(X$ or more) for the first is at least as large as $P(X$ or more) for the second for all values of X. Compare acts d_1 and d_4 in Table 7–2. Note that for each value of X, the $P(X$ or more) probability for act d_4 is always at least as large (and is greater for X values of 1 and 2) as that for act d_1. Hence, d_4 dominates d_1 by probabilistic dominance.

Consider a fixed amount of money. Obviously, you prefer an alternative that has a greater chance of obtaining that amount or more. If, for any amount of money, one alternative has a uniformly equal or better chance of obtaining that amount or more, then that alternative dominates by probabilistic dominance.

Of the three forms of dominance, outcome dominance is the strongest, event dominance next. and probabilistic dominance the weakest. If act A dominates by outcome dominance, it will also dominate by event dominance and probabilistic dominance; but the reverse is not true. For example, act d_4 dominates d_1 by probabilistic

[2]This is also called *stochastic dominance.*

dominance, as we have shown above, but does not dominate by either event dominance or outcome dominance.[3]

Using the dominance criterion to choose among decision alternatives is indeed a sensible procedure. The difficulty is that there may be no single alternative that dominates all the others. In fact, such is usually the case. Hence, the dominance criterion may fail to select an action to take. This is the major limitation of dominance. However, it can be useful in eliminating some alternatives and thus narrowing down the decision process.

The dominance criterion is related to expected value in that, if one act dominates a second, this implies that the expected value of the first act is greater than the expected value of the second. The reverse, however, is not true.

Dominance in Decision Trees

It is also possible to check for dominance when a decision problem is structured as a decision tree. First, we must introduce the idea of a **strategy.** A strategy is a set of decisions that completely determines a course of action. Consider the example shown in Figure 7–1. A decision maker has a choice of introducing a product or abandoning it. If introduced, the dealer acceptance can be either quick or slow. In either case, the manager can go with the product or stop. If the decision is to go, sales can be either high, medium, or low. The payoffs and probabilities are shown in Figure 7–1.

Consider the possible strategies available to the decision maker in this example. One easy-to-identify strategy is "Abandon the product." A second strategy is "Introduce the product: if quick acceptance, then Go; if slow acceptance, then also Go." We'll call this the Go/Go strategy. Note that both these strategy statements completely describe the decisions that must be made under all circumstances. If the product is to be abandoned, then there are no more decisions, but if the product is introduced, a Go or Stop decision must be specified, depending on quick or slow acceptance. In determining if a strategy statement is complete, ask yourself if it would contain sufficient instructions to enable an assistant to make all the decisions in your absence. If not, the statement does not specify a complete strategy.

In addition to the Abandon strategy and the Go/Go strategy, there are three other possible strategies:

- The Go/Stop strategy—"Introduce the product; if quick acceptance, then Go; if slow acceptance, then Stop."
- The Stop/Go strategy—"Introduce the product; if quick acceptance, then Stop; if slow acceptance, then Go."
- The Stop/Stop strategy—"Introduce the product; if quick acceptance, then Stop; if slow acceptance, then Stop."

Since a strategy completely determines all the decisions, only events are left. We can redraw the decision tree for each strategy. The tree for the Go/Go strategy is

[3]There are special cases for all three forms of dominance where both acts are tied. For outcome dominance, all profits for both acts may have exactly the same value. For event dominance, all profits for each event are exactly the same. And for probabilistic dominance, the $P(X$ or more) probabilities are the same for all X. In each of these cases, there is no dominance and the acts are considered equivalent.

FIGURE 7–1 Decision Tree for New Product Introduction

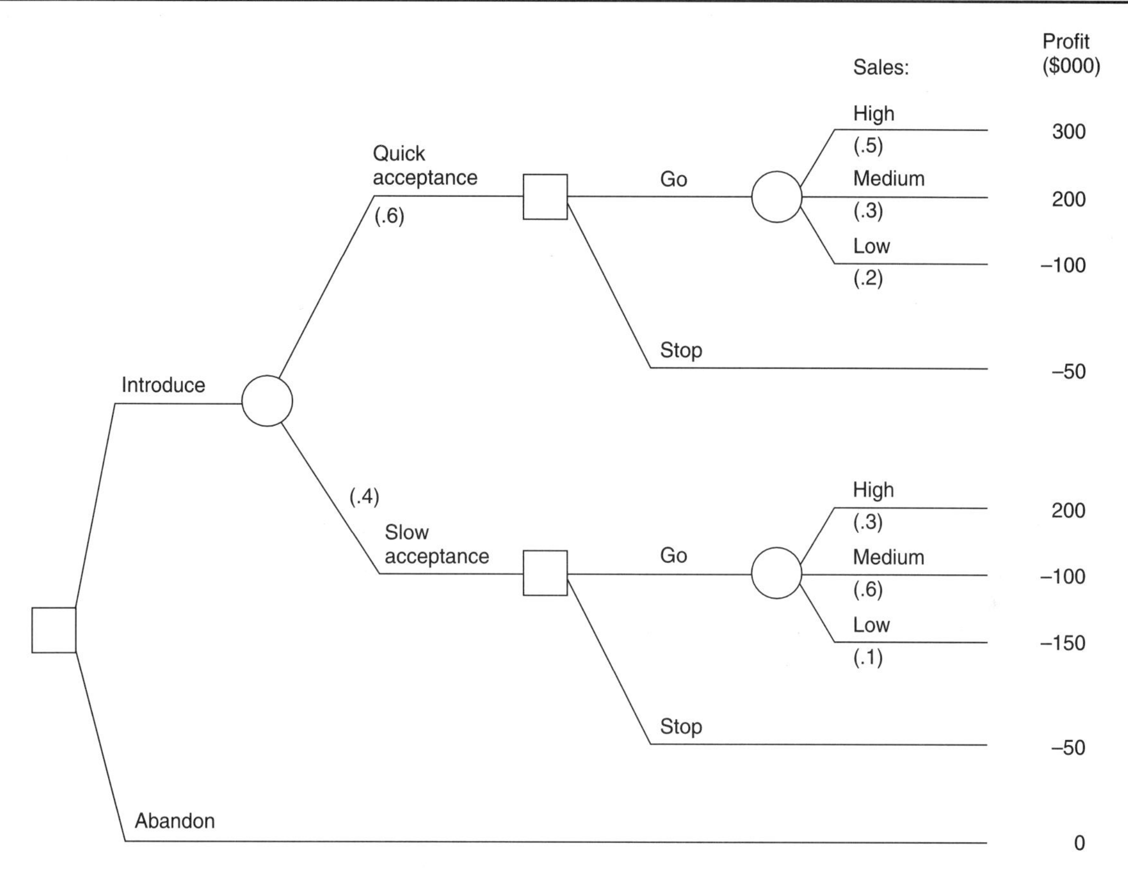

shown in Figure 7–2. The probabilities for each outcome are shown at the very end of the tree. For example, the probability for a $300,000 profit (the result of quick acceptance and high sales) is $0.6 \times 0.5 = 0.30$. The other probabilities are calculated similarly. The probability distributions for profit for this strategy (Go/Go) and for the Go/Stop and Stop/Go strategies are shown in Table 7–3.

The probability distributions for profit, such as those shown in Table 7–3, are sometimes called **profit lotteries** or **risk profiles,** since they describe compactly the risks that the decision maker faces.

The strategies "Abandon product" and Stop/Stop are not included in Table 7–3. The Abandon strategy has a sure profit of zero. The Stop/Stop strategy has a sure profit of −$50,000. Thus, the Abandon strategy dominates the Stop/Stop strategy by outcome dominance.

Note in Table 7–3 that strategy Go/Stop dominates strategy Stop/Go by probabilistic dominance, since the cumulative probability $P(X$ or more) is the same or greater in each case. No other dominance exists.

FIGURE 7–2 Abbreviated Tree for Go/Go Strategy

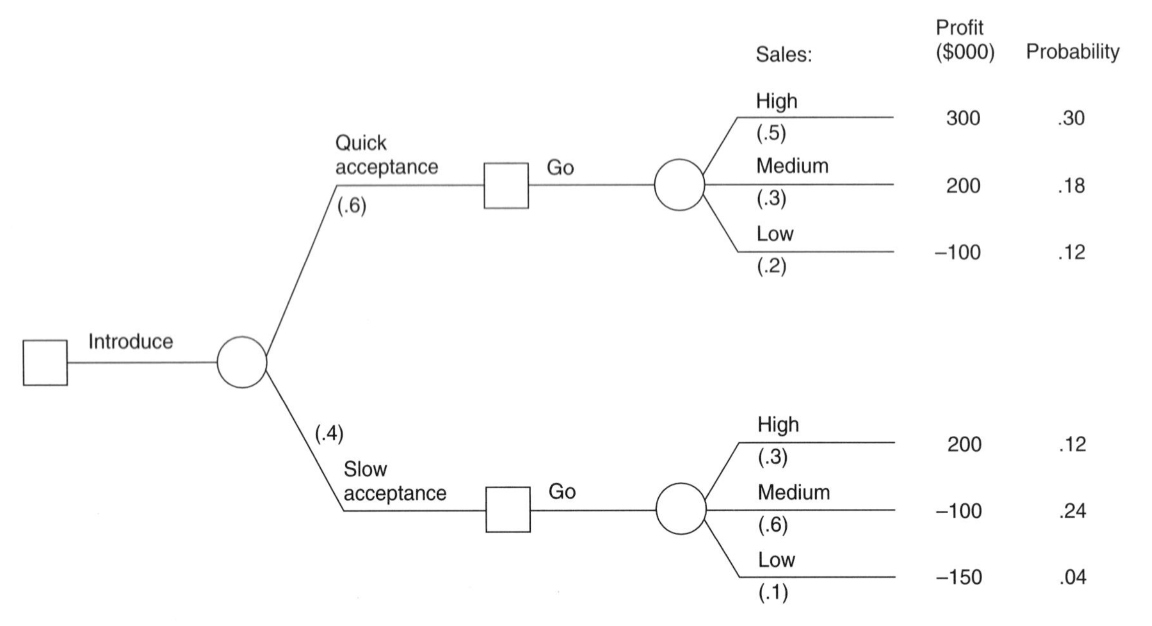

TABLE 7–3 Probability Distributions and Cumulative Distributions for Selected Strategies

	Go/Go Strategy		Go/Stop Strategy		Stop/Go Strategy	
Profit X	*P(X)*	*P(X or more)*	*P(X)*	*P(X or more)*	*P(X)*	*P(X or more)*
−150	.04	1.00	0	1.00	.04	1.00
−100	.36	.96	.12	1.00	.24	.96
−50	0	.60	.40	.88	.60	.72
200	.30	.60	.18	.48	.12	.12
300	.30	.30	.30	.30	0	0

It is sometimes easier to see probabilistic dominance by looking at a graph of the cumulative distributions, that is, a plot of *P*(*X* or more). *One strategy dominates another if its cumulative curve is everywhere the same or above the cumulative curve of the other.* Figure 7–3 shows the case of a dominated strategy in the left half. The Go/Stop strategy (the dashed line) dominates the Stop/Go strategy, since its curve is everywhere the same or above that for the Stop/Go strategy. On the other hand, when the curves cross, as in the right-hand part of Figure 7–3, there is no dominance. Neither distribution is always above (or the same) as the other.

When there are many outcomes in the decision tree, it is usually easier to check for dominance using cumulative curves than to use tables such as Table 7–3. Note in

FIGURE 7–3
Cumulative Profit Distributions

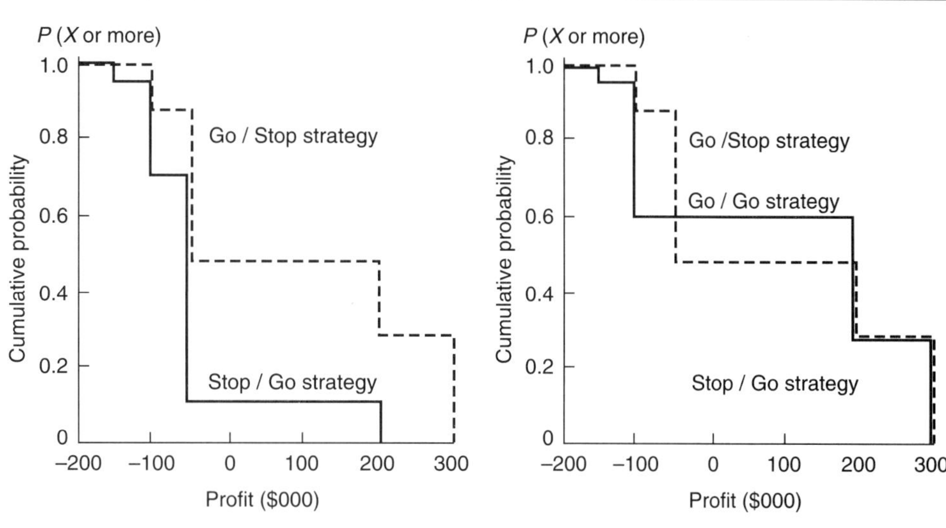

this example that we were able to eliminate only two dominated strategies (the Stop/Go and the Stop/Stop strategies). The dominance criterion does not provide a way to choose among the remaining three strategies. Hence, dominance is only a partial decision criterion.

Use of Risk Profiles in Decision Analysis

Cumulative probability distributions of profit such as those illustrated in Figure 7–3, are often called **risk profiles.** If the decision problem is relatively simple, involving only a few possible outcomes, the decision maker can readily understand the risk he or she is facing. On the other hand, real-world business decisions often involve many uncertainties, and obtaining an understanding of the risk is difficult. As an example, suppose a firm is facing a decision about a new product introduction. There may be uncertainty about the market size for the product, how fast the market will grow, the market share the firm will obtain, the price it will be able to charge, and the cost of producing the product. An abbreviated form of the decision tree for this decision is shown in Figure 7–4, in which the uncertain factors are shown. In the full tree, each uncertain node would be at the end of each branch. If, as shown, there are five levels for each uncertain factor, the full tree would be very bushy, with 3,125 end values. A decision maker would have a very difficult time understanding the risk associated with the decision to introduce the product.

However, the cumulative probability distribution, or risk profile, can be calculated as was illustrated in Table 7–3 and Figure 7–3. With 3,125 end values to calculate, this may seem a daunting task. However, modern decision analysis software routinely calculates such risk profiles.[4] There is also a technique called **Monte Carlo**

[4]See, for example, Peter McNamee and John Celona, *Decision Analysis for the Professional with Supertree,* 2nd ed. (Palo Alto, CA: Scientific Press, 1990); and *DPL, Decision Analysis Software for Microsoft Windows,* ADA Decision Systems (Belmont, CA: Duxbury Press, 1995).

FIGURE 7–4 Abbreviated Decision Tree for New Product Introduction

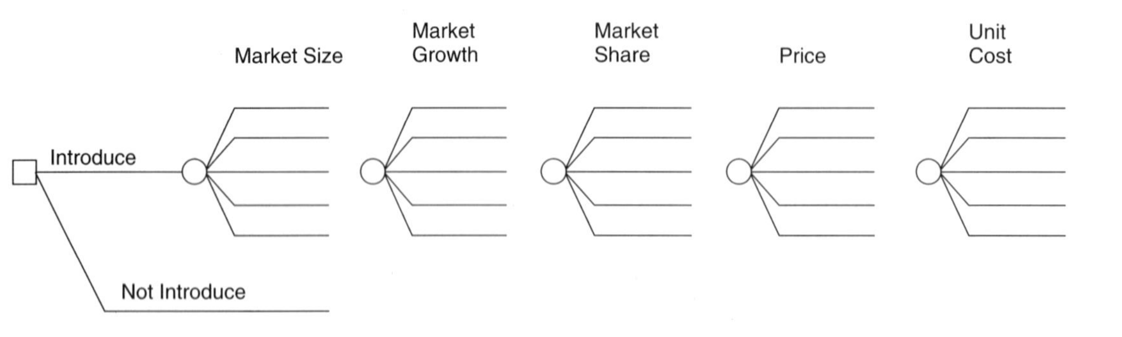

FIGURE 7–5 Risk Profile for New Product Decision

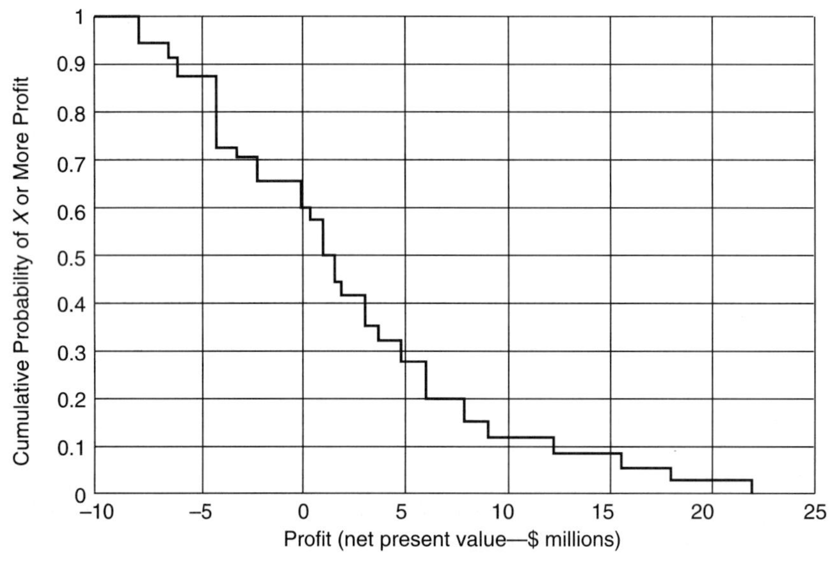

analysis that can be used; this technique is treated in a later chapter on Simulation. An example of the risk profile that might result is shown in Figure 7–5.

The value of such a risk profile is that it gives the decision maker an understanding of the riskiness of the decision. For example, from Figure 7–5, there is about a 40 percent chance that the new product will lose money (have a negative net present value) and a 60 percent chance that it will make money. There is approximately a 10 percent chance of losing more than $6 million, and a 10 percent chance of making more than $12 million. So if the firm decides to proceed with the new product introduction, it understands the risk it is taking.

An important extension of this analysis is to look at the contribution of the various factors to the risk. Consider the market share factor. By experimenting with different distributions for this factor, the firm may discover that the very large negative profits are the result of the firm obtaining a small market share. This might lead to consumer market research in which the firm's product is compared to competitors in order to obtain a better estimate of market share. Or the cost of producing the product may be a risk causing factor, and engineering research may be undertaken to more accurately estimate the cost.

In summary, developing the risk profile is an important step in the evaluation of major decisions. In the decision and risk analysis example at Du Pont at the beginning of this chapter, specific mention was made of the firm's use of the cumulative probabilities (risk profiles) to understand the uncertainties affecting the decision about the strategy for the business unit.

Summary

If a decision maker's attitude toward risk is not an important consideration in a decision problem, the expected value decision rule is generally preferred to other decision criteria. It is the only one that makes use of all the information available and that ensures a definite choice among the alternatives.

Even when risk is present, expected monetary value is a useful first step.

The use of dominance criteria can sometimes eliminate some inferior alternatives in a decision problem.

The calculation of the cumulative distribution or risk profile is a useful step in understanding the risk in a complex decision.

Utility as a Basis for Decision Making

At the beginning of this chapter, you were presented with several choices such as alternative A_1, which was the receipt of \$100,000 for sure, or alternative A_2, which was a lottery involving a one-half chance at nothing and a one-half chance of \$250,000. Most people—probably you also—would choose alternative A_1 over A_2 despite the fact that the expected value of the second choice was \$125,000, considerably more than the value of the first choice. Von Neumann and Morgenstern[5] constructed a framework consistent with choices such as preferring A_1 over A_2. They argued that decisions are made so as to maximize expected utility rather than expected monetary value. If you selected A_1 over A_2, we would conclude that alternative A_1 has more utility for you than alternative A_2. If you were indifferent between two alternatives, we would conclude that each alternative offered the same expected utility to you. Based on reasonable and logical assumptions about how people make choices between alternatives, von Neumann and Morgenstern developed a procedure for quantifying or measuring a person's utility function for commodities or money. This function can be used to calculate expected utility, and the decision maker can maximize expected utility rather than expected monetary value.

Derivation of a Utility Function for Money

To be of use in decision making, utility values must be assigned to all outcomes. In many circumstances, such outcomes are nonmonetary in nature. For example, in making a medical diagnosis, a physician has to weigh such factors as pain and

[5] J. von Neumann and O. Morgenstern, *Theory of Games and Economic Behavior* (Princeton: Princeton University Press, 1944).

suffering, loss of work from hospitalization, psychological effects, costs, and even death. It is possible using the von Neumann–Morgenstern approach to assign utility values to such outcomes. However, in most business decision problems, the monetary consequence is of major importance. Hence, we shall be concerned primarily with evaluating the utility function for money.

The Shape of Utility Functions

Some generalizations about the usual shape of a utility function are possible. People usually regard money as a desirable commodity and prefer more of it to less of it. The utility measure of a large sum is normally greater than the utility measure of a small sum, and the utility function rises over any relevant range of money. We can describe a utility function as having a positive slope over this relevant range. The slope in this case is the ratio of an incremental change in the utility index [$\Delta U(M)$] as a result of an incremental change in the stock of money (ΔM). The incremental changes will always have the same sign, so we may write:

$$\text{Slope} = \frac{\Delta U(M)}{\Delta M} > 0$$

This measure of the slope is called the **marginal utility of money** and, except for the algebraic sign, is an arbitrary measure.

The slope of a utility function is positive and probably does not vary in response to small changes in the stock of money. It follows that for small changes in the amount of money going to an individual, the utility function over that range has approximately a constant slope and may be regarded as linear. If the utility function is linear [$U(M)$ in Figure 7–6], the person maximizes expected utility by maximizing expected monetary value. Thus, expected monetary value may properly be used as a guide in decision making only when there is a reason to believe the pertinent utility function is linear over the range of possible outcomes. We have seen that for large variations in the amount of money, this is a most unlikely condition. At the extremes,

FIGURE 7–6
Linear Utility for Money

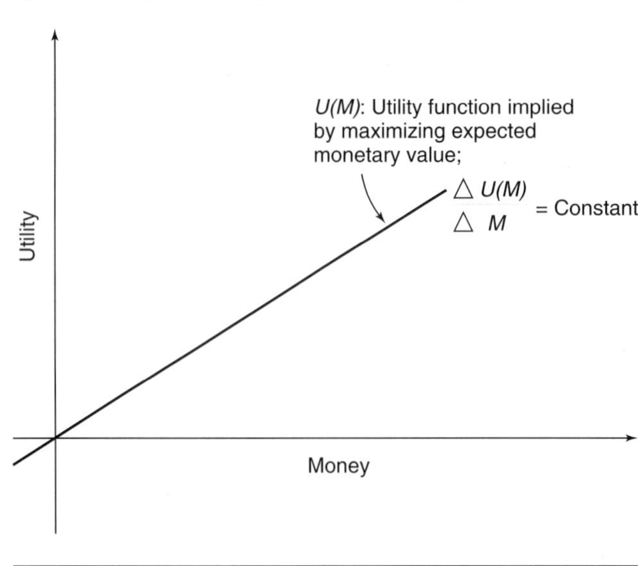

for large losses and large gains, the utility function is almost certain to approach upper and lower limits. The slope of the curve usually will increase sharply as the amount of the loss increases, implying that the disutility of a large loss is proportionately more than the disutility of a small loss, but the curve may flatten as the loss becomes very large. Similarly, for large stocks of money, the slope of the utility function grows smaller with further additions to that stock. These observations are consistent with the traditional "diminishing marginal utility" view of consumer psychology. They are also consistent with the notion of "risk aversion," which pervades most business decision problems. An example of a risk averse utility function is shown in Figure 7–7. If an individual is risk averse, then the expected utility of a gamble is less than the utility of the expected monetary value.

It is possible for a decision maker to be risk preferring, at least over a range of the utility function. In this case, the expected utility of a gamble is more than the utility of the expected monetary value. A risk preferring utility function is also shown in Figure 7–7.

Assessing a Utility Function

The first step in actually deriving a utility function is to determine two values to use as reference points. For convenience, these can be the largest and smallest monetary values involved in the decision problem. The utility values corresponding to these monetary values are arbitrarily selected—for convenience, we might assign utility values of 0 and 1 to these monetary values. For example, if the decision problem included monetary values ranging from −\$10,000 to +\$100,000, we would assign a 0 utility of −\$10,000 and a utility of 1.0 to \$100,000. That is:

$$U(-\$10{,}000) = 0 \quad \text{and} \quad U(\$100{,}000) = 1.0$$

The selection of utility values of 0 and 1 is arbitrary. Values of −29 and +132 or other values could have been selected. In this sense, the utility scale is like that for temperature. Both the Celsius and Fahrenheit scales measure temperature but have different readings for the freezing point of water (0° and 32°, respectively) and for the boiling point (100° and 212°, respectively).

FIGURE 7–7
Utility functions

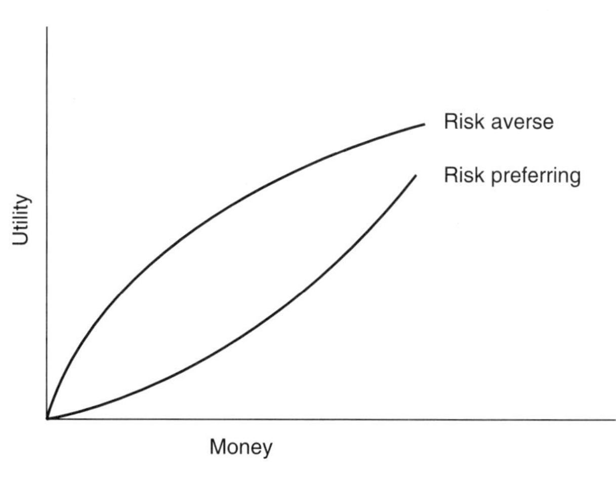

Next, formulate an alternative A_1 that offers a one-half chance at $-\$10,000$ and a one-half chance at $+\$100,000$. The expected utility of this alternative is the sum of the utility assignments to the possible events, weighted by the appropriate probabilities. In this case:

$$U(A_1) = \tfrac{1}{2}U(-\$10,000) + \tfrac{1}{2}U(\$100,000) = \tfrac{1}{2}(0) + \tfrac{1}{2}(1) = 0.5$$

Now formulate a second alternative (A_2) that yields some amount of money with certainty—say, \$25,000. You now have to choose between the two courses of action, A_1 and A_2. Say you choose A_2, or \$25,000 for certain. We infer that:

$$U(A_2) > U(A_1) = 0.5$$

or $U(\$25,000) > \tfrac{1}{2}U(-\$10,000) + \tfrac{1}{2}U(\$100,000) = 0.5$; that is, the utility of \$25,000 is greater than one-half. Because the \$25,000 is preferred to A_1, we conclude that the utility index of A_2 is greater than one-half. Assume next that you were offered \$5,000 for certain (A_3) and found that you preferred A_1 to A_3. This would imply that the utility index associated with \$5,000 should be less than one-half. If your patience held out, you could continue proposing alternative acts yielding sums of money with certainty until you discovered one that was exactly as attractive as A_1. Suppose this offer was \$15,000, so that we could infer that you were indifferent between \$15,000 for certain and the original proposal. Thus, the utility assignment to \$15,000 should be:

$$U(\$15,000) = \tfrac{1}{2}U(-\$10,0000) + \tfrac{1}{2}U(\$100,000) = 0.5$$

We now have three points through which your utility function passes. Additional utility evaluations may be made in a similar manner. For example, pose an alternative that offers a 0.5 probability of \$15,000 and a 0.5 probability of \$100,000. Find the sum that must be offered with certainty to make you indifferent to the opportunity involving risk. Say this amount is \$47,000. We could conclude that the appropriate utility assignment for \$47,000 is:

$$U(\$47,000) = \tfrac{1}{2}U(\$15,000) + \tfrac{1}{2}U(\$100,000)$$
$$= \tfrac{1}{2}(0.5) + \tfrac{1}{2}(1.0) = 0.75$$

Next, pose the alternative involving a one-half chance at \$15,000 and one-half chance at $-\$10,000$. You may consider this alternative unfavorable, and in fact be willing to pay some amount to be relieved of the alternative (in the same way that one buys insurance to be relieved of a risk). Suppose you are indifferent to $-\$2,500$ (that is, a payment of \$2,500) and the opportunity involving risk. Then:

$$U(-\$2,500) = \tfrac{1}{2}U(-\$10,000) + \tfrac{1}{2}U(\$15,000)$$
$$= \tfrac{1}{2}(0) + \tfrac{1}{2}(0.5) = 0.25$$

You now have the five points of the utility function shown in Table 7–4 and Figure 7–8. These can be connected by a smooth curve to give an approximation for the utility function over the entire range: $-\$10,000$ to \$100,000.

Note that:

$$U(\$15,000) = 0.5$$

and:

$$\tfrac{1}{2}U(-\$2,500) + \tfrac{1}{2}U(\$47,000) = \tfrac{1}{2}(0.25) + \tfrac{1}{2}(0.75) = 0.5$$

TABLE 7–4 Assessed Utility Points

Monetary Value M	*Utility Index* $U(M)$
\$−10,000	0
−2,500	0.25
15,000	0.50
47,000	0.75
100,000	1.0

FIGURE 7–8 Assessed Utility Function

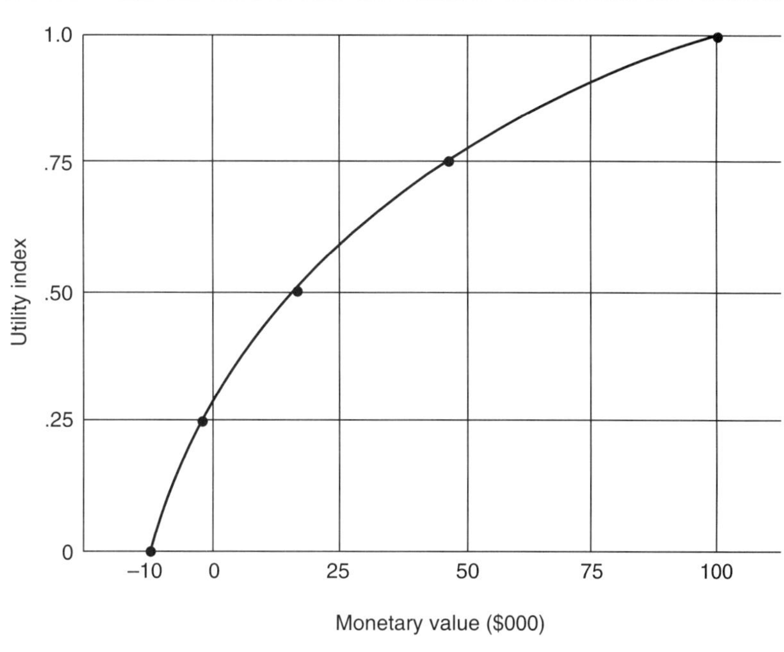

Hence, as a final check on your assessments, you should be indifferent between \$15,000 for sure and an alternative involving a one-half chance at −\$2,500 and a one-half chance at \$47,000. If this is not true, your assessments are not consistent and must be revised.

An alternative procedure for assessing the utility function is to pick a certain monetary value and then determine the probabilities that make a gamble involving the maximum and minimum values equivalent to the certain amount. For example, if we picked a certain amount L, we then formulate the equation:

$$pU(\$100{,}000) + (1 - p)U(-\$10{,}000) = U(L)$$

and we find the probability p that makes the decision maker indifferent between the two sides of this equation. As an illustration, if L were \$25,000, the decision maker would have to assess a probability p such that he was indifferent between \$25,000 for sure, and a p chance at \$100,000 and a $(1 - p)$ chance at −\$10,000. In this case, p might be 0.60. Then:

$$\begin{aligned} U(L) &= U(\$25{,}000) = 0.6U(\$100{,}000) + 0.4U(-\$10{,}000) \\ &= 0.6(1) + 0.4(0) = 0.6 \end{aligned}$$

[because we have set $U(\$100{,}000) = 1.0$ and $U(-\$10{,}000) = 0$, $U(L) = p$]. To obtain other values on the utility curve, other values of L would be selected and the p probability assessed. In this manner, a curve similar to that of Figure 7–8 could be obtained.

Using Utility Functions

A utility function represents the subjective attitude of a decision maker to risk. Hence, a utility function of a person can be used to evaluate decision alternatives involving uncertain outcomes.

Example
Suppose a decision maker has to make a choice between two alternatives. Alternative A involves a contract in which the company is sure to make a profit of \$20,000. Alternative B, on the other hand, is the introduction of a new product. The sales that the product would achieve, and hence the profit, are unknown. Management assigns the probabilities shown in Table 7–5 to the various profit possibilities.

The expected monetary value for alternative B is \$25,000. On this basis, B would be preferred to A. On the other hand, if the decision maker were risk averse, the preference might change. Note that there is a 30 percent chance of no profit and a 10 percent chance of a loss with alternative B. If the decision maker had the utility function given in Figure 7–8, we would evaluate this alternative by using utility values instead of monetary values. By interpolating in Figure 7–8, we could find the utility values associated with each profit amount. These are given in Table 7–5. Using the probabilities in the same table, the *expected utility* would be calculated (by multiplying the probabilities by the utility amounts and summing). The expected utility is calculated as 0.514. Note that the utility of \$20,000 is given in Table 7–5 as 0.55. Hence, the expected utility of alternative B is not as great as the utility of the contract involving \$20,000 for sure, and the sure contract should be accepted.

Certainty Equivalents

The notion of a certainty equivalent has been presented several times in this chapter. Let us now consider its meaning more explicitly. Consider an uncertain decision situation, which may be represented by a lottery, L, with dollar outcomes A_1 and A_2, and corresponding probabilities p and $(1 - p)$. The **certainty equivalent (CE)** is a

TABLE 7–5
Probabilities, Payoffs, and Utilities for Alternative B

Probability	*Profit (\$000s)*	*Utility*
0.1	−\$10	0
0.3	0	0.30
0.2	20	0.55
0.2	40	0.71
0.1	60	0.82
0.1	80	0.90
Expected values:	\$25	0.514

certain or sure dollar amount A^*, which is equivalent, for the decision maker, to the lottery L.

The certainty equivalent can be interpreted as the maximum insurance that the decision maker would pay to be freed of an undesirable risk (for example, the maximum premium to insure against a fire in one's house). Or we might consider the certainty equivalent as the minimum certain amount one would be willing to accept for selling a desirable but uncertain set of outcomes.

Once we have obtained the utility function for a decision maker and also obtained the probabilities in a given decision situation, the certainty equivalent can be obtained directly by the methods described earlier. In our example above, the alternative of introducing the new product has an expected utility of 0.514. If $17,500 also has a utility of 0.514, we can say that the amount of $17,500 is the *certainty equivalent* of the alternative involving the new product introduction. When faced with an uncertain decision situation, it would be beneficial to determine the certainty equivalent directly by asking the decision maker. If this does not agree with the value computed using the utility function and the probabilities, then we have come up with an inconsistency; it may be due either to the utility curve or to the probabilities assigned to the outcomes. Hence, the use of the certainty equivalent is a check on the validity of our analysis.

The certainty equivalent also has another use in analyzing complex decision situations. Our procedure so far has called for obtaining probabilities of various outcomes and a utility function as separate inputs to the decision-making process. Since both of these often represent subjective judgments on the part of the decision maker, it is sometimes convenient to shortcut the analysis and come up with a certainty equivalent directly.

Example

A firm is bidding on a contract to supply 1,000 units of a certain electronic component. It has to decide its bid price. One uncertain factor in the decision process is the possibility of a strike by its workers. If they do strike, it will mean delays and penalties associated with meeting the deadline on the contract. To simplify the decision analysis, we might ask our manufacturer how much it would be willing to pay for insurance against losses due to the possible strike. It might answer, for example, $3,000. This amount is the certainty equivalent to the uncertain situation related to the strike (the dollar outcomes with and without a strike *and* the related probabilities). The decision maker may not actually be able to purchase insurance of this type, but the certainty equivalent provides a figure that we can use in our analysis to determine the proper bid to be made by the manufacturer.

Utility Analysis in Decision Trees

Decision problems with multiple stages of decisions or events are represented by decision trees. When risk is a factor, utility values can be used directly in the tree. The utility function is assessed as discussed, and the utility values substituted for the payoff values at the end of the tree. The tree is then rolled back—the expected utility is calculated at every event node and the choice made for the higher utility at the decision nodes. In other words, it is treated exactly as a decision tree with monetary payoffs.

Figure 7–9 shows the decision tree for a decision about new product introduction that was used earlier (Figure 7–1). Suppose the firm has concerns about the

FIGURE 7–9 Decision Tree for New Product Introduction

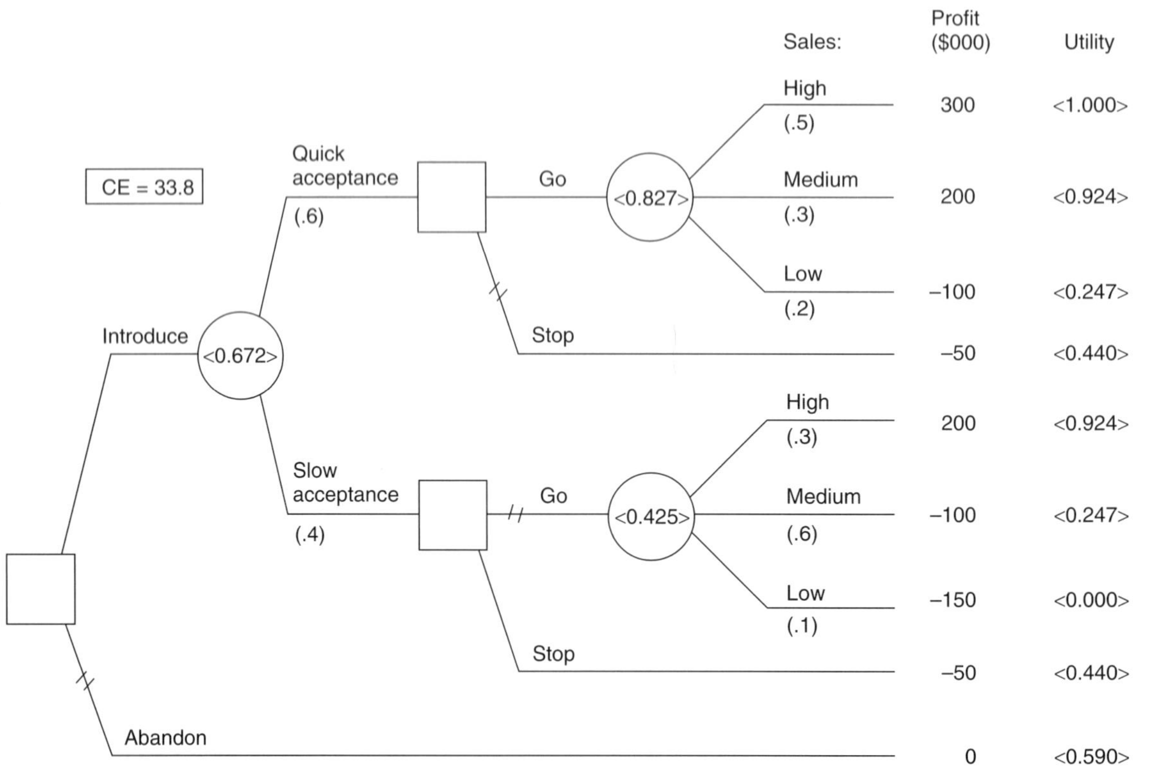

magnitude of the possible losses and has assessed its utility function for payoffs as shown in Figure 7–10. This utility function has been fit by a mathematical equation[6]:

$$u(x) = 1.118 - 0.5280e^{-x/200}$$

The utility values for the payoff are read from Figure 7–10 (or calculated from the function) and are shown at the end of the tree. The tree is rolled back using these values. For example, the value of <0.827> is the expected utility associated with the top event node (Introduce/Quick acceptance/Go).

As can be seen, the optimal strategy is to Introduce, and then Go if Quick acceptance, but Stop if Slow acceptance occurs. The expected utility of this strategy is <0.672>. The certainty equivalent of this (either reading from Figure 7–10 or from the function) is \$33,800. In contrast, the EMV strategy is to Go with the product regardless of Quick or Slow acceptance, and the EMV value is \$108,000.

Risk Premiums

Suppose an individual has a utility function $U(I)$ as shown in Figure 7–11. Consider first a gamble involving a one-half chance for the amount I_1 and a one-half chance for the amount I_3. The expected monetary value (EMV) of this gamble is I_2. The

[6]See the appendix to this chapter for a discussion of exponential utility functions of this type.

FIGURE 7–10
Utility Function for New Product Decision

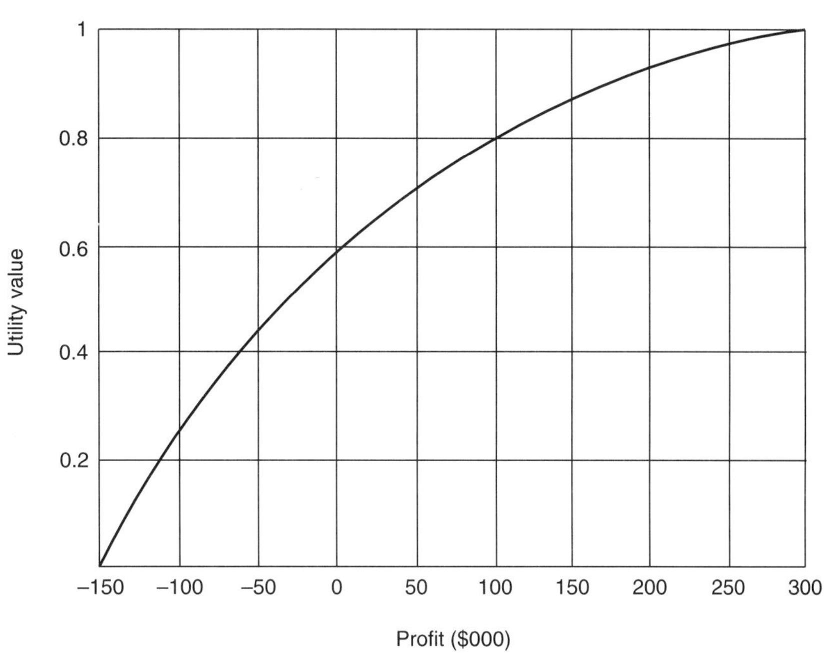

FIGURE 7–11
Utility Function

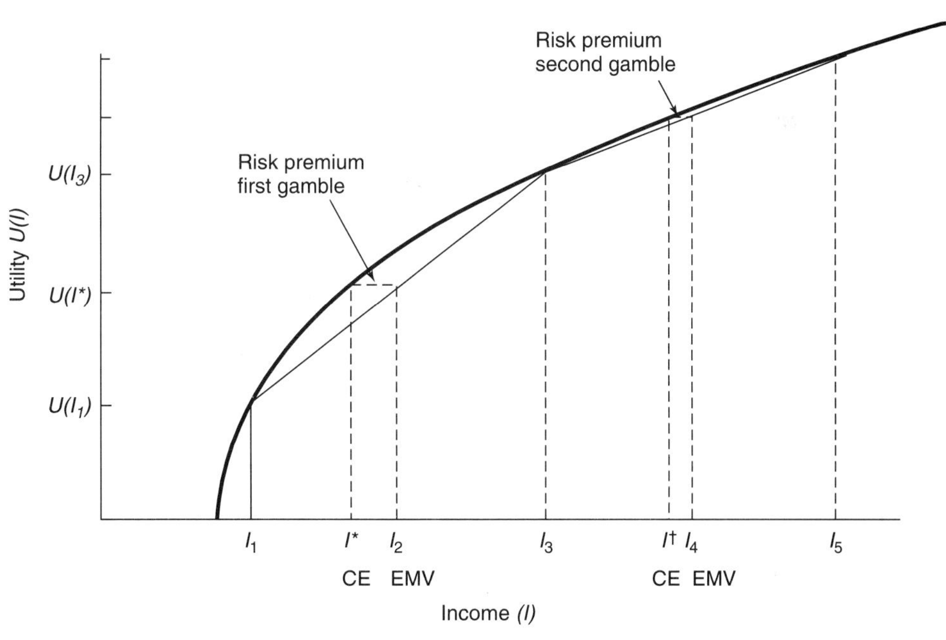

certainty equivalent of the gamble is I^*, the certain amount that has the same utility as the expected utility of the gamble [i.e., $\frac{1}{2}U(I_1) + \frac{1}{2}U(I_3) = U(I^*)$]. The difference between the EMV and the certainty equivalent (CE) of the gamble (i.e., $I_2 - I^*$) is the **risk premium** associated with the gamble for that individual. The risk premium is a measure of how much risk aversion there is in a given portion of an individual's utility function. For two individuals presented with the same gamble, the one with the higher risk premium is the more risk averse.

For a given individual, the risk premium will generally not be the same at different parts of the utility function. Consider a second gamble involving a one-half chance at I_3 and a one-half chance at I_5, where I_5 is such that the distance from I_3 to I_5 is the same as that from I_1 to I_3 (i.e., $I_5 - I_3 = I_3 - I_1$). We can think of this second gamble as if it were composed of a sure amount of $(I_3 - I_1)$ plus the first gamble above involving I_1 and I_3. In this sense, the second gamble is the same as the first, except for a different starting point (I_3 versus I_1). The expected value is I_4, and the certainty equivalent is $I\dagger$. Note that the risk premium in the second gamble ($I_4 - I\dagger$) is less than the risk premium of the first gamble. Thus, the utility function shown in Figure 7–11 has the property of **decreasing risk aversion.** In other words, the individual becomes less risk averse as the money amount I increases.

This property of decreasing risk aversion is one that seems reasonable for most business and many personal decisions. The possibility of a loss of a given size becomes less significant the more wealth the investor possesses.

Summary

When risk considerations are important, maximizing expected utility may be more appropriate than maximizing expected monetary value. A utility function can be assessed using lotteries and indifference points, or by certainty equivalents. The decision alternative that maximizes expected utility is the preferred alternative. Utility values may be used directly as payoff values in decision trees.

Cautions in the Use of Decision Analysis

The decision analysis approach to decision making involves identifying decision alternatives and events, calculating payoff values, and assessing probabilities for events. The expected monetary value (EMV) criterion is used when risk is not important; it is supplemented by utility theory and dominance when risk is involved. This approach has proved very useful at two levels. First, it provides a very valuable framework for thinking about uncertainty. Much of modern finance and economics theory relies on the basic concepts of EMV and utility. So decision analysis is an important component of the conceptual frameworks for other disciplines.

But decision analysis has also proved very valuable in solving practical business problems. For example, inventory and production scheduling systems use the EMV decision criterion to take into account the uncertainty associated with demand. Major investment decisions by firms often involve a formal decision analysis, including developing a risk profile for various alternatives. (See the Du Pont example at the beginning of the chapter.) In some industries, such as the oil drilling and electric utility industries, the use of decision analysis is routine. Nevertheless, its use is not always straightforward and there are some cautions about which a user should be aware.

Problem Framing

In all decision making, it is important to be solving the right problem. This is called *problem framing.* A very elaborate decision analysis about where to locate a factory, when the real problem the company faces is how to make its product meet consumer needs, is a waste of time and energy. An example of failure in problem framing was the Swiss watch industry. Swiss watchmakers were given the technology for electronic battery operated (digital) watches well before the Japanese. However, they did not think this new technology would replace the older spring-wound watches for which the Swiss are famous. Their decision frame did not include the idea of a whole new industry—digital watches. And they lost an opportunity to the Japanese.

What is the implication of this for decision analysis? The lesson is that the decision maker, before doing any detailed analysis, should step back and ask, "Are we solving the right problem?" "What are we trying to accomplish, and are there other ways of reaching that goal?" This may seem obvious, but experience has shown that it is a necessary step.

Biases in Estimating Probabilities

The expression of the decision maker's uncertainty in the form of probabilities is an important part of the decision analysis approach. Researchers have found that there may be important biases in elicited probabilities. To illustrate this point, please take a few minutes and answer the questions in Table 7–6. You are asked to estimate two

TABLE 7–6
Exercise in Estimating Probabilities

For each of the questions below, write down two estimates (a high and low end of an interval), such that, in your judgment, there is a 90 percent chance that the true value falls within the interval. For example, if the question asked for the population of California in 1993, you might estimate values of 25 million and 35 million, indicating that you believe there is a 90 percent chance that the true value is somewhere between 25 and 35 million—or alternatively, that there is only a 10 percent chance that it is outside that range.

Write down your estimates. When you have answered all questions, score yourself by looking up the answers in the footnote on the next page, and record the number of times your interval included the true value.

1. What is the length (in miles) of the Amazon River in South America?
2. What was the number of people who took the GMAT test worldwide in the 1995–1996 academic year? (The GMAT is the Graduate Management Admission Test, an admission requirement for most American MBA programs.)
3. What was the population of Singapore in 1994?
4. What is the airline distance (in miles) from San Francisco to Moscow?
5. What was the average daily circulation of the newspaper *USA Today* for the period January through March 1995?
6. What was the number of automobiles registered in the state of California in 1992?
7. What is the area of Alaska in square miles?
8. What was the number of MBA degrees awarded in the United States in 1994?
9. What was the total number of passengers passing through Chicago's O'Hare airport in 1994 (include both arriving and departing passengers.)
10. What is the average distance of the planet earth from the sun, in miles?

values on a probability distribution. For some of the questions, you may have a reasonable idea, but you may be quite uncertain about others. This should be reflected in the values you assess. **Please do not read on until you have completed the quiz.**

Have you finished? Good! Of the 10 questions, how many times were you surprised? That is, how many times did the true value fall outside the range you specified? If you are like most people, you got between 4 to 7 or 8 surprises. and yet, if you were properly calibrated, you should have only about one surprise. Remember that the intervals represented a 90 percent chance, hence only a 10 percent chance of being surprised (outside the interval). So you should expect only 10 percent times 10 questions or 1 question to be a surprise.

Researchers have done experiments like this many times, not just with students using almanac type questions but also with real businesspeople using questions about their industries and companies in which, presumably, they were experts.[7] Even professional statisticians exhibit the same tendency. It is called the **overconfidence bias.** We tend to think we know more than we do. We are too sure!

Researchers have identified some sources of overconfidence. One is called **availability.** We have experience with, perhaps, one or two ways in which events may happen (e.g., sales level of a new product), and we rely heavily on that. But there may be many things that can happen outside our direct experience. A related factor is our relying on easily available information. For example, most people substantially underestimate the number of deaths from lung cancer relative to that from murder, simply because the press gives the latter so much coverage (i.e., it is available information).

Another source of bias comes from **anchoring.** A procedure often followed in estimating is to first ask for a "best guess" value, and then to ask for ranges around this value. This tends to make the probability ranges much too narrow, perhaps exaggerating the effect you observed in the quiz.

Another factor is **selectivity.** We tend to filter information, accepting what confirms our ideas and estimates and ignoring what does not. This also leads to our being overconfident.

Does this mean that it is impossible to obtain reasonable probability estimates for use in decision analysis? No, indeed! But it is important to be aware of these biases. And we can take steps to overcome them. One important tactic that can be taken is **feedback.** If estimates are to be done repeatedly, providing feedback on how well previous estimates performed can lead to well-calibrated forecasters. The U.S. Weather Service forecasters do get feedback, for example, on their predictions for rain, and have become quite accurate. It rains 40 percent of the time when a 40 percent chance forecast is made. And Royal Dutch/Shell has a training program for its geologists to predict the presence of oil, using information from past sites.[8]

Answers to the quiz in Table 7–6. Count the number of times the actual value fell outside your interval. This is the number of "surprises" you experienced: 1) 4,007 miles; 2) 212,000; 3) 2.89 million people; 4) 5,871 miles; 5) 1.570 million; 6) 17.219 million; 7) 656,427 sq. miles; 8) 77,000; 9) 66.47 million passengers; and 10) 92.6 million miles. For the question used as the example, the population of California was 31.2 million (do not include this in your scoring).

[7]For a discussion of these results, see J. Russo and P. Schoemaker, "Managing Overconfidence," *Sloan Management Review,* Winter 1992. See Also A. Tversky and D. Kahneman, "Judgment under Uncertainty: Heuristics and Biases," *Science* 185 (1974), pp. 1124–31.

[8]These examples are described in Russo and Schoemaker, "Managing Overconfidence."

Another approach is to try to imagine scenarios or paths that result in different outcomes from the ones considered likely. As an example, suppose marketing managers were trying to estimate the first-year sales of a new product, and the 90 percent confidence interval was initially estimated as between 1 and 2 million cases. The managers imagine themselves a year into the future with the knowledge that sales actually were 4 million cases, and then try to think of scenarios that could lead to that outcome. Or, to combat the selectivity bias, the managers might deliberately review articles and sources with different views of the product or industry than normally read.

Limitations of Utility Theory

While utility analysis is a powerful framework for decisions involving risk, it does have some limitations. Our examples all have involved assessing utility functions for decisions that stand alone. However, in most business situations, and in many personal ones as well, the valuation of outcomes depends on other outside factors. For example, consider a firm making a major investment decision that has a potential loss of, say, \$20 million. Such a loss may be valued very differently if it were to occur in a year when other projects were successful, as opposed to one in which the firm was also suffering losses from the other projects. You may feel differently about a personal loss, depending on whether or not you get the pay raise you hope for. In other words, there is a *portfolio effect* that needs to be considered. In finance, the value of a stock depends not only on the variability of its return but also on how that is correlated with the returns of the portfolio of which it is a part. This complicates considerably the assessment of a utility function for a real decision problem. In finance, there is historical data that is used to estimate the correlation of returns of a stock with others. This is much more difficult to do for a decision, say, on building a new automated factory, or introducing a new product.

Another limitation of utility theory is that numerous experiments have shown that people sometimes violate the basic assumptions on which the approach is based. Consider, for example, the famous *Allais paradox.* Suppose you were faced with two decision situations as follows:

Situation 1: Choose either A or B:

A. You receive \$1 million for certain
B. You participate in a lottery that has a 10 percent chance of a \$5 million prize, and 89 percent chance for a \$1 million prize, and a 1 percent chance for nothing.

Situation 2: Choose either C or D:

C. You participate in a lottery that has an 11 percent chance of a \$1 million prize and an 89 percent chance for nothing.
D. You participate in a lottery that has a 10 percent chance of a \$5 million prize and a 90 percent chance for nothing.

Given such a choice, many people choose A over B in situation 1, and D over C in situation 2. If we put these in utility terms, preferring A over B implies:

$$u(1) > 0.10 \cdot u(5) + 0.89 \cdot u(1) + 0.01 \cdot u(0)$$

where $u(1)$ is the utility of \$1 million prize; $u(5)$ is the utility of the \$5 million prize, and $u(0)$ is the utility of obtaining nothing. Suppose we define the end points of the utility function at 0 and 1 and then set $u(0) = 0$ and $u(5) = 1$. With some algebraic manipulation, the above inequality becomes:

$$0.11u(1) > 0.10$$

Similarly, preferring D over C implies:

$$0.10 \cdot u(5) + 0.90 \cdot u(0) > 0.11 \cdot u(1) + 0.89 \cdot u(0)$$

Again, by substituting $u(5) = 1$ and $u(0) = 0$, we obtain:

$$0.10 > 0.11 \cdot u(1)$$

Note that these two choices give contradictory results. People who choose A over B in the first situation, and D over C in the second are acting inconsistently with the logical utility theory approach.

Researchers have performed many different experiments in which similar inconsistent behavior is observed.[9] They may relate to situations involving small differences in probabilities (such as 10 percent versus 11 percent, as above), with how the payoffs are viewed (a loss of \$600 versus a payment of an insurance premium of \$600), ambiguity in probabilities, looking at gains and losses rather than final asset position, and so on. The accumulated evidence is that utility theory has limitations as a *descriptive* theory of how people actually behave under uncertainty. On the other hand, it remains as a valuable *prescriptive* theory of how people should act to be consistent.

Because it is difficult to obtain accurate and consistent utility function values, utility is often incorporated in real applications in the following way: The problem is first analyzed in terms of EMV, including development of the risk profile. Very often, this provides an adequate basis for making the decision, and the utility function need not be assessed. However, if risk remains as an important part of the decision problem, then sensitivity analysis is done with different utility functions to determine how risk averse the decision maker would have to be before the selected decision changed. (See the appendix to this chapter for an example of this.) Recall that the purpose of decision analysis is to be an aid and provide insight to the decision maker, and this procedure has proven adequate.

Summary

In applying the decision analysis approach to solve real problems, certain cautions are in order. Care should be taken to avoid possible biases in estimating probabilities. While utility theory remains the most valuable prescriptive approach for the inclusion of risk in decision analysis, it has limitations as a descriptive model. In practice, utility considerations are often included as a final step by doing sensitivity analysis using utility functions with different levels of risk aversion.

[9]For a summary of this work, see Chapter 4 in P. R. Kleindorfer, H. C. Kunreuther, and P. J. H. Schoemaker, *Decision Sciences* (Cambridge: Cambridge University Press, 1993).

APPENDIX
THE EXPONENTIAL UTILITY FUNCTION

Figure 7–10 illustrated a type of utility function that is sometimes used in decision analysis–the exponential function. It has the form:

$$u(x) = a - be^{-x/R}$$

where $u(x)$ is the utility value for payoffs x, a and b are parameters that can be set to scale the function (to define the 0 and 1.0 points, for example), and R is the *risk aversion parameter.* This function has the property that it exhibits *constant risk aversion* over the whole range. That is, the risk premium does not change in different parts of the curve. As discussed earlier in the text, for individuals we might expect decreasing risk aversion (see Figure 7–11). However, the constant risk aversion assumption may be a reasonable approximation for many business decisions.

One advantage of using a mathematical form such as the exponential utility function is that it allows one to do sensitivity analysis with differing levels of risk aversion. In the case of the exponential utility function, this merely involves varying the risk aversion parameter, R. Let us use the example in Figures 7–9 and 7–10 to illustrate this. In that example, the values of the parameters were $a = 1.118$, $b = 0.5280$, and the risk premium parameter $R = 200$. Note that optimal strategy for a risk neutral or EMV decision maker would be the Go/Go strategy (Go regardless of quick or slow acceptance). As we saw in Figure 7–9, a risk premium parameter of $R = 200$ does change the decision to the Go/Stop strategy. We might ask how large the risk premium parameter would have to be to be just indifferent between the Go/Go strategy and the Go/Stop strategy. And we might go even further and ask how large the parameter would have to be for the decision maker to be indifferent between introducing and abandoning the product. By trying different values of R, these points can be found; they turn out to be $R = 234$ (indifference between Go/Go and Go/Stop) and $R = 105$ (indifference between Introduce and Abandon). The curves with these values are plotted in Figure 7–12.[10]

These curves can be used in the following fashion. Suppose a decision maker in this situation has difficulty estimating the appropriate utility function. Presented with the curves in Figure 7–12, the decision maker has only to decide in which range his or her risk aversion lies. This can be done by posing simple lotteries related to the curves. Consider, for example, a simple lottery involving a 50–50 chance of losing \$100,000 and winning \$200,000. Using the lower curve ($R = 234$) in Figure 7–12, the certainty equivalent of this lottery is about \$5,000. If decision makers value the lottery at more than \$5 thousand, they are less risk averse than the $R = 234$ curve, and hence should select the Go/Go strategy. The certainty equivalent for the same lottery using the $R = 105$ curve is about −\$34,000 (a payment of \$34,000 to avoid the lottery). If the decision maker values the lottery between \$5,000 and −\$34,000, the Go/Stop strategy is appropriate. A valuation of less than −\$34,000 implies that the Abandon strategy should be undertaken.

A word of caution! These sorts of analyses can be very valuable in practice, but they are not procedures to be followed mechanically. Rather, they are techniques that

[10]The parameter values for a and b are recalculated for these curves.

FIGURE 7–12
Utility Functions for Indifference Values of *R*

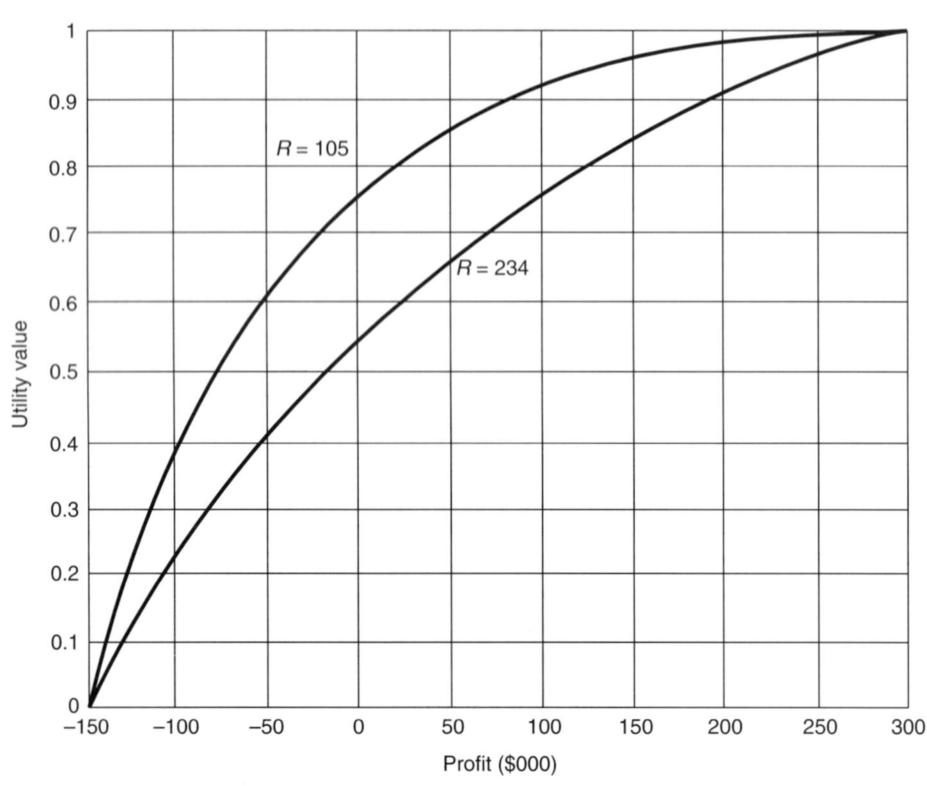

can aid judgment and provide insight to the decision maker. This sort of sensitivity analysis has been useful because of the difficulties mentioned in the chapter in actually assessing utility functions.

Bibliography

Bell, D. E.; H. Raiffa; and A. Tversky, eds. *Decision Making: Descriptive, Normative, and Prescriptive Interactions.* Cambridge: Cambridge University Press, 1988.

Bunn, D. W. *Applied Decision Analysis.* New York: McGraw-Hill, 1984.

Holloway, C. A. *Decision Making under Uncertainty.* New York: John Wiley & Sons, 1979.

Howard, R. H. "Decision Analysis: Practice and Promise." *Management Science* 34, no. 6 (June 1988).

Kahneman, D., and A. Tversky. "Judgment under Uncertainty: Heuristics and Biases," *Science* 185 (1974).

———. "The Psychology of Preferences," *Scientific American,* January 1982.

Kleindorfer, P.; H. Kunreuther; and P. Schoemaker. *Decision Sciences: An Integrated Perspective.* Cambridge: Cambridge University Press, 1993.

Russo, J., and P. Schoemaker. "Managing Overconfidence," *Sloan Management Review,* winter 1992.

———. *Decision Traps.* New York: Simon & Schuster, 1989.

Samson, D. *Managerial Decision Analysis.* Burr Ridge, IL: Richard D. Irwin, 1988.

Von Neumann, J., and O. Morgenstern. *Theory of Games and Economic Behavior.* Princeton NJ: Princeton University Press, 1944.

Practice Problems[11]

7–1. Consider the acts, the profits for which are shown in Table 7–7. Indicate which act or acts is best under the following criteria:

a. Which acts are involved in outcome dominance?

b. Which acts are involved in event dominance?

c. Which acts are involved in probabilistic dominance?

d. Which act are undominated by any form of dominance?

7–2. Refer to Figure 7–13. Assume that if no competitive product is introduced, you will set a high price. Given this assumption:

a. Make a list of all the complete strategies in the decision tree in Figure 7–13.

b. Calculate the profit lottery or risk profile for each strategy identified in (*a*).

c. Determine which, if any, strategies dominate others.

d. Plot the cumulative distributions for profit for all strategies.

7–3. Entrepreneur *W* has a utility index of 0 for a loss of \$1,000, and 1.0 for a profit of \$3,000. She says that she is indifferent between \$10 for certain and the following lottery: a 0.4 chance at a \$1,000 loss and a 0.6 chance at a \$3,000 profit. What is her utility index for \$10?

7–4. You have a date for the quantitative analysis ball; the admission is \$25, which you do not have. On the day of the dance, your psychology instructor offers you either \$20 for certain, or a 50–50 chance at nothing or \$30. Which choice would you make, assuming you had no other source of funds or credit? Why? If the utility of \$20 is 20, and the utility of zero dollars is 0, what does this imply about the utility of \$30?

7–5. A firm is facing a decision about a new product introduction and has diagrammed the problem as shown in Figure 7–13. Suppose that the utility for profit can be represented by the following function:

$$U(x) = 0.025\sqrt{500 + x}$$

where x is in thousands of dollars. Using this utility function for profit, roll back the tree of Figure 7–13 and indicate the strategy that maximizes expected utility. What is the certainty equivalent of this strategy?

7–6. The Iota Engineering Company does subcontracting on government contracts. Iota is a small company with limited capital. The utility function is approximated by the following function (where x is in thousands of dollars):

$$U(x) = 0.04364\sqrt{20 + x}$$

where $-20 \le x \le 500$ thousand \$.

a. Suppose Iota is considering bidding on a given contract. It will cost \$20,000 to prepare the bid. If the bid is lost, the \$20,000 cost is also lost. If Iota wins the bid, it will make \$400,000 and recover the \$20,000 bid preparation cost. Suppose Iota believes the probability of winning the contract is 0.2 if a bid is submitted. What should it do?

b. What would the probability of winning have to be before Iota would submit a bid?

c. Suppose there is another small engineering firm that proposes to partner with Iota in submitting a bid. The other firm would bear half the cost and receive half the profit if the bid was a winning bid. Assuming the probability of winning is still 0.2, should Iota take on this partner?

TABLE 7–7

		Act					
State of Nature	*Probability*	d_1	d_2	d_3	d_4	d_5	d_6
q_1	0.2	0	0	−4	5	−1	5
q_2	0.2	0	5	−4	0	2	5
q_3	0.4	0	2	3	3	5	0
q_4	0.2	0	−3	6	6	3	5

[11]Solutions are given at the end of this chapter.

FIGURE 7–13 Decision Tree (for Problems 7–2 and 7–5)

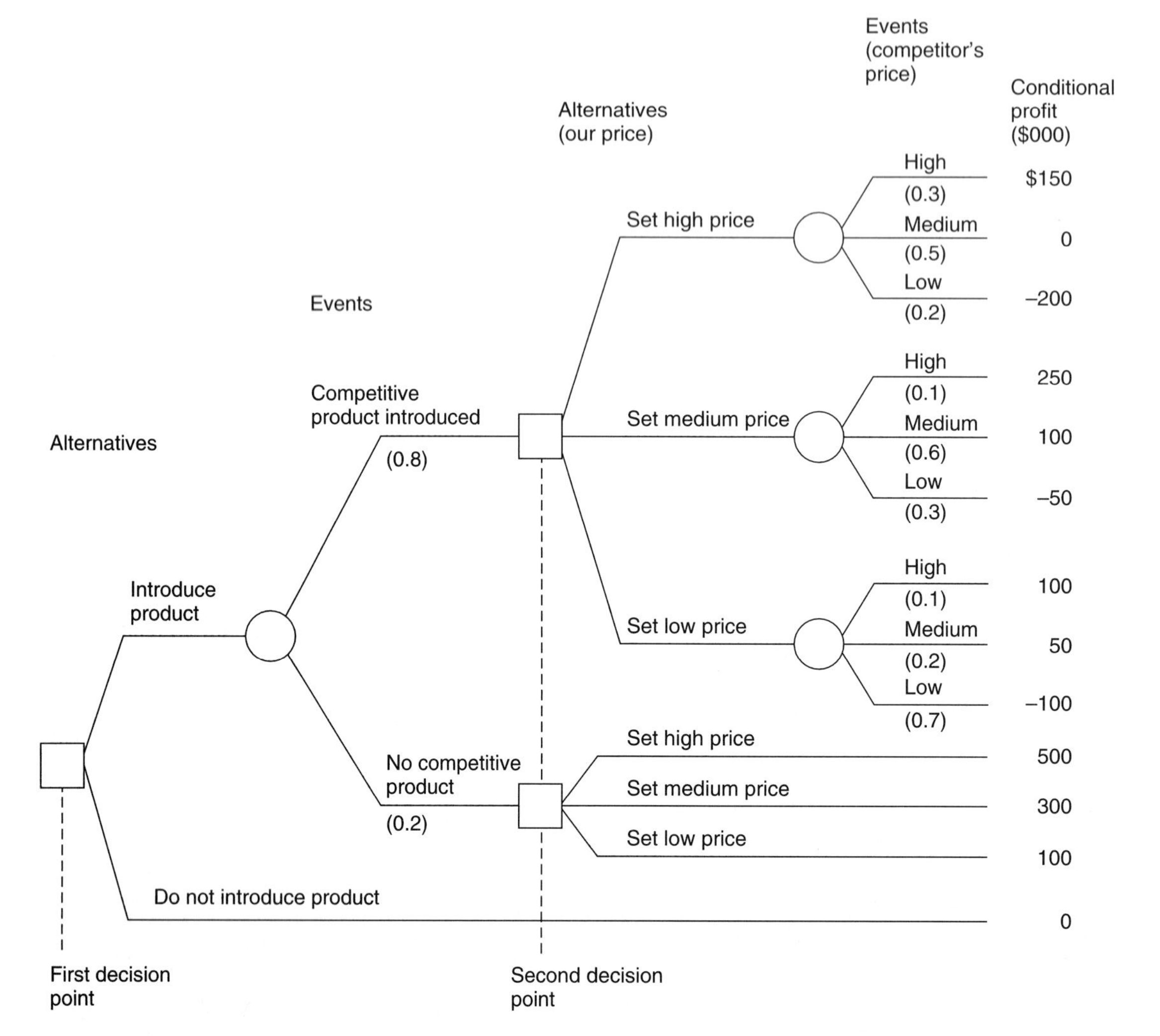

Problems

7–7. A decision maker has three possible investments with payoffs and probabilities as shown in the table on the next page.

a. Using the criterion of dominance, compare the alternatives. Can you find a preferred alternative? What form of dominance did you use to select your choice?

b. Using the expected value criterion, what choice would you make?

FIGURE 7–14 Decision Tree (for Problem 7–8)

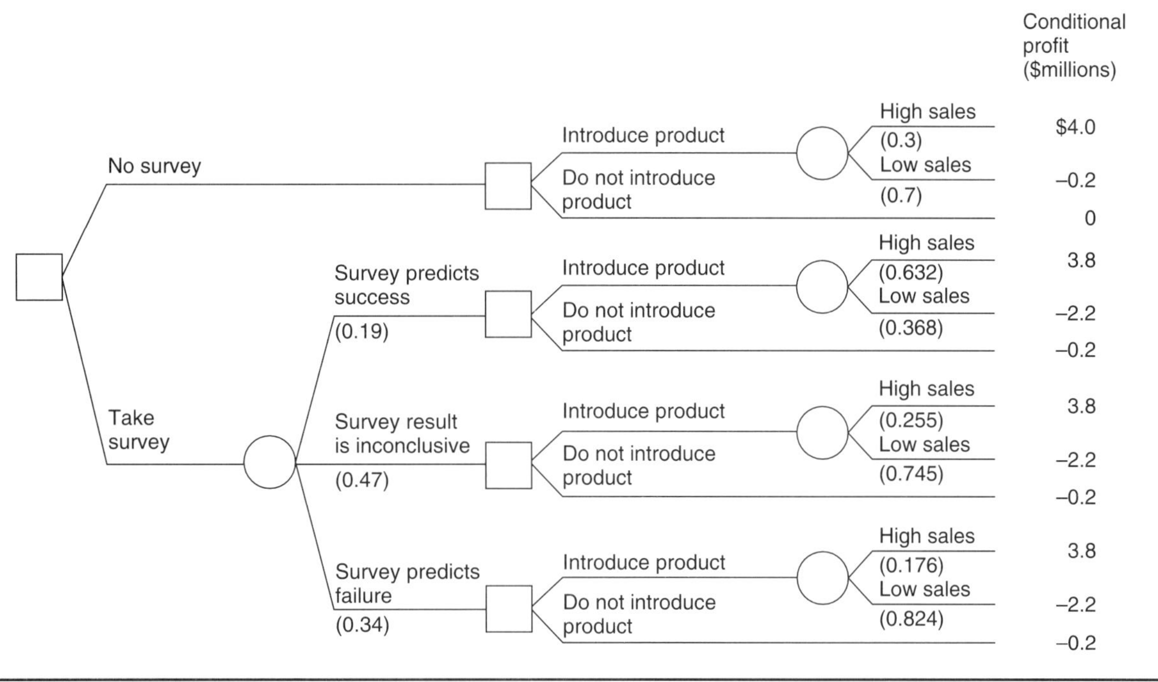

Probabilities for Investment Payoffs

Payoff ($000)	*Investment A*	*Investment B*	*Investment C*
−50	0.4	0.2	0.2
0	0.0	0.0	0.1
50	0.4	0.2	0.1
100	0.2	0.4	0.6
150	0.0	0.2	0.0

7–8. A firm is considering introduction of a new product. One alternative is to take a market survey before deciding. The problem has been diagrammed as shown in Figure 7–14.

a. List the strategies available in this decision tree. Include all the strategies, even ones that you might consider silly.

b. Find at least two strategies that are dominated by other strategies. Show the profit lotteries (risk profiles) for these dominated strategies and for the strategies that dominate them.

c. Some of the strategies in (*a*) may have seemed silly or unreasonable. What can you now say about why they seemed unreasonable?

7–9. Suppose a decision maker, when asked to find the certainty equivalents for the gambles shown in the first column below, responded with the answers in the second column.

Gamble	*Assessed Certainty Equivalent*
1. ½ chance at −$100,000 and ½ chance at $200,000	$ 10,000
2. ½ chance at $10,000 and ½ chance at $200,000	100,000
3. ½ chance at $10,000 and ½ chance at −$100,000	−55,000

a. Using graph paper, plot the utility points associated with the above gambles, and draw a smooth utility curve through the points.

b. Using this curve, find the certainty equivalent for the following gamble:

	Probability
−$ 80,000	0.2
0	0.4
80,000	0.2
160,000	0.2

7–10. The treasurer of a corporation is considering a decision to increase the deductible amount on the corporation's fire insurance from $20,000 per occurrence to $50,000 (meaning that the first $50,000 of fire loss would not be reimbursed under the policy). Such an increase in the deductible would lower the annual insurance premium from $25,000 to $14,000. Based on historical data, the treasurer estimates the probability of fire as follows:

Number of Fires in a Year	*Probability*
0	0.80
1	0.15
2	0.05
3 or more	0

If a fire occurs, the loss is certain to be above $50,000 because of the nature of the product produced.

When asked about risk aversion preferences, the following utility function was obtained:

Dollars	*Utility*
−$100,000	0.000
−40,000	0.300
0	0.490
10,000	0.537
30,000	0.620

Should the treasurer increase the deductible? Why or why not?

7–11. A company owns a lease granting it the right to explore for oil on certain property. It may sell the lease for $15,000, or it may drill for oil. The four possible drilling outcomes are listed below, together with probabilities of occurrence and dollar consequences:

Possible Outcome	*Probability*	*Consequences*
Dry well	0.16	−$100,000
Gas well only	0.40	50,000
Oil and gas combination	0.24	100,000
Oil well	0.20	200,000

Suppose that the utility function for money for the drilling problem is the same as that assessed in Problem 7–9.

a. Should the company drill or sell the lease?

b. Suppose, before the company began drilling, another firm offered to buy the lease. What is the minimum price the company should accept?

c. Suppose, before drilling began, an outside syndicate of investors offered the following proposition: The syndicate would pay the company $20,000 for a 50 percent share in the costs and revenues associated with drilling. (That is, revenues to the company would be $20,000 plus one-half of the values listed above.) Should the company accept the offer?

More Challenging Problems

7–12. The QPC Company is deciding whether to market product A or product B. The decision depends on the speed with which the distributors accept the product and the type of marketing strategy (promotion or advertising) employed by QPC. The company has diagrammed its decision problem as shown in Figure 7–15. The cash flows associated with the various decisions and events are shown at the end of the tree branches. Suppose QPC determines the following points on its utility function:

$ Millions	*Utility*
−4.00	0.0
−3.50	0.2
−2.00	0.4
0.75	0.6
5.00	0.8
10.00	1.0

FIGURE 7–15 QPC Decision Tree (for Problem 7–12)

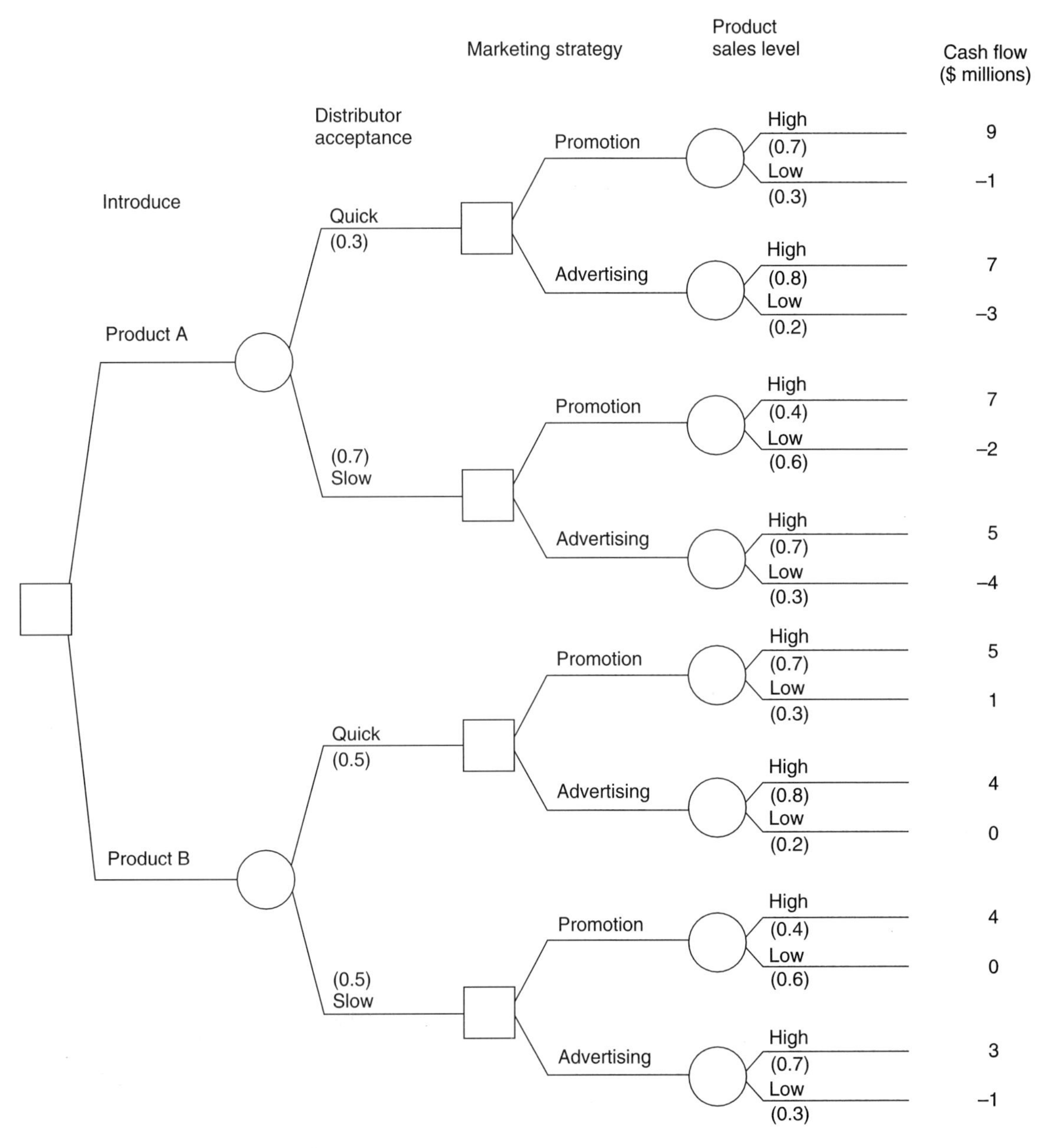

Graph these points and draw a smooth curve through them. Then use this curve to determine what decision QPC should make in the decision tree given in Figure 7–15.

7–13. Refer to Problem 7–12. Suppose QPC has another venture that involves a 0.50 chance for a gain of $10 million and a 0.5 chance for a $4 million loss. Use the utility curve through the points given in Problem 7–12.

Several investors offer to join with QPC in this venture. In particular, Investor *A* offers to share 50 percent of both the gains and losses with QPC. Investor *B* offers to accept a 40 percent share of the losses in return for a 30 percent share of the gains. Investor *C* offers to pay QPC $2 million in return for a 50 percent share of the gains, but no share of the losses. Which, if any, of these offers should QPC accept?

7–14. Little Electronics Company has initiated an antitrust and unfair trade practices lawsuit against Artex Computers, asking a settlement of $10 million in damages. On November 4, Little receives an offer from Artex to settle the suit for a payment to Little of $3.5 million.

The management at Little is trying to decide whether to accept the settlement or to proceed with the suit. The lawyers agree that the chances are about two in three that Little will win. They point out, however, that even if Little wins the suit, the chances are only about one in two that the judge will award the full $10 million; the judge is equally likely to grant a partial settlement of $5 million. The lawyers further estimate it will cost about $200,000 in legal fees between November and June (when the case is scheduled to be heard), plus another $10,000 in legal fees to try the case (which is expected to last three months).

In making the offer for the $3.5 million settlement, Artex stressed that it was a "final offer," and that the offer would be good for only 30 days. However, Little management and lawyers agree that Artex will probably make a new offer in June, just before the trial begins. After some thought, it is decided that 0.60 is a good estimate of the probability of a new Artex offer in June. And if there is a new offer, the chances are 7 in 10 that it will be $4.5 million and 3 in 10 for a $5.5 million settlement.

If Artex makes no last minute offer in June, Little itself can initiate a settlement. In this case, Little will have to settle for $2.5 million, because Artex will interpret the action as weakness in Little's case.

Suppose that Little Electronics, after careful consideration, has assessed its utility function for the cash flows resulting from the lawsuit. The utility function $U(X)$ can be described by the following function:

$$U(X) = 1 - \frac{1}{X + 2}$$

where X is the cash flow ($ millions) resulting from the lawsuit.

Develop the decision tree for Little's decision problem. Substitute the utility values in place of the cash flows at the ends of the tree. Analyze the tree using the utility values to determine what decision Little should make.

Solutions to Practice Problems

7–1. *a.* Both d_4 and d_6 dominate d_1 by outcome dominance.

b. Act d_4 dominates d_3 by event dominance. Also, of course, d_4 and d_6 dominate d_1 by event dominance, since they dominate by outcome dominance.

c. To investigate probabilistic dominance, the information must be rearranged as in Table 7–8. We need not consider acts d_1 and d_3, since we found that they were dominated by outcome or event dominance. Acts d_4, d_5, and d_6 all dominate d_2 by probabilistic dominance. Also, act d_4 dominates d_5.

d. This leaves acts d_4 and d_6 as undominated. The dominance criterion does not give us a choice between them.

7–2. *a.* There are four strategies (see Table 7–9):

(1) Do not introduce the product.

(2) Introduce the product; if a competitive product is introduced, set a high price (if no competitive product, set a high price).

(3) Introduce the product; if a competitive product is introduced, set a medium price (if no competitive product, set a high price).

(4) Introduce the product; if a competitive product is introduced, set a low price (if no competitive product, set a high price.)

b. Strategy 1 has a 1.0 probability for zero profit. For the remaining strategies:

c. Strategy 3 (set medium price) dominates strategy 4 (set low price). Every value for the cumulative probability $P(X$ or more) in Table 7–9 is at least as large or larger for strategy 3. This can also be seen in the plots shown in Figure 7–16. There is no other dominance.

d. See Figure 7–16.

7–3. $0.4(1) + 0.6(1.0) = 0.6$

7–4. Most would take the gamble, despite the fact that the EMV is higher for the sure $20. Taking the lottery

TABLE 7–8 (for Problem 7–1)

	Acts							
	d_2		d_4		d_5		d_6	
Profit X	*P(X)*	*P(X or more)*	*P(X)*	*P(X or more)*	*P(X)*	*P(X or more)*	*P(X)*	*P(X or more)*
−4	0	1.0	0	1.0	0	1.0	0	1.0
−3	.2	1.0	0	1.0	0	1.0	0	1.0
−1	0	.8	0	1.0	.2	1.0	0	1.0
0	.2	.8	.2	1.0	0	.8	.4	1.0
2	.4	.6	0	.8	.2	.8	0	.6
3	0	.2	.4	.8	.2	.6	0	.6
5	.2	.2	.2	.4	.4	.4	.6	.6
6	0	0	.2	.2	0	0	0	0

TABLE 7–9 (for Problem 7–2)

Profit ($000s) X	Strategy 2		Strategy 3		Strategy 4	
	P(X)	*P(X or more)*	*P(X)*	*P(X or more)*	*P(X)*	*P(X or more)*
−200	.16	1.00	0	1.00	0	1.00
−100	0	.84	0	1.00	.56	1.00
−50	0	.84	.24	1.00	0	.44
0	.40	.84	0	.76	0	.44
50	0	.44	0	.76	.16	.44
100	0	.44	.48	76	.08	.28
150	.24	.44	0	.28	0	.20
250	0	.20	.08	.28	0	.20
500	.20	.20	.20	.20	.20	.20

implies that 0.5 $U(\$0) + 0.5U(\$30) > U(\$20)$ or $0.5(0) + 0.5U(\$30) > 20$. This implies that the $U(\$30)$ must be > 40.

7–5. The tree with utility values is shown in Figure 7–17. The optimum strategy is to introduce the product and set a medium price if a competitive product is introduced and a high price otherwise. This is strategy 3 in problem 7–2 above. The expected utility of this strategy is 0.634, and the certainty equivalent of this is $143 thousand.

7–6. *a.* Alternative 1: Do not bid.

$$U(0) = 0.2182$$

Alternative 2: Bid.

$$\text{Expected utility} = 0.2\,U(400) + 0.8\,U(-20)$$
$$= 0.2(0.8897) + .8(0)$$
$$= 0.1799$$

$U(\text{Bid}) < U(\text{not Bid})$. Therefore, do not bid.

b. Let p be the probability of winning.

$$p(0.8897) + (1 - p)(0) = 0.2182$$

Solving for p, gives $p = 0.2425$

c. The payoffs are now −10 and 200 and the expected utility is

$$\text{Expected utility} = 0.2\,U(200) + 0.8U(-10)$$
$$= 0.2(0.6597) + .8(0.1912)$$
$$= 0.2839$$

Since this is greater than the utility of not bidding, Iota should partner with the other engineering firm. This is an example of risk sharing.

FIGURE 7–16 (for Problem 7–2*d*)

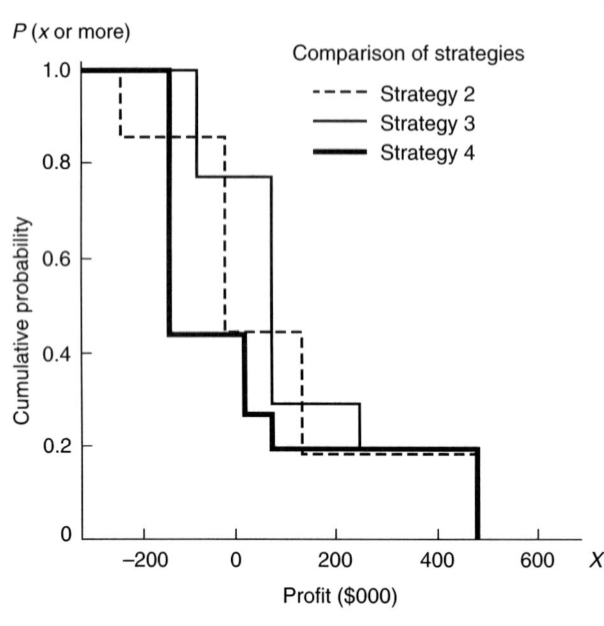

FIGURE 7–17 Tree with Utility Values (for Problem 7–5)

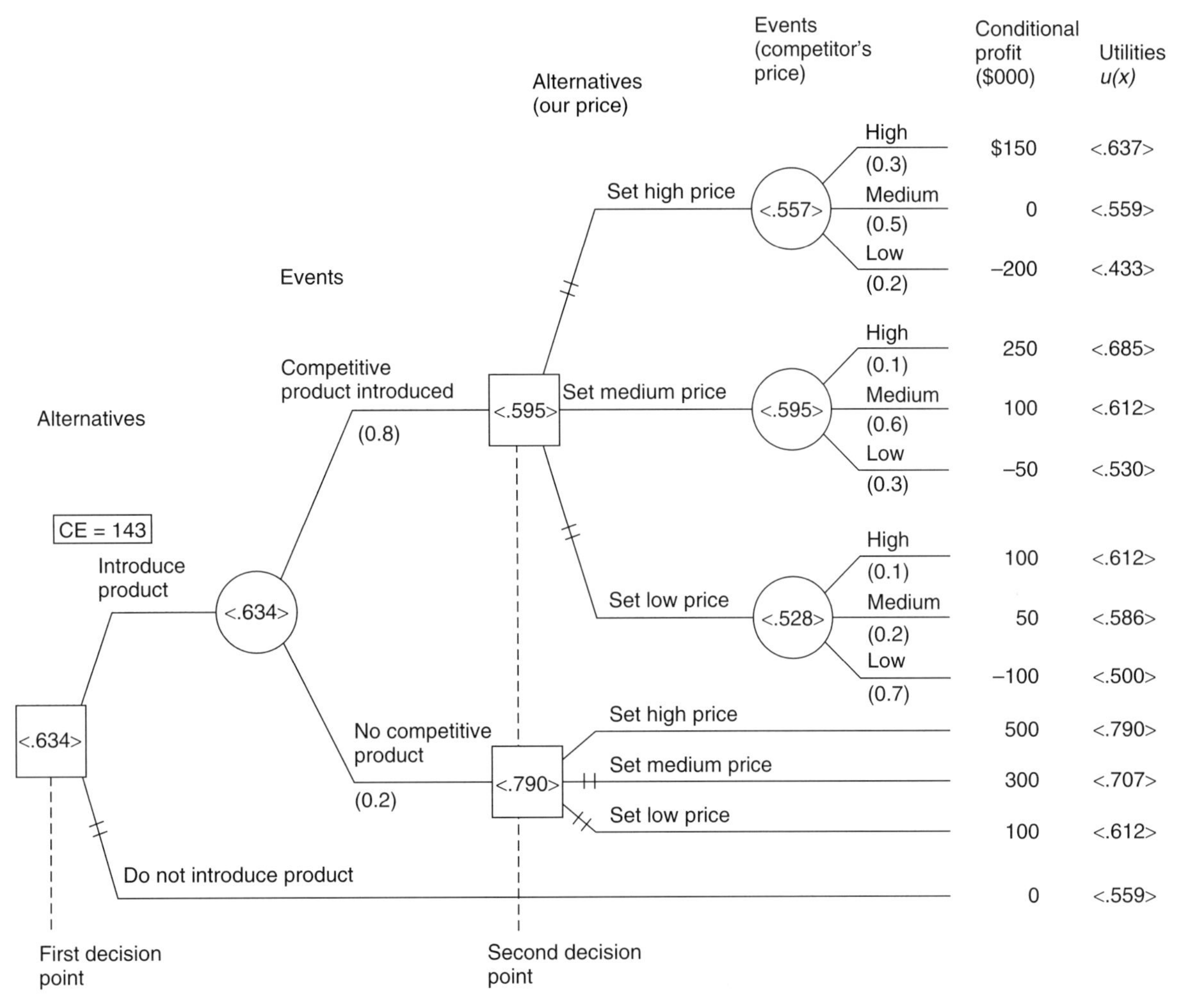

PART

III Application Areas

Motivating Example

Supply Chain Management at Hewlett-Packard[1]

Hewlett-Packard Corporation has made extensive use of the models presented in this chapter. They are used to evaluate and implement innovative product designs that enable customer demand worldwide to be fulfilled more effectively while at the same time enabling HP to hold less inventory. This "win–win" result can be achieved when inventory models are combined with a total, integrated view of the entire product supply chain, including all functional areas of the firm.

The problem faced by HP's Vancouver Division was a common problem: excessive inventory coupled with stockouts. This problem accompanies the so-called "curse of variety," where there is a proliferation of model types in a product family and difficulty in forecasting demand on an individual model basis. The problem was exacerbated in HP's case since it was manufacturing Deskjet Printers in the United States and shipping them to Europe. The different languages, power supplies, and electrical plug configurations required over two dozen models of each printer. Invariably, when the demand for printers from France was below forecast, for example, the demand for Spanish printers was above forecast; the former created excess inventory while the latter created stockouts.

HP's answer to this continuing and widespread dilemma was to use inventory modeling and analysis to assess the costs and benefits of redesigning its printers so that the steps needed to "localize" the printer could actually be postponed and performed in Europe at its distribution center. This meant it could produce and ship "plain Vanilla" printers to Europe and then adjust the localization operations rapidly to deal with shifting demand patterns.

One of the most difficult challenges in this entire project was trying to convince the HP product design engineers of the need to redesign a product that had proved very popular in the marketplace. Among other things, the redesign involved removing the power supply from the printer itself and placing it in a separate power cord. The distribution center in Europe also needed to be convinced that it should perform some light assembly operations that were foreign to its past responsibilities and capabilities. Having a quantitative model of the costs and benefits of this design change enabled HP managers from many different functional areas of responsibility to avoid emotional reactions to the suggestion and evaluate it on its quantitative merits.

HP estimates that millions of dollars have been saved annually by this improvement, and its Vancouver Division is now the company's showcase for "Design for Localization."

[1]See H. L. Lee, C. Billington, and C. Carter, "Hewlett-Packard Gains Control of Inventory and Service through Design for Localization," *Interfaces,* July–August 1993, pp. 1–11.

CHAPTER

8 Inventory Control and Management

Inventory control represents an important management function that has been very successfully treated by quantitative methods. The concepts in this chapter have been applied in numerous organizations, large and small, with favorable results. Nevertheless, there are additional business situations (even in well-managed companies) where the insights gained from inventory control models can be extremely useful in seeking improved operating decisions.

Before we introduce specific models to solve some common inventory problems, we will present a multi-item inventory classification technique called *ABC analysis* that is helpful in focusing management attention on the most important items in any multi-item inventory system.

Section I

ABC Analysis

Any significant inventory is always composed of more than one type of item. Each individual item requires control and management, but it is useful at the outset to recognize that not all items are equally important to the organization. **ABC analysis** is a way of classifying items based on some measure of importance. Frequently, a readily available measure of importance is annual dollar sales for each item.

Figure 8–1 illustrates a typical ABC curve obtained by ranking each of a group of items by their dollar sales (in descending order) and then plotting the cumulative dollar sales versus the number of different items in the inventory. The well-known "20–80 rule" is demonstrated in this figure; 20 percent of the items are responsible for approximately 80 percent of the total dollar sales of the company.

The shape of any ABC curve will be similar to that shown in Figure 8–1; this is because the items are *ranked* on the importance measure (annual dollar sales) before cumulating. It is impossible to avoid the type of curvature illustrated unless every item in a multi-item inventory system has exactly the same dollar-sales rate; this is highly unlikely.

FIGURE 8–1
ABC Analysis Example

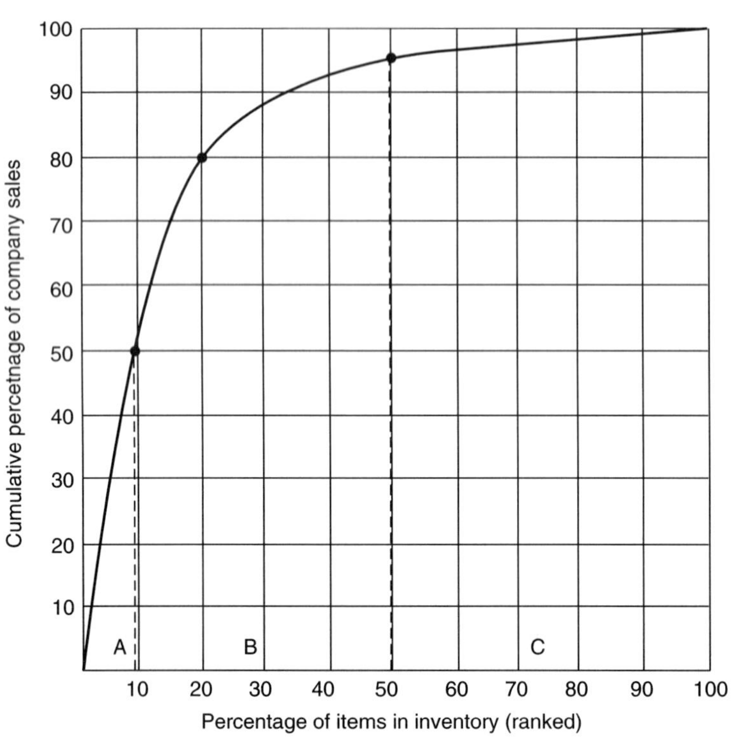

The ABC curve is used by managers to determine where detailed analysis will pay off, and conversely, where improved accuracy at a large cost may be unwarranted. The usual procedure is to divide the curve into three regions or groups, as follows:

- A items—the top 50 percent of dollar sales.
- C items—the bottom 50 percent of items.
- B items—the items in between.

Figure 8–1 illustrates these three regions for the example. It should be emphasized that these particular breakdowns are not rigid; some companies divide their inventory into four groups (ABCD), and others use slightly different cutoffs for the various regions. The key point is that whatever the definitions, the typical A item is quite a bit more important than the typical B item, which in turn is much more important than the typical C item.

For management purposes, the A items should receive the maximum analysis, monitoring, and review, since they rank highest on the importance measure. The B items should receive reasonable attention, but less than the A items. The C items represent many different items, but each individual C item has such low sales that C items can be managed more casually, with a tendency toward "high" inventory levels, since not much money is involved. If improved inventory control is being implemented in a company, the initial focus should be on the A items, since this is where the maximum leverage can be obtained.

FIGURE 8–2
ABC Analysis of Random Sample of 200 Items

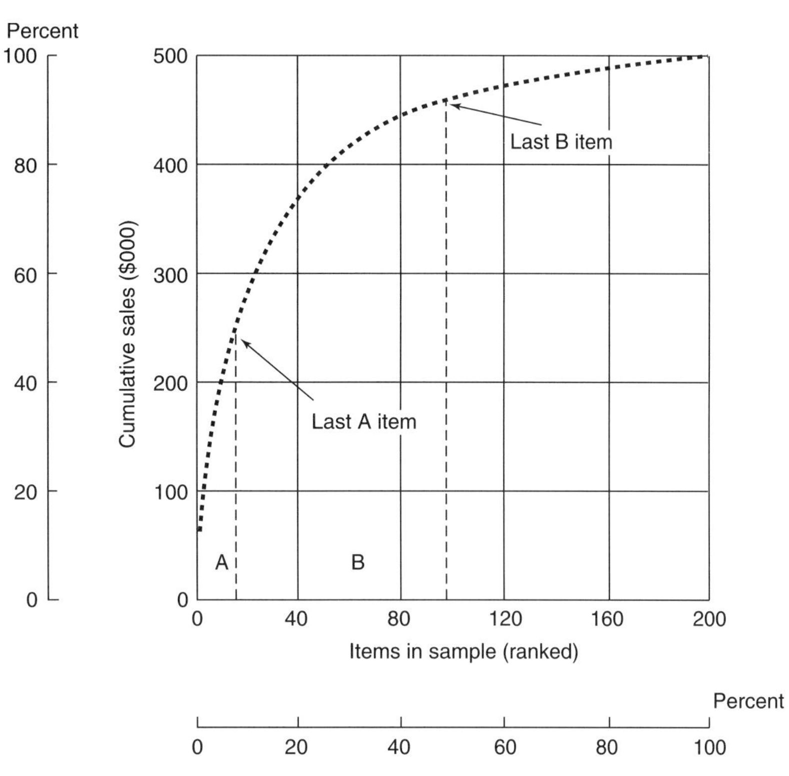

Performing an ABC Analysis

The precise way to do an ABC analysis is to select a measure of importance and then rank all items in inventory on that measure, producing a curve similar to Figure 8–1. Alternatively, one can do an ABC analysis on a *sample* of items. Although the sample curve will not be 100 percent accurate, it is likely to be accurate enough for decision purposes. For example, a random sample of 200 items from a 20,000-item inventory could be selected and plotted cumulatively, as shown in Figure 8–2. Note that the vertical scale in Figure 8–2 is cumulative dollar sales; after all points have been plotted, we can add another scale (on the left) indicating percentages. In Figure 8–2, total dollar sales of all 200 items is $500,000; this quantity represents 100 percent of sales in the sample, thereby determining all other percentages (see added vertical scale in Figure 8–2).

It is critical that the sample for the analysis be drawn *randomly,* so that there is a good likelihood that the outcome is representative. One way to do this would be to take every 100th item, for example, in a 20,000-item inventory listed by product number. This would produce a representative sample if there were nothing unusual about the 100th item, the 200th, and so on, in the listing by item number.

Once the sample is plotted, as in Figure 8–2, the ABC classifications can be made and the cutoff points determined as shown. If the ABC classifications described earlier are used, then the last A item is the one that brings cumulative dollar sales to the 50 percent mark. Suppose the actual dollar sales for that item were $8,561; then we might classify as an A item any item whose annual dollar sales exceed $8,500. Similarly, the last B item is the item at the 50 percent point on the horizontal scale; suppose its dollar sales were $983. Then we could classify as a B any item with dollar sales below $8,500 but above $1,000. The C items would be items with sales below $1,000. In this manner, the information gained from our sample of 200 items can be applied to all 20,000 items in inventory, and the "error" caused by our sample not being perfect is likely to be very small.

Cautions Regarding ABC Analysis

There are two potential pitfalls in using ABC analysis. The first relates to the performance measure. Although dollar sales are frequently used as a performance measure, this is often due to the fact that this data is readily available. One should guard against selecting the wrong performance measure simply because it is easily available. Depending on the decision to be made, the performance measure should be selected as the scale that is the best available measure of importance for the decision. For instance, if one is concerned about decisions regarding inventory investment, the dollar-sales measure is likely to be appropriate; but if the decision will affect the company's ability to meet customer orders without delay, then some measure of profitability (rather than simply sales) may be more desirable.

The second problem is that often a company has items that ordinarily would be classified as C items on a dollar-sales or profitability measure but are highly important to the company's customers. An example is sales of spare parts for complex machinery. The dollar value of the sales of parts may be low compared with the sales of new machinery, but the spare parts are critical to the operation of the machinery already sold, and poor performance on customer orders for spare parts could have an extremely bad effect on future machinery sales. Thus, one should carefully consider other attributes of C items that might make them subject to more careful management, such as that given to B and A items.

Summary

ABC analysis classifies items based on a measure of importance. Management can then focus maximum attention on the A items and spend less effort on the B and C items. Taking a random sample of 100 or 200 items is often the simplest way to perform an ABC analysis.

SECTION II

The Economic Order Quantity with Known Demand

In an ongoing inventory control system, there are two operating decisions to be made:

1. *When to place an order.* We must find the optimum *order point,* so that when the inventory level falls to the order point,[2] we place a replenishment order. We shall

[2]If there is any inventory on order, then the total of inventory on hand plus that on order is compared with the order point.

FIGURE 8–3
Reordering and Known Demand

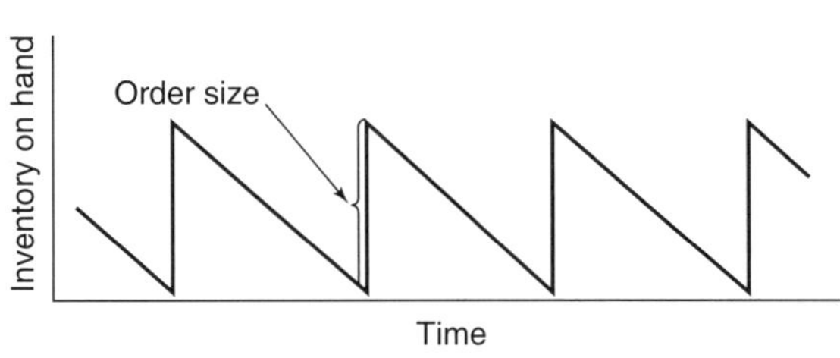

assume the order point is determined by the units on hand rather than a passage of calendar time (for example, placing an order every month).

2. *The size of the order.* We must find the optimum *order quantity.* In this section, we will assume that future demand for an item is known and constant; in succeeding sections, we will allow demand to be uncertain.

There are two general types of costs to be considered when demand is known and constant: (1) the cost of placing an order, and (2) the cost of carrying inventory in stock. The optimum order size and optimum order point will, in general, be a function of these two costs plus the intensity or rate of use (quantity used during a unit time period).

We assume that both the replenishment lead time and the demand rate are known and constant. With this assumption, the computation of the other point is not complicated. If the usage rate is 3 units per day and the lead time for replenishment is 40 days, we set an order point of 40 times 3, or 120 units. This allows us no room for error, but it is consistent with the assumptions of known demand and known lead time. Figure 8–3 illustrates the inventory behavior of the system under our assumption of known and constant demand rate and lead time.

The optimum order size is determined by analyzing total costs. The total cost (TC) for a period will be equal to the sum of the ordering costs (or setup costs) plus the costs of carrying the inventory during the period.[3] Assume that the units will be received all at once.

Let:

K = Incremental cost of placing an order (or setting up production)
k_c = Annual cost of carrying one unit of inventory
D = Annual total usage (demand) in units
Q = Optimum order size in units (the unknown)

Note that the annual number of orders placed depends on D and Q:

$$\frac{D}{Q} = \text{Annual number of orders}$$

Also:

$$\frac{Q}{2} = \text{Average inventory (assuming linear usage)}$$

[3]We need not consider shortage costs, since our assumptions of known demand and known lead time imply that shortages will not occur. The assumption of known demand will be relaxed in the next section.

Then:

$\frac{Q}{2}k_c =$ Annual cost of carrying inventory (average inventory $Q/2$, times k_c, the annual holding cost per unit)

$\frac{D}{Q}K =$ Annual cost of placing orders (annual number of orders, D/Q, times the cost of placing an order, K)

The total annual cost is:

$$TC = \frac{Q}{2}k_c + \frac{D}{Q}K \qquad (8\text{–}1)$$

These costs are plotted as a function of order size in Figure 8–4. The minimum total cost of Figure 8–4 occurs when the slopes of the two cost components (ordering and carrying cost) are equal and opposite in sign. In this particular case, this occurs where the two cost components are equal (where the curves cross). We may use this fact to obtain a formula for the optimal order quantity Q by setting the two costs equal and solving for Q.[4] At the optimum:

$$\frac{Q}{2}k_c = \frac{D}{Q}K$$

or:

$$Q^2 = \frac{2KD}{k_c}$$

so that:

$$Q = \sqrt{\frac{2KD}{k_c}} \qquad (8\text{–}2)$$

Equation 8–2 is often called the **economic order quantity** or **EOQ formula.**

Example 1
An example follows:

$D = 3{,}000$ units (expected annual demand)
$k_c = \$3$ per unit per year
$K = \$5$ per order

$$Q = \sqrt{\frac{2KD}{k_c}} = \sqrt{\frac{2 \cdot 5 \cdot 3{,}000}{3}} = \sqrt{10{,}000} = 100 \text{ units}$$

---

[4]This formula may also be obtained by using calculus to minimize total cost with respect to Q. Take the first derivative of Equation 8–1 with respect to Q, set it equal to 0, and solve for Q:

$$TC = \frac{Q}{2}k_c + \frac{DK}{Q}$$

$$\frac{dTC}{dQ} = \frac{1}{2}k_c - \frac{DK}{Q^2} = 0$$

Solving,

$$Q = \sqrt{\frac{2KD}{k_c}}$$

Since $\frac{d^2TC}{dQ^2} = \frac{2DK}{Q^3} > 0$, this solution does produce a minimum TC.

FIGURE 8–4
Inventory Costs

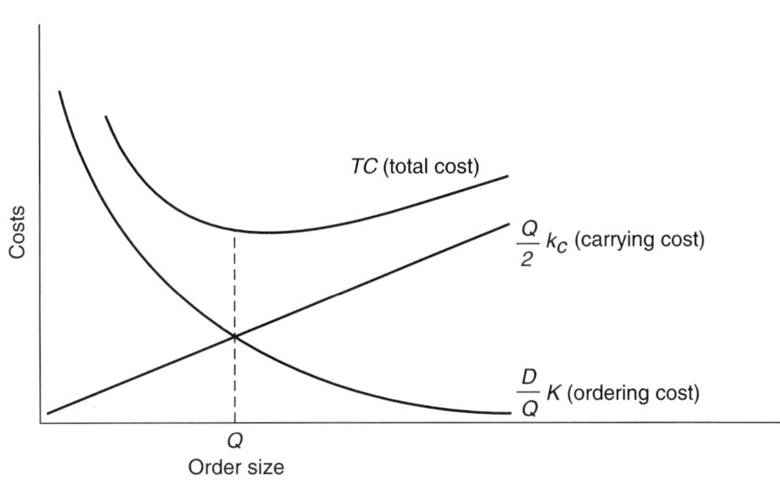

The optimum order size is 100 units. The total cost of using the optimal order size can be computed by substituting $Q = 100$ into the total cost Equation 8–1:

$$TC(Q = 100) = \frac{100}{2}(3) + \frac{3{,}000}{100}(5) = 150 + 150 = \$300$$

If D is measured in dollars instead of units, and if k_c is measured per dollar instead of per unit, then Q will also be in dollars. To illustrate this using the example above, let the price be \$15 per unit. The annual demand in dollars is $\$15 \cdot (3{,}000) = \$45{,}000$. Measuring k_c in dollars per dollar rather than dollars per unit, k_c is now $\$3/\$15 = \$0.20$ per dollar per year. The formula is now:

$$Q\text{ (in \$)} = \sqrt{\frac{2 \cdot \$5 \cdot \$45{,}000}{\$0.20/\$}} = \$\sqrt{2{,}250{,}000} = \$1{,}500$$

The optimal order quantity in dollars is \$1,500, corresponding to the optimal order quantity calculated above as 100 units (each unit is worth \$15).

Even when the demand is not known with certainty, the above model is very helpful in approximating a solution for the problem of optimum order size.

Sensitivity of Costs to Errors in Q

It is possible to use the cost model of Equation 8–1 to demonstrate that total costs in this model are not very sensitive to errors in determining Q. For example, suppose in the example just considered that the expected annual demand was incorrectly stated as 4,500 units instead of 3,000 units (a 50 percent overstatement). Then, using the optimal formula for Q, we would obtain the following (incorrect) order quantity:

$$Q = \sqrt{\frac{2 \cdot 5 \cdot 4{,}500}{3}} = \sqrt{15{,}000} = 123 \text{ units}$$

Note that because of the square root in the formula, a 50 percent error in estimating demand produces only a 23 percent error in the order size as compared with the optimal $Q = 100$. However, the true test of an error is how much it costs. Substituting $Q = 123$ into the total cost Equation 8–1 produces:

$$TC(Q = 123) = \frac{123}{2}(3) + \frac{3{,}000}{123}(5)$$

$$= 184.5 + 122 = 306.5$$

Comparing this total cost with the total cost of the optimal order size derived above ($TC = 300$), we see that the percentage increase in cost, or penalty for our error, is only $6.5/300 = 2.2$ percent. The same reasoning applies to a 50 percent error in either the order-processing cost or the inventory holding cost. Thus, as long as the costs and demand rate are reasonably estimated, it is likely that very little will be gained by making the estimates more precise.

Quantity Discounts

The preceding analysis ignored the possibility of quantity discounts (a lower price per unit if a larger quantity is purchased at one time). There are three basic elements to consider in evaluating whether or not to pursue a quantity discount.

1. The benefit of the discount in reduced purchase costs.
2. The cost of the discount in increased carrying costs.
3. The benefit of reduced numbers of orders per year.

It is always possible to evaluate quantity discounts by considering all possible alternatives, using the square root order quantity formula (8–2) and the equation for total cost (8–1) together with the stated discount. Incremental analysis can also be used to decide whether to take a discount or not. Consider the first example of this section. Suppose we were told by our supplier that a price discount of $1 per unit would be given if we purchased in quantities of 1,000 units or more. We would evaluate the *incremental* results of the three elements as follows:

1. Incremental benefit of discount:

$$(\$1 \text{ per unit}) \cdot (\text{Annual demand of 3,000 units}) = \$3{,}000 \text{ per year}$$

2. Incremental cost of higher inventory (assuming $Q = 1{,}000$ units)—Let:

$$k_c' = \text{Holding cost of items purchased with discount}$$

Then, since the original price was $15 and the discount is $1, if the carrying cost is a function solely of the price, then $k_c' = (14/15)k_c = (14/15)\$3 = \$2.80$. The incremental cost of holding inventory is:

$$k_c' \text{ (new average inventory)} - k_c \text{ (old average inventory)}$$

$$= \$2.80\left(\frac{1{,}000}{2}\right) - \$3\left(\frac{100}{2}\right) = \$1{,}400 - \$150 = \$1{,}250$$

3. Incremental benefit of reduced ordering costs:

$$K \cdot (\textit{Decrease} \text{ in annual orders}) = K\left(\frac{3{,}000}{100} - \frac{3{,}000}{1{,}000}\right)$$

$$= \$5(30 - 3) = \$5(27) = \$135$$

The net incremental benefit is \$3,000 − \$1,250 + \$135 = \$1,885. Since this value is positive, the discount should be taken.

Example 2

Annual demand for an item is 1,000 units. The item costs \$10 per unit, and the annual inventory holding charge is 25 percent of the cost of the item. The order-processing cost is \$50. If 500 or more units are ordered at once, a discount of \$0.40 per unit will be given. What should the order quantity be?

We first compute the usual economic order quantity using Equation 8–2, noting that the holding cost $k_c = 0.25(\$10) = \$2.50$:

$$Q = \sqrt{\frac{2KD}{k_c}} = \sqrt{\frac{2 \cdot 50 \cdot 1{,}000}{2.50}} = \sqrt{40{,}000} = 200 \text{ units}$$

Now we evaluate the discount, using the three elements described:

1. Incremental price benefit: We assume that the discount, if taken, will always be taken. Thus, the annual benefit of the discount is:

   $$(\$0.40 \text{ per unit})(1{,}000 \text{ units per year}) = \$400$$

2. Incremental holding cost: $k_c' = (\$9.60/\$10)k_c = \$2.40$, so that the incremental holding cost of ordering 500 units compared with ordering 200 units is:

   $$\$2.40\left(\frac{500}{2}\right) - \$2.50\left(\frac{200}{2}\right) = \$600 - \$250 = \$350$$

3. Incremental benefit of reduced orders:

   $$\$50\left(\frac{1{,}000}{200} - \frac{1{,}000}{500}\right) = \$50(5 - 2) = \$150$$

The net incremental benefit is \$400 − \$350 + \$150 = \$200, and the discount should be taken. (Note that as soon as we discovered that the price break benefit more than compensated for the increased carrying costs, we could have opted for the discount then, without calculating the benefit of reduced orders.)

Blanket Orders

It may be possible to obtain a price discount by agreeing to purchase a specific level of annual volume from a supplier while maintaining the flexibility of frequent delivery of small quantities. This procedure is called a *blanket order.* In this section, we assumed that demand is known and constant; hence, blanket orders would always be favored, and the size of the delivery quantity could be calculated according to EOQ calculations (refer also to the just-in-time section below). In practice, when demand is not known and constant, there is some risk of accepting an annual commitment that would have to be balanced against the price discount available.

Just-in-Time Inventory Systems

There has been much attention given to Japanese "just in time" or "Kanban" inventory systems. *Kanban* refers to a card that allows one department of the organization to produce some minimum quantity of items in response to another department's immediate requirement. The idea is to use very small order (or production) quantities, with relatively low order points so that replenishment inventory arrives "just in time."

The just-in-time concept strives for very low inventory levels, thereby lowering inventory holding cost. However, if order quantities are lowered below the economic order quantity level (see Equation 8–2), then ordering costs will increase and the total cost will be higher than optimal (see Figure 8–4). Thus, in order to implement the just-in-time concept, it is necessary for the ordering (or setup) cost somehow to be lowered from its earlier value. An important contribution of the Japanese was to realize that K, the "setup cost," could be changed. We illustrate these concepts with an example based on Example 1.

Example 3

Consider Example 1, but suppose that the firm can lower its ordering cost from $5 per order to $1.25 per order by purchasing a membership in a special group buying club. The annual membership fee is $50. Should the firm join the buying club, and if so, in what quantities should it order?

First, assume the firm joins the buying club. Then:

D = 3,000 units
k_c = $3 per unit per year
K = $1.25 per order

From Equation 8–2:

$$Q = \sqrt{\frac{2KD}{k_c}} = \sqrt{\frac{2 \cdot 1.25 \cdot 3{,}000}{3}} = \sqrt{2{,}500} = 50 \text{ units}$$

The optimum order size has dropped from the earlier value of 100 units (when the ordering cost was $5 per order) to 50 units. The total cost of using this order size with the lower ordering cost can be computed by substituting $Q = 50$ into the total cost equation (8–1):

$$TC(Q = 50) = \frac{50}{2}(3) + \frac{3{,}000}{50}(1.25) = 75 + 75 = 150$$

The previous total cost (using the $5 per order cost) was calculated in Example 1 to be $300, so the annual saving in total cost is $300 − $150, or $150. Since this saving exceeds the membership cost of $50, the firm should join the buying club and purchase in quantities of $Q = 50$.

Inventory Turnover

A related concept sometimes used by management to monitor inventory levels is inventory *turnover.* Inventory turnover is the ratio of annual demand divided by average inventory. In symbols:

$$\text{Turnover} = \frac{\text{Annual demand}}{\text{Average inventory}} = \frac{D}{Q/2} \tag{8–3}$$

For inventories involving multiple items, turnover is calculated using the aggregate cost of goods sold (COGS) and the aggregate value of inventory in dollars:

$$\text{Turnover} = \frac{\text{COGS}}{\$\ \text{inventory}}$$

It is sometimes suggested that if a firm's inventory turnover is lower than that of its competitors, then its inventory level is too high and should be reduced. The difficulty with this measure is that it focuses on only one type of cost, namely, inventory holding cost; it ignores ordering costs and shortage costs, as well as quantity discounts. In an environment in which quantity discounts are extremely important, a firm that takes appropriate advantage of them will certainly have higher average inventory and hence lower turnover than a firm that ignores such discounts. However, the first firm will also have lower *total* costs and hence higher profitability.

Thus, turnover is too narrow a measure of inventory performance; it omits important cost factors and may lead to unprofitable actions.

Example 4

Consider the quantity discount example based on Example 1 with $D = 3{,}000$ units. Let us compute the inventory turnover before and after the quantity discount is taken into consideration.

Before the quantity discount is offered, $Q = 100$. Using Equation 8–3:

$$\text{Turnover} = \frac{D}{Q/2} = \frac{3{,}000}{100/2} = \frac{3{,}000}{50} = 60$$

Thus, initially there were 60 "turns" per year.

After the quantity discount is analyzed and found to be profitable, the order quantity changes to $Q = 1{,}000$ units in order to earn the discount. Now, the turnover becomes:

$$\text{Turnover} = \frac{3{,}000}{1{,}000/2} = \frac{3{,}000}{500} = 6$$

Hence, the turnover has been reduced from 60 turns a year to 6 turns a year. Using the "turnover" measure, this change sounds very unprofitable, but we have previously shown that the total cost has been reduced by \$1,885 (see quantity discount example) by taking the discount. Therefore, the turnover measure is incomplete and misleading.

Summary

Under constant demand, the economic order quantity (EOQ) formula will minimize order processing plus inventory holding costs. Some deviation from the calculated EOQ is possible, since total costs are not very sensitive to the precise optimal value. Quantity discounts must be analyzed using incremental analysis. Just-in-time inventory concepts must still deal with the fundamental costs of inventory: ordering and holding. Inventory turnover may be a misleading performance measure, since it deals with only one of these costs (the holding cost).

Section III

Inventory Control with Reordering and Uncertain Demand

In this section, we expand the treatment of inventory control situations by allowing for uncertainty in demand.

Instead of assuming that the demand rate is known and constant, let us hypothesize that we know only the probability distribution of demand during the lead time, but not the actual demand during that period. When we set the order point, there is some probability that we shall run out of inventory and encounter a cost of shortage. We assume any leftover units can be used in the following period.

Figure 8–5 illustrates the behavior of inventory under this assumption. Note that an order of size Q is placed when inventory reaches a level R. Because of the uncertainty of demand during the lead time, a stockout sometimes occurs (such as during the third cycle in Figure 8–5). The annual expected cost of shortage will be affected by the choice of both the order point (R) and the order size (Q).

Before proceeding with the analysis, it is important to emphasize that the models of this section are appropriate only when the demand shown in Figure 8–5 comes from a reasonably large number of **independent** sources. Typically, this will occur for inventories of finished goods but will not occur for raw materials or purchased components in a manufacturing situation. In the latter case, for example, various sizes of electric motors may be purchased for assembly into air conditioners.

Figure 8–5 Illustration of Inventory Pattern

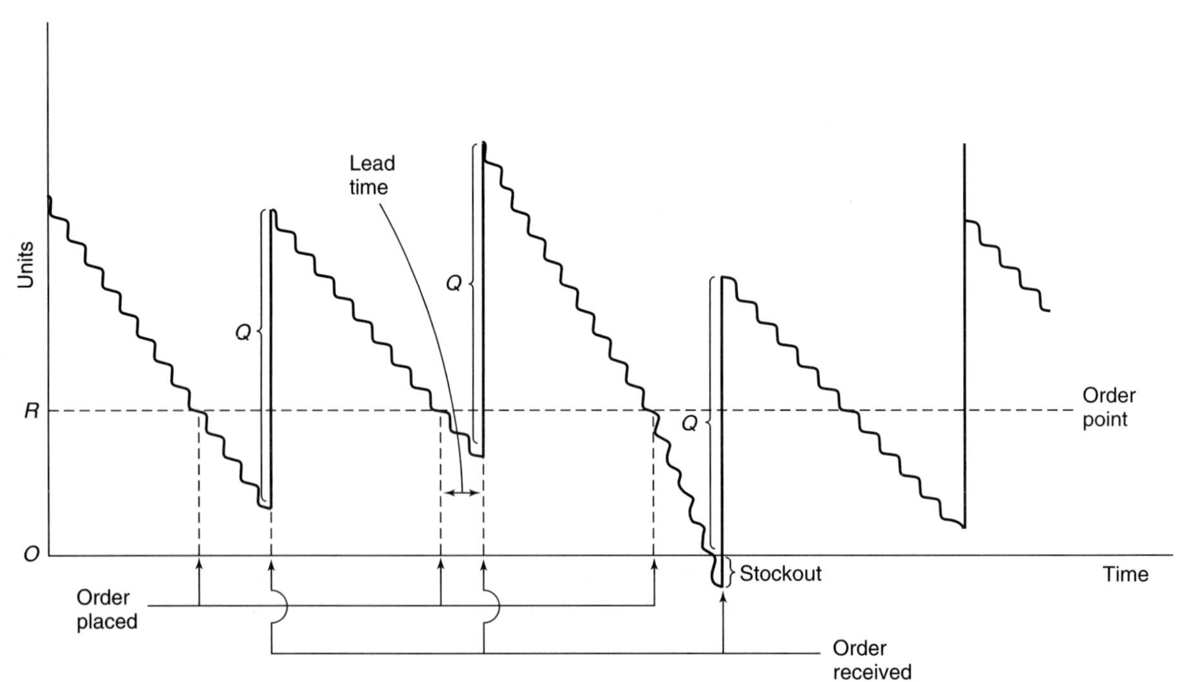

Since the "demand" for motors is completely dependent on the assembly schedule for air conditioners, such demand is called **dependent** rather than independent. For dependent-demand situations, a schedule-planning technique called **material requirements planning (MRP)** has been developed.[5] The models presented in this chapter should be used only in situations with independent demand.

We now wish to divide the inventory into two types: cycle stock and safety stock. **Cycle stock** is the inventory that was considered in the previous section: $Q/2$ on average. It is the inventory required to be carried as a function of the order size (Q). **Safety stock** refers to the difference between the order point (R) and the average demand during the replenishment lead time ($\overline{M}$). See Figure 8–6. The larger the safety stock (and the corresponding order point), the lower the chance that a stock-out will occur, and vice versa.

It is interesting to look at the interaction between the various costs and the two variables (order point and order size) shown in Table 8–1.

A change in order size affects the frequency of reaching the ordering point (thus, the frequency of encountering a chance of shortage). A change in the order point affects the likelihood of shortages and affects the optimum number of times the order point should be encountered. Thus, the total cost is affected by both the order point and the order size, and the optimum order point and the optimum order size are related.

FIGURE 8–6
Cycle Stock and Safety Stock under Average Demand Rate

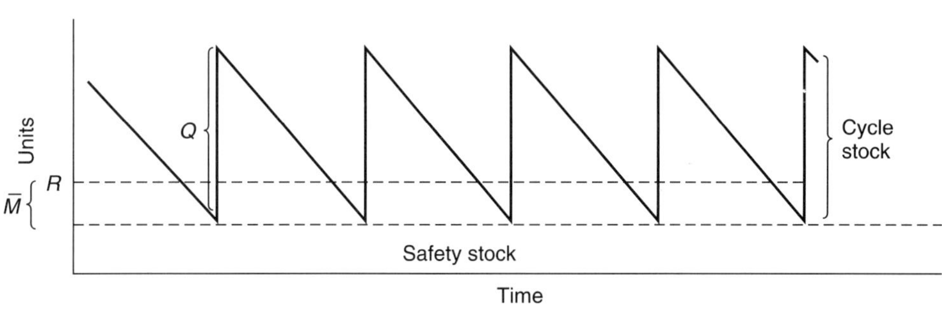

TABLE 8–1
Actions and Results

Action	*Result*
Decrease order point (i.e, place order when fewer units on hand).	Decrease carrying costs of safety stock and increase shortage cost.
Decrease order size.	Decrease carrying costs of cycle stock ($Q/2$), and increase shortage and ordering costs.
Increase order point.	Increase carrying costs of safety stock, and decrease shortage cost.
Increase order size.	Increase carrying costs of cycle stock, and decrease shortage and ordering costs.

[5]For a discussion of MRP, see S. Nahmias, *Production and Operations Analysis,* 3rd ed. (Burr Ridge, IL: Richard D. Irwin, 1997).

In order to model this inventory situation, we must decide how to evaluate shortages. Our first approach will be to assume we can estimate the cost of being out of stock one unit (the cost of shortage). While estimation of this type of cost is difficult and requires managerial assessment and judgment, frequently management is willing to set a range on this cost, such as "it is below \$20" or "it is definitely above \$5." Furthermore, once such a cost is estimated, every item will be consistently treated. Recognizing the potential difficulty of this approach, we will subsequently present an alternative model that allows management to specify the fraction of annual demand to be satisfied from stock.

Shortage Cost Model

Again, we want to minimize the total cost incurred during a given period. There are now three costs to consider:

K = Cost of placing one order
k_c = Cost of carrying one unit in inventory for one year
k_u = Cost of being out of stock one unit (cost of shortage)

The optimum order size and optimum order point will be, in general, a function of these three costs plus the average rate of demand over the lead time and the variability of demand over the lead time.

The Assumptions

We shall first assume that the replenishment lead time is known and constant. Second, the cost of shortage is assumed to be a cost per unit, independent of the duration of the out-of-stock position.[6] The third assumption is that M, the demand during the lead time, is normally distributed. This is the least essential of the assumptions and may be changed; it is chosen to simplify the computations. Next, we assume that the optimal order point R is larger than average lead time demand $\overline{M}$, so that the corresponding safety stock $(R - \overline{M})$ is positive. Finally, we assume safety stock, on the average, is always carried in inventory. We want to determine how much to order (Q) and when to order (R).

The Model

Let:

R = Order point (the total number of units on hand and on order that triggers the reorder)
Q = Order quantity (the number of units ordered at one time)
D = Average demand per year

[6]This measurement of shortage is most appropriate where sales are lost if inventory is not available. In this case, the cost of shortage would represent the opportunity cost of forgone profit plus any cost of ill will.

K = Cost of placing one order
k_c = Cost of carrying one unit in inventory for one year
k_u = Penalty cost of being out of stock one unit (cost of shortage)
M = Number of units of demand over the replenishment lead time (a random variable)
$\overline{M}$ = Average number of units demanded during the lead time
σ_M = Standard deviation of demand over the lead time

We want to determine the optimum order quantity (Q) and the optimum order point (R). We will assume that, as a reasonable approximation, the optimal order quantity for this situation (random demand) is the same as the economic order quantity (EOQ) for the case of constant demand covered in the previous section. That is, we will recommend use of the same square root EOQ formula derived there:

$$Q = \sqrt{\frac{2KD}{k_c}} \tag{8–2}$$

This recommendation is made for two reasons. First, as shown in the previous section, the sum of annual order-processing costs plus annual inventory holding costs is not very sensitive to moderate errors in Q; as long as the order quantity is reasonably close to the optimal value, extreme precision is not required. Second, a number of studies have indicated that—although Q and R should theoretically be determined *simultaneously*—in most practical situations, no serious cost penalty occurs if Q is *independently* determined by the square root EOQ formula of Equation 8–2. Thus, we will advocate Equation 8–2 as the basic formula for Q, even when demand is probabilistic.[7]

Once Q is chosen, however, it is important to take its value into account in determining R, since the size of Q directly influences the number of times per year that we will be exposed to a possible stockout position.

Optimal Order Point—A Marginal Approach

It is possible to obtain the formula for the optimal order point by applying marginal analysis as follows: We start with some value of the order point R; for example, $R = \overline{M}$, average lead time demand. We then ask if it is worthwhile to increase R by one unit. That is, we compare the expected annual cost of adding another unit to R, versus the expected annual cost of *not* adding the additional unit.

The annual incremental cost of *adding* an additional unit to R is approximately equal to k_c, since the additional unit will be added to safety stock ($R - \overline{M}$) and therefore held in inventory almost all of the time.[8]

The annual incremental expected cost of *not adding* the additional unit to R will equal the probability that the additional unit (or more) will be demanded during the

[7]R. G. Brown has shown that the only time the penalty for using the EOQ formula above is serious occurs when the EOQ is less than the standard deviation of demand over the lead time (σ_M). In that case, an excellent heuristic is to simply set the order quantity equal to σ_M. For details, see R. G. Brown, *Materials Management Systems* (New York: John Wiley & Sons, 1977).

[8]This is a reasonable approximation, since the additional unit will always be represented in inventory except during stockout (which is a small part of the time).

lead time, multiplied by the unit stockout cost k_u, all multiplied by the number of inventory cycles per year (D/Q):

$$\begin{array}{l}\text{Incremental cost}\\ \text{of not adding}\\ \text{incremental unit}\end{array} = \text{Prob}\begin{bmatrix}\text{Next unit}\\ \text{(or more)}\\ \text{demanded}\end{bmatrix} \cdot k_u \cdot \left[\frac{D}{Q}\right]$$

Suppose we define $F(R)$ to be the probability that the demand (M) during the lead time will be less than or equal to our current value of R:

$$F(R) = \text{Prob}(M \leq R)$$

Then the probability that the next unit (or more) will be demanded is $1 - F(R)$. The costs of adding and not adding the incremental unit are graphed in Figure 8–7.

Note that as R increases, the probability of the additional unit (or more) being demanded falls, and eventually the two lines cross in Figure 8–7. At this point, we stop adding units to R, since the cost of adding a unit exceeds the cost of not adding the unit. Where the lines cross, the two incremental costs are equal:

$$k_c = [1 - F(R)] \cdot k_u \cdot \frac{D}{Q}$$

or:

$$[1 - F(R)] = \frac{k_c Q}{k_u D}$$

so that:

$$F(R) = 1 - \frac{k_c Q}{k_u D} \qquad (8\text{–}4)$$

Equation 8–4 may be used as follows to obtain the optimal value for R:

1. Compute Q from the square root EOQ formula (Equation 8–2).
2. Compute the right-hand side of Equation 8–4; this is the *desired* probability of lead time demand being less than or equal to R.

FIGURE 8–7

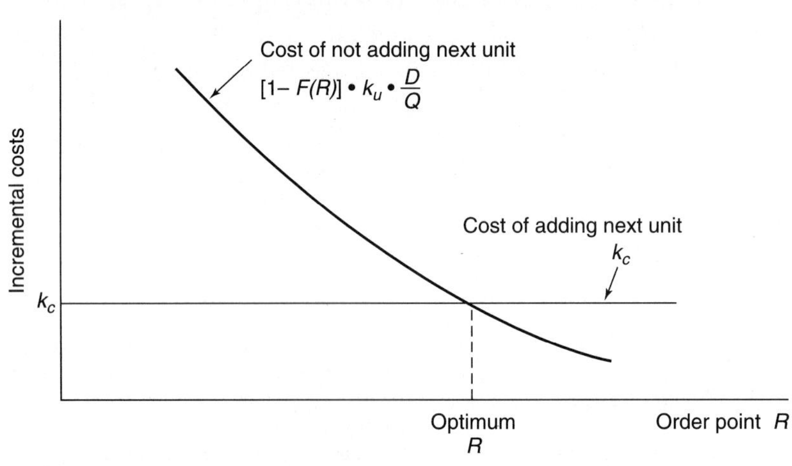

3. From normal tables, find the value of R for which the stated probability applies.

The term $F(R)$ in Equation 8–4 means: "Set R so that there is:

$$1 - \frac{k_c Q}{k_u D}$$

probability of M being equal to or less than R."[9]

Let Z be the number of standard deviations we must go from the mean sales, $\overline{M}$, before the probability is $F(R)$ that the lead time demand, M, is equal to or less than R. We can obtain R, the optimum order point, as follows (see Figure 8–8):

$$R = \overline{M} + Z\sigma_M \tag{8–5}$$

Note that by definition, the order point is equal to average lead time demand plus safety stock. Thus, the safety stock is $Z\sigma_M$.

Example 5

The following example illustrates the computation of the optimum order size and order point.

- The amount expected to be used (D) is 1,800 units per year.
- The cost of making one order (K) is \$10.
- The cost of carrying one unit for one year is 60 cents (this is k_c).
- The replenishment lead time is 20 days; and the mean usage, $\overline{M}$, during the lead time is 100 units, with a standard deviation of 30 units, and is normally distributed.
- The cost of shortage is \$5 per unit out of stock (this is k_u).

Using Equation 8–2, we can determine Q:

$$Q = \sqrt{\frac{2KD}{k_c}} = \sqrt{\frac{2 \cdot 10 \cdot 1{,}800}{0.60}} = \sqrt{60{,}000} = 245 \text{ units}$$

From Equation 8–4 we obtain:

$$F(R) = 1 - \frac{k_c\, Q}{k_u\, D} = 1 - \frac{0.6(245)}{5(1{,}800)} = 0.98367$$

FIGURE 8–8

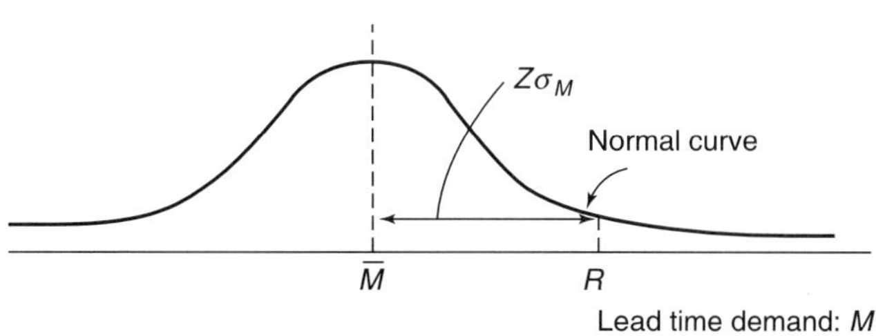

[9] $F(R)$ is the *left* tail of a probability distribution; that is, the Prob ($M \leq R$). In most business situations, the shortage cost will be substantially higher than the carrying cost, so the ratio will usually be greater than 0.50, and safety stock ($R - \overline{M}$) will be positive.

Referring to a table of cumulative probabilities for the normal distribution (Table A in the appendix at the end of the text), $F(R) = 0.98367$ is equivalent to:

$$Z = 2.14 \text{ standard deviations}$$

Thus:

$$R = 100 + 2.14 \cdot 30 = 164 \text{ units}$$

The safety stock is 64 units.

Computing the Standard Deviation of Lead Time Demand (σ_M)

The replenishment lead time is usually different from the standard time period (for example, weekly or monthly) used to collect demand data. We need a way to compute σ_M from σ_1, where σ_1 refers to the standard deviation of demand over the standard time period. For example, suppose the lead time is three weeks and the standard time period is one week. Consider the lead time demand as the sum of three weekly random demands. Then, if the weekly demands are independent, the variance of the sum equals the sum of the variances:

$$\sigma_M^2 = \sigma_1^2 + \sigma_1^2 + \sigma_1^2 = 3\sigma_1^2$$

so that:

$$\sigma_M = \sqrt{3}\,\sigma_1$$

If L is the length of the lead time, then the general formula is:

$$\sigma_M = \sqrt{L}\,\sigma_1 \qquad (8\text{–}6)$$

Example 6

Suppose weekly demand for an item has a mean of 100 units and a standard deviation of 10 units ($\sigma_1 = 10$). If the lead time is four weeks, what is the mean ($\overline{M}$) and the standard deviation (σ_M) of lead time demand?

$$\overline{M} = 4(100) = 400$$
$$\sigma_M = \sqrt{4}(10) = 2(10) = 20$$

Total Expected Cost

The total cost for an inventory policy of (Q, R) is:[10]

$$\text{Total cost }(Q, R) = [K + k_u\sigma_M N(Z)]\frac{D}{Q} + \left[\frac{Q}{2} + (R - \overline{M})\right]k_c \qquad (8\text{–}7)$$

where $N(Z)$ refers to the unit-loss function for the standard normal distribution (Table B in the appendix at the end of the text), and Z is equal to R converted into standard deviation units from the mean demand over the lead time:

$$Z = \frac{R - \overline{M}}{\sigma_M}$$

[10]See the appendix at the end of this chapter for a derivation of this formula.

Continuing with Example 5, the total cost of a policy of ordering 245 units at an order point of 164 units is:

$$TC(Q, R) = [K + k_u \cdot \sigma_M \cdot N(2.14)]\frac{D}{Q} + \left[\frac{Q}{2} + (R - \overline{M})\right]k_c$$

$$TC(Q, R) = [10 + 5 \cdot 30 \cdot 0.0058]\frac{1{,}800}{245} + \left[\frac{245}{2} + 164 - 100\right](0.6)$$

$$= (10.87)7.35 + (186.5)0.6$$

$$= 79.89 + 111.90 = 191.79$$

Recall that the above values for Q and R were determined using the square root EOQ formula (Equation 8–2) for Q. Let us now explore what the total cost is without this approximation. By trial and error, it is possible to find the precise pair of values for Q and R that minimizes the total cost; they are $Q = 255$ and $R = 164$. The (minimum) total cost of these optimal values is:

$$TC(Q, R) = [10 + 5 \cdot 30 \cdot 0.0058]\frac{1{,}800}{255} + \left[\frac{255}{2} + 164 - 100\right](0.6)$$

$$= (10.87)7.06 + (191.5)0.6 = 76.74 + 114.90 = 191.64$$

The more precise values result in an expected annual cost that is only 15 cents less (or 0.08 percent less) than the decision rule in which the order quantity is calculated independently of the order point.

For our example, the total cost is not very sensitive to the order quantity if an amount in the general magnitude of 250 units is ordered. Thus, we suggest using Equation 8–2 to obtain an approximate order quantity Q, and then using Equation 8–4 to solve for the corresponding order point R. Usually, the effect of this approximation on total cost is minor, as in our example.

Service Level Model

The previous model is recommended when the cost of a shortage (per unit) can be reasonably determined. As an alternative, it is possible to satisfy a specified fraction of demand (e.g., 95 percent) at minimum cost. Here, the burden of estimating a shortage cost is changed to the problem of assessing the desired service level, where service level is defined as the percentage of demand filled off-the-shelf (without backordering). Service levels may be set based on those provided by the competition (management may decide to meet or exceed the competition's service levels).

We will make the same assumptions as before and use the same notation, with one addition:

$$P = \text{Service level (fraction of demand filled from stock)}$$

It is recommended that the square root EOQ formula again be used to determine the order quantity, for the same reasons given previously. Regarding the order point, we first write down the expression[11] for the expected number of unfilled orders during a lead time as a function of Z, the number of standard deviations of protection:

[11]See the appendix at the end of the chapter for a derivation of this formula.

$$\text{Expected unfilled orders in a lead time} = \sigma_M N(Z) \tag{8–8}$$

where $N(Z)$ is the unit normal loss table presented in Table B in the appendix at the end of the book.

Next, we observe that average demand over a replenishment cycle must equal average supply in the long run, and since the amount supplied is Q, average demand over the cycle is also Q. Now we can write down the expected fraction of unfilled orders in a cycle:

$$\text{Fraction of unfilled orders per cycle} = \frac{\sigma_M N(Z)}{Q} = 1 - P \tag{8–9}$$

Since our desired service level is P, Equation 8–9 can be set equal to $1 - P$, as shown. Rearranging, we obtain:

$$N(Z) = \frac{Q(1 - P)}{\sigma_M} \tag{8–10}$$

Equation 8–10 is used as follows to obtain the optimal value for R:

1. Compute Q from the square root EOQ formula (Equation 8–2).
2. Compute the right-hand side of Equation 8–10.
3. From the unit normal loss table $N(Z)$ (Table B in the appendix at the end of the text), find the value of Z satisfying Equation 8–10.[12]
4. Then $R = \overline{M} + Z\sigma_M$.

Example 7
Consider Example 5 above, but instead of a shortage cost of \$5 per unit short, suppose management desires that 97 percent of all demands be met from stock ($P = 0.97$). From Equation 8–10:

$$\frac{Q(1 - P)}{\sigma_M} = \frac{245 \cdot 0.03}{30} = 0.245$$

From Table B, the corresponding value of $Z = 0.36$, so that the optimal order point is:

$$R = \overline{M} + Z\sigma_M = 100 + (0.36)(30) = 110.8 = 111 \text{ units}$$

Note that safety stock is 11 units. With an order point of 111 units, we shall satisfy approximately 97 percent of the demand.

It is important to note that the term *service level* defined here is *not* the same as the probability of no stockout in a lead time. Unfortunately, some writers use service level to refer to this probability. To illustrate the difference, consider Example 7, where the optimal $Z = 0.36$. Using Table A in the appendix at the end of the text, this value of Z will produce a probability 0.6406 of no stockout in a lead time. The reason that the percentage of demand filled off-the-shelf (our definition of service level) can be as high as 97 percent when the probability of no stockout in a lead time is only 64 percent relates to the size of the order quantity Q relative to the size of

[12]If the value of Equation 8–10 exceeds the highest value in the table (0.3989), then Z is set equal to zero, and the actual service level will exceed the specified value. This situation is due to a large value of Q relative to σ_M.

the standard deviation of lead time demand σ_M (see Equation 8–10). Intuitively, when stockouts do occur, the number of demands that are not met from stock is small, so that on average, 97 percent of all demands are met from stock.

When one reads or hears the expression "service level," one should ask how it is defined in order to avoid confusion and misunderstanding. The definition used here is more useful to management than the alternative definition.

Trade-Off Curves

A good way to illustrate the relationship between aggregate safety stock and customer service for a collection of items is through a trade-off curve; this is an illustration of feasible points representing various combinations of inventory investment in safety stock versus achieved service level. Suppose we consider a collection of 20 items, each of which is identical to the item in Example 7. Then, if a 97 percent service level were implemented for all 20 items, the total safety stock (in units) would be 20(11) = 220 units, and the total holding cost of this safety stock would be 220($0.60) = $132. These values, 97 percent and $132, are plotted as point A in Figure 8–9.

Also plotted in Figure 8–9 are a series of points that represent different service levels and corresponding safety stock holding costs. As one would expect, higher service levels require higher safety stocks (and hence, higher holding costs). The points in Figure 8–9 were generated in the same way as we calculated the first point (A); namely, select a service level (e.g., 99 percent), calculate the safety stock needed to provide that service level for one item, and then multiply the safety stock by 20 (representing the collection of 20 items) × $0.60 (the unit holding cost).

The same type of calculation can be performed when items do not have identical parameters (demand rates, standard deviations, holding costs, etc.)

When performing calculations for required safety stock, the following approximation for the unit normal loss table (Table B in the appendix at the end of the book) can be useful, especially when using a spreadsheet:[13]

$$Z = \frac{-1.19 + \sqrt{0.0545 - 1.48 \cdot ln(N(Z))}}{0.74} \tag{8–11}$$

where $N(Z)$ is the required unit normal loss value determined from equation (8–10) and *ln* is the natural logarithm.

Using Equation 8–11, one can program all these calculations in a spreadsheet and generate the set of points that trace out the aggregate trade-off curve (sometimes called an *exchange curve*) for any given collection of items comprising an inventory.

Trade-off curves are very useful in demonstrating to management the costs of providing various levels of customer service. The specific axes of measurement can vary; for inventory investment, one could use holding cost, as done here, total

[13]The formula as it would appear on a spreadsheet would be:

$$Z = (-1.19+(0.0545-1.48*LN(N(Z)))\hat{}0.5)/0.74$$

This is derived from the following approximation formula from J. O. Parr, "Formula Approximations to Brown's Service Function," *Production and Inventory Management* 13 (1972), pp 84–86:

$$N(Z) = e^{(-0.92-1.19Z-0.37Z^2)}$$

FIGURE 8–9
Trade-Off Curve Example

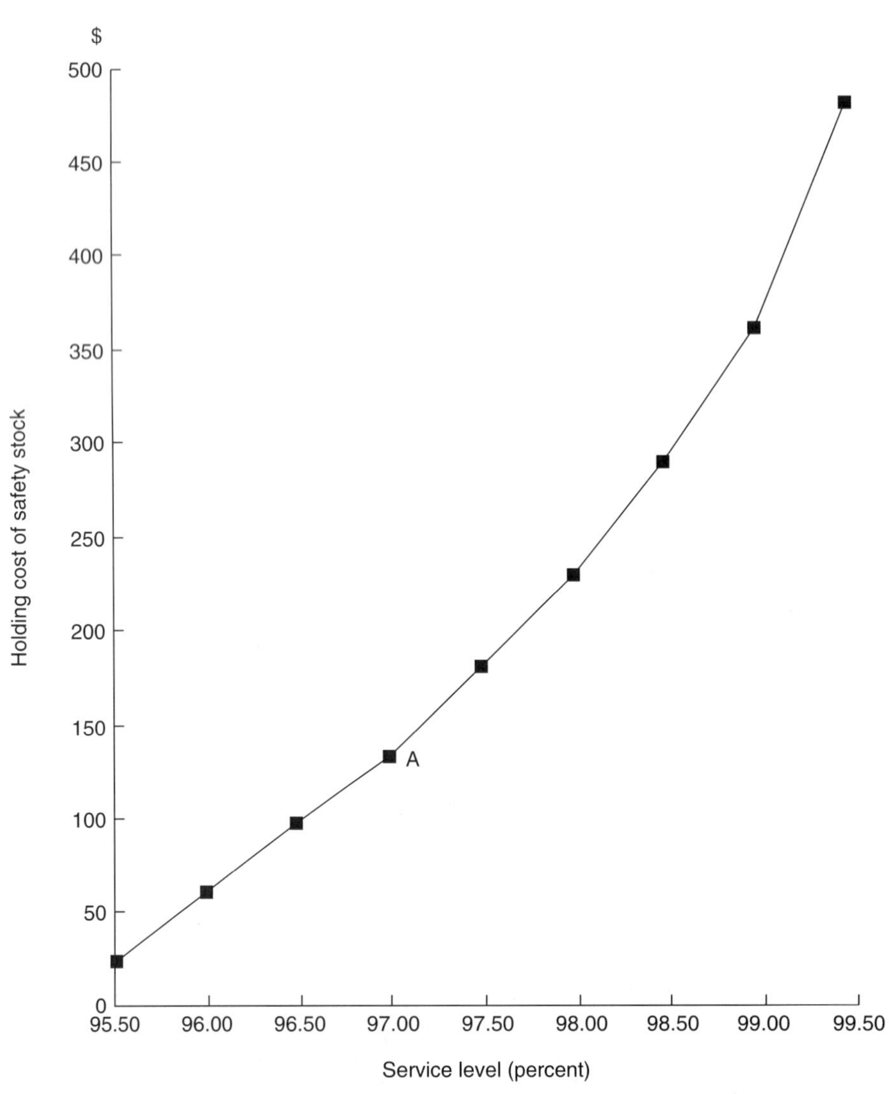

inventory investment, or inventory investment converted into average weeks of supply. For service, a weighted-average fill rate based on demand rates could be used, as done here; in other situations, one might use other measures of service.

Cautions on Using Service Level Models

There are times when, even though management has difficulty assessing a shortage cost k_u per unit stocked out, turning to a service level model may not be the best choice. Consider a collection of spare parts for industrial equipment. Here, a stockout of any part will cause downtime of the equipment, which may be very costly. Suppose management cannot easily assess the shortage cost of a stockout and instead decides to maintain a 98 percent service level for all parts. Is this the best policy when the fundamental goal is to minimize downtime of the corresponding equipment? In other words, how do you allocate safety stock dollars to maximize the *availability* of the equipment?

To answer this question, consider two parts with unit costs of $10 and $1,000, respectively, and suppose all other parameters (demand rates, standard deviations, etc.) are the same. The common service level model would set identical safety stock quantities to ensure 98 percent service for each part. Could you do better? Common sense suggests stocking fewer of the $1,000 item and (many) more of the $10 item, so that less money is invested in inventory and the weighted-average service level could actually exceed 98 percent, thus achieving a win–win situation. This is correct: Using the shortage cost approach of Equation 8–4 would treat a stockout of either item as equally costly, but since their unit costs are not the same, Equation 8–4 would stock much more of the $10 item and much less of the $1,000 item. The final result would be a reduction in total safety stock inventory levels and, at the same time, an improvement in equipment availability (as measured by the resulting weighted-average fill rate).

Other Shortage Measures

In addition to a dollar cost per unit short and a stated percentage of service, a number of other measures of shortage performance have been modeled and "solved" for the corresponding formulas for optimal order points. The reader is referred to the bibliography for this chapter for further information.

Just-in-Time Systems

The Japanese have developed inventory planning to a fine art. Their just-in-time (JIT) inventory policy is a very attractive alternative in concept.

Note that if the ordering or setup cost is driven toward zero, the inventory order quantity is driven as small as possible. (See the EOQ formula in Equation 8–2.) In that case, average cycle stock will be very small.

Also, if the lead time is close to zero (the setup or ordering time is extremely short), again the inventory level can be very low. If a unit is needed, it can be bought or produced in a very short time. Furthermore, if expected sales during the lead time has a very small (almost zero) variance, then there is no need for a large safety stock.

Thus, there can be situations in which the just-in-time inventory policy is consistent with the models of this chapter. In particular, JIT policy is the special case when setup costs are very small and lead times are very short. However, if there is considerable uncertainty about the level of sales during the lead time, or if the lead time until replenishment is very uncertain, and there is a high cost of being short of inventory, there is sufficient justification for having safety stock inventory. One would not want a just-in-time policy if there were a large probability of being short and if there were a large cost associated with being short.

In summary, the Japanese have done an excellent job of forcing us to consider ways of reducing inventory and inventory carrying costs. Earlier, we discussed how the just-in-time (JIT) concept leads one to find ways of lowering the ordering cost. Here, we see that if the replenishment lead time can be reduced, this will cause a reduction in the standard deviation of demand over the lead time (σ_M) and hence, a reduction in safety stock inventory. Again, one must always bear in mind all three types of costs in an inventory system: ordering costs, holding costs, and shortage costs.

Supply Chain Management

A supply chain refers to a network of production and distribution facilities, including material supply from suppliers (and their suppliers), transformation of materials to semifinished and finished products, and distribution of finished products to customers (and their customers). A sample supply chain for Hewlett-Packard Deskjet Printers is shown in Figure 8–10.

Recently, many companies have found that focusing on their supply chains enables them to find and implement improved operations, which can simultaneously reduce cost and improve customer service. One important principle of supply chain management is the concept of *postponement,* whereby the final tailoring or localization of products is postponed as long as possible. A simplified example is given below.

Suppose the ABC company sells three similar products in France, Germany, and Spain. While the products are similar, they have to be localized for each country's unique language, electrical power, and electrical plug requirements. Currently, the localization occurs at the U.S. factory. Shipping time to Europe takes five weeks.

The mean weekly demands and the standard deviation of weekly demands for each country's sales are as follows:

Country	*Mean Weekly Demand*	*Standard Deviation of Weekly Demand*
France	500	200
Germany	600	250
Spain	400	150

Assume that sales across countries are statistically independent.

FIGURE 8–10
HP Deskjet Supply Chain

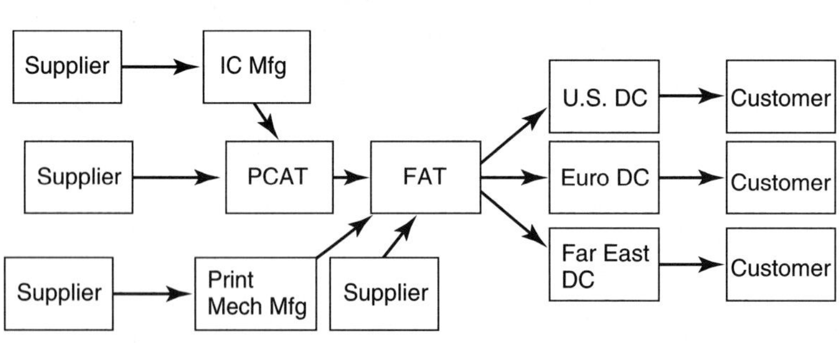

IC Mfg—Integrated Circuit Manufacturing
PCAT—Printed Circuit Assembly and Test
FAT—Final Assembly and Test
Print Mech Mfg—Print Mechanism Manufacturing
DC—Distribution Center

Given the five-week shipping lead time, the company maintains a distribution center (DC) in Europe that stocks finished goods. It can meet customer orders immediately as long as it has stock available.

Suppose the company uses independent *Q, R* policies to manage these separate inventories at the DC; also suppose *Q* is set at a one-week supply for each product. What levels of *R* (the reorder point) and safety stock for each product would ensure 95 percent service levels?

To solve this problem, we use Equations (8–6), (8–10), (8–11), and (8–5). All parameters except σ_M are given. Using Equation (8–6):

$$\sigma_M = (5)^{1/2}(\sigma_1)$$

The calculations for Equations (8–10), (8–11), and (8–5) are carried out in Table 8–2.

If each product cost $100, then the total investment in safety stock to provide 95 percent service would be $161,300.

Now suppose the product could be redesigned and produced in a plain vanilla fashion in the United States and shipped to Europe in generic form. Also, suppose the localization could be performed instantaneously. Then the end result of such a product redesign would be that the demand for the separate products would be pooled or aggregated together. Table 8–3 calculates the level of safety stock of the generic product that would be required for 95 percent service:

Note that in Table 8–3, the variance of weekly demand is calculated, then the variances are added (this assumes independence of demand across the three countries), then the square root is taken to obtain the standard deviation of the sum of product demands over a weekly time period. The remaining calculations are as before.

The result is highly instructive. Instead of 1,613 units of safety stock of the localized product, in the generic-product case only 739 units are required to satisfy the same service level! This result is based on the variance of a sum of random

TABLE 8–2
Risk Pooling Example
Separate Products

Country	*Mean*	*Standard Deviation*	σ_M	*N(Z)*	*Z*	*R*	*Safety Stock*
France	500	200	447.21	0.0559	1.2016	3,037	537
Germany	600	250	559.02	0.0537	1.2212	3,683	683
Spain	400	150	335.41	0.0596	1.1704	2,393	393
Totals							1,613

TABLE 8–3
Risk Pooling Example
Generic Product, 95 Percent Service Level

Country	*Mean*	*Standard Deviation*	*Variance*	*Standard Deviation of Sum*	σ_M	*N(Z)*	*Z*	*R*	*Safety Stock*
France	500	200	40,000						
Germany	600	250	62,500						
Spain	400	150	22,500						
Totals	1,500		125,000	353.55	790.57	0.0949	0.93	8,239	739

TABLE 8–4 Risk Pooling Example
Generic Product, 97 Percent Service Level

Country	Mean	Standard Deviation	Variance	Standard Deviation of Sum	σ_M	N(Z)	Z	R	Safety Stock
France	500	200	40,000						
Germany	600	250	62,500						
Spain	400	150	22,500						
Totals	1,500		125,000	353.55	790.57	0.0569	1.19	8,443	943

variables equaling the sum of the variances, which means that the standard deviation of a sum is always less than the sum of the standard deviations. The reduction in safety stock investment is (1,613 − 739) × \$100 = \$87,400, or 54 percent.

Instead of taking all the gain by lowered inventory, the company might choose to raise the service level somewhat—say, from 95 percent to 97 percent; these results are shown in Table 8–4.

This is an example of the typical win–win situation, in which both inventory reduction and improvement in customer service can result from risk pooling. Here, inventory has been reduced from 1,613 units to 943 units, a reduction of 41 percent, while at the same time customer service has been improved from 95 percent to 97 percent. (These data ignore the need for increased inventory of the localized materials, which would be much less expensive than inventory of the major product.)

Summary

When demand is uncertain, we may continue to use the square root EOQ formula for order size. For the order point, we can either assess a shortage cost per unit, or a desired level of service can be specified. In either case, an optimal formula for the order point has been obtained. Trade-off curves are a useful tool to demonstrate the relationship between inventory levels and customer service. Supply chain management focuses on the entire supply chain and quantifies the costs and benefits of potential improvements to the chain.

SECTION IV

Inventory Control with Uncertainty and No Reordering

This section introduces methods of solving a "one shot" inventory problem when there is no opportunity for reordering and the item cannot economically be stored for future orders. This situation is faced by firms producing highly seasonal or style goods, goods that are perishable (flowers, foods), goods that become obsolete (magazines), and services that are perishable (for example, airline seats on a given date).

Increasingly, this situation is also faced by electronics and computer companies whose major sales occur during the Christmas selling season, where planning for the right amount of materials and production is difficult due to sales uncertainty.

TABLE 8–5 Demand Distribution

Demand	Probability
0	0.10
1	0.30
2	0.40
3	0.20
	1.00

TABLE 8–6 Computation of Expected Profit*

		Order One Unit		Order Two Units		Order Three Units	
Event: Demand	*Probability of Demand*	*Conditional Profit*	*Expected Profit*	*Conditional Profit*	*Expected Profit*	*Conditional Profit*	*Expected Profit*
0	0.10	$(20)	$(2)	$(40)	$(4)	$(60)	$(6)
1	0.30	30	9	10	3	(10)	(3)
2	0.40	30	12	60	24	40	16
3	0.20	30	6	60	12	90	18
	1.00	Expected profit:	$25		$35		$25

*Amounts in parentheses are negative.

We will assume that demand is uncertain but that the probability distribution of demand is known. This is analogous to knowing that a fair coin has a tail and a head but not knowing which will come up on the next toss.

Example 8
Let us assume that the demand for a product is known to have the distribution shown in Table 8–5. Assume that units cost $25 each and that leftovers may be sold for salvage for $5. The sales price is $55 per unit. We know the probability distribution of demand for our product, but we do not know before the period begins how much will be demanded in this period. In this situation, how many units should be ordered?

One possibility would be to compute the different expected profits that would occur with different ordering plans. Table 8–6 presents this computation. Remember that if no units are purchased, no units may be sold; if one unit is purchased, no more than one unit may be sold, even if the amount demanded is greater.

Based on expected profit, the optimum act is to order two units, since the expected profit of $35 is higher than the expected profit resulting from any other strategy.

A Marginal Approach

In the above analysis, we computed the different total profits that would be expected following different ordering policies. A solution easier to compute uses a marginal approach. We compute the effect on profit of adding one more unit to the order size.

Let the probability of selling an additional unit (or more) be designated by p; then $(1 - p)$ is the probability of not selling the additional unit (or more). The values of p in our example are shown in Table 8–7.

The column headed Cumulative Probabilities is p, since it indicates the probability of selling zero or more (1.00), one or more (0.90), two or more (0.60), or three or more (0.20) units. It is the *right tail* of the probability distribution.

Let c_o be defined as the unit **cost of overage;** that is, the cost of having one unit left over. For example, if a unit costs \$25 and leftover units can be sold for \$5, then the cost of overage is \$20 per unit.

Let c_u be defined as the unit **cost of underage;** that is, the cost of not having any units to sell when a customer wants one. In our example, a unit costs \$25 and sells for \$55. Thus, the firm loses \$30 of profit for each unit that it is short; that is, c_u is \$30. We assume there is no cost beyond the present period because of the underage.

The relationship between the costs of overage and underage and the probability of demand for the next unit is shown in Table 8–8.

Table 8–8 shows that if a unit is ordered but there is no demand, the conditional cost is c_o. Similarly, if the unit is not ordered and there is a demand for it, the conditional cost is c_u. Note that the underage cost c_u is an **opportunity cost,** representing the cost of a lost opportunity to earn profit.

The expected cost for the act "do not order" is pc_u; and that for the act "order" is $(1 - p)c_o$. The additional unit should be ordered provided the expected cost of doing so is less than the expected cost of not ordering. That is, order if:

$$(1 - p)c_o < pc_u$$

For example, consider initially ordering zero units, with the act "order" representing the order for one unit. Then:

$$\text{Expected cost (do not order)} = pc_u = (0.9)(\$30) = \$27$$

TABLE 8–7

Demand	*Probability of Demand*	*Cumulative Probabilities (p)*
0	0.10	1.00
1	0.30	0.90
2	0.40	0.60
3	0.20	0.20
	1.00	

TABLE 8–8
Conditional and Expected Costs

Event: Demand for Next Unit (or more)	*Probability of Event*	*Act*	
		Do Not Order	*Order*
No	$1 - p$	0	c_o
Yes	p	c_u	0
Expected costs of acts		pc_u	$(1 - p)c_o$

and:

$$\text{Expected cost (order)} = (1 - p)c_o = (0.1)(\$20) = \$2$$

The expected cost of ordering is less than the expected cost of not ordering, so the unit should be ordered. The same comparison must be made to see if the second unit should be ordered, and so on. Table 8–9 and Figure 8–11 illustrate these calculations.

A negative cost in column 4 of Table 8–9 is a net expected profit. Ordering the first unit increases profit by \$25; ordering the second unit increases profit by \$10 (to \$35); and ordering the third unit decreases profit by \$10 (to \$25). It would not be desirable to stock three units, since there is an expected marginal cost of \$10 associated with stocking the third unit.

Using this rule, the decision maker will keep adding additional units until the expected cost of "order" equals or exceeds the cost of "do not order." Recall that as more units are added, the probability of demand for the next unit (or more), p, will decline, and $(1 - p)$ will increase. Ultimately, the expected cost from ordering will exceed that of not ordering (see Figure 8–11).

Instead of completing a table such as Table 8–9 to find the optimal solution, there is an important shortcut we can use. Suppose we let p_c be the probability at which the cost of ordering *equals* the cost of not ordering. We call p_c the **critical probability** and can find it by solving the following equation:

$$(1 - p_c)c_o = p_c c_u$$

TABLE 8–9

(1) Policy: Go from Ordering	*p*	*(2) Expected Cost of Ordering the Next Unit: $(1 - p)c_o$*	*(3) Expected Cost of Not Ordering the Next Unit: pc_u*	*(4) Net Incremental Cost of Ordering: (2) − (3)*
0 to 1	0.90	0.10 · 20 = 2	0.90 · 30 = 27	−25
1 to 2	0.60	0.40 · 20 = 8	0.60 · 30 = 18	−10
2 to 3	0.20	0.80 · 20 = 16	0.20 · 30 = 6	10

FIGURE 8–11
Expected Costs of Acts

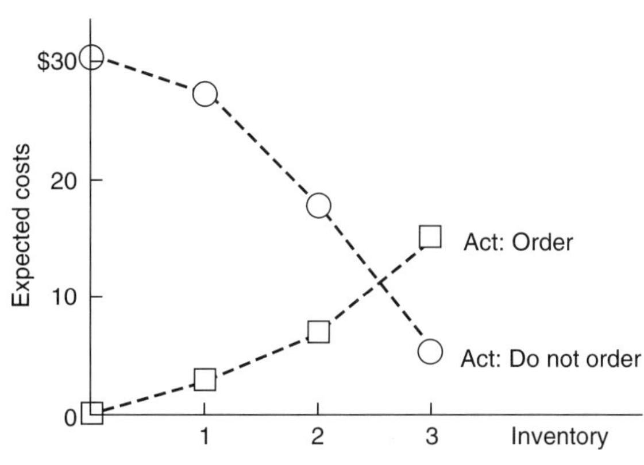

or:

$$p_c = \frac{c_o}{c_o + c_u} \qquad (8\text{–}12)$$

The ratio $c_o/(c_o + c_u)$ is called the **critical ratio.**

If the events are not continuous (for example, demand can be either 1,000 or 2,000 units, but not in between), it is not always possible to find the marginal sales with an exact probability of p_c. The following rules are useful in finding the optimum in the discrete case:

1. As long as the probability of selling one or more additional units is greater than p_c, the critical ratio, we should order that unit.
2. If the probability of selling the additional unit is equal to p_c, we are indifferent to including it in our order or leaving it out.
3. If the probability is less than p_c, do not order that unit.

In our example, c_o equals \$20, and c_u is \$30; thus:

$$p_c = \frac{c_o}{c_o + c_u} = \frac{20}{20 + 30} = \frac{20}{50} = 0.40$$

Referring to Table 8–7, we see that the decision maker would order two units (because $p = 0.60$ for the second unit, and this is greater than $p_c = 0.40$) but would not order the third unit (because $p = 0.20$ and this is less than 0.40).

Note that the inventory model we have developed assumed linearity in the costs of overage and underage. That is, it has assumed that the per unit costs are the same for all units. In some cases, these assumptions are not realistic, and more appropriate, but more complex, functions for the marginal costs can be used.

Cost of Ill Will

Thus far, we have assumed that the only cost of an underage (i.e., of being out of stock) was the profit that was lost in the one period. But it is possible to modify the model to include customer ill will that might result from not finding the goods on hand. Estimating the cost of ill will can be a very difficult process. One approach is to assume you could buy a magic wand and use it only once to avoid one unit of stockout; how much would you be willing to pay for the magic wand? In any event, it is necessary that an estimate of this factor be made in terms of the present value of future profits lost because of a unit underage. This amount can then be included in determining the critical ratio, and hence, in setting the optimal ordering policy.

Continuing Example 8 of this section, let us assume there is an additional ill will cost of \$7.50 associated with every unit of demand not filled because of an inventory shortage. Consider these definitions and data:

c_o = Unit cost of overage = \$20. The \$20 is the difference between the cost per unit (\$25) and the distress price (\$5).

c_u = Unit cost of underage = \$37.50. The \$37.50 is equal to the sum of the profit lost by one unfilled demand (\$55 − \$25 = \$30) and the cost of ill will ($7.50) for each unit of underage; that is, when there is demand and there are no units to sell.

The definition of the underage cost has been altered to include ill-will effects; however, the critical ratio equation still applies (Equation 8–12):

$$p_c = \frac{c_o}{c_o + c_u}$$

In our modified example:

$$p_c = \frac{c_o}{c_o + c_u} = \frac{20}{20 + 37.50} = 0.35$$

The increased penalty for not filling an order has had the same effect as an increase in the profit margin (i.e., an increase in the regret of not having a unit on hand when a unit is demanded), and it will tend to increase the size of the order by decreasing p_c.

Using a Continuous Probability Distribution

Instead of assuming that sales can take on only a few discrete values, we can make use of a continuous probability distribution. Such a distribution will make it possible to consider all feasible values of the random variable, demand. For illustrative purposes, assume that the random variable, tomorrow's demand, is normally distributed.

As in the previous section on the discrete case, we begin by computing p_c, where p_c is the critical ratio. This critical ratio is the probability at which the cost of ordering equals the cost of not ordering. In terms of the normal distribution, p_c can be represented by the shaded area shown in Figure 8–12. It should be noted that p_c is the *right tail* of the distribution.

Figure 8–12 shows an optimum order of 50 units. If fewer than 50 units are ordered, *p,* the probability of selling an additional unit or more, will be greater than p_c; the same arguments presented for the discrete case hold in the continuous case.

In the computation of optimum order size, the first step is to find *Z,* the number of standard deviations from the mean, that will equate the right tail of the normal

FIGURE 8–12

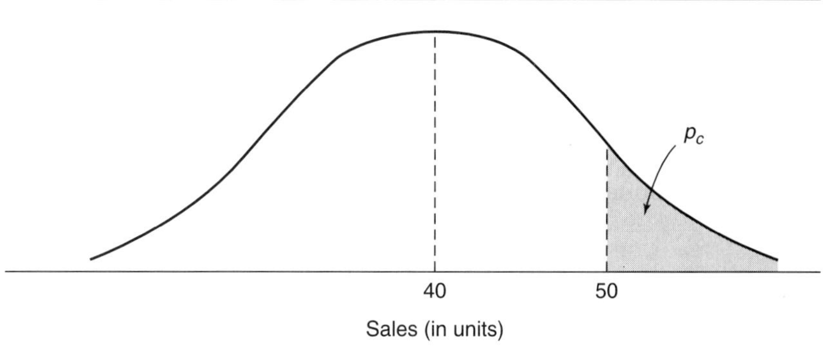

density function and p_c. It is then necessary to convert Z to units by multiplying Z by the standard deviation of the sales distribution.[14] This number of units is then added to mean sales, if $p_c < 0.50$ (as shown in Figure 8–12), or subtracted, if $p_c > 0.50$. If $p_c = 0.50$, then $Z = 0$.

Example 9
Assume that the distribution of demand is normal, c_o is equal to \$64, and c_u is equal to \$336. The critical ratio is:

$$p_c = \frac{c_o}{c_o + c_u} = \frac{64}{64 + 336} = 0.16$$

The 0.16 probability corresponds to the right tail of a normal distribution. Referring to Table A (in the appendix at the end of the text), we find that the left tails are given. The left-tail complement of a 0.16 right tail is 0.84, and this is approximately one standard deviation from the mean (with one standard deviation, the value in the table is 0.8413). If we move out one standard deviation to the right of the mean, the probability of making an additional sale or more will be equal to 0.16.

Assume mean sales for the coming period are 40 units and the standard deviation of the distribution is 10. We want to increase the order size until the probability of making an additional sale is equal to 0.16. We have to move one standard deviation to the right of the mean ($Z = 1$). In order to convert Z to units, we multiply by the standard deviation:

$$Z\sigma = 1 \cdot 10 = 10 \text{ units}$$

Since $p_c < 0.50$, we have to *add* 10 units to the mean sales to obtain Q, the optimum order size. We can write the following equation:

$$\begin{aligned} Q &= \text{Mean sales} \pm Z\sigma \\ &= 40 + 10 = 50 \end{aligned}$$

The sign is plus if $p_c < 0.50$ and minus if $p_c > 0.50$.

Example 10
Assume that demand has the same normal distribution as in Example 9. Suppose we have now computed p_c and found it to be 0.25. Figure 8–13 shows this situation.

The left-tail complement of a 0.25 right tail is 0.75; Table A shows that the Z value corresponding to $F(Z) = 0.75$ is approximately $Z = 0.67$. Then the optimal order size is:

$$\begin{aligned} Q &= \text{Mean sales} + Z\sigma \\ &= 40 + 0.67(10) = 46.7 \text{ or } 47 \end{aligned}$$

Example 11
Consider the same problem as Example 10, but now suppose that the forecast of sales is less certain; the standard deviation of the distribution is 25 instead of 10.

---

[14]Use the following formulas:

$$Z = \frac{X - \mu}{\sigma} \quad \text{and} \quad X = Z\sigma + \mu$$

FIGURE 8–13

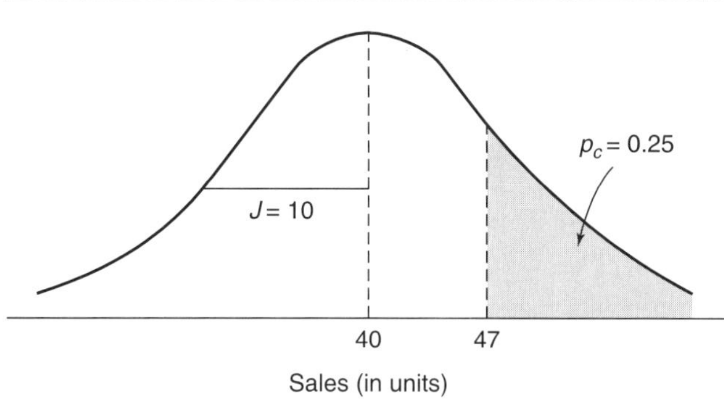

In Example 10, the critical ratio p_c was 0.25, and the corresponding Z value was approximately $Z = 0.67$. Using the larger standard deviation, the optimal order size is now:

$$\begin{aligned} Q &= \text{Mean sales} + Z\sigma \\ &= 40 + 0.67(25) = 56.75 \text{ or } 57 \end{aligned}$$

It is interesting to compare this result with that of Example 10, where the standard deviation of sales was 10. Note that as the forecast uncertainty increases (when the standard deviation increases), it is optimal to move even further away from the mean sales forecast of 40 units. This strategy may seem counterintuitive at first consideration, but it is a direct consequence of the critical ratio properly taking the costs of overage and underage into account. If we wish to have a 0.25 probability of underage, a higher standard deviation requires that a larger inventory be carried.

Normal Probabilities on Spreadsheets

The Excel and Quattro spreadsheet function NORMSINV is related to Table A.[15] It will give the value of Z corresponding to a given $1 - p_c$ value; that is, given a left-tail cumulative probability, it provides the value of the standardized Z. For example, for $1 - P_c = F(Z) = 0.75$, use:

$$=\text{NORMSINV}(0.75) = 0.6745 = Z$$

Relevant Costs

It is important to obtain correct estimates of relevant costs of overage and underage when using this solution procedure. These costs should be *incremental* or *marginal costs;* they should not contain any allocations of overhead or other fixed costs that

[15]The related function NORMSDIST gives the corresponding left-tail cumulative probability for a specified value of Z. Functions NORMDIST and NORMINV also provide normal probabilities using the values of X, μ and σ.

would be unaffected by the decision under consideration. For example, suppose in Example 8 the unit cost of the item was as follows:

Raw materials	\$20	(variable costs)
Direct labor	5	
Allocated overhead	25	(allocation of fixed cost)
Total	\$50	

From an accountant's viewpoint, the fully allocated cost of the item is \$50, but for inventory decision-making purposes, the *incremental* unit cost is only \$25 (the sum of raw material and direct labor, both of which are usually variable costs). We assume that the fixed overhead will not change whether or not we produce a marginal unit. Similarly, the unit underage cost should not contain any allocations of fixed costs.

Note that since the underage cost is an opportunity cost, it does not show up on the firm's profit-and-loss statements. Thus, a "conservative" management that focuses only on reported profit and loss may be missing significant opportunities for profit improvement if the underage cost is ignored.

Summary

One-shot inventory problems can be analyzed by determining the underage cost, the overage cost, and the critical ratio p_c. The order size is increased until the probability of selling the next unit or more falls to p_c. If ill will is a consideration, it must be estimated and included in the unit cost of underage.

Appendix
The Determination of the Optimum Order Point and Order Size

Let:

Q = Order size
R = Order point
D = Average demand per year
M = Amount demanded during lead time ($\overline{M}$ = Mean amount); a random variable
$f(M)$ = Probability density function for M
$R - \overline{M}$ = Safety stock
σ_M = Standard deviation of demand over lead time
$R - M$ = Units unsold when new units are received (if $M < R$)
$M - R$ = Amount by which demand during lead time exceeds order point (if $M > R$)
K = Cost of placing order
k_c = Carrying cost per unit per year
k_u = Penalty cost for being out of stock one unit (cost of shortage)

The Total Annual Expected Cost

The total cost of a policy involving a specific order size, *R*, and a specific order quantity, *Q*, is equal to the sum of the costs of ordering, the costs of being out of stock, and the costs of carrying inventory:

$$\text{Total cost }(Q, R) = K\left(\frac{D}{Q}\right) + \left[k_u\int_R^{\infty}(M - R)f(M)dM\right]\frac{D}{Q} + \left[\frac{Q}{2} + (R - \overline{M})\right]k_c \quad (8\text{–}13)$$

where $K(D/Q)$ is the cost of ordering: K is the cost per order; D/Q is the annual number of orders:

$$\left[k_u\int_R^{\infty}(M - R)f(M)dM\right]\frac{D}{Q}$$

is the cost of being out of stock; k_u is the cost per unit; the integral is the expected number of units out of stock per cycle; D/Q is the annual number of replenishment cycles—that is, the annual number of orders; $[(Q/2) + (R - \overline{M})]k_c$ is the cost of carrying inventory; and k_c is the cost of carrying one unit for one year. The remainder of the term is the average inventory; $Q/2$, the average inventory of cycle stock, plus the average safety stock $(R - \overline{M})$. The term $(R - \overline{M})$ only approximates the average level of safety stock, but the approximation is valid in most practical instances (see footnote 8 in this chapter).

The equations for Q and $F(R)$ are obtained from Equation 8–13, the equation for the total cost, by taking the partial derivatives with respect to R and with respect to Q and setting them equal to zero.[16]

$$\begin{aligned}\text{Total cost }(Q, R) &= K\frac{D}{Q} + \left[\frac{Q}{2} + (R - \overline{M})\right]k_c + \left[k_u\int_R^{\infty}(M - R)f(M)dM\right]\frac{D}{Q}\\ &= K\frac{D}{Q} + k_c\left[\frac{Q}{2} + (R - \overline{M})\right]\\ &\quad + \frac{D}{Q}k_u\left[\overline{M} - \underset{-\infty}{\overset{R}{\mathrm{E}}}(M)[1 - F(R)]\right]\end{aligned}$$

Differentiating with respect to *R:*

$$\begin{aligned}\frac{\partial\,\text{Total cost}}{\partial R} &= k_c - \frac{D}{Q}k_uRf(R) + \frac{D}{Q}k_u[F(R) + Rf(R) - 1]\\ &= k_c - \frac{D}{Q}k_u + \frac{D}{Q}k_uF(R)\end{aligned}$$

Setting the derivative equal to zero and solving for $F(R)$:[17]

$$F(R) = 1 - \frac{k_cQ}{k_uD} \quad (8\text{–}4)$$

---

[16]The symbol $\underset{-\infty}{\overset{R}{E}}(M)$ in the equations is the partial expectation. It equals $\int_{-\infty}^{R} Mf(M)dM$.

[17]Second-order conditions must also be checked.

Differentiating total cost with respect to Q:

$$\frac{\partial \text{ Total cost } (Q, R)}{\partial Q} = -\frac{KD}{Q^2} + \frac{k_c}{2} - \frac{D}{Q^2} k_u \int_R^\infty (M - R) f(M) dM$$

Setting the derivative equal to zero and solving for Q:

$$Q = \sqrt{\frac{2D\left[K + k_u \int_R^\infty (M - R) f(M) dM\right]}{k_c}} \tag{8–14}$$

Equation 8–14 can be converted into a form that is more susceptible to computation. We make use of the fact that if M is normally distributed and if R is larger than the expected sales ($\overline{M}$) during the reorder period, then:

$$\int_R^\infty (M - R) f(M) dM = \sigma_M N(Z) \tag{8–15}$$

where $N(Z)$ is the unit normal-loss integral valued for Z (R converted to standard deviations from the mean). The σ_M is the standard deviation of the distribution of demand during the lead time. Equation 8–15 is the expected number of unfilled orders in a lead time.

Equation 8–14 now becomes:

$$Q = \sqrt{\frac{2D[K + k_u \sigma_M N(Z)]}{k_c}} \tag{8–16}$$

Note that R is in the formula for Q (Equation 8–14), and Q is in Equation 8–4 for R. Theoretically, the two equations must be solved simultaneously. This can be done by the use of an iterative procedure, which starts with an estimate of Q, solves for R, then solves for a new Q, and repeats this process until a Q and an R are found to satisfy both equations. However, for practical purposes, it is sufficient to determine the value of Q by using the EOQ formula, where certain demand was assumed:

$$Q = \sqrt{\frac{2KD}{k_c}} \tag{8–2}$$

The equation for total cost can be simplified (assuming $R > \overline{M}$) by making use of Equation 8–15. Substituting into Equation 8–13, we obtain:

$$\text{Total cost } (Q, R) = [K + k_u \sigma_M N(Z)] \frac{D}{Q} + \left[\frac{Q}{2} + (R - \overline{M})\right] k_c \tag{8–17}$$

Bibliography

Brown, R. G. *Decision Rules for Inventory Management.* New York: Holt, Rinehart & Winston, 1967.

———. *Materials Management Systems.* New York: John Wiley & Sons, 1977.

Hall, R. W. *Zero Inventories.* Burr Ridge, IL: Richard D. Irwin, 1983.

Hillier, F., and G. J. Lieberman. *Introduction to Operations Research.* 6th ed. New York: McGraw-Hill, 1995.

Lee, H. L., and C. Billington, "The Evolution of Supply-Chain-Management Models and Practice at Hewlett-Packard," *Interfaces,* September–October 1995, pp. 42–63.

McClain, J. O., and L. J. Thomas. *Operations Management: Production of Goods and Services.* 2nd ed. Englewood Cliffs, NJ: Prentice Hall, 1985.

Nahmias, S. *Production and Operations Analysis.* 3rd ed. Burr Ridge, IL: Richard D. Irwin, 1997.

Parr, J. O., "Formula Approximations to Brown's Service Function," *Production and Inventory Management* 13 (1972), pp. 84–86.

Schonberger, J. *Japanese Manufacturing Techniques.* New York: Free Press, 1982.

Silver, E. A., and R. Peterson. *Decision Systems for Inventory Management and Production Planning.* 2nd ed. New York: John Wiley & Sons, 1985.

Practice Problems[18]

8–1. A random sample of 10 items has been taken from a 20,000-item inventory. (Ten is too small a sample, but it keeps the arithmetic simple.) The 10 dollar-sales amounts are: 170, 320, 49, 94, 530, 125, 2, 70, 225, 30.

a. Plot the ranked data on an ABC curve.

b. Based on your sample, what is the percentage of total sales for the 20,000-item inventory that would be represented by the first 4,000 items?

c. What percentage of sales is represented by the first 50 percent of the items?

d. Suppose management wanted A items to represent the first 50 percent of sales, C items to represent the last 50 percent of items, and B items to be in between. What dollar-sales rates would you use to separate the A, B, and C ranges?

8–2. The ABC Company uses 100,000 units per year of a product. The carrying cost per unit is \$3 per year. The cost of ordering a batch is \$60.

a. What is the optimum order size?

b. If the ordering costs were 60 cents per order, how many units should be ordered at one time?

8–3. Assume the same situation as in (*a*) of Problem 8–2, with the added information that the ordering cost can be reduced from \$60 to \$15 per batch if the company joins a cooperative buying organization with annual membership fee of \$2,000.

a. What would be the optimum order size if the company decided to join the cooperative buying organization?

b. Should the company join the co-op?

8–4. An oil company is drilling for oil in Alaska and is concerned about its inventory of spare parts. It takes a month to receive orders. Consider part 8J2N. This part is expected to be needed at a rate of 100 per month (1,200 per year). Demand during the lead time (one month) is approximately normal with a standard deviation of 40. The order cost is \$1,000 per order; the holding cost is \$20 per year; and the shortage cost is \$200 per unit. Determine the order size Q and the order point R.

[18]Solutions to these problems are at the end of this chapter.

8–5. Lead time demand for an item averages 100 units, with a standard deviation of 30. The order quantity is 200 units. Management desires that 99 percent of all demand be met from stock.

a. What is the optimal order point?

b. Suppose management wanted a 98 percent service level; what would the optimal order point be?

c. Suppose management wanted a 90 percent service level. Compute the optimal order point.

8–6. The probability distribution of the demand for a product has been estimated to be:

Demand	*Probability of Demand*
0	0.05
1	0.15
2	0.30
3	0.35
4	0.10
5	0.05
6	0.00
	1.00

Each unit sells for \$50, and if the product is not sold, it is completely worthless. The purchase costs of a unit are \$10.

a. Assuming no reordering is possible, how many units should be purchased?

b. If customer ill will is estimated to be \$20 for every unit for which there is unfilled demand, how many units should be ordered?

8–7. Given the following information, compute the optimum order size (reordering is not possible):

Sales price	$100
Incremental cost per unit sold (including purchase cost)	70
Purchase cost per unit	50
Salvage value (if not sold)	10
Loss in goodwill for each unit of demand not satisfied	50

The probability distribution of demand is normal; mean, 140; standard deviation, 20.

8–8. Refer to Problem 8–7. Recompute the optimum order size, assuming the standard deviation of the probability distribution is 50.

8–9. Refer to Problem 8–7. Recompute the optimum order size, assuming there is *no* loss in goodwill with unfilled orders.

a. Assume a standard deviation of 20.
b. Assume a standard deviation of 50.
c. Compare the above answers with those of Problems 8–7 and 8–8.

Problems

8–10. A random sample of 10 items has been taken from a 40,000-item inventory. (Ten is too small a sample but it keeps the arithmetic simple.) The 10 dollar-sales amounts are: 350, 600, 120, 30, 175, 1100, 5, 50, 200, 90.

a. Plot the ranked data on an ABC curve.
b. Based on your sample, what is the percentage of total sales for the 40,000-item inventory that would be represented by the first 4,000 items?
c. What percentage of items would represent the first 25 percent of sales?
d. Suppose management wanted A items to represent the first 50 percent of sales, C items to represent the last 50 percent of items, and B items to be in between. What dollar-sales rates would you use to separate the A, B, and C ranges?

8–11. Select a random sample of 10 items from your refrigerator. Estimate your annual expenditures on each item, and then plot your ranked data on an ABC curve. Do you tend to pay more attention to the one or two items at the top of your ranking?

8–12. The costs of placing an order are $150. It is estimated that 1,000 units will be used in the next 12 months. The carrying cost per unit per month is $2.50.

a. Compute the optimum order size.
b. Now suppose that the company could lower the ordering cost to $50; the cost of the effort to accomplish this change is $1,000. Assume the product will be sold only for the next two years. Compute the new optimal order quantity if the lower ordering cost were implemented, and determine if the company should invest $1,000 in the ordering-cost reduction program.

8–13. A company uses a certain part in the assembly of sets of electronic equipment at the rate of 8,000 per year. Each part has a value of $18. The company estimates that the cost of holding inventory is 20 percent of the value of the item per year.

The company can produce the part on either of two machines. Machine A has a setup cost of $200; machine B has a setup cost of only $100. However, it costs 10 cents more per unit to produce using machine B than it does using machine A.

Which machine should the company use? What is the optimum lot size?

8–14. A newly appointed inventory manager was given the following information for an item:

Annual usage in dollars = $100,000
Order-processing cost = $25
Carrying cost per dollar per year = 0.20

When asked to compute an optimal purchase amount for the item, the manager complained that he wasn't told the value per unit. Can you complete an optimal purchase amount for the item with the data provided? If so, do so; if not, explain why not.

8–15. Refer to (*a*) of Problem 8–2. Suppose the ABC Company was offered a discount of 12 cents per unit by its supplier if it ordered in lots of 10,000 units. Should ABC take the discount?

8–16. Father's Cookies produces chocolate-chip cookies in a large oven that holds up to 2,000 pounds of cookies at a time. Annual demand is constant at 200,000 pounds; variable cost is 25¢ per pound. Oven cleanout is required after the oven processes 2,000 or fewer pounds in a batch; the cleanout takes one hour's time for four workers, each of whom is paid $7 per hour. The inventory holding cost is 20 percent per dollar per year; spoilage occurs if inventory is held by Father's Cookies more than 12 months. There is a substantial unused oven capacity.

In what quantity should these cookies be produced? Why?

8–17. An item is consumed at the rate of 1,000 per year; ordering costs are $20 per order; and holding costs are 25 percent per year. Unit purchase cost is a function of quantity purchased at one time, as follows:

Quantity	*Cost per Unit*
1–100	$10.00
101–200	9.75
Above 200	9.50

What purchase quantity should be used for the item?

8–18. A retailer feels that the mean demand for an item in inventory for the coming year is 1,800 units. The lead time on orders is 20 days, and the mean demand during the lead time is 100 units. The lead time demand is assumed to be normally distributed, with $\sigma = 30$ (there is a 50–50 chance that the lead time demand could be less than 80 units or more than 120 units). The cost per unit of lost sales is $5, the cost of placing an order is $10, and the cost of carrying a unit in inventory for one year is $50.

a. Compute the approximate optimum order size (round to nearest whole unit).

b. Compute the approximate optimum order point.

8–19. The mean demand for an item in inventory for the next year is 4,000 units. The lead time on orders is 10 days. The demand for the product during the lead time is normally distributed and has a standard deviation of 30 units. The cost per unit of lost sales is $5, the cost of placing an order is $10, and the cost of carrying a unit in inventory for one year is 50 cents.

a. Compute the square root estimate of Q.

b. Compute the order point.

c. Compute the optimum order size after iterating (see the appendix for this chapter).

d. Compute the total cost of the initial order size and reorder point.

e. Compute the total cost of the optimum order size and reorder point.

8–20. The order-processing cost for an item is $50. Annual demand is 10,000 units. The item unit cost is $5; inventory holding cost is 20 percent per dollar per year.

a. Compute the economic order quantity in units.

b. Suppose the replenishment lead time is two weeks. Weekly demand averages 200 units (assume 50 weeks a year) with a standard deviation of 41 units; assume weekly demands are normally distributed and mutually independent. Management has determined that a unit backordered has a penalty cost of $3. Determine the optimal reorder point (R).

c. An analyst no longer with the company has previously recommended a reorder point of 603 units. What unit penalty cost (k_u) is implied by such a value for the reorder point?

8–21. An item is replenished 10 times per year, on the average. The annual unit holding cost is one-half the unit cost of being short. Weekly demand is normally distributed with a mean of 100 and a standard deviation of 20.

a. Compute the desired probability of not running out of stock during a lead time.

b. Suppose the replenishment lead time is *four* weeks. Compute the optimum order point.

8–22. Refer to Problem 8–21. Suppose that an error is made in estimating one of the values used to compute the order point. Specifically, suppose that a 50 percent error is made in estimating the shortage cost, with the result that the ratio k_c/k_u is erroneous.

a. Suppose the erroneous ratio is $k_c/k_u = 1.0$ instead of the true value of one-half. Compute the probability of not running out of stock during a lead time and the associated order point.

b. Suppose the erroneous ratio is $k_c/k_u = 1/4$. Again, compute the probability of not running out, and the order point.

c. Comment on the relative sensitivity of the order quantity versus the order point.

8–23. An item averages 2,400 demands annually. The lead time is one month; the standard deviation of monthly demand is 50 units. The order quantity is 300 units; management desires that 99 percent of demands be met from stock.

a. What is the optimal order point?

b. Suppose management wanted a 98 percent service level. What is the optimal order point?

c. If management were satisfied with a 90 percent service level, what would the optimal order point be?

8–24. A wholesaler of stationery is deciding how many desk calendars to stock for the coming year. It is impossible to reorder, and leftover units are worthless. The following table indicates the possible demand levels and the wholesaler's prior probabilities:

Demand (in 000s)	*Probability of Demand*
100	0.10
200	0.15
300	0.50
400	0.25
	1.00

The calendars sell for $100 per thousand, and the incremental purchase cost is $70. The incremental cost of selling (commissions) is $5 per thousand.

a. Use the analysis of this chapter to find how many calendars should be ordered.

b. Check this calculation by preparing conditional and expected value tables and computing expected values for each act.

c. How much of an ill-will cost would have to exist to justify an order of 400,000 calendars?

8–25. Demand for a product is approximately normal with mean 40 units and standard deviation 12 units. The product costs $2 per unit and sells for $5. Unsold units have no value.

a. Assuming there is no goodwill loss due to unfilled demand, what is the optimum order size?

b. Suppose that the manager in charge of the product has usually ordered 60 units. She defends the policy on the ground that there is loss of customer goodwill associated with unfilled demand. What is the implied goodwill loss associated with the manager's policy?

8–26. A camera manufacturer makes most of its sales during the Christmas selling season. For each camera sold, it makes a unit profit of $20; if a camera is unsold after the major selling season, it must be sold at a reduced price, which is $5 less than the variable cost of manufacturing the camera. The manufacturer estimates that demand is normally distributed with a mean of 10,000 units and a standard deviation of 1,000 units.

a. Ignoring ill-will costs of a stockout, what is the optimum order size?

b. What ill-will cost per stockout would justify an order size of 11,500 units?

8–27. The Green Garden Store must order its allotment of spring plants by March 23 (there is no opportunity to reorder later in the season). Due to the impending drought, Green Garden has revised its sales forecast downward and now expects to sell about $100,000 (retail) worth of spring plants; the standard deviation of forecast error for this forecast is 15 percent (i.e., $15,000). Assume forecast errors are normally distributed.

For every $1 of retail sales, the store pays $0.30 for plants that it purchases wholesale. Leftover plants after the selling season cannot be sold; furthermore, Green Garden must pay to have them removed, at a cost of $0.05 per $1 retail sales value. All other costs of operating the store are unaffected by the sales volume that materializes.

In retail dollars' worth, how many dollars' worth of spring plants should the store order?

8–28. The Peninsula Pumpkin Store (PPS) purchases pumpkins for resale prior to Halloween. PPS sells pumpkins for $0.50 per pound, while its wholesale purchase cost is $0.30 per pound. Its suppliers require firm orders by September 1, so PPS must make a commitment before demand is known. As of September 1, PPS forecasts pumpkin demand at 10,000 pounds; its forecast error is normally distributed with a standard deviation equal to 15 percent of its forecast. Forecasts have been unbiased, however. Leftover pumpkins (after Halloween) can be sold for an average of $0.20 per pound without limit on volume. Customer orders that cannot be filled are assumed lost.

a. What total amount of pumpkins should PPS order on September 1?

b. Assume that PPS has found a backup supplier who will fill subsequent replenishment orders *immediately*, so that if PPS begins to run out of pumpkins, it can reorder in small quantities as needed from the second suppliers. (PPS continues to use the original supplier for its initial order.) The new supplier charges $0.42 per pound for this expedited service, and guarantees supply.

Now, what is the desired initial purchase order on September 1?

More Challenging Problems

8–29. Consider Equation 8–1, total annual cost, and Equation 8–2, the economic order quantity formula. Suppose an error in data gathering creates an erroneous Q that is 20 percent smaller than the "true" Q^* (i.e., $Q_{error} = 0.80\ Q^*$). Substitute this error back into Equation 8–1 and find the percentage cost penalty that results from the 20 percent error in Q. (*Hint:* Use the fact that with the optimum Q^* the two terms of Equation 8–1 are equal, and each is one-half of optimal (minimum) total annual cost.)

8–30 A company uses 2,000 units of a product each year (constant usage). The product is purchased from a supplier at a unit cost of $4; however, the company must pay the freight from the supplier's plant. Each unit weighs 5 pounds; the shipping cost is 20 cents per pound. The company estimates the order-processing cost is $25 per order; inventory holding costs are 20 percent per dollar per year.

a. Find the optimal order quantity.

b. Suppose that for shipments above 300 pounds but less than 10,000 pounds, a flat charge of $50 *per shipment* (not per pound) is charged, while for shipments below 300 pounds that rate remains at 20 cents per pound. Now, what order quantity should be used to minimize the sum of all relevant variable costs?

8–31. The Bancroft Press publishes a wide variety of books. One of their steady sellers is *Imaginative Cooking,* now in its fourth edition. Bancroft expects that the next edition of this book will sell approximately 12,500 copies annually for the next few years.

In past years, Bancroft has always printed and bound a one-year supply of this type of book. Recently, increased inventory costs have forced a reconsideration of this policy. In particular, Bancroft is considering binding only half the printing quantity at the time of printing, and keeping the remaining printed sheets as unbound stock. When needed, the remaining half of the lot would be bound.

Costs are as follows (omitting typesetting costs, distribution costs, and other costs not affected by this decision):

	Printing	*Binding*
Setup cost	$5,000	$1,000
Variable cost per unit	4	2

Bancroft now charges inventory at 25 percent per dollar per year.

a. If a complete printing lot is bound at time of printing, what is the optimal quantity? What are the total annual costs?

b. If only half the printed quantity is bound, what is the optimal quantity to print? What are the total annual costs?

8–32. The ACME Dairy produces 15 flavors of ice cream, each of which is packaged in pints, quarts, and half gallons. Change-over time for packing *size* is two hours, and the variable cost associated with this changeover is $80. Cleanout from one *flavor* to another takes 30 minutes, with a variable cost of $20. The amount of ice cream produced and packaged in one hour of run time is approximately 1,000 gallons (irrespective of flavor or package size), and the variable cost associated with that amount of product (materials plus direct labor) is $500. Inventory holding cost is 25 percent per dollar per year.

a. Should ACME produce all sizes of a given flavor before changing to the next flavor, or should it produce all flavors in a given size before changing to the next size? Why?

b. Suppose demand in gallons for each combination of flavor and size (45 products) is identical, equaling 40,000 gallons a year each. Assume there are 2,200 hours the dairy is in operation annually. What is the economic batch size in which all of the products should be produced?

c. The union has recently negotiated a new contract with ACME that limits operating hours to 1,940 hours per year (and no overtime is allowed). What effect will this restriction have, if any, on your answer to (*b*)? What cost, if any, has this restriction placed on ACME?

8–33. Complex wood shapes used to form a bookcase are produced on an expensive automatic shaping machine. In order to set up the machine to produce the shapes, a cost of $500 is incurred. Once the machine is set up, it produces shapes at a rate of 200 bookcases per day at a cost of $5 (including raw materials) per bookcase. After the shapes are produced, they must be assembled. The first-line supervisor feels there is some "setup" time involved in assembly, due to the learning curve phenomenon whereby each successive bookcase in an assembly batch is assembled more rapidly than the last. He estimates this effect can be represented by a $50 assembly setup charge. Once assembly of bookcases begins, the assembly rate is 100 bookcases per day; the cost of the finished bookcase is $15 (including the $5 cost of the shaped parts).

Annual demand for bookcases is constant at 2,500 bookcases. Holding cost is 20 percent per dollar per year.

a. Suppose the shaper department is separate from the assembly department and is separately controlled financially. If you were to set the production run size for the *shaper,* ignoring the fact that your product is only an intermediate one, how would you set it?

b. If you were to determine the *assembly* lot size without regard to the shaping department, how would you set it?

c. The supervisor has said, "Unassembled shaped pieces do us no good. Whenever the shaper is run, we should run the entire quantity of shaped pieces through the assembly stage into finished-goods inventory so they will be useful to us." Given this suggested policy, what is the economic *quantity* in which shapes and assembled bookcases should be produced?

8–34. A firm has a choice of manufacturing a part internally or purchasing it from an outside supplier. The variable cost per unit is the same in either case. However, if the part is made internally, there is a setup cost of $100. If the part is purchased, there is a fixed order cost of $20. If the part is made internally, there is zero lead time; if purchased from outside, the lead time is 25 days (usage during the lead time is normally distributed with a mean of 100 units and a standard deviation of 20 units). The cost of carrying one unit in inventory is $2 per year. The cost of being short one unit is $18 (this is k_u). Annual requirements for this part are 1,000 units.

Should the firm make this part internally or purchase it on the outside? What other considerations besides inventory costs would actually go into a decision of this type?

8–35. A vaccine marketed by a drug company has a known and constant demand of 1,200 units per year (or 100 a month). The production cost is $120 per unit, the setup cost is $400 per batch, and the holding cost of inventory is 20 percent per year. Lead time for production is constant and known (one month).

a. What is the economic production quantity per batch?

b. The company has recently discovered that its vaccine has a shelf life of only 1.5 months. Determine the lowest-cost production strategy for this situation (i.e., that which minimizes total costs of setup, holding, and spoilage).

c. Now assume that the company's demand averages 100 units per month, but is no longer constant. The demand is normally distributed, with standard deviation of 20. The unit cost of a shortage is $640 (lost profit plus ill will). Ignoring the shelf-life problem of (*b*), what is the optimal inventory policy?

8–36. Aggregated Air Lines (AAL) maintains spare parts to repair jet engines, which fail randomly. As an example, consider part #7654, one of which is on each engine of a Boeing 747. When engines are brought to the maintenance base for disassembly, diagnosis, and repair, this part is examined carefully and is diagnosed as "needing repair" if necessary. Failures of this part per month occur according to a normal distribution with a mean of 5 and a standard deviation of 1.5.

The setup time for repair is very small compared with the value of the part itself, so whenever a part needs repair, it is sent to the repair shop (i.e., no "batching" takes place). Assume the repair shop takes exactly three months to repair this part. Suppose the airline has a target inventory of 30 spare parts; then the 30 parts must be able to cope with random demand over a three-month replenishment cycle or there will be a stockout.

AAL has determined that the cost of a shortage is $50 (this is the cost of expediting the delivery of a spare part from Boeing). You are asked to review its target number of 30 spares. How would you determine the optimal target quantity if the parts cost $125 each and annual inventory holding cost is 25 percent per year?

8–37. Refer to Problem 8–20. Suppose that for an annual fee of $100, it is possible to reduce the replenishment lead time from two weeks to one week to implement the just-in-time concept.

a. Assuming the fee is paid, compute the new economic order quantity (Q).

b. Assuming the fee is paid, compute the new optimal reorder point (R).

c. Compute the reduction in safety stock both in units and in dollars. Should the firm pay the fee? Explain.

8–38. The Friendly Computer Store currently orders packages of floppy disks from its suppliers. Orders are received one month after they are placed. The unit cost of a package of disks is $3; annual inventory holding costs are 25 percent; the unit shortage cost for being stocked out of a package is assessed as $7. Monthly demand for packages of disks is a normally distributed random variable with a mean of 1,000 packages and a standard deviation of 200 packages.

a. A new employee has asked what the order-processing cost is to order disks; she is told it is $5. She then proposes that the company adopt a continuous review policy of the type described in this chapter. What would the optimal values for Q and R be for such a policy?

b. A second new employee discovered that the $5 order-processing cost can be reduced to $1 if the store is willing to invest $100 in a software package for order processing. Analyze whether or not the investment should be made.

8–39. An item has a unit cost of $20 when purchased under normal replenishment conditions involving a two-week lead time. If a stockout threatens an immediate emergency replenishment can be obtained by paying $22 per unit (i.e., a $2 premium cost) and ordering units as needed (one unit at a time) when inventory falls to zero. There is no order-processing cost when ordering emergency replenishments; the order-processing cost for normal replenishments is $20 per order. Carrying costs are 25 percent annually. Annual demand averages 10,400 units; weekly demand is normally distributed with a mean of 200 units and a standard deviation of 30 units.

a. Compute the desired replenishment quantity and reorder point for normal replenishments.

b. Suppose that the option of immediate emergency replenishment is no longer available. Also, suppose the company must satisfy 98 percent of demand off-the-shelf without backorder. What should the reorder point be now?

8–40. Consider the data for the six items listed in Table 8–10.

a. Use a spreadsheet to calculate the individual reorder points for each item in order to achieve a 98 percent service level for each item. Then sum the investment in safety stock inventory for all six items taken together.

TABLE 8–10 (for Problem 8–40)

Weekly Demand	Lead Time (weeks)	Standard Deviation of Weekly Demand	Unit Cost	Order Quantity
10	3	1.1	$400	9
15	5	1.3	75	26
1,000	2	120	3	1,075
50	2	6	150	34
75	3	9	30	93
100	5	12	1,000	19

b. Repeat part (*a*) for the following service levels: 97 percent, 96 percent, and 95 percent. Plot your results on a trade-off curve showing how total safety stock inventory investment varies with the service level desired.

8–41. Consider Problem 8–40.

a. By trial and error, find a set of safety stock levels for these six items that has a weighted-average fill rate of 98 percent or better and that has lower inventory investment in safety stock.

b. Now apply a common cost of shortage k_u to this data. For each possible value of k_u, calculate both the weighted-average service level and also the total investment in safety stock. By trial and error, find k_u values that correspond approximately to the following weighted-average service levels: 98 percent, 97 percent, 96 percent, and 95 percent. Plot your results on a trade-off curve. Contrast these results with those of problem 8–40, part (*b*).

8–42. Consider the supply chain example in this chapter, but now assume all three countries (France, Germany, and Spain) have mean weekly demand of 500 and standard deviation of 200.

a. Calculate the required safety stock under a separate-products policy providing 95 percent service.

b. Calculate the required safety stock under a generic-product policy providing 95 percent service.

c. Calculate the required safety stock under a generic-product policy providing 97 percent service.

d. Now assume there are 10 identical countries (rather than three). Repeat parts (*a*), (*b*), and (*c*) for this situation. What happens to the magnitude of the improvement due to risk pooling when the number of items pooled increases from 3 to 10?

8–43. The ACME Company produces air conditioners. Due to limited production capacity and the desire to maintain steady employment throughout the year, production of particular models must be determined prior to the heavy summer selling season. The junior model costs $60 to produce (incremental cost) and sells for $100, while the super model costs $120 to produce and sells for $210. Any units unsold at the end of the summer must be sold for a sacrifice price of 80 percent of the incremental production cost.

Seasonal demand for the junior model is estimated as normal, with a mean of 10,000 and a standard deviation of 3,000; for the super model, estimated demand is normal with a mean of 6,000 and standard deviation of 2,000. The company feels that since the two models sell in different price ranges, the demands are independent.

a. Ignoring ill-will costs, compute optimal production sizes for the two models.

b. Suppose that the demands are no longer independent. As an extreme case, suppose that the number of units of the super model sold is precisely 60 percent of the number of units of the junior model sold. Also, suppose the mean sales of the junior model are estimated to be 10,000, with a standard deviation of 3,000 (ignore the other mean and standard deviation). Now, compute the optimal order size. (*Hint:* Given the strict dependence assumed, consider a *composite product* that contains 1 unit of the junior and 0.6 unit of a super.)

8–44. The Cox Photo Company is a mail-order firm specializing in 24-hour service on special photo developing and making presentation quality slides and prints. The general policy is that orders arriving in the morning mail must be finished and in the outgoing mail before the midnight mail pickup. This has usually involved little difficulty. Six full-time technicians work an eight-hour day from 8 AM to 5 PM and are paid at a rate of $12 per hour (including fringe benefits). These technicians can process an average of five orders an hour. When, on occasion, more than about 240 orders arrive on a given day, one or more of the technicians work overtime at a rate of $16 per hour.

Cox Photo has recently bought out a competitor in the same community and plans to consolidate operations. Mr. Cox is undecided, however, on how many technicians to add to the six he now employs. By adding together the past order data of his competitor to his, Mr. Cox has the following frequency data to ponder.

Number of Incoming Orders	*Fraction of Days*
Under 220	0.03
220–39	0.03
240–59	0.09
260–79	0.16
280–99	0.18
300–19	0.20
320–39	0.15
340–59	0.10
360–79	0.05
380 and above	0.01
	1.00

One of the technicians at Cox Photo was taking a night course in statistics at a local college and tried her hand at analyzing the above data. She told Mr. Cox that the data closely fit a normal distribution, with a mean of 300 and a standard deviation of 40; but she was unable to answer the question of how many to employ.

a. How many technicians should Cox employ? What is the expected cost?
b. What additional factors should be included in making this decision?

8–45. The ABC Office Supply Company maintains a spare parts warehouse in Alaska to support its office equipment maintenance needs. Once every six months, a major shipment of replenishment parts is shipped from the contiguous United States to Alaska. Between these planned shipments, emergency air shipments are used as needed to resupply spare parts when inventory falls short of demand.

ABC must determine the optimal inventory level for its spare parts. As an example, part #123456 has exhibited demand over past six-month intervals that is normally distributed with a mean of 100 and a standard deviation of 10. The cost of overage per unit (representing the cost of inventorying the unneeded item for six months) is $5; the incremental production and shipping cost of the item is $40 per unit.

ABC is having difficulty determining its underage cost per unit, for two reasons. First, it prices spare parts at cost and does not take any markup on them. Second, it will always satisfy demand, using the emergency air shipments to resupply if demand exceeds inventory. Emergency air shipments have a cost per unit shipped of $25 above normal shipping costs.

What should the optimal target inventory for this part be?

8–46. You are in charge of the annual banquet for the Football Boosters Club at your college. Although a large attendance is expected, you will not know until the evening of the banquet exactly how many dinners will be served. Your arrangement with the hotel where the banquet is being held provides that one week before the banquet, you must make a commitment for the number of dinners. The price for these dinners will be $21 each. If fewer people show up than the committed number, you are still required to pay for the full number. If more people attend than your committed number, they will be served at a cost of $36 each. For example, if you commit for 200 people and 200 or fewer show up, you still have to pay $4,200. If more than 200 attend, you pay $4,200 plus $36 for each dinner in excess of 200.

Your judgment about the number attending can be described by a normal probability distribution with mean of 400 people and standard deviation of 100.

a. Suppose the cost of the banquet is being borne entirely by the Alumni Association, and your objective is to minimize the cost, given that all who attend will be served. How big a prior commitment for dinners should you make to the hotel?
b. Suppose there is a charge of $30 for every person attending. Your objective is to maximize the profit from the banquet. In this case, how large a prior commitment should you make to the hotel?

8–47. The Dresden Glass Company (DGC) produces high-quality decorative glass sculptures and distributes the products through department and specialty stores catering to the upper-income segment of the market. Virtually all orders and shipments take place in October, in preparation for the retail Christmas-gift market. All items left unsold at the retailer level in January are returned to DGC for full credit, but the retailer pays the freight cost for the returns.

The economics for item #123C are as follows:

Standard manufacturing cost (per piece):	
Raw materials	$ 5.00
Direct labor	30.00
Variable overhead	5.00
Allocated overhead	15.00
Standard cost	55.00
Wholesale selling price from DGC to retailer	85.00
Retail selling price	170.00
Freight cost for returns from retailer to DGC (5 percent of $85)	4.25

If any retailer stocks out of this item, the unfilled orders are "lost" (as opposed to the customer waiting or buying a different gift item from the retailer). They are willing to ignore ill will but are not willing to ignore forgone profit.

What inventory level should a retailer have for DGC item #123C if mean seasonal demand is estimated at 100 units and the standard deviation is 20 units? (Assume a normally distributed random variable).

8–48. The Wyler Wine Company produces champagne fermented in the bottle. The fermentation process takes one year. The variable cost of initially producing a case of champagne (*not* including holding cost for the one-year fermentation period) is $10. The net selling price wholesalers pay is $18 per case. Cases unsold after their "target" year (year 1) are carried over into the next year, with no degradation in quality; however, money continues to be tied up in inventory. The company estimates inventory holding costs are 20 percent per dollar per year. Since the grapes ripen only once a year in the company's upstate New York location, Wyler must make a production commitment once a year for the entire amount of champagne it plans to produce.

Wyler's decision for this year's production (for next year's sales) is approaching. The marketing forecast for next year's sales is 100,000 cases ($\sigma = 8{,}000$); anticipated inventory carryover is 15,000 cases. No ill-will costs are assessed for out-of-stock situations, but profit is forgone in those instances.

How many cases should the company plan to produce?

8–49. The Alpine Valley Ski Area (AVSA) must make a decision at 5 PM each afternoon whether to call in crews for snowmaking that evening or not. Snowmaking beings at 11 PM and continues until 3 AM. However, snowmaking requires the temperature to be no higher than 27 degrees Fahrenheit. If, at 11 PM, the temperature is above 27 degrees, AVSA must pay its crews but does not make any snow; the cost to pay the crews is $1,000 per night. If AVSA decides at 5 PM not to make snow, but the temperature falls below 27 degrees at 11 PM, AVSA recognizes that it has lost an evening's opportunity to make snow, which has a gross value estimated at $4,000, and a net value (after paying the crews) of $3,000.

AVSA uses the following forecasting rule: forecasted temperature at 11 PM is equal to temperature at 5 PM less 10 degrees. A historical comparison of forecasted and actual 11 PM temperatures indicates that these forecasts are unbiased and that forecast errors are normally distributed with a standard deviation of 9 degrees.

What cutoff temperature at 5 PM should AVSA use in making its decision?

Hint: Find the desired probability (i.e., the optimal target gamble) that the crews will not be called when they would have been able to make snow.

8–50. An airline has found that the number of people not showing up for a flight (no-shows) is normally distributed with a mean of 20 and a standard deviation of 10. The airline estimates the opportunity cost of an empty seat to be $100; the ill-will and penalty costs associated with not being able to board a passenger holding a confirmed reservation are estimated to be $400.

The airline wishes to set a limit on "overbooking" for this flight. There are 150 seats. What should be its upper cutoff on confirmed reservations? Why?

Solutions to Practice Problems

8–1. *a.* The ranked data are: 530, 320, 225, 170, 125, 94, 70, 49, 30, 2. Cumulative data are: 530, 850, 1,075, 1,245, 1,370, 1,464, 1,534, 1,583, 1,613, 1,615. See the plot of cumulative data in Figure 8–14.

Note: After the total cumulative sales data of $1,615 are plotted, the vertical scale can be labeled 100 percent and then divided into percentages as shown.

b. 4,000/20,000 = 20 percent of the items; in the sample, this represents 850/1,615 = 52.6 percent of sales.

c. About 85 percent of dollar sales.

d. In the sample ABC curve, the point representing 50 percent of sales falls between items with sales of 530 and 320, but is very close to the latter. Hence, we might say any item with sales above 350 would be classified as an A item. We could similarly note that at the 50 percent point on the item scale, the sales rate is 125, and use 125 as the upper limit on the C items, although a slightly more accurate method would be to average the data points (125, 94) as an estimate of the median sales rate of the sample; this averaging would produce 109.5 as the upper limit on C items. B items would be between these values.

8–2. *a.* $Q = \sqrt{\dfrac{2DK}{k_c}} = \sqrt{\dfrac{2 \cdot 100{,}000 \cdot 60}{3}} = \sqrt{4 \cdot 10^6}$

$= 2{,}000$ units

FIGURE 8–14

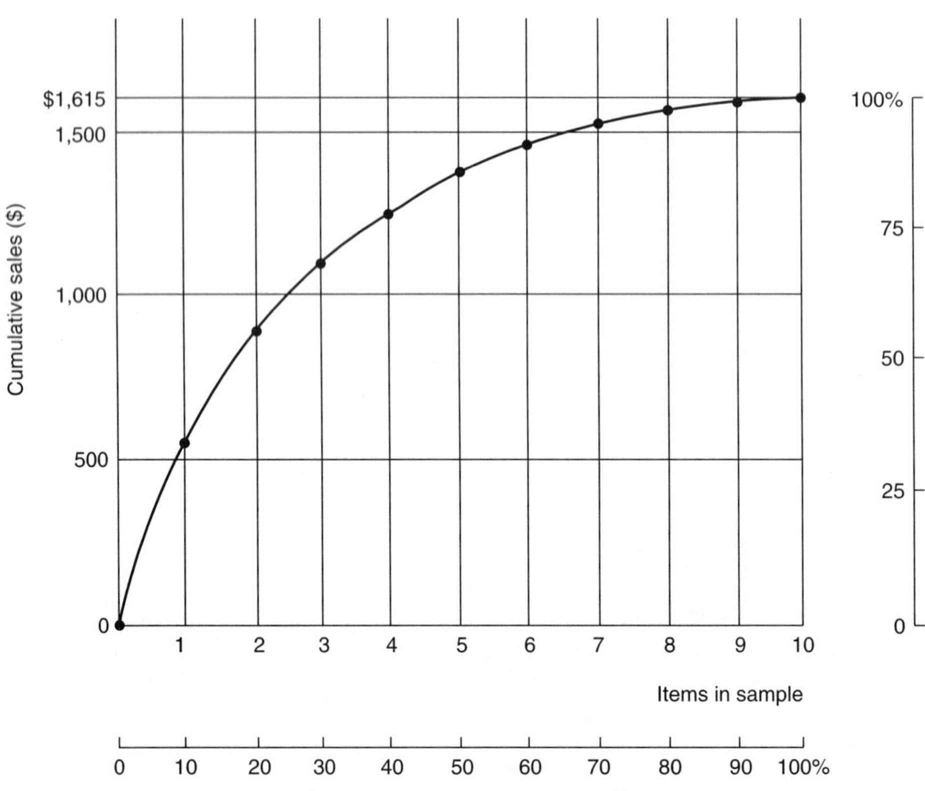

b. $Q = \sqrt{\dfrac{2 \cdot 100{,}000 \cdot 0.60}{3}} = \sqrt{40{,}000} = \sqrt{4 \cdot 10^4}$

$= 200$ units

Note: Daily use is 100,000/360 = 277 units per day. Would we order 200 or 277, or more?

8–3. *a.* $Q = \sqrt{\dfrac{2 \cdot 100{,}000 \cdot 15}{3}} = \sqrt{1{,}000{,}000}$

$= 1{,}000$ units

b. The total cost using the original ordering cost is, using Equation 8–1:

$$TC(Q = 2{,}000) = \frac{2{,}000}{2}(3) + \frac{100{,}000}{2{,}000}(60)$$

$$= 3{,}000 + 3{,}000 = \$6{,}000$$

The total cost using the new reduced ordering cost is:

$$TC(Q = 1{,}000) = \frac{1{,}000}{2}(3) + \frac{100{,}000}{1{,}000}(15)$$

$$= 1{,}500 + 1{,}500 = \$3{,}000$$

The reduction in costs is $6,000 − $3,000 = $3,000; since this $3,000 reduction exceeds the membership fee of $2,000, the company should join the co-op and order in batches of $Q = 1{,}000$ units.

8–4. $Q = \sqrt{\dfrac{2KD}{k_c}} = \sqrt{\dfrac{2(1{,}000)(1{,}200)}{20}} = 346$

$$F(R) = 1 - \frac{k_c Q}{k_u D} = 1 - \frac{20(346)}{200(1{,}200)} = .9712$$

From Table A, this corresponds to a $Z = 1.90$

$R = \text{mean} + Z\sigma = 100 + 1.90(40) = 176$

8–5. *a.* From Equation 8–10, $\dfrac{Q(1-P)}{\sigma_M} = \dfrac{200(.01)}{30}$

$= 0.0667$

from Table B, $Z = 1.11$, so $R = 100 + 1.11(30) = 133.3$ or 134

b. Similarly, $\dfrac{200(.02)}{30} = 0.1333$; from Table B, $Z = 0.74$, so:

$R = 100 + .74(30) = 122.2$ or 123

c. Similarly, $\frac{200(.10)}{30} = 0.667$

Since this exceeds the upper limit of Table B (.3989), this means that $Z = 0$ and R is set equal to $\overline{M}$ of 100. The stated service level will actually be exceeded, due to the size of the order quantity.

8–6.

Sales	$P(X = x)$	$P(X \geq x)$
0	0.05	1.00
1	0.15	.95
2	0.30	.80
3	0.35	.50
4	0.10	.15
5	0.05	.05
6	0.00	.00

a. $c_o = \$10; c_u = \$40$

$$P_c = \frac{c_o}{c_u + c_o} = \frac{10}{40 + 10} = .20$$

Three units should be ordered: $p_c = .20 > .15$; $p_c = .20 < .50$, where .15 is the probability that demand is four units or more, and .50 is the probability that demand is three units or more.

b. $c_u = \$40 + 20 = \$60; C_o = \$10$

$$p_c = \frac{c_o}{c_o + c_u} = \frac{10}{70} = .143$$

Four units should be ordered: $p_c = .14 < .15.$; $p_c = .14 > .05$

8–7. Note: Assume that the purchase cost of $50 is lost if an item is not sold, but the remaining incremental cost of $20 is not incurred unless the item is sold.

$p_c = \frac{c_o}{c_o + c_u}$; $c_o = \$50 - 10 = \$40$; $c_u = (\$100 - 70) + 50 = \$80$:

$$p_c = \frac{40}{40 + 80} = \frac{40}{120} = .33; Z = .44 \text{ standard deviations}$$

$140 + .44(20) = 140 + 8.8 = 148.8$ optimum order size

8–8. $140 + .44(50) = 140 + 22 = 162$ optimum order size. Note the increase in optimum order size caused by the increase in the standard deviation of the sales distribution. See Problem 8–9 for another comparison.

8–9. $p_c = \frac{c_o}{c_o + c_u} = \frac{40}{40 + 30} = .571$

a. $Z = .18$; $140 - .18(20) = 140 - 3.6 = 136.4$

b. $140 - .18(50) = 140 - 9 = 131.0$

Note: In this problem, the larger standard deviation decreased the order size; in Problem 8–8, the larger deviation increased the optimum order size. The effect depends on whether $p_c > .50$ or $p_c < .50$.

Motivating Example

Appointment Scheduling at Lourdes Hospital[1]

Lourdes Hospital in Binghamton, New York, created a centralized system to schedule appointments for hospital services. Telephone calls arrived at the scheduling center from individuals (outpatients and inpatients) as well as from physicians and hospital staff. Appointments were arranged for hospital services, including, for example, X ray, various laboratory services, and physical therapy.

Although the system was effective for coordinating the schedule of patients through a set of related appointments, the hospital was receiving many complaints about the busy signals encountered when calling into the system. Patients and physicians alike were frustrated about the delays.

Because this was an important activity, the hospital set as a goal that 90 percent or more of the calls should be answered immediately. A study of the system was also initiated in which the number of calls arriving in the system at various times of the day was measured.

Using the simple queuing models presented in this chapter, the hospital staff manager was able to determine the staffing needed to satisfy the goal for each of various time periods during the day. She was then able to rearrange the staffing schedule to meet these requirements. The result was a reduction of complaints about telephone delays to almost zero, without an increase in the staff required.

---

[1]See S. R. Agnihothri and P. F. Taylor, "Staffing a Centralized Appointment Scheduling Department at Lourdes Hospital," *Interfaces* 21, no. 5 (September–October 1991).

CHAPTER

9 QUEUING THEORY

Congestion in Processing Systems

Queues or waiting lines are very common in everyday life. There are few individuals in modern society who have not had to wait in line for a bus, a taxi, a movie ticket, a grocery checkout, a haircut, or registration material at the beginning of a school year. The system becomes congested and we wait. Most of us consider congestion with more or less good humor. Occasionally, the size of a line we encounter discourages us, we abandon the activity, and a sale is lost. This chapter is concerned with the decision-making process of the business firm (or government agency) that has charge of the operation of these systems and makes decisions relative to the number and capacity of service facilities and the scheduling of jobs in the system.

Systems such as described above are commonly called *queuing systems.* But a better term is *processing systems.* This broader term includes factories in which jobs move through several steps in the process of being manufactured, or offices in which paperwork (for example, a loan application in a bank) is handled by several individuals or committees. These are *networks of queues.* It also includes *loss systems* in which there is no queue at all. An example is a telephone reservation system with no "on-hold" feature; a customer who gets a busy signal cannot enter the system and is *lost.* The basic ideas of this chapter apply to all processing systems, whether they be simple queuing systems, loss systems, or more complicated processing systems.

Queuing theory is primarily concerned with processes that have variability in arrivals of *jobs* into the system. For example, jobs can be people needing service, manufacturing jobs, paper flows (e.g., applications for credit), or equipment needing repair. The time taken to service these jobs is also generally variable. The result is congestion or waiting lines. This can be measured by the average number of jobs in the queue and by the average waiting time of arrivals. There are costs associated with having jobs wait. There are also costs associated with adding more service capacity. The management challenge is to balance these costs.

Queuing theory may be used to determine the optimum number of:

- Toll booths for a bridge or toll road.
- Doctors available for clinic calls.
- Repair persons servicing machines.

- Landing strips for aircraft.
- Docks for ships.
- Paramedic units available for emergency calls.
- Clerks for a spare-parts counter.
- Service windows for a post office.

It may also be used to aid in decisions about:

- The order in which customers should be processed (should there be an express lane?).
- The scheduling of jobs through a manufacturing facility.
- Increasing the service speed of certain operations (by automation, for example).
- The value of reengineering whole processes.

An Example of a Processing System

Suppose you are operating a medical care center for a large factory. Workers come to the center if they become ill during working hours or if they have an accident requiring medical care. Table 9–1 is a history of 30 workers arriving at the clinic over a period of about eight hours. The left part of the table shows the actual times of arrival, when the patients actually started service (met with the doctor), and when they were finished. The numbers at the right are calculated from these data: the length of waiting line ahead of the arrival (excluding the person being serviced), the interarrival time (time since prior arrival), the actual time taken to service the patient, and the amount of time each patient spent waiting (not including service time).

Note that there is considerably variability in arrival patterns and in service time needed. For example, seven patients arrived in the hour between 13:00 to 14:00 (1 to 2 PM), and yet there was only one arrival in the hour between 10:00 and 11:00. Similarly, some patients needed only 6 or 7 minutes of service time, while one patient took 19 minutes.

As can be seen, the first arrivals had zero or short waits. However, after patient number 11, the line and waiting times began to build up. Several arrivals had to wait more than 50 minutes, and the waiting line built up to as many as 6 patients by the time patient 26 arrived. But the line shortened again, so that patient number 30 had a short wait.

Table 9–1 illustrates patterns that are typical in most queuing systems. There is variability in the interarrival times and in the service times for patients, and this results in lines and waits for service. Note that while the average waiting time was 28.4 minutes, this number doesn't fully capture the waiting time pattern. Eight of the 30 arrivals had to wait 50 minutes or more, and three people an hour or more.

In terms of service capacity, note that the table covered a period of 7 hours and 54 minutes—474 minutes. The average service time was 12.1 minutes. Thus, the total service time for all 30 arrivals was $30 \cdot 12.1 = 363$ minutes. Capacity utilization was thus $363/474 = 77$ percent. The clinic was servicing patients only about three-fourths of the time. And yet there was substantial congestion with long waits for patients.

TABLE 9–1
Factory Medical Clinic Example

Patient Number	*Arrival Time*	*Start Service Time*	*Finish Service Time*	*Length of Queue*	*Time Since Prior Arrival (minutes)*	*Service Time (minutes)*	*Waiting Time (minutes)*
0	8:00						
1	8:07	8:07	8:13	0	7	6	0
2	8:11	8:13	8:28	0	4	15	2
3	8:19	8:28	8:40	0	8	12	9
4	8:46	8:46	8:58	0	27	12	0
5	9:06	9:06	9:22	0	20	16	0
6	9:49	9:49	9:56	0	43	7	0
7	9:51	9:56	10:11	0	2	15	5
8	10:06	10:11	10:21	0	15	10	5
9	11:24	11:24	11:30	0	78	6	0
10	11:31	11:31	11:47	0	7	16	0
11	11:35	11:47	12:04	0	4	17	12
12	11:41	12:04	12:19	1	6	15	23
13	11:52	12:19	12:35	1	11	16	27
14	12:02	12:35	12:48	2	10	13	33
15	12:12	12:48	13:07	2	10	19	36
16	12:39	13:07	13:24	1	27	17	28
17	12:40	13:24	13:40	2	1	16	44
18	12:45	13:40	13:49	3	5	9	55
19	12:59	13:49	13:59	3	14	10	50
20	13:02	13:59	14:06	4	3	7	57
21	13:29	14:06	14:16	3	27	10	37
22	13:42	14:16	14:23	3	13	7	34
23	13:46	14:23	14:34	4	4	11	37
24	13:48	14:34	14:46	5	2	12	46
25	13:52	14:46	14:58	5	4	12	54
26	13:54	14:58	15:10	6	2	12	64
27	14:15	15:10	15:18	5	21	8	55
28	14:18	15:18	15:30	5	3	12	60
29	14:23	15:30	15:39	5	5	9	67
30	15:27	15:39	15:54	1	64	15	12
Average				2.0	14.9	12.1	28.4

Experience and Queues

Fortunately for the busy manager, reasonable decisions about processing systems can frequently be based on past experience or on the facts of the current situation. Thus, the management of a grocery chain knows approximately how many check-out counters should be installed in a new store by looking at the experience of comparable stores. At any time of the day, the store manager can tell how many of the installed counters should be open by noting the lengths of the queues and adding personnel from other chores, or sending the present check-out personnel to other tasks. Similarly, the manager of a medical clinic such as illustrated in Table 9–1 could use past experience as an aid in scheduling staffing for the clinic.

Although a number of problems encountered by an executive can be reasonably solved by the use of intuition or past experience, there will be many situations that are too complex for our intuition. In these situations, the problem can be approached by either simulation or by a mathematical model procedure. In this chapter, we examine several mathematical models of processing systems. A later chapter demonstrates how simulation can be used to study more complex systems.

System Structure

Processing systems may be distinguished from one another in many different ways. The most important structural distinctions and some of the common measures of system performance are:

Loss Systems versus Queuing Systems

Loss systems are those in which arrivals into the system (customers calling, for example) simply exit the system when they encounter delay. In queuing systems, arrivals wait in line for service. Of course, there can be systems that mix these two elements—potential customers may leave the system (called *balking*) if the waiting line is too long, for example.

Arrivals

Jobs come into the system for service. Jobs may be people, machines needing repair, telephone calls to be answered, manufacturing orders to be filled, mortgage applications to be approved, or, as in the example in Table 9–1, patients arriving at a medical center. They may come singly or in batches; they may come evenly spaced in time or in a random pattern; they may come from an infinite or very large population of possible arrivals (all the people in a city) or from a finite set (for example, the 10 machines in a shop that might break down and need repair).

Services

Each job must be serviced. This may mean making an airline reservation for a person, manufacturing a part, repairing a broken machine, or dispatching fire trucks to put out a fire. The service time required may be the same for each job, or service times may vary considerably in a random fashion.

Single Station or Network of Stations

The service may be completed by a single unit, such as the physician in the medical care example above. In some systems, completing a job requires having an order processed by several work units. This is common in manufacturing, where an order may pass through several manufacturing steps, or in paperwork flows where, for example, a loan request at a bank may require several levels of analysis or approval. Systems that involve more than one station are called *queuing networks.* Examples of these will be given later. At each station, some service time is required, and these times generally vary by station.

Number of Servers

At each station, there may be only one server or *channel* or many. As an example, there may be several positions open at an airline check-in counter. An arrival is processed by only one of the servers. Servers may have different service rates (some airline personnel may be speedier than others).

Queue Discipline

While jobs wait for service, they are in a waiting line or queue. There may be only one line or separate lines for each server. There may be a space limit on the waiting line, and jobs that arrive when the line is full may be turned away. The order in which jobs are served is often by **FIFO,** or **F**irst-**I**n, **F**irst-**O**ut. But there may be express or priority service for some jobs; an example is the express line at many supermarkets for customers with 10 items or less. Service may be in random order.

Measures of Performance

There are various ways of judging how well a processing system is performing. Results may be evaluated over a short period of time once the system opens, or they may be based on the long-run or equilibrium results. Generally, the time jobs spend waiting is important, and we may look at the average waiting time or at a measure such as the percent of jobs that wait longer than, say, 10 minutes. A related measure is the *throughput time* for a job (waiting time plus service time). The length of the waiting line is another common measure of performance. These are measures of how well the system is performing from the customer point of view.

Other measures relate to the cost of operating the system. The system load factor or capacity utilization measures the ability of the system to handle the arrival load. Management has the option of adding more capacity.

A given processing system can have any combination of the elements described above. Hence, there are a very large number of possible systems, and no one mathematical model can describe them all. In this chapter, we focus on a few simple models that have wide applicability and that give us insight into queuing system behavior in general. Another chapter describes simulation, which can be used to model processing systems in a very general way.

Notation

Before considering mathematical models of processing systems, first consider some notation:

$$A = \text{Time between arrivals}$$

This is a random variable. As an example, consider the sixth column in Table 9–1, which gives the time between arrivals at the factory medical care center.

$$\mu_A = \text{Mean of distribution of } A \text{ (i.e., mean interarrival time)}$$
$$\sigma_A = \text{Standard deviation of } A$$
$$cv_A = \frac{\sigma_A}{\mu_A} = \begin{array}{l}\text{Coefficient of variation of } A\\ \text{(a relative measure of the variability in interarrival times)}\end{array}$$
$$S = \text{Service time}$$

This is also a random variable, representing the time taken to service a job. See the seventh column of Table 9–1 as an example.

μ_S = Mean of distribution of S (i.e., mean service time)
σ_S = Standard deviation of S

$$cv_S = \frac{\sigma_S}{\mu_S} = \begin{array}{l}\text{Coefficient of variation of } S \\ \text{(a relative measure of the variability in service times)}\end{array}$$

W = Waiting time in the queue for an arrival

This does not include the time taken to service the arrival.

L = Length of the waiting line for an arrival

This does not include any job being serviced.

As examples, see the eighth and fifth columns in Table 9–1. These also are random variables.

μ_W = Mean of the distribution of W (mean waiting time)
μ_L = Mean of the distribution of L (mean line length)

ρ = System load factor (or *system utilization*)

This is a ratio of the arrival load into the system compared to the capacity of the system to service that load.

WTM = Waiting time multiple

This is the average waiting time for an arrival divided by the average service time. It is a standardized measure of waiting time and will be our basic measure of congestion in the system.

$$WTM = \frac{\mu_W}{\mu_S}$$

There are two important probability distributions that appear often in queuing models. The *Poisson* distribution assumes a very large (infinite) number of possible arrivals, with each having a small probability of occurrence. Arrivals are independent and the number of arrivals in one period of time does not affect the number in the next. The Poisson distribution is a good approximation for many processes that are considered "random," such as calls arriving at a switchboard, customers at a check-in counter, or fire alarms.

The random variable in the Poisson distribution is the number of arrivals or services per unit of time. The *exponential* distribution is a complementary distribution to the Poisson that has as the random variable the interarrival time or the service time. This type of distribution corresponds to the random variables A and S defined above. Both of these distributions are called *Markov* distributions. The details of these distributions are given in Appendix A at the end of this chapter.

It has become standard practice to denote queuing models by a short-hand notation as follows:

Arrival time Distribution / Service time distribution / Number of servers or channels

where

M = Markov (Poisson or exponential) distribution
D = Deterministic (i.e., constant) distribution
G = General distribution with specified mean and standard deviation

A Single-Server Queuing Model (*M/G/1*)

For this model, we shall consider the case in which:[2]

1. Arrivals are random, and the interarrival times come from an exponential (or Markov) probability distribution.
2. Service times are also assumed to be random following a general distribution with mean μ_S and standard deviation σ_S. Service times are assumed to be independent of each other and independent of the arrival process.
3. There is a single server or channel.
4. The queue discipline is FIFO, and there is no limit on the size of the line.
5. The average interarrival and service times do not change over time. The process has been operating long enough to remove effects of the initial conditions. We are interested in the long-run or equilibrium conditions.

Using the notation above; this is the ***M/G/1*** queue.

Note first that the system load factor (or capacity utilization) for this queuing model is:

$$\rho = \frac{\mu_S}{\mu_A}$$

Thus, the capacity utilization of the system (the percent of time the facility is busy serving arrivals) is the average service time divided by the average interarrival time. This number must be less than 1.0—if the service time is longer than the interarrival time, the queue will continue to grow without limit.

It is possible to solve this model mathematically for the long-run equilibrium distribution of waiting time and number waiting in line.

For this *M/G/1* model, our basic measure, the waiting time multiple (*WTM*), is given by:

$$WTM = \left(\frac{\rho}{1-\rho}\right)\left(\frac{1 + cv_S^2}{2}\right) \tag{9–1}$$

From this, the mean of the distribution of waiting times can be calculated as:

$$\mu_W = \mu_S \cdot WTM \tag{9–2}$$

And the average length of the queue is:[3]

$$\mu_L = \frac{\mu_W}{\mu_A} \tag{9–3}$$

Example 1

Consider a situation like that described in Table 9–1—the medical office of a very large factory. Assume patients for the medical office arrive randomly following a Markov process (that is, interarrival times are exponentially distributed). Patients arrive individually with a mean interarrival time of 15 minutes. The office can treat

[2]This model is often called the Pollaczek-Khintchine model.

[3]This relationship between the line length and average waiting time is called Little's Formula: John D. C. Little, "A Proof for the Queuing Formula: $L = \lambda W$," *Operations Research* 9 (1961).

patients in an average time of 12 minutes, but some take longer and others less. Suppose the standard deviation of service time is 3 minutes. There is one medical team available to see arriving patients.

That is:

$$\mu_A = 15;\ \mu_S = 12;\ \sigma_S = 3;\ \text{and}\ cv_S = \frac{\sigma_S}{\mu_S} = \frac{3}{12} = 0.25$$

And the system load factor:

$$\rho = \frac{\mu_S}{\mu_A} = \frac{12}{15} = 0.80$$

This means that the medical team will be treating patients 80 percent of the time and idle (perhaps doing other tasks) 20 percent of the time.

The waiting time multiple is:

$$WTM = \left(\frac{\rho}{1-\rho}\right)\left(\frac{1+cv_S^2}{2}\right) = \left(\frac{0.8}{1-0.8}\right)\left(\frac{1+(0.25)^2}{2}\right) = 2.125$$

And the average waiting time of an arrival is:

$$\mu_W = \mu_S \cdot WTM = (12)(2.125) = 25.5 \text{ minutes}$$

Remember that this is the average waiting time. Some arrivals will find the line empty when they arrive and have zero waiting time (actually 20 percent will, since the facility is busy 80 percent and idle 20 percent of the time), while others may spend hours waiting.

The average length of the waiting line is:

$$\mu_L = \frac{\mu_W}{\mu_A} = \frac{25.5}{15} = 1.70 \text{ persons}$$

Although an arrival spends, on average, 25.5 minutes waiting, he or she also must spend an average of 12 minutes being treated, or a total time in the system of 37.5 minutes, on average.

All of the above measures assume that the process has been operating long enough for the probabilities to reach an equilibrium condition.

Let us look at the cost associated with this system. If we assume a 24-hour work day (3 shifts), there will be an average of 96 patients arriving per day (15 minutes apart, on average, is 4 per hour). As indicated above, each patient will spend 37.5 minutes in the system (waiting plus service time). Suppose the cost of lost time for each worker is \$60 per hour (or \$1 per minute). Then the total cost per day from lost time for this system is:

$$\begin{aligned}\text{Total cost} &= (\text{Number of arrivals}) \times (\text{Average time in system}) \times (\text{Cost per minute})\\ &= (96)(37.5)(\$1) = \$3{,}600 \text{ per day}\end{aligned}$$

This is a substantial cost, over a million dollars per year. There is plenty of opportunity for management to reduce this cost.

Example 1 Extended

Consider again our example of the medical office in a factory. Suppose the number of arrivals for service increased (because more workers were hired) so that the mean interarrival time was 13.33 minutes. The mean (12 minutes) and standard deviation (3 minutes) of service time remain the same. The system load factor ρ increases from 80 to 90 percent ($\rho = \mu_S/\mu_A = 12/13.33 = 0.9$). Consider what would happen to waiting time and queue length. Before reading the next paragraph, make a rough intuitive guess at what would happen. Certainly waiting times would increase, but by how much? The system load factor increased by about 12 percent. Do you think waiting time would increase also by 12 percent, by 25 percent, by 50 percent, or more?

Using our formula (Equation 9–1), we have:

$$WTM = \left(\frac{\rho}{1-\rho}\right)\left(\frac{1 + cv_S^2}{2}\right) = \left(\frac{0.9}{1-0.9}\right)\left(\frac{1 + (0.25)^2}{2}\right) = 4.78$$

That is, an arriving patient will wait 4.78 times the average service time. Since the average service time is 12 minutes, the average waiting time is:

$$\mu_W = \mu_S \cdot WTM = (12)(4.78) = 57.4 \text{ minutes}$$

This is more than double the previous waiting time of 25.5 minutes. This is probably much more than you expected—a counterintuitive result. Queuing phenomena can produce surprising results, which is why it is valuable to have models to gain these insights for designing systems before they are put in practice.

How realistic is the model? The *M/G/1* model with the Markov or exponential distribution for arrivals and a general distribution for service times is applicable to many situations. The Markov process describes many real situations in which arrivals are random. And since the service time distribution is general, it can be customized to fit the situation. Hence, it has broad applicability.

However, our specific example also assumes that the arrival rate is the same over the day, and this may not be true if there are more medical problems during some shifts (say, the night shift) or toward the end of a shift (more accidents as workers get tired). This would cause some longer delays during higher arrival periods, and shorter waits at other times.

Table 9–1 is a short history of this system, with values close to those used in the model above (interarrival time of 14.9 and service time of 12.1). Note that the results in terms of delays are approximately the same. Such a short history would not be adequate to represent the long-run pattern of delays. However, one can see how the delays occur.

Some Special Cases for the Single-Server Queue

The M/M/1 Queue. There are two special cases of the general queuing formulas above that merit consideration. First, consider the case in which the distribution of service times is also exponential (that is, Markov). This is the ***M/M/1*** queue.

One feature of the exponential distribution is that the standard deviation equals the mean (i.e., $\sigma_S = \mu_S$). If we make this substitution back in the basic formula for the WTM (Equation 9–1), we obtain the following:

$$\textit{For M/M/1 queue: } WTM = \frac{\rho}{1-\rho}$$

The M/D/1 Queue. A second special case is that in which the service is deterministic, the ***M/D/1*** case. That is, service time is a constant with zero standard deviation. Substituting $\sigma_S = 0$ in the basic formula (Equation 9–1), we obtain:

$$\text{For } M/D/1 \text{ Queue: } WTM = \frac{\rho}{2(1-\rho)}$$

The equations for the average waiting time and average queue length are the same as in the basic case.

Queuing System Behavior

The formulas presented for the single-channel case enable us to study the behavior of the system as a function of the system load factor or system utilization ρ. Figure 9–1 shows a graph of the waiting time multiple (WTM) as a function of load factor for two of the models presented above, the *M/M/1* queue and the *M/D/1* queue. The curve for the general case, the *M/G/1* queue, would be in between the other two, with specific values depending on the standard deviation of service time.

A characteristic of these curves is the steep upward slope once the system becomes utilized above 60 or 70 percent. Waiting times increase exponentially. An example of this was given in Example 1 Extended (pages 388–89). In the *M/M/1* queue, for example, the WTM is 2.33 at 70 percent capacity utilization, increases to 4.0 at 80 percent utilization, and more than doubles to 9.0 at 90 percent utilization. If a manager were to try to get 95 percent utilization of the system, it would require a WTM of 19.0—customers or jobs would wait almost 20 times their service time. The implication is that *if prompt service is desired in a single-server system, there must be "excess" capacity (much less than 100 percent utilization) in order to avoid excessive waiting.*

There is pressure in most organizations to be efficient and to reduce idle time as much as possible. Managers do not like to see personnel or equipment standing idle. Yet we see the need to have excess capacity to avoid long waits for customers. This is a very important insight about queuing systems and one that is not obvious.

FIGURE 9–1
System Load Factor versus WTM for the *M/M/1* and *M/D/1* Queues

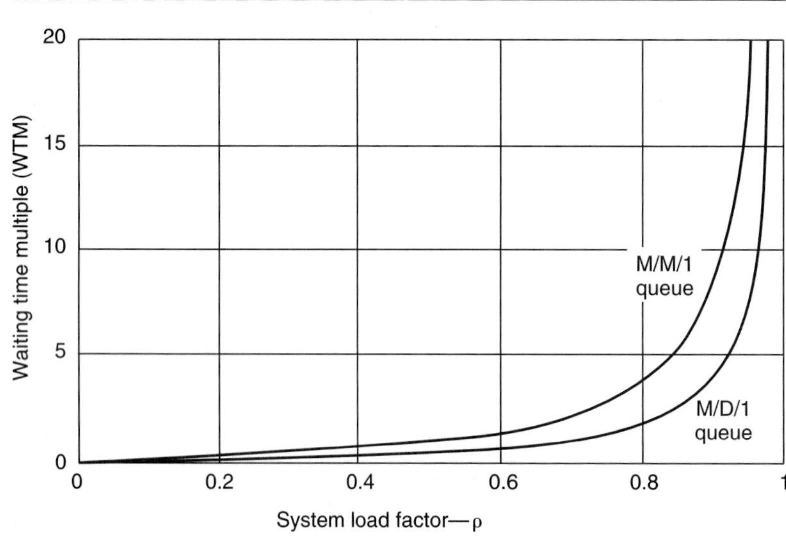

A More General Model for the Single-Channel Queue—The G/G/1 Queue

Suppose we make no assumptions about the distributions for interarrival time and for service time—they can be general probability distributions with specified means and standard deviations. We continue to assume that the distributions are independent and that the single queue has a FIFO discipline.

There is no mathematical model that can solve this case exactly. However, there is an approximation model for this situation called the *heavy-traffic approximation.* It is an accurate estimation for waiting time when the system is heavily loaded (values of ρ close to 100 percent) and a reasonable approximation in other cases. The waiting time multiple in this case is:

$$WTM \cong \left(\frac{\rho}{1-\rho}\right)\left(\frac{cv_A^2 + cv_S^2}{2}\right) \qquad (9\text{–}4)$$

In this formula, cv_A and cv_S are the coefficients of variation and measure the relative variability of interarrival and service times. The formulas for average waiting time (Equation 9–2) and average queue length (Equation 9–3) are the same as in the basic case.

Effects of Variability in Arrivals and Services

Recall the example of the medical office in a plant that was given in Table 9–1 earlier in the chapter. It was the variability in the interarrival times and service times that created the congestion and waiting in the system. If patients arrived exactly 15 minutes apart, and if it took exactly 12 minutes to treat them, there never would be any waiting or anyone in line.

The second term of Equation 9–4 highlights the effect of variability as measured by the coefficients of variation of interarrival time (cv_A) and service time (cv_S). Variability in either arrivals or service times has an equal and additive effect. This can also be seen in Figure 9–1, which compares the *M/M/1* queue, which has highly variable service times (exponential or Markov), with the *M/D/1* queue, which has no variability in service times. Waiting times are exactly double in the highly variable case.

This effect has important implications for the management of queuing systems. Because variability has such a big impact, it may be possible to substantially reduce waiting and congestion by reducing the variability. This may be done by redesigning service operations to reduce the variability in service time with the use of information technology or by other means. It may also be possible to reduce the variability in the arrival pattern. For example, having different prices for differing times of the day is one way telephone companies spread out the load on the telephone system.

Multiple Servers: The *M/M/c* Model

In many queuing situations, there is more than one server (or channel) waiting on customers. A check-in counter at the airport with several clerks or multiple check-out stands at the supermarket are examples. In such situations, the waiting line discipline is important—there may be only one line for all channels (common at airport checkpoints) or each channel may have its own line (the usual supermarket case).

TABLE 9–2
Waiting Time Multiple for the *M/M/c* Queue

System Load Factor	Number of Service Channels, c					
	c = 1	c = 2	c = 3	c = 4	c = 5	c = 10
0.10	0.1111	0.0101	0.0014	0.0002	0.0000*	0.0000*
0.20	0.2500	0.0417	0.0103	0.0030	0.0010	0.0000*
0.30	0.4286	0.0989	0.0333	0.0132	0.0058	0.0002
0.40	0.6667	0.1905	0.0784	0.0378	0.0199	0.0015
0.50	1.0000	0.3333	0.1579	0.0870	0.0521	0.0072
0.60	1.5000	0.5625	0.2956	0.1794	0.1181	0.0253
0.70	2.3333	0.9608	0.5470	0.3572	0.2519	0.0739
0.80	4.0000	1.7778	1.0787	0.7455	0.5541	0.2046
0.90	9.0000	4.2632	2.7235	1.9694	1.5250	0.6687
0.95	19.0000	9.2564	6.0467	4.4571	3.5112	1.6512

*Less than 0.00005.

For the simple model described below, we shall assume that there is a single waiting line. Customers arrive into the system with mean interarrival time μ_A. There are c servers, and each has the same average service time μ_S. The single line is serviced in a FIFO (first-in, first-out) manner, and arrivals and services are independent. The distributions for both interarrival times and service times are assumed to be Markov (exponential).

The formula for the waiting time multiple (WTM) in this case is, unfortunately, very messy and complicated. Instead of providing it, Table 9–2 gives the WTM for a number of useful cases: number of channels from 1 through 5 and 10, and for various levels of the system load factor. Note that the system load factor or utilization in a system with c channels is:

$$\text{System load factor} = \rho_c = \frac{\mu_S}{c\mu_A}$$

A More General Model—The G/G/c Queue

As in the case for a single channel, there is no mathematically exact formula for the case in which the arrival and service times can have a general distribution. However, there is an estimation formula (the *heavy-traffic approximation*) that provides accurate approximations when the system is heavily loaded (load factor close to 100 percent), and rough estimates in other cases. This formula provides an adjustment to the waiting time multiple for the *M/M/c* queue given in Table 9–2. If we let $WTM_{M/M}$ represent the values in Table 9–2 for the appropriate system load factor and number of channels, then the waiting time multiple for the *G/G/c* queue is given by:[4]

$$WTM = WTM_{M/M}\left(\frac{cv_A^2 + cv_S^2}{2}\right) \tag{9–5}$$

[4]Equation 9–5 is exact for the case of exponential (Markov) arrivals and general service time distribution.

The second term is an adjustment that allows for different variability in the arrival and service times. The formulas for average waiting time and queue length are the same as in the single-channel case:

$$\text{Average waiting time: } \mu_W = \mu_S \cdot WTM$$

$$\text{Average length of waiting line: } \mu_L = \frac{\mu_W}{\mu_A}$$

Pooling Efficiencies in Queuing Systems

Pooling refers to combining separate systems into a common pool or group. As an example, consider an airport with two wings, A and B, each containing a group of departure gates. And consider the design of the security system used to screen passengers and their carry-on bags. One approach might be to have a security system for each wing, so that passengers for the A wing would go through one system and passengers for the B wing would go through a second one. An alternative approach would be to pool the two security systems so that passengers for both wings would form a single queue and pass through one or the other before going on to their gates. See Figure 9–2. Before reading on, you might consider which system you think would result in less congestion.

Example 2—Airport Security Checks

In fact, let us be specific about the airport security example discussed above and diagrammed in Figure 9–2. Suppose passengers going to Gate A have a mean interarrival time (μ_A) of 1.25 minutes, and similarly those for Gate B also have the same mean interarrival time of 1.25 minutes. Furthermore, these arrivals are random—that is, have an exponential (Markov) distribution. Suppose it takes an average of 1 minute to pass an arrival through the security system, and the standard deviation of this service time is 0.5 minute. Thus, the coefficient of variation for service time is $cv_S = \frac{\sigma_S}{\mu_S} = \frac{0.5}{1.0} = 0.5$.

Individual Facilities for Each Gate. If there are individual security systems for each gate, each is a single-channel queue of the *M/G/1* variety. The system load factor is:

FIGURE 9–2
Individual versus Pooled Security Checking Facilities

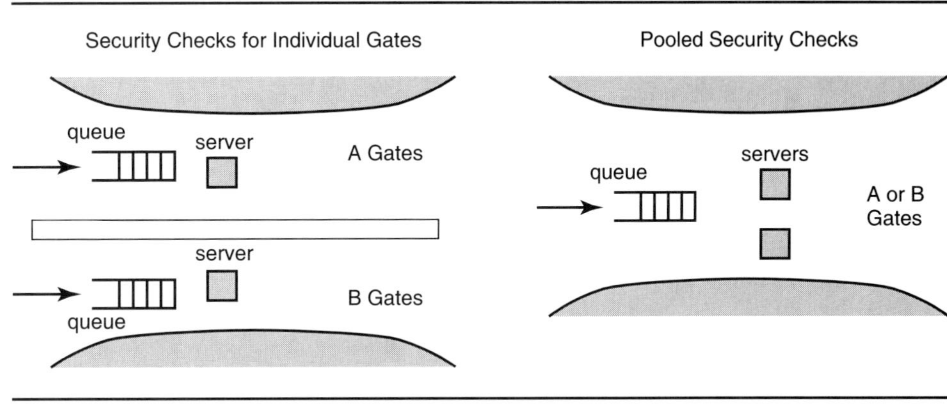

$$\rho = \frac{\mu_S}{\mu_A} = \frac{1.0}{1.25} = 0.80$$

That is, each gate is operating at 80 percent of capacity. From Equation 9–1, we can obtain the waiting time multiple as:

$$WTM = \left(\frac{\rho}{1-\rho}\right)\left(\frac{1 + cv_S^2}{2}\right) = \left(\frac{0.8}{1-0.8}\right)\left(\frac{1 + 0.5^2}{2}\right) = 2.50$$

Thus, on average, a passenger waits in line 2.5 times the average service time (1 minute)—or 2.5 minutes—before reaching the security station to be passed through. This is true for each gate, since they are identical.

Pooled System. Now consider the case in which the two security systems are pooled, and there is a single line for all passengers for both gates. Mean interarrival time for passengers for each gate is 1.25 minutes; hence, when pooled, the mean interarrival time will be 0.625 minutes. Another way to see this is that a mean interarrival time of 1.25 minutes corresponds to 48 arrivals per hour. Twice this, or 96 arrivals, is the combined total, and this represents an interarrival time of 0.625 minutes. The system load factor is the same as it was with separate systems:

$$\text{System load factor} = \rho_c = \frac{\mu_S}{c \cdot \mu_A} = \frac{1.0}{(2)(0.625)} = 0.80$$

This is a two-channel system, and with a system load factor of 80 percent, the WTM from Table 9–2 is 1.7778. Also note that, since interarrival times are exponential (Markov), the standard deviation of interarrival times equals the mean, so that $cv_A = 1$. And cv_S remains 0.5. Now, from our general formula (Equation 9–5):

$$WTM = WTM_{M/M}\left(\frac{cv_A^2 + cv_S^2}{2}\right) = (1.7778)\left(\frac{1 + 0.5^2}{2}\right) = 1.11$$

Now a passenger waits 1.11 times the average service time (one minute) or 1.11 minutes. *Note that this is less than half the waiting time from the separate facilities case.* Pooling had a substantial effect. And note that there was no reduction in number of arrivals, and the service capacity was exactly the same.

Why is there this effect? With separate facilities, one may be sitting idle while the other has a long waiting line. When they are pooled, this cannot happen since there is a common queue. So it is not surprising that pooling reduces congestion. What is surprising is the magnitude of the effect. It can be very effective!

Figure 9–3 is a graphic way of representing this. It shows the waiting time multiple as a function of the system load factor, comparing a system with individual servers versus those with two pooled servers and five pooled servers. This represents the *M/M/c* type of queue, but the general effect applies to other types as well. There are big differences, particularly for systems that are heavily loaded.

Loss Systems

In some processing systems, arriving jobs cannot enter the system because there is no waiting line or queue. These are called *loss systems.* As an example, consider a towing service that has one tow truck for towing disabled vehicles to repair facilities. The towing service is one of several under contract with an auto club. When the auto

FIGURE 9–3 Waiting Time in Single- and Pooled-Server Systems for *M/M/c* Queues

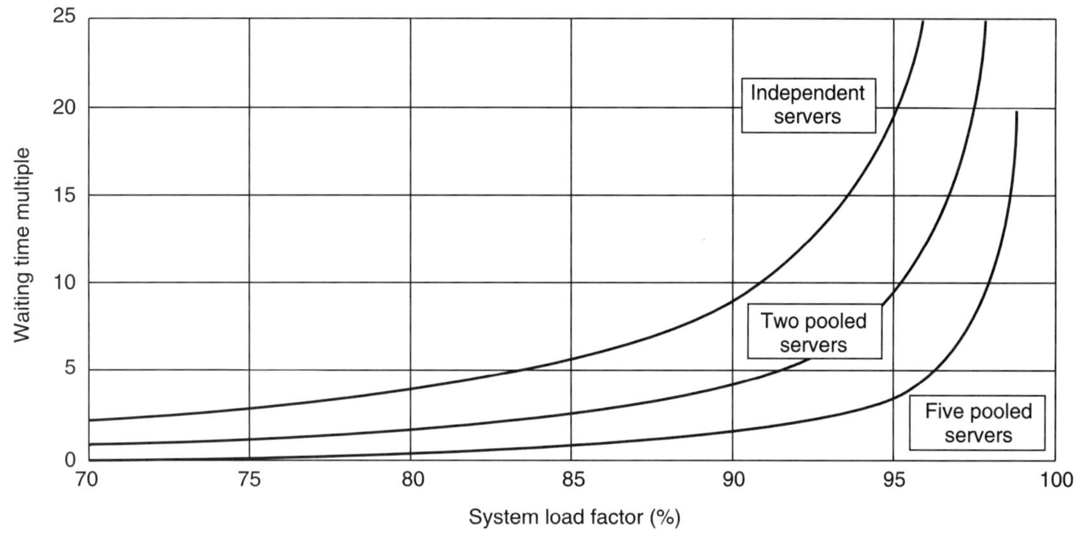

club gets a call for emergency service, it contacts the closest towing service. If all the trucks at that service are busy, it contacts another of the towing services under contract.

From the towing company's perspective, this is a loss system. If a call comes from the auto club while its truck is busy servicing another customer, the job is lost.

The M/G/c Loss system

Consider a system in which jobs arrive in a random or Markov process (that is, interarrival times are exponential) and service times can have a general distribution. There are c service channels. Jobs that arrive when all c channels are busy are lost.

The mean interarrival time is μ_A and the mean service time is μ_S. The system load factor is:

$$\rho = \frac{\mu_S}{c \cdot \mu_A}$$

In loss systems, this may be greater than 100 percent since some arrivals actually do not enter the system for service. An important measure of performance for loss systems is the fraction of arriving jobs that are lost. The formula for this is:

$$\text{Fraction lost} = \frac{\dfrac{(c\rho)^c}{c!}}{\displaystyle\sum_{k=0}^{c} \frac{(c\rho)^k}{k!}} \qquad (9\text{–}6)$$

For the single-channel case ($c = 1$), this becomes:

$$\text{Fraction lost} = \frac{\rho}{1 + \rho}$$

For the two-channel case ($c = 2$), it simplifies to:

$$\text{Fraction lost} = \frac{2\rho^2}{1 + 2\rho + 2\rho^2}$$

For the three-channel case ($c = 3$):

$$\text{Fraction lost} = \frac{\dfrac{(3\rho)^3}{3!}}{1 + (3\rho) + \dfrac{(3\rho)^2}{2} + \dfrac{(3\rho)^3}{3!}}$$

and so on.

Example 3

Consider the towing service described above. Suppose calls for service from the auto club arrive with mean interarrival time of 2 hours (μ_A), and the average service time (μ_S) is 3 hours (time used in getting to a disabled vehicle, towing it, and becoming ready for the next call). There is only one tow truck, so $c = 1$ (single channel). The system load factor is:

$$\rho = \frac{\mu_S}{c \cdot \mu_A} = \frac{3}{1 \cdot 2} = 1.50$$

That is, the available work is 150 percent of the capacity of this towing service to handle it. The fraction of jobs lost is:

$$\text{Fraction lost} = \frac{\rho}{1 + \rho} = \frac{1.5}{1 + 1.5} = 0.60$$

In a given period of, say, 100 hours, 50 calls for service would arrive, on average. The towing service would lose 60 percent and actually service the other 40 percent, or 20 jobs. At 3 hours per job, the tow truck would be busy 60 out of the 100 hours, or 60 percent of the time.[5]

Suppose our towing service were to add a second tow truck, with arrivals and service times the same. It is now a two-channel system ($c = 2$). The system load factor is:

$$\rho = \frac{\mu_S}{c \cdot \mu_A} = \frac{3}{2 \cdot 2} = 0.75$$

And the fraction of jobs lost is:

$$\text{Fraction lost} = \frac{2\rho^2}{1 + 2\rho + 2\rho^2} = \frac{2(0.75)^2}{1 + 2(0.75) + 2(0.75)^2} = 0.310$$

Now only about 31 percent of jobs would be lost. Again, over a 100-hour period, 50 jobs would arrive, and ($1 - 0.31 = 0.69$) or 69 percent would be accepted, resulting in 34.5 towing jobs. Compare this to the result with only one tow truck above. *Adding a second truck significantly increased (34.5 versus 20) the number of jobs handled.*

[5]In the single-channel loss system, the fraction of the time the system is busy is exactly equal to the fraction of jobs lost. This is because a job is lost whenever it arrives when the only channel is busy. The loss formula (9–6) is known as *Erlang's Loss Formula*.

Scheduling and Priorities in Processing Systems

In all the models discussed above, we have assumed a FIFO queue discipline. All jobs are treated equally on a first-come, first-served basis. But it may be possible to reduce congestion in systems by the use of priorities in scheduling. Consider a simple example—a homeowner insurance underwriting desk at an insurance agency. Requests for insurance policies are faxed in by agents. There are two types of requests: requests for new policies and requests for renewals of existing policies. Suppose requests for new policies arrive on average every 2 hours and requests for renewals also have a mean interarrival time of 2 hours (120 minutes). And these arrival distributions are exponential (Markov). Also suppose it takes an average of 80 minutes to process a request for a new policy and the distribution of service time is exponential. However, it takes only 20 minutes, on average, to process a renewal request (distribution is normal, with standard deviation of 8 minutes).

One approach would be to treat all requests equally and process them in the order of arrival. Consider an alternative: Give priority to renewals and process them first. That is, any renewal request in the queue is processed before any new policy request. A comparison of these alternatives is shown in Table 9–3. These results are based on simulating the system, not on a mathematical model.

As you might expect, giving priority to renewals reduces the waiting time for those requests and increases the waiting time for the new policies. However, this increase for the new policies is rather small (about 10 percent), whereas the reduction for the renewals is about 80 percent. And the overall average waiting time drops considerably. So the renewals benefit with very little cost to the new policy requests.

Thus, scheduling can have significant effects. We see examples similar to that above every day. For example, most supermarkets have express lines for those having 10 items or less, and banks sometimes have express lines for those making only one transaction (a deposit, for example).

Networks of Queues

In many important applications in the real world, queues exist not just as a single station but as a part of a network of queues. In manufacturing, for example, a job order may be processed at many work stations in a factory before being shipped to a customer. Paper processing, such as processing accounts payable, will have many stations through which the transaction will pass before it is finished. Because these

TABLE 9–3
Waiting Time for Insurance Agency Example

	Average Waiting Time (minutes)	
	FIFO	*Priority to Renewals*
New policies	344	374
Renewals	344	66
Average	344	218

FIGURE 9–4 Network of Queues in a Manufacturing Facility

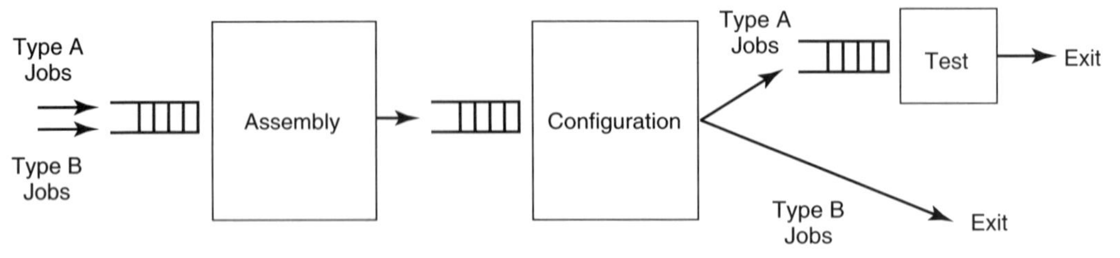

TABLE 9–4
Interarrival and Service Times for Manufacturing Operation

	Job Type B	*Job Type A*
Interarrival time		
Mean	16 hours	16 hours
Distribution	Exponential	Exponential
Assembly operation		
Mean of service time	6.4 hours	6.4 hours
Standard deviation	3.0 hours	3.0 hours
Distribution	Normal	Normal
Configuration operation		
Mean of service time	4.0 hours	10.4 hours
Standard deviation	1.6 hours	4.0 hours
Distribution	Normal	Normal
Test operation		
Mean of service time	—	14.0 hours
Standard deviation	—	6.0 hours
Distribution	—	Normal
Sum of mean service times	10.4 hours	30.8 hours

systems are so varied and complex, there are no simple mathematical models to describe them as there are for single-station queuing situations. Our purpose here is to introduce the idea, give an example, and point out that the ideas and insights learned from single-station queues can generally be carried over to networks.

Consider a manufacturing operation as described in Figure 9–4. There are two types of jobs that the manufacturing facility can accept. Both types go through assembly and configuration steps, and Type A jobs also go through a testing step. Each process can work on only one job at a time, and job orders wait in a queue before each step in the process.

Suppose an equal number of Type A and Type B orders arrive at the manufacturing operation. Further, suppose the information about the interarrival times and service times for each type of job at each station is as given in Table 9–4.

Note that both types of jobs take the same amount of time for assembly. However, B type jobs take much less time in configuration and, of course, do not need to have a test step.

This system is heavily loaded. The assembly operation has a system load factor of 80 percent, that for the configuration operation is 90 percent, and 87.5 percent

TABLE 9–5
Results of Simulation of Manufacturing Operation (in hours)

	Base Case: No Priority	*Alternate Case I: Priority to Type B Jobs*	*Alternative Case II: Reduced Variability and Priority to Type B*
Average total throughput time			
Type A jobs	117	121	57
Type B jobs	61	31	23
Average waiting time in queue			
Assembly queue	15.5	15.5	7.1
Configuration queue	35.2	23.2	7.2
Test queue (A jobs only)	34.5	32.2	10.8

for the test operation.[6] From what we learned earlier in the chapter, we should expect congestion and waiting lines, particularly at the configuration operation.

This system has been simulated, and the results are shown as the base case in the first column in Table 9–5. Since it is simulated, the results are approximations. As expected, there is considerable congestion, particularly in the queue waiting for configuration. Note that it took Type A jobs an average of 117 hours to move through the system, although the total time required for the actual operations (on average) was only 30.8 hours. Type B jobs were even worse, taking 61 hours through the system, when only 10.4 hours of operations were needed (on average).

There is plenty of opportunity for management to improve this system. Increasing the capacity of the various operations, especially configuration, would reduce the congestion. Management might find ways to increase the number of channels. Consider the assembly operation as an example. Suppose management could reorganize into two separate parallel assembly operations, each taking perhaps twice as long as the previous one. But assembly now becomes a two-channel server system. This would cut the congestion at that stage roughly in half.

An alternative is to modify the scheduling of jobs through the system. As an example, consider an alternative in which Type B jobs are given priority at the configuration station. That is, any Type B job waiting for configuration is given priority over any Type A job. This case also has been simulated and the results are shown in the Alternate Case I column of Table 9–5. Note the major improvements. The average throughput time for Type B jobs dropped almost in half at very little change in throughput time for Type A jobs. The average dropped significantly. *Scheduling does matter.*

Another alternative open to management is to reduce the variability within the operation. There is considerable variation both in the arrival of jobs into the system as well as how long it takes to perform each of the assembly, configuration, and test operations. Consider a specific example. Suppose management could make an arrangement with the customer who orders Type A jobs so that orders, instead of coming randomly, arrive exactly 16 hours apart. That is, there is no variability in

[6]For assembly, the overall mean interarrival time is 8.0 hours. With a service rate of 6.4, the load factor is 80 percent. The mean interarrival time for configuration is also 8.0 hours. Since on average there are equal numbers of each type of job, the average service time is 7.2 hours, making 90 percent utilization. For test, the interarrival time for type A jobs is 16 hours and service time is 14 hours, or 87.5 percent utilization.

arrivals of Type A jobs. Type B jobs continue to arrive randomly. Further, suppose that by an improvement in work methods management is able to reduce the standard deviation of service time for the assembly operation from 3.0 hours to 1.5 hours. Both of these actions reduce variability in the system. Suppose priority to Type B jobs at the configuration step is also maintained. This alternative also has been simulated and is shown in Table 9–5 as Alternate Case II.

Note the dramatic improvement, especially in how long it takes a Type A job to be processed in the system. Note that reduction of variability in upstream operations (input into the system and variability in assembly) reduced congestion even in the downstream operations of configuration and test. *Reducing variability can have a major effect on congestion.*

Summary

Processing systems are an important part of most business and public sector operations. They can represent flows of goods and parts through a manufacturing process or flows of paperwork through back-office systems. They can represent flows of people through reservation and check-in systems or telephone inquiries. They can even represent flows of information in computer networks. Congestion is a significant and costly component of many of these systems.

This chapter presented models for representing some simple types of systems: single- and multiple-channel queuing systems and loss systems. These may be used to make estimates of congestion in real-world systems.

But more important is that these models (and the simulation results presented in the later part of the chapter) provide insights that can be applied to a great variety of processing systems and that are not at all obvious. These insights are:

- *There is a need for planned excess capacity.* Management might like to see facilities as close to 100 percent utilized as possible. But waiting time and congestion is very sensitive to the system load factor, particularly when it gets above 70 to 80 percent. (Recall the shape of the curves in Figures 9–1 and 9–3.) So one must plan for some idle capacity in processing systems.
- *Variability is a major culprit in congestion.* The amount of congestion in a processing system is directly related to the amount of variability in interarrival and service times. Management can significantly improve congestion by reducing these sources of variability.
- *Pooling can lead to significant improvements.* Pooling of resources, so that jobs can be serviced by alternate service facilities, was shown by formulas and examples to significantly reduce congestion. There are many opportunities for pooling, some of which are not obvious. Cross-training of personnel on multiple tasks is one example. If a firm has a mechanic who specializes in one type of repair (engines, for example) and a second who only handles a second type of repair (brakes and struts, for example), there will be situations when one has a big backlog and the other is idle. However, if they can be cross-trained to handle either type of job, it becomes a two-channel system with significant reduction in congestion. This is just one example of the many opportunities for pooling.
- *Scheduling matters.* The examples in the chapter illustrated that how jobs are scheduled through the system can significantly impact congestion.

- *These factors can have big impacts.* They can have orders of magnitude effects on the congestion in systems. Management can significantly improve processes.
- *They are not intuitively obvious.* Our intuition about processing systems is not adequate to understand the size of these effects. Hopefully, the models and examples in this chapter will lead to a better understanding.

APPENDIX
MARKOV DISTRIBUTIONS:
Poisson and Exponential

The two probability distributions, the Poisson discrete distribution and the exponential continuous distribution, are complementary distributions. They are used in queuing theory to represent "random" arrivals or services. Both are called Markov distributions.

The Poisson Process and Distribution

In a Poisson process, the probability of occurrence of an event is constant, and the occurrence of an event is independent of what has happened immediately preceding the present observation. We may be interested in what happens over a continuous interval. This interval may be a measure of distance—for example, a yard—or a unit of time such as a day. Printing errors per page of a book is an example of a process that may be Poisson; other examples are the manufacturing of textiles, rolled steel, pipe, wire, and so on, where there are X defects per unit measure of product.

The sales for a product may behave like a Poisson process. Suppose we have had 80 individual sales of one unit of product per person during the past 50 weeks, or an average sale of 1.6 units per week. We may wish to know the probability of different weekly sales in the next five weeks.

The Poisson probability distribution applied to a Poisson process gives the probability of a number of events in a measure of distance or time, given that we know (1) the expected number of events *per unit* of distance or time and (2) the length of distance or time. Suppose we use the symbol λ to be the expected number of events per unit measure; that is, the *rate* or *intensity* of the process. Examples of λ are 1.6 units of sales per week, 25 telephone calls per hour, 3 defects per 100 feet of pipe, and so forth. We shall let T be the unit of time or space during which events are to be counted. Then the Poisson probability of exactly r events occurring during time T, given the average number of events per unit of time is λ, is given as:[7]

$$P(R = r|\lambda,T) = \frac{e^{-\lambda T}(\lambda T)^r}{r!} \tag{9–7}$$

In using the Poisson probability distribution, we may combine λ and T by multiplication to obtain m; that is, $m = \lambda T$, where m is the expected number of events

[7] $e = 2.718\ldots$, the base for natural logarithms.

in the specified time period. We *expect* m events in a specified time, T. For example, if $\lambda = 2$ (the average number of events per week) and $T = 5$ (the time period is five weeks), the average number of events per five-week period is $2 \cdot 5 = 10$. A Poisson distribution has the special property that its variance is always equal to its mean, m, so the standard deviation is $\sqrt{m}$.

The Exponential Distribution

In connection with the Poisson process, we have discussed the Poisson probability distribution, which gives the probability of the number of occurrences of an event, given an intensity λ and a certain time period T. *For the same Poisson process,* we could ask about the waiting time between successive events (that is, the interarrival time). In other words, what is the probability distribution of time, t, *between* events? This probability distribution is called the **exponential distribution** (see Figure 9–5). The exponential probability density function is:

$$f(t) = \lambda e^{-\lambda t}, \qquad 0 \leq t < \infty \tag{9–8}$$

The mean of the exponential distribution is $E(t) = (1/\lambda)$ and the variance is $(1/\lambda)^2$.

The right-hand tail of the exponential distribution is:[8]

$$p(t > T) = e^{-m}$$

where

$$m = \lambda T$$

FIGURE 9–5
Exponential Probability Density Function

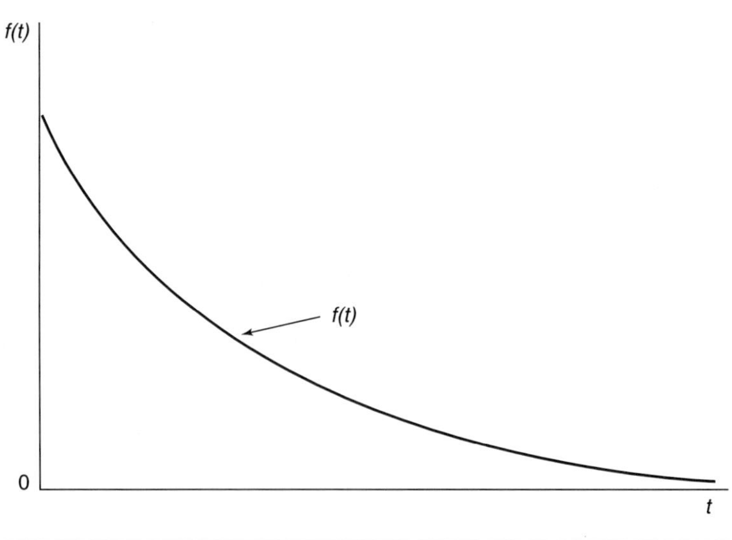

[8] $$\int_T^\infty \lambda e^{-\lambda x} dx = -e^{-\lambda x}\Big|_T^\infty = 0 + e^{-\lambda T} = e^{-\lambda T} = e^{-m}$$

That is, the probability that the time between events (arrivals) is greater than T is e^{-m}. Note that this is also the value of a Poisson mass function for zero occurrences (arrivals) in a time period T.[9]

Thus, the Poisson distribution for arrivals per unit of time and the exponential distribution for interarrival times provide two alternative ways of describing the same thing. We can say that the number of arrivals per unit is Poisson with mean rate $\lambda = 5$ per hour, for example; alternatively, we can say that the interarrival times are exponentially distributed with mean interarrival time $\mu_A = (1/\lambda) = 1/5$ hour; each statement implies the other.

Bibliography

Gross, D., and C. M. Harris. *Fundamentals of Queuing Theory.* 2nd ed. New York: John Wiley & Sons, 1985.

Hall, R. W. *Queuing Methods for Services and Manufacturing.* Englewood Cliffs, NJ: Prentice Hall, 1991.

Hillier, F., and G. J. Lieberman. *Introduction to Operations Research.* 6th ed. New York: McGraw-Hill, 1995.

Lee, A. M. *Applied Queuing Theory.* New York: Macmillan, 1966.

Newell, G. F. *Applications of Queuing Theory.* 2nd ed. London: Chapman & Hall, 1982.

Papadopoulos, H. T., C. Heavey, and J. Browne. *Queuing Theory in Manufacturing Systems Analysis and Design.* London: Chapman & Hall, 1993.

Walrand, J. *An Introduction to Queueing Networks.* Englewood Cliffs, NJ: Prentice Hall, 1988.

Practice Problems[10]

9–1. Ace Airlines has one reservation clerk on duty at a time. He handles information about flight schedules and makes reservations. All calls to Ace Airlines are answered by a voice messaging system. If the clerk is available, the call is transferred to him. If he is busy, the caller is put on hold. When the clerk becomes free, the voice messaging system transfers the caller who has been waiting the longest.

Assume that arrivals follow a Markov process (interarrival times are exponential) with an average interarrival time of 6 minutes. On average, it takes 4 minutes for the clerk to service a customer, and the standard deviation for this service time is 2 minutes.

a. What is the average time a caller must wait before reaching the reservation clerk?

b. What is the average number of calls waiting to be connected to the reservation clerk?

c. What is the average time for a caller to complete a call (i.e., waiting time plus service time)?

9–2. Refer to Problem 9–1. Suppose that the manager of Ace Airlines is considering installing a new reservations system. One of the benefits of this system is that it will reduce the average time required to service a call from four to three minutes (assume that the standard deviation remains the same).

[9]The Poisson mass function is:

$$P(R = r|\lambda,T) = e^{-m}\frac{m^r}{r!}$$

where $m = \lambda T$. If $r = 0$, then:

$$P(R = 0|\lambda,T) = e^{-m}$$

That is, the probability of no arrivals in time T is e^{-m}.

[10]Solutions for these problems are at the end of this chapter.

a. What is the average time a caller must wait before reaching the reservation clerk under this new system?
b. What is the average number of calls waiting to be connected to the reservation clerk under this new system?

9–3. Refer to Problems 9–1 and 9–2. Suppose that instead of reducing the average time required to service a call, the new system will reduce the variability of service time. The service time distribution will have a mean of 4 minutes (as before) but a new standard deviation of 0.75 minutes.

a. What is the average time a caller must wait before reaching the reservation clerk under this system?
b. What is the average number of calls waiting to be connected to the reservation clerk under this system?
c. Now suppose the new system could reduce the variability in service time entirely, so that all calls could be serviced in exactly 4 minutes. Answer (*a*) and (*b*) for this case.

9–4. Refer to Problem 9–1. Suppose that instead of installing a new reservation system, Ace Airlines was considering adding a second reservation clerk. The telephone messaging system would then refer calls to whichever clerk was free. Assume service time for both clerks was the same (mean of 4 minutes, standard deviation of 2 minutes).

a. What is the average time a caller must wait before reaching a reservation clerk under this system?
b. What is the average number of calls waiting to be connected to a reservation clerk under this system?

9–5. Refer to Problems 9–1 and 9–4. Suppose that the cost of adding the second reservation clerk was $500 per day. Ace operates its reservations system for 12 hours per day. Ace considers that there is some goodwill cost per minute of having a customer wait before receiving service.

a. What would this goodwill cost per minute have to be to make Ace airlines indifferent as to whether or not to add the second clerk?
b. What assumption is made about the expected number of calls for each hour of the day?

9–6. You are the manager of a local supermarket. As a part of your operation, you rent out equipment for homeowners to steam clean their carpets. You get requests from customers to rent these units at a rate of 2 per day on average (that is, the mean interarrival time is one-half day). Assume that the requests for the machines follow a Markov process (exponential distribution). You have two of the machines available. Customers rent them for a maximum 2-day period, but on average they are returned in one day. Assume that if you do not have a machine available for rent, the customer goes to another store to rent one (customers do not wait).

a. What is the probability that a customer will request a machine when none is available?
b. How many machines would you need to have available in order to reduce to less than 0.05 the probability of turning a customer away?

Problems

9–7. Two typists have identical jobs. Each types letters dictated by a particular manager. Suppose that letters to be typed arrive at random (exponential interarrival times) with a mean interarrival time of 20 minutes. Suppose each typist can type a letter in 15 minutes, on average (also an exponential distribution).

a. Assuming that each typist does his or her own work, what is the expected waiting time for a letter (time before work is started on a letter)?
b. Suppose that the two typists are pooled. That is, letters are sent to the two together and are done by whoever is free, in order of arrival. What is the expected waiting time for a letter under this arrangement?
c. Comment on this example.

9–8. An integrated petroleum company is considering expansion of its one unloading facility at its Singapore refinery. Due to random variations in weather, loading delays, and other factors, the interarrival times for ships arriving at the refinery to unload crude oil follow an exponential distribution with average $\mu_A = 1.4$ days. Service time is also exponential with average $\mu_S = 0.7$ days.

a. What is the average number of ships waiting to deliver crude oil?
b. What is the average time a ship must wait before beginning to deliver its cargo to the refinery?
c. What is the average total time (waiting plus actual delivery) that a ship spends at the refinery?

9–9. Refer to Problem 9–8. The company has under consideration a second unloading berth, which could be rented for $1,500 per day. The service time for this berth would also be exponential, with the same mean service time as the company's own berth. For each day of a ship spent idle waiting, the company loses $4,000.

a. If a second berth is rented, what would be the average time a ship would wait?
b. What would be the average number of ships waiting?
c. Is the benefit of reduced waiting time (in dollars) worth the rental cost for the second berth?

9–10. Refer to Problem 9–8. An alternative way to improve unloading facilities is for the company to rent a high-speed unloading device. With the new device, the service time would have a distribution with $\mu_S = 0.5$ day and $\sigma_S = 0.3$ day. The daily rental cost of the new device is $1,500.

a. If this new device were rented, what would be the average time a ship would wait?
b. What would be the average total time a ship would spend (waiting plus unloading)?
c. What would be the average number of ships waiting?
d. Is the benefit of the reduced total time (in dollars) worth the rental cost for the new device?

9–11. Refer to Problems 9–9 and 9–10. An analyst for the company, after studying the costs and benefits of the two suggested modifications, suggests, "In each case, the benefit exceeds the cost, so let's install *both* the high-speed unloading device on our own berth *and* rent the second berth." Unfortunately, there are no formulas in the chapter that are appropriate for a two-channel queue with differing mean service times. Find a way to calculate an upper limit on the potential savings from this approach, and use this limit to comment on the analyst's suggestion.

More Challenging Problems

9–12. A bank has established the following processing system for requests for automobile and other personal loans. See Figure 9–6. One customer representative specializes in auto loans, and a customer who comes or calls is directed to this desk. Another customer representative handles other types of personal loans. These representatives help the customer prepare the necessary applications. They then review them to be

FIGURE 9–6
Bank Loan Processing System

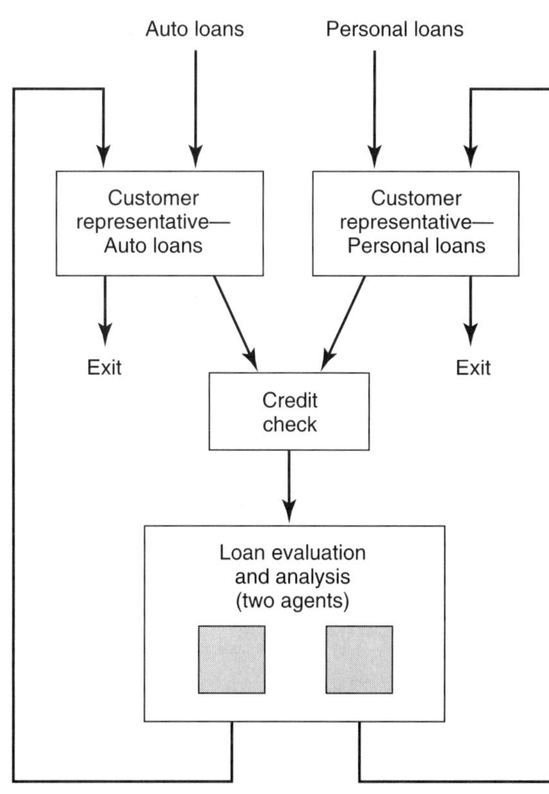

sure they are complete. Each representative handles only the particular type of loan (auto versus other personal loans), and a customer who arrives when the representative is busy is asked to wait.

After the applications have been checked by the customer representative, they are sent to a credit check desk, staffed by one clerk. This clerk collects the necessary credit history of the applicant from the bank's records and from credit agencies. Applications are processed in FIFO order.

When finished at the credit check desk, applications are passed on to the loan evaluation and analysis department where the loan application is evaluated and a final decision is made. This is staffed by two agents, either of whom can handle either type of loan application. Applications are also processed here in FIFO order.

Finally, the applications are returned to the customer representative desk from which they started so that the customer can be informed of the decision and can provide final signatures if necessary. Note that the customer representative is handling two different tasks. Assume they are all done in FIFO order.

Suppose auto loan applications arrive at the customer representative desk 80 minutes apart, on average. It takes the customer representative an average of 43 minutes to process the loan through the first stage, and an additional 20 minutes, on average, to process the second stage (informing about decision and signatures). For other personal loans, the mean interarrival time is 90 minutes, and the service representative takes 60 minutes to process the first stage and 15 minutes for the second stage, on average.

For both types of loans, it takes an average of 26 minutes to do the credit check and 76 minutes to do the loan evaluation and analysis.

All of these times are averages, and actual times vary considerably from the average depending on the complexity of the loan and the applicant's credit history.

The purpose of this problem is to apply some of the insights about processing systems from this chapter. Formulas for networks of queues have not been given so you cannot calculate waiting times in the system.

a. Where do you think will be the bottlenecks in this system? That is, at what station(s) will there be backlogs of applications and congestion? (*Hint:* Look at the system load factor for each station.)

b. What suggestions might you make for improving the operation of this system? What is the basis for your suggestions?

9–13. The public works director for the city is examining a request for an additional building inspector. The request indicates that building inspections are expected to increase from 118 to 154 per month, a 30 percent increase. (Assume 22 working days in a month.) The department currently has four inspectors, and the proposal requests one additional, "only a 25 percent increase that will enable the department to maintain its policy of an average wait of less than one day for those requesting an inspector's services." The director knows that it takes about half a day, on the average, for an inspector to complete an inspection and file a report.

Assuming that requests for inspections and services are Markov (i.e., exponential distributions for interarrival and service times), is the additional person necessary to meet the department policy?

9–14. Many banks and post offices have switched from a system having a line at each teller or clerk to a single waiting line cordoned off by a set of ropes or chains. Examine this change by considering the following two cases:

a. *Case 1.* Customers arrive at a bank at an average rate of 80 per hour (i.e., average interarrival is 0.75 minutes) and form a single line. There are five tellers, and the average service time is 3.0 minutes for each teller. Assuming exponential interarrival and service times, how long is the average wait in line?

b. *Case 2.* Customers arrive at a teller's window at a rate of 16 per hour (mean interarrival time of 3.75 minutes). There are five tellers so the total arrival rate is 80 per hour. There is a separate line at each window (with no switching between lines). As in Case 1, the average service time for each teller is 3.0 minutes. How long is the average wait in line?

c. Comment on the results of Cases 1 and 2. What additional factors might affect waiting times in a real banking situation?

9–15. A tool crib in a factory is a room where special tools, jigs, and other equipment are stored for general use by mechanics. An attendant signs the equipment in and out as the mechanics request it or return it.

Assume that mechanics arrive randomly at the tool crib on an average of one a minute (60 per hour). It takes an attendant an average of 2.5 minutes to locate and sign out the equipment (or to check it in). Mechanics are paid at a rate of $32 per hour and attendants at a rate of $20 per hour. How many attendants should be hired to staff the tool crib? Assume that interarrival times are exponentially distributed and that service times have a distribution with standard deviation of 1.5 minutes.

9–16. Listen-Up is a company that sells music CDs over the telephone. A caller dials the company's toll-free number and a computerized system, operated by the Touch-Tone keys on the phone, allows the caller to listen to samples of music on various CDs and then order them if desired. The computerized system has the limitation that at most three callers can be active at any one time. Suppose that during the peak period calls arrive randomly at an average rate of 20 per hour (i.e., interarrival time is exponentially distributed with mean of 3.0 minutes). If a call arrives when three previous callers are actively using the system, the caller is turned away and told to call at some other time. Assume that callers spend an average of 12 minutes listening to music and making choices (with standard deviation of 6 minutes).

a. What fraction of arriving calls are turned away?

b. Suppose the system were modified so that calls arriving when all three previous users were actively using the system were put in a queue until a slot was available. What would be the average number in the queue?

9–17. Chicago's O'Hare International Airport uses two runways when demand is heavy. Assume that one runway is dedicated to takeoffs only, and the other is dedicated to landings only. Under this method of operation, the service times are exponentially distributed with a mean of two minutes per request on each of the runways. Assume no interference from one runway to the next, so that they can operate independently of one another. Assume requests for takeoff are Markov, with a rate of 25 per hour, and requests for landings are also Markov, with a rate of 25 per hour.

a. Calculate the average number of minutes spent waiting prior to service for takeoffs and for landings.

b. Suppose now that the O'Hare controllers can use both runways for takeoff and landings, interspersed; however, safety requirements under this mode of operation lengthen the average service time for both takeoffs and landings from 2 minutes to 2.16 minutes per request. (Actual service times are exponentially distributed, with mean = 2.16 minutes.) Pooling the two request arrival streams (takeoff requests and landing requests) results in Markov arrivals with a rate of 50 per hour.

Now calculate average waiting time per request. Which arrangement is better—two separate systems or one pooled system?

9–18. The Santa Clon Transit System (SCTS) has 380 buses. On average, each bus requires maintenance (scheduled and unscheduled) once a month. Average maintenance time is two hours. SCTS has five skilled mechanics on duty to perform maintenance; they each work 160 hours per month. Assume interarrival times and service times are exponentially distributed.

a. What is the average time a bus spends waiting for maintenance to begin?

b. What is the average number of buses that are inoperable at any time (i.e., either waiting for service or in service)?

c. Suppose an analyst randomly observes the number of inoperable buses; the average number observed was 95. What might account for the discrepancy between this observation and your answer to (*b*)?

Solutions to Practice Problems

9–1. $\mu_A = 6.0$, $\mu_S = 4.0$, $\sigma_S = 2.0$, $cv_S = \dfrac{\sigma_S}{\mu_S} = 0.5$, $c = 1$, $\rho = \dfrac{\mu_S}{\mu_A} = 0.667$

$$WTM = \frac{\rho}{1-\rho}\left(\frac{1+cv_S^2}{2}\right) = 1.25$$

a. Average waiting time: $\mu_W = \mu_S \cdot WTM = 5.0$ minutes.

b. Average line length: $\mu_L = \dfrac{\mu_W}{\mu_A} = 0.83$.

c. Average total time: $\mu_W + \mu_S = 5.0 + 4.0 = 9.0$ minutes.

9–2. Now $\mu_S = 3.0$, $cv_S = \dfrac{\sigma_S}{\mu_S} = \dfrac{2}{3} = 0.667$, $\rho = \dfrac{\mu_S}{\mu_A} = 0.5$

$$WTM = \frac{\rho}{1-\rho}\left(\frac{1+cv_S^2}{2}\right) = 0.72$$

a. Average waiting time: $\mu_W = \mu_S \cdot WTM = 2.16$ minutes.

b. Average line length: $\mu_L = \dfrac{\mu_W}{\mu_A} = 0.36$.

9–3. Now $\mu_S = 4.0$, $\sigma_S = 0.75$, $cv_S = \dfrac{\sigma_S}{\mu_S} = \dfrac{0.75}{4.0} = 0.1875$, $\rho = \dfrac{\mu_S}{\mu_A} = 0.667$.

$$WTM = \frac{\rho}{1-\rho}\left(\frac{1+cv_S^2}{2}\right) = 1.04$$

a. Average waiting time: $\mu_W = \mu_S \cdot WTM = 4.16$ minutes.

b. Average line length: $\mu_L = \dfrac{\mu_W}{\mu_A} = 0.69$.

c. This becomes a *M/D/1* queue and:

$$WTM = \frac{\rho}{2(1-\rho)} = 1.0 \text{ and}$$

Average waiting time: $\mu_W = \mu_S \cdot WTM = 4.0$ minutes.

Average line length: $\mu_L = \dfrac{\mu_W}{\mu_A} = 0.667.$

9–4. Now this is a *M/G/2* queuing system and:

$$\mu_A = 6.0, \mu_S = 4.0, \sigma_S = 2.0, cv_S = \frac{\sigma_S}{\mu_S} = 0.5,$$

$$c = 2, \rho = \frac{\mu_S}{2\mu_A} = 0.333$$

Table 9–2 does not have a row for system load factor of 0.333. However, we can interpolate and an approximate value (for $c = 2$) is $WTM_{M/M} \approx 0.129$. Also note that arrivals are exponential, so that $\sigma_A = \mu_A$ and $cv_A = 1$. Thus:

$$WTM = WTM_{M/M}\left(\frac{cv_A^2 + cv_S^2}{2}\right)$$

$$= (0.129)\left(\frac{1 + 0.5^2}{2}\right)$$

$$= 0.081$$

a. Average waiting time: $\mu_W = \mu_S \cdot WTM = 0.32$ minutes.

b. Average line length: $\mu_L = \dfrac{\mu_W}{\mu_A} = \dfrac{0.32}{6.0} = 0.054.$

9–5. *a*. An average interarrival time of 6 minutes implies 10 calls per hour, or 120 in the 12-hour day. The reduction in waiting time is from 5 minutes to 0.32, a reduction of 4.68 minutes per caller. For the 120 callers, this is 562 minutes. It would take a goodwill cost of \$0.89 per minute to make a total of \$500 per day for the second clerk.

b. The assumption is that the average rate of arrivals is the same throughout the day. This probably would not be true, as calls would tend to be bunched at certain times.

9–6. This is a loss system with two channels (i.e., two machines available).

$$\mu_A = 0.5 \text{ day}, \mu_S = 1.0 \text{ day}, c = 2, \text{ and}$$

$$\rho = \frac{\mu_S}{c \cdot \mu_A} = 1.0 \text{ or } 100\%$$

a. Fraction lost $= \dfrac{2\rho^2}{1 + 2\rho + 2\rho^2} = 0.40$. That is, the probability is 40 percent.

b. Consider the case with three machines; $c = 3$ and

$$\rho = \frac{\mu_S}{c \cdot \mu_A} = 0.667.$$

$$\text{Fraction lost: } \frac{\dfrac{(3\rho)^3}{3!}}{1 + 3\rho + \dfrac{(3\rho)^2}{2} + \dfrac{(3\rho)^3}{3!}} = 0.211$$

With four machines, $c = 4$ and $\rho = \dfrac{\mu_S}{c \cdot \mu_A} = 0.50.$

$$\text{Fraction lost} = \frac{\dfrac{(4\rho)^4}{4!}}{1 + 4\rho + \dfrac{(4\rho)^2}{2} + \dfrac{(4\rho)^3}{3!} + \dfrac{(4\rho)^4}{4!}} = 0.095$$

With five machines, $c = 5$ and $\rho = \dfrac{\mu_S}{c \cdot \mu_A} = 0.40.$

$$\text{Fraction lost} = \frac{\dfrac{(5\rho)^5}{5!}}{1 + 5\rho + \dfrac{(5\rho)^2}{2} + \dfrac{(5\rho)^3}{3!} + \dfrac{(5\rho)^4}{4!} + \dfrac{(5\rho)^5}{5!}} = 0.037$$

So it would take five machines in order to reduce the probability of turning away a customer to less than 0.05.

Three Applications of Simulation

Simulation is applied to a variety of systems in business and the public sector, from very large to small operations. Here are three applications, selected out of the many presented at the annual *Winter Simulation Conference,* December 1994.

Paramount Farm Pistachio Nut Production[1]

Pistachio nuts are harvested from trees and then hauled by truck to a facility called a huller. The nuts go through several steps: weigh-in, precleaning, hulling, drying, storing, sorting, roasting, drying and packaging. Paramount Farms wished to increase production of pistachios from the current level of 66 million pounds of nuts by 20 percent over a two-year horizon and by 40 percent over four years. The firm developed simulation models for its two major hulling facilities. These models tracked the nuts through the various steps and included random or uncertain factors such as truck arrivals. Based on the simulation analysis, the firm identified the bottlenecks in the process and determined how to reconfigure the existing equipment to obtain the needed 20 percent increase in capacity. Similarly, the firm was able to determine what minimal equipment must be added to obtain the goal of a 40 percent increase in output.

Port of Singapore[2]

Singapore is a major hub for Pacific Ocean container traffic. With over 11 million containers in 1995, Singapore is a very close second to Hong Kong in the world in terms of number of containers handled. Over the past nine years, the Port of Singapore has increased the number of containers handled sixfold, while simultaneously reducing the work force by 11 percent. This spectacular productivity gain has been accomplished partially by investment in the latest handling equipment and information technology. But the port management has also been a very advanced user of the quantitative techniques described in this book. Of particular note is a simulation model developed to analyze the operations in detail.

Port operations start with the arrival of a ship, which is allocated a berth and a number of quay cranes for unloading. Containers are moved from the quay crane by vanlike motor carriers called *prime movers (PMs).* The containers are sent to various parts of the shipyard where they are handled by yard cranes and stacked six or seven feet high. The process is reversed as the ship is reloaded with outgoing containers—yard cranes to PMs to quay cranes to ship. While this is going on, trucks arrive to deliver and pick up containers from the outside. Also, there is movement of containers within the yard to make them more easily available for future ship loading.

The simulation model captures all of this and allows the planners to spot bottlenecks and to make changes in scheduling and allocation of resources (such as cranes or PMs) before the bottlenecks actually occur. This model is a significant part of the decision support system for the port operations.

Taco Bell[3]

Taco Bell is a chain of about 4,000 fast-food restaurants worldwide. Providing good customer service is a challenge. Customer arrivals are random and vary during the day. Customer orders are also random, as well as the time needed to take the order and to prepare it. Walk-in customers have different order patterns than drive-through ones. And, as new menu items are introduced, these patterns change.

Taco Bell built a simulation model that included all these elements and that could be customized for each restaurant. It enables the manager to determine the amount of labor needed to meet customer requirements and how to organize that labor (how to assign tasks, for example). The model has been implemented at the Taco Bells in the United States at an estimated savings of $7.6 million per year in labor costs.

---

[1] Y. Dessouky, G. Maggioli, and D. Szeflin, "A Simulation Approach to Capacity Expansion for the Pistachio Hulling Process," *Proceedings of the 1994 Winter Simulation Conference.*

[2] P. H. Koh, J. L. K. Koh, H. S. Ng, and H. C. Ng, "Using Simulation to Preview Plans of a Container Port Operation," *Proceedings of the 1994 Winter Simulation Conference.*

[3] M. Godward and W. Swart, "An Object Oriented Simulation Model for Determining Labor Requirements at Taco Bell," *Proceedings of the 1994 Winter Simulation Conference.*

CHAPTER

10 SIMULATION

Simulation implies building a replica of some real system and using it under test conditions. Thus, engineers may test out models of new aircraft in wind tunnels, and airline pilots and astronauts train in flight simulators. In management, mathematical models are constructed and used to test the results of decisions before they are implemented in actuality. In a general way, any model of a business decision problem could be called a simulation, since it represents or simulates some aspects of the real problem. For example, a linear programming model may be designed to represent a product-mix problem or a transportation-planning problem. The simulation models considered in this chapter differ from other models in three respects:

1. Simulation models are typically not designed to find optimal or best solutions, as in linear programming or decision analysis. Instead, several proposed alternatives are evaluated and a decision is made on the basis of a comparison of the results. In other words, they evaluate performance of given prespecified systems.
2. Simulation models typically focus on the detailed operations, either physical or financial, of the system. The system is studied as it operates over time, and the effects of one time period's results on the next are included.
3. Random or probabilistic elements are included in the simulation models in this chapter. This includes examples of queuing systems, inventory systems, and risk analysis models, often called Monte Carlo simulation.

To illustrate these differences, consider building a model of a factory that produces a series of products. A linear programming model might develop the optimal product mix. A more detailed simulation model might be concerned with the specifics of how the factory is scheduled to achieve the desired product mix, taking into account machine setup times, waiting time before processing, and other details that cannot be included in the linear programming formulation.

Probabilistic Simulation

In many situations, uncertainty plays a key part in the operations of the system, and it is important to take this randomness into account in the model. Waiting-line problems can be analyzed by building such a simulation model. Where we can adequately solve the problem by mathematical methods, it is generally preferable to do so. However, there are many queuing (and other) situations that cannot be solved easily by mathematics, and hence, we resort to simulation.

Example 1

Consider a warehouse that has one dock used to unload railroad freight cars. Incoming freight cars are delivered to the warehouse during the night. It takes exactly half a day to unload a car. If more than two cars are waiting to be unloaded on a given day, the unloading of some of the cars is postponed until the following day.

Past experience has indicated that the number of cars arriving during the night have the frequencies shown in Table 10–1. Furthermore, there is no apparent pattern, so that the number arriving on any night is independent of the number arriving on any other night.

This is a one-channel queuing problem with an average service rate of 2 per day and an average arrival rate of 1.5 per day. However, it can be shown that the arrivals are not Poisson; hence, none of the standard queuing models apply directly.

The first step in simulating this queuing process is to generate a history or time series of arrivals for a number of nights. This is done using a randomized or **Monte Carlo** process. One way to do this would be to take 100 chips and write the number 0 on 23 of them; the number 1 on 30 of them; the number 2 on 30 of them; and so on, corresponding to the frequencies in Table 10–1. We could then draw a chip from a hat, and the number on the chip would indicate the number of freight cars arriving in a given simulated period.

A simpler procedure is to use a table of random numbers, such as Table 10–2. Each entry in the table was drawn in such a way that each digit (zero through nine) had an equal chance of being drawn.

We could then assign two-digit random numbers to each of the possible outcomes (i.e., to the number of arrivals), as shown in Table 10–3.

There are 100 two-digit pairs of numbers. Note that 23 are assigned to the event "zero cars arrive"; 30 to the event "one car arrives"; 30 to the event "two cars arrive"; and so on. Since each two-digit number has a 1/100 chance of coming up, the probability that the event "zero cars arrive" will occur is 23/100, or 0.23, as desired.

We are now prepared to simulate the queuing process. This is done in Table 10–4.

TABLE 10–1

Number of Cars Arriving	*Relative Frequency*
0	0.23
1	0.30
2	0.30
3	0.10
4	0.05
5	0.02
6 or more	0.00
	1.00

Average = 1.5 cars per night

TABLE 10–2
Table of Random Digits

97	95	12	11	90	49	57	13	86	81
02	92	75	91	24	58	39	22	13	02
80	67	14	99	16	89	96	63	67	60
66	24	72	57	32	15	49	63	00	04
96	76	20	28	72	12	77	23	79	46
55	64	82	61	73	94	26	18	37	31
50	02	74	70	16	85	95	32	85	67
29	53	08	33	81	34	30	21	24	25
58	16	01	91	70	07	50	13	18	24
51	16	69	67	16	53	11	06	36	10
04	55	36	97	30	99	80	10	52	40
86	54	35	61	59	89	64	97	16	02
24	23	52	11	59	10	88	68	17	39
39	36	99	50	74	27	69	48	32	68
47	44	41	86	83	50	24	51	02	08
60	71	41	25	90	93	07	24	29	59
65	88	48	06	68	92	70	97	02	66
44	74	11	60	14	57	08	54	12	90
93	10	95	80	32	50	40	44	08	12
20	46	36	19	47	78	16	90	59	64
86	54	24	88	94	14	58	49	80	79
12	88	12	25	19	70	40	06	40	31
42	00	50	24	60	90	69	60	07	86
29	98	81	68	61	24	90	92	32	68
36	63	02	37	89	40	81	77	74	82
01	77	82	78	20	72	35	38	56	89
41	69	43	37	41	21	36	39	57	80
54	40	76	04	05	01	45	84	55	11
68	03	82	32	22	80	92	47	77	62
21	31	77	75	43	13	83	43	70	16
53	64	54	21	04	23	85	44	81	36
91	66	21	47	95	69	58	91	47	59
48	72	74	40	97	92	05	01	61	18
36	21	47	71	84	46	09	85	32	82
55	95	24	85	84	51	61	60	62	13
70	27	01	88	84	85	77	94	67	35
38	13	66	15	38	54	43	64	25	43
36	80	25	24	92	98	35	12	17	62
98	10	91	61	04	90	05	22	75	20
50	54	29	19	26	26	87	94	27	73

TABLE 10–3

Number of Cars Arriving	*Random Digits*	*Relative Frequency*
0	00 to 22	0.23
1	23 to 52	0.30
2	53 to 82	0.30
3	83 to 92	0.10
4	93 to 97	0.05
5	98 and 99	0.02
		1.00

Table 10–4
Queuing System Simulation

Day Number	*Random Number*	*Number of Arrivals*	*Total Number to Be Unloaded*	*Number Unloaded*	*Number Delayed to Following Day*
x	97	4	4	2	2
x	02	0	2	2	0
x	80	2	2	2	0
1	66	2	2	2	0
2	96	4	4	2	2
3	55	2	4	2	2
4	50	1	3	2	1
5	29	1	2	2	0
6	58	2	2	2	0
7	51	1	1	1	0
8	04	0	0	0	0
9	86	3	3	2	1
10	24	1	2	2	0
11	39	1	1	1	0
12	47	1	1	1	0
13	60	2	2	2	0
14	65	2	2	2	0
15	44	1	1	1	0
16	93	4	4	2	2
17	20	0	2	2	0
18	86	3	3	2	1
19	12	0	1	1	0
20	42	1	1	1	0
21	29	1	1	1	0
22	36	1	1	1	0
23	01	0	0	0	0
24	41	1	1	1	0
25	54	2	2	2	0
26	68	2	2	2	0
27	21	0	0	0	0
28	53	2	2	2	0
29	91	3	3	2	1
30	48	1	2	2	0
31	36	1	1	1	0
32	55	2	2	2	0
33	70	2	2	2	0
34	38	1	1	1	0
35	36	1	1	1	0
36	98	5	5	2	3
37	50	1	4	2	2
38	95	4	6	2	4
39	92	3	7	2	5
40	67	2	7	2	5
41	24	1	6	2	4
42	76	2	6	2	4
43	64	2	6	2	4
44	02	0	4	2	2
45	53	2	4	2	2
46	16	0	2	2	0
47	16	0	0	0	0
48	55	2	2	2	0
49	54	2	2	2	0
50	23	1	1	1	0
Totals		79			45
Average		1.58			0.90

Three days are used to start the process (marked x). For the first day, the random number (taken from Table 10–2) is 97. Since 97 corresponds to the event "four cars arrive" in Table 10–3, we list four in the third column. Of these four cars, two are unloaded, and the unloading of the other two is postponed until the following day. The random number for the second day is 02 (again from Table 10–2). This means zero cars arrive, and the two cars from the previous day are unloaded. We continue in the same fashion. However, we do not count the results of the first three days; this is the **initialization period.** The simulation starts with no freight cars, which is not typical. The initialization period gives the simulation a chance to reach typical or "steady state" behavior before results are counted.

Table 10–4 simulates 50 days of operation (in addition to the three days to get started). During most of the period, there is little delay. Note, however, that there is considerable delay starting around period 36. The average number of arrivals per day (1.58) over the sample period of 50 days is slightly larger than the expected number per day (1.50). On the average, 0.90 cars are delayed per day. For more accurate results, the simulation should be carried on for more days.

We could use the simulation model to compare the effects of feasible alternatives on waiting time and cost. For example, in this case we could compare delays under the current service rate of two per day with a service rate of three per day. Or we could introduce one or more additional channels.

Simulation and Computers

The calculations in Table 10–4 are tedious; in an actual application a computer model would be built to perform the analysis. There are now several simulation packages available for personal computers that have the capability of building very complex models, can generate random values from a wide range of distributions, and accumulate statistics and summary measures of the results.[4] Many even have a graphical user interface and animation, allowing the user to observe the simulation as it occurs.

It is also possible to build relatively simple models of systems on spreadsheets. Appendix 2 of this chapter is a tutorial in building such systems. And for risk analysis or Monte Carlo models, such as that illustrated in Example 3 below, spreadsheets are quite effective and can handle even quite complex models. There are popular software add-ins to spreadsheets that make this even easier.[5]

Computers, of course, make it quite easy to generate many simulated periods or trials—not just the 50 or so used in the manual examples in this chapter. A large number of trials is essential in order to obtain valid results when simulating systems that involve randomness, especially queuing and waiting line systems.

However, it is instructive to go through the manual examples of this chapter in order to understand the basic ideas involved. Examples 2 and 3 below continue this pattern.

---

[4]For a recent survey of simulation software see James J. Swain, "Simulation Survey: Tools for Process Understanding and Improvement," *OR/MS Today,* August 1995.

[5]See, for example, the programs @RISK (Newfield, NJ, Palisade Corp., 1994) and Crystal Ball (Boulder, CO, Decisioneering, Inc., 1994).

Simulation and Inventory Control

The use of simulation is not restricted to queuing processes. Many phases of business operations have been simulated with successful results. We shall illustrate by a brief example how simulation could be applied to the solution of an inventory problem.

Example 2
Suppose that the weekly demand of a certain product has the distribution shown in Table 10–5.

When an order is placed to replenish inventory, there is a delivery lag, which is a random variable, as shown in Table 10–6.

We want to determine an order quantity, Q, and an order point, R. We can do this by trying several values of Q and R, and simulating to determine the best values.

An illustration with $Q = 15$ and $R = 5$ is shown in Table 10–7. Note that the opening inventory is set to 10, and five weeks are used for initialization before the results are counted. We assume no backorders are allowed. If we established the cost of ordering, the cost of holding inventory, and the cost of being out of stock, we could estimate the cost of the inventory system under the rule $Q = 15$ and $R = 5$. Alternative rules could be compared to this. For example, formulas for optimal order quantity and optimum reorder point could be used, even though the assumptions needed for such formulas are not met in our example (the replenishment lead time is not constant). The amount of error introduced by using the formulas may be estimated by the simulation. Frequently, a method of solution may be operationally useful even when it is not strictly applicable theoretically.

TABLE 10–5
Probability Distribution for Weekly Demand

Number Demanded	*Probability*	*Random Numbers Assigned*
0	0.10	00 to 09
1	0.40	10 to 49
2	0.30	50 to 79
3	0.20	80 to 99
	1.00	

TABLE 10–6
Probability Distribution for Delivery Lag

Number of Weeks from Order to Delivery	*Probability*	*Random Numbers Assigned*
2	0.20	00 to 19
3	0.60	20 to 79
4	0.20	80 to 99
	1.00	

Table 10–7 Inventory Simulation Illustration

Week Number	Receipts	Beginning Inventory	Random Number	Sales (units)	Ending Inventory	Lost Sales (outages)	Orders	Random Number for Orders	Number of Weeks Hence When Order Will Arrive
x		10	37	1	9				
x		9	51	2	7				
x		7	68	2	5		15	45	3
x		5	83	3	2				
x		2	56	2	0				
0	15	15	11	1	14				
1		14	91	3	11				
2		11	99	3	8				
3		8	57	2	6				
4		6	28	1	5		15	61	3
5		5	70	2	3				
6		3	33	1	2				
7	15	17	91	3	14				
8		14	67	2	12				
9		12	97	3	9				
10		9	61	2	7				
11		7	11	1	6				
12		6	50	2	4		15	86	4
13		4	25	1	3				
14		3	06	0	3				
15		3	60	2	1				
16	15	16	80	3	13				
17		13	19	1	12				
18		12	88	3	9				
19		9	25	1	8				
20		8	24	1	7				
21		7	68	2	5		15	37	3
22		5	78	2	3				
23		3	37	1	2				
24	15	17	04	0	17				
25		17	32	1	16				
26		16	75	2	14				
27		14	21	1	13				
28		13	47	1	12				
29		12	40	1	11				
30		11	71	2	9				
31		9	85	3	6				
32		6	88	3	3		15	15	2
33		3	24	1	2				
34	15	17	61	2	15				
35		15	19	1	14				
36		14	90	3	11				
37		11	24	1	10				
38		10	16	1	9				
39		9	32	1	8				
40		8	72	2	6				
Totals		412				0			
Average		10.3							

Summary

Probabilistic simulation models include random variables for uncertain events. Random numbers are assigned in accordance with the probabilities for the uncertain events, and the Monte Carlo process is used to generate a history of events for simulating the system under study. Queuing and inventory systems are examples of probabilistic simulation applications.

Risk Analysis

Consider the decision on a major capital investment such as the introduction of a new product. The profitability of the investment depends on several factors that are generally uncertain. Estimates of total market for the product; the market share that the firm can attain; the growth in the market; the cost of producing the product; the selling price; the life of the product; and even the cost of the equipment needed—all are generally subject to substantial uncertainty.

One common approach would be to make single-number "best estimates" for each of the uncertain factors above and then to calculate a measure of profitability. This approach has two drawbacks:

1. There is no guarantee that using the "best estimates" will give the true expected profitability of the project.
2. There is no way to measure the risk associated with the investment. In particular, the manager has no way of determining the probability that the project will lose money or the probability that very large profits will result. For example, using only the one-number approach, a manager would not be able to distinguish between the two projects shown in Figure 10–1. And yet such information is necessary if techniques for dealing with risk, such as utility measures, are to be applied.

Risk analysis is a technique designed to circumvent these two disadvantages. The general approach is to assign a subjective probability distribution to each un-

FIGURE 10–1 Comparison of Two Projects

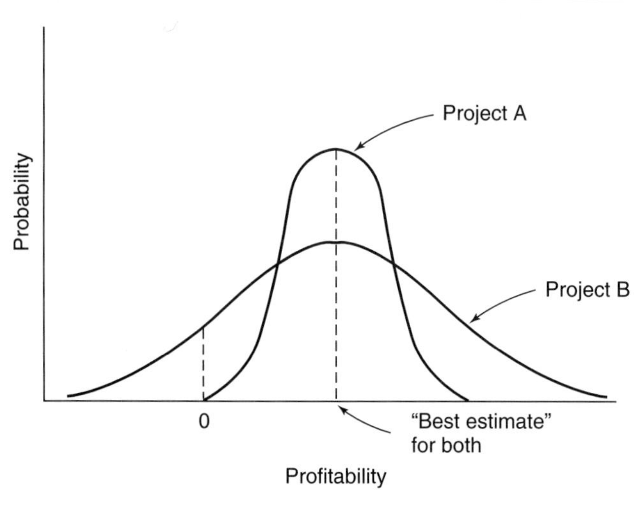

known factor and to combine these, using the Monte Carlo simulation approach, into a probability distribution for the project profitability as a whole. This can be shown with a simple example.

Example 3
Suppose we are considering marketing a new product. The investment required is $5 million. There are three uncertain factors: selling price, variable cost, and annual sales volume. The product has a life of only one year. Table 10–8 contains the various possible levels of these factors, together with the estimated probability of each. We will assume that the factors in Table 10–8 are statistically *independent.* (This is an important assumption. If it were not true, we would want to modify our simulation to include whatever probabilistic dependence we felt appropriate.)

Because this is a very simple example, it is possible to use decision tree and probability tree techniques to calculate the various outcomes and probabilities. In this case, we have only $3 \cdot 3 \cdot 3 = 27$ possible distinct outcomes. However, in a more realistic problem with many uncertain factors each having 10 or 20 levels, we could easily have a million possible outcomes. In these circumstances, the technique of simulation can be very useful in estimating both the average profitability of the investment and its "riskiness" as described by the probability of achieving various levels of profit.

We first need a way of generating random values for the elements of Table 10–8 according to the stated probabilities. As before, we associate various random numbers with various outcomes, as in Table 10–9.

Now we can begin the simulation. We generate single-digit random numbers from the random number table (Table 10–2) and, in turn, determine a price, a cost, and a volume. Once these elements have been determined, profit (in millions of dollars) is computed as follows:

$$\text{Profit} = (\text{Price} - \text{Cost}) \cdot \text{Volume} - 5.0$$

Then the process is repeated a large number of times to generate a large number of profit outcomes. See Table 10–10 for a sample of 25 trials. Note that in the risk analysis type of simulation, each trial is separate from the rest; thus, there is no need for any initialization period.

TABLE 10–8
Factors in Risk Analysis Example

Selling Price	*Probability*	*Variable Cost*	*Probability*	*Sales Volume (million units)*	*Probability*
$4	0.3	$2	0.1	3.0	0.2
5	0.5	3	0.6	4.0	0.4
6	0.2	4	0.3	5.0	0.4

TABLE 10–9
Random Number Assignments in Risk Analysis Example

Selling Price	*Random Numbers*	*Variable Cost*	*Random Numbers*	*Sales Volume (million units)*	*Random Numbers*
$4	0–2	$2	0	3.0	0, 1
5	3–7	3	1–6	4.0	2–5
6	8, 9	4	7–9	5.0	6–9

TABLE 10–10
Risk Analysis Example— 25 Trials

Trial	Random Number	Price	Random Number	Cost	Random Number	Volume (million units)	Profit ($ million)
1	8	$6	0	$2	6	5	15
2	0	4	4	3	3	4	−1
3	6	5	3	3	2	4	3
4	1	4	4	3	0	3	−2
5	3	5	6	3	0	3	1
6	5	5	6	3	9	5	5
7	1	4	6	3	7	5	0
8	3	5	8	4	6	5	0
9	2	4	8	4	8	5	−5
10	1	4	6	3	1	3	−2
11	5	5	7	4	3	4	−1
12	9	6	9	4	6	5	5
13	4	5	9	4	7	5	0
14	7	5	2	3	6	5	5
15	9	6	5	3	3	4	7
16	0	4	5	3	0	3	−2
17	1	4	1	3	8	5	0
18	0	4	6	3	4	4	−1
19	8	6	8	4	6	5	5
20	9	6	2	3	4	4	7
21	0	4	7	4	7	5	−5
22	0	4	0	2	8	5	5
23	4	5	0	2	1	3	4
24	6	5	5	3	8	5	5
25	4	5	0	2	1	3	4
							Average = 2.08

Twenty-five trials is not enough to make a precise estimate of the average profitability or of the probability distribution of profits. If this process were programmed on a computer, a thousand or more trials could be easily simulated. However, for illustrative purposes, we will base our discussion on the results of these 25 trials.

Note that the average profit is $2.08 million. It is interesting to compare this with simpler methods of analysis. For example, if we had used the one-number approach and used the most likely value for each factor, our estimate of profit would have been:

$$\text{Most likely profit} = (\$5 - \$3) \cdot (4.0) - \$5.0 = \$3.0 \text{ million}$$

Thus, the simple one-number approach, in this case, significantly overstates the expected profitability of the investment.

Because it is a simple case, computation of the expected profit (the profit of each of the 27 possible outcomes, weighted by the probabilities) can be performed;[6] this expected profit is $2.14 million. Thus, as one would expect, our sample average for 25 trials is not precisely equal to expected profit. However, the expected profit cal-

[6]In this case, since the factors are independent and related by simple multiplication and addition, we can compute the expected profit from the expected values of price, cost, and volume. If, however, these elements were not linearly related or independent, then the complete set of branches of the probability tree would have to be evaluated.

FIGURE 10–2
Risk Profile: Sample Cumulative Probability Function

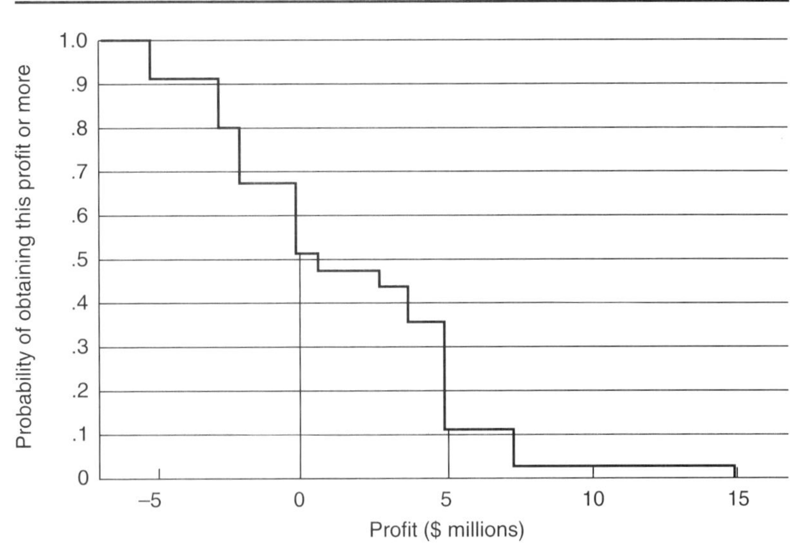

culation sheds no light on the *risk* associated with the investment, whereas the set of 25 sample outcomes clearly indicates that one may actually incur a loss (for example, trial 2 in Table 10–10).

A convenient way to represent the results of a risk analysis is to list the outcomes by profitability and plot a graph of the sample cumulative probability function (see Figure 10–2). This is called a *risk profile.* From Figure 10–2 we see that there is a 68 percent chance of making 0 profit or more (and a 32 percent chance of incurring a loss); there is a 36 percent chance of making $5 million or more, and no chance of making more than $15 million. As larger numbers of trials are simulated, the curve of Figure 10–2 would smooth out somewhat (although it would continue to have the staircase shape because there is a finite number of alternative outcomes rather than an infinite number).

Summary

Risk analysis is an application of simulation to evaluation of investment projects. Probability distributions are assessed for the uncertain factors involved in a project and combined, using the Monte Carlo process, to obtain the probability distribution for overall project profitability.

Simulation with Continuous Probability Distributions

In the risk analysis example above, the random variables were discrete (e.g., selling price took on only three distinct possible values: $4, $5, and $6). There may be situations in which we would like to assume that elements are random variables drawn from some continuous probability distribution. Suppose, for example, that we felt that annual sales volume in the risk analysis example would be normally distributed, with mean $\mu = 3.0$ million units and standard deviation $\sigma = 0.5$ million units. How can we generate random values of sales volume for use in a simulation?

Graphical Method

One way to generate random variables from continuous distributions is to plot the cumulative distribution function. For the normal distribution just mentioned, the cumulative distribution function is shown in Figure 10–3.

In order to use the cumulative distribution function, we first use a table of random numbers (like Table 10–2) to generate a random decimal between 0 and 1. This can be done by taking three random numbers from Table 10–2 and placing the decimal point in front of them. For example, if the random numbers 7, 3, and 6 were drawn, the corresponding decimal would be 0.736.

Then the cumulative curve of Figure 10–3 is *entered on the vertical axis* at the corresponding decimal value (0.736 in our example). Draw a horizontal line over to the cumulative curve, and when the line at height 0.736 hits the curve, drop straight down to the horizontal axis. Then read off the value reached; this value will be the particular random value desired. In our case, this value is approximately 3.30.

This method of generating random values works because the choice of a random decimal between 0 and 1 is equivalent to choosing a random *percentile* of the distribution. Then the figure is used to convert the random percentile (in our case, the 73.6 percentile) to a particular value (3.30). The method is general and can be used for *any* cumulative probability distribution, either continuous or discrete.

For a normal random variable, the process just described can be performed using standard normal tables (see Table A at the end of the text). We enter the table with the random decimal 0.736 and find the corresponding Z value is $Z = 0.63$. Then the random estimate of sales volume is:

$$\text{Sales volume} = \mu + Z\sigma = 3.0 + 0.63(0.5) = 3.315 \text{ million units}$$

FIGURE 10–3
Cumulative Normal Distribution ($\mu = 3.0, \sigma = 0.5$)

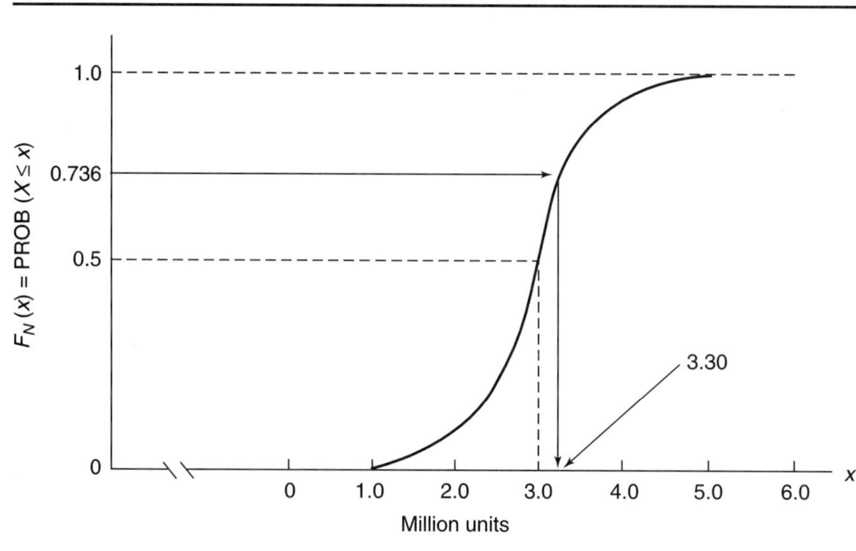

Sometimes it is possible to perform the above process algebraically. See Appendix 1 to this chapter for an illustration of the algebraic method.

Computer Generation of Random Variables

Spreadsheet programs have the capability of generating random values from various probability distributions. For example, Excel can generate random draws from the normal, binomial, exponential, Poisson and other distributions. It also has a function RAND( ), which generates a uniform random value between zero and 1. Some of these are illustrated in the tutorial in Appendix 2.

Summary

Simulation may be performed with continuous random variables either by graphic, tabular look-up, or computer generation using the appropriate cumulative probability distribution.

Simulation of Complex Systems

Although simulation is a useful tool in dealing with queuing, inventory, risk analysis, and other problems, perhaps its greatest contribution is in the analysis of complex systems. Many real-world problems involve systems made up of many component parts that are interrelated; the system may be dynamic and changing over time; and the system may involve probabilistic or uncertain events. Simulation may be the only technique for quantitative analysis of such problems.

We shall use an example to illustrate the use of simulation for such problems. Consider the operations of a barge line down the Ohio–Mississippi river system.[7] This barge company is a subsidiary of a steel company and receives barge loads of steel at its home port in Pittsburgh for shipment down the river to various ports, and to Gulf Coast ports by another barge line. Figure 10–4 sketches the operations of this system. Barge loads of steel arrive at the Pittsburgh port in a random fashion represented by a probability distribution in Figure 10–4. The destinations of these barges also vary from time to time, shown by the frequency distribution in the figure. If a barge is available, the steel is loaded. Otherwise, it must be shipped by another (i.e., a foreign) barge company. A tug will start with a tow of full barges (tow size is limited because of the locks in the river system) and calls on the various ports downstream. The number of ports is simplified to six in the illustration. At each port, barges designated for that port are dropped. At New Orleans, barges destined for Gulf ports of Pascagoula (P) and Orange (O) are transferred to another barge line and then the tug turns upstream and picks up available empty barges from the ports as it goes. These empty barges are available after a turnaround time (for unloading), which is a random event. Back at the home port, the tug returns to the

[7]This example was adapted from G. G. O'Brien and R. R. Crane, "The Scheduling of a Barge Line," *Operations Research* 7 (1959), pp. 561–70.

FIGURE 10–4 Operations of Barge Company

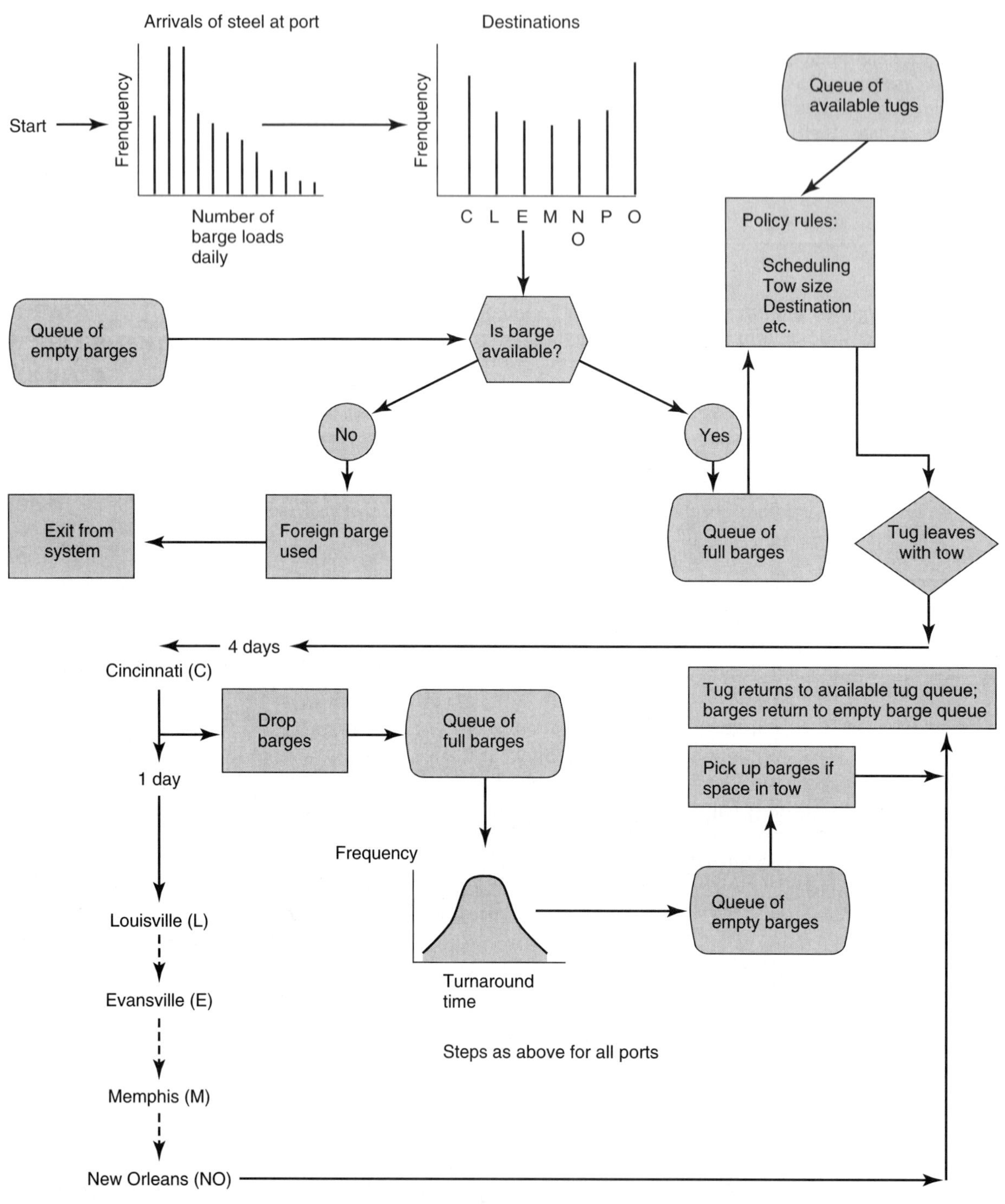

available tug queue (after taking a short time for restocking, repairs, etc.) and the barges go to the empty barge queue, both ready to move back into the system again.

The company has 4 tugs and 127 barges, and at any one time these may be scattered throughout the system.

A simulation model of this system has been constructed and programmed on a computer. The probabilistic elements (arrivals of steel, destinations for barges, and turnaround times) are incorporated using the Monte Carlo simulation technique. The computer model must also keep track of time in the system; keep track of the barges, tugs, and physical limitations in the system; move the tugs and barges from port to port in accordance with travel distances (four days from Pittsburgh to Cincinnati, for example); and so on.

Once such a simulation model is developed, management can use it to try out possible alternative policies. Several scheduling rules might be tried, including:

1. Having a tug leave Pittsburgh at fixed intervals—8 or 10 days apart—regardless of how many barges it has.
2. Having a tug leave when it has a tow of at least so many barges—16, for example.

Other scheduling policies are, of course, possible. In addition, the company could examine the effects on the system of additional equipment—more barges or tugs, or faster tugs.

The simulation model allows the company to experiment with these and other changes without having to try them out on the real system. Besides the cost of disruption that would be incurred, it is difficult to evaluate results of an experiment in the real world because other external factors are constantly changing. It is hard to know if the observed results are attributable to the external factors or to the changes in the system. This problem does not exist in simulation models because the external factors can be controlled.

Simulation has been used extensively to deal with a great variety of problems. Simulation models have been built for transportation systems, factories, and airport operations; for the processing of defendants in court systems; for ambulance and fire services; for computer and communications systems; and for studying urban and world population and economic growth.

Although simulation models of complex systems can be very valuable, there are some disadvantages. They tend to be relatively costly to build. It may also be difficult to validate a complex simulation (i.e., ensure that the desired model framework is properly represented without any "bugs" in the computer program or logic). Also, one must determine an appropriate initialization period and run length for the simulation. Statistical methods can be useful in determining how long a simulation should be run in order to determine whether a particular result is due to chance or is a systematic result. And, of course, like all models, simulations are simplifications of the real world and may fail to adequately represent important elements or relationships.

Summary

An important application of simulation is the study of complex operation systems that cannot be analyzed by optimization or other mathematical methods.

Appendix 1
Algebraic Method to Generate Random Variables

Suppose the cumulative distribution function of interest can be expressed in closed form (i.e., in a formula as a function of x without any integration signs); then the graphical process can be replaced by an equivalent algebraic relationship. For example, consider the exponential probability density function:

$$f(t) = \lambda e^{-\lambda t}, \quad 0 < t < \infty$$

The cumulative distribution function of the exponential distribution is:

$$F(t) = 1 - e^{-\lambda t}$$

Now we set a hypothetical random decimal (R.D.) equal to the cumulative distribution function and solve for t:

$$\text{R.D.} = 1 - e^{-\lambda t}$$

$$e^{-\lambda t} = 1 - \text{R.D.}$$

Since our random decimal is between 0 and 1, so is 1 − R.D.; thus, *this* quantity (1 − R.D.) can be considered directly as a random decimal. So we can define:

$$e^{\ \lambda t} = \text{R.D.}$$

Taking natural logarithms:

$$-\lambda t = \log_e(\text{R.D.})$$

or:

$$t = -(1/\lambda)\log_e(\text{R.D.})$$

This equation can be used directly to generate values from an exponential distribution with parameter λ. First, a random decimal (R.D.) is obtained from a random number table such as Table 10–2; then the particular value obtained is substituted into the right-hand side of the equation and solved to produce a particular value for t. The value obtained will be a random draw from an exponential distribution with parameter λ.

For example, if $\lambda = 5$ and the random decimal were R.D. = 0.475, then from tables of natural logarithms, $\log_e(0.475) = -0.744$; and $t = -(1/5)(-0.744) = 0.1488$. This value would be a random draw from an exponential distribution with parameter $\lambda = 5$ (mean $1/\lambda = 1/5$).

Appendix 2
Monte Carlo Simulation on Spreadsheets

Modern spreadsheet software is quite flexible, and it is possible to use a spreadsheet to build and analyze simple simulations. This appendix is designed to be a short tutorial for using Excel to build such models. The best way to use this tutorial is to sit down at a personal computer with Excel and work through the steps as instructed. The tutorial presumes that you know at least the basics of Excel spreadsheet usage.

We shall work through two of the examples in the chapter, so you should review them before beginning. In the warehouse example, a variable number of rail cars arrive during the night and are unloaded during the day. It takes exactly one-half day to unload a rail car, so a maximum of two can be unloaded each day. The probability distribution for the number of arrivals is a discrete distribution and is given in Table 10–11. We shall simulate 500 days of operation.

Step 1. To start the simulation, open an Excel workbook and enter the headings as shown in Figure 10–5. Also enter the information for the probability distribution of arrivals in columns H and I as indicated. Fill in all the numbers as shown, including a value of 2 in cell B2, which is the unloading capacity of the dock.

Step 2. Fill in column A with the number for each day. To do this, type the number 1 in cell **A7.** If the cursor has moved from cell A7, move it back there. Then click on the *Edit* item at the top of the spreadsheet. Then click on the *Fill* item in the menu. Then click on *Series* in the side menu. The dialogue box, as shown in Figure 10–6, appears; fill it in as shown.

TABLE 10–11
Distribution of Rail Car Arrivals

Number of Cars Arriving (X)	*Probability of X Arrivals*
0	0.23
1	0.30
2	0.30
3	0.10
4	0.05
5	0.02

FIGURE 10–5 Headings for Columns of Model and Probability Distribution

	A	B	C	D	E	F	G	H	I
1			Warehouse Simulation Model						
2	Dock Cap.	2							
3									
4	Day	Number of	No. to	Actually	No.			No. of	Probability
5		Arrivals	Unload	Unloaded	Delayed			Arrivals	
6	0				0			0	0.23
7	1							1	0.30
8	2							2	0.30
9								3	0.10
10								4	0.05
11								5	0.02
12									

FIGURE 10–6
Data Fill Dialogue Box

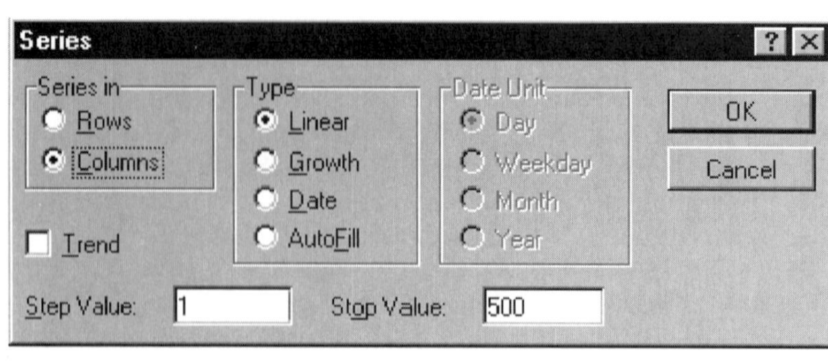

In particular, click on the circle next to *Columns* and on the circle beside *Linear.* Make the step value 1 and enter 500 in the stop value. Then click **OK.** The column from A7 down should fill with the numbers 1 to 500.

Generating Random Values from Probability Distributions

Excel has a built-in feature that makes generating random values from probability distributions relatively easy. Samples can be randomly drawn from certain continuous probability distributions (the normal distribution and the uniform distribution) and from the binomial and Poisson discrete distributions. A related feature is to allow random draws from a discrete distribution defined by a table such as Table 10–11 and incorporated in columns H and I in the spreadsheet created in step 1.

Step 3. Click on the *Tools* menu item at the top of the spreadsheet. A dropdown menu will appear and an item near the bottom will be *Data Analysis.* Click on this. (*Note:* If the *Data Analysis* item does not appear on the *Tools* menu, it may not have been added into the spreadsheet. Go to the *Help* menu and look under "add-ins" to see how to include this in your spreadsheet.)

Step 4. The menu shown in Figure 10–7 should appear. Click on the item *Random Number Generation.* (You may need to scroll down a few items.)

Step 5. The dialogue box shown as Figure 10–8 should appear. Fill it in as shown. The explanations for the various items are as follows:

- Number of Variables is 1 since we wish to generate only one column of random draws from the probability distribution.
- Number of Random Numbers is 500—we are going to take a sample of 500 draws from the probability distribution.
- The distribution to be used is a discrete distribution, as defined. Clicking on the down arrow shows what other options are available.
- The Value and Probability Input Range is H6 to I11. It contains two columns, the first with the values of the random variable and the second with the probabilities. The probabilities must add to 1.0. You can type in the values as **H6:I11** (Excel will add the $s) or highlight the cells on the spreadsheet.

FIGURE 10–7
Menu

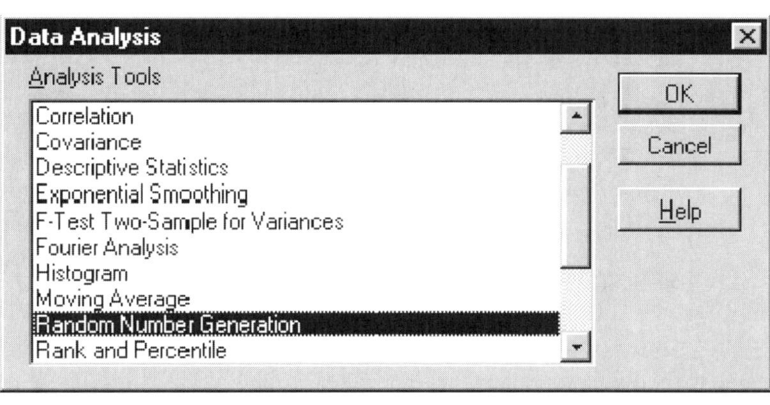

FIGURE 10–8
Dialogue Box

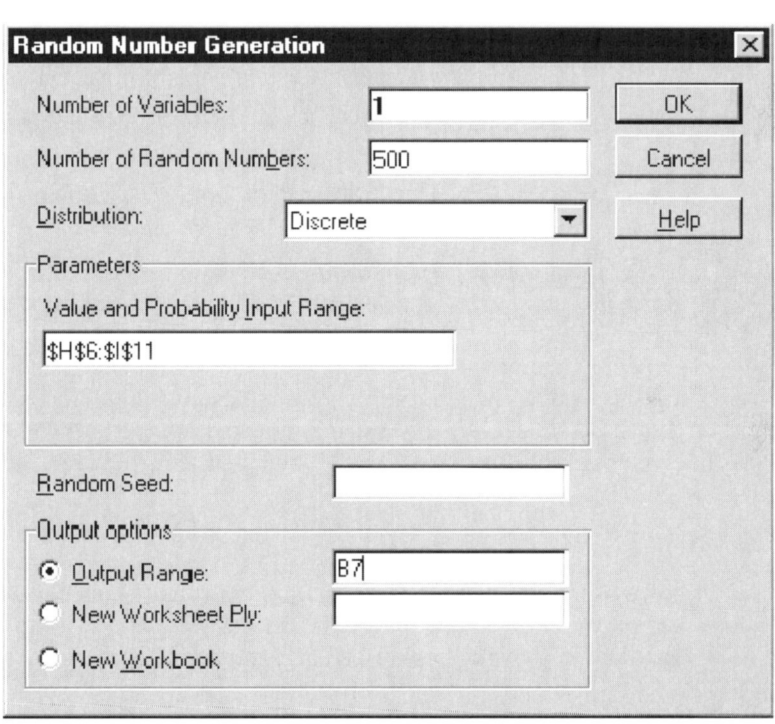

- No random seed is needed.
- Click the circle next to *Output Range,* and enter the value **B7.** This is the top cell in the column in which the 500 random sample of values will be placed.
- When you have finished, click **OK.**

At this point, Column B on the spreadsheet (from cell B7 down to B506) will be filled with values for number of rail cars arriving each evening, drawn with the probabilities from the table in the spreadsheet.

Step 6. Move to cell C7 and type **=B7+E6** This indicates that the number of cars to be unloaded on a given day is the number delayed from the previous day plus the arrivals that night.

Step 7. Move to cell D7 and type **=Min($B$2,C7)** This indicates that the number of cars unloaded on a given day is the smaller of the dock's capacity (contained in the cell B2) or the number available to be unloaded. This is not immediately obvious, so think about why this is so. Also note the absolute reference to cell B2 using the $. This is because we want the reference to stay fixed when we copy, as we shall do shortly.

Step 8. Move to cell E7 and type **=C7−D7** The number of cars delayed to the following day equals the number to be unloaded less those actually unloaded.

You should pause at this point to survey what you have done—created the first day of our model. Be sure you understand it. We are now going to copy the first day model 500 times in order to simulate 500 days' operations.

Step 9. Copy cells **C6** through **E6** to cells **C7** to **E506.** There is more than one way to do this. Use the way you know, or follow the steps below:

- Highlight cells **C6** through **E6** and click on the *Copy* icon at the top of the spreadsheet.
- Highlight cells **C7** through **E506.**
- Click on the *Paste* icon at the top of the spreadsheet.

You have now completed the simulation model. The company is concerned about the number of cars delayed because it is costly to have cars waiting. The values in column E show this. You should move up and down through the results. Generally, there will be periods with little or no delay, and then a day with 4 or 5 arrivals, so that the number delayed builds up, with perhaps 10 or more railroad cars delayed. The delays may last for a period of several days, and then work down to zero again. This is exactly how queuing systems behave.

Summarizing the Results

To be useful, we need to summarize the results. We shall calculate the average number of cars delayed and determine the cost of this delay. Further, we shall produce a distribution showing how often each number of cars was delayed. But first:

Step 10. Move to cells **G14** and **G15** and type in the headings as shown in Figure 10–9. Then move to cell I14 and type **=Average(E7:E506)**

This will give you the average number of rail cars delayed per day for the 500 days simulated.

Step 11. Move to cell I15 and type **=100*365*I14**

This is the cost of the delay at $100 per day per rail car for a 365-day year.

Step 12. Fill in the cells G19 through G39 with the values of 0 through 20, as shown in Figure 10–9. These are the "bins" for tabulating the number delayed each day. They are used in step 14 below.

FIGURE 10–9
Headings for Summary Information

	F	G	H	I	J
13					
14		Average Delay		=Average(E7:E506)	
15		Annual Cost		= 100*365*I14	
16					
17					
18					
19		0			
20		1			
21		2			
22		3			
23		4			
24		5			
25		6			
26		7			
27		8			
28		9			
29		10			
30		11			
31		12			
32		13			
33		14			
34		15			
35		16			
36		17			
37		18			
38		19			
39		20			
40					

Step 13. We are now going to determine the distribution of cars delayed. Click on the *Tools* item at the top of the spreadsheet, and then click on the *Data Analysis* item on the menu. Next, click on the *Histogram* item on the Data Analysis menu.

Step 14. The Histogram dialogue box, as shown in Figure 10–10, will appear. Fill it in as shown. In particular:

- The Input Range is **E7:E506**—the column for the number of cars delayed.
- The Bin Range is **G19:G39**—these are the tabulation bins (step 12).
- Click on the circle next to *Output Range.*
- The Output Range is **H18**—the corner for the output.
- Then click **OK.**

FIGURE 10–10

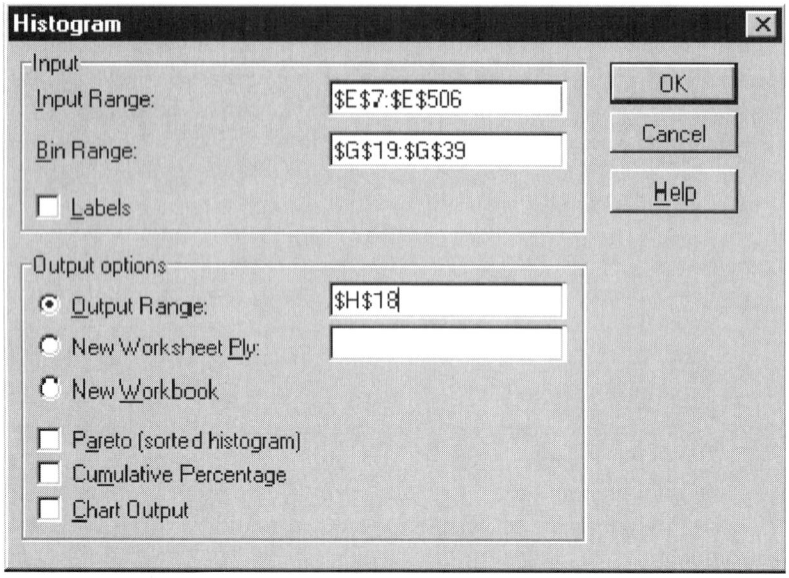

Histogram

Input
Input Range: $E$7:$E$506
Bin Range: $G$19:$G$39
☐ Labels

Output options
◉ Output Range: $H$18
○ New Worksheet Ply:
○ New Workbook
☐ Pareto (sorted histogram)
☐ Cumulative Percentage
☐ Chart Output

OK
Cancel
Help

At this point, the distribution for the number of cars delayed will appear. Note that on many days there were zero or no delayed cars, but that there were some days with 5 or 6 or more delays.

Changing the Capacity

The results obtained above were based on the assumption that the warehouse dock has the capacity to unload two railroad cars per day. Suppose the company could add new equipment that would increase the unloading capacity to three cars per day. This should reduce the delays. Let us see how much saving would result.

Step 15. Write down the current estimate for the average number of cars delayed per day (in cell I14) and the annual cost (cell I15).

Step 16. Move to cell **B2,** and enter the number 3. Note that new values are shown for the average delay and the annual cost—rather substantial reductions. To obtain the distribution of delays, do the following:

Step 17. Click on the *Tools* item at the top of the spreadsheet. Then click on *Data Analysis,* and then on *Histogram.* A dialogue box like that of Figure 10–10 should appear. It may even have retained the values entered in step 14. If so, click on **OK.** If not, enter the values the same as described in step 14. Then click **OK.** You will get a warning that you will overwrite existing data, but this is expected, so click **OK.**

You can see how the simulation model could be an aid in management decision making. The benefits of increasing the unloading capacity from two to three railroad cars per day have been estimated from the model. This would be compared to the cost of adding these facilities.

Monte Carlo Risk Analysis

Example 3 in this chapter described a firm considering the introduction of a new product, with uncertainty about the market size, price, and unit cost. In this tutorial, we shall expand that example. First, we shall assume that the product to be introduced has a three-year life. New products typically have a product life cycle in which sales increase and then decline. We shall assume that there is uncertainty about first-year sales, but then sales increase by 20 percent in the second year and then decline by 50 percent in the third year. Further, we shall assume that the uncertainty about first-year sales can be described by a normal distribution with mean of 2.0 million cases and standard deviation of 0.6 million cases. The cost of producing the product is also uncertain, and we shall assume that this uncertainty can be represented by a uniform distribution between $2.00 and $4.00 per unit. The uncertainty about the price for the product is represented by a discrete distribution (same as Example 3) as follows:

Selling Price (dollars per unit)	*Probability*
$4	0.3
5	0.5
6	0.2

We shall assume that there are fixed costs associated with introducing the product of $3.0 million in the first year and $1.0 million for each of years 2 and 3. Finally, we shall assume that the firm has the ability to abandon the product after the first year if it is not profitable (in which case there would be no fixed costs for later years). As suggested, this is a more complicated model than illustrated in Example 3 in the chapter; however, it is still quite simplified compared to one that might be used for new product introduction analysis.

Step 1. Open a new spreadsheet and set it up as shown in Figure 10–11. The top part contains values for the uncertain factors—unit sales, price, and unit cost. For the moment, enter the fixed values as shown (we shall deal with random values shortly). The main part of the model—cells C8 through F12—contains equations, and the explanations for these are shown in the figure. Take care in checking that the model is correct—you might try different values for price or cost or sales and see the result. In particular, be sure you understand the profit equations for years 2 and 3. The model assumes that the firm can project sales and profits for years 2 and 3 based on the year 1 results, and that, if profit is forecast to be negative, it will abandon the product and have zero profit.

Enter the values for the look-up table (rows 14 through 19) exactly as shown. They will be explained shortly.

Step 2. We are now ready to enter the functions to generate the random values for price, sales, and cost. There are two ways this can be done on spreadsheets. The first way involves generating a set of random draws and putting them in a column of the spreadsheet. This approach was illustrated in the previous model in this tutorial modeling railroad car arrivals.

FIGURE 10–11 Spreadsheet with the New Product Introduction Model

	A	B	C	D	E	F	G	H	I
1	Uncertain Factors:								
2	Price (dollars/unit)			5.00					
3	Cost (dollars/unit)			3.00					
4	Initial Sales (million units)			2.00					
5									
6		Income Statements (all units in million)							
7			Year 1	Year 2	Year 3	Total			
8	Units Sold		2.00	2.40	1.20				
9	Dollar Sales		10.00	12.00	6.00				
10	Cost of Sales		6.00	7.20	3.60				
11	Fixed Costs		3.00	1.00	1.00				
12	Profit		1.00	3.80	1.40	6.20			
13									
14	Lookup Table for Price								
15		Cum. Prob	Price						
16		0	4						
17		0.3	5						
18		0.8	6						
19		1	7						
20									
21				Cell	Equation		Explanation		
22				C8	=D4		Year 1 sales units		
23				C9	=C8*D2		price * unit sales		
24				C10	=C8*D3		unit cost * unit sales		
25				C12	=C9-C10-C11		revenue - cost of units - fixed cost		
26				D8	=1.2*C8		Year 2 sales increase 20%		
27				D9	=D8*D2		price * unit sales for year 2		
28				D10	=D8*D3		unit cost * unit sales for year 2		
29				D12	=MAX(0,D9-D10-D11)		If profit (D9-D10-D11) is projected		
30							to be zero or less, the product		
31							is abandoned and profit is 0.		
32				E8	=0.5*D8		Year 3 sales decline by 50%		
33				E9	=E8*D2		price * unit sales for year 3		
34				E10	=E8*D3		unit cost * unit sales for year 3		
35				E12	=MAX(0,E9-E10-E11)		see explanation for cell D12		
36				F12	=C12+D12+E12		sum of profit for the three years		
37									

The second approach involves the random number generating function RAND( ). This function returns a uniform random value between 0 and 1.0. To try it out, move to a blank cell in the spreadsheet—say, cell **G2**—and type **=RAND( )** This function is a "hot" function in the sense that it draws a new random value each time the spreadsheet is recalculated. To illustrate this, push the recalculate key (key **F9**) a few times, noticing how the value changes. Then delete the function.

Step 3. Move to Cell D3 and type **=2+2*RAND( )**
Recall that the probability distribution for unit cost is assumed to be uniform between $2.00 and $4.00. Since RAND( ) generates a random value between 0 and 1, two times this (i.e., 2*RAND( )) will generate a value between 0 and 2.0, and by adding 2 more, we have a function that will generate the required uniform distribution from $2.00 to $4.00 for unit cost.

After typing it in, push the **F9** recalculate key a few times to see the result.

Step 4. Move to cell D4 and type **=NORMINV(RAND( ),2.0,0.6)**
The NORMINV function in Excel calculates the inverse value for a normal probability distribution. Three arguments must be specified: the cumulative normal probability, the mean of the normal distribution, and its standard deviation. The function RAND( ), which generates values from 0 to 1.0, supplies the cumulative normal value, and the values 2.0 and 0.6 are the mean and standard deviation for the uncertainty about sales. This function, as specified, will generate random draws from the required normal distribution. Press the **F9** recalculate key a few times and note the result.

Step 5. Move to cell D2 and type **=VLOOKUP(RAND( ),B16:C19,2)**
This is the table look-up function in Excel. Cells B16:C19 contain the table giving the cumulative probability distribution for our uncertain variable unit price. The value 2 in the function specifies that the second column contains the values of interest (the prices). The RAND( ) function determines which row is selected. When the random value drawn is less than 0.3, the first row is selected (and price of $4.00 returned by the function). If the random value is 0.3 or more but less than 0.8, the second row of the table is selected and a price of $5.00 is returned; if the random value is 0.8 or greater, the third row is chosen and the price of $6.00 is returned. As before, press the **F9** recalculate key to see the result.

Note: The three functions in steps 3, 4, and 5 are not usually used in spreadsheet work, so you may be a little puzzled at how they work. You can get more information by using the Excel Help function. In any case, note that they work by generating random draws from the three different probability distributions.

Each time the spreadsheet is recalculated, new values for each uncertain variable are created, and a new value for the profitability of the new product introduction is calculated. Use the recalculate F9 key a few times and note the very different values for three-year profitability that result.[8]

But the result of a single trial is not useful by itself. We need to generate and record a large sample of trials—say, 1,000. We will do that now. We shall create two

---

[8]Since the profit occurs over three years, it should be discounted using the appropriate discount rate. This was omitted to keep the analysis simple.

columns of values. The trial number from 1 to 1000 will be in column H, and the results of the thousand trials will be in column I.

Step 6. Move to cell H2 and enter the number **1.** If the cursor has moved from cell H2, move it back there.

Step 7. Click on the *Edit* item at the top of the spreadsheet. Then click on the *Fill* item in the menu. Then click on *Series* in the side menu. The dialogue box, as shown in Figure 10–12, appears; fill it in as shown.

In particular, click on *Columns* and on *Linear.* Make the step value 1 and enter 1000 in the stop value. Then click **OK.** The column from H2 down should fill with the numbers 1 to 1000.

To fill in the values for profit for the 1,000 trials, we are going to use the Excel data table command but in a unique and clever way.

Step 8. Move to cell I1 and type **=F12** This refers to the cell containing the total three-year profit.

Step 9. Highlight the whole area from cell H1 through I1001. That is, we want to select the whole of both columns H and I, including the very top cells and the cells in row 1001.

Step 10. Click on the *Data* item at the top of the spreadsheet, and then select *Table* from the dropdown menu. A dialogue box appears. **Leave empty** the box next to *Row Input Cell.* Enter **G10** in the box next to *Column Input Cell.* Then click **OK.** Column I will now fill with the results of 1,000 trials of the simulation.

Ordinarily the data table command will substitute the values in the first column into the designated cell in the model and put the result in the second column. We were tricky in that the reference cell (G10) was a blank cell not used by our model. But the spreadsheet is recalculated each time, so we obtained different values for our unknown factors. That is, column I now contains 1,000 replications or trials of our model. However, these values are still "hot" in the sense that a recalculation will change all of them. We want to change that, so:

FIGURE 10–12
Data Fill Dialogue Box

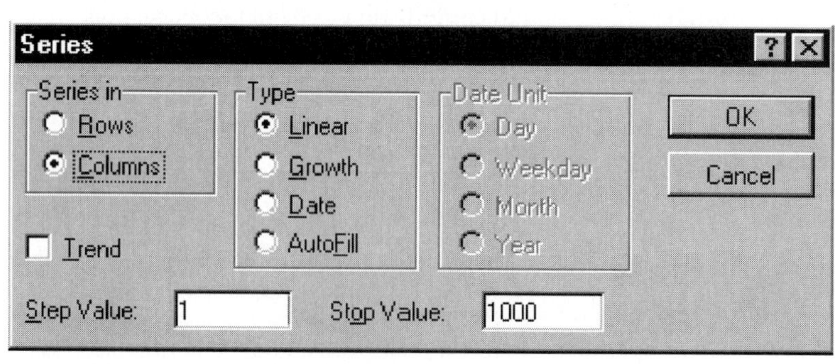

Step 11. Highlight cells **I2** through **I1001.**

Step 12. Click on the *Edit* item at the top of the spreadsheet. From the dropdown menu click on *Copy.*

Step 13. Again click on the *Edit* item at the top of the spreadsheet. From the drop-down menu click on *Paste Special.* A dialogue box should appear on the screen. Click in the circle next to *Values* in the first column. Then click **OK.**

We have replaced the hot numbers by their values, unconnected to the model.

Graphing the Results

We can now use the numbers for further analysis, including graphing. But first, let us calculate the average three-year profit over the 1,000 trials.

Step 14. Move to cell F3 in the worksheet and type **=AVERAGE(I2:I1001)** We next set up the data for graphing. This involves two steps. First, we create a column of values for the cumulative probability (the Y-axis of the plot). Then we sort the values of our 1,000 trials.

Step 15. Move to cell **J2** and enter into the cell **0.001** Move the cursor back to cell J2, if it moved when you entered the number. Then click on the *Edit* item at the top of the spreadsheet. From the dropdown menu select *Fill.* From the side menu that appears, select *Series.*

A dialogue box appears. Do the following:

- Click on the circle next to *Columns.*
- Click on the circle next to *Linear.*
- Enter **0.001** in the box labeled *Step.*
- Enter **1.0** in the box labeled *Stop.*
- Click **OK.**

Column J should fill with cumulative probability values, starting with 0.001, 0.002, 0.003 . . . on up to 1.000

Step 16. Highlight cells **I2** through **I1001.**

Step 17. Click on the *Data* item at the top of the spreadsheet. From the dropdown menu, click on the *Sort* item.

You will get a box warning you that there are other columns nearby. Click on the circle next to *Continue with the current selection,* and then click **OK.**

Another dialogue box appears. Click on the circle next to *Descending* in the first box. Then click **OK.**

The results of the 1,000 trials should now be sorted from highest to lowest.

Step 18. Move the cursor so that a blank part of the spreadsheet appears on the screen. This could be, for example, columns L through Q.

Step 19. Click on the Chart Wizard icon (shown in the margin) in the top row of icons. Move the cursor to the upper left corner of the screen and hold down the mouse button while you create the box for the graph.

Step 20. The first of five Chart Wizard boxes should appear. In the box next to *Range* type **=I2:J1001** Then click on *Next.*

Step 21. On the next Wizard box, click on the picture labeled *X-Y (Scatter),* and then click on *Next.*

Step 22. In the next Wizard box, click on the box with the graphs showing smooth curves. Then click on *Next.*

Step 23. Simply click on *Next* in the fourth Wizard box.

Step 24. In the final Wizard box, do the following (or use your own options):

- Click on the *no* circle next to *Legend.*
- Type in **Risk Profile** in the *title* box.
- Type in **Million $** in the *X-axis* box.
- Type in **Cumulative Probability** in the *Y-axis* box.
- Then click on *Finish.*

A chart graphing the probability of obtaining *X* or more profit should result. For example, there is approximately an 80 percent chance that the product will show a positive profit and a 20 percent chance of a loss.

You may wish to modify the graph by, for example, adding grid lines and moving the *Y*-axis to the left, but these options are beyond the scope of this tutorial.

Summary

The purpose of this tutorial was to step you through building a simplified example. A model of a real business decision may be much more complex and involve more uncertainties. But the basic ideas of this exercise should enable you to build and analyze these more complicated problems.

Bibliography

Hertz, D. B., and H. Thomas. *Risk Analysis and its Applications.* New York: John Wiley & Sons, 1983.

Hillier, F., and G. J. Lieberman. *Introduction to Operations Research.* 6th ed. New York: McGraw-Hill, 1995.

Khoshnevis, B. *Discrete Systems Simulation.* New York: McGraw-Hill, 1994.

Law, A. M., and W. D. Kelton. *Simulation Modeling and Analysis.* 2nd ed. New York: McGraw-Hill, 1991.

Plane, D. R. *Management Science: A Spreadsheet Approach for Windows.* Danvers, MA: boyd & fraser publishing co., 1996.

Ragsdale, C. T. *Spreadsheet Modeling and Decision Analysis.* Cambridge, MA: Course Technology, Inc. 1995.

Savage, S. *Fast QM.* New York: McGraw-Hill, 1993.

Schriber, T. J. *An Introduction to Simulation.* New York: John Wiley & Sons, 1991.

Practice Problems[9]

10–1. *a.* Using the same history of arrivals shown in Table 10–4, simulate the waiting line process of the warehouse–railroad car example with a constant service rate of three per day.

b. Assuming that the warehouse company pays $100 per day for freight cars kept over one day, estimate the annual savings (365 days = 1 year) from a service rate of three per day (instead of two per day).

10–2. Continue Table 10–10 to 50 trials, using random numbers from Table 10–2. Plot your results on a diagram similar to Figure 10–2. Out of your sample of 25 trials, what is the probability of the profit being less than zero? What is the average profit for your sample of 25 trials? Compare your answer with those obtained in Table 10–10 and with the expected profit of $2.14 million.

10–3. Refer to Problem 10–2. Suppose that the selling price and annual sales volume were *not* independent variables but were jointly distributed with the following probabilities. Note that the marginal probabilities are the same as in the chapter; but now, the assumption of independence does not apply.

a. Simply by studying the accompanying joint probability table, can you predict whether expected profit under the new assumption will be higher or lower than previously? Why or why not?

Price \ Sales Volume*	$3	$4	$5	Row Sums
$4	0	0	0.3	0.3
$5	0	0.4	0.1	0.5
$6	0.2	0	0	0.2
Column Sums	0.2	0.4	0.4	1.0

*$ millions.

b. Devise a scheme similar to Table 10–9 that uses random numbers to produce random values for price and volume when they are related as specified.

c. Use your scheme in (*b*) to generate 25 trials of the investment as in Table 10–10, but now assuming price and volume are dependent as specified.

d. Plot a figure similar to Figure 10–2 for your data in (*c*).

e. Compare your figure of (*d*) to Figure 10–2. Which investment would you prefer? Why?

[9] Solutions for these problems are at the end of this chapter.

Problems

10–4. Continue Table 10–7 to 100 periods, using random numbers from Table 10–2. Estimate the total annual cost (1 year = 50 weeks) if the cost of placing an order is $10, the cost of holding one unit of inventory is 50 cents per year, and the cost of outage is $3 per unit of lost sales. (Use average beginning inventory in determining cost of holding inventory.)

10–5. Pick an inventory rule that you consider good for the situation described in Problem 10–4. (That is, pick a number Q and a number R.) Simulate for 100 periods, and compare the cost of your rule with the cost in Problem 10–4.

10–6. An Idaho potato farmer is studying the risks associated with planting his potato crop. Based on past experience, he assesses the probabilities associated with potato prices per hundredweight (cwt.), yields in cwt. per acre, and costs (for fertilizer, water, seed, and labor) per acre (see Table 10–12).

TABLE 10–12
Probabilities for Problem 10–6

Price (per cwt.)	Probability	Yield (cwt. per acre)	Probability	Cost (per acre)	Probability
$2	0.10	210	0.10	$400	0.70
3	0.20	220	0.10	500	0.20
4	0.50	230	0.40	600	0.10
5	0.10	240	0.30		1.00
6	0.05	250	0.10		
7	0.05		1.00		
	1.00				

The profit per acre is (Price · Yield) − Cost. Assume all probabilities are independent. Using the Monte Carlo method for 25 trials, estimate the expected profit per acre and the probability distribution for profit per acre. What is the estimated probability that the farmer makes less than $100 per acre on his crop?

More Challenging Problems

10–7. Refer to Problem 10–6. In reality, the price and yield are not independent variables. A low yield generally means a shortage of potatoes, and the price rises; a high yield means low prices. However, this relationship is not exact, as there are other factors besides yields that affect prices. Suppose that the yield and cost per acre are the same as given in Problem 10–6 and are independent. Suppose, further, that price is related to yield by the following equation:

$$\text{Price} = 15.5 - 0.05(\text{Yield}) + D$$

where D is a random variable indicating a deviation from the equation. D has the following distribution (independent of yield and cost):

D	*Probability*
−$1.00	0.10
− 0.50	0.20
0	0.40
0.50	0.20
1.00	0.10
	1.00

Estimate the expected profit per acre and the distribution of profit per acre using the Monte Carlo method with 25 trials.

10–8. An analyst for International Widgets Corp. (IWC) was working on the corporate financial plan for the next year. IWC has two major divisions, one in the United States and the other in the United Kingdom. From the management of each division, the analyst had obtained an assessment of the probability distribution for net profit for the next year. Table 10–13 (next page) lists these assessments. Suppose it is reasonable to assume the distributions are independent.

a. Set up a procedure, using Monte Carlo methods, to estimate the probability distribution for combined net profit for IWC. Carry out the procedure for five Monte Carlo trials to illustrate how it is done.

b. Indicate how you would obtain the probability distribution of combined net profit from the Monte Carlo results.

c. Suppose the distributions were not considered independent (world economic conditions tend to affect all countries to some extent). To handle this problem, the analyst proposes to use the same random number in determining Monte Carlo sampled value both for U.S. and U.K. profit. Do you agree with the procedure? Comment briefly.

10–9.[10] The Acme Airline Company (AAC) is concerned about scheduling its engine repair shop. Under alternative A, engine repair times would be exponentially distributed with a mean time of 40 days. Under alternative B (a more complex procedure), engine repair times would be normally distributed with a mean of 40 days and a standard deviation of 5 days.

When an engine arrives for repair, a spare engine is sent out to take its place. The engine requiring repair is then sent to the shop; all engines under repair are worked on simultaneously. When repairs have been completed, the repaired engine enters the "spares pool" to be used to satisfy a subsequent requirement. Engine arrivals for repair are Poisson, with rate $\lambda = 0.5$ per day.

If an engine arrives when there are no spare engines to take its place, a spare engine is expedited from another location; this costs $10,000 per request. AAC has purchased 25 spare engines in order to keep the likelihood of expediting low.

Note that since engine repair times are not constant, engines may "cross" in time; that is, an engine that arrived at the repair facility later may actually be completed earlier.

Describe carefully how you would simulate this situation, including each of the following:

Random engine arrivals.

Random engine repair times (under each alternative).

The number of spares available at all times.

The number of occurrences of expediting.

Your initialization process.

10–10.[11] An Automatic Storage/Retrieval System (AS/RS) is a computer-controlled device for

[10]This problem requires knowledge of material in Appendix 1 to this chapter.

[11]This problem is adapted from W. H Hausman, S. C. Graves, and L. B. Schwarz, "Simulation Tests of Automatic Warehousing Systems," *AIEE Transactions,* September 1978.

TABLE 10–13 (for Problem 10–8)

U.S. Net Profit		U.K. Net Profit	
Amount ($ millions)	*Probability of This Much Profit or Less*	*Amount (converted to U.S. $ in millions)*	*Probability of This Much Profit or Less*
−$ 1.0	0.00	$0.5	0.00
3.0	0.10	0.7	0.10
6.0	0.25	0.9	0.25
8.0	0.50	1.0	0.50
10.0	0.75	1.3	0.75
15.0	0.90	2.0	0.90
20.0	1.00	3.0	1.00

warehousing that can store pallets of material by picking one up at a conveyorized pickup/delivery point and moving both vertically and horizontally down an aisle until an open storage location for the pallet is found. When a retrieve request occurs, the AS/RS travels to the location in which the designated pallet is stored, pulls out the pallet, and delivers it to the pickup/delivery point.

The AS/RS can be described as a pallet loader that can be moved up or down a "mast," which rolls down a storage aisle. There are locations on either side of the aisle for storage. Consider an AS/RS with a single aisle.

a. Suppose arrivals of pallets to be stored are Poisson, as are requests for retrievals of pallets already stored. Also, suppose the "service times" (i.e., the time for the system to perform a store or a retrieve) are exponential. Suppose stores and retrieves are done separately, and suppose a single queue exists covering both stores and retrieve requests; also, priority is first-come, first-served. How would you *approach* the problem of analyzing such a system? (*Note:* The sum of two Poisson processes is again Poisson.)

b. Now suppose that two separate queues are maintained, one for stores and one for retrieve requests. Assume the operating policy is that stores and retrieves are now combined (as long as both queues are not empty) so that the AS/RS does not return to the pickup/delivery point empty. This combining of stores and retrieves naturally increases the performance of the system. Assume service times are still exponentially distributed, but with a smaller mean. How would you approach the problem of analyzing this system?

c. Consider the situation in (*b*), but now assume that the AS/RS can select retrieve requests "out of order" in order to try to minimize wasted travel time. That is, given a decision to store a pallet in a given location, it may be more efficient to do one retrieve rather than another because of the location of the retrieves in the rack. How would you approach the problem of analyzing this system?

Problems for Computer Simulation

The problems in this section assume that the tutorial in Appendix 2 has been done. They are designed for the Excel spreadsheet.

10–11. A software company has introduced a new game, called *Build-a-City*. The company offers a telephone help line for users of the program. The help desk is staffed by one person knowledgeable about the game. If that person is busy answering a call, the telephone system puts the caller on hold until the help person is free. On average, the mean interarrival time between calls is 4 minutes, and on average it takes 3 minutes to answer the caller's question. However, there is considerable variability in both arrival and service times, and these are independently distributed, both with exponential distributions. The company wants to estimate the average waiting time for a caller. (For purposes of this question, assume the rate of arrivals is the same throughout the day, and that no caller hangs up before being helped.)

Note: The *M/M/1* queuing model is a classical model for the single server queue. The model assumes interarrival times that are distributed as an exponential or *M*arkov distribution, and service times that are independently distributed, also by an exponential or

Markov distribution with one service channel. See Appendix 1 for a discussion of this distribution. This model can be solved mathematically.

Let: μ_A be the mean of the distribution of interarrival times ($1/\mu_A$ is the arrival rate)
μ_S be the mean of the distribution of service times ($1/\mu_S$ is the service rate)

$\rho = \frac{\mu_S}{\mu_A}$ be the system load factor or utilization

Then the long run average waiting time, μ_W, is given by the formula:

$$\mu_W = \frac{\mu_S \cdot \rho}{1 - \rho}$$

The simulation model set up for this simulation is shown in Figure 10–13. Enter the headings and fill in the equations as shown. Set up the model to simulate 1000 job arrivals (i.e. calls to the help desk). Refer to Appendix 1 for the method for simulating the exponential distribution. Fill in the first column with job numbers, and copy cells B10 through H10 down to B1009 through H1009.

a. Set up the simulation model as described. Using the model, simulate 1,000 job arrivals (calls). Use the first 200 as startup, and calculate the average waiting time for the other 800 calls. Compare this to the theoretical value calculated from the formula above. Are they exactly the same? Should they be?

FIGURE 10–13 Setup for Simulation of a One-Channel Queue

	A	B	C	D	E	F	G	H
1				One-Channel Queuing System				
2								
3	Mean Interarrival Time			4				
4	Mean Service Time			3				
5								
6				Clock	Start	Finish		
7	Job	Interarrival	Service	Arrival	Service	Service	Waiting	Time in
8	Number	Time	Time	Time	Time	Time	Time	System
9	0			0	0	0		
10	1	3.59	3.35	3.59	3.59	6.94	0.00	3.35
11	2	1.82	2.83	5.41	6.94	9.77	1.53	4.36
12	3	2.12	0.40	7.53	9.77	10.17	2.24	2.64
13	4	4.67	0.38	12.20	12.20	12.58	0.00	0.38
14	5	0.56	5.16	12.76	12.76	17.92	0.00	5.16

Cell	Equation	Meaning
B10	=–($D$3)*LN(RAND( ))	Random Draw from Exponential Distribution (see Appendix 1)
C10	=–($D$4)*LN(RAND( ))	Random Draw from Exponential Distribution
D10	=D9+B10	Actual clock arrival time = arrival time of previous job plus interarrival time
E10	=MAX(D10,F9)	Job starts service either at time of arrival or when previous job finishes,
		whichever is later
F10	=E10+C10	Finish time is start time plus service time
G10	=E10-D10	Waiting time is time between arrival and start of service
H10	=G10+C10	Time in the system is waiting plus service time
	Copy Cells B10 to H10 down to B1009 to H1009.	

b. Simulate another 1,000 arrivals by pushing the recalculate key (F9). As in part *a,* disregard the first 200 trials and calculate the average of the last 800. Compare this to your result in (*a*), and to the theoretical result.

10–12. Refer to Problem 10–11. Suppose the software producer could develop a support system for the person on the help desk. This might take the form of a computerized expert system, for example. Assuming that this would reduce the average service time to 2 minutes, what would be the effect on the average waiting time of callers? Answer by both simulating the situation and using the theoretical model.

10–13. Refer to Problem 10–11 and Figure 10–13.

a. Simulate the queuing system for 1,000 trials for each of the following average interarrival rates (keeping the average service rate of 3 minutes unchanged):

3.5 minutes.
6.0 minutes.
9.0 minutes.

b. The utilization of the queuing system is defined to be $\rho = \frac{\mu_S}{\mu_A}$ or the average service time divided by the average interarrival time. Using the results of each of the cases in part (*a*), and the results of Problem 10–11, plot the average waiting time versus the system utilization factor ρ.

10–14. Refer to Problem 10–11 and Figure 10–13. Suppose the time between arrivals can be represented by a normal distribution with mean of 4 minutes and standard deviation of 1.5 minutes. Further suppose that the service time can also be represented by a normal distribution, with mean of 3 minutes and standard deviation of 1.0 minute.

a. Modify the model to incorporate this change. In particular:

Replace cell **B10** by **=NORMINV(RAND( ),4,1.5)**
Replace cell **C10** by **=NORMINV(RAND( ),3,1)**

and copy these cells down through B1009 and C1009. Note the change in the average waiting time.

b. Keep the mean service time at 3 minutes but decrease the standard deviation of service time to 0.5. (Do this by changing cell C10 to =NORMINV(RAND( ),3,0.5) and copying it down through C1009.) Note what has happened to the average waiting time.

c. Keep the mean service time at 3 minutes but decrease the standard deviation to zero (constant service time). Do this by replacing C10 by the value 3, and copying this down through C1009. Note what has happened to the average waiting time.

d. What conclusion would you draw from this about the effect of variability in service time on waiting time in a queue?

10–15. Refer to Problem 10–11. Suppose the calls for help to *Build-a-City* double, so that the average interarrival time is 2 minutes (still exponentially distributed). The company decides to add a second help desk, with a telephone system that will feed the call to whichever help desk is free or keep the caller on hold until one is free. This is called a two-channel system. Figure 10–14 shows how to set up the simulation of this system. Set it up as directed in Figure 10–14. Note that service time remains exponentially distributed with mean of 3 minutes.

a. Simulate this system for 1,000 arrivals; discard the first 200 and calculate the average waiting time for the subsequent 800.

b. Compare this to the result you got in Problem 10–11 (either the theoretical or calculated value). Note that both the arrivals and the service capacity doubled. Do you get the same result as in Problem 10–11? Should you? (*Note:* what you observed is called the effect of pooling of servers, or *risk pooling.*)

10–16. Example 2 in this chapter was a simulation of an inventory system. Figure 10–15 (pages 445–46) indicates how such a simulation can be set up on a spreadsheet. Use the steps below:

- Set up the spreadsheet headings as shown in Figure 10–15. Include the probability distributions for Demand and Delivery Lag in columns L and M, as shown.
- In column A, put in four startup weeks indicated by "x" and then fill in the week numbers from 1 through 500 (for simulation of 500 weeks).
- In column B put in 500 sampled values from the distribution of Demand in columns L and M. Do this using the procedure in steps 3, 4, and 5 in the first example in the tutorial in Appendix 2.
- In column C, put in 500 sampled values from the distribution on Delivery Lag time, using the same procedure.
- Fill in the values of zero in cell E10, in cells I7:I10 and cells J7:J10.
- Fill in the value 10 in cell G10, the value 5 in cell C2, and the value 5 in cell C3.
- Enter the equations for the model as shown at the bottom of Figure 10–15.
- Copy cells D11 through J11 down to D12 through J510.

FIGURE 10–14 Setup for Simulation of a Two-Channel Queue

	A	B	C	D	E	F	G	H	I	J	K
1				Two-Channel Queuing System							
2		Mean Interarrival Time			2						
3		Mean Service Time			3						
4											
5				Clock	Service	Channel 1	Channel 1	Channel 2	Channel 2		
6	Job	Interarrival	Service	Arrival	Channel	Start	Complete	Start	Complete	Waiting	Time in
7	Number	Time	Time	Time	Used	Service	Service	Service	Service	Time	System
8	0			0		0	0	0	0		
9	1	1.17	2.30	1.17	1	1.17	3.47	0.00	0.00	0.00	2.30
10	2	0.98	0.97	2.15	2	1.17	3.47	2.15	3.12	0.00	0.97
11	3	0.53	1.97	2.68	2	1.17	3.47	3.12	5.10	0.44	2.42
12	4	0.73	1.25	3.41	1	3.47	4.73	3.12	5.10	0.07	1.32
13	5	1.25	0.03	4.66	1	4.73	4.76	3.12	5.10	0.07	0.10
14	6	0.40	0.48	5.06	1	5.06	5.54	3.12	5.10	0.00	0.48
15	7	1.17	3.80	6.24	2	5.06	5.54	6.24	10.03	0.00	3.80
16	8	0.59	1.23	6.83	1	6.83	8.05	6.24	10.03	0.00	1.23
17	9	0.03	1.35	6.86	1	8.05	9.40	6.24	10.03	1.19	2.54
18	10	0.03	2.26	6.88	1	9.40	11.67	6.24	10.03	2.52	4.78
19	11	5.87	2.74	12.76	2	9.40	11.67	12.76	15.50	0.00	2.74

Equations:

Cell	Equation	Meaning
B9	=–($E$2)*LN(RAND( ))	Random draw from Exponential Distribution
C9	=–($E$3)*LN(RAND( ))	Random draw from Exponential Distribution
D9	=D8+B9	Arrival time = arrival time of previous job + interarrival time
E9	=IF(G8<=I8,1,2)	Job goes to channel 1 or 2 whichever is free first
F9	=IF(E9=1,MAX(D9,G8),F8)	If channel 1, start service either at arrival time or time of finish of previous job being served; if otherwise (i.e., if channel is 2), start service time is same as line above
G9	=IF(E9=1,F9+C9,G8)	If channel is 1, finish time is start time plus service time; otherwise (i.e., if channel is 2), finish service is copied from above line
H9	=IF(E9=2,MAX(D9,I8),H8)	Same as explanation for cell F9, but for channel 2
I9	=IF(E9=2,H9+C9,I8)	Same as explanation for cell G9, but for channel 2
J9	=IF(E9=1,F9-D9,H9-D9)	Waiting time is start service time minus arrival time, for channel 1 or 2
K9	=J9+C9	Time in the system is waiting time plus service time
	Cell A9 through A1008 are filled with numbers 1 through 1000	
	Cells B9 through K9 are copied down to cells B1008 to K1008	

a. Calculate the average values for Lost Sales Outages and for Ending Inventory.

b. Try different values for Q and R (values in cells C2 and C3) and note the result on the averages.

10–17. Refer to Problem 10–16. Note that in Problem 10–16, any demands that could not be met from inventory were lost (the so-called lost sales case). Now suppose that unfilled demands can be backordered. Relabel cells H5:H6 as Units Backordered, and describe how you would modify your spreadsheet to deal with this situation.

FIGURE 10–15 Setup for Inventory Simulation Example

	A	B	C	D	E	F	G	H	I	J	K	L	M	N
1		Simulation of Inventory System												
2	Order Size - Q		5									Weekly Demand Distribution		
3	Order Level - R		5									Demand	Probability	
4										Order		0	0.1	
5	Week	Sales	Order	Receipts	Amount	Beginning	Ending	Lost Sales	Order	Delivery		1	0.4	
6	Number	Units	Delay		on Order	Inventory	Inventory	Outages	Amount	Week		2	0.3	
7	x								0	0		3	0.2	
8	x								0	0				
9	x								0	0				
10	x				0		10		0	0		Delivery Lag		
11	1	1	3	0	0	10	9	0	0	0		Weeks	Probability	
12	2	1	3	0	0	9	8	0	0	0		2	0.2	
13	3	2	3	0	0	8	6	0	0	0		3	0.6	
14	4	3	3	0	0	6	3	0	5	7		4	0.2	
15	5	3	3	0	5	3	0	0	5	8				
16	6	3	2	0.	10	0	0	3	0	0				
17	7	0	3	5	5	5	5	0	0	0				
18	8	1	2	5	0	10	9	0	0	0				
19	9	3	3	0	0	9	6	0	0	0				
20	10	1	3	0	0	6	5	0	5	13				
21	11	1	4	0	5	5	4	0	0	0				
22	12	0	3	0	5	4	4	0	0	0				

(continued)

Figure 10–15 *(concluded)*

Cell	Equation	Meaning
Equations:		
D11	=IF(J7=A11,$C$2,0)+IF(J8=A11,$C$2,0)	If delivery week for the last three periods equals the current
	+IF(J9=A11,$C$2,0)	week, order is received
E11	=E10-D11+I10	Previous amount on order minus receipts plus orders from
		last week
F11	=G10+D11	Prior ending inventory plus receipts
G11	=MAX(0,F11-B11)	Beginning Inventory minus Sales (not less than zero)
H11	=MAX(0,B11-F11)	Excess of Sales over Inventory, if any
I11	=IF(G11+E11<=$C$3,$C$2,0)	If Ending Inventory plus Amount on Order
		is <= reorder level R, order amount Q
J11	=IF(I11=0,0,A11+C11)	If there is no order, delivery week is set to 0; otherwise it is
		current week number plus order delay

Solutions to Practice Problems

10–1 *a*. The total number delayed to the following day is 6 (an average of 0.12 per day).

b. Cost of waiting with service rate of 2 cars per day is:

$$\$100(0.90)(365) = \$32{,}850$$

Cost of waiting with service rate of 3 cars per day is:

$$\$100(0.12)(365) = \$4{,}380$$

Savings is $32,850 − $4,380 = $28,470 per year.

10–2. Results will depend on the random numbers drawn. As stated in the chapter, expected profit is $2.14 million. Also a negative profit results when Price = $4 and Cost = $4 (regardless of the volume), and the probability of a loss in this fashion is (0.3)(0.3) = 0.09. Also, a loss can occur when Cost is $4 and Price is $5 and Volume is 3 or 4 million. Probability = (0.3)(0.5)(0.6) = 0.09. There is also a loss when Cost is $3 and Price is $4 and Volume is 3 or 4 million. Probability = (0.3)(0.6)(0.6) = 0.108. Total probability = 0.09 + 0.09 + 0.108 = 0.288.

10–3. *a*. Since the higher price is associated with the lower volume and vice versa, this indicates that when the higher price occurs, profits will be lower than before; and when the lower price occurs, low profit margins (or negative margins) will be multiplied by larger volumes. The general effect should be to *lower* expected profit.

b. Use the following table:

Price \ *Sales Volume**	*$3*	*$4*	*$5*
$4	—	—	0,1,2†
$5	—	3–6	7
$6	8.9	—	—

*$ millions.
†Random numbers.

c, d, and *e* are straightforward, using (*b*). Results depend on random numbers drawn. The expected profit can be calculated as $1.66 million.

Motivating Example

Oil Platforms in the North Sea[1]

Since 1966, there have been major oil exploration activities in the North Sea off the coast of Norway. Each individual platform project may take from three to five years to construct, at a cost of about $700 million. Critical path methods such as those described in this chapter have been used extensively to plan and control such large construction projects. The initial focus was on project completion time, but current approaches also include elements of cost and resource requirements. Monte Carlo simulation has been applied, both on completion time and on project cost estimates. Integrating time, cost, and resource requirements has been shown to be very important; limited resources often play a major role in determining which activities can be performed at what times.

[1]See Per Willy Hetland, "Toward Ultimate Control of Megaprojects in the North Sea," in *Global Project Management Handbook*, Chapter 30, ed. D. I. Cleland and R. Garies (New York: McGraw-Hill, 1994).

CHAPTER

11 PERT

Program Evaluation and Review Technique

This chapter presents tools to manage the planning and control of major projects with many separate activities that require coordination. In many business situations, a number of different activities must be performed in a specified sequence in order to accomplish some major project. Some of the activities may be in series (for example, market research cannot be performed before the research design is planned), whereas others may be in parallel (for example, the engines for a ship can be built at the same time the hull is being constructed.) For a large, complex project, the complete set of activities will usually contain a combination of series and parallel elements. The technique of PERT (Program Evaluation and Review Technique) is designed to aid a manager in planning and controlling such a project. For planning purposes prior to the start of the project, the PERT technique allows a manager to calculate the expected total amount of time the entire project will take to complete. The technique highlights the bottleneck activities in the project so that the manager may either allocate more resources to them or keep a careful watch on them as the project progresses. For purposes of control after the project has begun, the technique provides a way of monitoring progress and calling attention to those delays in activities that will cause a delay in the project's completion date.

This chapter presents the basic concepts of PERT under conditions of both known and uncertain activity times.

Information Requirements

In order to use PERT, two types of information are needed for each activity in the project.[2] The *sequencing requirements* for an activity must be known. For example, we need to know the set of activities that must be completed prior to the beginning of each specific activity. In addition, we require an estimate of the *time* each activity will take.

[2]A closely related procedure called CPM (Critical Path Method) also exists. In this chapter, the terminology of PERT is used, although the network diagram procedure follows the convention of CPM.

Case I: Known Activity Times

In the first part of this chapter, we will assume that there is a precise, known amount of time that each activity in the project will take. In the second part, we will assume that the time to perform each activity is uncertain (i.e., a random variable).

Network Diagram

The **network diagram** is a graphical representation of the entire project. Each activity in the project is represented by a circle, and arrows are used to indicate sequencing requirements.[3]

Example

Table 11–1 contains a list of six activities that constitute a project, together with the sequencing requirements and the estimated times for each activity. The immediate predecessor of activity B is activity A; this means that activity A must be completed before activity B can begin. Figure 11–1 shows the network diagram for our example, with the activities represented by circles. The arrows in the network

TABLE 11–1

Activity	*Immediate Predecessors*	*Estimated Time (days)*
A	None	2
B	A	3
C	A	4
D	B, C	6
E	None	2
F	E	8

FIGURE 11–1
Network Diagram

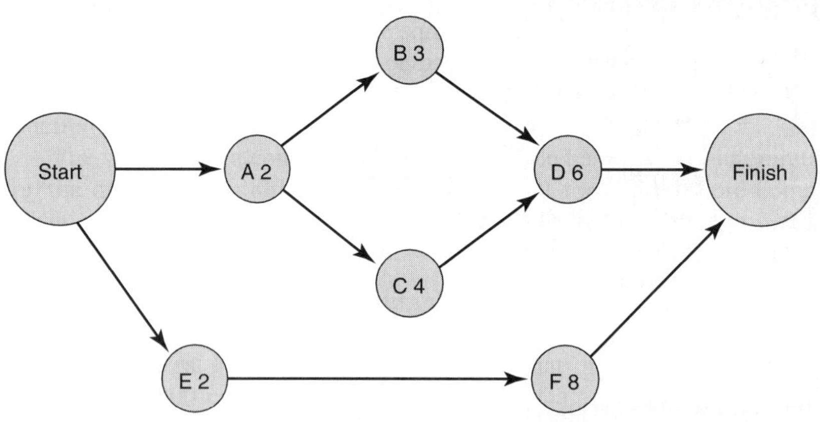

[3]In PERT, the arrows are used to represent activities; however, the CPM convention used here is easier to understand.

diagram illustrate the sequencing requirements of the problem. For example, the arrow from circle A to circle B indicates that activity A must be completed before activity B can begin. Similarly, activities B and C must *both* be completed before activity D can begin.

The estimated time for each activity has been placed in the circle representing that activity. Once the network diagram is completed, it may be used to develop the critical path for the project.

The Critical Path

A **path** is defined as a sequence of connected activities in the project. In our example, there are only three possible paths: *ABD*, which has a length of 11 days; *ACD*, which has a length of 12 days; and *EF*, which has a length of 10 days. The **critical path** is the path that has the largest amount of time associated with it. In our example, it is *ACD*, with a length of 12 days. The length of the critical path determines the minimum time in which the entire project may be completed. The activities on the critical path are the bottleneck activities in the project.

The critical path is important for two reasons. First, the completion time for the project cannot be reduced unless one or more of the activities on the critical path can be completed in less time than the initial time estimate. The critical path highlights those activities that must be performed more rapidly if the total project completion time is to be reduced. Second, any delays in activities that are on the critical path will produce delays in completion of the project, whereas delays in noncritical activities may not actually delay the completion of the project. In our example, the estimated project completion time is 12 days. If we desire to reduce this time, we must reduce the time to complete one of the three activities on the critical path—A, C, or D. We obtain no benefit from reducing the time required to perform activities B, E, and F, since these activities are not on the critical path. Also, a delay of up to one day in the time required to perform activity B could be tolerated, since this would have no effect on the project completion time. On the other hand, any delay in activities A, C, or D would directly lengthen the project completion time. If activity C were delayed 3 days, the project would take 15 days rather than 12 to be completed.

For simple projects such as the one in our example, the critical path may be found by inspection of the network diagram. However, the PERT technique is typically used for planning and control of a large-scale, complex project (e.g., the construction of a 50-story building, the development and implementation of a new military defense systcm, or the design and installation of major new manufacturing processes). In such a situation, there may be hundreds or thousands of activities that must be performed to complete the project, and some systematic way of finding the critical path is needed.

Finding the Critical Path

One way to find the critical path in a network is presented below. Let:

ES_i = Earliest start time for activity *i*

EF_i = Earliest finish time for activity *i*

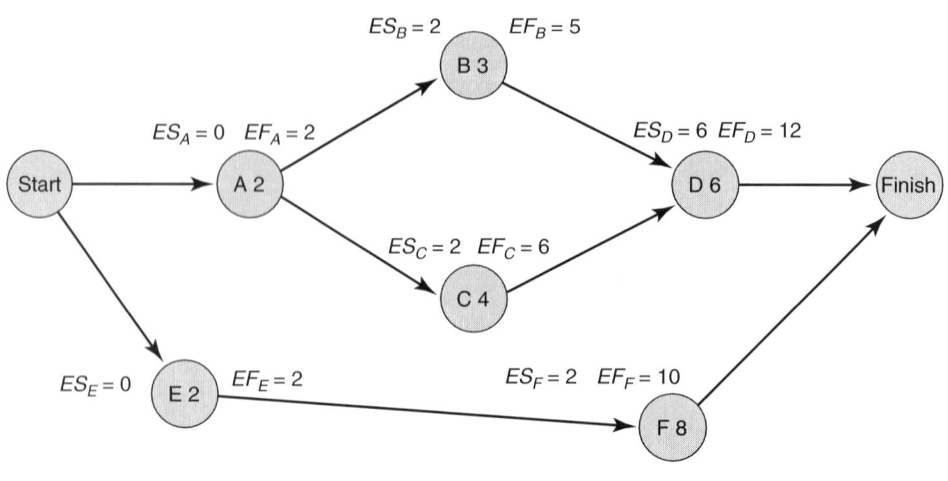

FIGURE 11–2
Earliest Start, Earliest Finish Time

where the earliest start time for an activity is the earliest possible time that the activity can begin, assuming that all of its predecessors also started at the earliest possible times. The earliest finish time for an activity is the sum of the earliest start time and the estimated time to perform the activity. The earliest finish time represents the earliest possible time that an activity could be finished, assuming all of its predecessors started at their earliest start times.

The *ES* and the *EF* for each activity in the network are obtained as follows. First, set the *ES* of the first activity equal to zero. Then add the estimated time to perform the first activity to its *ES* (zero), obtaining the *EF* for the first activity. Now consider any activity for which all its immediate predecessors have *ES* and *EF* values. The *ES* of such an activity is equal to the largest of the *EF* values of its immediate predecessors, because all have to be finished before that activity can be started again. Again, the *EF* is obtained by adding the estimated time to perform the activity to its *ES* time.

Figure 11–2 contains *ES* and *EF* times for the activities in our first example. Activities A and E are the first activities, so the *ES* for A and E is zero. Since activity A takes two days, the *EF* for activity A is 2. Similarly, the *EF* for activity E is 2. Then the *ES* for activities B and C is 2. The *EF* for B is 2 + 3, or 5; and the *EF* for C is 2 + 4, or 6. Since activity D requires both B and C to be completed before it can begin, the *ES* for activity D is the larger of 5 or 6; namely, 6. The *EF* for D is 6 + 6, or 12. The *ES* for activity F is 2, and the *EF* for activity *F* is 10.

Continuing with our algorithm, define:

LS_i = Latest start time for activity i
LF_i = Latest finish time for activity i

where the latest finish time for an activity is the latest possible time an activity can finish without delaying the project beyond its deadline, assuming all of the subsequent activities are performed as planned. The latest start time for an activity is the difference between the latest finish time and the estimated time for the activity to be performed.

FIGURE 11–3
Latest Start, Latest Finish Time

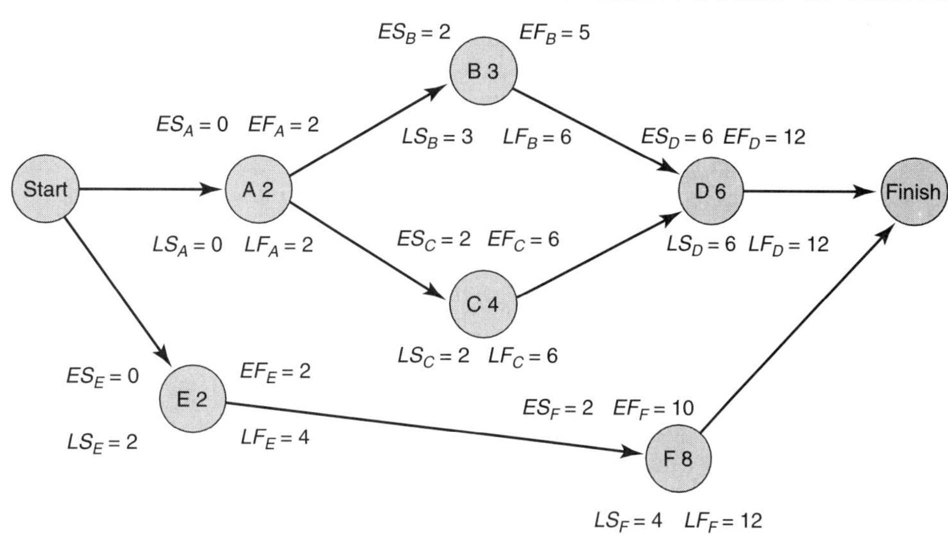

To obtain the *LS* and *LF* for each activity, we start at the end of the network diagram and first set the *LF* for the last activity equal to the *EF* for that activity.[4] Then we subtract the estimated time to perform the last activity from the *LF* to obtain the *LS*. Now consider any activity for which all of its immediate successors have *LS* and *LF* values. The *LF* of such an activity is equal to the smallest of the *LS* values of its immediate successors. Then the *LS* is obtained by subtracting the estimated time to perform the activity from its *LF* time. Figure 11–3 contains *LS* and *LF* times for the activities in our example, assuming the deadline for project completion is 12 days. Activities D and F are the last activities, so the *LF* for D and for F is set equal to the project deadline of 12 days. Since activity D takes 6 days, the *LS* for activity D is 12 − 6, or 6. Activity F takes 8 days, so the *LS* for F is 12 − 8, or 4. The *LF* for both B and C is 6, since they both have the same successor activity. The *LS* for activity B is 6 − 3, or 3; and the *LS* for activity C is 6 − 4, or 2. Activity A's *LF* is the smallest of the *LS* values of its immediate successors; the smaller of 3 and 2 is 2. Since activity A takes 2 days, the *LS* for A is 2 − 2, or 0. Finally, the *LF* for activity E is 4, and its *LS* is 2.

Slack and Critical Path

Slack refers to the number of days an activity can be delayed without forcing the total project to be delayed beyond its due date. After the *ES, EF, LS*, and *LF* have been calculated for each activity in the project, the slack for each activity is calculated as the difference between the *LS* and the *ES* for that activity (or equivalently, the difference between the *LF* and the *EF*). In our example, we specified that the

[4]In practice, the *LF* for the last activity is set equal to the project due date, or deadline. However, it is also instructive to set the *LF* of the last activity equal to its *EF* time, so that the critical path will have no slack.

TABLE 11–2
Slack for Activities

Activity	LS	ES	Slack
A	0	0	0
B	3	2	1
C	2	2	0
D	6	6	0
E	2	0	2
F	4	2	2

project deadline was the length of the critical path, or 12 days. Thus, there will be zero slack for those activities on the critical path. Table 11–2 presents the slack for each activity in our example. Activity B has slack of one day; activities E and F have slack of two days; and activities A, C, and D have zero slack. If the project deadline is set equal to the length of the critical path, then all activities with zero slack must be on the critical path, since the definition of the critical path implies that any delay in a critical activity will delay the total project. Conversely, any activity that has positive slack may be delayed beyond its *ES* by an amount of time up to the amount of slack, since such a delay will by itself have no effect on the duration of the total project.

The concept of slack for an activity assumes all other activities are completed in their planned times. Thus, if several activities are in series, any slack is shared among them. Once one such activity uses up the slack, the other activities in series will have zero slack. In our example, activities E and F share two days of slack.

The algorithm to compute slack and find the critical path for a network diagram has been programmed for computer calculations, and a number of software packages are available for personal computers. These packages offer many options in addition to calculating the critical path. The program may, for example, display the network diagram on the screen or print it. Most of the programs also incorporate other aspects of project management, such as recording the budgets for the various tasks, designating who is responsible for each task, indicating whether or not the budgets have been met, and creating charts showing the time sequence of the projects.

Summary

A network diagram shows the various tasks in a project, with arrows indicating which activities must precede others. The *ES, LS, EF*, and *LF* times are the early and late start and finish times for an activity. The *ES* and *EF* times are obtained by working through the network, starting from the first task. For each activity, *ES* is the largest of the *EF* times for all preceding activities, and *EF* is the *ES* plus the time for the activity itself. The *EF* of the last task is the minimum project completion time.

The *LS* and *LF* times are obtained by working backward through the network. For each activity, the *LS* is the *LF* minus the activity time, and the *LF* is the smallest *LS* of immediate successor activities.

Slack time is the difference between *ES* and *LS* for each activity. Activities with zero slack time are on the critical path.

Time–Cost Tradeoffs

In the analysis above, we have assumed that the time needed to complete any activity was fixed. Sometimes this is true, but more generally, management can alter the time needed to complete an activity by allocating more resources to the task. For example, an activity—the painting of a house—may be assigned six days. However, this time can be shortened if more painters are assigned to the task or if they are scheduled to work overtime. The time for most activities may be thus shortened, usually at an increase in cost.[5] In this section, we shall examine how a manager might allocate resources to shorten the total project time.

To do this, let us consider the same example that we have been using. However, we shall allow the possibility that each activity may be done on a hurry-up or "crash" basis.[6] The times and costs for the regular and crash programs are given in Table 11–3.

Recall that the critical path is *ACD,* and it has a length of 12 days. This is under the assumption that the regular programs are used for each activity. In this case, the cost may be obtained by adding the figures in the fourth column of Table 11–3. The total is $2,280. Now, suppose that the manager of the project decides that 12 days is too long and that the project has to be completed in a shorter period. A shorter project completion time can be obtained by doing some of the activities on a crash basis, while incurring the additional cost of doing so. But which activities should be done on a crash basis?

The activities *not* on the critical path already have slack time. Cutting down the time needed for these activities would have no effect on the total project time. So the manager needs to examine only those activities *on* the critical path. Shortening the time of any activity on the critical path will shorten total project time. The three critical path activities, their incremental savings in days due to a crash program, and the incremental costs are shown in Table 11–4.

TABLE 11–3
Activity Times and Costs

	Time Required		Cost (dollars)	
Activity	*Regular Program*	*Crash Program*	*Regular Program*	*Crash Program*
A	2	1½	$ 100	$150
B	3	2	200	250
C	4	3	300	375
D	6	4½	500	740
E	2	1½	180	210
F	8	5½	1,000	1,200
			$2,280	$2,925

[5]Note that the activity times are now assumed to be controllable but are still deterministic; that is, they still have no random components. Case II will consider the situation in which activity times are random variables.

[6]Here, we assume an activity is either crashed or not. However, if activity crashing can occur proportionately (for example, a 40 percent crashing effort), then it is possible to formulate the deterministic time–cost tradeoff problem (Case I) as a linear programming problem; see J. O. McClain, L. J. Thomas and J. B. Mazzola, *Operations Management: Production of Goods and Services*, 3rd ed. (Englewood Cliffs, NJ: Prentice Hall, 1992).

TABLE 11–4
Incremental Costs for Crash Program

Activity	Days Shortened by Crash Program	Incremental Cost of Crash Program	Incremental Cost per Day Shortened
A	½	$ 50	$100
C	1	75	75
D	1½	240	160

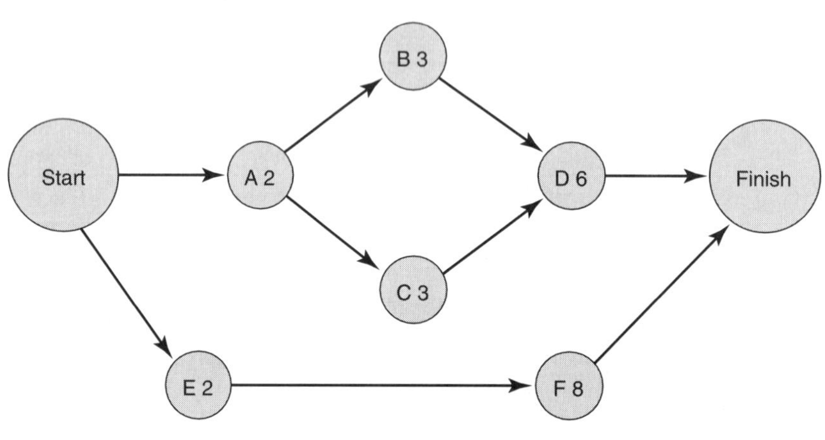

FIGURE 11–4
Network with Activity C Shortened to Three Days

The last column of Table 11–4 contains the incremental cost per day shortened. This is obtained by dividing the incremental cost of the crash program for each activity by the number of days shortened. From Table 11–4, we can see that the activity that can be shortened most inexpensively on a per day basis is activity C. The cost per day for this is only $75, compared with $100 and $160 for activities A and D, respectively. If activity C is done on a crash basis, the total project completion time is cut by one day. The network now looks as shown in Figure 11–4. Both paths *ACD* and *ABD* are now critical, each being 11 days long. The cost of this crash program is $2,355, the additional $75 being the incremental cost of putting activity C on a crash basis.

If the manager wished to cut the project completion time further, more activities could be placed on a crash basis. The critical activities are now A, B, C, and D. Activity C cannot be shortened further. Shortening B would shorten the path *ABD* but would leave the path *ACD* unchanged at 11 days and hence, would not cut total project time. The project time can be cut only by reducing activities A or D. Referring to Table 11–4, we see that activity A is the less expensive. This reduction amounts to one-half day, with an additional cost of $50, making the total cost $2,405. The two reductions are summarized in the second and third rows of Table 11–5.

If the manager wished to reduce the project time even further, activity D would be placed on a crash basis. However, this would eliminate the need to have *both* A and C on a crash basis, since the critical path would shift to *EF*; path *EF* takes 10 days, whereas if A, C, and D are all crashed, path *ACD* takes only nine days. Thus, after deciding that activity D must be crashed to reduce the project time below 10½ days, the manager must review tentatively crashed activities A and C to ascertain which of these should be moved back to the regular program.

TABLE 11–5
Critical Paths and Costs for Alternative Programs

Activities on:				
Regular Program	*Crash Program*	*Critical Path(s)*	*Project Completion Time*	*Project Total Cost*
All	None	*ACD*	12	$2,280
A, B, D, E, F	C	*ABD, ACD*	11	2,355
B, D, E, F	A, C	*ABD, ACD*	10½	2,405
B, C, E, F	A, D	*ACD, EF*	10	2,570
A, B, F	C, D, E	*ABD, ACD, EF*	9½	2,625
B, E	A, C, D, F	*ABD, ACD*	9	2,845

Assuming D and C are crashed (and A is not), then path *ACD* takes 9½ days, and path *EF* with 10 days is the critical path; the cost of crashing D and C is $2,280 + $75 + $240 = $2,595. However, suppose that D and A are crashed, and C is restricted to the regular program. Then path *ACD* takes 10 days, and there are two critical paths: *ACD* and *EF*. The cost of crashing A and D is $2,280 + $50 + $240 = $2,570. Thus, for a target of 10 project days, this alternative meets the target at lower cost. This example illustrates the complexity of making optimal time–cost tradeoffs.

Since there are now two critical paths (*ACD* and *EF*), the manager must simultaneously shorten *both* of these paths in order to reduce further the project time. Consider each of these paths in turn. For path *EF*, activity E can be reduced by one-half day at a cost of $60 per day or activity F by 2½ days at a cost of $80 per day. Activity E is the less expensive, and the manager tentatively plans to crash activity E. Since this reduces path *EF* to 9½ days, the manager next considers ways to lower path *ACD* to 9½ days (or less). Path *ACD* will take precisely 9½ days if activities C and D are crashed. Now we must check to see whether any other paths have become critical. If activities C, D, and E are crashed, then path *ABD* becomes critical with time 9½ days. The fifth row in Table 11–5 shows this situation. All three paths are now critical; total project time is 9½ days, and total cost is $2,625.

In order to reduce the total project time further, all three critical paths must be shortened simultaneously. This can be done by doing both activity A and activity F on a crash basis. Note that once activity F is crashed, activity E can be moved back to the regular program. The sixth line in Table 11–5 shows this situation. Total project time is nine days, with total cost of $2,845. It is not possible to reduce project time further. Activities B and E are at the regular program level; all others are on a crash basis.

Figure 11–5 summarizes the results of our analysis. The curve can be labeled a **time–cost tradeoff**, indicative of the fact that the manager can have different project completion times, depending on how much the firm is willing to pay.[7]

The determination of the time–cost tradeoffs above has been deliberately simplified in order to increase understanding of what is happening. But there is no reason why only two possible programs should be considered for each activity. There may be many alternative levels in addition to regular and crash programs. In fact, one could assume a continuum of possibilities, expressed by a straight line or other

[7]Under our assumption that an activity is either crashed or not, only the points indicated in Figure 11–5 are feasible alternatives. The lines connecting the points are drawn only to give a proper graphic effect.

FIGURE 11–5
Time–Cost Tradeoffs

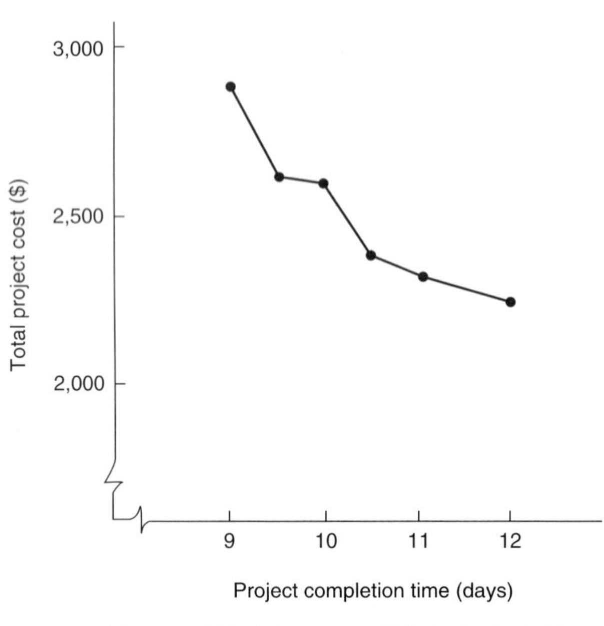

curve between the cost and time of the regular and crash programs. Some PERT or critical path computer programs allow the user to find these resource-allocation or tradeoff alternatives as a part of the solution of the critical path network.

Summary

Management can allocate resources and incur additional costs to reduce total project time. By selectively reducing the time for critical path activities with the smallest incremental cost, the optimal tradeoff function relating project time and cost can be developed.

Case II: Uncertain Activity Times

We now make a more realistic assumption concerning activity times; namely, that they are not known (or controllable) with certainty. Suppose activity times are treated as random variables. Then we need to obtain information concerning the probability density functions of these random variables before we may begin manipulating them. One technique to obtain such information is called the multiple-estimate approach.

Multiple Time Estimates for Uncertain Activity Times

Instead of asking for an estimate of expected activity time directly, three time estimates are requested, as follows:

a_i = Most optimistic time for activity i
b_i = Most pessimistic time for activity i
m_i = Most likely time for activity i (i.e., the mode)

Then Equation 11–1 is used to estimate the expected (mean) activity time:

$$t_i = (1/6)(a_i + 4m_i + b_i) \qquad (11\text{–}1)$$

where t_i is the expected activity time for activity i. For example, suppose the estimates for activity B are:

$$a_B = 1$$
$$b_B = 8$$
$$m_B = 3$$

Then the expected activity time for activity B is:

$$t_B = (1/6)(1 + 4 \cdot 3 + 8) = (1/6)(21) = 3.5$$

The most likely or modal estimate for activity B is 3, but the expected time for the completion is 3.5. This occurs because the pessimistic time is quite large. The formula for expected time in Equation 11–1 is used because this formula approximates the mean of a beta distribution whose end points are a_i and b_i and whose mode is m_i. It is not possible to justify the use of the beta distribution in a rigorous sense, but the distribution has the following characteristics: it is unimodal, it is continuous, and it has a finite range. Intuitively, the formula in Equation 11–1 gives some weight to the end points (a_i and b_i) as well as the mode (m_i) in calculating the mean time for completion.[8]

The multiple-estimate approach is supposed to produce improved estimates of the expected time to complete an activity. In practice, it is not obvious that the multiple-estimate approach leads to a better expected value than the single-estimate approach; however, the multiple-estimate approach allows us to consider the variability of the time for completion of an activity. Equation 11–2 is used to estimate the standard deviation of the time required to complete an activity, based on the optimistic and pessimistic time estimates:

$$\sigma_i = (1/6)(b_i - a_i) \qquad (11\text{–}2)$$

where σ_i represents the standard deviation of the time required to complete activity i. Again, this formula is only an approximation used if the time to complete an activity is beta distributed. The value of the standard deviation is that it may be calculated for each activity on a path and used to obtain an estimate of the standard deviation of the duration of the path. For instance, suppose the multiple time estimates shown in Table 11–6 were made for the project in our example. The numbers in the table were chosen so that the estimated time, t_i, would be the same as the initial estimates in Figure 11–1. Thus, the critical path is still *ACD*, with an expected length of 12 days. Path *ABD* has an expected length of 11 days, and path *EF* has an expected length of 10 days. Table 11–6 contains the expected time for each activity and the standard deviation of time for each activity.

---

[8]Sasieni has demonstrated that the well-known formula in Equation 11–1 cannot be derived in general from the beta distribution; see M. W. Sasieni, "A Note on PERT Times," *Management Science* 32, no. 12 (December 1986), pp. 1652–53. Hence, Equation 11–1 should be interpreted as one reasonable way to estimate expected activity time from the three separate estimates a_i, b_i, and m_i.

TABLE 11–6
Multiple Time Estimates

Activity	a_i	b_i	m_i	t_i	$\sigma_i = (1/6)(b_i - a_i)$	σ_i^2
A	1	3	2	2	0.33	0.11
B	1	5	3	3	0.67	0.45
C	2	6	4	4	0.67	0.45
D	4	8	6	6	0.67	0.45
E	1	3	2	2	0.33	0.11
F	1	15	8	8	2.33	5.43

Some authors suggest computing the standard deviation of the length of each path. Starting with the critical path, if we assume that the activity times are independent random variables, then the variance of time to complete the critical path may be computed as the sum of the variances of the activities on the critical path.[9] In our example, the path *ACD* is the critical path. If we add the variances along this path, we obtain:

$$\sigma^2_{ACD} = 0.11 + 0.45 + 0.45 = 1.01$$

The standard deviation of the length of path *ACD* is:

$$\sigma_{ACD} = \sqrt{1.01} = 1.005$$

If there is a large number of independent activities on the critical path, the distribution of the total time for the path can be assumed to be normal.[10] Our example has only three activities, so the assumption of normality would not be strictly appropriate; but for illustration, our results may be interpreted as follows: The length of time it takes to complete path *ACD* is a normally distributed random variable with a mean of 12 days and a standard deviation of 1.005 days. Given this information, it is possible to use tables of the cumulative normal distribution to make probability statements concerning various completion times for the critical path.[11] For example, the probability of path *ACD* being completed within 14 days is:

$$F\left(\frac{X-\mu}{\sigma}\right) = F\left(\frac{14-12}{1.005}\right) = F(2) = 0.977$$

from Table A in the Appendix of Tables at the end of the book.

However, there is a major problem in performing this type of analysis on the critical path. Apart from the difficulties involved in assuming that all activity times are independent and beta distributed, it is not necessarily true that the longest *expected* path (i.e., the critical path) will turn out to be the longest *actual* path. In our example, the noncritical path *EF* has an expected length of 10 days. The variance of that path is:

$$\sigma^2_{EF} = 0.11 + 5.43 = 5.54$$

[9]The variance of a sum of random variables equals the sum of the variances of each random variable if the variables are independent.

[10]The sum of n independent variables with finite mean and variance tends toward normality by the central limit theorem as n tends toward infinity.

[11]Use the standardized normal variate:

$$Z = \frac{X-\mu}{\sigma}$$

The standard deviation is:

$$\sigma_{EF} = \sqrt{5.54} = 2.35$$

If we assume that the distribution of the length of path *EF* is normal, then the probability of path *EF* being completed within 14 days is:

$$F\left(\frac{14 - 10}{2.35}\right) = F(1.70) = 0.955 \text{ from Table A}$$

Path *ACD* and path *EF* must both be completed within 14 days for the project to be completed within 14 days, since the project is not completed until all activities are completed. The probability that both paths (*ACD* and *EF*) are completed within 14 days is:

$$(0.977)(0.955) = 0.933$$

If we had considered only the critical path, the probability of not completing the project in 14 days would have been 1 − 0.977, or 0.023. After path *EF* is also considered, the probability of not completing the project in 14 days is 1 − 0.933, or 0.067, almost three times the probability of the critical path not being completed. Another way of describing the situation is to say that if the project takes more than 14 days, path *EF* has a larger chance of causing the delay than path *ACD* does.

A final difficulty remains. Path *ABD* may also turn out to be the most constraining path, and we could compute the variance of that path, as we did above for paths *ACD* and *EF*. However, there are two activities in common between path *ABD* and path *ACD* (activities A and D), and thus the lengths of the two paths are not independent variables. In order to calculate the probability that both path *ABD* and path *ACD* are completed in less than 14 days, we must deal with the joint probability of dependent events, and this is beyond the method of calculation presented in this chapter. The problems we have encountered in a six-activity sample project are greatly magnified when a realistic project with hundreds of activities is considered. Thus, there is a serious danger in using the mean and variance of the length of the critical path to estimate the probability that the project will be completed within some specified time. Since some "noncritical" paths may in fact turn out to be constraining, the mean estimate of project completion time obtained by studying the critical path alone is *too optimistic* an estimate; it is biased and always tends to *underestimate* the average project completion time.

Fortunately, even though the analytical calculation of the distribution of the project completion time is exceedingly difficult in real-sized network, it is relatively easy to use the technique of Monte Carlo simulation to obtain information about the likelihood of project duration when activity times are uncertain.

Simulation of PERT Networks: Project Duration

To overcome the problem described above, it is possible to simulate any PERT network. In general terms, the steps would proceed as follows:

1. Using (for example) a normal distribution of activity times for each activity, and using each activity's calculated mean and standard deviation from Equations 11–1 and 11–2, generate a random value (a realization) for the time to complete each activity in the network.

FIGURE 11–6 Cumulative Frequency Distribution for Project Duration

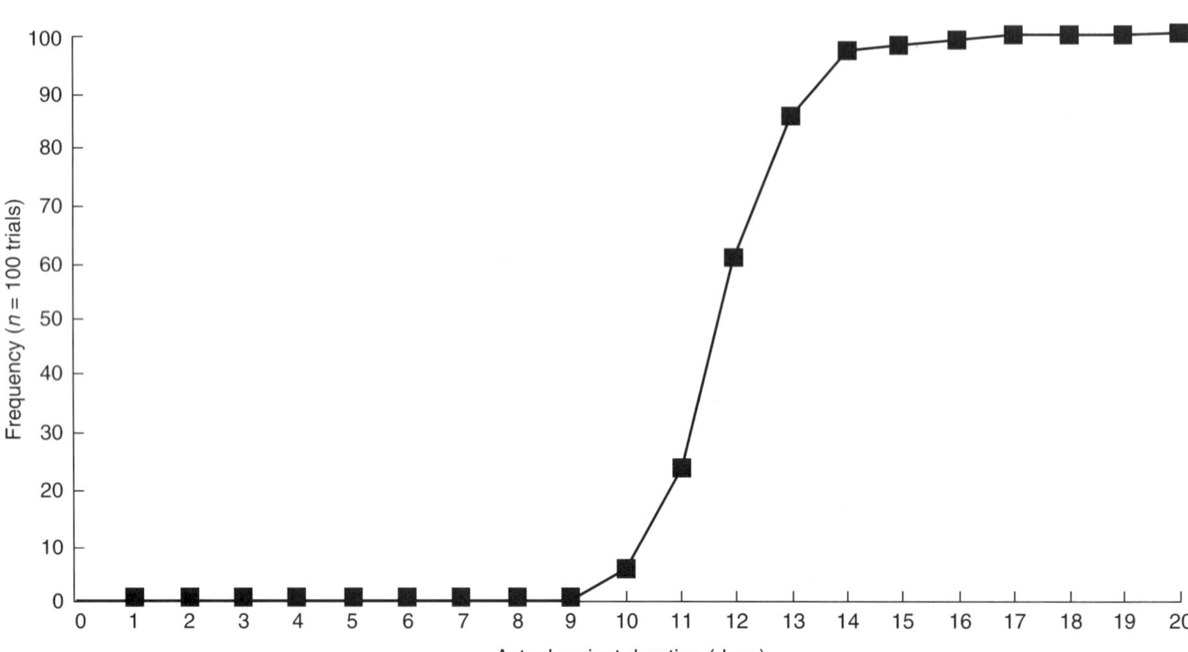

2. Treat the generated times as actual times for each activity, and use the critical path algorithm described earlier to find both the "actual critical path" (*ex post*) and the actual project duration.
3. Repeat steps 1 and 2 for some large number of trials, recording a histogram of project completion times and the percentage of time each activity was on the *ex post* critical path.

Example

Suppose a simulation were run 100 times for the sample network of the chapter, using means and standard deviations from Table 11–6. Figure 11–6 contains a representative cumulative distribution of the type that might be produced from the simulation. Although the information contained in Figure 11–6 would be useful in deciding whether or not the risk of project lateness were tolerable, it is of no direct help in deciding how to crash activities so as to speed the project. For this purpose, the simulation can record the percentage of times each activity was on the *ex post* critical path (that is, the path that actually turned out to be critical in a given simulation run). Table 11–7 is an example of such a record.

Activities E and F constitute one potentially critical path, and thus have identical percentages in Table 11–7. Activities A and D are in series in two paths (*ABD* and *ACD*), and hence also have identical percentages. Activities B and C are in parallel, and thus, the sum of their percentages (5 percent + 66 percent) must add to 71 percent, which is the percentage for activities A and D in series with the B–C parallel link.[12]

[12]This is true only if it is not possible for both paths *ABD* and *ACD* to be critical.

TABLE 11–7
Percentage of Time Activities Were Critical

A	71%
B	5
C	66
D	71
E	30
F	30

TABLE 11–8
Percentage of Time Activities Were Critical, Given Project Duration > 12 Days

A	49%
B	3
C	46
D	49
E	54
F	54

Table 11–7 has been calculated using the entire simulation output. When considering which activities should be crashed to reduce the project completion time, it makes sense to consider only those simulation outcomes where the project was delayed beyond some desired target. Considering 12 days (the expected length of the critical path) as our target, Table 11–8 contains illustrative data on the percentage of time each activity was critical, *given that the project took longer than 12 days to complete*. Note that these percentages will be different from those given in Table 11–7. Since we are less interested in "crashing" a project when it is completed prior to its expected date, the results of Table 11–8 would be more useful in determining which activity crashing would produce the largest reduction in delays beyond 12 days.

For a large network, a simulation of the regular program would produce a distribution like Figure 11–6. If the project performance needed to be improved, study of a table like Table 11–8 would indicate the set of activities that, on the average, were causing delays various percentages of the time. Then, after some of the critical activities were crashed, the simulation could be repeated to see whether or not project performance had been sufficiently improved.

Summary

If the activity times in a PERT network are uncertain, then the length of the critical path calculated using deterministic estimates will understate the true expected project time. The probability distribution of the actual project time and the probability that each activity will be on the *ex post* actual critical path can be obtained by simulation. Conditional on the project being late, the simulation can also show the percentage of time each activity was on the actual critical path.

Simulation of PERT Networks: Total Cost

If there are uncertain cost estimates for each activity, it is possible to use exactly the same approach to simulate the cost performance of any PERT network. Proceeding as above, one would generate random values for the cost of each activity and simply sum them to obtain a realized value for project cost for that trial. This process could be repeated for some large number of trials, and the cumulative distribution of total cost could be plotted. However, it turns out there is a simpler way to obtain the cumulative distribution of total cost, as shown in the following example.

Example

Consider the cost entries in Table 11–3 under the regular (not crash) program. Now suppose those costs are the mean values, and each activity's cost is actually a normal random variable with standard deviation and variance as specified in Table 11–9.

If all the cost uncertainty was independent from activity to activity, then we know from basic probability that the expected cost of the project is just the sum of the expected costs of each activity, and the variance of project cost is the sum of the variances of activity costs. The standard deviation of project cost is $\sqrt{56{,}896} = 238.53$, and the mean is $2,280. A cumulative frequency distribution of project cost outcomes based on the normal distribution with these parameters is illustrated in Figure 11–7, labeled *Independence* case.

However, in this situation the assumption of statistical independence of the different cost elements may not be valid. Suppose you were told that the first three activities each cost 30 percent more than expected. Would you want to revise your estimate of the cost of the last three activities? If so, then we say the cost elements are not independent, and in order to proceed further one would have to make explicit assumptions about the dependencies among the costs of the various activities. Suppose as an extreme case we assumed that the six costs were perfectly positively correlated. Then, for example, if the cost for activity A were at its mean, the cost for each of the other activities would also be at its mean. If the cost for activity A was at the 20th percentile of its distribution of costs, then the cost of each of the other activities would also be at its 20th percentile point.

In this case, the expected total project cost is also the sum of the expected costs of the individual activities. That is, from Table 11–9, expected total cost = $2,280.

It can also be shown that in this extreme case of perfect positive correlation, the standard deviation of total cost is equal to the sum of the standard deviations of cost for each activity. From Table 11–9, this is standard deviation of total project cost = $\sigma = \$456$. A cumulative frequency distribution of project cost outcomes based on the normal distribution with these parameters is also illustrated in Figure 11–7, labeled *Perfect Correlation* case. Note that although the means of the two distributions are the same, with perfect positive correlation among all cost elements, the likelihood of the total project cost being well above or well below the mean increases considerably (the distribution is more spread out or has more variability in the perfect correlation case).

TABLE 11–9
Uncertain Activity Costs

Activity	*Expected Cost*	*Standard Deviation*	*Variance*
A	$ 100	20	400
B	200	40	1,600
C	300	60	3,600
D	500	100	10,000
E	180	36	1,296
F	1,000	200	40,000
Total	$2,280	456	56,896

The cases of independence (no correlation) and perfect positive correlation are two extreme cases; the general situation probably falls somewhere between these extremes. It is beyond the scope of this text to deal with multivariate correlated distributions, but the simple exercise performed above of calculating the cumulative frequency distribution of project cost outcomes under these two extremes may be a useful one.

Evaluation of PERT

The PERT technique forces the planner to specify in detail the set of activities that constitute the project and to estimate their times and state their sequencing requirements. The construction of the network diagram can often point out major problems in the project. If the critical path is longer than desired, the project can be replanned, with more resources committed to critical activities. Once the project has begun, the PERT technique may be used to provide periodic reports on the status of the project, including any changes in the critical path. If there is a path that is almost critical, the PERT technique can provide this information by pointing out activities with a small amount of slack.

The time estimates to perform activities constitute a major potential problem in the PERT technique. If the time estimates are poor, then the initial network diagram and initial critical path will have little real meaning after the project begins. Also, if there is uncertainty in how long it will take to complete the tasks, then this uncertainty must be taken into account in estimating the probability of project completion within any specified time. As we have seen, when activity times are random, one may compute the probability of the critical path being completed in any given time; but with random activity times, the actual *ex post* critical path may differ from the *ex ante* critical path. One way of dealing with this complexity involves simulation of

FIGURE 11–7
Project Cost Distributions: Two Extreme Cases

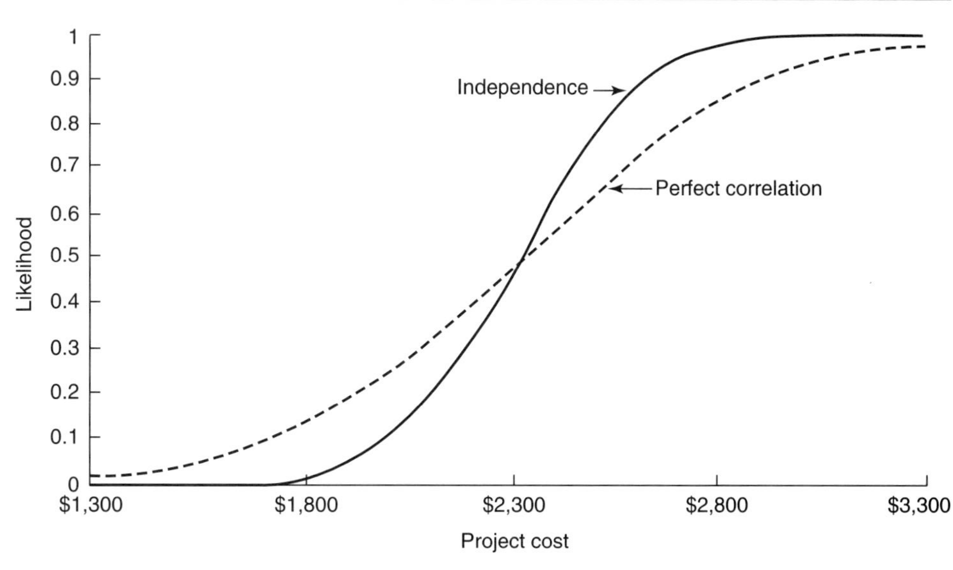

the network. In the simulation, both the probability of project lateness and the probability that each activity will be critical can be estimated, thereby providing guidance to the project planner.

Finally, the simple PERT technique does not consider the resources required at various stages of the project. For example, if a certain resource must be used to perform both activity B and C in our example, and if it can only be used for one activity at a time, then the diagram in Figure 11–3 is infeasible because activity C cannot be performed in parallel with activity B. Various extensions of the PERT technique have been developed that allow for resource constraints and that keep track of costs as well as time as the project progresses.

Many project managers experienced in using PERT and CPM now feel that the major advantages of the technique are in the planning stage of a project. Using PERT for active control of a project requires frequent updating and rerunning of the PERT calculations, whereas often a simple bar chart of progress to date can provide an adequate record for control purposes at much less cost.

Bibliography

Cleland, D. I., and R. Gareis, eds. *Global Project Management Handbook.* New York: McGraw-Hill, 1994.

Cleland, D. I., and W. R. King, eds. *Project Management Handbook.* New York: Van Nostrand Reinhold, 1983.

McClain, J. O., L. J. Thomas, and J. B. Mazzola. *Operations Management: Production of Goods and Services.* 3nd ed. Englewood Cliffs, NJ: Prentice Hall, 1992.

Moder, J.; C. R. Phillips; and E. W. Davis, *Project Management with CPM, PERT, and PRECEDENCE Diagramming.* 3rd ed. New York: Van Nostrand Reinhold, 1983.

Wiest, J. D., and F. K. Levy. *A Management Guide to PERT/CPM.* 2nd ed. Englewood Cliffs, NJ: Prentice Hall, 1977.

Practice Problems[13]

11–1. Consider the following data for the activities in a project:

Activity	*Immediate Predecessors*	*Estimated Time (days)*
A	—	5
B	A	4
C	—	7
D	B, C	3
E	B	4
F	D, E	2

a. Draw a network diagram for the project.

b. Compute the *ES, EF, LS,* and *LF* for each activity, assuming the *EF* and the *LF* for the last activity are the same. What is the minimum project completion time?

c. List the activities that are on the critical path.

11–2. Consider the data in Problem 11–1, but suppose now that activity C takes nine days to complete rather than seven days.

a. Does the critical path change?

b. If activity C were to take 11 days to complete, would the critical path change?

11–3. You are given the following data concerning the activities in a project (numbers refer to days):

Activity	*Immediate Predecessor*	a_i	b_i	m_i
A	—	2	6	4
B	—	6	10	8
C	A	1	15	5
D	C	1	9	5
E	B	6	10	8

[13]Solutions for these problems are at the end of this chapter.

a. Compute the expectation (t_i) and the variance (σ_i^2) of the time required to complete each activity.
b. Draw a network diagram, and find the critical path by inspection. What is the expected length of the critical path?
c. Assume the times for each activity are independent and that the time required to complete a path is normally distributed. Compute the probability that path *ACD* will be completed in less than 16 days. Also compute the probability that path *BE* will be completed in less than 16 days.
d. What is the probability that the project will be completed in less than 16 days?

Problems

11–4. Table 11–10 contains a list of activities and sequencing requirements as indicated, which comprise necessary activities for the completion of a thesis.
a. Draw a network diagram illustrating the sequencing requirements for the set of activities in the table. Be sure to portray activities by circles and sequencing requirements by arrows.
b. Compute the *ES, EF, LS,* and *LF* for each activity, assuming the *EF* and *LF* for the last activity are the same. What is the minimum project completion time?
c. List the activities that are on the critical path.

11–5. Consider the following data for a project:

Activity	*Immediate Predecessor*	t_i*(days)*	σ_i
A	—	4.0	0
B	A	6.0	1.0
C	A	3.0	0
D	C	7.0	1.0
E	B, C	2.0	2.0

a. Draw a network diagram for the project.
b. Find the "critical path" (*ex ante*) by inspection. What is its expected length?
c. What is the probability that path *ABE* will be completed no later than day 15, assuming independence among activity times?
d. What is the probability that the entire project will be completed no later than day 15?

11–6. Consider the estimate of total project duration as calculated by the usual PERT algorithm (adding up expected time estimates of all activities that are on the critical path).
a. Suppose you are dealing with a pure series network:

START →Ⓐ →Ⓑ →Ⓒ→ . . .
→Ⓧ →Ⓨ →Ⓩ→ FINISH

Can you argue logically that the PERT estimate of total project duration is unbiased? (*Hint:* Recall that the expectation of a sum equals the sum of the expectations.)

TABLE 11–10 (for Problem 11–4)

Activity	*Description*	*Prerequisite Activity*	*Expected Time (weeks)*
A	Literature search	None	6
B	Topic formulation	None	5
C	Committee selection	B	2
D	Formal proposal	C	2
E	Company selection and contact	A, D	2
F	Progress report	D	1
G	Formal research	A, D	6
H	Data collection	E	5
I	Data analysis	G, H	6
J	Conclusions	I	2
K	Rough draft (without conclusions)	G	4
L	Final copy	J, K	3
M	Oral examination	L	1

TABLE 11–11 (for Problem 11–7)

Activity	Predecessor Activities	Time (weeks) Regular Program	Time (weeks) Crash Program	Cost ($000s) Regular Program	Cost ($000s) Crash Program
A (start)	—	0	—	0	—
B	A	5	3	10	22
C	A	2	1	6	15
D	B, C	3	2	6	15
E	B	4	2	10	25
F (finish)	D, E	0	—	0	—

b. Suppose you are dealing with a pure parallel network:

START
↓

↓ ↓ ↓ ↓ ↓ ↓
Ⓐ Ⓑ Ⓒ . . . Ⓧ Ⓨ Ⓩ
↓ ↓ ↓ ↓ ↓ ↓

↓
FINISH

Assume that all activities in this network have the same expected time for completion. Can you argue logically that the PERT estimate of total project duration is biased in this case? In which direction is the estimate biased?

c. From your conclusions in (*a*) and (*b*), make a valid generalization about the bias (or lack thereof) inherent in a PERT project duration estimate when we have a large, complex network combining series and parallel portions.

11–7. A project is characterized by activities A through F. The predecessor activities and the times required, and costs for both a regular and a crash program for each activity, are shown in Table 11–11.

a. Using only the time for the regular program activities, draw a PERT network for this problem. What is the critical path? How long will it take to complete the total project?

b. What is the cost of the project as given in (*a*)?

c. Find the time–cost tradeoff points that are possible. What is the minimum time in which the project can be completed? What is the cost of this program?

More Challenging Problems

11–8. The Ocean Hardware Company is a chain of retail hardware and appliance stores. The company is considering the installation of a new computer system to do the payroll for the company, the sales accounting (paying for purchases and sending bills), and inventory recordkeeping. The company controller is trying to lay out a schedule for the various tasks involved in putting the new computer system into operation.

The company plans to hire programmers to develop the payroll and accounting programs. However, an outside consulting firm is to be hired to do the inventory control program. Certain aspects of the inventory control program depend on the accounting program and hence it has to be developed after the accounting program is completed.

The job of completing each program involves preliminary work, final work, testing, revising, writing of manuals, and implementation. The new manager of the computer operations has identified the list of tasks (activities) shown in Table 11–12 that have to be performed, together with the times needed to accomplish each and the activities that have to be completed before the given activity can begin (the predecessor activities).

a. How long will it take before the computer system with the three programs is completed? What activities are critical in achieving this time?

b. Suppose that management is concerned only with minimizing the time to get the accounting and payroll programs implemented. How long will this take? What activities are critical in this case?

11–9. Refer to Problem 11–3. Assume for purposes of this exercise that each activity time is equally likely between its a_i and b_i time estimates (i.e., ignore the m_i column, and consider activity times to be uniformly distributed over the appropriate range). Using random digits, perform a hand simulation of the network for 10 trials, recording for each trial the project completion time and the activities that were critical. Which activities were critical the largest percentage of the time? Also compute the percentage of time each activity was critical, conditional on the project being delayed beyond 16 days.

TABLE 11–12 (for Problem 11–8)

Activity	*Description*	*Predecessor Activity*	*Time to Complete (in months)*
A	Analyze alternative computer systems, and order computer from the manufacturer	—	2
B	Wait for delivery of computer from manufacturer	A	4
C	Hire computer programmers	A	1
D	Do preliminary work on payroll program	C	1½
E	Do preliminary work on accounting program	C	2½
F	Do final work on both payroll and accounting programs	D, E	2
G	Hire outside consultant for work on inventory control program	A	1
H	Do preliminary work on inventory control program	E, G	2
I	Do final work on inventory control program	F, H	2
J	Do preliminary testing of payroll and accounting programs on rented machine	F	½
K	Revise payroll and accounting programs	J	½
L	Install and test computer on delivery from manufacturer	B	½
M	Test payroll and accounting programs on installed computer	K, L	½
N	Prepare manuals describing payroll and accounting programs	J	1
O	Implement payroll and accounting programs	M, N	½
P	Test inventory control program on installed computer	I, L	½
Q	Prepare manuals describing inventory control programs	I	1
R	Implement inventory control program	P, Q	½
S	Done	O, R	0

FIGURE 11–8 (for Problem 11–10)

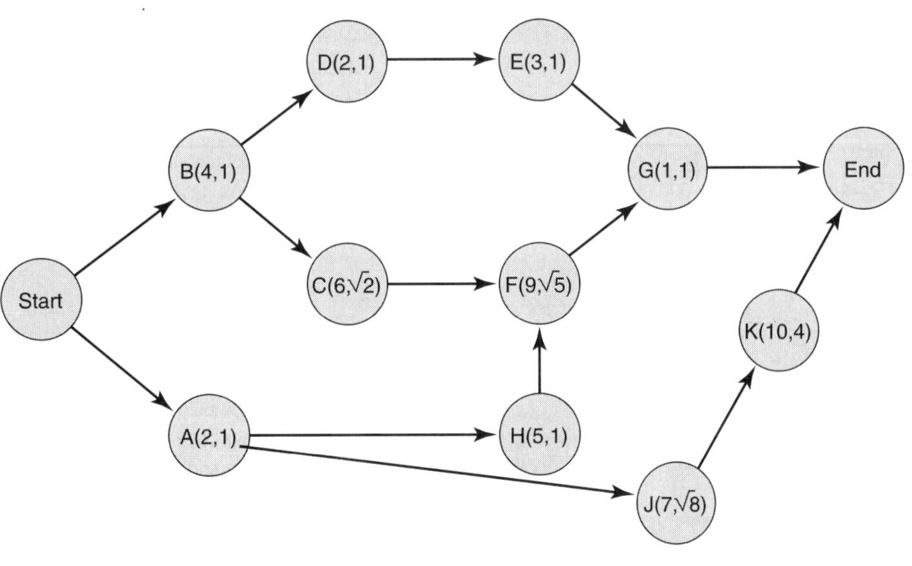

11–10. A network for a project is shown in Figure 11–8. The t_i and σ_i attached to each node in parentheses represent the expected time and standard deviation, respectively, in months, of this segment of the project.

a. Identify the critical path, and calculate its expected length.

b. Assuming independent activities and that the length of the critical path is normally distributed, calculate the probability that the *path* of (*a*) will be completed in less than 23 months.

c. Will the actual *project* be completed by 23 months:
(1) With the same probability as in (*b*)?
(2) With lower probability?
(3) With higher probability? Why?

d. Suppose you wish to reduce the probability that the project will take longer than 23 months. You can crash *one* of the following activities, and *only one*, by one month: A, C, E, or H. Which one would you choose to crash? Why? (*Note:* Assume that crashing will reduce the *mean* activity time by one month and leave the variance unchanged.)

11–11. In the project considered here, activity crashing can take place over a wide range of reduction times. The cost per day of reduction is given:

Activity	*Immediate Predecessor*	*Normal Time (days)*	*Cost per Day to Crash*	*Lower Time Limit*
A	None	3	$450	1
B	None	4	300	2
C	A	3	200	1
D	E	2	100	1
E	A, B	2	500	1
F	C, D	4	600	3

For example, activity C can be crashed from its normal time of three days down to as little as one day, or anywhere between; the cost per day to crash C is $200.

a. Draw a network diagram for this project. What is the critical path? How long will the project take, if no crashing takes place?

b. Determine the least-cost way to crash activities in order to complete the project in 11 days; in 10 days; in 9 days; in 8 days. Draw your results on a time–cost tradeoff diagram.

c. Suppose the due date for the project is five days, and a penalty of $500 per day is assessed for each day late. What is the optimal number of days to crash the project? Why?

11–12. A firm is building a plant to produce a new frozen convenience food. The activities in Table 11–13 have been identified, the times estimated, and the precedence relationships established. How long will the project take? What activities are on the critical path(s)?

11–13. A project is composed of the five activities shown in Table 11–14. Probabilities have been assessed for the length of time in weeks that each activity will take, as shown in Table 11–14. Thus, for example, there is a 0.6 chance that activity A will take four weeks, a 0.1 chance that it will be completed in five weeks, a 0.1 chance that it will take six weeks, and so on.

a. Draw the network for this project. Note that there are four paths through the network. Using the expected times, calculate the time for each path. Which is the longest or critical expected path?

b. Assign random numbers to each outcome (number of weeks) for each activity in accordance with the probabilities in the table.

c. Using random numbers, randomly select a time for each activity. Calculate the time for each of the four paths in the network, and record the time of the

TABLE 11–13 (for Problem 11–12)

Activity	*Description*	*Immediate Predecessors*	*Estimated Time (months)*
A	Engineering design of the building	None	1.5
B	Design of production line	None	1.0
C	Design of oven	B	2.0
D	Design of freezer	B	1.0
E	Design of packaging equipment	C, D	1.0
F	Order and manufacture of oven	C	9.0
G	Order and manufacture of freezer	D	8.0
H	Order and manufacture of packaging equipment	E	3.0
I	Submission and awarding of bids on building construction	A	2.0
J	Building construction (first phase)	I	9.0
K	Building construction (final phase)	J	1.5
L	Installation of oven	F, J	2.0
M	Installation of freezer	J, L	0.5
N	Installation of packaging equipment	H, J	0.5
O	Baking tests	K, L	1.0
P	Freezing tests	M, O	0.5
Q	Entire system test	N, P	0.5
R	USDA inspection	N, P	0.5

TABLE 11–14 (for Problem 11–13)

	Time in Weeks								
Activity	*4*	*5*	*6*	*7*	*8*	*9*	*10*	*Expected Time*	*Predecessor Activities*
A	0.6	0.1	0.1	0.1	0.1			5	None
B		0.1	0.2	0.4	0.2	0.1		7	None
C		0.1	0.1	0.1	0.3	0.2	0.2	8	A, B
D	0.1	0.4	0.2	0.1	0.1	0.1		6	A, B
E	0.1	0.8	0.1					5	C, D

longest path and the activities on the longest path.

d. Repeat (*c*) 25 times (or the number of times assigned by your instructor). Calculate the average time for the longest path. Does it differ from that calculated in (*a*)? Why?

e. Calculate the percentage of time that each activity was on the longest path.

f. Conditional on the project being delayed beyond 21 days, compute the percentage of time that each activity was on the longest path.

Solutions to Practice Problems

11–1. *a.* Network diagram:

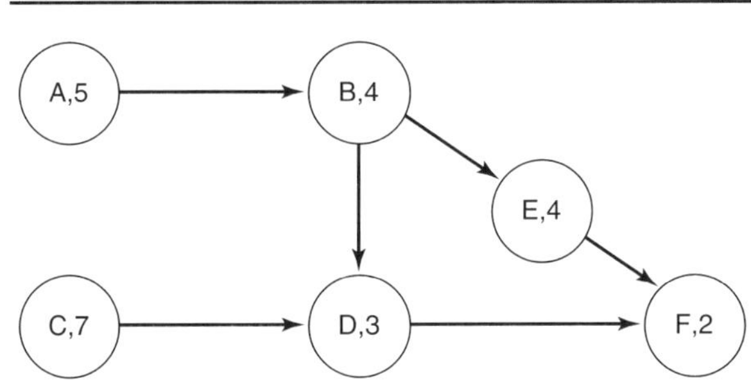

b.

Activity	*ES*	*LS*	*EF*	*LF*
A	0	0	5	5
B	5	5	9	9
C	0	3	7	10
D	9	10	12	13
E	9	9	13	13
F	13	13	15	15

Project completion time is 15 days.

c. A, B, E, F.

11–2. *a.* No; there is a three-day slack in activity C.

b. Yes; the critical path is now *CDF*, with a project completion time of 16 days.

11–3. *a.*

Activity	t_i	σ_i^2
A	4	0.44
B	8	0.44
C	6	5.44
D	5	1.78
E	8	0.44

b. Network diagram:

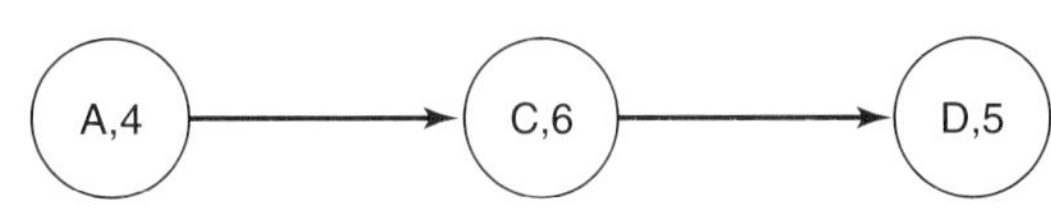

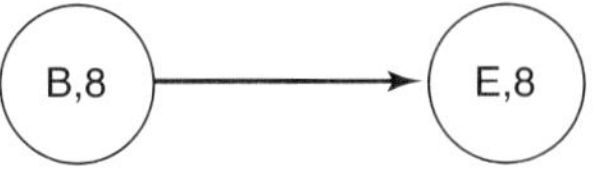

Critical path is *BE*, with a length of 16 days.

c. For path *ACD*, the expected length is 15 days and the variance is $.44 + 5.44 + 1.78 = 7.67$. Standard deviation is 2.77.
$P(\text{Time} < 16) = 1 - P(Z < 1/2.77) = .64$
For path *BE*, the variance is $.44 + .44 = .89$. Standard deviation is .94.
$P(\text{Time} < 16) = .50$.

d. $P(\text{Total project} < 16) = .64 \cdot .50 = .32$.

Motivating Example

Forecasting at L. L. Bean[1]

L. L. Bean, the successful mail-order house, requires forecasts of telephone orders to plan appropriate staffing levels three weeks in advance. Of total sales, 72 percent are from phone calls to its call center. Major factors affecting daily telephone volume are the day of the week (volume is highest on Mondays and generally declines throughout the week), time of the year (December holiday volume is much higher than an average month's volume), holiday influences (which reduce call volume), and catalog mailings (which sharply increase call volume the day a new catalog is received and for the next several days).

The company recently completed a successful project to improve the forecasts of call-center calls, using concepts to be described in this chapter. All the elements cited above have been incorporated into the forecasting system, which has proven to be much more accurate than the previous forecasting procedure.

Forecasts that are more accurate translate directly into cost savings for L. L. Bean. If a forecast is too high, then the resulting overstaffing results in wasted personnel costs; if it is too low, then not only is customer service lower than desired, the company also incurs additional telephone charges due to waits (it provides an 800-number service) and also loses some sales because some potential customers will not wait when they cannot get through immediately. The company estimates that the improved forecasting system is saving about $300,000 annually; this figure excludes the savings from avoiding much of the labor formerly involved in generating the previous forecasts.

[1]See Andrews, Bruce H., and Cunningham, Shawn M., "L. L. Bean Improves Call-Center Forecasting," *Interfaces*, November–December 1995, pp. 1–13.

CHAPTER

12 FORECASTING

Forecasts are essential for effective business operations. They enable different parts of an organization to work together more smoothly. While the saying is true that "forecasts are always wrong," it doesn't make any sense at all for the manufacturing portion of an organization to plan, say, for sales of 1 million computers this year, for sales and marketing to plan on sales of 2 million, and for finance and accounting to plan on sales of .5 million.

This chapter discusses a number of different forecasting concepts and tools. The concepts presented here are quantitative and are generally most suitable when past data on orders, demands, or shipments is available. Forecasts can be at different levels of aggregation. Sometimes what is of interest is aggregate dollar sales over a year, while at other times it is necessary to forecast short-term demand for a particular model of a product or for a particular spare part. Business firms have systems for inventory control and stock replenishment, and forecasts of future demand are a key element of such systems.

The first part of this chapter presents *time series* forecasting methods that use past data to estimate future values. We first consider *moving averages* and then present a forecasting technique called *exponential smoothing,* which is most useful for forecasting sales of a product, a part, or a product line over time. The second part of the chapter discusses *regression,* which is a statistical technique that can be used for forecasting, often at a more aggregated level such as quarterly or annual dollar sales of a division or company. We close with a discussion of forecasting approaches for new products where past data on historical sales is not available; regression analysis can also be useful here.

SECTION I. TIME SERIES METHODS

Moving Averages

Consider the sales data presented in Table 12–1 and Figure 12–1. These are monthly sales (in thousands of dollars) for a cereal product sold by one company. Sales

TABLE 12–1
Monthly Cereal Sales

Month	*Sales ($000)*
January	$1,212
February	1,321
March	1,278
April	1,341
May	1,257
June	1,287
July	1,189
August	1,111
September	1,145
October	1,150
November	1,298
December	1,331
Average	$1,243.33

FIGURE 12–1
Monthly Cereal Sales

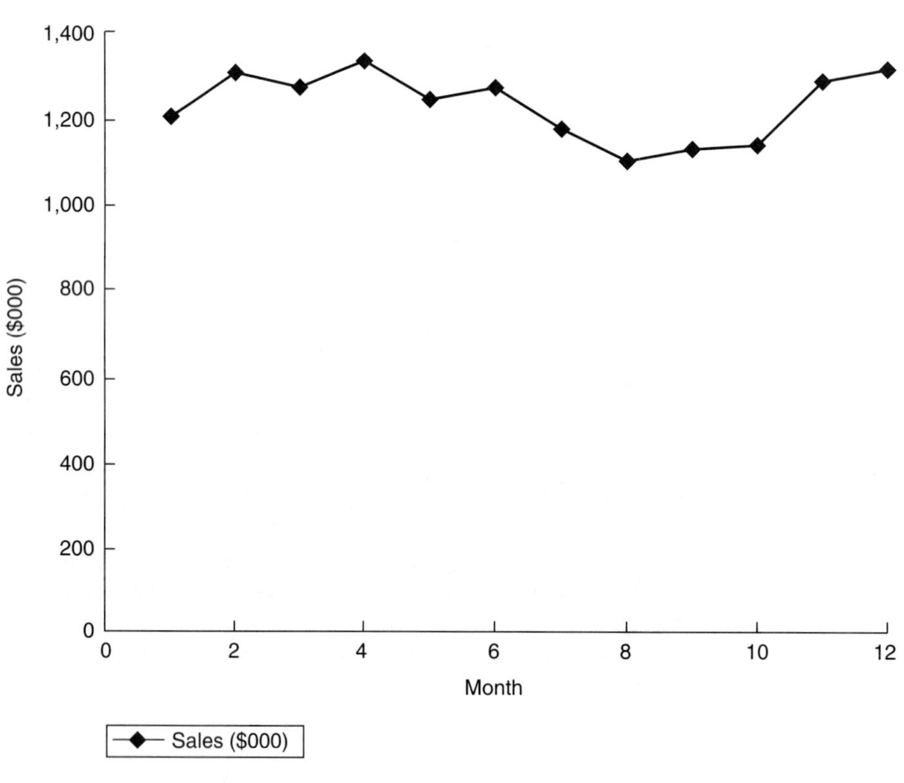

forecasts for the next several months are needed in order to plan for raw material purchases, factory labor and plant equipment utilization, and financial projections.

The simplest forecast based on past data would be to calculate the average monthly sales and use that average value ($1,243.33) as a forecast for future months. However, as time passes and new data is obtained each month, ideally one would like to update that average. A *moving average* is an average that is calculated over a

TABLE 12–2
Three-Month Moving Average Forecast

Month	*Sales ($000)*	*Three-Month Moving Average*
January	$1,212	
February	1,321	
March	1,278	
April	1,341	$1,270.33
May	1,257	1,313.33
June	1,287	1,292.00
July	1,189	1,295.00
August	1,111	1,244.33
September	1,145	1,195.67
October	1,150	1,148.33
November	1,298	1,135.33
December	1,331	1,197.67
		1,259.67

certain number of past data points; for example, a three-month moving average would be calculated by taking the most recent three months of data, averaging them, and then using that average as the forecast for the next month. Table 12–2 contains these calculations, starting with April, since three months of initial data are needed to calculate the first moving average.

For example, the April forecast of $1,270.33 is obtained from:

$$(1{,}212 + 1{,}321 + 1{,}278)/3 = 1{,}270.33$$

That is, the average of the first three months of actual sales would be used as a forecast for the fourth month's sales. Figure 12–2 illustrates these forecasts:

In our cereal sales data there is a downturn in sales in July, August, and September, and then an increase in November and December. Note how the moving average forecast lags behind the actual changes. While one cannot expect any time series forecasting method to predict turning points ahead of time, we would like forecasts that can react rapidly to short-term trends. One way to do this is to shorten the period of the moving average—say, from three months to two months; this is illustrated in Figure 12–3, which presents both three-month moving average forecasts and two-month moving average forecasts. Note that the two-month moving average forecasts show less lag in following short-term trends than the three-month moving average forecasts.

One disadvantage of moving average forecasts is that they place equal weight on each data point when they are calculated. One might argue that the most recent data deserve a higher weight in forecasting. A method that systematically places highest weight on most recent data and progressively less weight on older data is called *exponential smoothing*; we now present it and apply it to the cereal forecasting example.

Exponential Smoothing

Exponential smoothing makes use of a smoothing constant, which is the percentage of the forecast affected by the most recent data point or sales observation. We will select a smoothing constant value of 0.20; this means that 20 percent of the forecast

Figure 12–2
Three-Month Moving Average

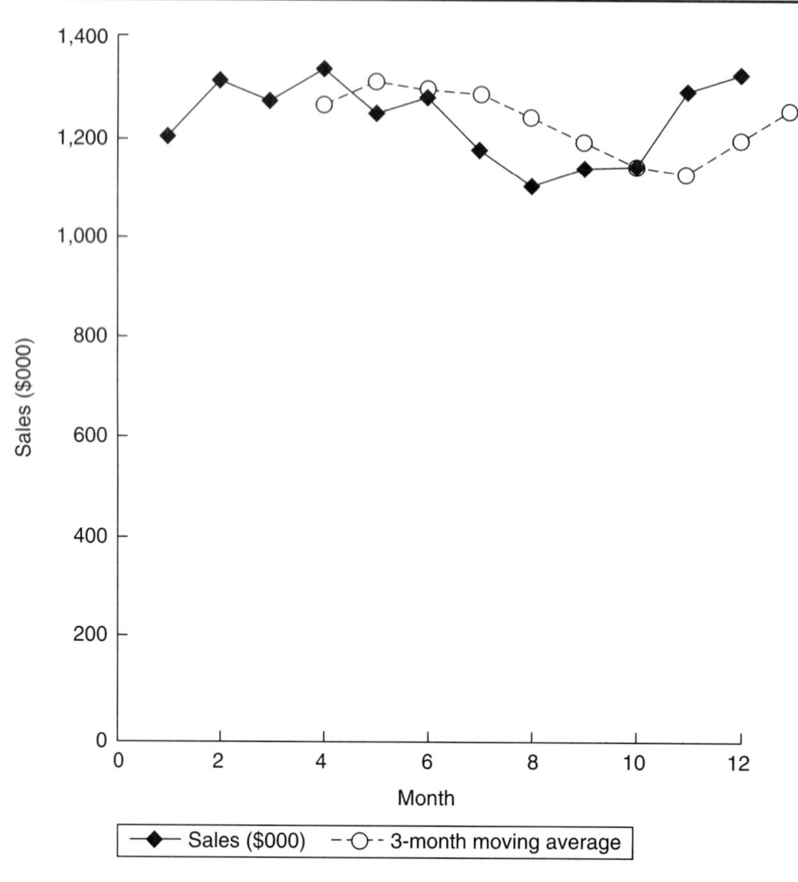

will be affected by the last data point and 80 percent of the forecast will be affected by earlier data points. With this value of the smoothing constant, the basic equation of exponential smoothing is:

New forecast = .20 (latest data point) + .80 (previous forecast) (12–1)

Let us use this equation from February onward, assuming that the previous forecast for January is taken as January's sales of $1,212. Then the February forecast would be:

February forecast = .20 (January actual sales) + .80 (previous January forecast)
= .20 (1,212) + .80 (1,212) = 1,212

Now we observe actual February sales of $1,321; we will use this data to create a forecast for March:

March forecast = .20 (February actual sales) + .80 (previous February forecast)
= .20 (1,321) + .80 (1,212) = 264.2 + 969.6 = 1,233.8

Next, we observe actual March sales of $1,278 ; we will use this data to create a forecast for April:

April forecast = .20 (March actual sales) + .80 (previous March forecast)
= .20 (1,278) + .80 (1,233.8) = 255.6 + 987.04 = 1,242.64

FIGURE 12–3
Two-Month Moving Average

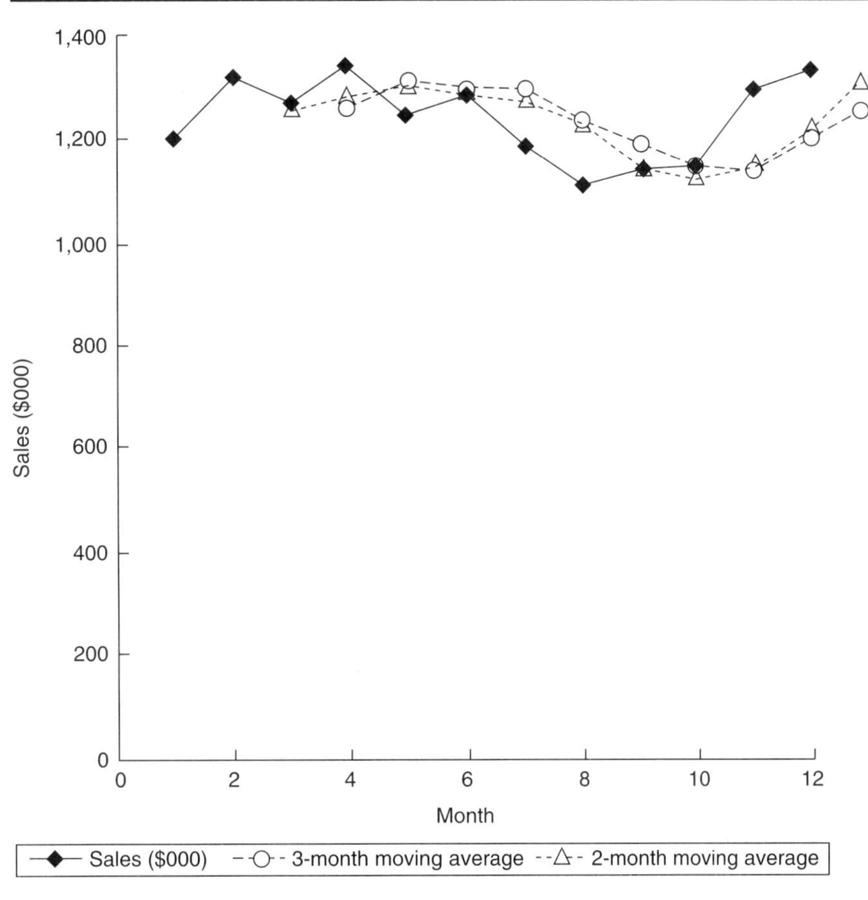

These calculations are completed in Table 12–3, and the forecasts are illustrated in Figure 12–4.

Note that in Figure 12–4, the value .20 of the smoothing constant makes the forecast respond rather slowly to the July–September decrease in sales. Let's try a higher value of the smoothing constant—say, .40; the results are plotted in Figure 12–5.

Notice in Figure 12–5 that a high value of the smoothing constant makes the forecast respond somewhat more rapidly to the July–September decrease in sales. Of course, while an even higher value of the smoothing constant would be more responsive, it would also react to what may turn out to be simply random movements in sales from one month to the next, so the usual range of values for the smoothing constant is between .10 and .30.

The calculations for Equation 12–1 are, of course, simple to perform in a spreadsheet.[2] We performed them in detail above simply to demonstrate how they

[2]Excel includes a feature to do single-equation exponential smoothing. Click on the *Tools* menu, then *Data Analysis*, then *Exponential Smoothing*. Excel uses the term *Damping factor*; this is 1 − the smoothing constant in our notation. A plot option is available. Smoothing with trend and seasonal factors is currently not included in Excel.

TABLE 12–3
Exponential Smoothing Forecast
(Smoothing Constant = .20)

Month	*Sales ($000)*	*Exponential Smoothing Forecast*
January	$1,212	$1,212.00
February	1,321	1,212.00
March	1,278	1,233.80
April	1,341	1,242.64
May	1,257	1,262.31
June	1,287	1,261.25
July	1,189	1,266.40
August	1,111	1,250.92
September	1,145	1,222.94
October	1,150	1,207.35
November	1,298	1,195.88
December	1,331	1,216.30
		1,239.24

FIGURE 12–4
Exponential Smoothing Forecast
(Smoothing Constant = .20)

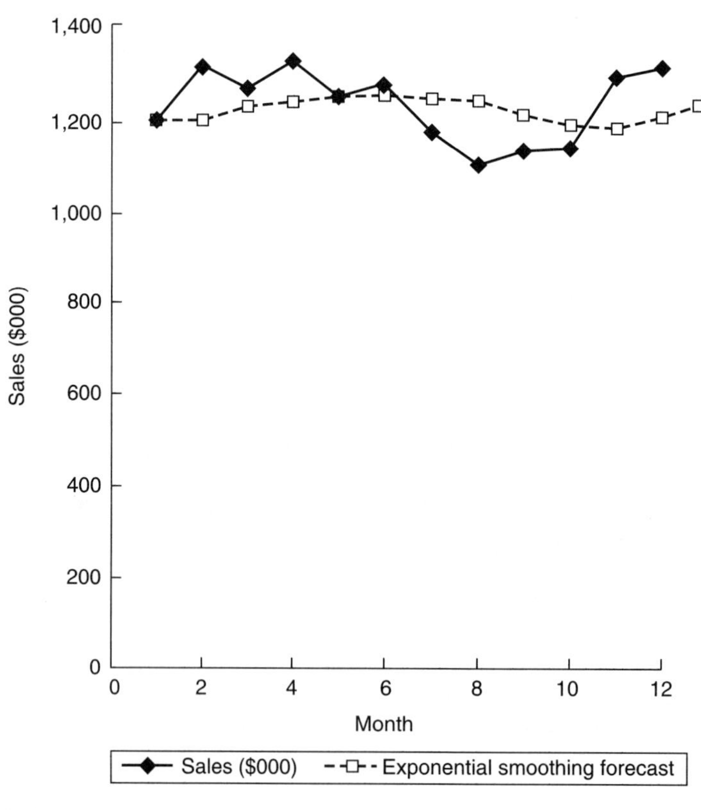

work. Appendix 1 to this chapter illustrates the details of exponential smoothing computations in spreadsheets.

Now let us restate Equation 12–1 in symbols, which will be simpler to use when more complex models are presented. Let:

FIGURE 12–5
Exponential Smoothing Forecast
Smoothing Constant = .40

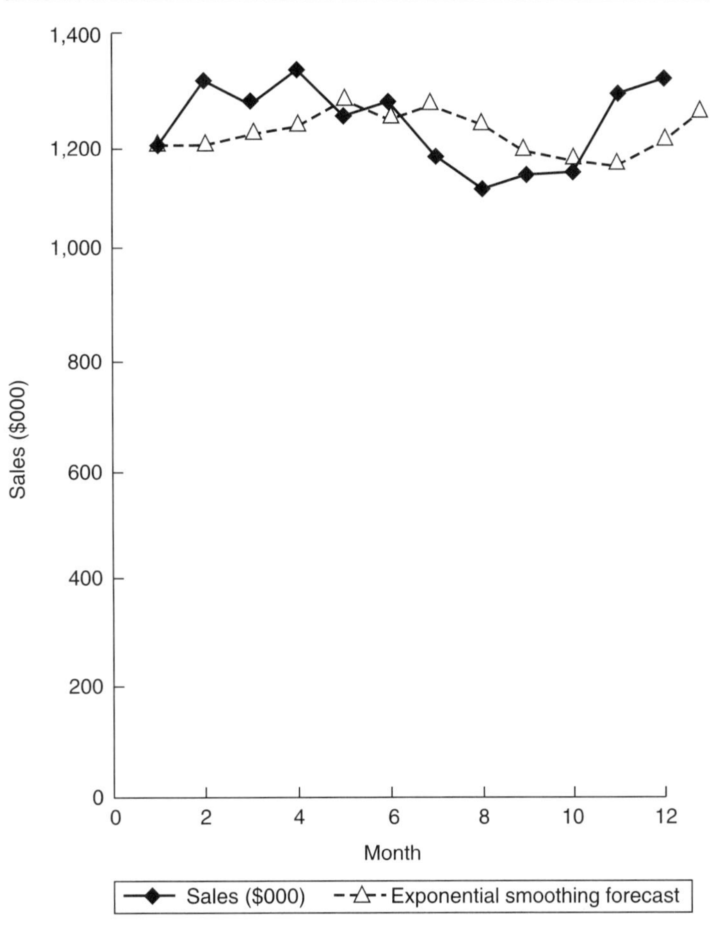

D_t = Sales (demand) in period t

F_{t+1} = Forecast for period $t+1$ (i.e., knowing sales in period t)

α = Smoothing constant

Then Equation 12–1 in symbols is:

$$F_{t+1} = \alpha D_t + (1 - \alpha)F_t \tag{12–2}$$

You should verify that Equation 12–2, using symbols, represents the same calculations as described in Equation 12–1.

Why the Name?

There is a reason for the unusual name *exponential smoothing*. It turns out that an actual observation on monthly sales is given less and less weight as time passes and as more recent data is accumulated. Figure 12–6 shows how the weights for any given data point decline as that data point becomes older (i.e., as newer data is put into updating Equations 12–1 or 12–2).

FIGURE 12–6
Weights for Past Data
Smoothing Constant = .20

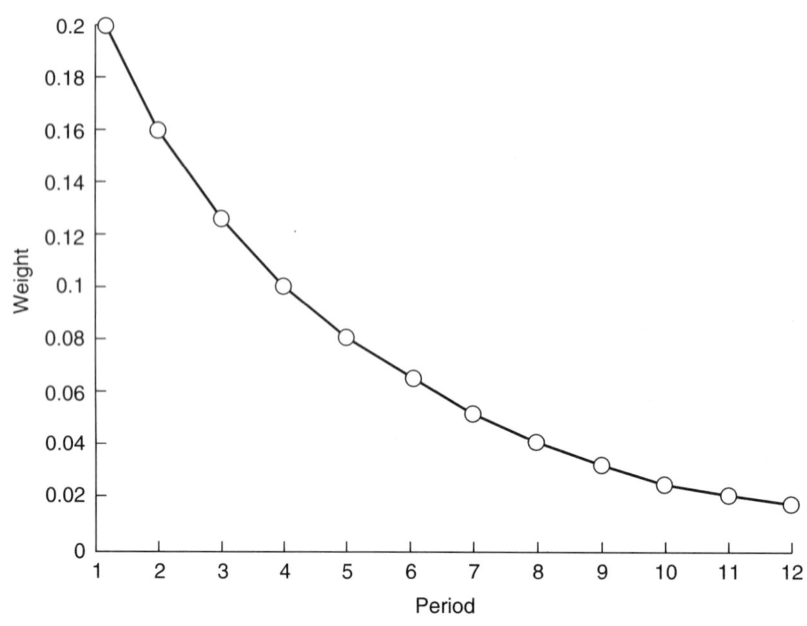

Since the smoothing constant is .20, when a particular month (say March) occurs, its sales are initially given the weight of .20 by the basic smoothing equation (12–1 or 12–2). Then, one month later, when April's sales become the new data point, March sales are "buried" in the previous period's forecast; note that by the smoothing equations (12–1 or 12–2), the previous forecast is multiplied by 1 minus the smoothing constant, or $1 - .2 = .8$. Thus, the original weight of .20 gets multiplied by .8 to become .16 for period 2, as shown in Figure 12–6. Successive months each cause another multiplication by .8 and result in the declining curve shown in Figure 12–6. These weights are exponentially declining; hence the name exponential smoothing.

Add Linear Trend

The basic smoothing model presented above will always lag behind any systematic increase or decrease in sales data. Consider Table 12–4, which contains monthly sales data for a popular spreadsheet program.

Exponential smoothing has been applied to this data with a smoothing constant of 0.20; the results are presented in Figure 12–7.

Notice that the general upward trend in sales is not well captured by the single-equation exponential smoothing model. While a higher smoothing constant would track the data better, an alternative is to use a different model, called exponential smoothing with linear trend, which explicitly allows for a linear trend (either up or down) through time. Let:

G_t = One-period trend estimate

TABLE 12–4
Monthly Sales for a Spreadsheet Program ($ thousands of dollars)

Month	*Sales*
January	$1,214
February	1,252
March	1,304
April	1,384
May	1,279
June	1,583
July	1,470
August	1,739
September	1,573
October	1,836
November	2,041
December	1,983

FIGURE 12–7
Monthly Software Sales

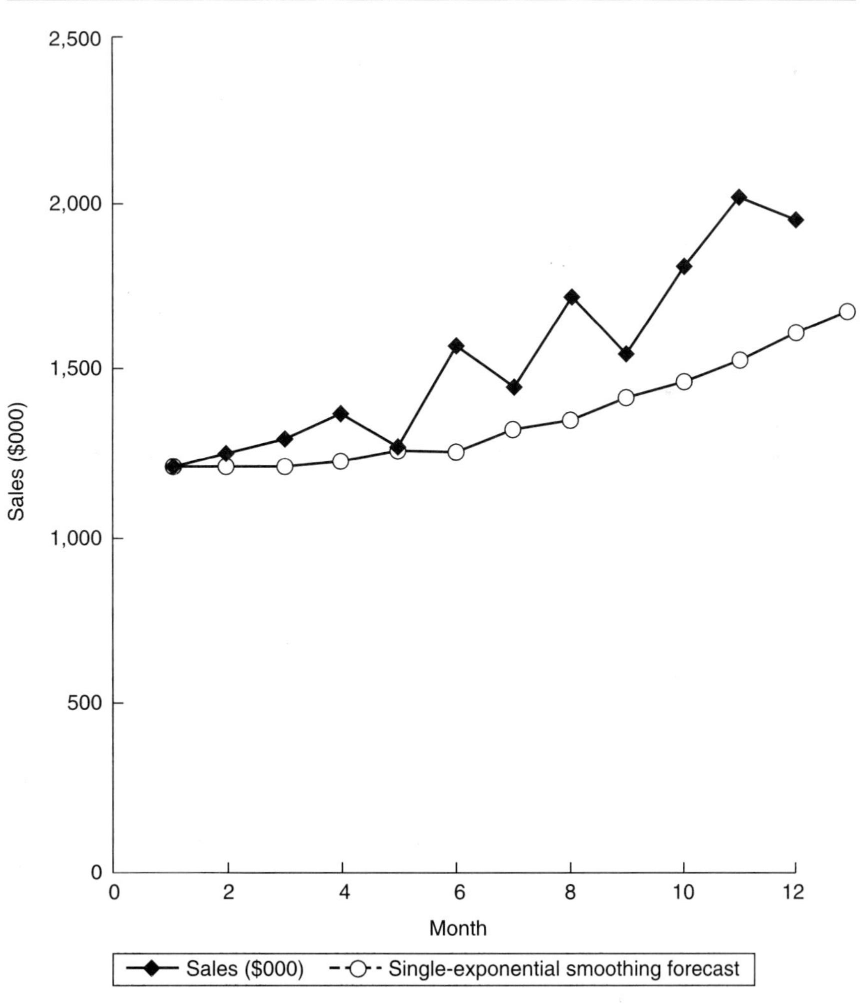

Then the basic equation 12–1 or 12–2 is modified to include the trend estimate as follows:

$$S_t = \alpha D_t + (1 - \alpha)(S_{t-1} + G_{t-1}) \tag{12–3}$$

This equation follows the basic notion of Equation 12–1; it is a weighted average of the latest data point (D_t) and the previous forecast. Note in Equation 12–3 that the previous period value has the previous value of the one-period trend value (G_{t-1}) added to it. This is how the trend gets included in the model. Also, we use a new symbol, S_t, which is like an updated baseline forecast except it doesn't project forward the trend for the following period.

For the data in Figure 12–7, a rough estimate of the trend (increase) each month is about 70 (in thousands of dollars), since sales go from 1,214 to 1,983 over an 11-month period. However, a more convenient way to update the trend factor is to use exponential smoothing again; see Equation 12–4.

$$G_t = \beta (S_t - S_{t-1}) + (1 - \beta) G_{t-1} \tag{12–4}$$

In Equation 12–4, the previous value of the trend, G_{t-1}, plays a role similar to the previous value of the forecast in the basic equation (12–1 or 12–2); and the latest data value in Equation 12–1 is represented by the difference between the last two baseline forecasts, $S_t - S_{t-1}$. This difference is the latest information on trend. Thus, the general structure of Equation 12–4 follows that of the earlier equations. We allow for a different smoothing constant, β instead of α, to provide some flexibility. Since there are two equations now, this model is called a *two-equation model with linear trend*, or simply a two-equation model.

For this two-equation model, the forecast for one period ahead is calculated as follows:

$$F_{t+1} = S_t + G_t \tag{12–5}$$

Equation 12–5 calculates a one-period-ahead forecast by adding the one-period trend value (G_t) from Equation 12–4 to the baseline forecast S_t calculated in Equation 12–3.

Equations 12–3, 12–4, and 12–5, when used with smoothing constant values of $\alpha = .20$ and $\beta = .20$, produce the forecasts shown in Figure 12–8. Notice that these forecasts track the increase in sales much better than the single-equation model in Figure 12–7.

Table 12–5 contains the calculations for Equations 12–3 through 12–5 underlying Figure 12–8.

Note that in order use Equations 12–3 and 12–4, the previous values of S and G are required. In Table 12–5, we delay one month and start calculations as of February. Then the previous value of S is taken as January actual sales, and the previous value of the monthly trend, G, is initially estimated as 70 (from the aggregate increase from 1,214 to 1,983 over 11 months). You should verify that Equations 12–3 through 12–5 produce the numbers indicated for S_{Feb} and G_{Feb} and the forecast for March.

Seasonal Factors

In many situations, demand may follow a seasonal pattern. In cold climates, more chicken soup is consumed in the winter than in the summer; more houses tend to be

FIGURE 12–8
Two-Equation Exponential Smoothing Forecast

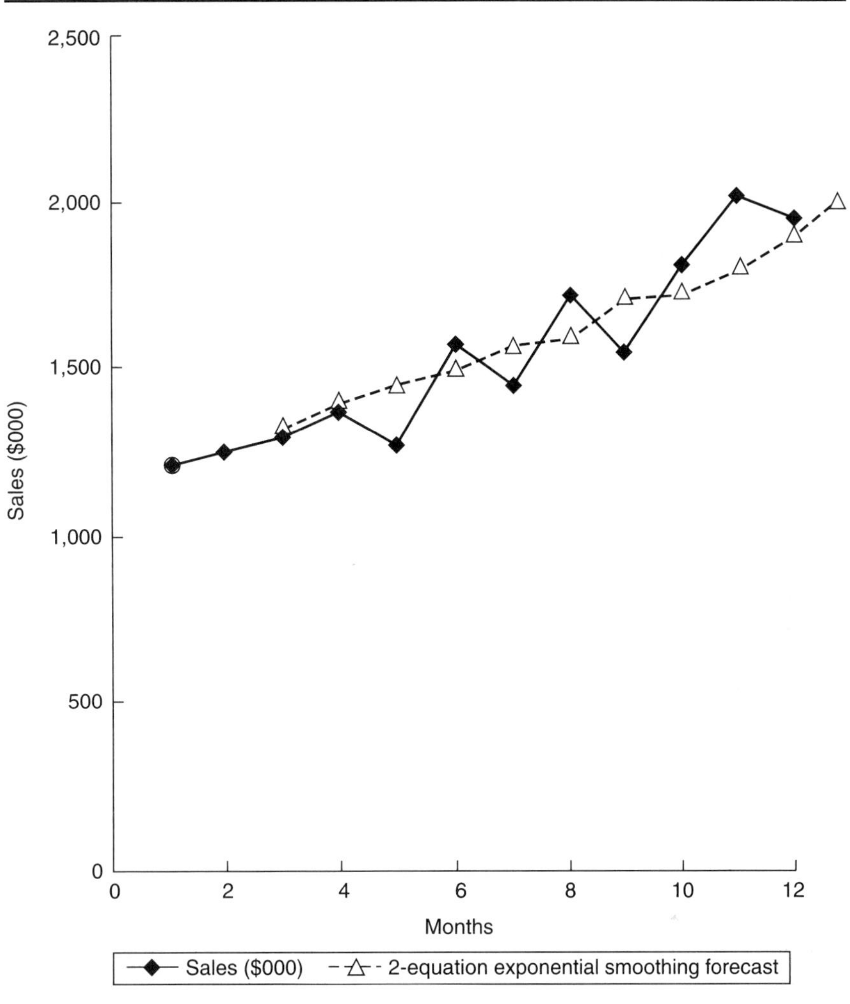

TABLE 12–5
Calculations for Two-Equation Exponential Smoothing Model for Software Sales

Month	*Sales ($000)*	S_t	G_t	*Two-Equation Exponential Smoothing Forecast*
January	$1,214	1,214	70.00	
February	1,252	1,277.60	68.72	$1,284.00
March	1,304	1,337.86	67.03	1,346.32
April	1,384	1,400.71	66.19	1,404.88
May	1,279	1,429.32	58.68	1,466.90
June	1,583	1,507.00	62.48	1,487.99
July	1,470	1,549.58	58.50	1,569.47
August	1,739	1,634.26	63.73	1,608.07
September	1,573	1,673.00	58.73	1,697.99
October	1,836	1,752.58	62.91	1,731.73
November	2,041	1,860.59	71.93	1,815.49
December	1,983	1,942.61	73.95	1,932.52
				2,016.56

TABLE 12–6
Monthly Sales of Chicken Soup

	Sales (000 cases)			
	1994	*1995*	*1996*	*Seasonal Factors*
January	219	236	243	1.3278
February	216	239	238	1.3183
March	218	221	224	1.2613
April	185	194	194	1.0900
May	154	161	162	0.9074
June	147	131	153	0.8199
July	124	110	138	0.7077
August	93	101	128	0.6126
September	127	131	151	0.7781
October	148	157	165	0.8941
November	161	189	194	1.0349
December	198	217	241	1.2479

Three-year average = 175.2222

purchased in the spring and early summer; and retail toy sales and computer sales are higher in the United States in December than in other months of the year, due to holiday gift purchases. Thus, it is desirable to be able to take advantage of this information in adjusting forecasts obtained by basic exponential smoothing or exponential smoothing with trend.

Table 12–6 contains monthly sales (thousands of cases) of a national brand of chicken soup for three years. Figure 12–9 plots these data. Note that sales are higher than average during the winter months December–March and lower than average during the summer months July and August.

We include seasonality by defining individual seasonal factors for each seaon of the cycle. In this case, the data are monthly sales, so we will have 12 seasonal factors C_1 to C_{12}. In general, the seasonal factor for a season equals the average demand or sales for that period divided by the overall average sales. Thus, the seasonal factors for the winter months will be larger than 1.0, and those for the summer months will be less than 1.0.

Using Seasonal Factors

The seasonal factors C_t are included in Equations 12–3 through 12–5 as follows:

Equation (12–3) becomes:

$$S_t = \alpha\,(D_t/C_{t-N}) + (1 - \alpha)(S_{t-1} + G_{t-1}) \qquad (12\text{–}6)$$

where N is the number of periods in a complete seasonal cycle (here, $N = 12$ months per year). The reason we use C_{t-N} rather than C_t is that the latest information available on a particular month is one "cycle" old.

Equation (12–4) remains the same:

$$G_t = \beta\,(S_t - S_{t-1}) + (1 - \beta)G_{t-1} \qquad (12\text{–}4)$$

FIGURE 12–9
Monthly Sales of Chicken Soup

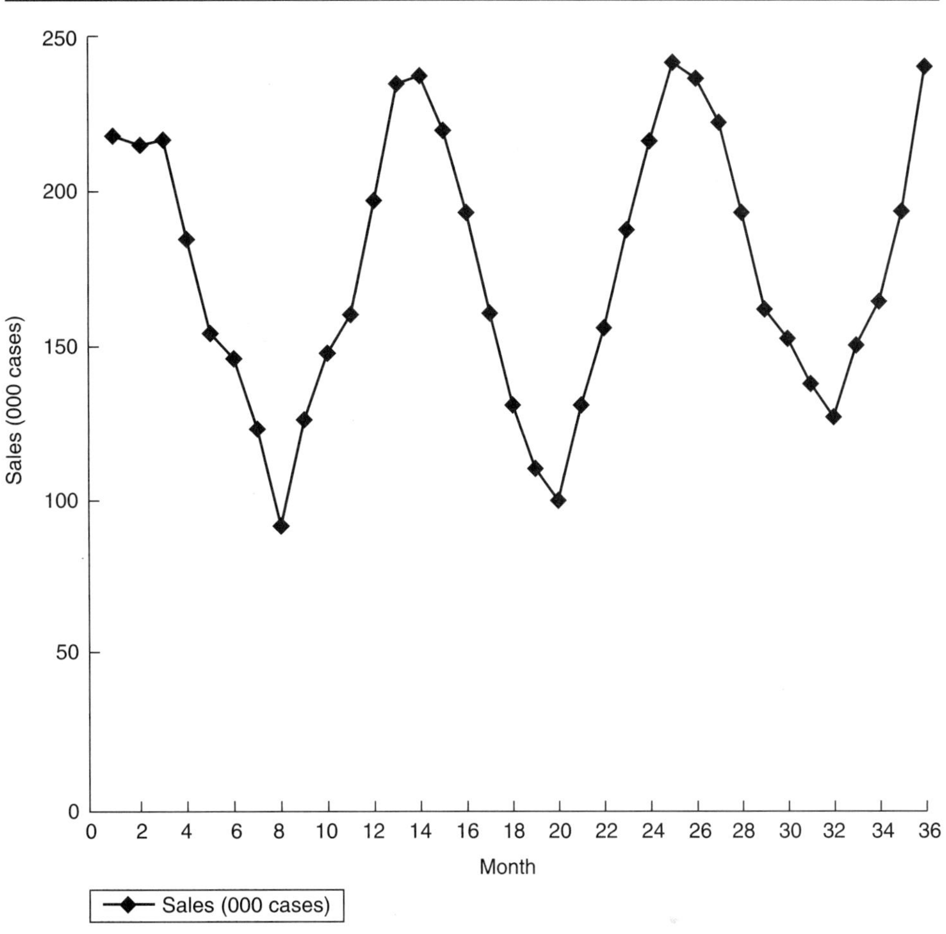

However, we need a procedure to update (revise) the seasonal factors themselves as new data becomes available. As we did with the trend term, we will again use exponential smoothing to update seasonal factors as follows:

$$C_t = \gamma\,(D_t/S_t) + (1 - \gamma)C_{t-N} \tag{12–7}$$

We use a third Greek letter, γ, to allow for a different smoothing constant for updating the seasonal factors. Since the number of new observations of the seasonal factor is only one per year, generally the smoothing constant γ for the seasonal factor updating in Equation 12–7 would be somewhat higher than the values used in the other equations.

Finally, Equation 12–5 becomes:

$$F_{t+1} = (S_t + G_t)C_{t+1-N} \tag{12–8}$$

Equation 12–8 takes the baseline forecast S_t, adds a one-period trend G_t, and then multiplies that result by the seasonal factor corresponding to the next month (the one being forecasted). For example, if one has just observed the demand for December 1996 and wishes to forecast the demand for the first month of 1997, then the appropriate seasonal factor to use is the January factor, and the one available is from January 1996; this is why the subscript for the C is $t + 1 - N$ in Equation 12–8.

Example

Suppose we consider the seasonal factors in the chicken soup data in Table 12–6. A simple way to get estimates of the seasonal factors is to calculate the average monthly sales over the entire sample and then calculate, for each individual month, the ratio of that month's average sales to the overall average. In Table 12–6, overall average monthly sales is 175.2222. Considering the three January data points, the average January sales are:

$$\text{Average January sales} = (219 + 236 + 243)/3 = 698/3 = 232.67$$

Thus, the January seasonal factor, C_{Jan} or C_1, equals 232.67/175.2222 = 1.3278. Table 12–6 contains the value of the 12 seasonal factors calculated in this manner.

We will initially estimate the trend by taking the increase in sales from January 1994 to January 1996 (243 − 219 = 24) and dividing by 24 months, to obtain an estimate of $G = 1$ unit per month. To estimate the initial S value, we will calculate average 1994 monthly sales = 161 units and then subtract one-half year of trend (since $G = 1$, one-half year of trend is 6 units; 161 − 6 = 155 units) and use 155 as our initial estimate of the previous S value before January 1994.

Then we can use Equations 12–6, 12–4, 12–7, and 12–8 to compute new S values, new G values, new forecasts, and updated seasonal factors.[3] For example, using .20 for all smoothing factors, consider the updating we can perform once the January 1994 sales of 219 units is known. Equation 12–6 becomes:

$$S_1 = .20\ (219/1.3278) + (.80)(155 + 1) = 32.987 + 124.8 = 157.787$$

Equation 12–4 becomes:

$$G_1 = .20\ (157.787 - 155) + (.8)(1) = 0.5574 + .8 = 1.3574$$

Equation 12–7 becomes:

$$C_1 = .20\ (219/157.787) + (.8)(1.3278) = 0.2776 + 1.0622 = 1.3398$$

Finally, Equation 12–8 becomes:

$$F_2 = (157.787 + 1.3574)C_{t+1-N}$$

Here, we must use the approximate initial value of $C_2 = 1.3183$ for the seasonal factor, since we don't have a year-earlier factor when we start out. Thus:

$$F_2 = (157.787 + 1.3574)(1.3183) = 209.8$$

Table 12–7 illustrates these calculations from January 1994 through December 1996.[4] The resulting one-month-ahead forecasts are plotted in Figure 12–10.

---

[3]For the case with seasonals, it is simpler to start the calculations with the first (e.g., January) data point rather than the second (February) point, as we did earlier.

[4]Since the table calculations use more decimal places, the text calculations do not agree precisely with the table values.

Table 12–7
Forecasting of Chicken Soup with Seasonal Factors and Trend

	Sales (000 cases)	S_t	G_t	C_t	F_t
		155	1		
January 1994	219	157.7860	1.3572	1.3399	
February	216	160.0834	1.5452	1.3245	209.803
March	218	163.8716	1.9938	1.2751	203.855
April	185	166.6359	2.1479	1.0941	180.801
May	154	168.9695	2.1851	0.9082	153.158
June	147	172.7812	2.5104	0.8261	140.332
July	124	175.2777	2.5076	0.7076	124.049
August	93	172.5928	1.4691	0.5978	108.903
September	127	171.8949	1.0357	0.7702	135.431
October	148	171.4503	0.7396	0.8879	154.618
November	161	168.8668	0.0750	1.0186	178.195
December	198	166.8857	−0.3362	1.2356	210.829
January 1995	236	168.4672	0.0473	1.3521	223.153
February	239	170.9001	0.5245	1.3393	223.201
March	221	171.8045	0.6004	1.2773	218.578
April	194	173.3877	0.7970	1.0990	188.624
May	161	174.8018	0.9204	0.9108	158.197
June	131	172.2936	0.2347	0.8129	145.162
July	110	169.1124	−0.4485	0.6962	122.086
August	101	168.7210	−0.4371	0.5980	100.829
September	131	168.6437	−0.3651	0.7715	129.614
October	157	169.9862	−0.0236	0.8951	149.419
November	189	173.0804	0.6000	1.0333	173.121
December	217	174.0678	0.6775	1.2378	214.606
January 1996	243	175.7413	0.8767	1.3582	236.266
February	238	176.8350	0.9201	1.3406	236.546
March	224	177.2774	0.8245	1.2746	227.051
April	194	177.7852	0.7612	1.0975	195.741
May	162	178.4109	0.7341	0.9102	162.617
June	153	180.9574	1.0966	0.8194	145.633
July	138	185.2873	1.7432	0.7059	126.745
August	128	192.4357	2.8243	0.6114	111.839
September	151	195.3511	2.8425	0.7718	150.648
October	165	195.4238	2.2885	0.8849	177.396
November	194	195.7208	1.8902	1.0249	204.289
December	241	197.0277	1.7736	1.2349	244.611

Notice how well the monthly sales of chicken soup are forecasted by this model with a small trend and monthly seasonal factors. This is because the seasonality of the data is very pronounced and very systematic (i.e., stable through time).

Model Initialization

There are a variety of ways to take past data and initialize any of these exponential smoothing models. One suggested procedure is to simply run through the data twice; that is, use averages over the entire set of data to obtain average sales per period, average trend per period, and average seasonal factors; and then go back to the first

FIGURE 12–10 Forecasting Chicken Soup Sales with Seasonal Factors and Trend

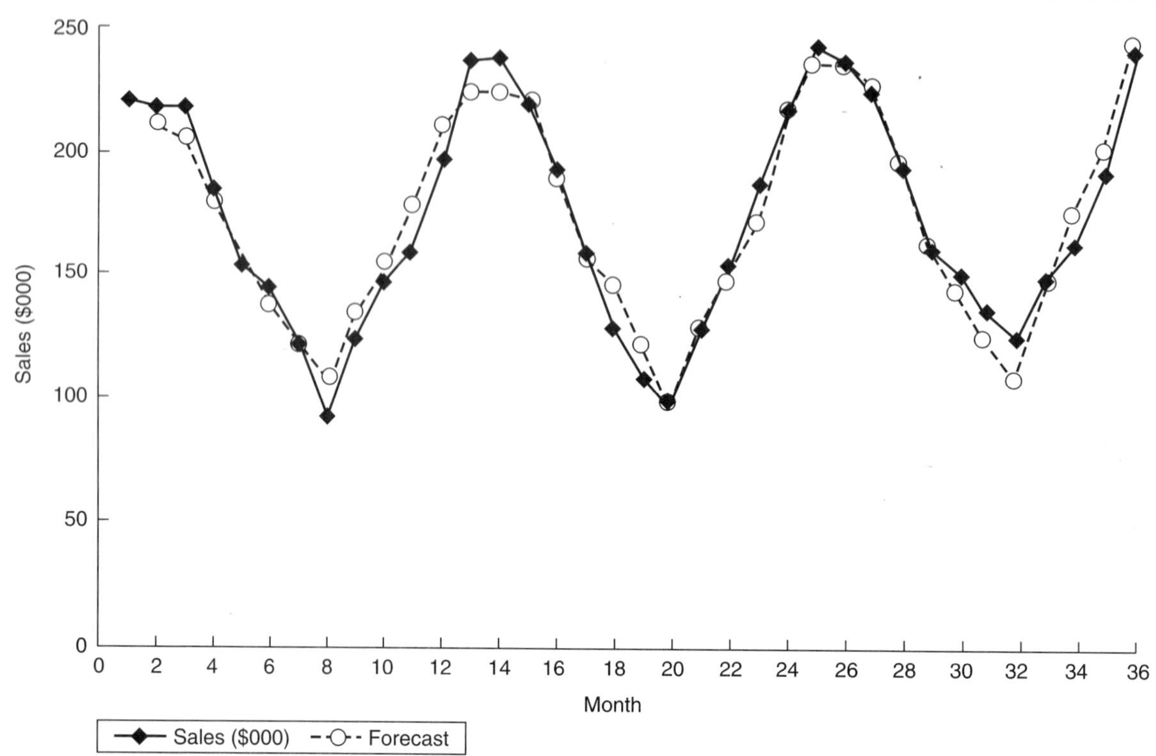

data point and use the equations to bootstrap forward just as you would if the data became available over time. This is what we did above in the chicken soup example. In order to do this, you would need at least two and preferably three (or more) seasonal cycles, to get good estimates of the seasonal factors.

Also, periodically the seasonal factors could be renormalized so that they add precisely to N (they will drift away from this relationship as they are updated).

Smoothing Constant Values

Values for the α and β smoothing constants generally are set between .10 and .30. The larger the value of the smoothing constant, the more the forecast will respond to recent changes in sales. However, sometimes the response will simply be a response to random changes in sales from month to month, and it is undesirable to have forecasts leaping around a great deal from month to month. For this reason, the α and β smoothing values are kept at or below .30, as noted above.

The seasonal smoothing factor γ often may have a higher value, perhaps .20 to as high as .60; this is because each seasonal factor C_i is updated only once in a complete seasonal cycle. For example, considering 12 months as a seasonal cycle, the baseline and trend formulas get updated 12 times in a year, whereas the December seasonal factor C_{12} is updated only once; hence, the higher smoothing factor.

Summary

Exponential smoothing provides a mechanistic way of generating forecasts from past data. The basic single-equation model can be extended to include a second equation for trend and a third set of coefficients to deal with seasonal fluctuations. The method is suited for situations where a large number of products or parts require forecasting in an automated manner.

SECTION II. REGRESSION MODELS

Simple Linear Regression Models

Another technique to analyze data and generate forecasts involves the use of regression models. The simplest regression model will fit a straight line through a series of data points. For example, given the data on software sales in Figure 12–7, a linear regression model will produce the line shown in Figure 12–11.

A regression model fits a straight line to data. In simple linear regression, there is one independent variable (here, it is months) and one dependent variable (sales, the variable being forecasted). The general form of the simple linear regression equation is:

$$Y_t = a + bX_t \tag{12–9}$$

where X_t is the independent variable (month) and Y_t is the corresponding dependent variable (sales in that month). The coefficient a is called the *intercept*; the coefficient b is the *slope* of the line. The principle behind linear regression is that coefficients a and b are determined so as to produce a "best linear fit" of the line through all the data points.[5]

For Figure 12–11, the values of the fitted or estimated coefficients in Equation 12–9 are $a = 1{,}066.3$ and $b = 75.161$; this indicates that the linear upward trend of sales adds about 75 units of additional sales each month.[6]

In using linear regression for forecasting purposes, it is necessary to select a certain number of data points in order to "fit" the regression line and then use the line to determine a forecast of sales in the next period. Figure 12–11 doesn't do this; in that figure, all 12 observations were used to fit the line as drawn. (The line in Figure 12–11 has been extended to month 13, and that is the forecast for month 13—January of the following year.) Thus, to compare regression forecasts to those of exponential smoothing or other alternatives, one must perform a *series* of regressions, one for each forecast data point. For example, a forecast for month 7 (July) would ordinarily be made using only the available data points prior to July (i.e.,

[5]The usual fitting criterion is to minimize the sum of squared vertical deviations from the line to the observations—hence, the name *least-squares regression* is often used.

[6]The months January, February, and so on must be replaced with numbers 1, 2 and so forth to perform the regression.

FIGURE 12–11
Regression Line for Software Sales

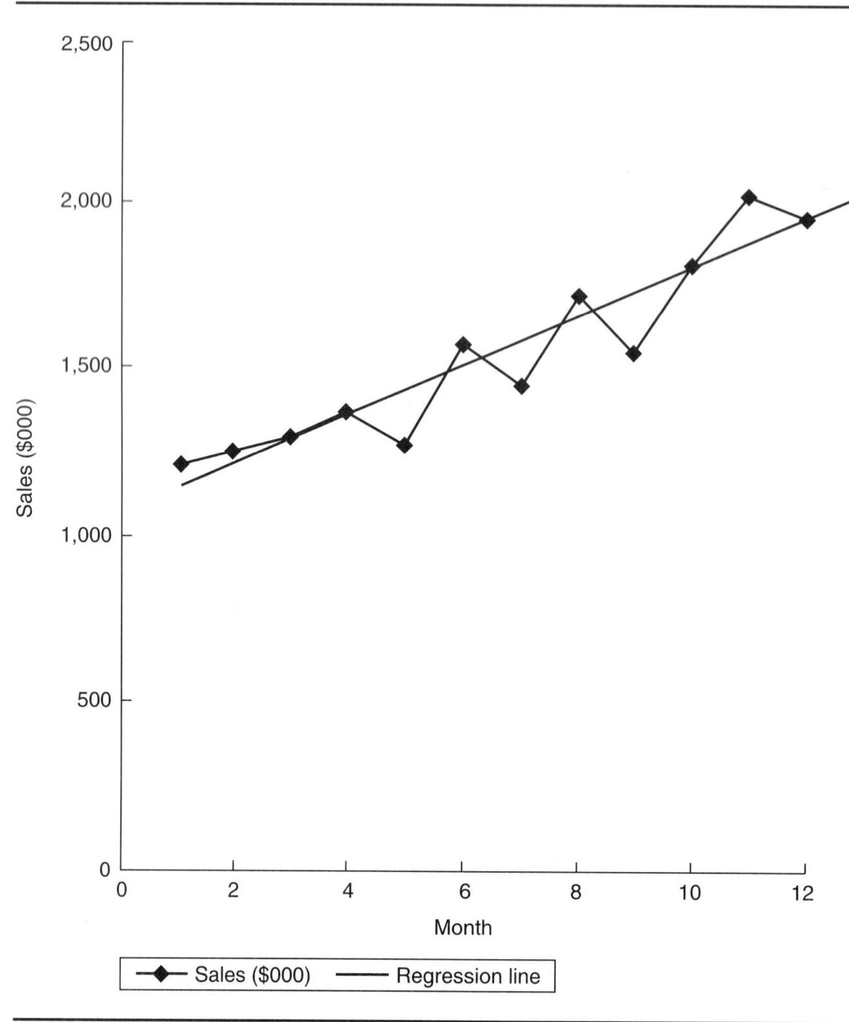

January to June, or months 1–6). Thus, whenever a regression model is fitted, one must always ask *what data points are being used to fit the regression.*

Figure 12–12 shows a regression line fitted to the first six months of data and its forecast for month 7 (July). One would have to generate a series of such figures, one each for July, August, and so on, in order to obtain forecasts as they would have been generated using available data prior to each month. In many circumstances, this work is not undertaken, and one is simply shown the results of an overall regression such as Figure 12–11. For forecast evaluation purposes, Figure 12–11 only shows how well a fitted straight line fits the past data, not how well the regression approach can forecast.

Fortunately, modern spreadsheets have regression calculations built into their tools or options. They produce a wealth of output, including a measure of how good the model (the regression line) fits the data. We will now describe how to use Excel to perform regression calculations.

FIGURE 12–12
Regression Line after First Six Months

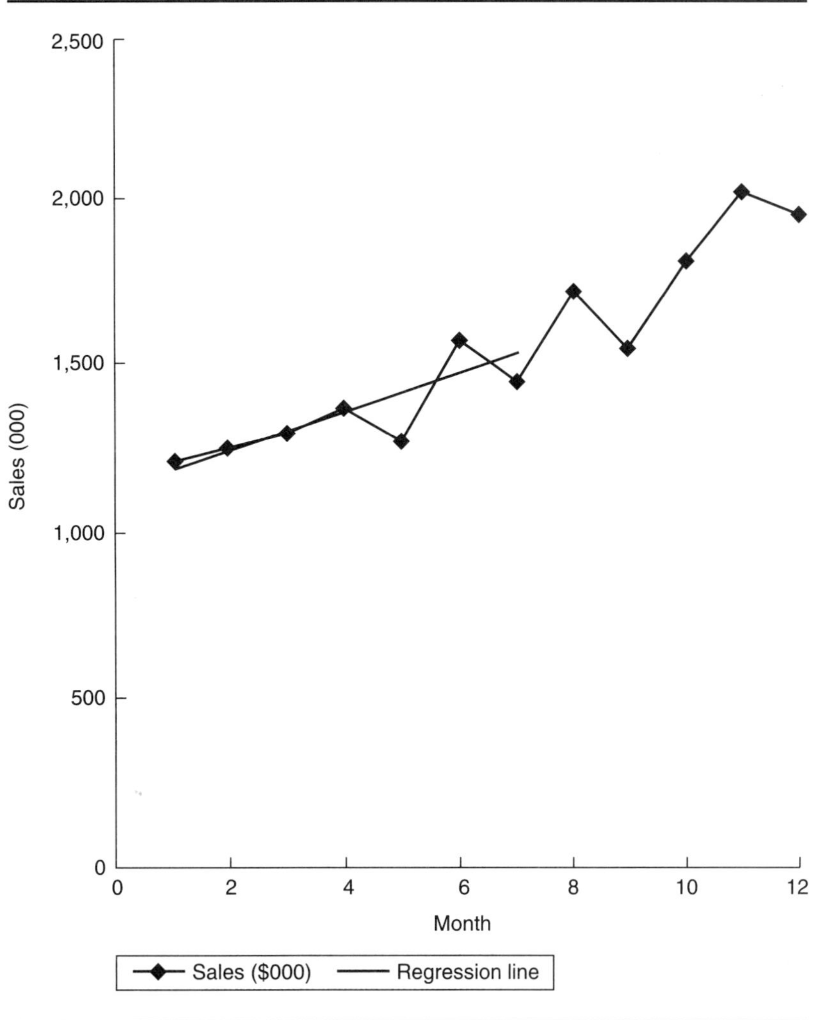

Performing Regression Using Excel

Suppose the data in Table 12–4 are in the first two columns of an Excel spreadsheet so that the column titles (Month, Sales) are in cells A1 and B1 and the data are in cells A2:A13 and B2:B13. We first change the Month entries from January, February, and so on to 1, 2, ···, 12 since regression requires numerical inputs. Next, to perform a regression analysis, go to the Tools Menu and select Data Analysis. A separate window will open; in that window, select Regression. Another window will open; in this window you must complete the boxes for the input Y range (the dependent variable, the one we're trying to forecast), the input X variable (the independent variable, the one we're using to forecast), and the location for the output to be presented.

For our data, the Y range is B2:B13 and the X range is A2:A13, so we enter that information. Suppose we ask the output range to start at cell A16. Also check the box next to *Residuals* and that next to *Line Fit Plot*. Select OK, and, after a moment, the spreadsheet will look like Figure 12–13.

Reviewing Figure 12–13, note that the values for the a and b coefficients are presented in cells B32 for the intercept ($a = 1066.29$) and B33 for the slope coefficient ($b = 75.16$).[7] These values can be used to obtain the forecasts (Predicted Y) that are shown in cells B40 through B51. These values are also plotted in the accompanying line fit plot.

The *Residuals*, which are shown in cells C40 through C51, are the differences between the actual sales values and those predicted using the regression equation. The smaller these values, the closer the fit. One overall measure of how well the regression equation fits the data is the standard deviation of these values. This is the *Standard Error* value shown in cell B22 in the *Regression Statistics* part of the output. In our example, this value is 104.5 (thousands of dollars). If the residual values followed approximately a normal bell-shaped distribution, then in about two-thirds of the months the forecasted sales would be within $\pm$ 104.5 of the actual value.

Another measure of goodness of fit of the regression equation is the adjusted R-square. This value ranges from 0 (no fit at all) to 1.0 (perfect fit), and, in general, indicates the percentage of data variation that is explained or fitted by the straight line. In our example, the adjusted R-square value is 0.869 (cell B21), indicating that 87 percent of the total variation in sales data are explained by a linear trend upward over the 12 months. The forecasts or *Predicted Y* values given at the bottom of the table are for the 12 months of historical data. To make a forecast for the next month (month 13), put this value in the regression equation:

$$\text{Forecast (month 13)} = a + bX = 1{,}066 + 75.16(13) = 2{,}043$$

Similar calculations can produce forecasts for any future month, although as one gets farther and farther away from the last data point, one would expect that the forecast error would increase.

Multiple Regression Models

It is possible to extend the framework of Equation 12–9 to allow for more than one independent variable. This extension, called *multiple linear regression*, has the form (for two independent variables):

$$Y_t = a + b_1X_{1t} + b_2X_{2t} \quad (12\text{–}10)$$

For example, suppose a software company wants to forecast the number of customer support telephone calls per month. Data is as given in Table 12–8, where installed base is the cumulative number of sales of the software package and customer support calls are the number of telephone calls for customer assistance each month. Suppose we fit a multiple regression model to this data, where the two independent variables are time (months) and the size of the installed base. Fitting a multiple regression line to this data, the coefficients obtained are:

$$a = 2{,}177.53;\ b_1 = 821.86;\ \text{and } b_2 = 0.1212$$

[7]Note that spreadsheet output may show an excessive number of decimal places relative to the input data and to the number appropriate for computational significance.

Figure 12–13 Regression Example

	A	B	C	D	E	F	G	H	I
1	**Month**	**Sales**							
2	1	1214							
3	2	1252							
4	3	1304							
5	4	1384							
6	5	1279							
7	6	1583							
8	7	1470							
9	8	1739							
10	9	1573							
11	10	1836							
12	11	2041							
13	12	1983							
14	13								
15									
16	SUMMARY OUTPUT								
17									
18	*Regression Statistics*								
19	Multiple *R*	0.938568667							
20	*R* Square	0.880911143							
21	Adjusted *R* Square	0.869002258							
22	Standard Error	104.5030944							
23	Observations	12							
24									
25	ANOVA								
26		*df*	*SS*	*MS*	*F*	*Significance F*			
27	Regression	1	807828.6993	807828.7	73.97091	6.21166E-06			
28	Residual	10	109208.9674	10920.9					
29	Total	11	917037.6667						
30									
31		*Coefficients*	*Standard Error*	*t Stat*	*P-value*	*Lower 95%*	*Upper 95%*		
32	Intercept	1066.287879	64.3172085	16.57858	1.33E-08	922.9801829	1209.596		
33	*X* Variable 1	75.16083916	8.73898777	8.600634	6.21E-06	55.68915761	94.63252		
34									
35									
36									
37	RESIDUAL OUTPUT								
38									
39	*Observation*	*Predicted Y*	*Residuals*						
40	1	1141.448718	72.55128205						
41	2	1216.609557	35.39044289						
42	3	1291.770369	12.22960373						
43	4	1366.931235	17.06876457						
44	5	1442.092075	-163.0920746						
45	6	1517.252914	65.74708625						
46	7	1592.413753	-122.4137529						
47	8	1667.574592	71.42540793						
48	9	1742.735431	-169.7354312						
49	10	1817.89627	18.1037296						
50	11	1893.05711	147.9428904						
51	12	1968.217949	14.78205128						

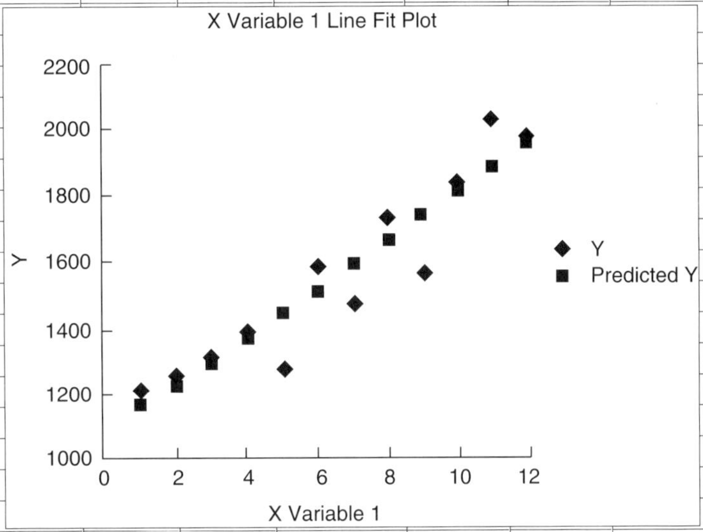

X Variable 1 Line Fit Plot

Y

2200
2000
1800
1600
1400
1200
1000

0 2 4 6 8 10 12

X Variable 1

Y
Predicted Y

TABLE 12–8
Data on Customer Support Calls and Installed Base

Month	*Installed Base*	*Customer Calls*
1	12,436	4,507
2	13,725	5,604
3	14,991	7,035
4	15,732	7,184
5	16,497	7,493
6	20,381	9,723
7	30,743	11,837
8	45,938	14,783
9	52,834	14,927
10	55,394	17,294
11	56,836	18,026
12	57,489	19,473

Thus, the fitted regression line is:

$$Y_t = 2{,}177.53 + 821.86\ (\text{month}) + 0.1212\ (\text{installed base})$$

The values b_1 and b_2 are called *net regression coefficients*; they represent the effect of the given variable while simultaneously adjusting for the effect of the other. Thus, 821.86 is the monthly increase in calls after adjusting for the effect of the installed base, and 0.1212 (or 12.12 percent) is the effect on calls due to the installed base after adjusting for the effect of monthly trend.

How good a fit is this multiple regression? The standard error of the regression is 541 calls, indicating small prediction error. In addition, the adjusted R-square = 0.9894, which is close to 1 (100 percent), indicating a good fit for these 12 data points. Thus, if the software company can anticipate its future installed base numbers, this model would be a good one to use to forecast the demand placed on customer support lines.

The actual regression output for this model is reproduced in Figure 12–14. The top panel of Figure 12–15 illustrates the forecasts obtained by the multiple regression approach.

Of particular importance to us are the values of the so-called *t-statistics* for the regression coefficients. A *t*-statistic greater than about 2.0 indicates statistical significance, whereas *t*-values less than 2.0 indicate the true value of the coefficient may actually be zero with reasonable probability. In Figure 12–14, all three *t*-values (one for the intercept and two for the independent variable coefficients) are well above 2.0, indicating that all three coefficients are significantly different from zero.

Figure 12–15 shows three different regression models: the multiple regression model just presented, and two single-regression models, each using one of the independent variables (months and installed base). Note that the single-equation models using either time (months) or the installed base data do not track the number of calls as well as the multiple regression model does.

Summary

Regression models fit lines to past data. They provide equal weight to recent and less-recent data, in contrast to exponential smoothing models, which weight recent data more heavily. Regression models can have more than one independent variable.

FIGURE 12–14
Output of Multiple Regression Analysis

Summary Output

Regression Statistics	
Multiple R	0.995648908
R-square	0.991316748
Adjusted R-square	0.989387136
Standard error	541.3993753
Observations	12

ANOVA

	df	*SS*	*MS*	*F*	*Significance F*
Regression	2	301167449.4	150583724.7	513.7389984	5.2975E-10
Residual	9	2638019.552	293113.2836		
Total	11	303805469			

	Coefficients	*Standard Error*	*t Stat*	*P-value*	*Lower 95%*	*Upper 95%*
Intercept	2177.53471	333.2602084	6.534037596	0.000107133	1423.647189	2931.422273
X Variable 1	821.8606606	143.88483	5.711934056	0.000289896	496.3703137	1147.351007
X Variable 2	0.121249203	0.026927404	4.502818185	0.001482931	0.060335137	0.182163268

Residual Output

Observation	*Predicted Y*	*Residuals*
1	4507.250478	-0.250477611
2	5485.401361	118.5986394
3	6460.763512	574.236488
4	7372.469832	-188.4698318
5	8287.086133	-794.0861326
6	9579.878697	143.1213032
7	11658.1236	178.8764033
8	14322.36589	460.6341063
9	15980.36106	-1053.361057
10	17112.61968	181.3803235
11	18109.32169	-83.32168749
12	19010.35808	462.6419225

Cautions

Regression models have proved very useful as a basis for forecasting. However, there are some cautions that apply, particularly to multiple regression. First, to be useful as a forecasting tool, there must be some reliable way to predict the values of the independent variables. In our example above of calls to a software company, there must be some way to estimate future installed base. Without this value, the model hsa limited value as a forecaster for calls.

A second caution is that a regression model, like other models, is to some extent a matter of judgment. Judgment has to do with what variables are used as predictor variables. With enough searching, it may be possible to find some variable that is

FIGURE 12–15
Customer Support Calls

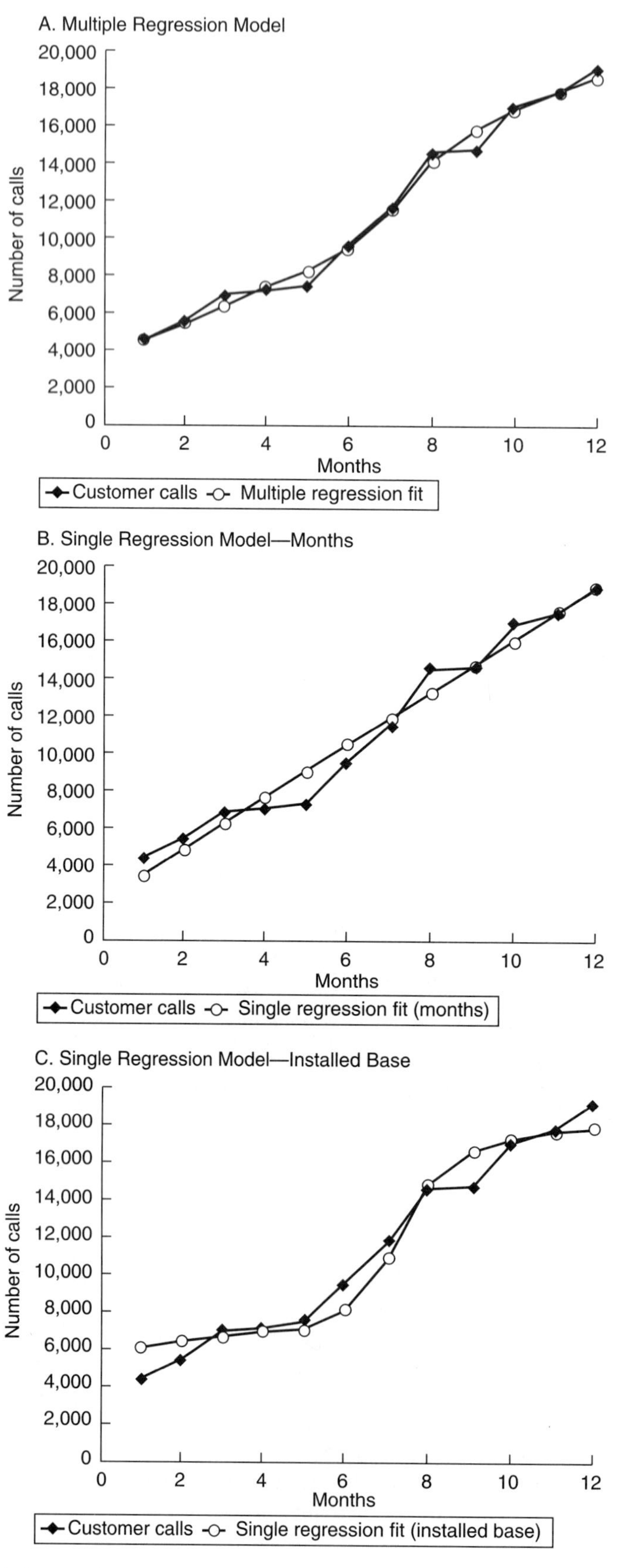

highly correlated with the one we are trying to predict. But that variable should not be included in the regression model unless it makes sense as a predictor variable. In our example, the occurrences of sunspots might coincidentally correlate with calls, but that would not be a sensible variable to include in the regression model.

A third caution relates to the fact that regression and other forecasting models are based on historical data and implicitly assume that past forces will continue into the future. But things do change: New competitors come into the marketplace; consumers' tastes change; new technology emerges; and the old trends may not continue.

SECTION III. NEW PRODUCT FORECASTING

For new products, there is generally no past data of the sort we have been using for both exponential smoothing and also regression analysis. In such cases, companies often analyze data from similar products. As an example, suppose a company is marketing a new software package. They might have data on monthly sales for four other packages, as shown in Table 12–9.

The company could convert this data to the fraction of 12-month demand sold in each month. This data is presented in Table 12–10 and Figure 12–16. Note that there is a generally similar trend for sales to peak in the first month after introduction and then decline at a decreasing rate as time passes, but the pattern of decline is not precisely identical across products.

The company would have to decide which of the existing products were perhaps most similar to the new product and then select an initial sales forecast for month 1 based qualitatively on the data in Table 12–9. Then, after one month of initial sales data were obtained for the new product, the percentage data of Table 12–10 and Figure 12–16 could be used to extrapolate from the first month of initial sales. For example, suppose the new product is closest to Product D in its attributes. Then the

TABLE 12–9
Software Sales for Four Products

Month after Introduction	*Product A*	*Product B*	*Product C*	*Product D*
1	11,392	35,483	20,847	46,839
2	8,432	28,374	15,849	32,849
3	5,385	17,007	11,876	30,483
4	4,685	15,293	9,723	28,495
5	2,797	16,290	8,243	22,740
6	1,734	12,746	7,034	24,059
7	1,479	9,074	6,293	19,483
8	1,148	8,264	6,823	17,304
9	754	6,283	4,293	16,303
10	479	4,018	3,027	14,302
11	357	2,794	2,057	11,922
12	164	1,947	1,749	7,003
Total	38,806	157,573	97,814	271,782

TABLE 12–10
Software Sales for Four Products: Fraction of Total

Month after Introduction	*Product A*	*Product B*	*Product C*	*Product D*
1	0.294	0.225	0.213	0.172
2	0.217	0.180	0.162	0.121
3	0.139	0.108	0.121	0.112
4	0.121	0.097	0.099	0.105
5	0.072	0.103	0.084	0.084
6	0.045	0.081	0.072	0.089
7	0.038	0.058	0.064	0.072
8	0.030	0.052	0.070	0.064
9	0.019	0.040	0.044	0.060
10	0.012	0.025	0.031	0.053
11	0.009	0.018	0.021	0.044
12	0.004	0.012	0.018	0.026

FIGURE 12–16
Fraction of Sales by Month for Software Products

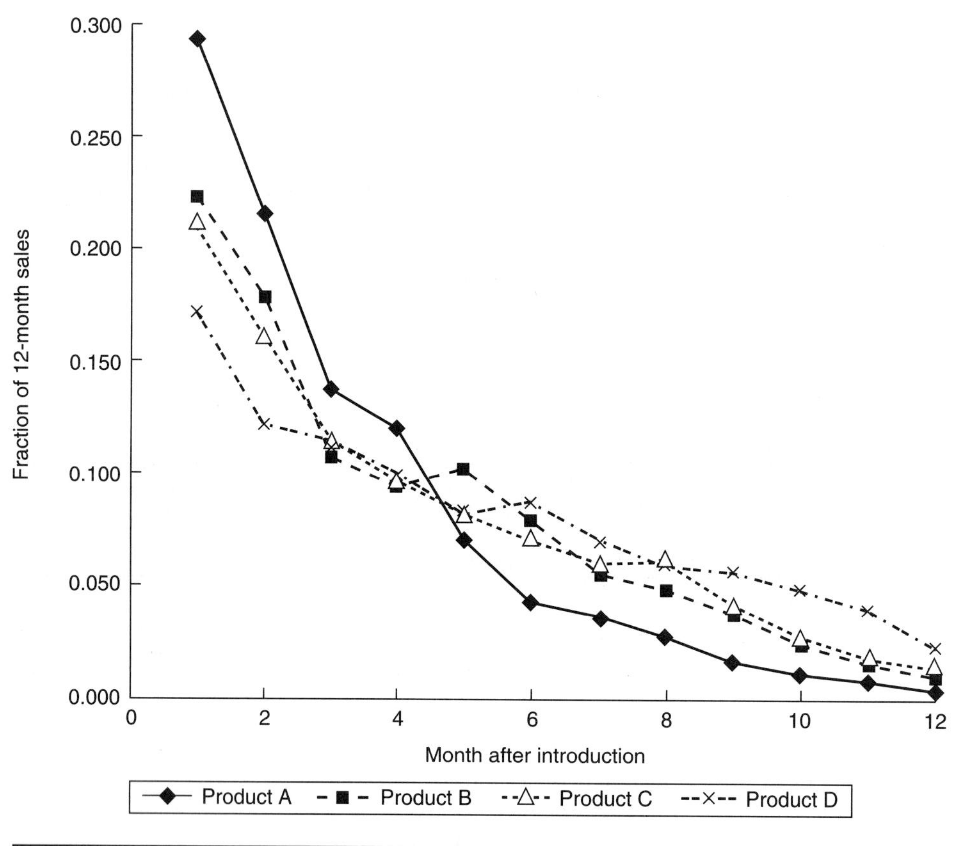

initial forecast for month 1 might be 47,000 units taken from Table 12–9. Then suppose actual sales for the new product in month 1 were only 30,500 units. We divide 30,500 by the expected fraction of 12-month demand occurring in month 1 (0.172, from Table 12–12, column D) to obtain a 12-month forecast of 30,500/.172 = 177,300 units for our new product.

Summary

Forecasting of sales for new products is particularly difficult since there is no direct historical data available. Generally, companies make comparisons based on related or similar products, using past data on those products to make both initial and updated forecasts as sales data comes in for the new product.

SECTION IV. FORECAST ERROR MEASUREMENT

Since forecasts are "always wrong," we need to analyze forecast error in order to make optimal decisions when using forecasts in decision situations. Forecast error is defined as:

$$\text{Error} = \text{Forecast} - \text{Actual}$$

or in symbols:

$$\text{Error} = e_t = F_t - D_t \qquad (12\text{–}11)$$

Consider the forecast errors in our first example in this chapter; these are presented in Table 12–11.

There are a number of different ways of measuring forecast error. The first, mean squared error (MSE), involves taking each error, squaring it, and then taking the average.[8] For the errors in Table 12–11, this value would be 7,520. Note that squaring the errors gives much higher weight or penalty to the larger errors. Squaring also removes the sign of the error, counting large errors in either direction as equally serious.

TABLE 12–11 Forecast Errors, First Example—Cereal Product Sales

Month	*Sales ($000)*	*Exponential Smoothing Forecast*	*Error*	*Mean Squared Error*	*MAD*	*MAPE*
January	$1,212	1,212.00				
February	1,321	1,212.00	−109.00	11,881.00	109.00	8.25%
March	1,278	1,233.80	−44.20	1,953.64	44.20	3.46
April	1,341	1,242.64	−98.36	9,674.69	98.36	7.33
May	1,257	1,262.31	5.31	28.22	5.31	0.42
June	1,287	1,261.25	−25.75	663.08	25.75	2.00
July	1,189	1,266.40	77.40	5,990.71	77.40	6.51
August	1,111	1,250.92	139.92	19,577.53	139.92	12.59
September	1,145	1,222.94	77.94	6,073.99	77.94	6.81
October	1,150	1,207.35	57.35	3,288.87	57.35	4.99
November	1,298	1,195.88	−102.12	10.428.72	102.12	7.87
December	1,331	1,216.30	−114.70	13,155.37	114.70	8.62
				MSE = 7,519.62	MAD = 77.46	MAPE = 6.26%

[8]This measure is related to the standard deviation of forecast errors.

A second measure is the mean absolute deviation (MAD).[9] Here, we first take the absolute value of each error and then average these values. For the data in Table 12–11, we obtain MAD = 77.46. The MAD measure of forecast error doesn't weight large errors in a disproportional manner, as the MSE measure does. Also, taking the absolute values again treats negative and positive forecast errors symmetrically.

Both the MSE and MAD measures of forecast error are scale-dependent; if we change the unit of measurement from, say, units to dozens, then these values will also change. Thus, we don't have any way of calibrating these measures when using them to compare two or more different forecasting approaches across different products. A third measure, the mean absolute percentage error (MAPE), avoids this shortcoming by using the absolute percentage errors and averaging them. For the Table 12–11 data, this value would be MAPE = 6.26 percent.

Summary

Forecast errors are measured as mean squared error (MSE), mean absolute deviation (MAD), or mean absolute percentage error (MAPE). The latter metric, being a percentage, is most useful when comparing forecasting techniques across more than one product.

Appendix 1 Exponential Smoothing on Spreadsheets

Spreadsheets are excellent instruments for implementing smoothing methods. Once the basic equations are set up, it is only a matter of copying them down using the standard spreadsheet copy command.

Figures 12–17 through 12–19 show how to set up the three smoothing models in the Excel spreadsheet format. The examples are those used in the chapter. Note that the smoothing constants are set up as parameters so they can be changed without redoing the whole model. The equations for key cells are shown, and these can be copied down to fill out the model.

Appendix 2 Trend Estimation in Excel

In this chapter, the focus is on linear regression. However, in some circumstances, trends may be nonlinear. For example, in new product introductions there may initially be a high sales growth but then a leveling off, followed by a decline. One approach to such situations is to use a nonlinear trend line to fit the data.

[9] If forecast errors are normally distributed, which they often are, then there is a relationship between the standard deviation of forecast error σ_e and MAD: σ_e = 1.25 MAD.

FIGURE 12–17 Simple Exponential Smoothing

	A	B	C	D	E	F	G	H
1	smoothing constant (alpha)			0.2				
2								
3	Period	Sales	Forecast					
4	1	1212						
5	2	1321	1212		Cell	Equation		
6	3	1278	1233.8		C6	=$D$1*B5+(1-$D$1)*C5		
7	4	1341	copy					
8	5	1257	down					
9	6	1287	↓					
10	7	1189						
11	8	1111						

FIGURE 12–18 Exponential Smoothing with Trend

	A	B	C	D	E	F	G	H	I	J
1	smoothing constant (alpha)			0.2						
2	smoothing constant (beta)			0.2						
3										
4	Period	Sales	Baseline Forecast	Trend	Forecast					
5	t	D_t	S_t	G_t	F_t					
6	1	1214	1214	70			Cell	Equation		
7	2	1252	1277.6	68.72			C7	=$D$1*B7+(1-$D$1)*(C6+D6)		
8	3	1304	copy	copy	1346.32		D7	=$D$2*(C7-C6)+(1-$D$2)*D6		
9	4	1384	down	down	copy		E8	=C7+D7		
10	5	1279	↓	↓	down					
11	6	1583			↓					
12	7	1470								
13	8	1739								
14										

Excel has the capability to fit several trend lines of this sort. In particular, the following are available:

Linear: $Y = a + bX$
Logarithmic: $Y = a + b \ln(X)$
Polynomial: $Y = a + bX + cX^2$
Power: $Y = aX^b$
Exponential: $Y = ae^{bX}$

FIGURE 12–19 Exponential Smoothing with Trend and Seasonals

	A	B	C	D	E	F	G	H	I	J	K	L
1	smoothing constant (alpha)			0.2								
2	smoothing constant (beta)			0.2								
3	smoothing constant (gamma)			0.2								
4												
5	Period	Sales	Baseline F/C	Trend	Seasonal	Forecast						
6	t	D_t	S_t	G_t	C_t	F_t						
7	*Jan*				1.3278							
8	*Feb*				1.3183							
9	*Mar*				1.2613							
10	*Apr*				1.0900							
11	*May*				0.9074							
12	*Jun*				0.8199							
13	*Jul*				0.7077							
14	*Aug*				0.6126							
15	*Sep*				0.7781							
16	*Oct*				0.8941							
17	*Nov*				1.0349							
18	*Dec*		155	1	1.2479			Cell	Equation			
19	1	219	157.78596	1.3572	1.3399			C19	=$D$1*(B19/E7)+(1-$D$1)*(C18+D18)			
20	2	216	copy	copy	copy	209.803		D19	=$D$2*(C19-C18)+(1-$D$2)*D18			
21	3	218	down	down	down	copy		E19	=$D$3*(B19/C19)+(1-$D$3)*E7			
22	4	185	↓	↓	↓	down		F20	=(C19+D19)*E8			
23	5	154	↓	↓	↓	↓						
24	6	147	↓	↓	↓	↓						
25	7	124	↓	↓	↓	↓						
26	8	93	↓	↓	↓	↓						

FIGURE 12–20

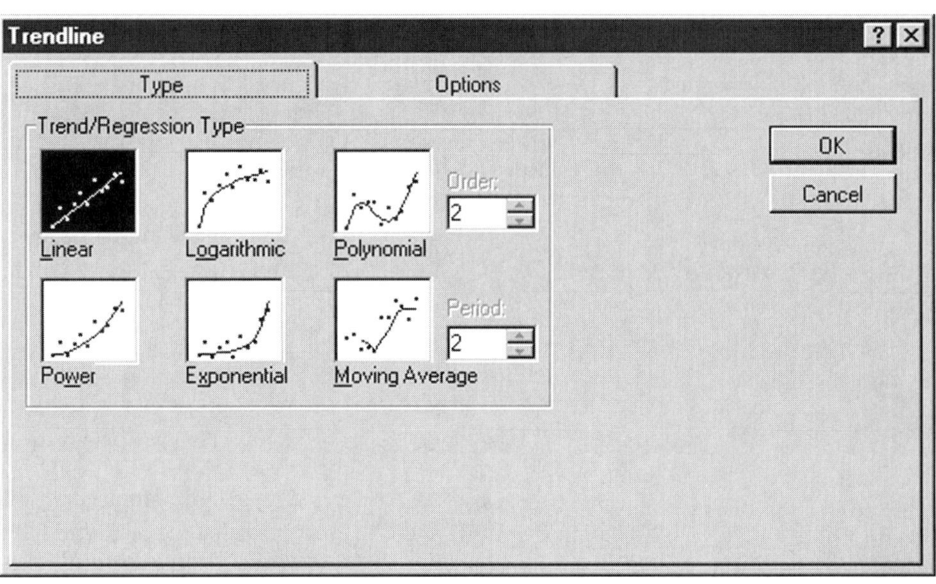

To access these functions, first plot the data using the line plot format. Then click on the data points to highlight them. Click on the *Insert* menu item, and on *Trendline* from the dropdown menu. Choices such as shown in Figure 12–20 will appear. The Options include the ability to have the fitted equation and R-squared value on the plot.

A word of caution! There should be a good rationale for choosing a particular shape of function for forecasting. Avoid the temptation to try every possibility and pick the one with the best fit (highest R-squared).

Bibliography

Nahmias, S. *Production and Operations Analysis.* 3rd ed. Burr Ridge, IL: Richard D. Irwin, 1997.

Makridakis, S.; S. C. Wheelwright; and V. E. McGhee. *Forecasting: Methods and Applications.* 2nd ed. New York: John Wiley & Sons, 1983.

Silver, E. A., and R. Peterson. *Decision Systems for Inventory Management and Production Planning.* 2nd ed. New York: John Wiley & Sons, 1985.

Practice Problems[10]

12–1. Consider the data in Table 12–1 for monthly cereal sales ($000). Input this data into an Excel spreadsheet and do the following:

a. Calculate a four-month moving average forecast. What is your forecast for month 13?

b. Use exponential smoothing with a smoothing factor of 0.30 to calculate the forecast for month 13.

12–2. Although the data in Table 12–1 (Figure 12–1) do not seem to show a trend, fit an exponential smoothing model with linear trend to this data. For smoothing constants, use .20; for initial values, use $S = 1{,}212$ and $G = 0$. What is your forecast for month 13?

12–3. Fit a simple regression model to the data in Table 12–1. What is your forecast for month 13?

12–4. Consider the data in Table 12–11. Suppose the company has a new product that is most similar to Product A and the sales of the new product one month after introduction are 6,489 units. What is your forecast of total sales over a 12-month period for the new product?

[10]Solutions for these problems are at the end of this chapter.

Problems

12–5. Consider the following data representing monthly retail sales of athletic shoes:

Month	*Sales ($000)*
January	$328
February	337
March	341
April	367
May	385
June	403
July	389
August	376
September	428
October	305
November	278
December	450

Input this data into an Excel spreadsheet and do the following:

a. Calculate a three-month moving average forecast. What is your forecast for month 13?

b. Use exponential smoothing with a smoothing factor of 0.20 to calculate the forecast for month 13.

12–6. Fit an exponential smoothing model with linear trend to the data in Problem 12–5. For smoothing constants, use 0.20; for initial values, use $S = 328$ and $G = 0$. What is your forecast for month 13?

12–7. Fit a simple regression model to the data in Problem 12–5. What is your forecast for month 13?

12–8. Consider the data in Problem 12–5. Based on the product, can you explain why sales in April, May, and June are higher than average? September? December?

12–9. A publisher tracks book sales in half-year increments. Based on long experience, the publisher knows sales in the second half of the calendar year represent about two-thirds of total annual sales. Consider the data below for a basic accounting text:

Period	*Sales (units)*
January–June 1992	4,075
July–December 1992	8,239
January–June 1993	3,284
July–December 1993	6,194
January–June 1994	2,582
July–December 1994	5,183
January–June 1995	1,968
July–December 1995	4,023
January–June 1996	1,798
July–December 1996	3,522

Fit an exponential smoothing model to this data, using as initial values $S = 6{,}000$ and $G = -600$; and for seasonal factors, $C_1 = 0.667$ and $C_2 = 1.333$. Use smoothing constants of .20 throughout. What is your forecast for the January–June 1997 period?

12–10. Consider the data in Problem 12–9.

a. Fit a simple linear regression to this data. What is your forecast for the January–June 1997 period?

b. Now divide the data into two sets: the first half of the year, and the second half of the year. Perform a simple regression on the data for sales in the first half-year. What is your forecast for the January–June 1997 period? Do you think this answer is more likely to be accurate than the answer to part (*a*)? Why?

12–11. Consider the data in Problem 12–9. Now suppose that the publisher has also obtained data on the number of students enrolled in U.S. colleges and universities for each of those time periods.

Period	*Sales (units)*	*Number of Students (millions)*
January–June 1992	4,075	72
July–December 1992	8,239	71
January–June 1993	3,284	76
July–December 1993	6,194	75
January–June 1994	2,582	74
July–December 1994	5,183	73
January–June 1995	1,968	69
July–December 1995	4,023	68
January–June 1996	1,798	65
July–December 1996	3,522	64

a. Perform a multiple regression on all this data. What is your forecast for the January–June 1997 period? (Assume that the publisher estimates there will be 66 million students enrolled then.)

b. Perform a multiple regression on the data for sales in the first half-year of each year. What is your forecast for the January–June 1997 period? Do you think this answer is more likely to be accurate than the answer to part (*a*)? Why?

12–12. A company is marketing a new video. Forecasts of sales in the first 10 weeks are needed for inventory planning purposes. The closest past product has experienced the following sales in its first 10 weeks:

Week	*Sales (thousands of units)*
1	$63
2	46
3	34
4	27
5	24
6	20
7	18
8	16
9	15
10	13

a. Calculate the fraction of the total sales occurring in each week.

b. Suppose week 1 sales of the new video are 81,000. Use your result in part (*a*) to forecast total sales of the new video over the 10 weeks.

12–13. Consider Problem 12–1. Compute the MSE, the MAD, and the MAPE for:

a. The four-month moving average forecast (from May through December)

b. The exponential smoothing forecast (from March through December). For this data, is one forecasting method always better than the other on all these measures?

More Challenging Problems

12–14. Reproduce Figure 12–6 for the case where the smoothing constant is 0.10.

12–15. Consider the following retail sales data for ski-wear, in thousands of dollars:

Month	*1994*	*1995*	*1996*
January	$342	$382	$402
February	423	548	592
March	278	402	479
April	156	283	328
May	65	94	118
June	15	21	24
July	8	8	9
August	5	4	6
September	47	69	85
October	95	129	148
November	204	308	384
December	573	642	749

a. Estimate the 12 seasonal factors $C_1, C_2, \cdots, C_{12}$ using all the data.

b. Estimate the monthly trend factor G using all the data.

c. Estimate the initial S value by taking the average monthly sales in the first year and then subtracting six months' worth of trend.

d. Perform exponential smoothing with trend and seasonality on this data. Use 0.20 for all smoothing constants. What is your forecast for the next month (January 1997 sales)?

12–16. You are the owner of a vineyard in the Napa Valley of California. The yield from your vineyard, in tons of grapes per acre for the past 21 years, is shown in the last column of the following table.

Year	*Rainfall (inches)*	*Degree-Days (hundreds)*	*Freeze*	*Yield (tons per acre)*
1	14.2	28.57	0	2.72
2	16.8	28.83	0	2.42
3	25.0	29.30	0	2.99
4	37.4	28.18	0	2.88
5	41.2	29.44	1	2.42
6	33.9	27.81	0	2.84
7	28.2	26.96	0	2.74
8	16.0	25.76	1	1.56
9	11.9	26.66	0	2.19
10	16.3	28.41	0	2.45
11	28.7	27.32	0	2.57
12	38.0	28.66	0	2.65
13	38.3	27.05	1	1.96
14	35.8	29.38	0	3.09
15	29.8	28.24	1	1.67
16	18.6	27.89	0	2.63
17	12.2	26.94	0	2.38
18	15.4	27.72	0	2.53
19	24.1	28.55	0	2.66
20	37.6	28.37	0	2.76
21	38.2	29.10	0	2.95

a. Build an exponential smoothing model to provide forecasts of yield (tons per acre) for the various years.

TABLE 12–12
Total Visitor Arrivals to the Hawaiian Islands

	Thousands of Persons				
Year	*First Quarter*	*Second Quarter*	*Third Quarter*	*Fourth Quarter*	*Annual Visitors*
1980	1,004.8	942.9	1,047.3	939.5	3,934.5
1981	959.0	984.5	1,042.3	948.8	3,934.6
1982	1,054.0	1,048.7	1,110.7	1,029.5	4,242.9
1983	1,069.9	1,071.5	1,146.4	1,080.2	4,368.1
1984	1,218.5	1,206.8	1,222.9	1,207.4	4,855.6
1985	1,301.5	1,129.6	1,266.9	1,186.2	4,884.1
1986	1,393.2	1,421.2	1,450.9	1,341.8	5,607.0
1987	1,448.9	1,370.0	1,555.2	1,425.8	5,799.8
1988	1,484.9	1,488.2	1,635.6	1,533.7	6,142.4
1989	1,683.7	1,605.1	1,754.8	1,598.3	6,641.8
1990	1,714.8	1,724.4	1,879.9	1,652.2	6,971.2
1991	1,509.5	1,727.2	1,958.3	1,678.9	6,873.9
1992	1,622.2	1,598.0	1,703.6	1,590.1	6,513.9
1993	1,559.6	1,476.3	1,588.9	1,499.5	6,124.2
1994	1,615.6	1,527.7	1,692.7	1,594.3	6,430.3
1995	1,621.9	1,582.2	1,796.5	1,632.2	6,632.8

b. Suppose you know that in years 5, 8, 13, and 15 there was a hard freeze during the year. Such freezes tend to have a significant negative effect on grape yields. How might you take this into account in your forecasting model?

12–17. Consider the table in Problem 12–16. Also shown is the amount of rainfall (in inches) in the year, and degree-days. Degree-days represent a cumulative measure of the number of degrees and days that the average temperature exceeds 50°F. (A day in which the average temperature was 74°F would contribute 24 degree-days to the total; a day with 60°F would contribute 10 degree-days; any day with average temperature below 50°F would contribute zero to the total.) The column labeled Freeze indicates if there was a hard frost in that year (value = 1) or not (value = 0).

a. Build a regression model to forecast the grape yield in your vineyard. Use the first 18 years to build the model and then forecast years 19 through 21.

b. Explain the meaning of the coefficients in your regression model in verbal terms. How well do you think the model fits the data?

c. Compare the results of your forecasts for the last three years with those obtained by the moving average method in Problem 12–16.

12–18. The data shown in Table 12–12 represent visitors to the Hawaiian Islands over the past several years, by quarter.[11] Use the data for the first five years to estimate the seasonal and trend factors. Then build an exponential smoothing model (incorporating both trend and seasonal factors) to provide forecasts for the remaining period. Plot the actual visitors and the forecasts. Compare the accuracy of the forecasts in the 1985 to 1990 period with those subsequent to that period.

CASE 12–19

QUALITY KITCHENS MEAT LOAF MIX

Amalgamated Food Products (AFP) markets a meat loaf mix under the brand name Quality Kitchens in the far western United States. The mix is packaged in foil packets and contains cracker crumbs, meal, seasonings, and other ingredients. The purchaser mixes the ingredients together with an egg and ground beef to make a meat loaf. The mix has the effect of stretching the meat loaf as well as seasoning it.

[11]Source: World Wide Web site: http://kumu.icsd.hawaii.gov/tourism.

TABLE 12–13
Quality Kitchens Meat Loaf Mix

	Thousands of Dollars			
Quarter	*Sales*	*Promotion*	*Advertising*	*Index*
1	$504.72	$15.6	$30	100
2	406.59	22.2	36	102
3	398.55	.0	45	104
4	587.76	.0	57	104
5	598.92	.0	39	104
6	703.62	31.8	21	100
7	387.24	21.3	12	98
8	365.67	3.9	6	96
9	388.71	.0	6	98
10	372.96	8.4	30	103
11	603.30	45.3	30	105
12	614.73	50.1	33	107
13	484.38	39.6	6	107
14	227.76	4.2	33	107
15	329.13	.0	6	108
16	308.25	.0	3	105
17	433.86	.0	45	103
18	514.98	13.8	48	108
19	404.70	17.7	0	110
20	245.43	.0	15	112
21	433.20	17.4	9	113
22	627.24	37.8	54	112
23	647.61	42.3	36	113
24	342.81	11.4	39	114

Sales: Quarterly sales of Quality Kitchens meat loaf mix.
Promotion: Funds spent on promotion activities in quarter.
Advertising: Funds spent on advertising during the quarter.
Index: Economic index of general economic conditions in Quality Kitchens market area—calculated by the AFP Economic Research department.

The Quality Kitchen meat loaf mix is an established brand, and although its sales are not large, it is a consistently profitable item. Sally Franklin has just joined AFP as brand manager, and the meat loaf product was assigned to her. Her first task is to prepare a sales forecast and a budget for promotion and advertising for the next year. She collected the historical data shown in Table 12–13. The data included sales of the meat loaf mix and also the expenditures for promotion and advertising over the past 24 quarters, all in thousands of dollars. Also included is an index of general economic conditions in the meat loaf market area. High values of the index indicate good economic times.

The meat loaf mix is sold through food brokers in Seattle, San Francisco, Los Angeles, and Denver. Advertising expenditures are directed at the consumer in magazines such as *Woman's Day* and in newspapers. Promotion expenditures, on the other hand, are directed at the food broker or store manager. These consist of special deals such as getting a fifth case free if four are purchased, short-term increases in broker commissions, or sales contests among broker salespeople (with prizes such as trips to Hawaii).

Sally Franklin was quite puzzled by the great variability in the sales of the meat loaf mix from quarter to quarter, and also at the great variations in past expenditures for promotion and advertising. On inquiry, the sales vice president explained that there was a general policy that the company should either promote or advertise in a given quarter but not both. However, there had been a long-standing dispute in the company about the relative effectiveness of promotion and advertising on meat loaf mix sales. Franklin's predecessors had tried various different strategies, but no one had been able to determine what had or had not been successful. Some skeptics felt that both promotion and advertising expenditures were wasted, since neither seemed to affect sales. Others felt that promotion was effective but the effect was merely to reduce future sales. That is, they felt that brokers and store managers bought heavily during promotion periods and then didn't order in subsequent periods until inventories were back to normal. The effect of advertising was equally confusing, since sales seemed to vary greatly even during periods when advertising was relatively constant. For example, in the last two quarters in the data shown in Table 12–13 (quarters 23 and 24), advertising had been about the same ($36,000 and $39,000, respectively), but sales were $647,610 in one quarter and only $342,810 in the other.

If this wasn't confusing enough, the economist in the Economic Analysis department insisted that the meat loaf mix was a countercyclical product, meaning that it sold better in bad times than in good. His theory was that meat loaf was a less expensive meal than other meats, and people ate more of it during tough times. Furthermore, he felt that there was a seasonal pattern in sales, with more being sold during colder months than in the summer.

Build a multiple regression model to aid Franklin in preparing her forecasts. Suppose AFP plans to spend $30,000 on advertising and $10,000 on promotion in the next quarter. Plans for the subsequent quarter call for $10,000 in advertising and $25,000 on promotion. The economic index is expected to remain at 115 for both quarters. Provide forecasts for sales for these next two quarters.

Solutions to Practice Problems

12–1. *a, b.*

		Four-Month	Exponential	
	Sales	Moving	Smoothing	
Month	($000)	Average	Forecast	
January	1,212		1,212.00	
February	1,321		1,212.00	
March	1,278		1,244.70	
April	1,341		1,254.69	
May	1,257	1,288.00	1,280.58	
June	1,287	1,299.25	1,273.51	
July	1,189	1,290.75	1,277.56	
August	1,111	1,268.50	1,250.99	
September	1,145	1,211.00	1,208.99	
October	1,150	1,183.00	1,189.79	
November	1,298	1,148.75	1,177.86	
December	1,331	1,176.00	1,213.90	
		1,231.00	1,249.03	

12–2.

				Two-Equation
				Exponential
	Sales			Smoothing
Month	($000)	S_t	G_t	Forecast
January	1,212	1,212.00	0	
February	1,321	1,233.80	4.36	
March	1,278	1,246.13	5.95	1,238.16
April	1,341	1,269.87	9.51	1,252.08
May	1,257	1,274.90	8.62	1,279.38
June	1,287	1,284.21	8.75	1,283.52
July	1,189	1,272.17	4.60	1,292.97
August	1,111	1,243.62	−2.03	1.276.77
September	1,145	1,222.26	−5.90	1,241.58
October	1,150	1,203.09	−8.55	1,216.37
November	1,298	1,215.23	−4.41	1,194.54
December	1,331	1,234.85	0.39	1,210.82
				1,235.25

12–3.

Month	Sales ($000)	Regression Forecast
1	$1,212	$1,268.53
2	1,321	1,263.95
3	1,278	1,259.36
4	1,341	1,254.78
5	1,257	1,250.20
6	1,287	1,245.62
7	1,189	1,241.04
8	1,111	1,236.46
9	1,145	1,231.88
10	1,150	1,227.30
11	1,298	1,222.72
12	1,331	1,218.14
13		1,213.56

Summary Output

Regression Statistics	
Multiple R	0.20796865
R-square	0.04325096
Adjusted R-square	-0.0524239
Standard error	81.4656319
Observations	12

ANOVA

	df	*SS*	*MS*	*F*	*Significance F*
Regression	1	3000.17483	3000.17483	0.45206169	0.51659108
Residual	10	66366.4918	6636.64918		
Total	11	69366.6667			

	Coefficients	*Standard Error*	*t Stat*	*P-value*	*Lower 95%*	*Upper 95%*
Intercept	1273.10606	50.1386305	25.3917199	2.0585E-10	1161.39021	1384.82191
X Variable 1	-4.5804196	6.81249838	-0.6723553	0.51659108	-19.759615	10.5987754

Forecast for month 13 = 1,273.106 + (−4.5804)*(13) = 1,213.56

12–4. 6489/0.294 = 22,071 units.

APPENDIX OF TABLES

TABLE A The Standardized Normal Distribution Function,* $F_N(Z)$

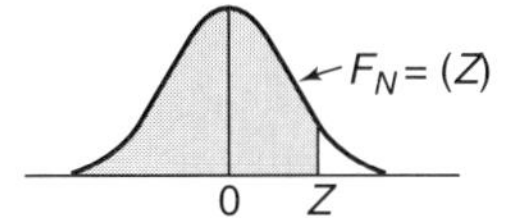

Z	0.00	0.01	0.02	0.03	0.04	0.05	0.06	0.07	0.08	0.09
0.0	0.5000	0.5040	0.5080	0.5120	0.5160	0.5199	0.5239	0.5279	0.5319	0.5359
0.1	0.5398	0.5438	0.5478	0.5517	0.5557	0.5596	0.5636	0.5675	0.5714	0.5753
0.2	0.5793	0.5832	0.5871	0.5910	0.5948	0.5987	0.6026	0.6064	0.6103	0.6141
0.3	0.6179	0.6217	0.6255	0.6293	0.6331	0.6368	0.6406	0.6443	0.6480	0.6517
0.4	0.6554	0.6591	0.6228	0.6664	0.6700	0.6736	0.6772	0.6808	0.6844	0.6879
0.5	0.6915	0.6950	0.6985	0.7019	0.7054	0.7088	0.7123	0.7157	0.7190	0.7224
0.6	0.7257	0.7291	0.7324	0.7357	0.7389	0.7422	0.7454	0.7486	0.7517	0.7549
0.7	0.7580	0.7611	0.7642	0.7673	0.7703	0.7734	0.7764	0.7794	0.7823	0.7852
0.8	0.7881	0.7910	0.7939	0.7967	0.7995	0.8023	0.8051	0.8078	0.8106	0.8133
0.9	0.8159	0.8186	0.8212	0.8238	0.8264	0.8289	0.8315	0.8340	0.8365	0.8389
1.0	0.8413	0.8438	0.8461	0.8485	0.8508	0.8531	0.8554	0.8577	0.8599	0.8621
1.1	0.8643	0.8665	0.8686	0.8708	0.8729	0.8749	0.8770	0.8790	0.8810	0.8830
1.2	0.8849	0.8869	0.8888	0.8907	0.8925	0.8944	0.8962	0.8980	0.8997	0.90147
1.3	0.90320	0.90490	0.90658	0.90824	0.90988	0.91149	0.91309	0.91466	0.91621	0.91774
1.4	0.91924	0.92073	0.92220	0.92364	0.92507	0.92647	0.92785	0.92922	0.93056	0.93189
1.5	0.93319	0.93448	0.93574	0.93699	0.93822	0.93943	0.94062	0.94179	0.94295	0.94408
1.6	0.94520	0.94630	0.94738	0.94845	0.94950	0.95053	0.95154	0.95254	0.95352	0.95449
1.7	0.95543	0.95637	0.95728	0.95818	0.95907	0.95994	0.96080	0.96164	0.96246	0.96327
1.8	0.96407	0.96485	0.96562	0.96638	0.96712	0.96784	0.96856	0.96926	0.96995	0.97062
1.9	0.97128	0.97193	0.97257	0.97320	0.97381	0.97441	0.97500	0.97558	0.97615	0.97670
2.0	0.97725	0.97778	0.97831	0.97882	0.97932	0.97982	0.98030	0.98077	0.98124	0.98169
2.1	0.98214	0.98257	0.98300	0.98341	0.98382	0.98422	0.98461	0.98500	0.98537	0.98574
2.2	0.98610	0.98645	0.98679	0.98713	0.98745	0.98778	0.98809	0.98840	0.98870	0.98899
2.3	0.98928	0.98956	0.98983	$0.9^{2}0097$	$0.9^{2}0358$	$0.9^{2}0613$	$0.9^{2}0863$	$0.9^{2}1106$	$0.9^{2}1344$	$0.9^{2}1576$
2.4	$0.9^{2}1802$	$0.9^{2}2024$	$0.9^{2}2240$	$0.9^{2}2451$	$0.9^{2}2656$	$0.9^{2}2857$	$0.9^{2}3053$	$0.9^{2}3244$	$0.9^{2}3431$	$0.9^{2}3613$
2.5	$0.9^{2}3790$	$0.9^{2}3963$	$0.9^{2}4132$	$0.9^{2}4297$	$0.9^{2}4457$	$0.9^{2}4614$	$0.9^{2}4766$	$0.9^{2}4915$	$0.9^{2}5060$	$0.9^{2}5201$
3.0	$0.9^{2}8650$	$0.9^{2}8694$	$0.9^{2}8736$	$0.9^{2}8777$	$0.9^{2}8817$	$0.9^{2}8856$	$0.9^{2}8893$	$0.9^{2}8930$	$0.9^{2}8965$	$0.9^{2}8999$
3.5	$0.9^{3}7674$	$0.9^{3}7759$	$0.9^{3}7842$	$0.9^{3}7922$	$0.9^{3}7999$	$0.9^{3}8074$	$0.9^{3}8146$	$0.9^{3}8215$	$0.9^{3}8282$	$0.9^{3}8347$
4.0	$0.9^{4}6833$	$0.9^{4}6964$	$0.9^{4}7090$	$0.9^{4}7211$	$0.9^{4}7327$	$0.9^{4}7439$	$0.9^{4}7546$	$0.9^{4}7649$	$0.9^{4}7748$	$0.9^{4}7843$

For example: $F(2.41) = .9^{2}2024 = .992024$.

*From A. Hald, *Statistical Tables and Formulas* (New York: John Wiley & Sons, 1952); reproduced by permission of Professor A. Hald and the publishers.

Note: The values in this table can also be obtained from the Excel spreadsheet function NORMSDIST.

TABLE B $N(D)$—Standard Normal Distribution Loss Function*

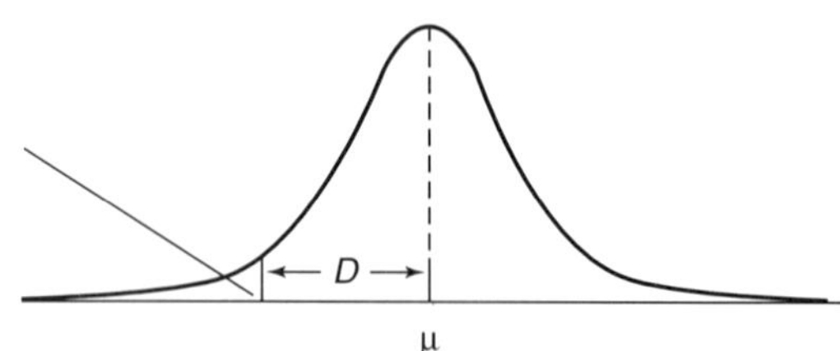

D or Z	.00	.01	.02	.03	.04	.05	.06	.07	.08	.09
.0	.3989	.3940	.3890	.3841	.3793	.3744	.3697	.3649	.3602	.3556
.1	.3509	.3464	.3418	.3373	.3328	.3284	.3240	.3197	.3154	.3111
.2	.3069	.3027	.2986	.2944	.2904	.2863	.2824	.2784	.2745	.2706
.3	.2668	.2630	.2592	.2555	.2518	.2481	.2445	.2409	.2374	.2339
.4	.2304	.2270	.2236	.2203	.2169	.2137	.2104	.2072	.2040	.2009
.5	.1978	.1947	.1917	.1887	.1857	.1828	.1799	.1771	.1742	.1714
.6	.1687	.1659	.1633	.1606	.1580	.1554	.1528	.1503	.1478	.1453
.7	.1429	.1405	.1381	.1358	.1334	.1312	.1289	.1267	.1245	.1223
.8	.1202	.1181	.1160	.1140	.1120	.1100	.1080	.1061	.1042	.1023
.9	.1004	.09860	.09680	.09503	.09328	.09156	.08986	.08819	.08654	.08491
1.0	.08332	.08174	.08019	.07866	.07716	.07568	.07422	.07279	.07138	.06999
1.1	.06862	.06727	.06595	.06465	.06336	.06210	.06086	.05964	.05844	.05726
1.2	.05610	.05496	.05384	.05274	.05165	.05059	.04954	.04851	.04750	.04650
1.3	.04553	.04457	.04363	.04270	.04179	.04090	.04002	.03916	.03831	.03748
1.4	.03667	.03587	.03508	.03431	.03356	.03281	.03208	.03137	.03067	.02998
1.5	.02931	.02865	.02800	.02736	.02674	.02612	.02552	.02494	.02436	.02380
1.6	.02324	.02270	.02217	.02165	.02114	.02064	.02015	.01967	.01920	.01874
1.7	.01829	.01785	.01742	.01699	.01658	.01617	.01578	.01539	.01501	.01464
1.8	.01428	.01392	.01357	.01323	.01290	.01257	.01226	.01195	.01164	.01134
1.9	.01105	.01077	.01049	.01022	$.0^{2}9957$	$.0^{2}9698$	$.0^{2}9445$	$.0^{2}9198$	$.0^{2}8957$	$.0^{2}8721$
2.0	$.0^{2}8491$	$.0^{2}8266$	$.0^{2}8046$	$.0^{2}7832$	$.0^{2}7623$	$.0^{2}7418$	$.0^{2}7219$	$.0^{2}7024$	$.0^{2}6835$	$.0^{2}6649$
2.1	$.0^{2}6468$	$.0^{2}6292$	$.0^{2}6120$	$.0^{2}5952$	$.0^{2}5788$	$.0^{2}5628$	$.0^{2}5472$	$.0^{2}5320$	$.0^{2}5172$	$.0^{2}5028$
2.2	$.0^{2}4887$	$.0^{2}4750$	$.0^{2}4616$	$.0^{2}4486$	$.0^{2}4358$	$.0^{2}4235$	$.0^{2}4114$	$.0^{2}3996$	$.0^{2}3882$	$.0^{2}3770$
2.3	$.0^{2}3662$	$.0^{2}3556$	$.0^{2}3453$	$.0^{2}3352$	$.0^{2}3225$	$.0^{2}3159$	$.0^{2}3067$	$.0^{2}2977$	$.0^{2}2889$	$.0^{2}2804$
2.4	$.0^{2}2720$	$.0^{2}2640$	$.0^{2}2561$	$.0^{2}2484$	$.0^{2}2410$	$.0^{2}2337$	$.0^{2}2267$	$.0^{2}2199$	$.0^{2}2132$	$.0^{2}2067$
2.5	$.0^{2}2005$	$.0^{2}1943$	$.0^{2}1883$	$.0^{2}1826$	$.0^{2}1769$	$.0^{2}1715$	$.0^{2}1662$	$.0^{2}1610$	$.0^{2}1560$	$.0^{2}1511$
3.0	$.0^{3}3822$	$.0^{3}3689$	$.0^{3}3560$	$.0^{3}3436$	$.0^{3}3316$	$.0^{3}3199$	$.0^{3}3087$	$.0^{3}2978$	$.0^{3}2873$	$.0^{3}2771$
3.5	$.0^{4}5848$	$.0^{4}5620$	$.0^{4}5400$	$.0^{4}5188$	$.0^{4}4984$	$.0^{4}4788$	$.0^{4}4599$	$.0^{4}4417$	$.0^{4}4242$	$.0^{4}4073$
4.0	$.0^{5}7145$	$.0^{5}6835$	$.0^{5}6538$	$.0^{5}6253$	$.0^{5}5980$	$.0^{5}5718$	$.0^{5}5468$	$.0^{5}5227$	$.0^{5}4997$	$.0^{5}4777$

$N(D)$ is defined as follows:

$$N(D) = \int_{-\infty}^{-D} (-D - X) f^*(X) dX = \int_{D}^{\infty} (X - D) f^*(X) dX$$

where $f^*(X)$ is the standardized normal density function, and D is positive.

*By permission from R. Schlaifer, *Probability and Statistics for Business Decisions* (New York: McGraw-Hill, 1959).

TABLE C Cumulative Binomial Distributions* $P(R \geq r \mid n, p)$

$n = 1$

p / r	01	02	03	04	05	06	07	08	09	10
1	0100	0200	0300	0400	0500	0600	0700	0800	0900	1000

p / r	11	12	13	14	15	16	17	18	19	20
1	1100	1200	1300	1400	1500	1600	1700	1800	1900	2000

p / r	21	22	23	24	25	26	27	28	29	30
1	2100	2200	2300	2400	2500	2600	2700	2800	2900	3000

p / r	31	32	33	34	35	36	37	38	39	40
1	3100	3200	3300	3400	3500	3600	3700	3800	3900	4000

p / r	41	42	43	44	45	46	47	48	49	50
1	4100	4200	4300	4400	4500	4600	4700	4800	4900	5000

$n = 2$

p / r	01	02	03	04	05	06	07	08	09	10
1	0199	0396	0591	0784	0975	1164	1351	1536	1719	1900
2	0001	0004	0009	0016	0025	0036	0049	0064	0081	0100

p / r	11	12	13	14	15	16	17	18	19	20
1	2079	2256	2431	2604	2775	2944	3111	3276	3439	3600
2	0121	0144	0169	0196	0225	0256	0289	0324	0361	0400

p / r	21	22	23	24	25	26	27	28	29	30
1	3759	3916	4071	4224	4375	4524	4671	4816	4959	6100
2	0441	0484	0529	0576	0625	0676	0729	0784	0841	0900

p / r	31	32	33	34	35	36	37	38	39	40
1	5239	5376	5511	5644	5775	5904	6031	6156	6279	6400
2	0961	1024	1089	1156	1225	1296	1369	1444	1521	1600

p / r	41	42	43	44	45	46	47	48	49	50
1	6519	6636	6751	6864	6975	7084	7191	7296	7399	7500
2	1681	1764	1849	1936	2025	2116	2209	2304	2401	2500

Note: For $p > 0.5$, the following identity holds:

$$P(R \geq r \mid n, p) = 1 - P(R \geq n - r + 1 \mid n, 1 - p)$$

For example, consider the probability of two or more heads in three tosses of a coin with P (head) = 0.60; this is identical to 1 minus the probability of two or more tails in three tosses, with P (tail) = 0.4, or 1 − 0.3520 = 0.6480.

*By permission from R. Schlaifer, *Probability and Statistics for Business Decisions* (New York: McGraw-Hill, 1959).

Note: The cumulative binomial values in this table, as well as the individual binomial values, can also be obtained from the Excel spreadsheet function BINOMDIST.

TABLE C *(continued)*

n = 3

p / r	01	02	03	04	05	06	07	08	09	10
1	0297	0588	0873	1153	1426	1694	1956	2213	2464	2710
2	0003	0012	0026	0047	0073	0104	0140	0182	0228	0280
3				0001	0001	0002	0003	0005	0007	0010
p / r	11	12	13	14	15	16	17	18	19	20
1	2950	3185	3415	3639	3859	4073	4282	4486	4686	4880
2	0336	0397	0463	0533	0608	0686	0769	0855	0946	1040
3	0013	0017	0022	0027	0034	0041	0049	0058	0069	0080
p / r	21	22	23	24	25	26	27	28	29	30
1	5070	5254	5435	5610	5781	5948	6110	6268	6421	6570
2	1138	1239	1344	1452	1563	1676	1793	1913	2035	2160
3	0093	0106	0122	0138	0156	0176	0197	0220	0244	0270
p / r	31	32	33	34	35	36	37	38	39	40
1	6715	6856	6992	7125	7254	7379	7500	7617	7730	7840
2	2287	2417	2548	2682	2818	2955	3094	3235	3377	3520
3	0298	0328	0359	0393	0429	0467	0507	0549	0593	0640
p / r	41	42	43	44	45	46	47	48	49	50
1	7946	8049	8148	8244	8336	8425	8511	8594	8673	8750
2	3665	3810	3957	4104	4253	4401	4551	4700	4850	5000
3	0689	0741	0795	0852	0911	0973	1038	1106	1176	1250

n = 4

p / r	01	02	03	04	05	06	07	08	09	10
1	0394	0776	1147	1507	1855	2193	2519	2836	3143	3439
2	0006	0023	0052	0091	0140	0199	0267	0344	0430	0523
3			0001	0002	0005	0008	0013	0019	0027	0037
4									0001	0001
p / r	11	12	13	14	15	16	17	18	19	20
1	3726	4003	4271	4530	4780	5021	5254	5479	5695	5904
2	0624	0732	0847	0968	1095	1228	1366	1509	1656	1808
3	0049	0063	0079	0098	0120	0144	0171	0202	0235	0272
4	0001	0002	0003	0004	0005	0007	0008	0010	0013	0016
p / r	21	22	23	24	25	26	27	28	29	30
1	6105	6298	6485	6664	6836	7001	7160	7313	7459	7599
2	1963	2122	2285	2450	2617	2787	2959	3132	3307	3483
3	0312	0356	0403	0453	0508	0566	0628	0694	0763	0837
4	0019	0023	0028	0033	0039	0046	0053	0061	0071	0081

TABLE C *(continued)*

p / r	31	32	33	34	35	36	37	38	39	40
1	7733	7862	7985	8103	8215	8322	8425	8522	8615	8704
2	3660	3837	4015	4193	4370	4547	4724	4900	5075	5248
3	0915	0996	1082	1171	1265	1362	1464	1569	1679	1792
4	0092	0105	0119	0134	0150	0168	0187	0209	0231	0256

p / r	41	42	43	44	45	46	47	48	49	50
1	8788	8868	8944	9017	9085	9150	9211	9269	9323	9375
2	5420	5590	5759	5926	6090	6252	6412	6569	6724	6875
3	1909	2030	2155	2283	2415	2550	2689	2831	2977	3125
4	0283	0311	0342	0375	0410	0448	0488	0531	0576	0625

$n = 5$

p / r	01	02	03	04	05	06	07	08	09	10
1	0490	0961	1413	1846	2262	2661	3043	3409	3760	4095
2	0010	0038	0085	0148	0226	0319	0425	0544	0674	0815
3		0001	0003	0006	0012	0020	0031	0045	0063	0086
4						0001	0001	0002	0003	0005

p / r	11	12	13	14	15	16	17	18	19	20
1	4416	4723	5016	5296	5563	5818	6061	6293	6513	6723
2	0965	1125	1292	1467	1648	1835	2027	2224	2424	2627
3	0112	0143	0179	0220	0266	0318	0375	0437	0505	0579
4	0007	0009	0013	0017	0022	0029	0036	0045	0055	0067
5				0001	0001	0001	0001	0002	0002	0003

p / r	21	22	23	24	25	26	27	28	29	30
1	6923	7113	7293	7464	7627	7781	7927	8065	8196	8319
2	2833	3041	3251	3461	3672	3883	4093	4303	4511	4718
3	0659	0744	0836	0933	1035	1143	1257	1376	1501	1631
4	0081	0097	0114	0134	0156	0181	0208	0238	0272	0308
5	0004	0005	0006	0008	0010	0012	0014	0017	0021	0024

p / r	31	32	33	34	35	36	37	38	39	40
1	8436	8546	8650	8748	8840	8926	9008	9084	9155	9222
2	4923	5125	5325	5522	5716	5906	6093	6276	6455	6630
3	1766	1905	2050	2199	2352	2509	2670	2835	3003	3174
4	0347	0390	0436	0486	0540	0598	0660	0726	0796	0870
5	0029	0034	0039	0045	0053	0060	0069	0079	0090	0102

p / r	41	42	43	44	45	46	47	48	49	50
1	9285	9344	9398	9449	9497	9541	9582	9620	9655	9688
2	6801	6967	7129	7286	7438	7585	7728	7865	7998	8125
3	3349	3525	3705	3886	4069	4253	4439	4625	4813	5000
4	0949	1033	1121	1214	1312	1415	1522	1635	1753	1875
5	0116	0131	0147	0165	0185	0206	0229	0255	0282	0313

TABLE C *(continued)*

n = 6

r \ p	01	02	03	04	05	06	07	08	09	10
1	0585	1142	1670	2172	2649	3101	3530	3936	4321	4686
2	0015	0057	0125	0216	0328	0459	0608	0773	0952	1143
3		0002	0005	0012	0022	0038	0058	0085	0118	0159
4					0001	0002	0003	0005	0008	0013
5										0001

r \ p	11	12	13	14	15	16	17	18	19	20
1	5030	5356	5664	5954	6229	6487	6731	6960	7176	7379
2	1345	1556	1776	2003	2235	2472	2713	2956	3201	3446
3	0206	0261	0324	0395	0473	0560	0655	0759	0870	0989
4	0018	0025	0034	0045	0059	0075	0094	0116	0141	0170
5	0001	0001	0002	0003	0004	0005	0007	0010	0013	0016
6										0001

r \ p	21	22	23	24	25	26	27	28	29	30
1	7569	7748	7916	8073	8220	8358	8487	8607	8719	8824
2	3692	3637	4180	4422	4661	4896	5128	5356	5580	5798
3	1115	1250	1391	1539	1694	1856	2023	2196	2374	2557
4	0202	0239	0280	0326	0376	0431	0492	0557	0628	0705
5	0020	0025	0031	0038	0046	0056	0067	0079	0093	0109
6	0001	0001	0001	0002	0002	0003	0004	0005	0006	0007

r \ p	31	32	33	34	35	36	37	38	39	40
1	8921	9011	9095	9173	9246	9313	9375	9432	9485	9533
2	6012	6220	6422	6619	6809	6994	7172	7343	7508	7667
3	2744	2936	3130	3328	3529	3732	3937	4143	4350	4557
4	0787	0875	0969	1069	1174	1286	1404	1527	1657	1792
5	0127	0148	0170	0195	0223	0254	0288	0325	0365	0410
6	0009	0011	0013	0015	0018	0022	0026	0030	0035	0041

r \ p	41	42	43	44	45	46	47	48	49	50
1	9578	9619	9657	9692	9723	9752	9778	9802	9824	9844
2	7819	7965	8105	8238	8364	8485	8599	8707	8810	8906
3	4764	4971	5177	5382	5585	5786	5985	6180	6373	6563
4	1933	2080	2232	2390	2553	2721	2893	3070	3252	3438
5	0458	0510	0566	0627	0692	0762	0837	0917	1003	1094
6	0048	0055	0063	0073	0083	0095	0108	0122	0138	0156

n = 7

r \ p	01	02	03	04	05	06	07	08	09	10
1	0679	1319	1920	2486	3017	3513	3983	4422	4832	5217
2	0020	0079	0171	0294	0444	0618	0813	1026	1255	1497
3		003	0009	0020	0038	0063	0097	0140	0193	0257
4				0001	0002	0004	0007	0012	0018	0027
5								0001	0001	0002

Table C *(continued)*

p / r	11	12	13	14	15	16	17	18	19	20
1	5577	5913	6227	6581	6794	7049	7286	7507	7712	7903
2	1750	2012	2281	2556	2834	3115	3396	3677	3956	4233
3	0331	0416	0513	0620	0738	0866	1005	1154	1313	1480
4	0039	0054	0072	0094	0121	0153	0189	0231	0279	0333
5	0003	0004	0006	0009	0012	0017	0022	0029	0037	0047
6					0001	0001	0001	0002	0003	0004

p / r	21	22	23	24	25	26	27	28	29	30
1	8080	8243	8395	8535	8665	8785	8895	8997	9090	9176
2	4506	4775	5040	5290	5551	5796	6035	6266	6490	6706
3	1657	1841	2033	2231	2436	2646	2861	3081	3304	3529
4	0394	0461	0536	0617	0706	0802	0905	1016	1134	1260
5	0058	0072	0088	0107	0129	0153	0181	0213	0248	0288
6	0005	0006	0008	0011	0013	0017	0021	0026	0031	0038
7					0001	0001	0001	0001	0002	0002

p / r	31	32	33	34	35	36	37	38	39	40
1	9255	9328	9394	9454	9510	9560	9606	9648	9686	9720
2	6914	7113	7304	7487	7662	7828	7987	8137	8279	8414
3	3757	3987	4217	4447	4677	4906	5134	5359	5581	5801
4	1394	1534	1682	1837	1998	2167	2341	2521	2707	2898
5	0221	0380	0434	0492	0556	0625	0701	0782	0869	0963
6	0046	0055	0065	0077	0090	0105	0123	0142	0164	0188
7	0003	0003	0004	0005	0006	0008	0009	0011	0014	0016

p / r	41	42	43	44	45	46	47	48	49	50
1	9751	9779	9805	9827	9848	9866	9883	9897	9910	9922
2	8541	8660	8772	8877	8976	9068	9153	9233	9307	9375
3	6017	6229	6436	6638	6836	7027	7213	7393	7567	7734
4	3094	3294	3498	3706	3917	4131	4346	4563	4781	5000
5	1063	1169	1282	1402	1529	1663	1803	1951	2105	2266
6	0216	0246	0279	0316	0357	0402	0451	0504	0562	0625
7	0019	0023	0027	0032	0037	0044	0051	0059	0068	0078

$n = 8$

p / r	01	02	03	04	05	06	07	08	09	10
1	0773	1492	2163	2786	3366	3904	4404	4868	5297	5695
2	0027	0103	0223	0381	0572	0792	1035	1298	1577	1869
3	0001	0004	0013	0031	0058	0096	0147	0211	0289	0381
4			0001	0002	0004	0007	0013	0022	0034	0050
5							0001	0001	0003	0004

TABLE C *(continued)*

p / r	11	12	13	14	15	16	17	18	19	20
1	6063	6404	6718	7008	7275	7521	7748	7956	8147	8322
2	2171	2480	2794	3111	3428	3744	4057	4366	4670	4967
3	0487	0608	0743	0891	1052	1226	1412	1608	1815	2031
4	0071	0097	0129	0168	0214	0267	0328	0397	0476	0563
5	0007	0010	0015	0021	0029	0038	0050	0065	0083	0104
6		0001	0001	0002	0002	0003	0005	0007	0009	0012
7									0001	0001

p / r	21	22	23	24	25	26	27	28	29	30
1	8483	8630	8764	8887	8999	9101	9194	9278	9354	9424
2	5257	5538	5811	6075	6329	6573	6807	7031	7244	7447
3	2255	2486	2724	2967	3215	3465	3718	3973	4228	4482
4	0659	0765	0880	1004	1138	1281	1433	1594	1763	1941
5	0129	0158	0191	0230	0273	0322	0377	0438	0505	0580
6	0016	0021	0027	0034	0042	0052	0064	0078	0094	0113
7	0001	0002	0002	0003	0004	0005	0006	0008	0010	0013
8									0001	0001

p / r	31	32	33	34	35	36	37	38	39	40
1	9486	9543	9594	9640	9681	9719	9752	9782	9808	9838
2	7640	7822	7994	8156	8309	8452	8586	8711	8828	8936
3	4736	4987	5236	5481	5722	5958	6189	6415	6634	6846
4	2126	2319	2519	2724	2936	3153	3374	3599	3828	4059
5	0661	0750	0846	0949	1061	1180	1307	1443	1586	1737
6	0134	0159	0187	0218	0253	0293	0336	0385	0439	0498
7	0016	0020	0024	0030	0036	0043	0051	0061	0072	0085
8	0001	0001	0001	0002	0002	0003	0004	0004	0005	0007

p / r	41	42	43	44	45	46	47	48	49	50
1	9853	9872	9889	9903	9916	9928	9938	9947	9954	9961
2	9037	9130	9216	9295	9368	9435	9496	9552	9602	9648
3	7052	7250	7440	7624	7799	7966	8125	8276	8419	8555
4	4292	4527	4762	4996	5230	5463	5694	5922	6146	6367
5	1895	2062	2235	2416	2604	2798	2999	3205	3416	3633
6	0563	0634	0711	0794	0885	0982	1086	1198	1318	1445
7	0100	0117	0136	0157	0181	0208	0239	0272	0310	0352
8	0008	0010	0012	0014	0017	0020	0024	0028	0033	0039

***n* = 9**

p / r	01	02	03	04	05	06	07	08	09	10
1	0865	1663	2398	3075	3698	4270	4796	5278	5721	6126
2	0034	0131	0282	0478	0712	0978	1271	1583	1912	2252
3	0001	0006	0020	0045	0084	0138	0209	0298	0405	0530
4			0001	0003	0006	0013	0023	0037	0057	0083
5						0001	0002	0003	0005	0009
6										0001

Table C *(continued)*

r \ p	11	12	13	14	15	16	17	18	19	20
1	6496	6835	7145	7427	7684	7918	8131	8324	8499	8658
2	2599	2951	3304	3657	4005	4348	4685	5012	5330	5638
3	0672	0833	1009	1202	1409	1629	1861	2105	2357	2618
4	0117	0158	0209	0269	0339	0420	0512	0615	0730	0856
5	0014	0021	0030	0041	0056	0075	0098	0125	0158	0196
6	0001	0002	0003	0004	0006	0009	0013	0017	0023	0031
7						0001	0001	0002	0002	0003

r \ p	21	22	23	24	25	26	27	28	29	30
1	8801	8931	9048	9154	9249	9335	9411	9480	9542	9596
2	5934	6218	6491	7850	6997	7230	7452	7660	7856	8040
3	2885	3158	3434	3713	3993	4273	4552	4829	5102	5372
4	0994	1144	1304	1475	1657	1849	2050	2260	2478	2703
5	0240	0291	0350	0416	0489	0571	0662	0762	0870	0988
6	0040	0051	0065	0081	0100	0122	0149	0179	0213	0253
7	0004	0006	0008	0010	0013	0017	0022	0028	0035	0043
8			0001	0001	0001	0001	0002	0003	0003	0004

r \ p	31	32	33	34	35	36	37	38	39	40
1	9645	9689	9728	9762	9793	9820	9844	9865	9883	9899
2	8212	8372	8522	8661	8790	8908	9017	9118	9210	9295
3	5636	5894	6146	6390	6627	6856	7076	7287	7489	7682
4	2935	3173	3415	3662	3911	4163	4416	4669	4922	5174
5	1115	1252	1398	1553	1717	1890	2072	2262	2460	2666
6	0298	0348	0404	0467	0536	0612	0696	0787	0886	0994
7	0053	0064	0078	0094	0112	0133	0157	0184	0215	0250
8	0006	0007	0009	0011	0014	0017	0021	0026	0031	0036
9				0001	0001	0001	0001	0002	0002	0003

r \ p	41	42	43	44	45	46	47	48	49	50
1	9913	9926	9936	9946	9954	9961	9967	9972	9977	9980
2	9372	9442	9505	9563	9615	9662	9704	9741	9775	9805
3	7866	8039	8204	8359	8505	8642	8769	8889	8999	9102
4	5424	5670	5913	6152	6386	6614	6836	7052	7260	7461
5	2878	3097	3322	3551	3786	4024	4265	4509	4754	5000
6	1109	1233	1366	1508	1658	1817	1985	2161	2346	2539
7	0290	0334	0383	0437	0498	0564	0637	0717	0804	0898
8	0046	0055	0065	0077	0091	0107	0125	0145	0189	1095
9	0003	0004	0005	0006	0008	0009	0011	0014	0016	0020

n* = *10

r \ p	01	02	03	04	05	06	07	08	09	10
1	0956	1829	2626	3352	4013	4614	5160	5656	6106	6513
2	0043	0162	0345	0582	0861	1176	1517	1879	2254	2639
3	0001	0009	0028	0062	0115	0188	0283	0401	0540	0702
4			0001	0004	0010	0020	0036	0058	0088	0128
5					0001	0002	0003	0006	0010	0016
6									0001	0001

TABLE C *(continued)*

r \ p	11	12	13	14	15	16	17	18	19	20
1	6882	7215	7516	7787	8031	8251	8448	8626	8784	8926
2	3028	3417	3804	4184	4557	4920	5270	5608	5932	6242
3	0884	1087	1308	1545	1798	2064	2341	2628	2922	3222
4	0178	0239	0313	0400	0500	0614	0741	0883	1039	1209
5	0025	0037	0053	0073	0099	0130	0168	0213	0266	0328
6	0003	0004	0006	0010	0014	0020	0027	0037	0049	0064
7			0001	0001	0001	0002	0003	0004	0006	0009
8									0001	0001

r \ p	21	22	23	24	25	26	27	28	29	30
1	9053	9166	9267	9357	9437	9508	9570	9626	9674	9718
2	6536	6815	7079	7327	7560	7778	7981	8170	8345	8507
3	3526	3831	4137	4442	4744	5042	5335	5622	5901	6172
4	1391	1587	1794	2012	2241	2479	2726	2979	3239	3504
5	0399	0479	0569	0670	0781	0904	1037	1181	1337	1503
6	0082	0104	0130	0161	0197	0239	0287	0342	0404	0473
7	0012	0016	0021	0027	0035	0045	0056	0070	0087	0106
8	0001	0002	0002	0003	0004	0006	0007	0010	0012	0016
9							0001	0001	0001	0001

r \ p	31	32	33	34	35	36	37	38	39	40
1	9755	9789	9818	9843	9865	9885	9902	9916	9929	9940
2	8656	8794	8920	9035	9140	9236	9323	9402	9473	9536
3	6434	6687	6930	7162	7384	7595	7794	7983	8160	8327
4	3772	4044	4316	4589	4862	5132	5400	5664	5923	6177
5	1679	1867	2064	2270	2485	2708	2939	3177	3420	3669
6	0551	0637	0732	0836	0949	1072	1205	1348	1500	1663
7	0129	0155	0185	0220	0260	0305	0356	0413	0477	0548
8	0020	0025	0032	0039	0048	0059	0071	0086	0103	0183
9	0002	0003	0003	0004	0005	0007	0009	0011	0014	0017
10								0001	0001	0001

r \ p	41	42	43	44	45	46	47	48	49	50
1	9949	9957	9964	9970	9975	9979	9983	9986	9988	9990
2	9594	9645	9691	9731	9767	9799	9827	9852	9874	9893
3	8483	8628	8764	8889	9004	9111	9209	9298	9379	9453
4	6425	6665	6898	7123	7340	7547	7745	7933	8112	8281
5	3922	4178	4436	4696	4956	5216	5474	5730	5982	6230
6	1834	2016	2207	2407	2616	2832	3057	3288	3526	3770
7	0626	0712	0806	0908	1020	1141	1271	1410	1560	1719
8	0146	0172	0202	0236	0274	0317	0366	0420	0480	0547
9	0021	0025	0031	0037	0045	0054	0065	0077	0091	0107
10	0001	0002	0002	0003	0003	0004	0005	0006	0008	0010

TABLE C *(continued)*

n = 11

r \ p	01	02	03	04	05	06	07	08	09	10
1	1047	1993	2847	3618	4312	4937	5499	6004	6456	6862
2	0052	0195	0413	0692	1012	1382	1772	2181	2601	3086
3	0002	0013	0037	0083	0152	0248	0370	0519	0695	0896
4			0002	0007	0016	0030	0053	0085	0129	0185
5					0001	0003	0005	0010	0017	0028
6								0001	0002	0003

r \ p	11	12	13	14	15	16	17	18	19	20
1	7225	7549	7839	8097	9327	8531	8712	8873	9015	9141
2	3452	3873	4486	4689	5078	5453	5811	6151	6474	6779
3	1120	1366	1632	1915	2212	2521	2839	3164	3494	3826
4	0236	0341	0442	0560	0694	0846	1013	1197	1397	1611
5	0042	0061	0087	0119	0159	0207	0266	0334	0413	0504
6	0005	0008	0012	0018	0027	0037	0051	0068	0090	0117
7		0001	0001	0002	0003	0005	0007	0010	0014	0020
8							0001	0001	0002	0002

r \ p	21	22	23	24	25	26	27	28	29	30
1	9252	9350	9436	9511	9578	9636	9686	9730	9769	9802
2	7068	7333	7582	7814	8029	9227	8410	8577	8730	8870
3	4158	4488	4014	5134	5448	5753	6049	6335	6610	6873
4	1940	2081	2333	2596	2867	3146	3430	3719	4011	4304
5	0607	0723	0851	0998	1146	1313	1493	1685	1888	2103
6	0148	0186	0231	0283	0343	0412	0490	0577	0674	0782
7	0027	0035	0046	0059	0076	0095	0119	0146	0179	0216
8	0003	0005	0007	0009	0012	0016	0021	0027	0034	0043
9			0001	0001	0001	0002	0002	0003	0004	0006

r \ p	31	32	33	34	35	36	37	38	39	40
1	9831	9856	9878	9896	9912	9926	9938	9948	9956	9964
2	8997	9112	9216	9310	9394	9470	9537	9597	9650	9698
3	7183	7361	7587	7799	7999	8186	8360	8522	8672	8811
4	4596	4890	5179	5464	5744	6019	6286	6545	6796	7037
5	2328	8563	2807	3059	3317	3501	3850	4122	4397	4672
6	0901	1031	1171	1324	1487	1661	1847	2043	2249	2465
7	0860	0309	0366	0430	0501	0581	0670	0768	0876	0994
8	0054	0067	0082	0101	0122	0148	0177	0210	0249	0059
9	0008	0010	0013	0016	0020	0026	0032	0039	0048	0059
10	0001	0001	0001	0002	0002	0003	0004	0005	0006	0007

r \ p	41	42	43	44	45	46	47	48	49	50
1	9970	9975	9979	9983	9986	9989	9991	9992	9994	9995
2	9739	0887	9808	9836	9861	9882	9900	9916	9930	9941
3	8938	9055	9162	9260	9348	9428	9499	9564	9622	9673
4	7869	7490	7700	7900	8089	9266	8433	8588	8733	8867
5	4948	5283	5495	5764	6029	6288	6541	6787	7026	7256

TABLE C *(continued)*

6	2690	2924	3166	3414	3669	3929	4193	4460	4729	5000
7	1121	1260	1408	1568	1738	1919	2110	2312	2523	2744
8	0343	0399	0461	0532	0610	0696	0791	0895	1009	1133
9	0072	0087	0104	0125	0148	0175	0206	0241	0282	0327
10	0009	0012	0014	0018	0022	0027	0033	0040	0049	0059
11	0001	0001	0001	0001	0002	0002	0002	0003	0004	0005

n = 12

p / r	01	02	03	04	05	06	07	08	09	10
1	1136	2153	3062	3873	4596	5241	5814	6323	6775	7176
2	0062	0231	0486	0809	1184	1595	2033	2487	2948	3410
3	0002	0015	0048	0107	0196	1316	0468	0652	0866	1109
4		0001	0003	0010	0022	0043	0075	0120	0180	0256
5				0001	0002	0004	0009	0016	0027	0043
6							0001	0002	0003	0005
7										0001

p / r	11	12	13	14	15	16	17	18	19	20
1	7530	7843	8120	8363	8578	8766	8931	9076	9202	9313
2	3867	4314	4748	5166	5565	5945	6304	6641	6957	7251
3	1377	1667	1977	2303	2642	2990	3344	3702	4060	4417
4	0351	0464	0597	0750	0922	1114	1324	1552	1795	2054
5	0065	0095	0133	0181	0239	0310	0393	0489	0600	0726
6	0009	0014	0022	0033	0046	0065	0088	0116	0151	0194
7	0001	0002	0003	0004	0007	0010	0015	0021	0029	0039
8					0001	0001	0002	0003	0004	0006
9										0001

p / r	21	22	23	24	25	26	27	28	29	30
1	9409	9493	9566	9629	9683	9730	9771	9806	9836	9862
2	7524	7776	8009	8222	8416	8594	8755	8900	9032	9150
3	4768	5114	5450	5778	6093	6397	6687	6963	7225	7472
4	2326	2610	2904	3205	3512	3824	4137	4452	4765	5075
5	0866	1081	1192	1377	1576	1790	2016	2254	2504	2763
6	0245	0304	0374	0453	0544	0646	0760	0887	1026	1178
7	0052	0068	0089	0113	0143	0178	0219	0267	0322	0386
8	0008	0011	0016	0021	0028	0036	0047	0060	0076	0095
9	0001	0001	0002	0003	0004	0005	0007	0010	0013	0017
10						0001	0001	0001	0002	0002

p / r	31	32	33	34	35	36	37	38	39	40
1	9894	9902	9918	9932	9943	9953	9961	9968	9973	9978
2	9256	9350	9435	9509	9576	9634	9685	9730	9770	9804
3	7704	7922	8124	8313	8487	8648	8795	8931	9054	9166
4	5381	5681	5973	6258	6533	6799	7053	7296	7528	7747
5	3032	3308	3590	3876	4167	4459	4751	5043	5332	5618

TABLE C *(continued)*

r										
6	1343	1521	1711	1913	2127	2352	2588	2833	3087	3348
7	0458	0540	0632	0734	0846	0970	1106	1253	1411	1582
8	0118	0144	0176	0213	0255	0304	0359	0422	0493	0573
9	0022	0028	0036	0045	0056	0070	0086	0104	0127	0153
10	0003	0004	0005	0007	0008	0011	0014	0018	0022	0028
11				0001	0001	0001	0001	0002	0002	0003

p / r	41	42	43	44	45	46	47	48	49	50
1	9982	9986	9988	9990	9992	9994	9995	9996	9997	9998
2	9834	9860	9882	9901	9917	9931	9943	9953	9961	9968
3	9267	9358	9440	9513	9579	9637	9688	9733	9773	9807
4	7953	8147	8329	8409	8655	8801	8934	9057	9168	9270
5	5899	6175	6443	6704	6956	7198	7430	7652	7862	8062
6	3616	3889	4167	4448	4731	5014	5297	5577	5855	6128
7	1765	1959	2164	2380	2607	2843	3089	3343	3604	3872
8	0662	0760	0869	0988	1117	1258	1411	1575	1751	1938
9	0183	0218	0258	0304	0356	0415	0481	0555	0638	0730
10	0035	0043	0053	0065	0079	0095	0114	0137	0163	0193
11	0004	0005	0007	0009	0011	0014	0017	0021	0026	0032
12				0001	0001	0001	0001	0001	0002	0002

***n* = 13**

p / r	01	02	03	04	05	06	07	08	09	10
1	1225	2310	3270	4118	4867	5526	6107	6617	7065	7458
2	0072	0270	0564	0932	1354	1814	2298	2794	3293	3787
3	0003	0020	0062	0135	0245	0392	0578	0799	1054	1339
4		0001	0005	0014	0031	0060	0103	0163	0242	0342
5				0001	0003	0007	0013	0024	0041	0065
6							0001	0003	0005	0009
7									0001	0001

p / r	11	12	13	14	15	16	17	18	19	20
1	7802	8102	8364	8592	8791	8963	9113	9242	9354	9450
2	4270	4738	5186	5614	6017	6396	6751	7080	7384	7661
3	1651	1985	2337	2704	3080	3463	3848	4231	4611	4983
4	0464	0609	0776	0967	1180	1414	1667	1939	2226	2527
5	0097	0139	0193	0260	0342	0438	0551	0681	0827	0991
6	0015	0024	0036	0053	0075	0104	0139	0183	0237	0300
7	0002	0003	0005	0008	0013	0019	0027	0038	0052	0070
8			0001	0001	0002	0003	0004	0006	0009	0012
9								0001	0001	0002

p / r	21	22	23	24	25	26	27	28	29	30
1	9533	9604	9666	9718	9762	9800	9833	9860	9883	9903
2	7920	8154	8367	8559	8733	8889	9029	9154	9265	9363
3	5347	5699	6039	6364	6674	6968	7245	7505	7749	7975
4	2839	3161	3489	3822	4157	4493	4826	5155	5478	5794
5	1173	1371	1585	1816	2060	2319	2589	2870	3160	3457

TABLE C *(continued)*

r										
6	0375	0462	0562	0675	0802	0944	1099	1270	1455	1654
7	0093	0120	0154	0195	0243	0299	0365	0440	0527	0624
8	0017	0024	0032	0043	0056	0073	0093	0118	0147	0182
9	0002	0004	0005	0007	0010	0013	0018	0024	0031	0040
10			0001	0001	0001	0002	0003	0004	0005	0007
11									0001	0001

p / r	31	32	33	34	35	36	37	38	39	40
1	9920	9934	9945	9955	9963	9970	9975	9980	9984	9987
2	9450	9527	9594	9653	9704	9749	9787	9821	9849	9874
3	8185	8379	8557	8720	8868	9003	9125	9235	9333	9421
4	6101	6398	6683	6957	7217	7464	7698	7917	8123	8314
5	3760	4067	4376	4686	4995	5301	5603	5899	6188	6470
6	1867	2093	2331	2581	2841	3111	3388	3673	3962	4256
7	0733	0854	0988	1135	1295	1468	1654	1853	2065	2288
8	0223	0271	0326	0390	0462	0544	0635	0738	0851	0977
9	0052	0065	0082	0102	0126	0154	0187	0225	0270	0321
10	0009	0012	0015	0020	0025	0032	0040	0051	0063	0078
11	0001	0001	0002	0003	0003	0005	0006	0008	0010	0013
12							0001	0001	0001	0001

p / r	41	42	43	44	45	46	47	48	49	50
1	9990	9992	9993	9995	9996	9997	9997	9998	9998	9999
2	9895	9912	9928	9940	9951	9960	9967	9974	9979	9983
3	9499	9569	9630	9684	9731	9772	9808	9839	9865	9888
4	8492	8656	8807	8945	9071	9185	9288	9381	9464	9539
5	6742	7003	7254	7493	7721	7935	8137	8326	8502	8666
6	4552	4849	5146	5441	5732	6019	6299	6573	6838	7095
7	2524	2770	3025	3290	3563	3842	4127	4415	4707	5000
8	1114	1264	1426	1600	1788	1988	2200	2424	2659	2905
9	0379	0446	0520	0605	0698	0803	0918	1045	1183	1334
10	0096	0117	0141	0170	0203	0242	0287	0338	0396	0461
11	0017	0021	0027	0033	0041	0051	0063	0077	0093	0112
12	0002	0002	0003	0004	0005	0007	0009	0011	0014	0017
13							0001	0001	0001	0001

***n* = 14**

p / r	01	02	03	04	05	06	07	08	09	10
1	1313	2464	3472	4353	5123	5795	6380	6888	7330	7712
2	0084	0310	0645	1059	1530	2037	2564	3100	3632	4154
3	0003	0025	0077	0167	0301	0478	0698	0958	1255	1584
4		0001	0006	0019	0042	0080	0136	0214	0315	0441
5				0002	0004	0010	0020	0035	0059	0092
6						0001	0002	0004	0008	0015
7									0001	0002

Table C *(continued)*

p / r	11	12	13	14	15	16	17	18	19	20
1	8044	8330	8577	8789	8972	9129	9264	9379	9477	9560
2	4658	5141	5599	6031	6433	6807	7152	7469	7758	8021
3	1939	2315	2708	3111	3521	3932	4341	4744	5138	5519
4	0594	0774	0979	1210	1465	1742	2038	2351	2679	3018
5	0137	0196	0269	0359	0467	0594	0741	0907	1093	1298
6	0024	0038	0057	0082	0115	0157	0209	0273	0349	0439
7	0003	0006	0009	0015	0022	0032	0046	0064	0087	0116
8		0001	0001	0002	0003	0005	0008	0012	0017	0024
9						0001	0001	0002	0003	0004

p / r	21	22	23	24	25	26	27	28	29	30
1	9631	9691	9742	9786	9822	9852	9878	9899	9917	9932
2	8259	8473	8665	8837	8990	9126	9246	9352	9444	9825
3	5887	6239	6574	6891	7189	7467	7727	7967	8188	8392
4	3366	3719	4076	4432	4787	5136	5479	5813	6137	6448
5	1523	1765	2023	2297	2585	2884	3193	3509	3832	4158
6	0543	0662	0797	0949	1117	1301	1502	1718	1949	2195
7	0152	0196	0248	0410	0383	0467	0563	0673	0796	0933
8	0033	0045	0060	0079	0103	0132	0167	0208	0257	0315
9	0006	0008	0011	0016	0022	0029	0038	0050	0065	0083
10	0001	0001	0002	0002	0003	0005	0007	0009	0012	0017
11						0001	0001	0001	0002	0003

p / r	31	32	33	34	35	36	37	38	39	40
1	9945	9955	9963	9970	9976	9981	9984	9988	9990	9992
2	9596	9657	9710	9756	9795	9828	9857	9881	9902	9919
3	8577	8746	8899	9037	9161	9271	9370	9457	9534	9602
4	6747	7032	7301	7556	7795	8018	8226	8418	8595	8757
5	4486	4813	5138	5458	5773	6080	6478	6666	6943	7207
6	2454	2724	3006	3297	3595	3899	4208	4519	4831	5141
7	1084	1250	1431	1626	1836	2059	2296	2545	2805	3075
8	0381	0450	0545	0643	0753	0876	1012	1162	1325	1501
9	0105	0131	0163	0200	0243	0294	0353	0420	0497	0583
10	0022	0029	0037	0048	0060	0076	0095	0117	0144	0175
11	0003	0005	0006	0008	0011	0014	0019	0024	0031	0039
12		0001	0001	0001	0001	0002	0003	0003	0005	0006
13										0001

p / r	41	42	43	44	45	46	47	48	49	50
1	9994	9995	9996	9997	9998	9998	9999	9999	9999	9999
2	9934	9946	9956	9964	9971	9977	9981	9985	9988	9991
3	9661	9713	9758	9797	9830	9850	9883	9903	9921	9935
4	8905	9039	9161	9270	9368	9455	9532	9601	9661	9713
5	7459	7697	7922	8132	8328	8510	8678	8833	8974	9102
6	5450	5754	6052	6344	6627	6900	7163	7415	7654	7880
7	3355	3643	3937	4236	4539	4843	5148	5451	5751	6047
8	1692	1896	2113	2344	2586	2840	3105	3380	3663	3953
9	0680	0789	0910	1043	1189	1348	1520	1707	1906	2120
10	0212	0255	0304	0361	0426	0500	0583	0677	0782	0898

Table C *(continued)*

11	0049	0061	0076	0093	0114	0139	0168	0202	0241	0287
12	0008	0010	0013	0017	0022	0027	0034	0042	0053	0065
13	0001	0001	0001	0002	0003	0003	0004	0006	0007	0009
14										0001

n = 15

p r	01	02	03	04	05	06	07	08	09	10
1	1399	2614	3667	4579	5367	6047	6633	7137	7570	7941
2	0096	0353	0730	1191	1710	2262	2832	3403	3965	4510
3	0004	0030	0094	0203	0362	0571	0829	1130	1469	1841
4		0002	0008	0024	0055	0104	0175	0273	0399	0556
5			0001	0002	0006	0014	0028	0050	0082	0127
6					0001	0001	0003	0007	0013	0022
7								0001	0002	0003

p r	11	12	13	14	15	16	17	18	19	20
1	8259	8530	8762	8959	9126	9269	9389	9490	9576	9648
2	5031	5524	5987	6417	6814	7179	7511	7813	8085	8329
3	2238	2654	3084	3520	3958	4392	4819	5234	5635	6020
4	0742	0959	1204	1476	1773	2092	2429	2782	3146	3518
5	0187	0265	0361	0478	0617	0778	0961	1167	1394	1642
6	0037	0057	0084	0121	0168	0227	0300	0387	0490	0611
7	0006	0010	0015	0024	0036	0052	0074	0102	0137	0181
8	0001	0001	0002	0004	0006	0010	0014	0021	0030	0042
9					0001	0001	0002	0003	0005	0008
10									0001	0001

p r	21	22	23	24	25	26	27	28	29	30
1	9709	9759	9802	9837	9866	9891	9911	9928	9941	9953
2	8547	8741	8913	9062	9198	9315	9417	9505	9581	9647
3	6385	6731	7055	7358	7639	7899	8137	8355	8553	8732
4	3895	4274	4650	5022	5387	5742	6086	6416	6732	7031
5	1910	2195	2495	2810	3135	3469	3810	4154	4500	4845
6	0748	0905	1079	1272	1484	1713	1958	2220	2495	2704
7	0834	0298	0374	0463	0566	0684	0817	0965	1130	1311
8	0058	0078	0104	0135	0173	0219	0274	0338	0413	0500
9	0011	0016	0023	0031	0042	0056	0073	0094	0121	0152
10	0002	0003	0004	0006	0008	0011	0015	0021	0028	0037
11			0001	0001	0001	0002	0002	0003	0005	0007
12									0001	0001

p r	31	32	33	34	35	36	37	38	39	40
1	9962	9969	9975	9980	9984	9988	9990	9992	9994	9995
2	9704	9752	9794	9829	9858	9883	9904	9922	9936	9948
3	8893	9038	9167	9281	9383	9472	9550	9618	9678	9729
4	7314	7580	7829	8060	8273	8469	8649	8813	8961	9095
5	5187	5523	5852	6171	6481	6778	7062	7332	7587	7827

TABLE C *(continued)*

6	3084	3393	3709	4032	4357	4684	5011	5335	5654	5968
7	1509	1722	1951	2194	2452	2722	3003	3295	3595	3902
8	0599	0711	0837	0977	1132	1302	1487	1687	1902	2131
9	0190	0236	0289	0351	0422	0504	0597	0702	0820	0950
10	0048	0062	0079	0099	0124	0154	0190	0232	0281	0338
11	009	0013	0016	0022	0028	0037	0047	0059	0075	0093
12	0001	0002	0003	0004	0005	0006	0009	0011	0015	0019
13					0001	0001	0001	0002	0002	0003

p / r	41	42	43	44	45	46	47	48	49	50
1	9996	9997	9998	9998	9999	9999	9999	9999	10000	10000
2	9958	9966	9973	9979	9983	9987	9990	9992	9994	9995
3	9773	9811	9843	9870	9893	9913	9929	9943	9954	9963
4	9215	9322	9417	9502	9576	9641	9697	9746	9788	9824
5	8052	0261	8454	8633	8796	8945	9080	9201	9310	9408
6	6274	6570	6856	7131	7398	7641	7875	8095	9302	8491
7	4214	4530	4847	5164	5478	5789	6095	6394	6684	6964
8	2374	2630	2898	3176	3465	3762	4065	4374	4686	5000
9	1095	1254	1427	1615	1818	2034	2265	2510	2767	3036
10	0404	0479	0565	0661	0769	0890	1024	1171	1333	1509
11	0116	0143	0174	0211	0255	0305	0363	0430	0506	0592
12	0025	0032	0040	0051	0063	0079	0097	0119	0145	0176
13	0004	0005	0007	0009	0011	0014	0018	0023	0029	0037
14			0001	0001	0001	0002	0002	0003	0004	0005

***n* = 16**

p / r	01	02	03	04	05	06	07	08	09	10
1	1485	2762	3857	4796	5599	6284	6869	7366	7789	8147
2	0109	0399	0818	1327	1892	2489	3098	3701	4289	4853
3	0005	0037	0113	0242	0429	0673	0969	1311	1694	2108
4		0002	0011	0032	0070	0132	0221	0342	0496	0684
5			0001	0003	0009	0019	0038	0068	0111	0170
6					0001	0002	0005	0010	0019	0033
7							0001	0001	0003	0005
8										0001

p / r	11	12	13	14	15	16	17	18	19	20
1	8450	8707	8983	9105	9257	9386	9493	9582	9657	9719
2	5386	5805	6347	6773	7161	7513	7830	8115	8368	8593
3	2545	2999	3461	3926	4386	4838	5277	5698	6101	6482
4	0907	1162	1448	1763	2101	2460	2836	3223	3619	4019
5	0248	0348	0471	0618	0791	0988	1211	1458	1727	2018
6	0053	0082	0120	0171	0235	0315	0412	0527	0662	0817
7	0009	0015	0024	0038	0056	0080	0112	0153	0204	0267
8	0001	0002	0004	0007	0011	0016	0024	0036	0051	0070
9			0001	0001	0002	0003	0004	0007	0010	0015
10							0001	0001	0002	0002

TABLE C *(continued)*

p / r	21	22	23	24	25	26	27	28	29	30
1	9770	9812	9847	9876	9900	9919	9935	9948	9958	9967
2	8791	8965	9117	9250	9365	9465	9550	9623	9686	9739
3	6839	7173	7483	7768	8029	8267	8482	8677	8851	9006
4	4418	4814	5203	5583	5950	6303	6640	6959	7260	7541
5	2327	2652	2991	3341	3698	4060	4425	4788	5147	5501
6	0992	1188	1405	1641	1897	2169	2458	2761	3077	3402
7	0342	0432	0536	0657	0796	0951	1125	1317	1526	1753
8	0095	0127	0116	0214	0271	0340	0420	0514	0621	0744
9	0021	0030	0041	0056	0075	0098	0127	0163	0206	0257
10	0004	0006	0008	0012	0016	0023	0031	0041	0055	0071
11	0001	0001	0001	0002	0003	0004	0006	0008	0011	0016
12						0001	0001	0001	0002	0003

p / r	31	32	33	34	35	36	37	38	39	40
1	9974	9979	9984	9987	9990	9992	9994	9995	9996	9997
2	9784	9822	9854	9880	9902	9921	9936	9948	9959	9967
3	9144	9266	9374	9467	9549	9620	9681	9734	9778	9817
4	7804	8047	8270	8475	8661	8830	8982	9119	9241	9349
5	5846	6181	6504	6813	7108	7387	7649	7895	8123	8334
6	3736	4074	4416	4759	5100	5438	5770	6094	6408	6712
7	1997	2257	2531	2819	3119	3428	3746	4070	4398	4728
8	0881	1035	1205	1391	1594	1813	2048	2298	2562	2839
9	0317	0388	0470	0564	0671	0791	0926	1076	1242	1423
10	0092	0117	0148	0185	0229	0280	0341	0411	0491	0483
11	0021	0028	0037	0048	0062	0079	0100	0125	0155	0191
12	0004	0005	0007	0010	0013	0017	0023	0030	0038	0049
13		0001	0001	0001	0002	0003	0004	0005	0007	0009
14								0001	0001	0001

p / r	41	42	43	44	45	46	47	48	49	50
1	9998	9998	9999	9999	9999	9999	10000	10000	10000	10000
2	9974	9979	9984	9987	9990	9992	9994	9995	9997	9997
3	9849	9876	9899	9918	9934	9947	9958	9966	9973	9979
4	9444	9527	9600	9664	9719	9766	9806	9840	9869	9894
5	8529	9808	8869	9015	9147	9265	9370	9463	9544	9616
6	7003	7280	7543	7792	8024	8241	8441	8626	8795	8949
7	5058	5387	5711	6029	6340	6641	6932	7210	7476	7728
8	3128	3428	3736	4051	4371	4694	5019	5343	5665	5982
9	1619	1832	2060	2302	2559	2829	3111	3405	3707	4018
10	0687	0805	0936	1081	1241	1416	1607	1814	2036	2272
11	0234	0284	0342	0409	0486	0574	0674	0786	0911	1051
12	0062	0078	0098	0121	0149	0183	0222	0268	0322	0384
13	0012	0016	0021	0027	0035	0044	0055	0069	0086	0106
14	0002	0002	0003	0004	0006	0007	0010	0013	0016	0021
15					0001	0001	0001	0001	0002	0003

TABLE C *(continued)*

n = *17*

p / r	01	02	03	04	05	06	07	08	09	10
1	1571	2907	4042	5004	5819	6507	7088	7577	7988	8332
2	0123	0446	0909	1465	2078	2717	3362	3995	4604	5182
3	0006	0044	0134	0286	0503	0782	1118	1503	1927	2382
4		0003	0014	0040	0088	0164	0273	0419	0603	0826
5			0001	0004	0012	0026	0051	0089	0145	0221
6					0001	0003	0007	0015	0027	0047
7							0001	0002	0004	0008
8										0001

p / r	11	12	13	14	15	16	17	18	19	20
1	8621	8862	9063	9230	9369	9484	9579	9657	9722	9775
2	5723	6223	6682	7099	7475	7813	8113	8379	8613	8818
3	2858	3345	3836	4324	4802	5266	5711	6133	6532	6904
4	1087	1383	1710	2065	2444	2841	3251	3669	4091	4511
5	0321	0446	0598	0778	0987	1224	1487	1775	2087	2418
6	0075	0114	0166	0234	0319	0423	0548	0695	0864	1057
7	0014	0023	0037	0056	0083	0118	0163	0220	0291	0377
8	0002	0004	0007	0011	0017	0027	0039	0057	0080	0109
9		0001	0001	0002	0003	0005	0008	0012	0018	0020
10						0001	0001	0002	0003	0005
11										0001

p / r	21	22	23	24	25	26	27	28	29	30
1	9818	9854	9882	9906	9925	9940	9953	9962	9970	9977
2	8996	9152	9285	9400	9499	9583	9654	9714	9765	9807
3	7249	7567	7859	8123	8363	8578	8771	8942	9093	9226
4	4927	5333	5728	6107	6470	6814	7137	7440	7721	7981
5	2766	3128	3500	3879	4261	4643	5023	5396	5760	6113
6	1273	1510	1770	2049	2347	2661	2989	3329	3677	4032
7	0479	0598	0736	0894	1071	1268	1485	1721	1976	2248
8	0147	0194	0251	0320	0402	0499	0611	0739	0884	1046
9	0037	0051	0070	0094	0124	0161	0206	0261	0326	0403
10	0007	0011	0016	0022	0031	0042	0057	0075	0098	0127
11	0001	0002	0003	0004	0006	0009	0013	0018	0024	0032
12				0001	0001	0002	0002	0003	0005	0007
13									0001	0001

p / r	31	32	33	34	35	36	37	38	39	40
1	9982	9986	9989	9991	9993	9995	9996	9997	9998	9998
2	9843	9872	9896	9917	9933	9946	9957	9966	9973	9979
3	9343	9444	9532	9608	9673	9728	9775	9815	9849	9877
4	8219	8437	8634	8812	8972	9115	9341	9353	9450	9536
5	6453	6778	7087	7378	7652	7906	8142	8360	8559	8740
6	4390	4749	5105	5458	5803	6139	6465	6778	7077	7361
7	2536	2838	3153	3479	3812	4152	4495	4839	5182	5522
8	1227	1426	1642	1877	2128	2395	2676	2971	3278	3595
9	0498	0595	0712	0845	0994	1159	1341	1541	1757	1989
10	0162	0204	0254	0314	0383	0464	0557	0664	0784	0919

TABLE C *(continued)*

11	0043	0057	0074	0095	0120	0151	0189	0234	0286	0348
12	0009	0013	0017	0023	0030	0040	0051	0066	0084	0106
13	0002	0002	0003	0004	0006	0008	0011	0015	0019	0025
14				0001	0001	0001	0002	0002	0003	0005
15										0001

p	41	42	43	44	45	46	47	48	49	50
r										
1	9999	9999	9999	9999	10000	10000	10000	10000	10000	10000
2	9984	9987	9990	9992	9994	9996	9997	9998	9998	9999
3	9900	9920	9935	9948	9959	9968	9975	9980	9985	9988
4	9610	9674	9729	9976	9816	9849	9877	9901	9920	9936
5	8904	9052	9183	9301	9404	9495	9575	9644	9704	9755
6	7628	7879	8113	8330	8520	8712	8878	9028	9162	9283
7	5856	6182	6499	6805	7098	7377	7641	7890	8122	8338
8	3920	4250	4585	4921	5257	5590	5918	6239	6552	6855
9	2238	2502	2780	3072	3374	3687	4008	4335	4667	5000
10	1070	1236	1419	1618	1834	2066	2314	2577	2855	3145
11	0420	0503	0597	0705	0826	0962	1112	1279	1462	1662
12	0133	0165	0203	0248	0301	0363	0434	0517	0611	0717
13	0033	0042	0054	0069	0086	0108	0134	0165	0202	0245
14	0006	0008	0011	0014	0019	0024	0031	0040	0050	0064
15	0001	0001	0002	0002	0003	0004	0005	0007	0009	0012
16							0001	0001	0001	0001

***n* = 18**

p	01	02	03	04	05	06	07	08	09	10
r										
1	1655	3049	4220	5204	6028	6717	7292	7771	8169	8499
2	0138	0495	1003	1607	2265	2945	3622	4281	4909	5497
3	0007	0052	0157	0333	0581	0898	1275	1702	2168	2662
4		0004	0018	0050	0109	0201	0333	0506	0723	0982
5			0002	0006	0015	0034	0067	0116	0186	0282
6				0001	0002	0005	0010	0021	0038	0064
7							0001	0003	0006	0012
8									0001	0002

p	11	12	13	14	15	16	17	18	19	20
r										
1	8773	8998	9185	9338	9464	9566	9651	9719	9775	9820
2	6042	6540	6992	7398	7759	8080	8362	8609	8824	9009
3	3173	3690	4206	4713	5203	5673	6119	6538	6927	7287
4	1282	1618	1986	2382	2798	3229	3669	4112	4554	4990
5	0405	0558	0743	0959	1206	1482	1787	2116	2467	2836
r										
6	0102	0154	0222	0310	0419	0551	0708	0889	1097	1329
7	0021	0034	0054	0081	0118	0167	0229	0306	0400	0513
8	0003	0006	0011	0017	0027	0041	0060	0086	0120	0163
9		0001	0002	0003	0005	0008	0013	0020	0029	0043
10					0001	0001	0002	0004	0006	0009
11								0001	0001	0002

TABLE C *(continued)*

p / r	21	22	23	24	25	26	27	28	29	30
1	9856	9886	9909	9928	9944	9956	9965	9973	9979	9984
2	9169	9306	9423	9522	9605	9676	9735	9784	9824	9858
3	7616	7916	8127	8430	8647	8839	9009	9158	9288	9400
4	5414	5825	6218	6591	6943	7272	7578	7860	8119	8354
5	3220	3413	4012	4414	4813	5208	5594	5968	6329	6673
6	1586	1866	2168	2488	2885	3176	3538	3907	4201	4656
7	0645	0799	0974	1171	1390	1630	1891	2171	2469	2783
8	0217	0283	0363	0458	0569	0699	0847	1014	1200	1407
9	0060	0083	0112	0148	0193	0249	0316	0395	0488	0596
10	0014	0020	0028	0039	0054	0073	0097	0127	0164	0210
11	0003	0004	0006	0009	0012	0018	0025	0034	0046	0061
12		0001	0001	0002	0002	0003	0005	0007	0010	0014
13						0001	0001	0001	0002	0003

p / r	31	32	33	34	35	36	37	38	39	40
1	9987	9990	9993	9994	9996	9997	9998	9998	9999	9999
2	9886	9908	9927	9942	9954	9964	9972	9978	9983	9987
3	9498	9581	9652	9713	9764	9807	9843	9873	9897	9918
4	8568	8759	8931	9083	9217	9335	9439	9528	9606	9672
5	7001	7309	7598	7866	8114	8341	8549	8737	8907	9058
6	5029	5398	5759	6111	6450	6776	7086	7379	7655	7912
7	3111	3450	3797	4151	4509	4867	5224	5576	5921	6257
8	1633	1878	2141	2421	2717	3027	3349	3681	4021	4366
9	0720	0861	1019	1196	1391	1604	1835	2084	2350	2632
10	0264	0329	0405	0494	0597	0714	0847	0997	1163	1347
11	0080	0104	0133	0169	0212	0264	0325	0397	0480	0576
12	0020	0027	0036	0047	0062	0080	0102	0130	0163	0203
13	0004	0005	0008	0011	0014	0019	0026	0034	0044	0058
14	0001	0001	0001	0002	0003	0004	0005	0007	0010	0013
15						0001	0001	0001	0002	0002

p / r	41	42	43	44	45	46	47	48	49	50
1	9999	9999	10000	10000	10000	10000	10000	10000	10000	10000
2	9990	9992	9994	9996	9997	9998	9998	9999	9999	9999
3	9934	9948	9959	9968	9975	9981	9985	9989	9991	9993
4	9729	9777	9818	9852	9880	9904	9923	9939	9952	9962
5	9193	9313	9418	9510	9589	9658	9717	9767	9810	9846
6	8151	8372	8573	8747	8923	9072	9205	9324	9428	9519
7	6582	6895	7193	7476	7742	7991	8222	8436	8632	8811
8	4713	5062	5408	5750	6085	6412	6728	7032	7322	7597
9	2928	3236	3556	3885	4222	4562	4906	5249	5591	5927
10	1549	1768	2004	2258	2527	2812	3110	3421	3742	4073
11	0686	0811	0951	1107	1280	1470	1677	1902	2144	2403
12	0250	0307	0372	0449	0537	0658	0753	0883	1028	1189
13	0074	0094	0110	0147	0183	0225	0275	0334	0402	0481
14	0017	0022	0029	0038	0049	0063	0079	0100	0125	0154
15	0003	0004	0006	0007	0010	0013	0017	0023	0029	0038
16		0001	0001	0001	0001	0002	0003	0004	0005	0007
17									0001	0001

TABLE C *(continued)*

n = 19

r \ p	01	02	03	04	05	06	07	08	09	10
1	1738	3188	4394	5396	6226	6914	7481	7949	8334	8649
2	0153	0546	1100	1751	2453	3171	3879	4560	5202	5797
3	0009	0061	0183	0384	0665	1021	1439	1908	2415	2946
4		0005	0022	0061	0132	0243	0398	0602	0953	1150
5			0002	0007	0020	0044	0085	0147	0235	0352
6				0001	0002	0006	0014	0029	0051	0086
7						0001	0002	0004	0009	0017
8								0001	0001	0003

r \ p	11	12	13	14	15	16	17	18	19	20
1	8908	9119	9291	9431	9544	9636	9710	9770	9818	9856
2	6342	6835	7277	7669	8015	8318	8581	8809	9004	9171
3	3488	4032	4568	5089	5587	6059	6500	6910	7287	7631
4	1490	1867	2275	2708	3159	3620	4085	4549	5005	5449
5	0502	0685	0904	1158	1444	1762	2107	2476	2864	3267
6	0135	0202	0290	0401	0537	0700	0891	1110	1357	1631
7	0030	0048	0076	0113	0163	0228	0310	0411	0532	0676
8	0005	0009	0016	0026	0041	0061	0089	0126	0173	0233
9	0001	0002	0003	0005	0008	0014	0021	0032	0047	0067
10				0001	0001	0002	0004	0007	0010	0016
11							0001	0001	0002	0003

r \ p	21	22	23	24	25	26	27	28	29	30
1	9887	9911	9930	9946	9958	9967	9975	9981	9985	9989
2	9313	9434	9535	9619	9690	9749	9797	9837	9869	9896
3	7942	8222	8471	8692	8887	9057	9205	9333	9443	9538
4	5877	6285	6671	7032	7369	7680	7965	8224	8458	8668
5	3681	4100	4320	4936	5346	5744	6129	6498	6848	7178
6	1929	2251	2592	2950	3322	3705	4093	4484	4875	5261
7	0843	1034	1248	1487	1749	2032	2336	2657	2995	3345
8	0307	0396	0503	0629	0775	0941	1129	1338	1568	1820
9	0093	0127	0169	0222	0287	0366	0459	0568	0694	0839
10	0023	0034	0047	0066	0089	0119	0156	0202	0258	0326
11	0005	0007	0011	0016	0023	0032	0044	0060	0080	0105
12	0001	0001	0002	0003	0005	0007	0010	0015	0021	0028
13				0001	0001	0001	0002	0003	0004	0006
14									0001	0001

r \ p	31	32	33	34	35	36	37	38	39	40
1	9991	9993	9995	9996	9997	9998	9998	9999	9999	9999
2	9917	9935	9949	9960	9969	9976	9981	9986	9989	9992
3	9618	9686	9743	9791	9830	9862	9890	9913	9931	9945
4	8856	9022	9169	9297	9409	9505	9588	9659	9719	9770
5	7486	7773	8037	8280	8500	8699	8878	9038	9179	9304

Table C *(continued)*

r										
6	5641	6010	6366	6707	7032	7339	7627	7895	8143	8371
7	3705	4073	4445	4818	5188	5554	5913	6261	6597	6919
8	2091	2381	2688	3010	3344	3690	4043	4401	4762	5122
9	1003	1186	1389	1612	1855	2116	2395	2691	3002	3325
10	0405	0499	0608	0733	0875	1035	1213	1410	1626	1861
11	0137	0176	0223	0280	0347	0436	0518	0625	0747	0885
12	0038	0051	0068	0089	0114	0146	0185	0231	0287	0352
13	0009	0012	0017	0023	0031	0041	0054	0070	0091	0116
14	0002	0002	0003	0005	0007	0009	0013	0017	0023	0031
15			0001	0001	0001	0002	0002	0003	0005	0006
16									0001	0001

p r	41	42	43	44	45	46	47	48	49	50
1	10000	10000	10000	10000	10000	10000	10000	10000	10000	10000
2	9994	9995	9996	9997	9998	9999	9999	9999	9999	10000
3	9957	9967	9974	9980	9985	9988	9991	9993	9995	9996
4	9813	9849	9878	9903	9923	9939	9952	9963	9971	9978
5	9413	9508	9590	9660	9720	9771	9814	9850	9879	9904
6	8579	8767	8937	9088	9223	9342	9446	9537	9615	9682
7	7226	7515	7787	8039	8273	8488	8684	8862	9022	9165
8	5480	5832	6176	6509	6831	7138	7430	7706	7964	8204
9	3660	4003	4353	4706	5060	5413	5762	6105	6439	6762
10	2114	2385	2672	2974	3290	3617	3954	4299	4648	5000
11	1040	1213	1404	1613	1841	2087	2351	2631	6928	3238
12	0429	0518	0621	0738	0871	1021	1187	1372	1575	1796
13	0146	0183	0227	0280	0342	0415	0500	0597	0709	0835
14	0040	0052	0067	0086	0109	0137	0171	0212	0261	0318
15	0009	0012	0016	0021	0028	0036	0046	0060	0076	0096
16	0001	0002	0003	0004	0005	0007	0010	0013	0017	0022
17				0001	0001	0001	0001	0002	0003	0004

n = 20

p r	01	02	03	04	05	06	07	08	09	10
1	1821	3324	4562	5580	6415	7099	7658	8113	8484	8784
2	0169	0599	1198	1897	2642	3395	4131	4831	5484	6083
3	0010	0071	0210	0439	0755	1150	1610	2121	2666	3231
4		0006	0027	0074	0159	0290	0471	0706	0993	1330
5			0003	0010	0026	0056	0107	0183	0290	0432
6				0001	0003	0009	0019	0038	0068	0113
7						0001	0003	0006	0013	0024
8								0001	0002	0004
9										0001

p r	11	12	13	14	15	16	17	18	19	20
1	9028	9224	9383	9510	9612	9694	9759	9811	9852	9885
2	6624	7109	7539	7916	8244	8529	8773	8982	9159	9308
3	3802	4369	4920	5450	5951	6420	6854	7252	7614	7939
4	1710	2127	2573	3041	3523	4010	4496	4974	5439	5886
5	0610	0826	1083	1375	1702	2059	2443	2849	3271	3704

TABLE C *(continued)*

6	0175	0260	0370	0507	0673	0870	1098	1356	1643	1958
8	0041	0067	0103	0153	0219	0304	0409	0537	0689	0867
9	0001	0002	0005	0008	0013	0021	0033	0049	0071	0100
10			0001	0001	0002	0004	0007	0011	0017	0026
11						0001	0001	0002	0004	0006
12									0001	0001
p	21	22	23	24	25	26	27	28	29	30
r										
1	9910	9931	9946	9959	9968	9976	9982	9986	9989	9992
2	9434	9539	9626	9698	9757	9805	9845	9877	9903	9924
3	8230	8488	8716	8915	9087	9237	9365	9474	9567	9645
4	6310	6711	7085	7431	7748	8038	8300	8534	8744	8929
5	4142	4580	5014	5439	5852	6248	6625	6981	7315	7625
6	2297	2657	3035	3427	3828	4235	4643	5048	5447	5836
7	1071	1301	1557	1838	2142	2467	2810	3169	3540	3920
8	0419	0536	0675	0835	1018	1225	1455	1707	1982	2277
9	0138	0186	0246	0320	0409	0515	0640	0784	0948	1133
10	0038	0054	0075	0103	0139	0183	0238	0305	0385	0480
11	0009	0013	0019	0028	0039	0055	0074	0100	0132	0171
12	0002	0003	0004	0006	0009	0014	0018	0027	0038	0051
13			0001	0001	0002	0003	0004	0006	0009	0013
14							0001	0001	0002	0003
p	31	32	33	34	35	36	37	38	39	40
r										
1	9994	9996	9997	9998	9998	9999	9999	9999	9999	10000
2	9940	9953	9964	9972	9979	9984	9988	9991	9993	9995
3	9711	9765	9811	9849	9879	9904	9924	9940	9953	9964
4	9092	9235	9358	9465	9556	9634	9700	9755	9802	9840
5	7911	8173	8411	8626	8818	8989	9141	9274	9390	9490
6	6213	6574	6917	7242	7546	7829	8090	8329	8547	8744
7	4305	4693	5079	5460	5834	6197	6547	6882	7200	7500
8	2591	2922	3268	3624	3990	4361	4735	5108	5478	5841
9	1340	1568	1818	2087	2376	2683	3005	3341	3688	4044
10	0591	0719	0866	1032	1218	1424	1650	1897	2163	2447
11	0220	0279	0350	0434	0532	0645	0775	0923	1090	1275
12	0069	0091	0119	0154	0196	0247	0308	0381	0466	0565
13	0018	0025	0034	0045	0060	0079	0102	0132	0167	0210
14	0004	0006	0008	0011	0015	0021	0028	0037	0049	0065
15	0001	0001	0001	0002	0003	0004	0006	0009	0012	0016
16						0001	0001	0002	0002	0003
p	41	42	43	44	45	46	47	48	49	50
r										
1	10000	10000	10000	10000	10000	10000	10000	10000	10000	10000
2	9996	9997	9998	9998	9999	9999	9999	10000	10000	10000
3	9972	9979	9984	9988	9991	9993	9995	9996	9997	9998
4	9872	9898	9920	9937	9951	9962	9971	9977	9983	9987
5	9577	9651	9714	9767	9811	9848	9879	9904	9924	9941

TABLE C *(concluded)*

p / r	41	42	43	44	45	46	47	48	49	50
6	8921	9078	9217	9340	9447	9539	9619	9687	9745	9793
7	7780	8041	8281	8501	8701	8881	9042	9186	9312	9423
8	6196	6539	6868	7183	7480	7759	8020	8261	8482	8684
9	4406	4771	5136	5499	5857	6207	6546	6873	7186	7483
10	2748	3064	3394	3736	4086	4443	4804	5166	5525	5881
11	1480	1705	1949	2212	2493	2791	3104	3432	3771	4119
12	0679	0810	0958	1123	1308	1511	1734	1977	2238	2517
13	0262	0324	0397	0482	0580	0694	0823	0969	1133	1316
14	0084	0107	0136	0172	0214	0265	0326	0397	0480	0577
15	0022	0029	0038	0050	0064	0083	0105	0133	0166	0207
16	0004	0006	0008	0011	0015	0020	0027	0035	0046	0059
17	0001	0001	0001	0002	0003	0004	0005	0007	0010	0013
18						0001	0001	0001	0001	0002

INDEX